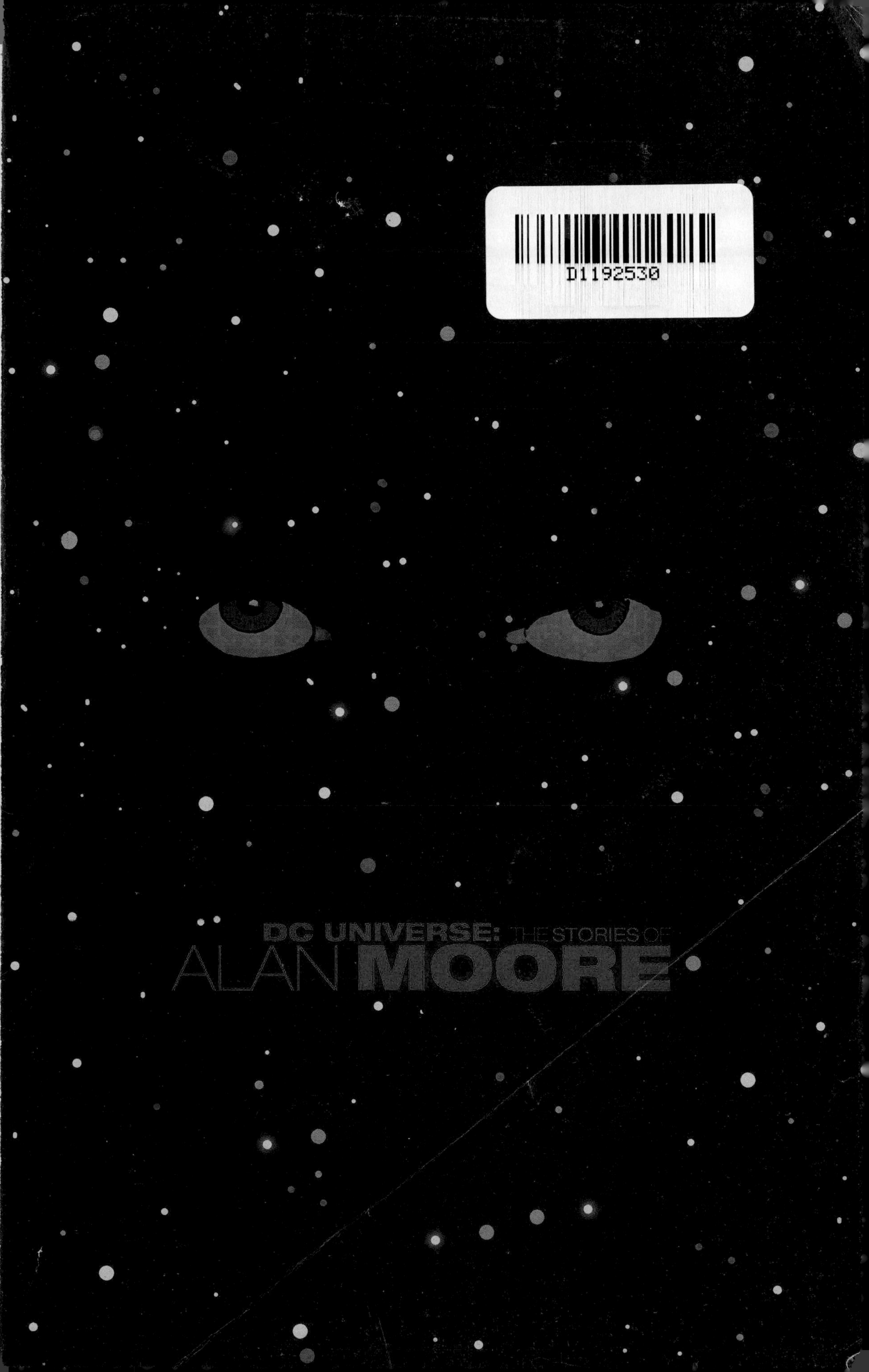
DC UNIVERSE: THE STORIES OF
ALAN MOORE

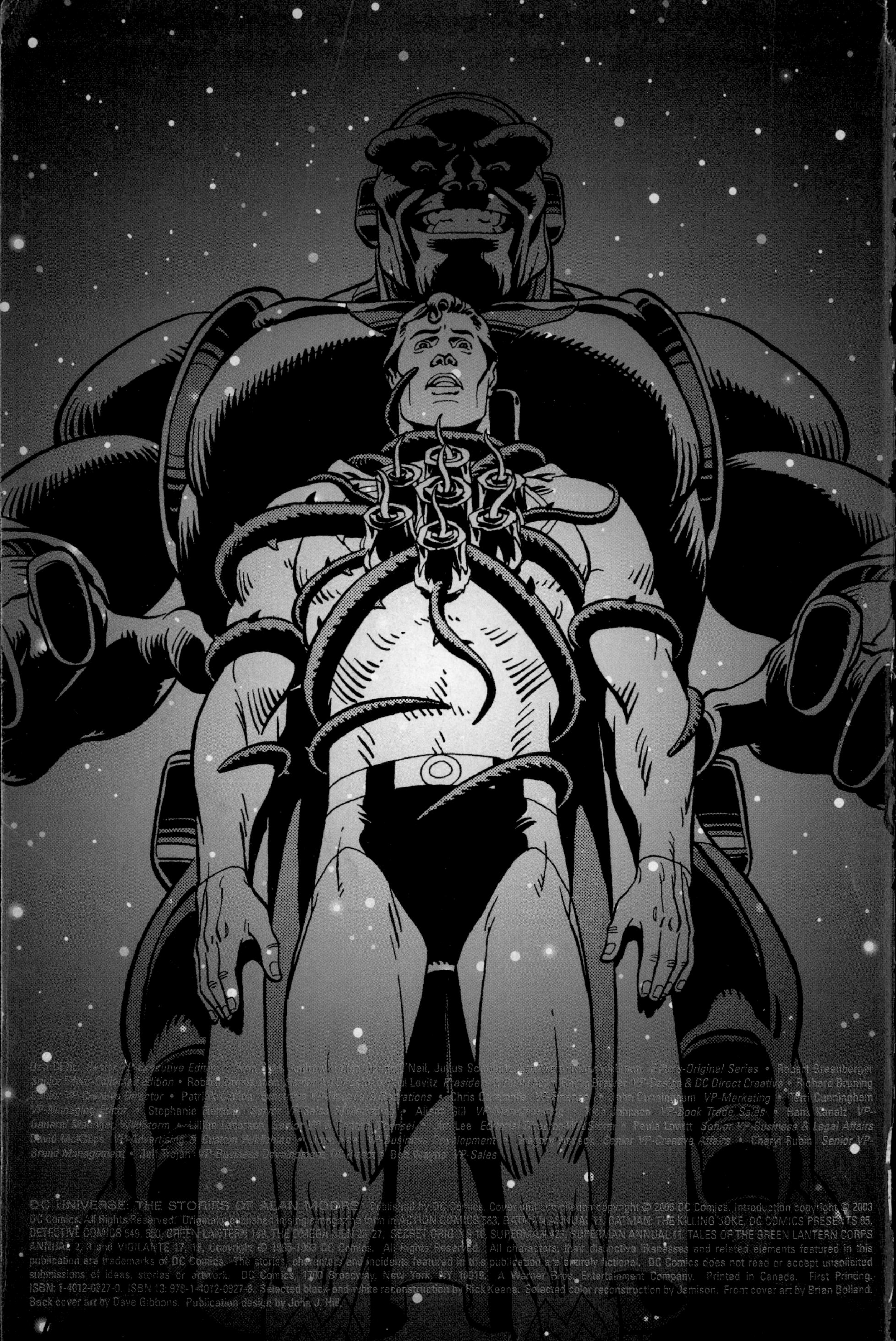

DC UNIVERSE: THE STORIES OF ALAN MOORE Published by DC Comics. Cover and compilation copyright © 2006 DC Comics. Introduction copyright © 2003 DC Comics. All Rights Reserved. Originally published in single magazine form in ACTION COMICS 583, BATMAN ANNUAL 11, BATMAN: THE KILLING JOKE, DC COMICS PRESENTS 85, DETECTIVE COMICS 549, 550, GREEN LANTERN 188, THE OMEGA MEN 26, 27, SECRET ORIGINS 10, SUPERMAN 423, SUPERMAN ANNUAL 11, TALES OF THE GREEN LANTERN CORPS ANNUAL 2, 3 and VIGILANTE 17, 18. Copyright © 1985-1988 DC Comics. All Rights Reserved. All characters, their distinctive likenesses and related elements featured in this publication are trademarks of DC Comics. The stories, characters and incidents featured in this publication are entirely fictional. DC Comics does not read or accept unsolicited submissions of ideas, stories or artwork. DC Comics, 1700 Broadway, New York, NY 10019. A Warner Bros. Entertainment Company. Printed in Canada. First Printing. ISBN: 1-4012-0927-0. ISBN 13: 978-1-4012-0927-8. Selected black-and-white reconstruction by Rick Keene. Selected color reconstruction by Jamison. Front cover art by Brian Bolland. Back cover art by Dave Gibbons. Publication design by John J. Hill.

TABLE OF CONTENTS

SUPERMAN created by JERRY SIEGEL and JOE SHUSTER.
BATMAN created by BOB KANE
WONDER WOMAN created by WILLIAM MOULTON MARSTON
SWAMP THING created by LEN WEIN and BERNI WRIGHTSON

INTRODUCTION

There's been a lot said about Alan Moore's writing talent. It's clear to anyone who's read even one of his stories that he possesses a remarkable command of language and is a master of description and dialogue. His work connects on both an intellectual and emotional level, in a way that's unmatched in today's comics. I share in the admiration of his writing skills, both as a reader and a frequent collaborator. As the latter, I've experienced firsthand his ability to write amazingly well, amazingly fast and have been privy to the parts of his writing that the reader never sees: namely, the extensive scene and mood-setting descriptions that have enabled me and his other artistic partners to produce perhaps the best work of our careers.

I could easily fill this introduction with praise for his creative prowess, but I'd rather talk about something else, the capacity without which his writing skills would be superfluous, the talent that is truly at the root of his genius. And that is his abilty to closely observe the universe around him.

Of course, the universe that surrounds Alan is the same universe that you and I also inhabit, but we just don't see the details that he sees. We don't hear the resonant chords he hears. We overlook the connections he makes us aware of. To one degree or another, we take things for granted, we go through the motions, we see what we expect to see.

But not Alan. Not in our "real" universe, and not in the fictional universes which he has given his attention to.

Now, it may be that "universe" is too grand a term for the interwoven comic-book narratives that, by their consensus, form the DC Universe. But, from the randomly conceived episodes of the nineteen forties to the deliberate constructions of later years, the stories of DC's heroic characters have, at least, aggregated into a wonderful, tantalizingly complex vista.

Alan, from an early age, was observing that imaginary continuum, absorbing the detail, the connections, the magic. For a boy in the Britain of the late fifties and early sixties, DC comics, even as mere objects, held an extraordinary appeal. They were vivid artifacts of a distant, more exciting civilization, a colorful land a million miles away from the grey uniformity of mundane reality.

And within their pages, there was a joyous escape into the gaudy, hard-focus proto-universes of the characters themselves. In those days, only the stories of the Superman and Batman "families" were widely available, with their B-list supporters, J'onn J'onzz, Green Arrow, Aquaman and the like. Back then, their worlds had not merged, beyond the pairing of Superman and Batman or the briefest of caption footnotes. But the potential was clearly there, although only dreamt-of by the readers, until the day that the first advertisement for the Justice League of America saw print:

"*Just Imagine… The Mightiest Heroes of Our Time have banded TOGETHER as the JUSTICE LEAGUE OF AMERICA.*"

It was comic books' equivalent of the Big Bang. And Alan was there, watching, listening, absorbing, and, no doubt, just imagining…

As the DC Universe rapidly expanded, to incorporate the earlier, more limited continuities of its forties' "Golden Age" stars, the characters of former four-color rivals from Quality Comics, and eventually

even the world of archcompetitor Captain Marvel himself, Alan kept vigil.

He didn't miss a thing. He wandered those imaginary worlds, taking in everything that he was shown but clearly also wondering about what he wasn't shown. Wondering just what it was really like to have super-powers, a Fortress of Solitude, a power ring, a secret identity, a kid sidekick. What it really felt like to be the last survivor of a doomed world, to want to strike fear into the hearts of evildoers, to be the fastest man alive, or the tiniest.

Like a lot of early fans and would-be professionals, Alan concocted his own stories and grandiose plotlines featuring DC characters, dreaming that one day, he might get his chance to guide their destinies himself.

As a near contemporary of Alan's, I shared the same dream and, like him, was one of those fortunate enough to realize it. It was a dream made all the more improbable by the real-world existence of the North Atlantic Ocean but, somehow, by luck and circumstance, it came true.

I managed to get my toe in DC's door a little ahead of Alan, although, by then, I'd already worked with him professionally on short stories for Britain's *2000 A.D.* weekly. I knew him and his work well enough to want to work with him more.

We'd talk often about doing something together for DC, and he even typed up a couple of outlines for proposed series that we could submit jointly. One, a complex continuity-ranging saga, prominently featuring the Challengers of the Unknown, made far-reaching changes to the entire DC Universe. I mentioned it to a contact at DC, prior to making a full proposal, but was told that the Challengers had been "promised" to another writer, and that there was no point in our continuing.

Another proposal, this time for the Martian Manhunter, was a much less ambitious notion, setting an alien being against a fifties backdrop of McCarthyism and small-town paranoia. Unfortunately, we learned that someone else was already revamping the character and so that, too, went no further.

After such a lot of unpaid and frustrated work on Alan's part, his eventual arrival at DC Comics was quite easily achieved. My phone rang one evening and Len Wein, then an editor/writer at DC, asked me if I had the number of a writer called Alan Moore. He'd read some of the work Alan had done for Britain's *Warrior* magazine and thought he might be able to revitalize Swamp Thing…

The rest, as they say, is comic-book history.

Before he eventually parted company with DC Comics, to explore and create other universes, Alan wrote some of the most resonant tales about their characters, both major and minor, that have ever seen print. All of those stories are presented here. They range from the whimsical to the poetic to the disturbingly real. They give some idea of the breadth of Alan's writing, his command of language and mastery of description and dialogue. But, above all, they show what magic there can be in the universe, if you really pay attention.

— Dave Gibbons
3/20/03

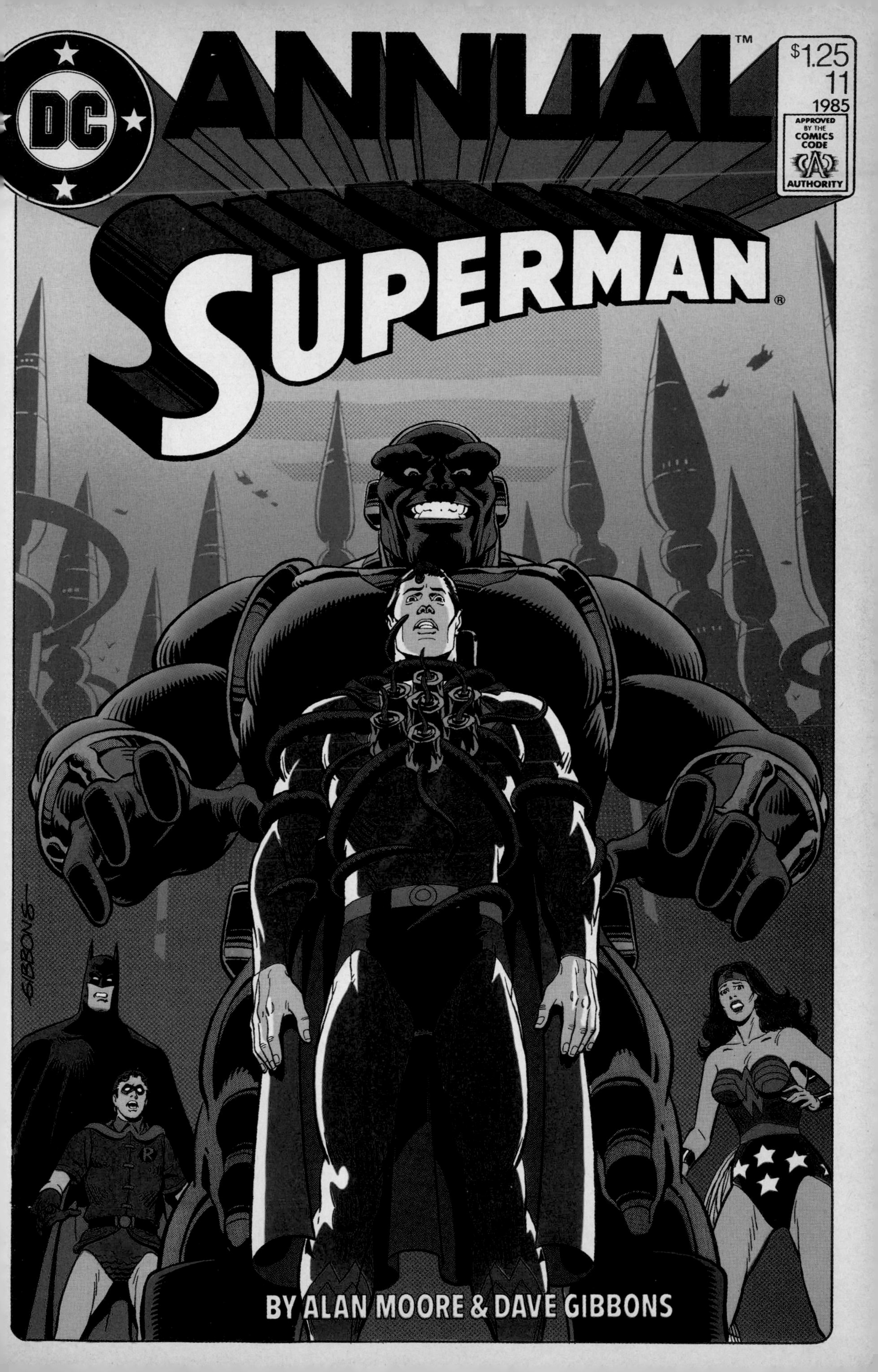

DC
ANNUAL™
$1.25
11
1985
APPROVED BY THE COMICS CODE AUTHORITY
SUPERMAN®
GIBBONS
BY ALAN MOORE & DAVE GIBBONS

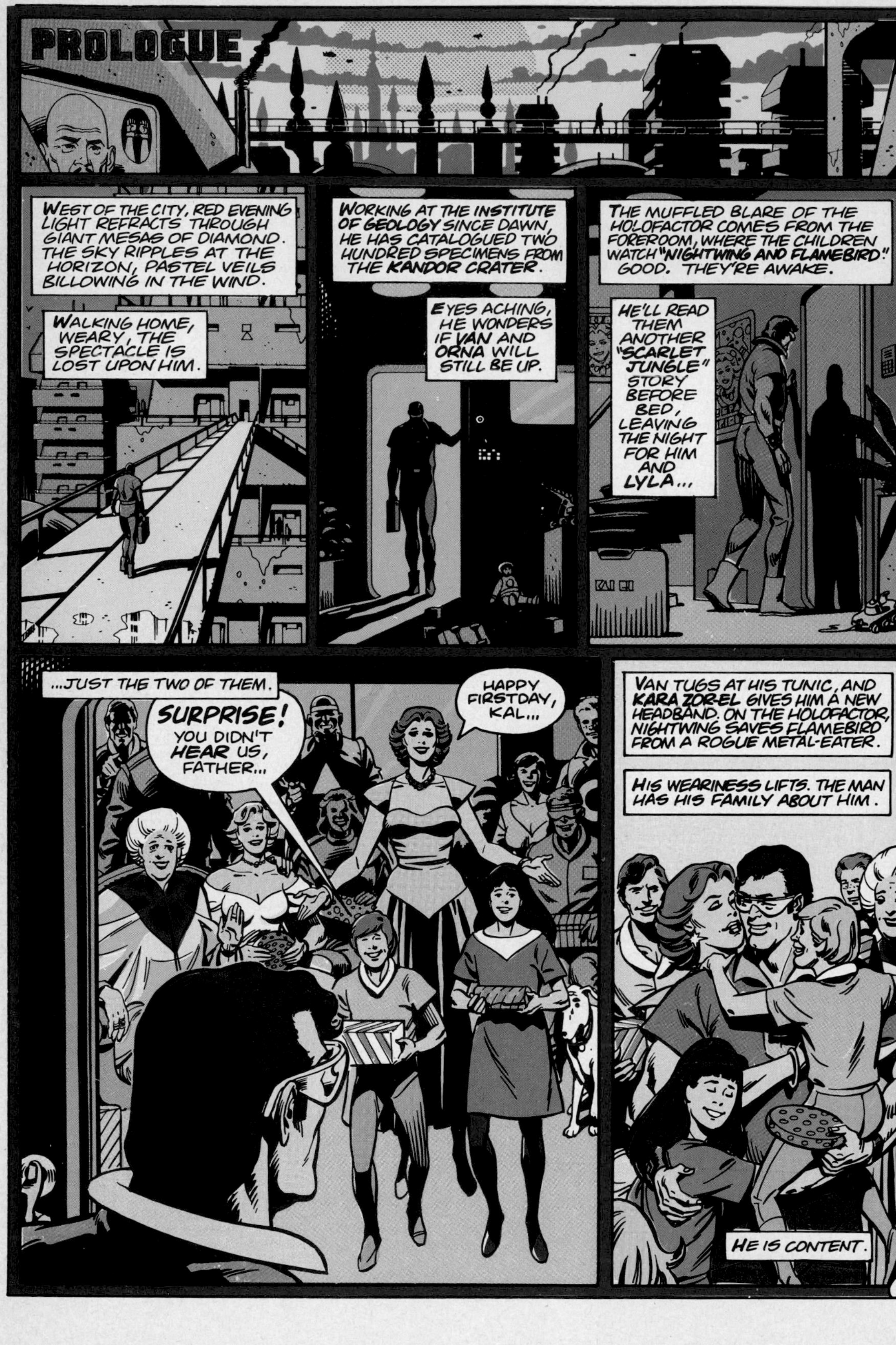

PROLOGUE
WEST OF THE CITY, RED EVENING LIGHT REFRACTS THROUGH GIANT MESAS OF DIAMOND. THE SKY RIPPLES AT THE HORIZON, PASTEL VEILS BILLOWING IN THE WIND.
WALKING HOME, WEARY, THE SPECTACLE IS LOST UPON HIM.
WORKING AT THE INSTITUTE OF GEOLOGY SINCE DAWN, HE HAS CATALOGUED TWO HUNDRED SPECIMENS FROM THE KANDOR CRATER.
EYES ACHING, HE WONDERS IF VAN AND ORNA WILL STILL BE UP.
THE MUFFLED BLARE OF THE HOLOFACTOR COMES FROM THE FOREROOM, WHERE THE CHILDREN WATCH "NIGHTWING AND FLAMEBIRD." GOOD. THEY'RE AWAKE.
HE'LL READ THEM ANOTHER "SCARLET JUNGLE" STORY BEFORE BED, LEAVING THE NIGHT FOR HIM AND LYLA...
...JUST THE TWO OF THEM.
SURPRISE! YOU DIDN'T HEAR US, FATHER...
HAPPY FIRSTDAY, KAL...
VAN TUGS AT HIS TUNIC, AND KARA ZOR-EL GIVES HIM A NEW HEADBAND. ON THE HOLOFACTOR, NIGHTWING SAVES FLAMEBIRD FROM A ROGUE METAL-EATER.
HIS WEARINESS LIFTS. THE MAN HAS HIS FAMILY ABOUT HIM.
HE IS CONTENT.
1

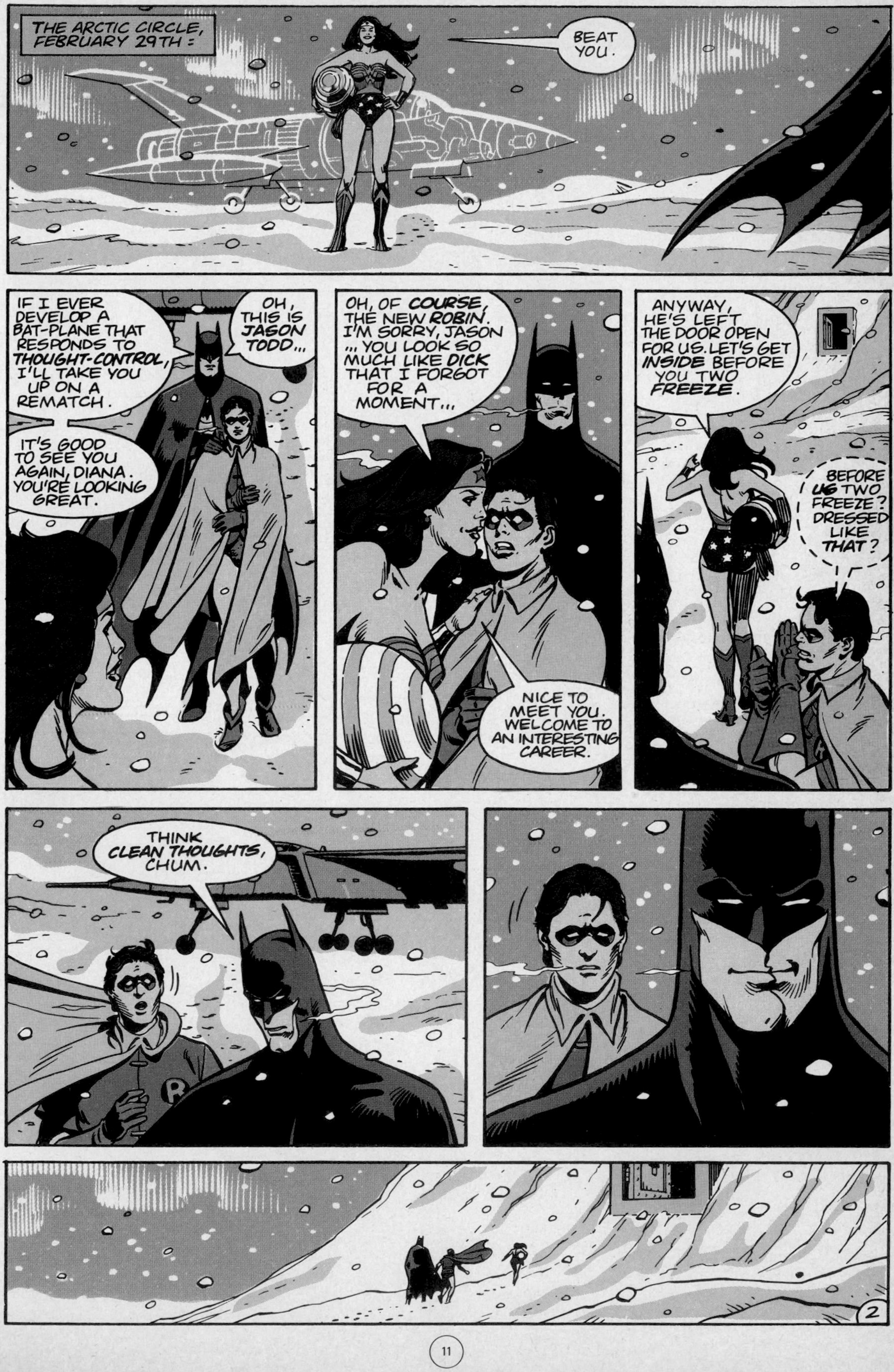
THE ARCTIC CIRCLE, FEBRUARY 29TH:
BEAT YOU.
IF I EVER DEVELOP A BAT-PLANE THAT RESPONDS TO THOUGHT-CONTROL, I'LL TAKE YOU UP ON A REMATCH.
IT'S GOOD TO SEE YOU AGAIN, DIANA. YOU'RE LOOKING GREAT.
OH, THIS IS JASON TODD...
OH, OF COURSE, THE NEW ROBIN. I'M SORRY, JASON ... YOU LOOK SO MUCH LIKE DICK THAT I FORGOT FOR A MOMENT...
NICE TO MEET YOU. WELCOME TO AN INTERESTING CAREER.
ANYWAY, HE'S LEFT THE DOOR OPEN FOR US. LET'S GET INSIDE BEFORE YOU TWO FREEZE.
BEFORE US TWO FREEZE? DRESSED LIKE THAT?
THINK CLEAN THOUGHTS, CHUM.
2

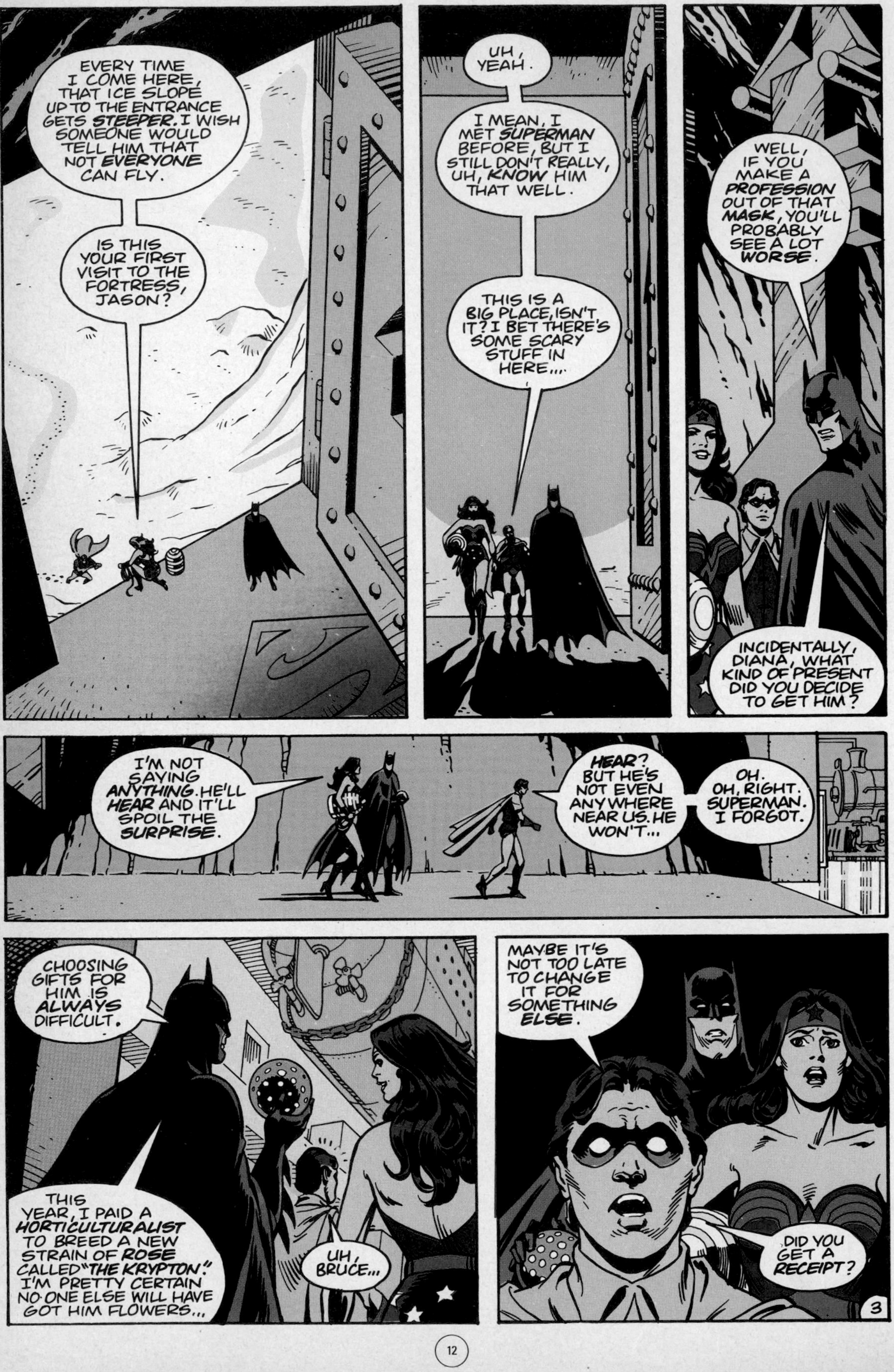
EVERY TIME I COME HERE, THAT ICE SLOPE UP TO THE ENTRANCE GETS STEEPER. I WISH SOMEONE WOULD TELL HIM THAT NOT EVERYONE CAN FLY.
IS THIS YOUR FIRST VISIT TO THE FORTRESS, JASON?
UH, YEAH.
I MEAN, I MET SUPERMAN BEFORE, BUT I STILL DON'T REALLY, UH, KNOW HIM THAT WELL.
THIS IS A BIG PLACE, ISN'T IT? I BET THERE'S SOME SCARY STUFF IN HERE....
WELL, IF YOU MAKE A PROFESSION OUT OF THAT MASK, YOU'LL PROBABLY SEE A LOT WORSE.
INCIDENTALLY, DIANA, WHAT KIND OF PRESENT DID YOU DECIDE TO GET HIM?
I'M NOT SAYING ANYTHING. HE'LL HEAR AND IT'LL SPOIL THE SURPRISE.
HEAR? BUT HE'S NOT EVEN ANYWHERE NEAR US. HE WON'T...
OH. OH, RIGHT. SUPERMAN. I FORGOT.
CHOOSING GIFTS FOR HIM IS ALWAYS DIFFICULT.
THIS YEAR, I PAID A HORTICULTURALIST TO BREED A NEW STRAIN OF ROSE CALLED "THE KRYPTON." I'M PRETTY CERTAIN NO ONE ELSE WILL HAVE GOT HIM FLOWERS...
UH, BRUCE...
MAYBE IT'S NOT TOO LATE TO CHANGE IT FOR SOMETHING ELSE.
DID YOU GET A RECEIPT?
3

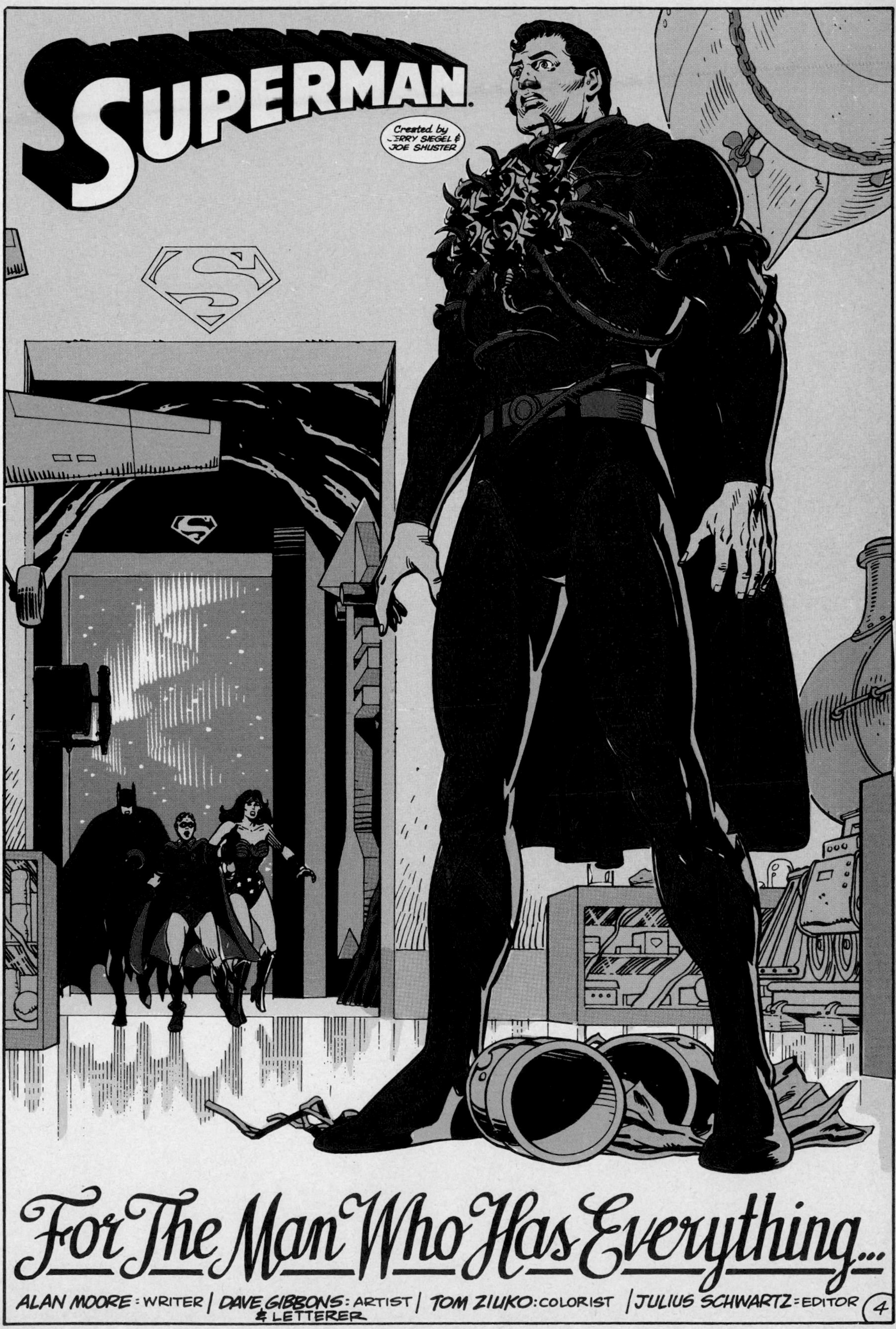
SUPERMAN
Created by JERRY SIEGEL & JOE SHUSTER
For The Man Who Has Everything...
ALAN MOORE: WRITER | DAVE GIBBONS: ARTIST & LETTERER | TOM ZIUKO: COLORIST | JULIUS SCHWARTZ: EDITOR
4

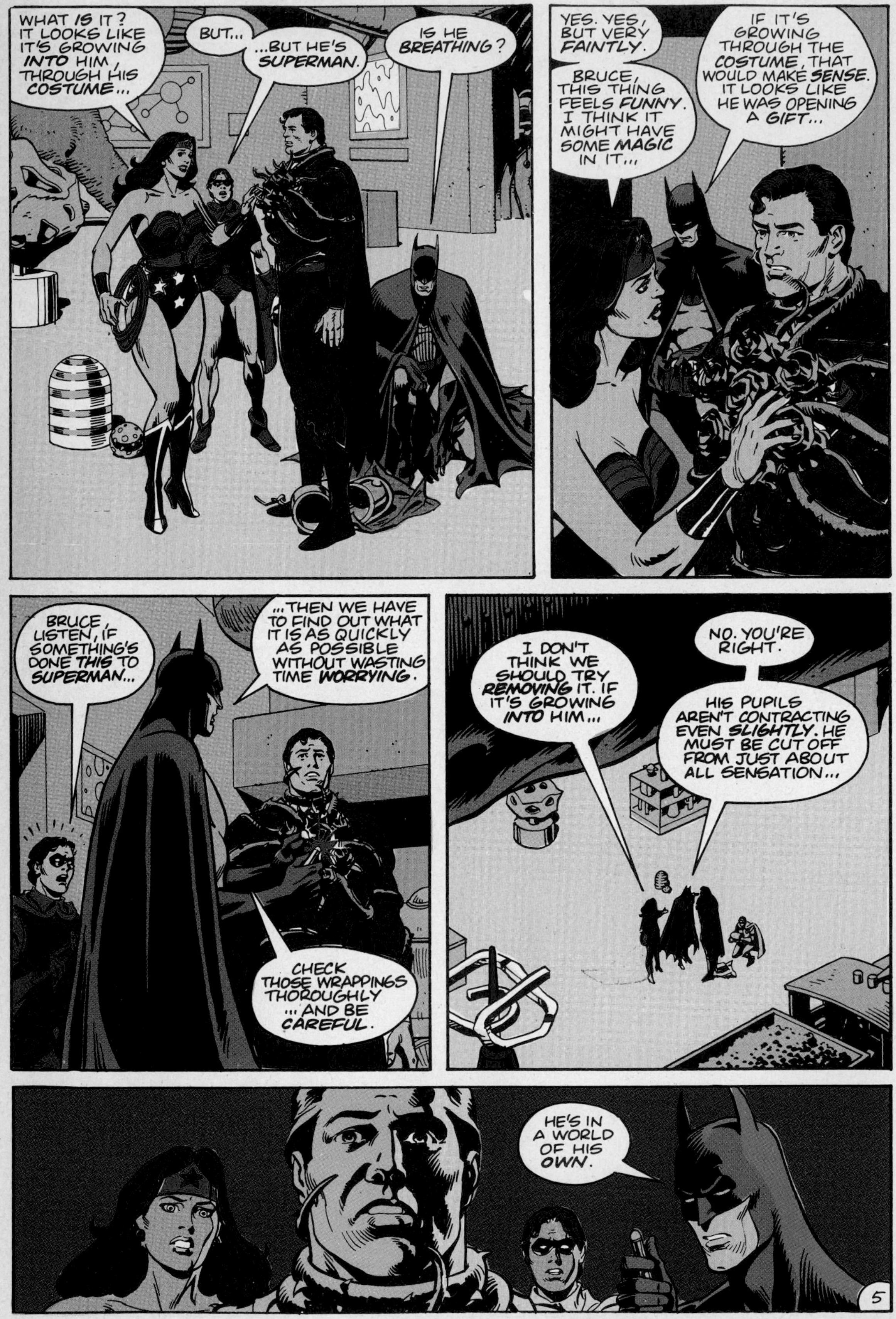
WHAT IS IT? IT LOOKS LIKE IT'S GROWING INTO HIM, THROUGH HIS COSTUME...
BUT...
...BUT HE'S SUPERMAN.
IS HE BREATHING?
YES. YES, BUT VERY FAINTLY.
BRUCE, THIS THING FEELS FUNNY. I THINK IT MIGHT HAVE SOME MAGIC IN IT...
IF IT'S GROWING THROUGH THE COSTUME, THAT WOULD MAKE SENSE. IT LOOKS LIKE HE WAS OPENING A GIFT...
BRUCE, LISTEN, IF SOMETHING'S DONE THIS TO SUPERMAN...
...THEN WE HAVE TO FIND OUT WHAT IT IS AS QUICKLY AS POSSIBLE WITHOUT WASTING TIME WORRYING.
CHECK THOSE WRAPPINGS THOROUGHLY ...AND BE CAREFUL.
I DON'T THINK WE SHOULD TRY REMOVING IT. IF IT'S GROWING INTO HIM...
NO. YOU'RE RIGHT.
HIS PUPILS AREN'T CONTRACTING EVEN SLIGHTLY. HE MUST BE CUT OFF FROM JUST ABOUT ALL SENSATION...
HE'S IN A WORLD OF HIS OWN.
5

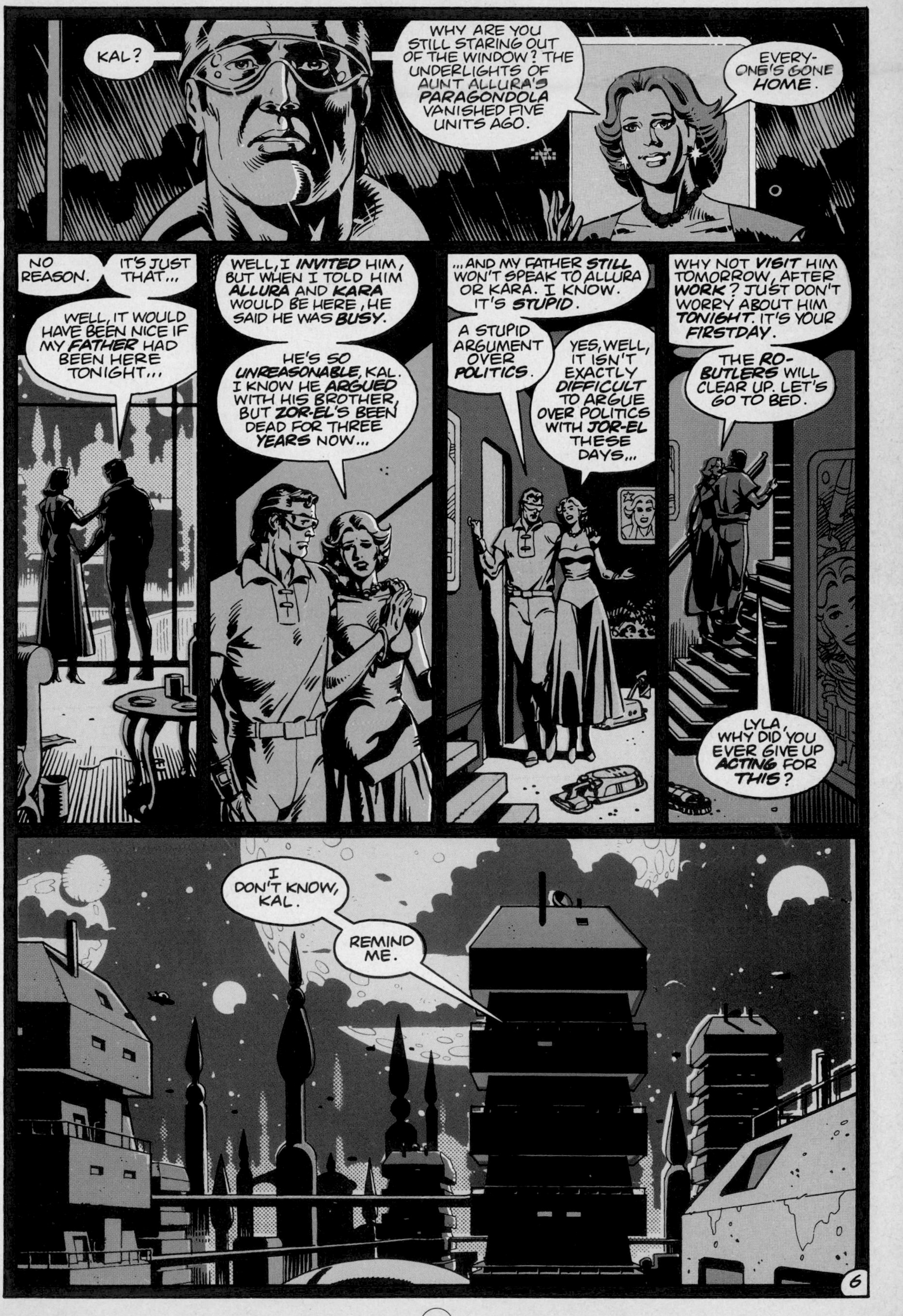
KAL?
WHY ARE YOU STILL STARING OUT OF THE WINDOW? THE UNDERLIGHTS OF AUNT ALLURA'S PARAGONDOLA VANISHED FIVE UNITS AGO.
EVERY-ONE'S GONE HOME.
NO REASON.
IT'S JUST THAT...
WELL, IT WOULD HAVE BEEN NICE IF MY FATHER HAD BEEN HERE TONIGHT...
WELL, I INVITED HIM, BUT WHEN I TOLD HIM ALLURA AND KARA WOULD BE HERE, HE SAID HE WAS BUSY.
HE'S SO UNREASONABLE, KAL. I KNOW HE ARGUED WITH HIS BROTHER, BUT ZOR-EL'S BEEN DEAD FOR THREE YEARS NOW...
...AND MY FATHER STILL WON'T SPEAK TO ALLURA OR KARA. I KNOW. IT'S STUPID.
A STUPID ARGUMENT OVER POLITICS.
YES, WELL, IT ISN'T EXACTLY DIFFICULT TO ARGUE OVER POLITICS WITH JOR-EL THESE DAYS...
WHY NOT VISIT HIM TOMORROW, AFTER WORK? JUST DON'T WORRY ABOUT HIM TONIGHT. IT'S YOUR FIRSTDAY.
THE RO-BUTLERS WILL CLEAR UP. LET'S GO TO BED.
LYLA, WHY DID YOU EVER GIVE UP ACTING FOR THIS?
I DON'T KNOW, KAL.
REMIND ME.
6

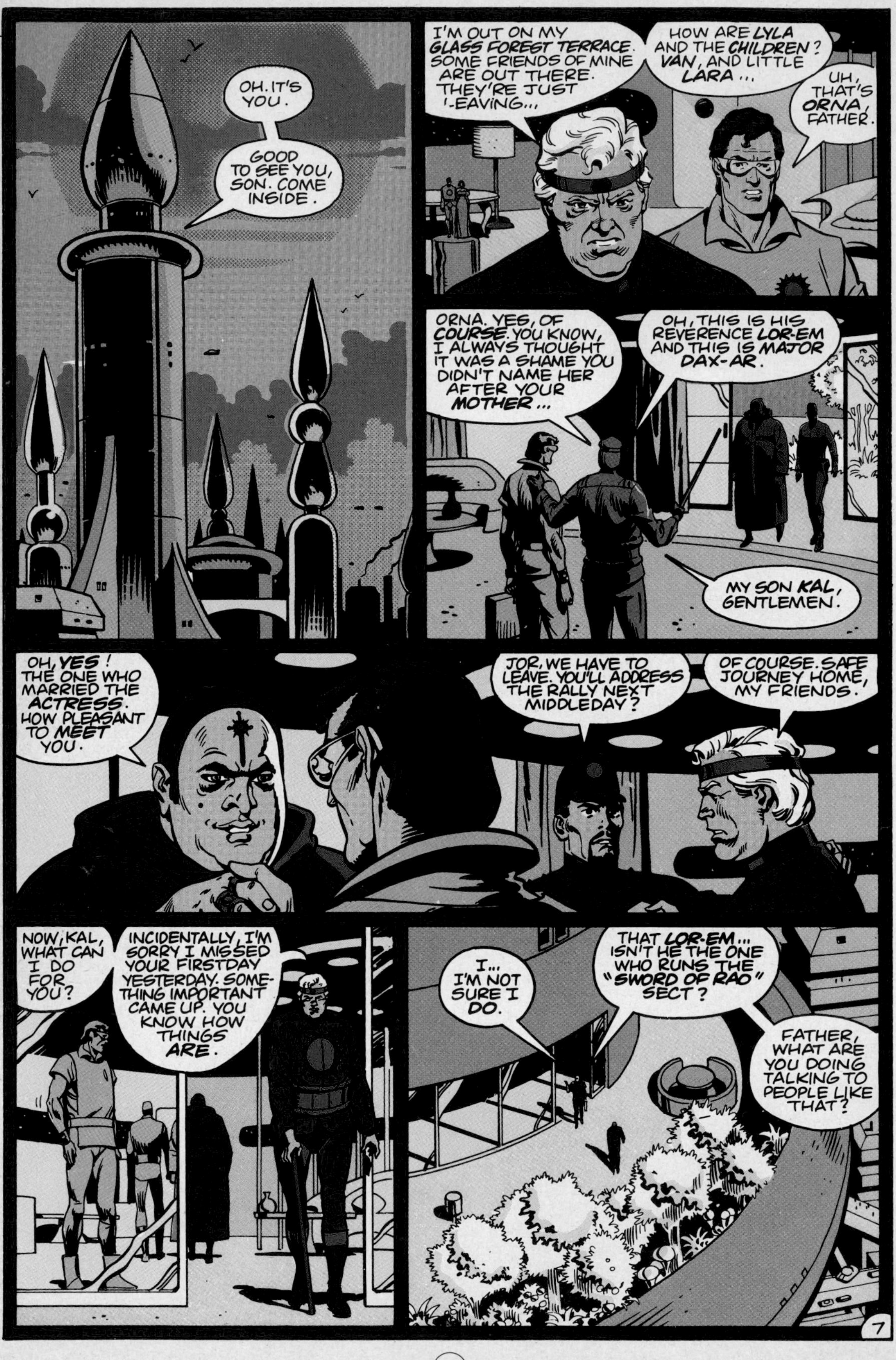
OH. IT'S YOU.
GOOD TO SEE YOU, SON. COME INSIDE.
I'M OUT ON MY GLASS FOREST TERRACE. SOME FRIENDS OF MINE ARE OUT THERE. THEY'RE JUST LEAVING...
HOW ARE LYLA AND THE CHILDREN? VAN, AND LITTLE LARA...
UH, THAT'S ORNA, FATHER.
ORNA. YES, OF COURSE. YOU KNOW, I ALWAYS THOUGHT IT WAS A SHAME YOU DIDN'T NAME HER AFTER YOUR MOTHER...
OH, THIS IS HIS REVERENCE LOR-EM AND THIS IS MAJOR DAX-AR.
MY SON KAL, GENTLEMEN.
OH, YES! THE ONE WHO MARRIED THE ACTRESS. HOW PLEASANT TO MEET YOU.
JOR, WE HAVE TO LEAVE. YOU'LL ADDRESS THE RALLY NEXT MIDDLEDAY?
OF COURSE. SAFE JOURNEY HOME, MY FRIENDS.
NOW, KAL, WHAT CAN I DO FOR YOU?
INCIDENTALLY, I'M SORRY I MISSED YOUR FIRSTDAY YESTERDAY. SOMETHING IMPORTANT CAME UP. YOU KNOW HOW THINGS ARE.
I... I'M NOT SURE I DO.
THAT LOR-EM... ISN'T HE THE ONE WHO RUNS THE "SWORD OF RAO" SECT?
FATHER, WHAT ARE YOU DOING TALKING TO PEOPLE LIKE THAT?
7

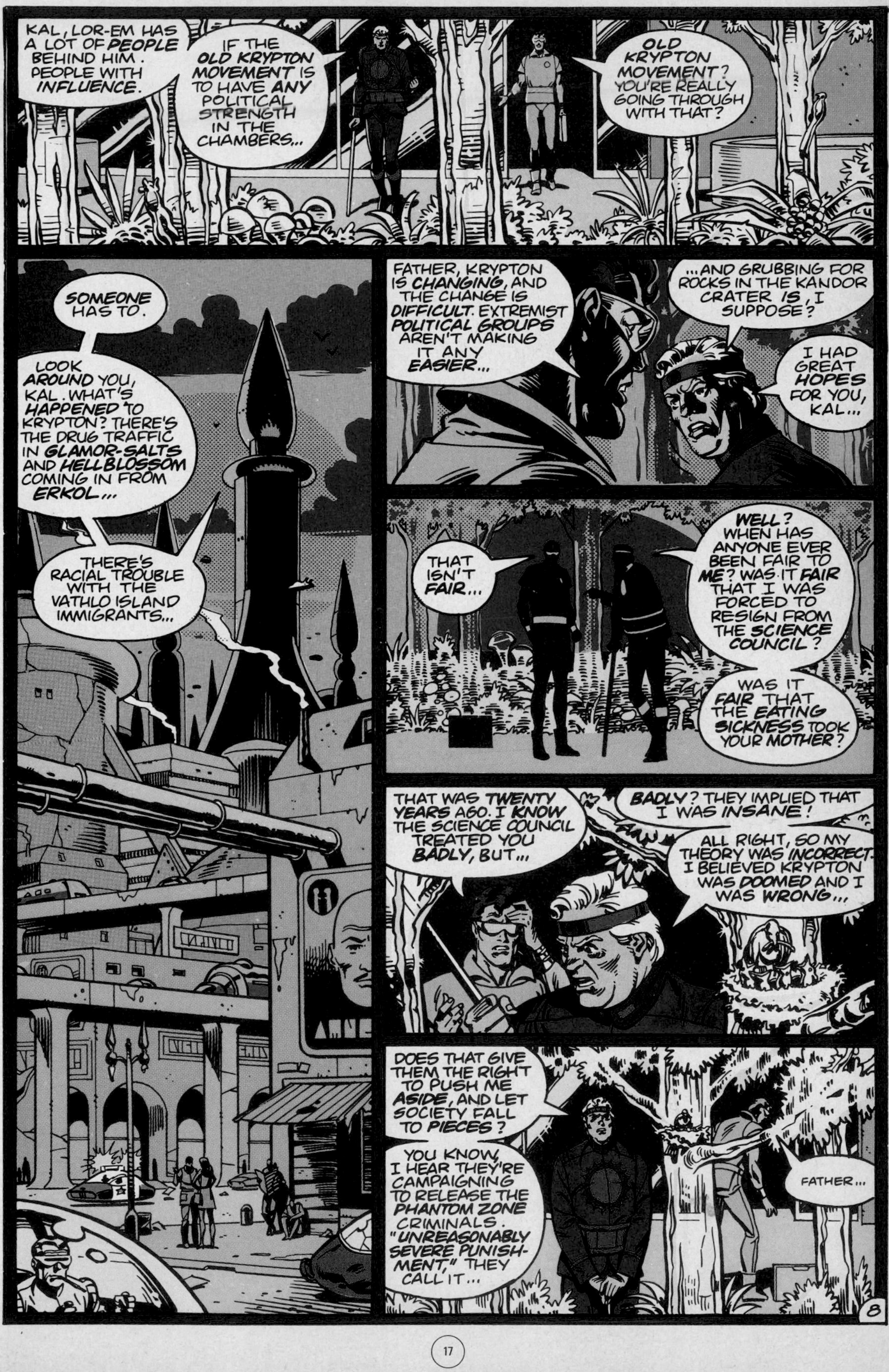
KAL, LOR-EM HAS A LOT OF PEOPLE BEHIND HIM. PEOPLE WITH INFLUENCE.
IF THE OLD KRYPTON MOVEMENT IS TO HAVE ANY POLITICAL STRENGTH IN THE CHAMBERS...
OLD KRYPTON MOVEMENT? YOU'RE REALLY GOING THROUGH WITH THAT?
SOMEONE HAS TO.
LOOK AROUND YOU, KAL. WHAT'S HAPPENED TO KRYPTON? THERE'S THE DRUG TRAFFIC IN GLAMOR-SALTS AND HELLBLOSSOM COMING IN FROM ERKOL...
THERE'S RACIAL TROUBLE WITH THE VATHLO ISLAND IMMIGRANTS...
FATHER, KRYPTON IS CHANGING, AND THE CHANGE IS DIFFICULT. EXTREMIST POLITICAL GROUPS AREN'T MAKING IT ANY EASIER...
...AND GRUBBING FOR ROCKS IN THE KANDOR CRATER IS, I SUPPOSE?
I HAD GREAT HOPES FOR YOU, KAL...
THAT ISN'T FAIR...
WELL? WHEN HAS ANYONE EVER BEEN FAIR TO ME? WAS IT FAIR THAT I WAS FORCED TO RESIGN FROM THE SCIENCE COUNCIL?
WAS IT FAIR THAT THE EATING SICKNESS TOOK YOUR MOTHER?
THAT WAS TWENTY YEARS AGO. I KNOW THE SCIENCE COUNCIL TREATED YOU BADLY, BUT...
BADLY? THEY IMPLIED THAT I WAS INSANE!
ALL RIGHT, SO MY THEORY WAS INCORRECT. I BELIEVED KRYPTON WAS DOOMED AND I WAS WRONG...
DOES THAT GIVE THEM THE RIGHT TO PUSH ME ASIDE, AND LET SOCIETY FALL TO PIECES?
YOU KNOW, I HEAR THEY'RE CAMPAIGNING TO RELEASE THE PHANTOM ZONE CRIMINALS. "UNREASONABLY SEVERE PUNISHMENT," THEY CALL IT...
FATHER...
8

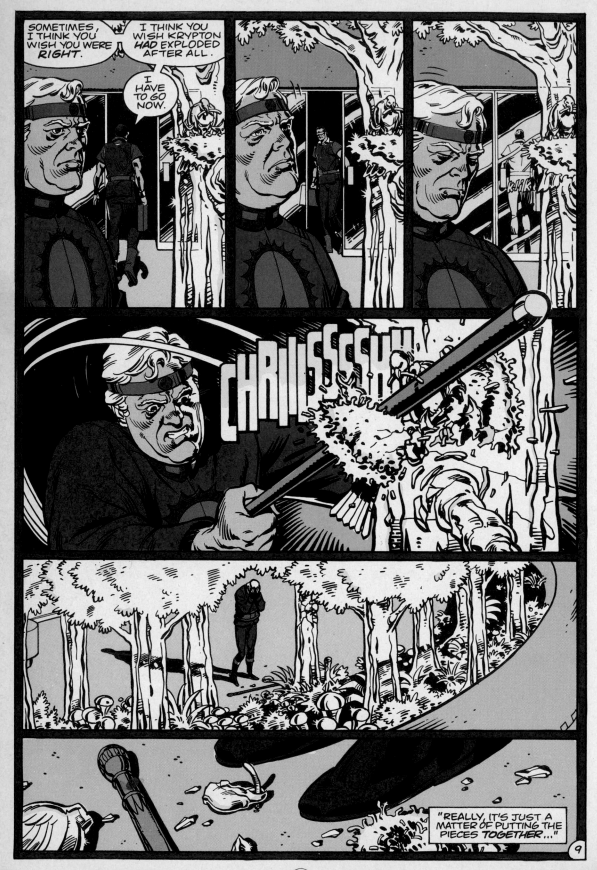

SOMETIMES, I THINK YOU WISH YOU WERE *RIGHT*. I THINK YOU WISH KRYPTON *HAD* EXPLODED AFTER ALL.

I HAVE TO GO NOW.

CHRIISSSSSH

"REALLY, IT'S JUST A MATTER OF PUTTING THE PIECES *TOGETHER*..."

9

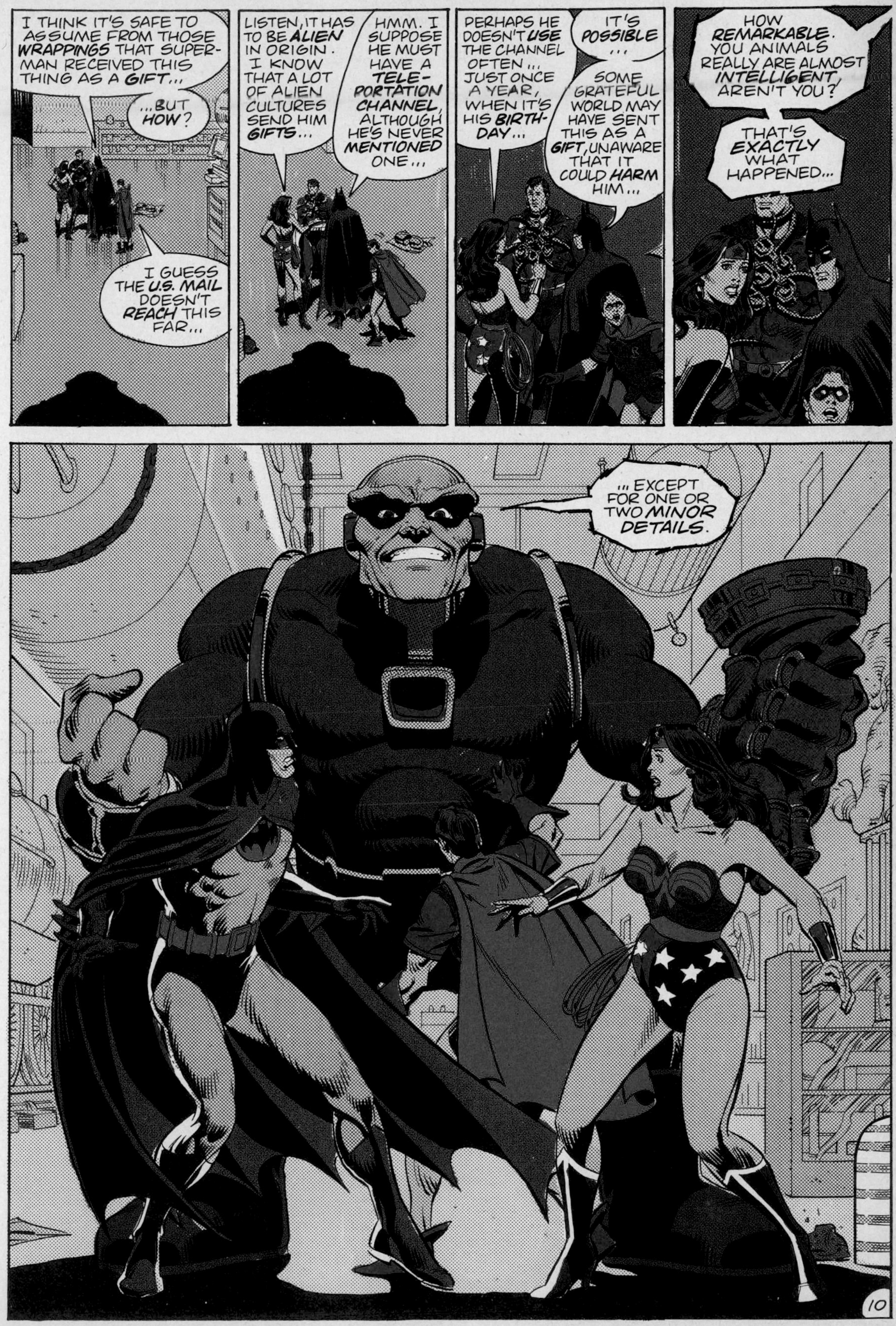
I THINK IT'S SAFE TO ASSUME FROM THOSE WRAPPINGS THAT SUPERMAN RECEIVED THIS THING AS A GIFT...
...BUT HOW?
I GUESS THE U.S. MAIL DOESN'T REACH THIS FAR...
LISTEN, IT HAS TO BE ALIEN IN ORIGIN. I KNOW THAT A LOT OF ALIEN CULTURES SEND HIM GIFTS...
HMM. I SUPPOSE HE MUST HAVE A TELE-PORTATION CHANNEL, ALTHOUGH HE'S NEVER MENTIONED ONE...
PERHAPS HE DOESN'T USE THE CHANNEL OFTEN... JUST ONCE A YEAR, WHEN IT'S HIS BIRTH-DAY...
IT'S POSSIBLE...
SOME GRATEFUL WORLD MAY HAVE SENT THIS AS A GIFT, UNAWARE THAT IT COULD HARM HIM...
HOW REMARKABLE. YOU ANIMALS REALLY ARE ALMOST INTELLIGENT, AREN'T YOU?
THAT'S EXACTLY WHAT HAPPENED...
...EXCEPT FOR ONE OR TWO MINOR DETAILS.
10

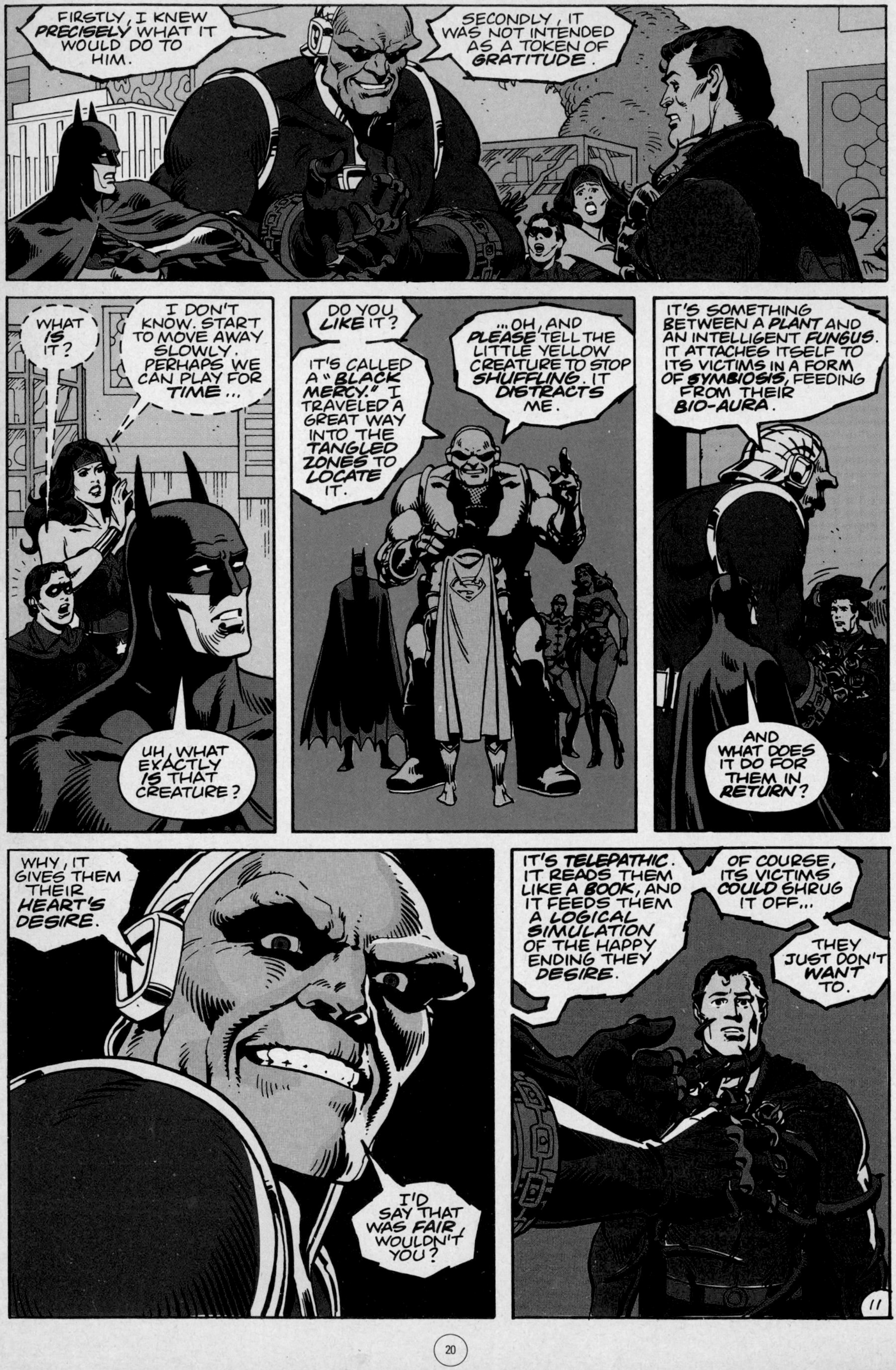
FIRSTLY, I KNEW PRECISELY WHAT IT WOULD DO TO HIM.
SECONDLY, IT WAS NOT INTENDED AS A TOKEN OF GRATITUDE.
WHAT IS IT?
I DON'T KNOW. START TO MOVE AWAY SLOWLY. PERHAPS WE CAN PLAY FOR TIME...
UH, WHAT EXACTLY IS THAT CREATURE?
DO YOU LIKE IT?
IT'S CALLED A "BLACK MERCY." I TRAVELED A GREAT WAY INTO THE TANGLED ZONES TO LOCATE IT.
...OH, AND PLEASE TELL THE LITTLE YELLOW CREATURE TO STOP SHUFFLING. IT DISTRACTS ME.
IT'S SOMETHING BETWEEN A PLANT AND AN INTELLIGENT FUNGUS. IT ATTACHES ITSELF TO ITS VICTIMS IN A FORM OF SYMBIOSIS, FEEDING FROM THEIR BIO-AURA.
AND WHAT DOES IT DO FOR THEM IN RETURN?
WHY, IT GIVES THEM THEIR HEART'S DESIRE.
I'D SAY THAT WAS FAIR WOULDN'T YOU?
IT'S TELEPATHIC. IT READS THEM LIKE A BOOK, AND IT FEEDS THEM A LOGICAL SIMULATION OF THE HAPPY ENDING THEY DESIRE.
OF COURSE, ITS VICTIMS COULD SHRUG IT OFF...
THEY JUST DON'T WANT TO.
11

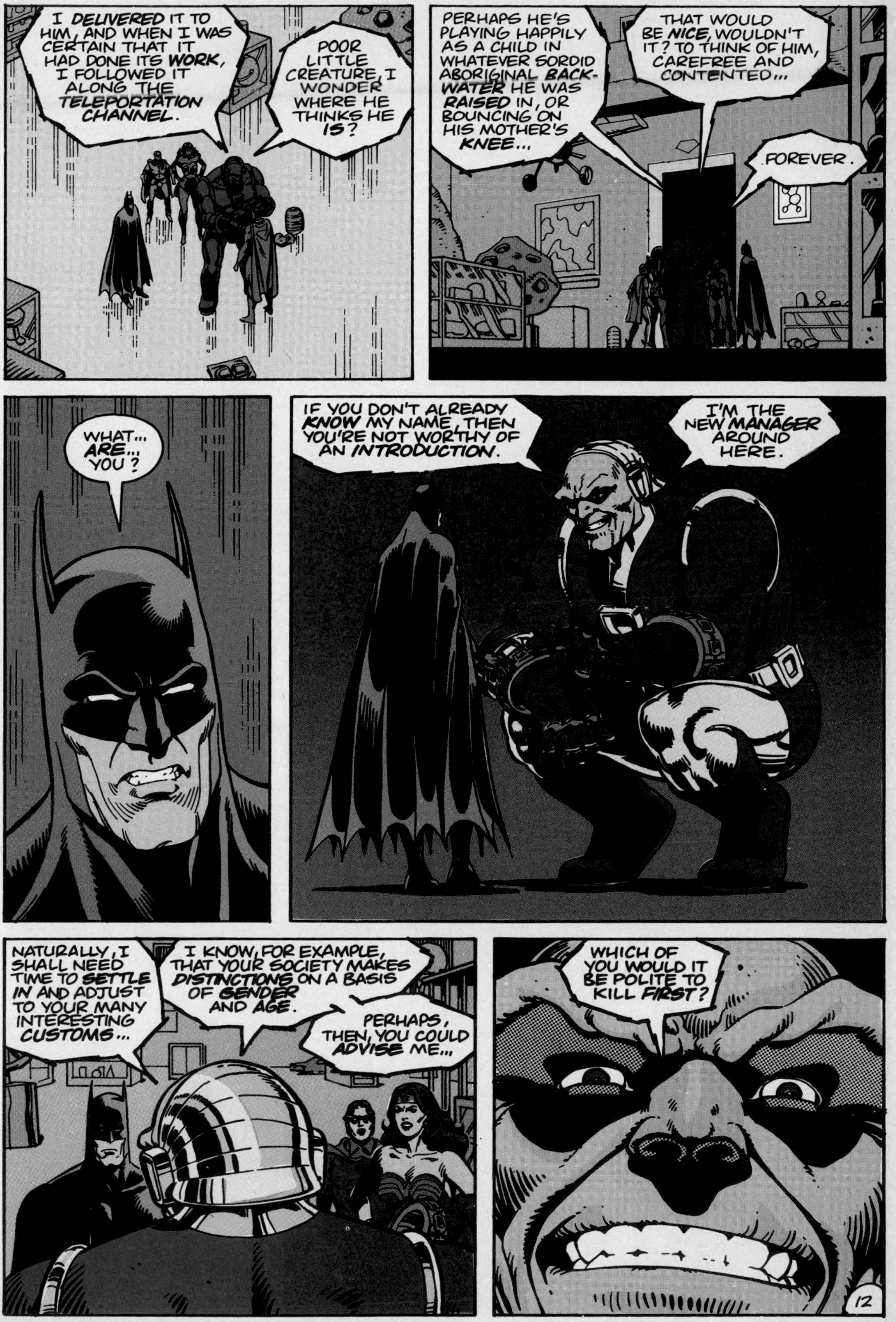
I DELIVERED IT TO HIM, AND WHEN I WAS CERTAIN THAT IT HAD DONE ITS WORK, I FOLLOWED IT ALONG THE TELEPORTATION CHANNEL.
POOR LITTLE CREATURE, I WONDER WHERE HE THINKS HE IS?
PERHAPS HE'S PLAYING HAPPILY AS A CHILD IN WHATEVER SORDID ABORIGINAL BACK-WATER HE WAS RAISED IN, OR BOUNCING ON HIS MOTHER'S KNEE...
THAT WOULD BE NICE, WOULDN'T IT? TO THINK OF HIM, CAREFREE AND CONTENTED...
...FOREVER.
WHAT... ARE... YOU?
IF YOU DON'T ALREADY KNOW MY NAME, THEN YOU'RE NOT WORTHY OF AN INTRODUCTION.
I'M THE NEW MANAGER AROUND HERE.
NATURALLY, I SHALL NEED TIME TO SETTLE IN AND ADJUST TO YOUR MANY INTERESTING CUSTOMS...
I KNOW, FOR EXAMPLE, THAT YOUR SOCIETY MAKES DISTINCTIONS ON A BASIS OF GENDER AND AGE.
PERHAPS, THEN, YOU COULD ADVISE ME...
WHICH OF YOU WOULD IT BE POLITE TO KILL FIRST?
12

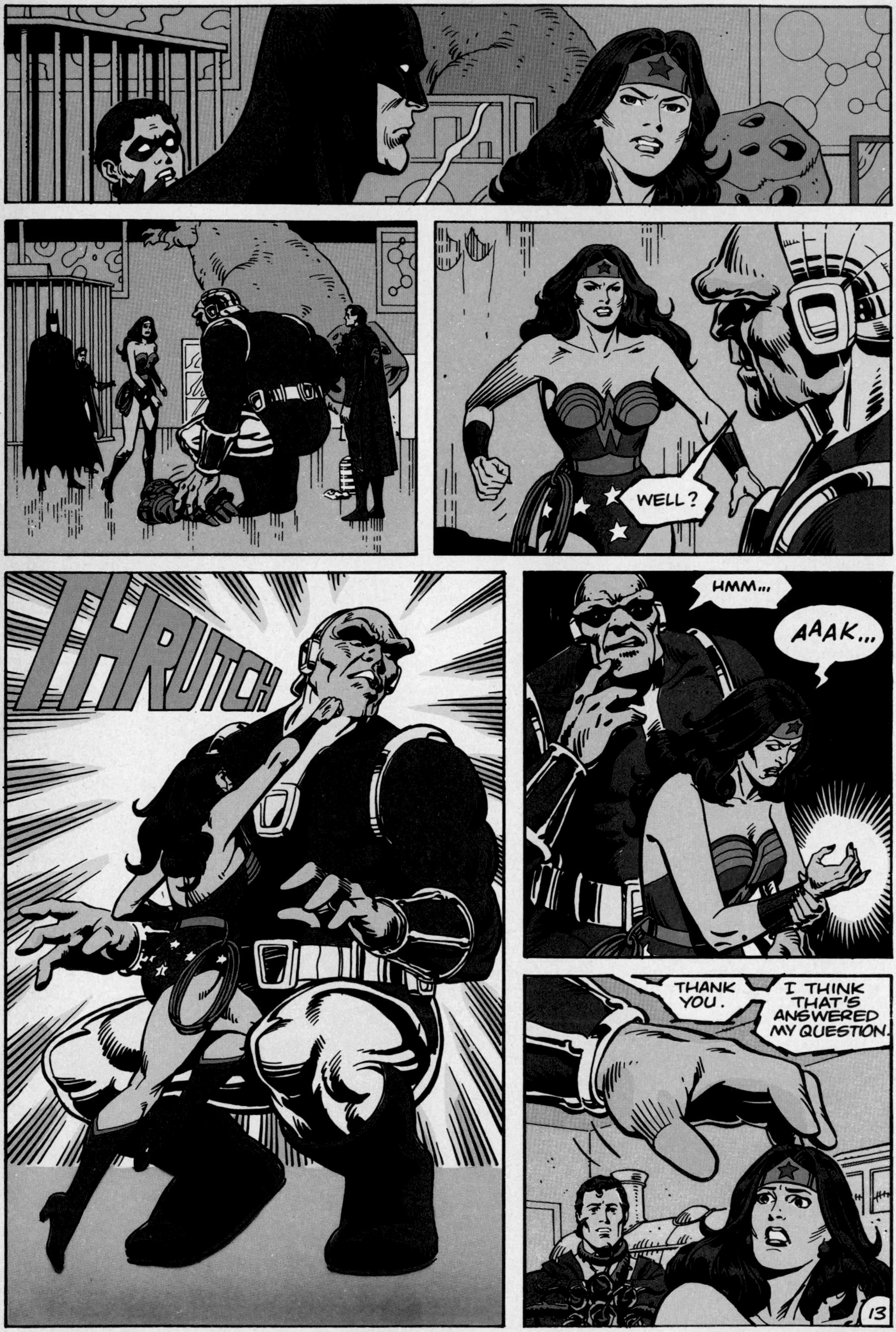
WELL?
THRUTCH
HMM...
AAAK...
THANK YOU.
I THINK THAT'S ANSWERED MY QUESTION!
13

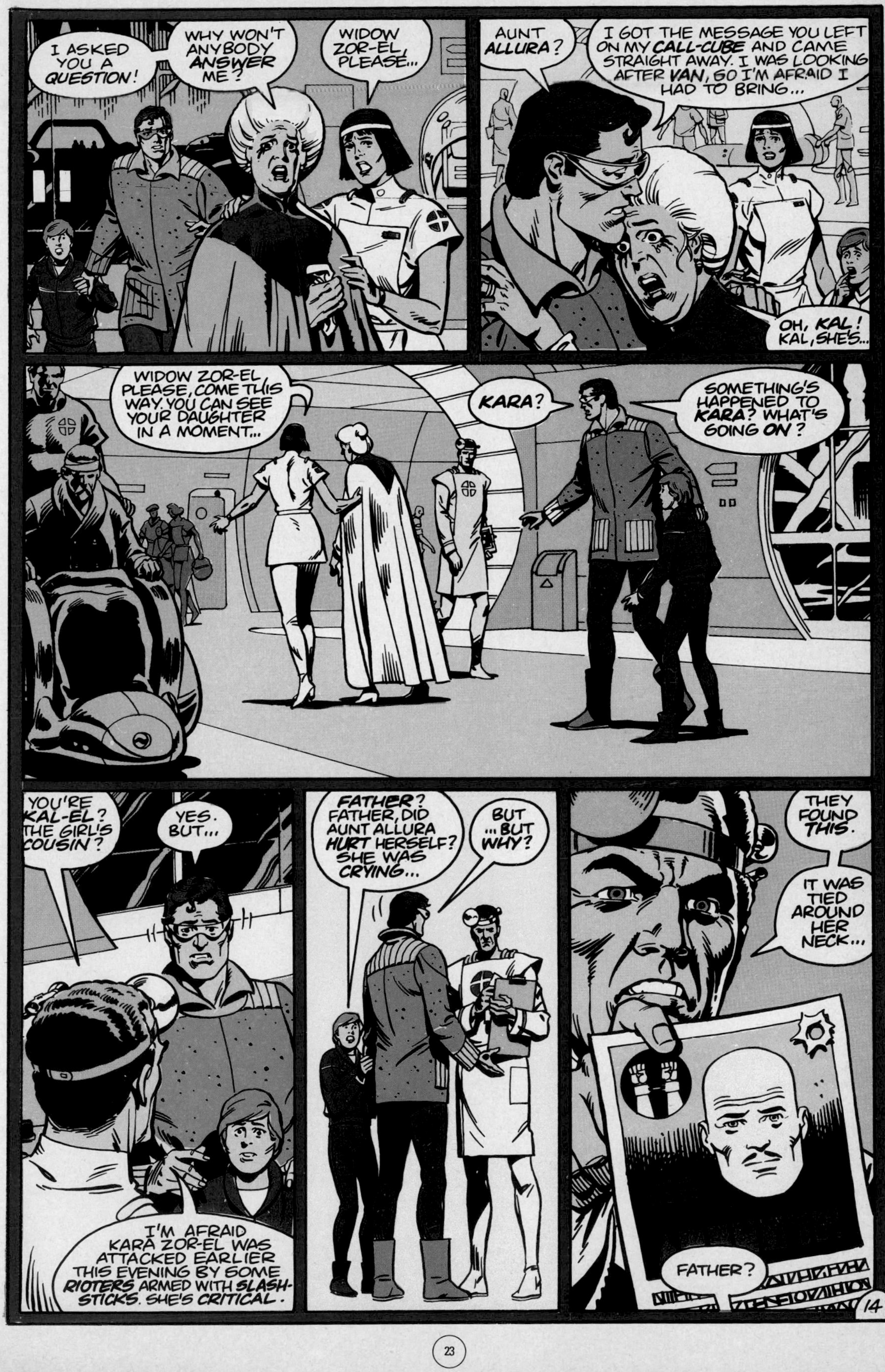
I ASKED YOU A QUESTION!
WHY WON'T ANYBODY ANSWER ME?
WIDOW ZOR-EL, PLEASE...
AUNT ALLURA?
I GOT THE MESSAGE YOU LEFT ON MY CALL-CUBE AND CAME STRAIGHT AWAY. I WAS LOOKING AFTER VAN, SO I'M AFRAID I HAD TO BRING...
OH, KAL! KAL, SHE'S...
WIDOW ZOR-EL PLEASE, COME THIS WAY. YOU CAN SEE YOUR DAUGHTER IN A MOMENT...
KARA?
SOMETHING'S HAPPENED TO KARA? WHAT'S GOING ON?
YOU'RE KAL-EL? THE GIRL'S COUSIN?
YES. BUT...
I'M AFRAID KARA ZOR-EL WAS ATTACKED EARLIER THIS EVENING BY SOME RIOTERS ARMED WITH SLASH-STICKS. SHE'S CRITICAL.
FATHER? FATHER, DID AUNT ALLURA HURT HERSELF? SHE WAS CRYING...
BUT ...BUT WHY?
THEY FOUND THIS.
IT WAS TIED AROUND HER NECK...
FATHER?
14

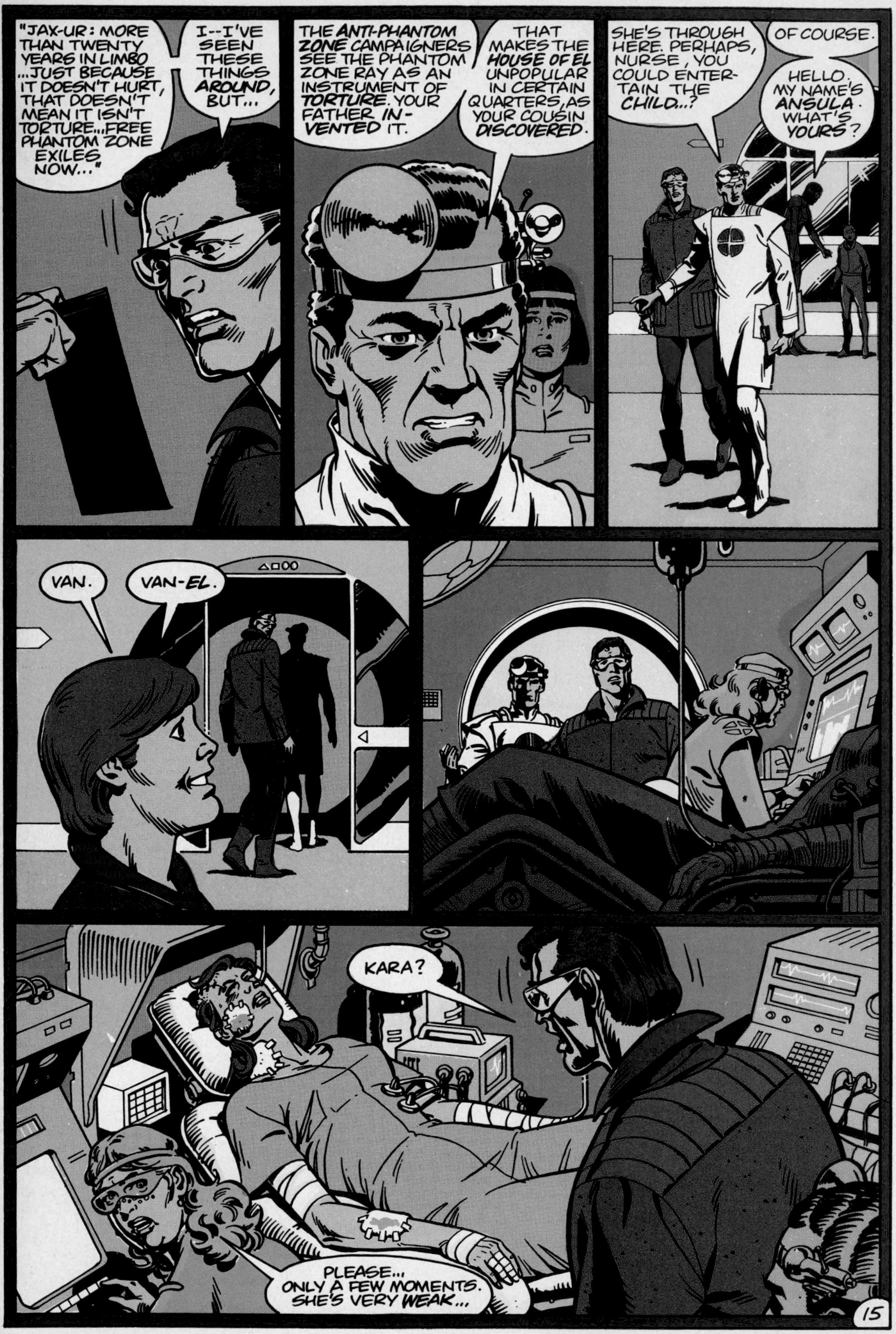
"JAX-UR: MORE THAN TWENTY YEARS IN LIMBO ...JUST BECAUSE IT DOESN'T HURT, THAT DOESN'T MEAN IT ISN'T TORTURE...FREE PHANTOM ZONE EXILES NOW..."
I--I'VE SEEN THESE THINGS AROUND, BUT...
THE ANTI-PHANTOM ZONE CAMPAIGNERS SEE THE PHANTOM ZONE RAY AS AN INSTRUMENT OF TORTURE. YOUR FATHER IN-VENTED IT.
THAT MAKES THE HOUSE OF EL UNPOPULAR IN CERTAIN QUARTERS, AS YOUR COUSIN DISCOVERED.
SHE'S THROUGH HERE. PERHAPS, NURSE, YOU COULD ENTER-TAIN THE CHILD...?
OF COURSE.
HELLO. MY NAME'S ANSULA. WHAT'S YOURS?
VAN.
VAN-EL.
KARA?
PLEASE... ONLY A FEW MOMENTS. SHE'S VERY WEAK...
15

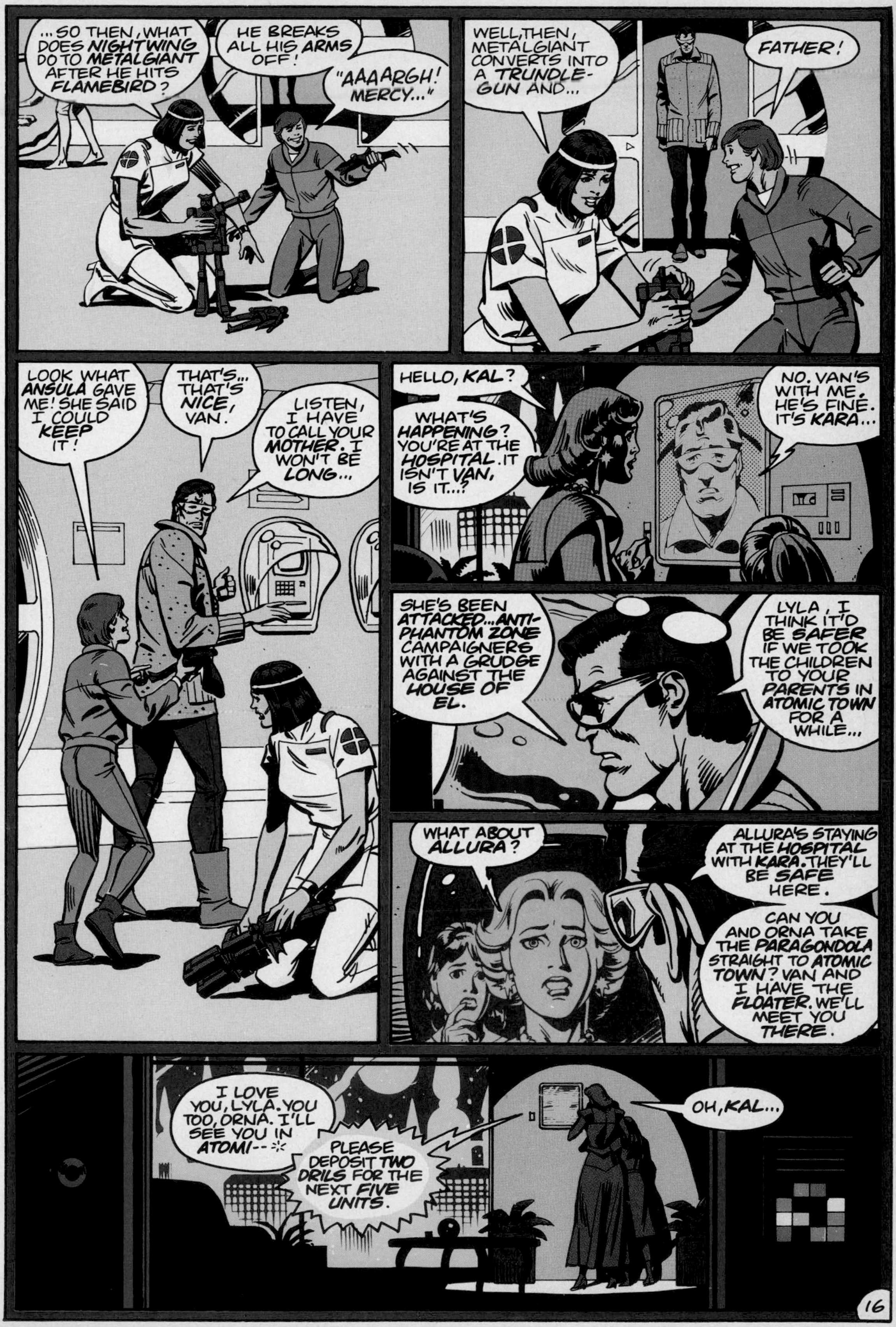
...SO THEN, WHAT DOES NIGHTWING DO TO METALGIANT AFTER HE HITS FLAMEBIRD?
HE BREAKS ALL HIS ARMS OFF!
"AAAARGH! MERCY..."
WELL, THEN, METALGIANT CONVERTS INTO A TRUNDLE-GUN AND...
FATHER!
LOOK WHAT ANSULA GAVE ME! SHE SAID I COULD KEEP IT!
THAT'S... THAT'S NICE, VAN.
LISTEN, I HAVE TO CALL YOUR MOTHER. I WON'T BE LONG...
HELLO, KAL?
WHAT'S HAPPENING? YOU'RE AT THE HOSPITAL. IT ISN'T VAN, IS IT...?
NO. VAN'S WITH ME. HE'S FINE. IT'S KARA...
SHE'S BEEN ATTACKED... ANTI-PHANTOM ZONE CAMPAIGNERS WITH A GRUDGE AGAINST THE HOUSE OF EL.
LYLA, I THINK IT'D BE SAFER IF WE TOOK THE CHILDREN TO YOUR PARENTS IN ATOMIC TOWN FOR A WHILE...
WHAT ABOUT ALLURA?
ALLURA'S STAYING AT THE HOSPITAL WITH KARA. THEY'LL BE SAFE HERE.
CAN YOU AND ORNA TAKE THE PARAGONDOLA STRAIGHT TO ATOMIC TOWN? VAN AND I HAVE THE FLOATER. WE'LL MEET YOU THERE.
I LOVE YOU, LYLA. YOU TOO, ORNA. I'LL SEE YOU IN ATOMI--
PLEASE DEPOSIT TWO DRILS FOR THE NEXT FIVE UNITS.
OH, KAL...
16

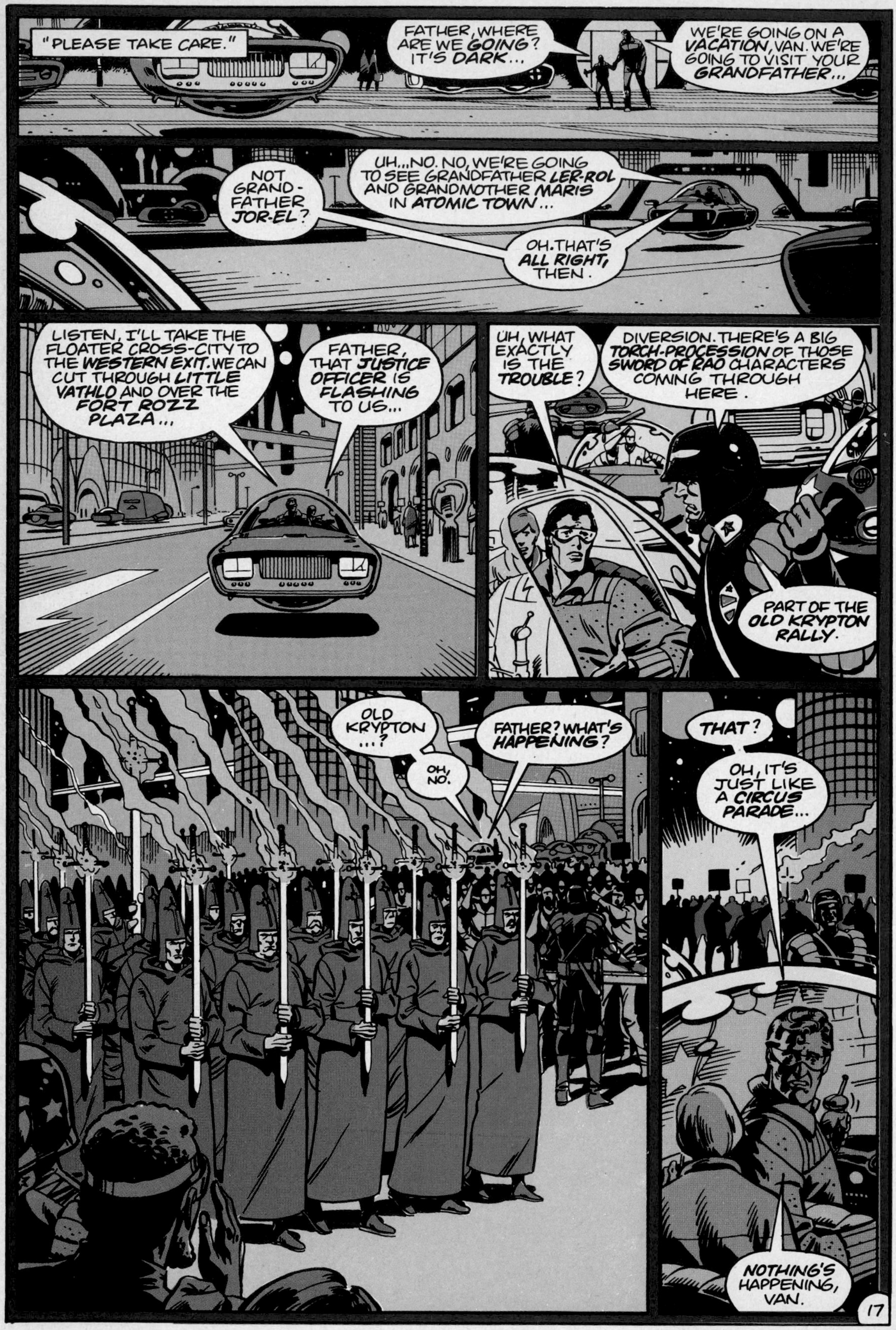
"PLEASE TAKE CARE."
FATHER, WHERE ARE WE GOING? IT'S DARK...
WE'RE GOING ON A VACATION, VAN. WE'RE GOING TO VISIT YOUR GRANDFATHER...
NOT GRAND-FATHER JOR-EL?
UH...NO. NO, WE'RE GOING TO SEE GRANDFATHER LER-ROL AND GRANDMOTHER MARIS IN ATOMIC TOWN...
OH. THAT'S ALL RIGHT, THEN.
LISTEN, I'LL TAKE THE FLOATER CROSS-CITY TO THE WESTERN EXIT. WE CAN CUT THROUGH LITTLE VATHLO AND OVER THE FORT ROZZ PLAZA...
FATHER, THAT JUSTICE OFFICER IS FLASHING TO US...
UH, WHAT EXACTLY IS THE TROUBLE?
DIVERSION. THERE'S A BIG TORCH-PROCESSION OF THOSE SWORD OF RAO CHARACTERS COMING THROUGH HERE.
PART OF THE OLD KRYPTON RALLY.
OLD KRYPTON...?
OH, NO.
FATHER? WHAT'S HAPPENING?
THAT?
OH, IT'S JUST LIKE A CIRCUS PARADE...
NOTHING'S HAPPENING, VAN.
17

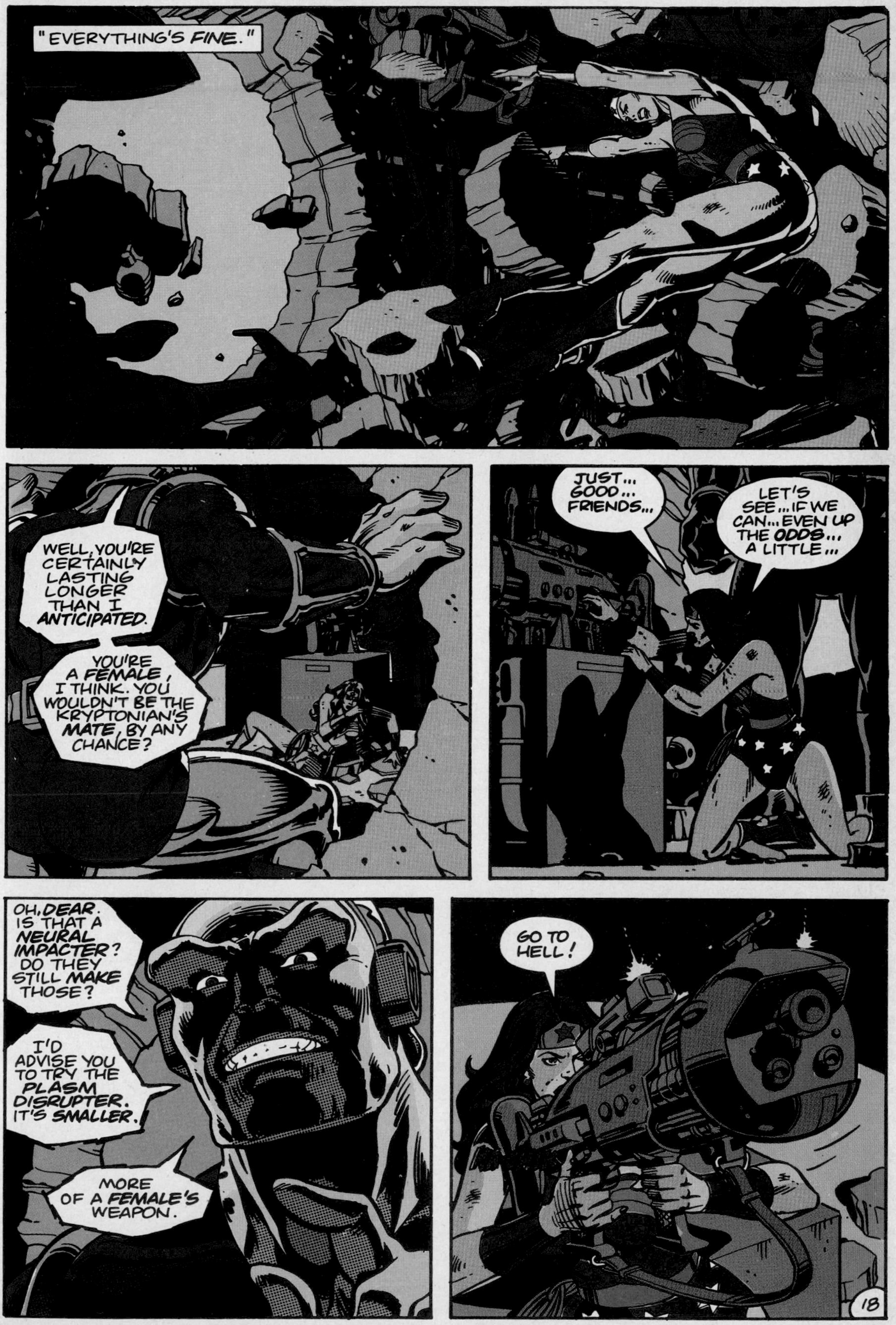
"EVERYTHING'S FINE."
WELL, YOU'RE CERTAINLY LASTING LONGER THAN I ANTICIPATED.
YOU'RE A FEMALE, I THINK. YOU WOULDN'T BE THE KRYPTONIAN'S MATE, BY ANY CHANCE?
JUST... GOOD... FRIENDS...
LET'S SEE... IF WE CAN... EVEN UP THE ODDS... A LITTLE...
OH, DEAR. IS THAT A NEURAL IMPACTER? DO THEY STILL MAKE THOSE?
I'D ADVISE YOU TO TRY THE PLASM DISRUPTER. IT'S SMALLER.
MORE OF A FEMALE'S WEAPON.
GO TO HELL!
18

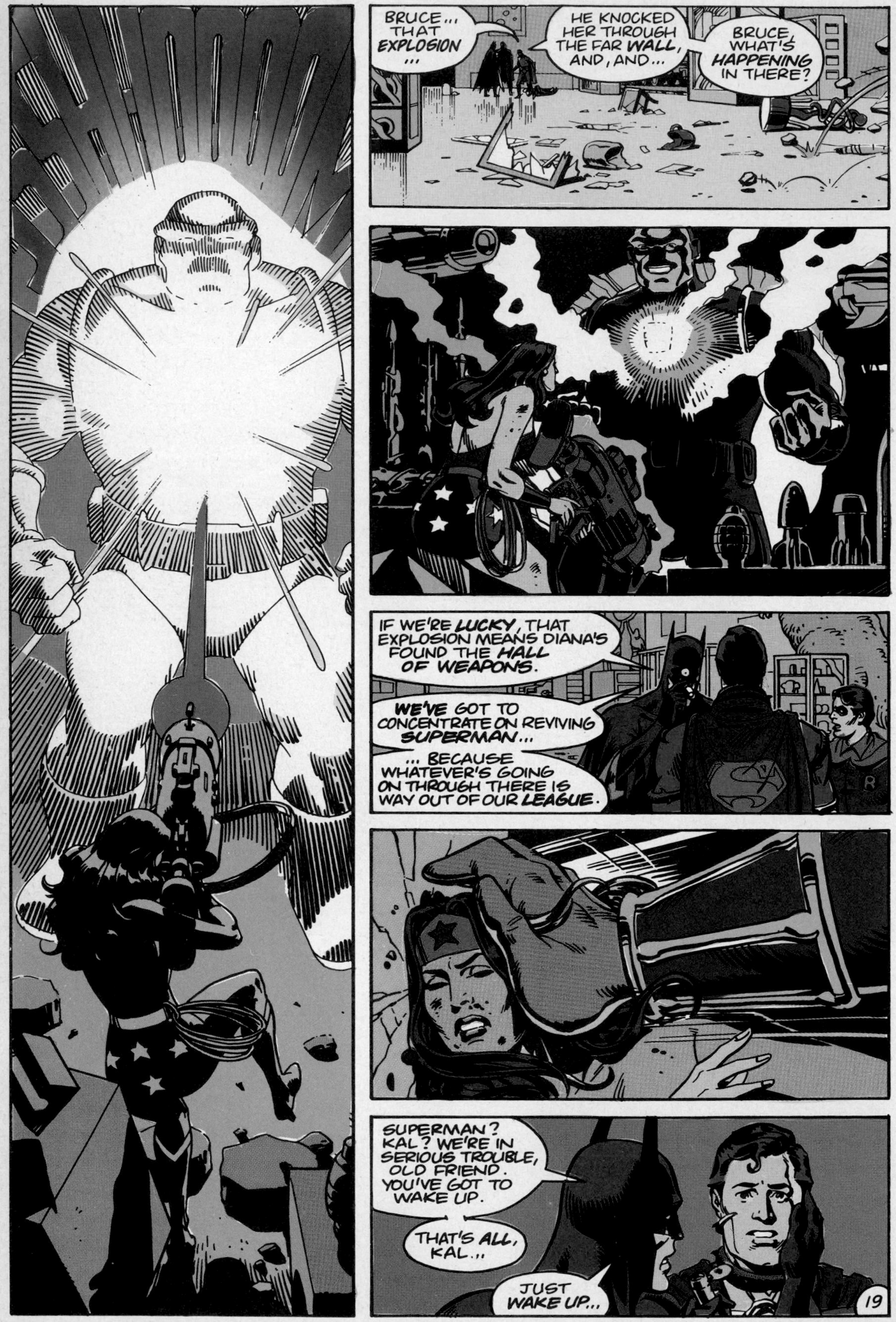
BRUCE... THAT EXPLOSION...
HE KNOCKED HER THROUGH THE FAR WALL, AND, AND...
BRUCE, WHAT'S HAPPENING IN THERE?
IF WE'RE LUCKY, THAT EXPLOSION MEANS DIANA'S FOUND THE HALL OF WEAPONS.
WE'VE GOT TO CONCENTRATE ON REVIVING SUPERMAN...
... BECAUSE WHATEVER'S GOING ON THROUGH THERE IS WAY OUT OF OUR LEAGUE.
SUPERMAN? KAL? WE'RE IN SERIOUS TROUBLE, OLD FRIEND. YOU'VE GOT TO WAKE UP.
THAT'S ALL, KAL...
JUST WAKE UP...
19

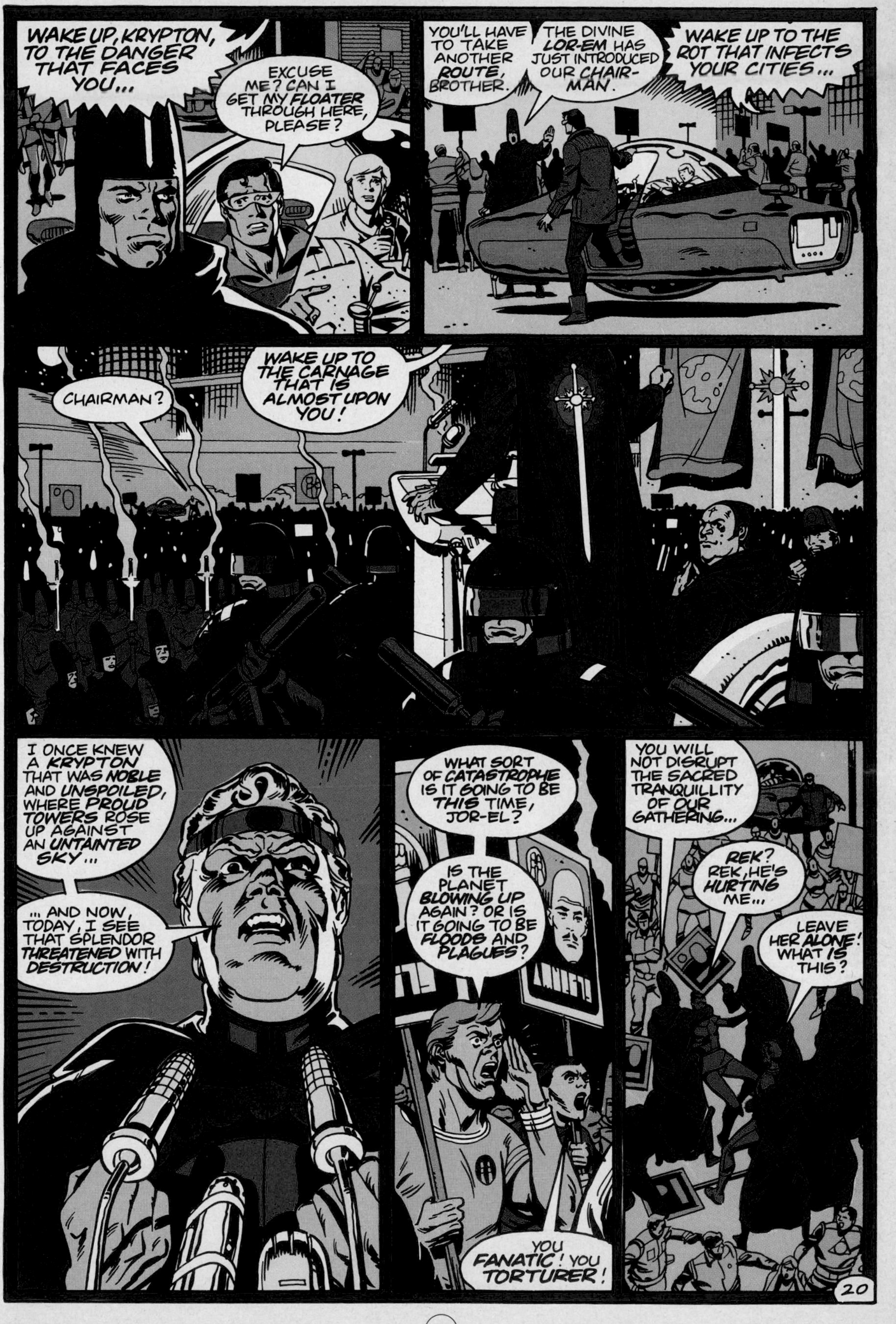

WAKE UP, KRYPTON, TO THE DANGER THAT FACES YOU...
EXCUSE ME? CAN I GET MY FLOATER THROUGH HERE, PLEASE?
YOU'LL HAVE TO TAKE ANOTHER ROUTE, BROTHER.
THE DIVINE LOR-EM HAS JUST INTRODUCED OUR CHAIRMAN.
WAKE UP TO THE ROT THAT INFECTS YOUR CITIES...
CHAIRMAN?
WAKE UP TO THE CARNAGE THAT IS ALMOST UPON YOU!
I ONCE KNEW A KRYPTON THAT WAS NOBLE AND UNSPOILED, WHERE PROUD TOWERS ROSE UP AGAINST AN UNTAINTED SKY...
... AND NOW, TODAY, I SEE THAT SPLENDOR THREATENED WITH DESTRUCTION!
WHAT SORT OF CATASTROPHE IS IT GOING TO BE THIS TIME, JOR-EL?
IS THE PLANET BLOWING UP AGAIN? OR IS IT GOING TO BE FLOODS AND PLAGUES?
YOU FANATIC! YOU TORTURER!
YOU WILL NOT DISRUPT THE SACRED TRANQUILLITY OF OUR GATHERING...
REK? REK, HE'S HURTING ME...
LEAVE HER ALONE! WHAT IS THIS?
20

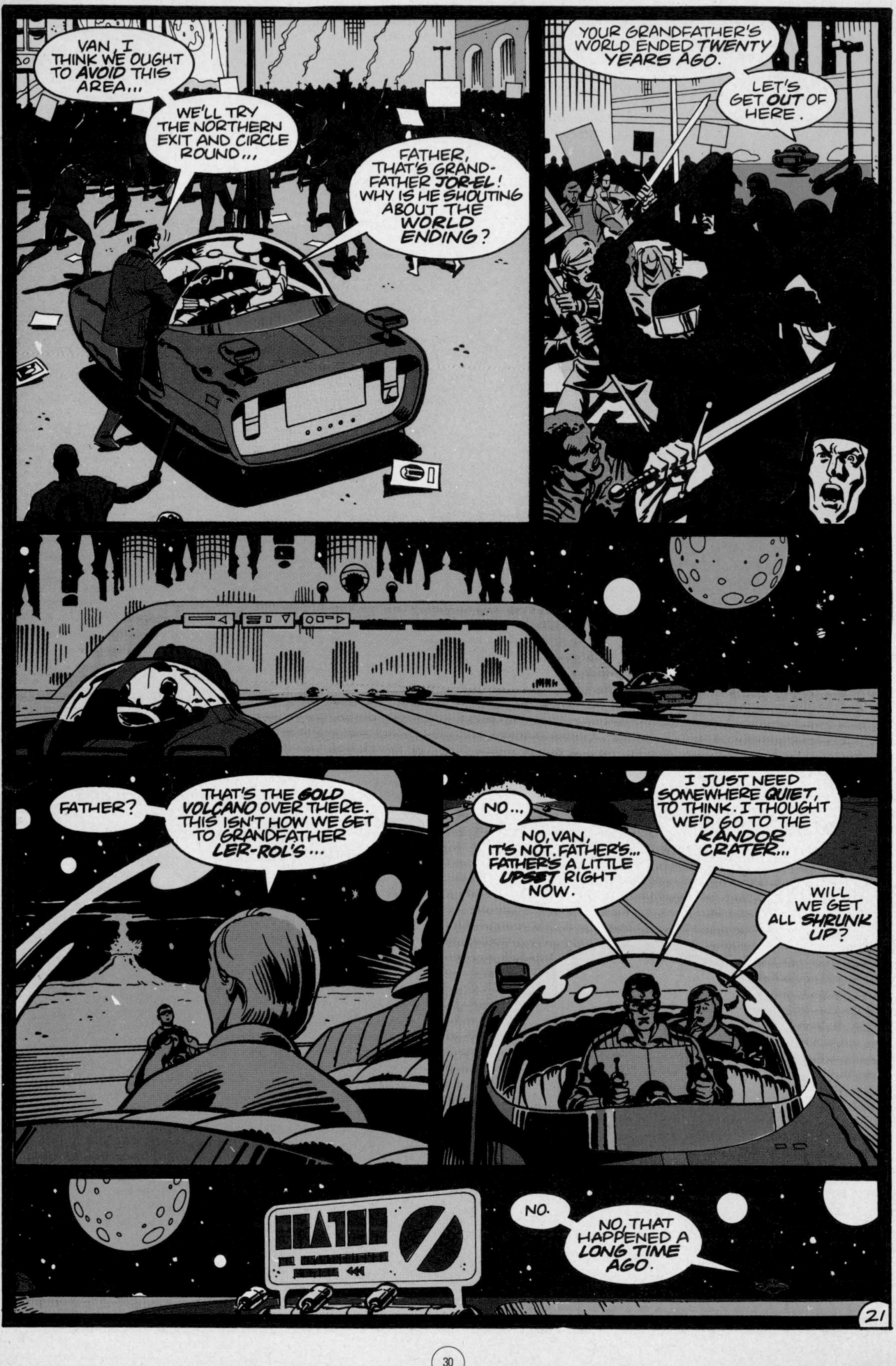
VAN, I THINK WE OUGHT TO AVOID THIS AREA...
WE'LL TRY THE NORTHERN EXIT AND CIRCLE ROUND...
FATHER, THAT'S GRAND-FATHER JOR-EL! WHY IS HE SHOUTING ABOUT THE WORLD ENDING?
YOUR GRANDFATHER'S WORLD ENDED TWENTY YEARS AGO.
LET'S GET OUT OF HERE.
FATHER?
THAT'S THE GOLD VOLCANO OVER THERE. THIS ISN'T HOW WE GET TO GRANDFATHER LER-ROL'S...
NO...
NO, VAN, IT'S NOT. FATHER'S... FATHER'S A LITTLE UPSET RIGHT NOW.
I JUST NEED SOMEWHERE QUIET, TO THINK. I THOUGHT WE'D GO TO THE KANDOR CRATER...
WILL WE GET ALL SHRUNK UP?
NO.
NO, THAT HAPPENED A LONG TIME AGO.
21

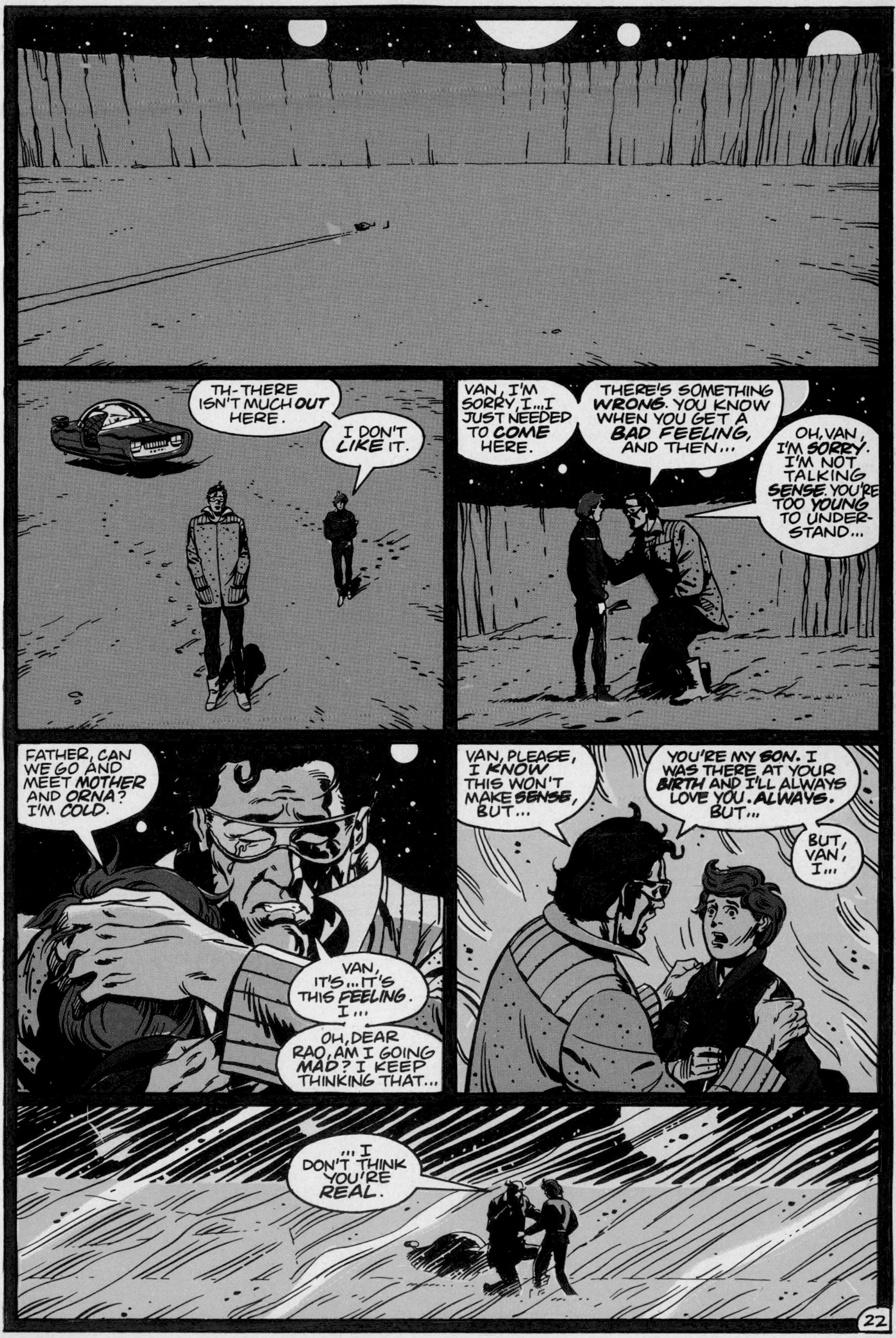
TH-THERE ISN'T MUCH OUT HERE.
I DON'T LIKE IT.
VAN, I'M SORRY, I...I JUST NEEDED TO COME HERE.
THERE'S SOMETHING WRONG. YOU KNOW WHEN YOU GET A BAD FEELING, AND THEN...
OH, VAN, I'M SORRY. I'M NOT TALKING SENSE. YOU'RE TOO YOUNG TO UNDERSTAND...
FATHER, CAN WE GO AND MEET MOTHER AND ORNA? I'M COLD.
VAN, IT'S...IT'S THIS FEELING. I...
OH, DEAR RAO, AM I GOING MAD? I KEEP THINKING THAT...
VAN, PLEASE, I KNOW THIS WON'T MAKE SENSE, BUT...
YOU'RE MY SON. I WAS THERE AT YOUR BIRTH AND I'LL ALWAYS LOVE YOU. ALWAYS. BUT...
BUT, VAN, I...
...I DON'T THINK YOU'RE REAL.
22

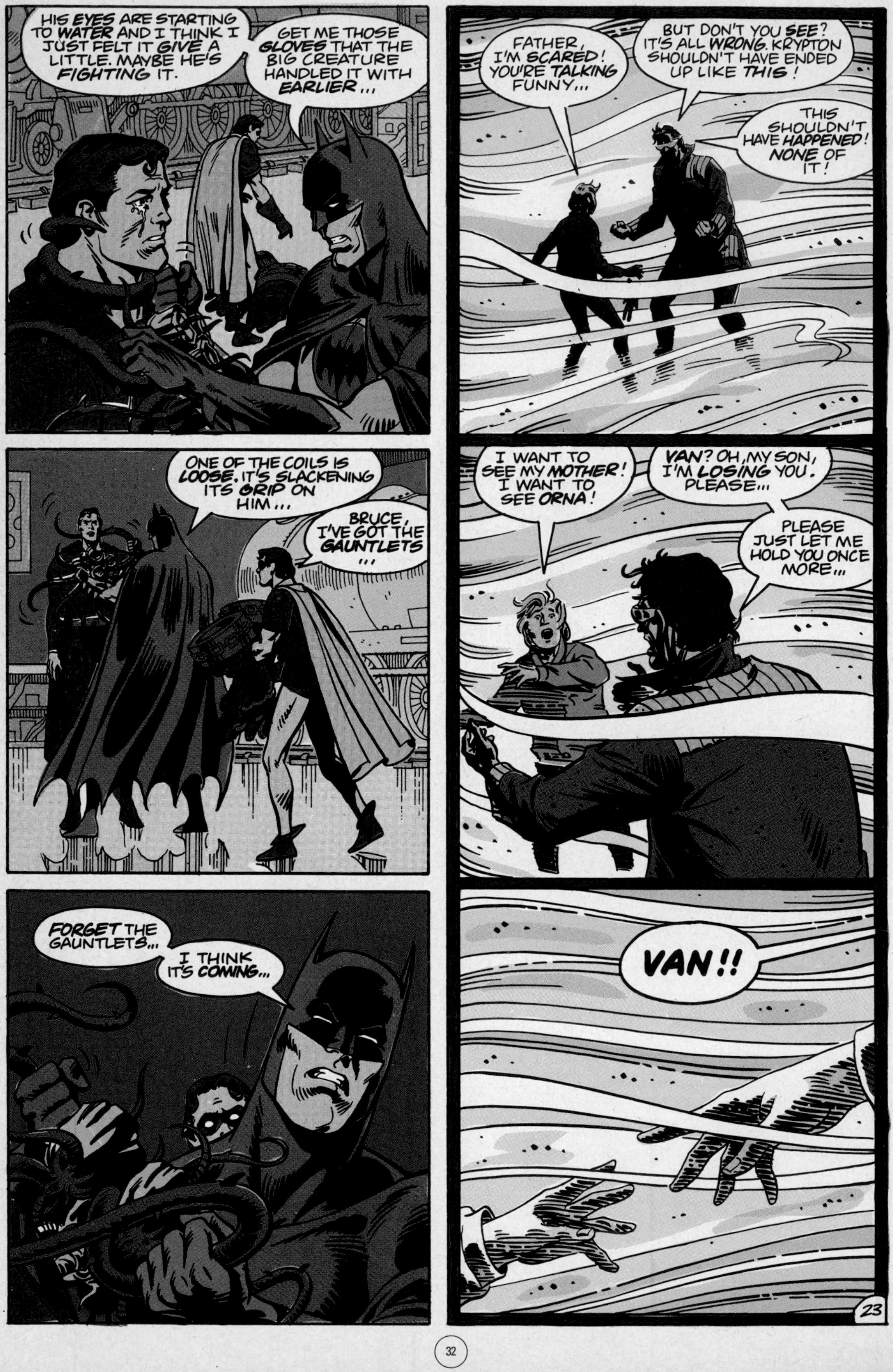
HIS EYES ARE STARTING TO WATER AND I THINK I JUST FELT IT GIVE A LITTLE. MAYBE HE'S FIGHTING IT.
GET ME THOSE GLOVES THAT THE BIG CREATURE HANDLED IT WITH EARLIER...
FATHER, I'M SCARED! YOU'RE TALKING FUNNY...
BUT DON'T YOU SEE? IT'S ALL WRONG. KRYPTON SHOULDN'T HAVE ENDED UP LIKE THIS!
THIS SHOULDN'T HAVE HAPPENED! NONE OF IT!
ONE OF THE COILS IS LOOSE. IT'S SLACKENING ITS GRIP ON HIM...
BRUCE, I'VE GOT THE GAUNTLETS...
I WANT TO SEE MY MOTHER! I WANT TO SEE ORNA!
VAN? OH, MY SON, I'M LOSING YOU. PLEASE...
PLEASE JUST LET ME HOLD YOU ONCE MORE...
FORGET THE GAUNTLETS...
I THINK IT'S COMING...
VAN!!
23

"...OFF?"

"BRUCE!"

"BRUCE, LOOK OUT! IT'S..."

THEY ARE IN THE DARK AND FAMILIAR STREETS OF OLD GOTHAM, WALKING HOME AFTER THE SHOW...

THERE IS THE SOUND OF HIS FATHER'S LAUGHTER, THE SMELL OF HIS MOTHER'S PERFUME...

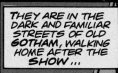

"OH, NO!"

"BRUCE? BRUCE, DON'T LET IT GET HOLD OF YOU..."

...AND THEN THE MAN WITH THE WEASEL FACE STEPS FROM THE SHADOWS, CARRYING AN UGLY-LOOKING GUN...

...AND HE FIRES...

"BRUCE?"

"...AND HE MISSES..."

...AND THOMAS WAYNE TAKES THE GUN AWAY FROM HIM WITH NO TROUBLE AT ALL.

24

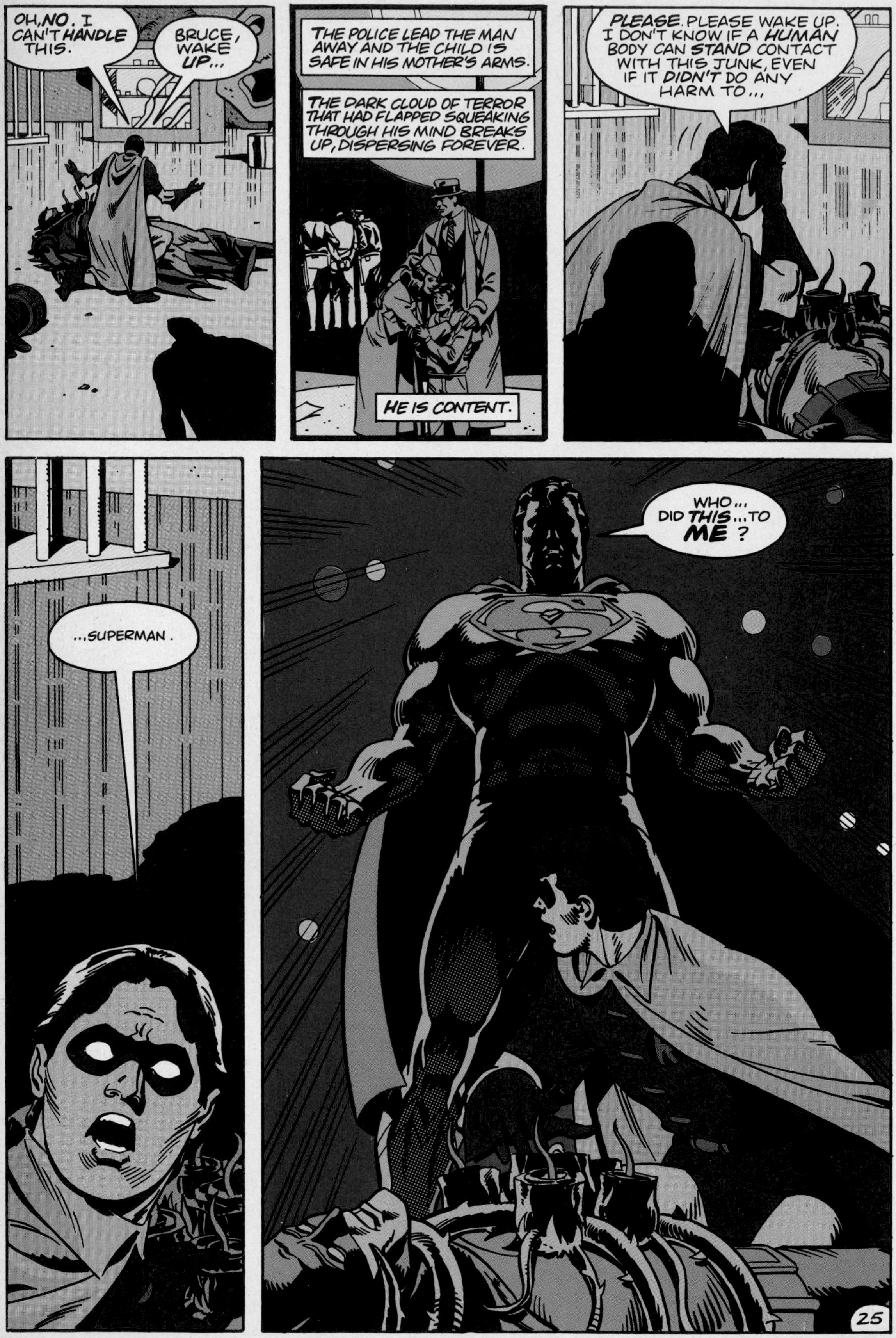
OH, NO. I CAN'T HANDLE THIS.
BRUCE, WAKE UP...
THE POLICE LEAD THE MAN AWAY AND THE CHILD IS SAFE IN HIS MOTHER'S ARMS.
THE DARK CLOUD OF TERROR THAT HAD FLAPPED SQUEAKING THROUGH HIS MIND BREAKS UP, DISPERSING FOREVER.
HE IS CONTENT.
PLEASE. PLEASE WAKE UP. I DON'T KNOW IF A HUMAN BODY CAN STAND CONTACT WITH THIS JUNK, EVEN IF IT DIDN'T DO ANY HARM TO...
...SUPERMAN.
WHO... DID THIS... TO ME?
25

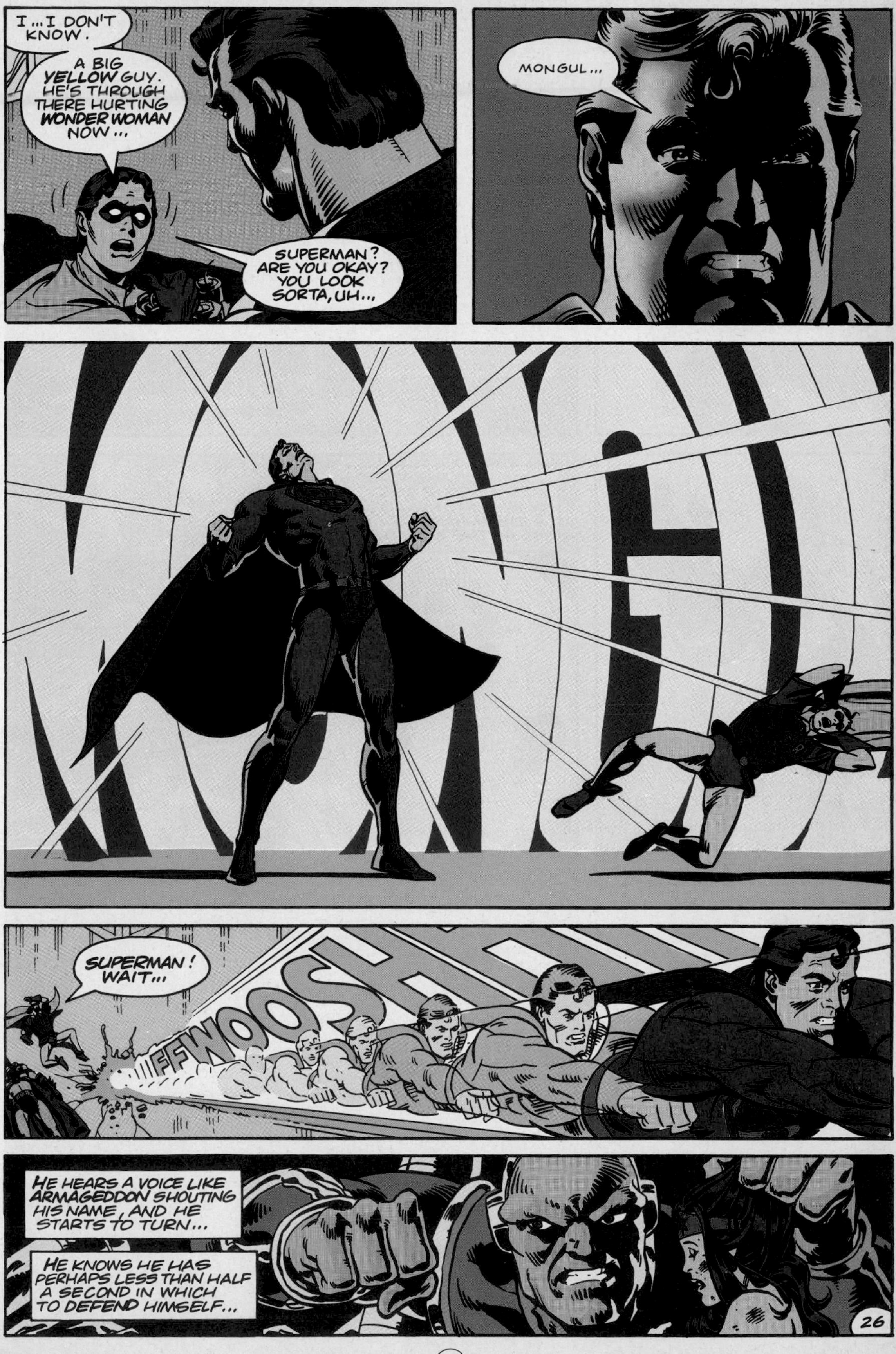
I... I DON'T KNOW.
A BIG YELLOW GUY. HE'S THROUGH THERE HURTING WONDER WOMAN NOW...
SUPERMAN? ARE YOU OKAY? YOU LOOK SORTA, UH...
MONGUL...
SUPERMAN! WAIT...
FFWOOSH
HE HEARS A VOICE LIKE ARMAGEDDON SHOUTING HIS NAME, AND HE STARTS TO TURN...
HE KNOWS HE HAS PERHAPS LESS THAN HALF A SECOND IN WHICH TO DEFEND HIMSELF...
26

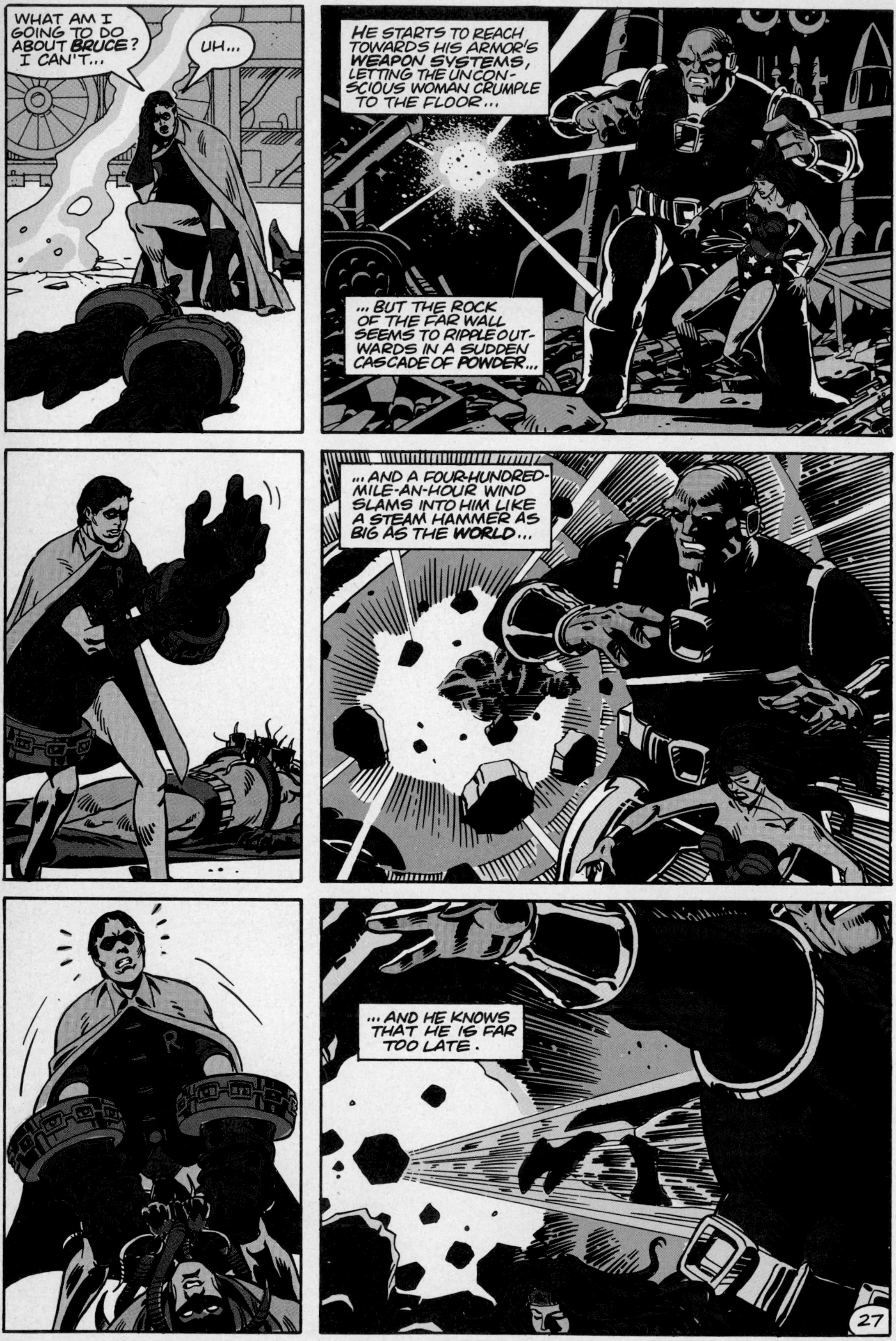
WHAT AM I GOING TO DO ABOUT BRUCE? I CAN'T...
UH...
HE STARTS TO REACH TOWARDS HIS ARMOR'S WEAPON SYSTEMS, LETTING THE UNCONSCIOUS WOMAN CRUMPLE TO THE FLOOR...
...BUT THE ROCK OF THE FAR WALL SEEMS TO RIPPLE OUTWARDS IN A SUDDEN CASCADE OF POWDER...
...AND A FOUR-HUNDRED-MILE-AN-HOUR WIND SLAMS INTO HIM LIKE A STEAM HAMMER AS BIG AS THE WORLD...
...AND HE KNOWS THAT HE IS FAR TOO LATE.
27

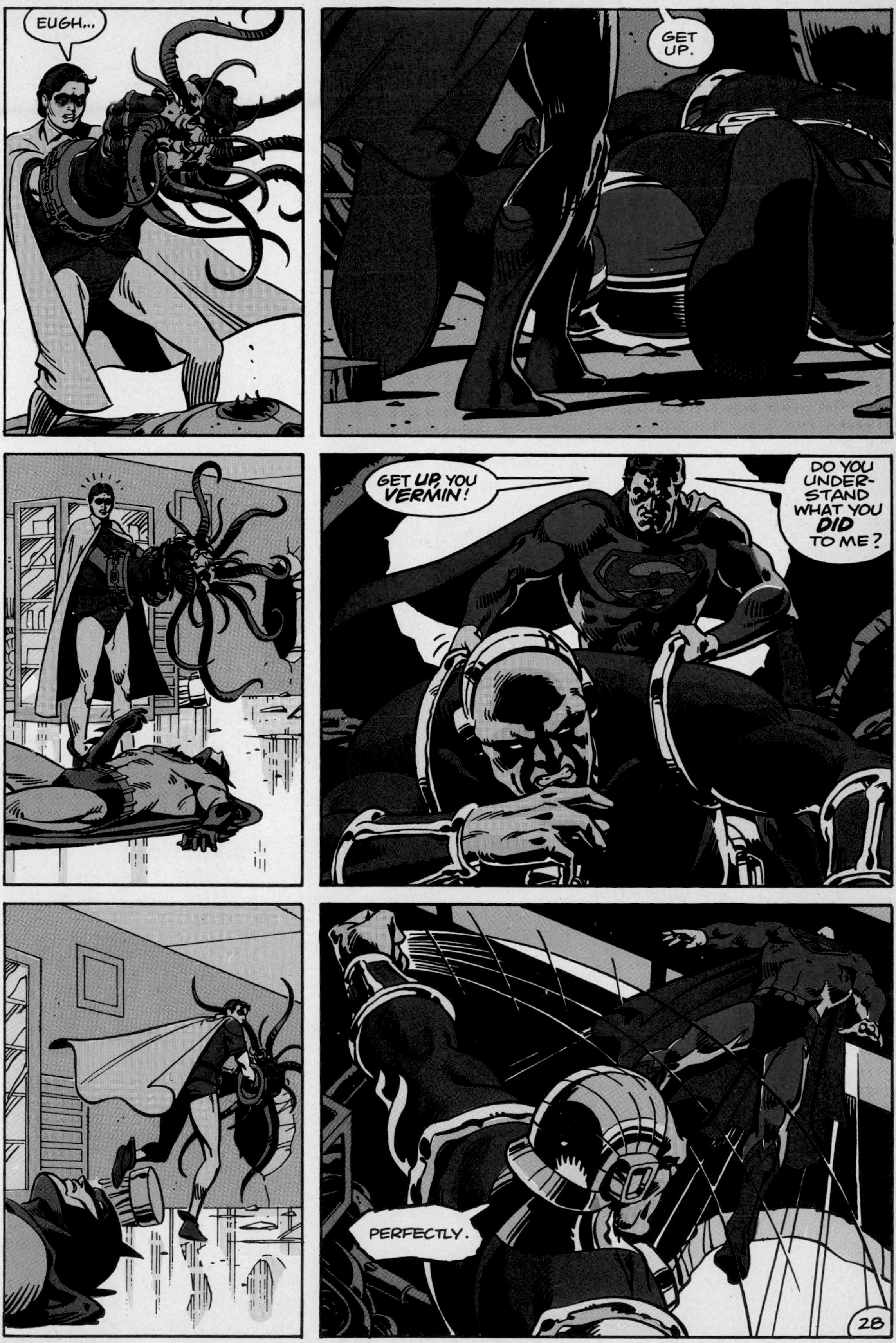
EUGH...
GET UP.
GET UP, YOU VERMIN!
DO YOU UNDERSTAND WHAT YOU DID TO ME?
PERFECTLY.
28

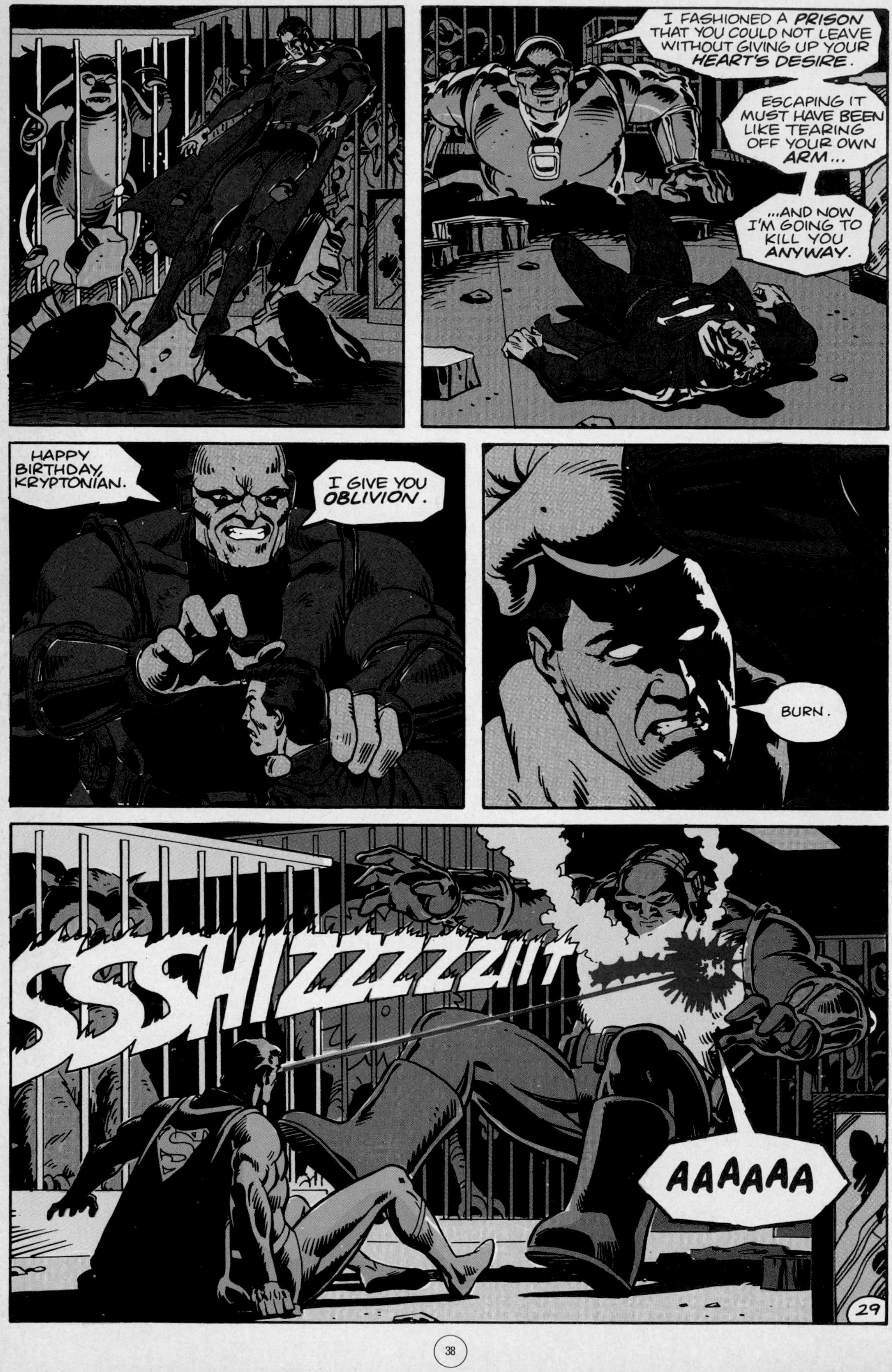
I FASHIONED A PRISON THAT YOU COULD NOT LEAVE WITHOUT GIVING UP YOUR HEART'S DESIRE.
ESCAPING IT MUST HAVE BEEN LIKE TEARING OFF YOUR OWN ARM...
...AND NOW I'M GOING TO KILL YOU ANYWAY.
HAPPY BIRTHDAY, KRYPTONIAN.
I GIVE YOU OBLIVION.
BURN.
SSHIZZZZZIIT
AAAAAA
29

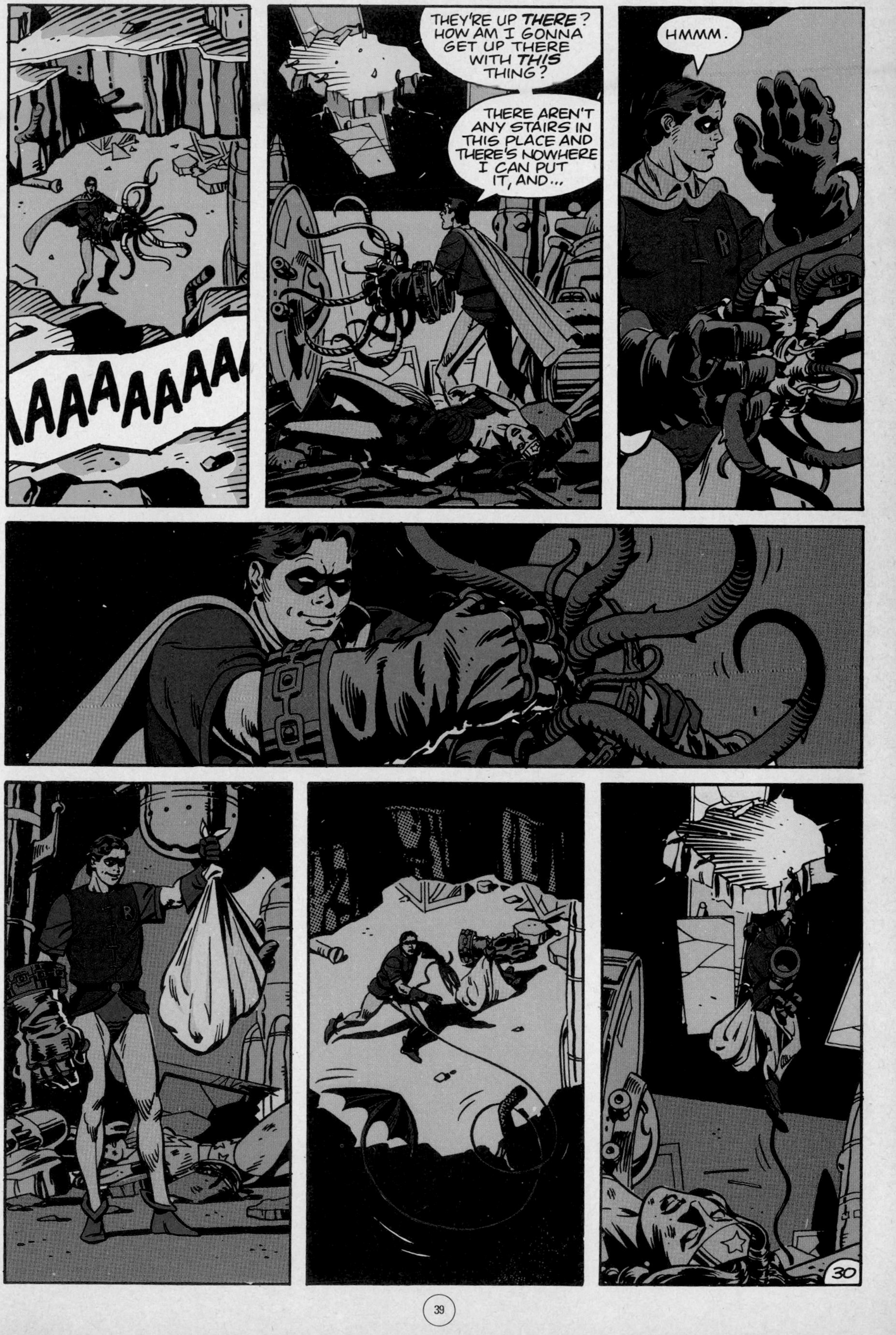
AAAAAAAAA
THEY'RE UP THERE? HOW AM I GONNA GET UP THERE WITH THIS THING?
THERE AREN'T ANY STAIRS IN THIS PLACE AND THERE'S NOWHERE I CAN PUT IT, AND...
HMMM.
30

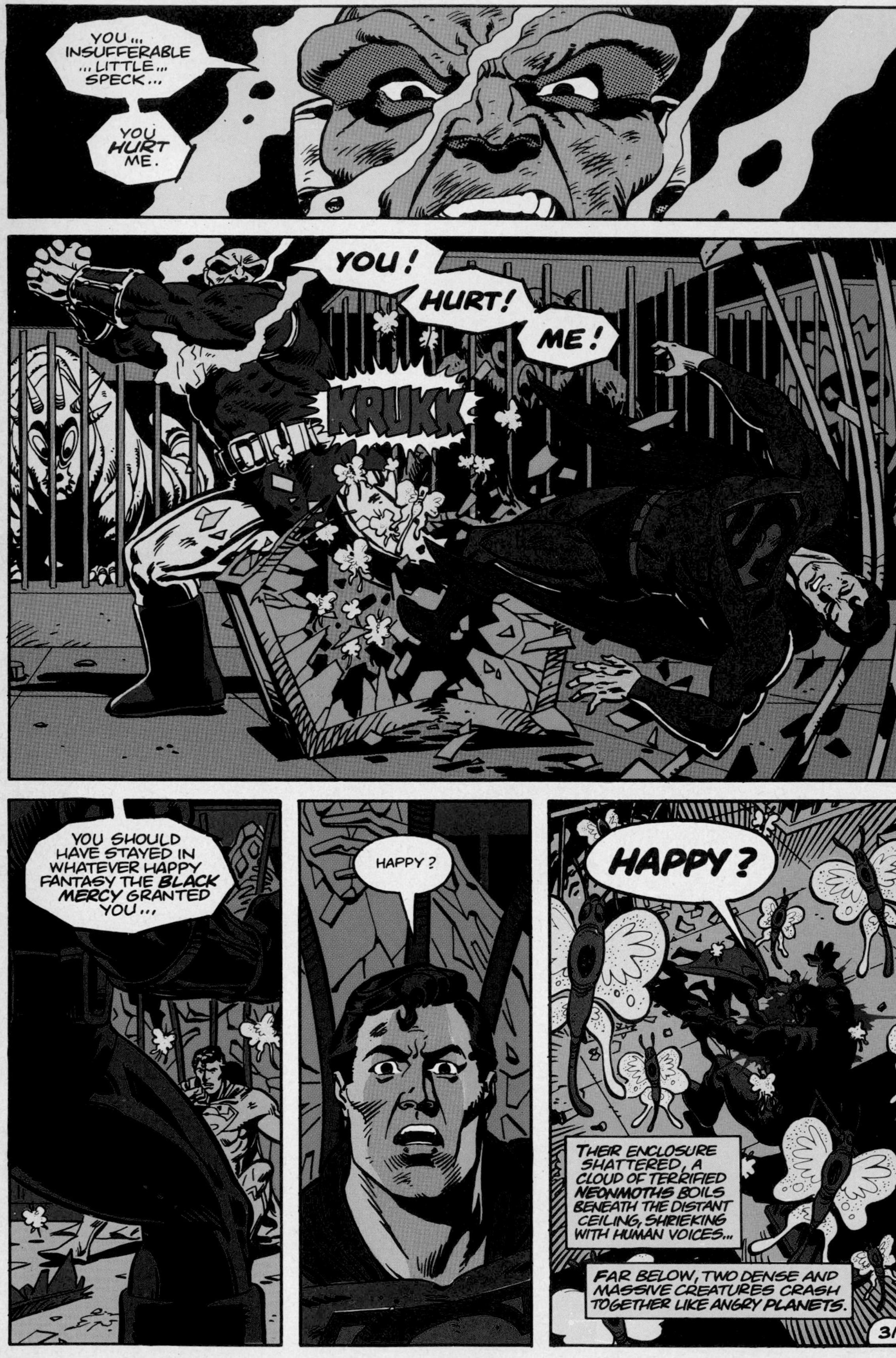
YOU... INSUFFERABLE ...LITTLE... SPECK...
YOU HURT ME.
YOU!
HURT!
ME!
KRUKK
YOU SHOULD HAVE STAYED IN WHATEVER HAPPY FANTASY THE BLACK MERCY GRANTED YOU...
HAPPY?
HAPPY?
THEIR ENCLOSURE SHATTERED, A CLOUD OF TERRIFIED NEONMOTHS BOILS BENEATH THE DISTANT CEILING, SHRIEKING WITH HUMAN VOICES...
FAR BELOW, TWO DENSE AND MASSIVE CREATURES CRASH TOGETHER LIKE ANGRY PLANETS.
31

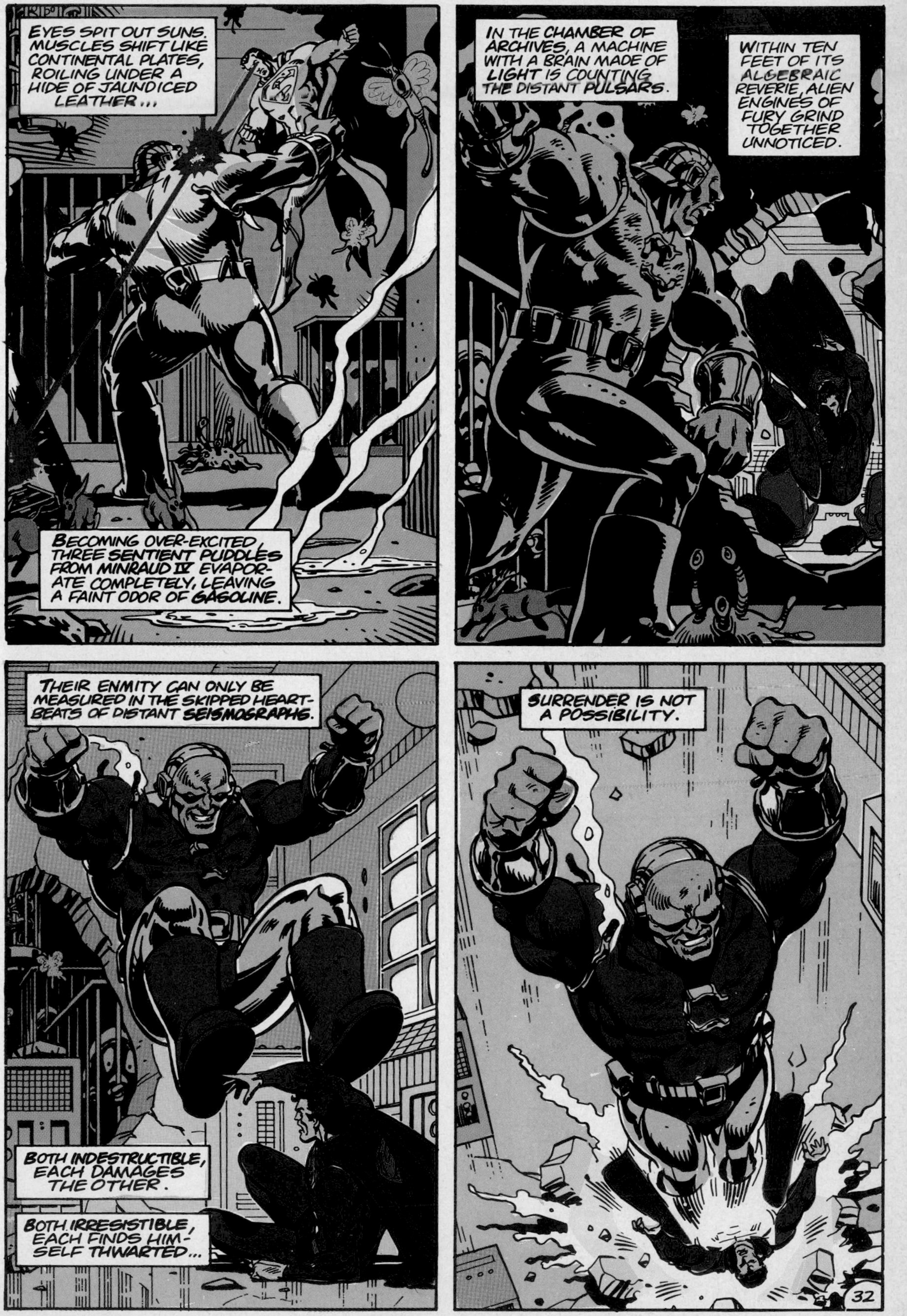
EYES SPIT OUT SUNS. MUSCLES SHIFT LIKE CONTINENTAL PLATES, ROILING UNDER A HIDE OF JAUNDICED LEATHER...
BECOMING OVER-EXCITED, THREE SENTIENT PUDDLES FROM MINRAUD IV EVAPORATE COMPLETELY, LEAVING A FAINT ODOR OF GASOLINE.
IN THE CHAMBER OF ARCHIVES, A MACHINE WITH A BRAIN MADE OF LIGHT IS COUNTING THE DISTANT PULSARS.
WITHIN TEN FEET OF ITS ALGEBRAIC REVERIE, ALIEN ENGINES OF FURY GRIND TOGETHER UNNOTICED.
THEIR ENMITY CAN ONLY BE MEASURED IN THE SKIPPED HEART-BEATS OF DISTANT SEISMOGRAPHS.
BOTH INDESTRUCTIBLE, EACH DAMAGES THE OTHER.
BOTH IRRESISTIBLE, EACH FINDS HIMSELF THWARTED...
SURRENDER IS NOT A POSSIBILITY.
32

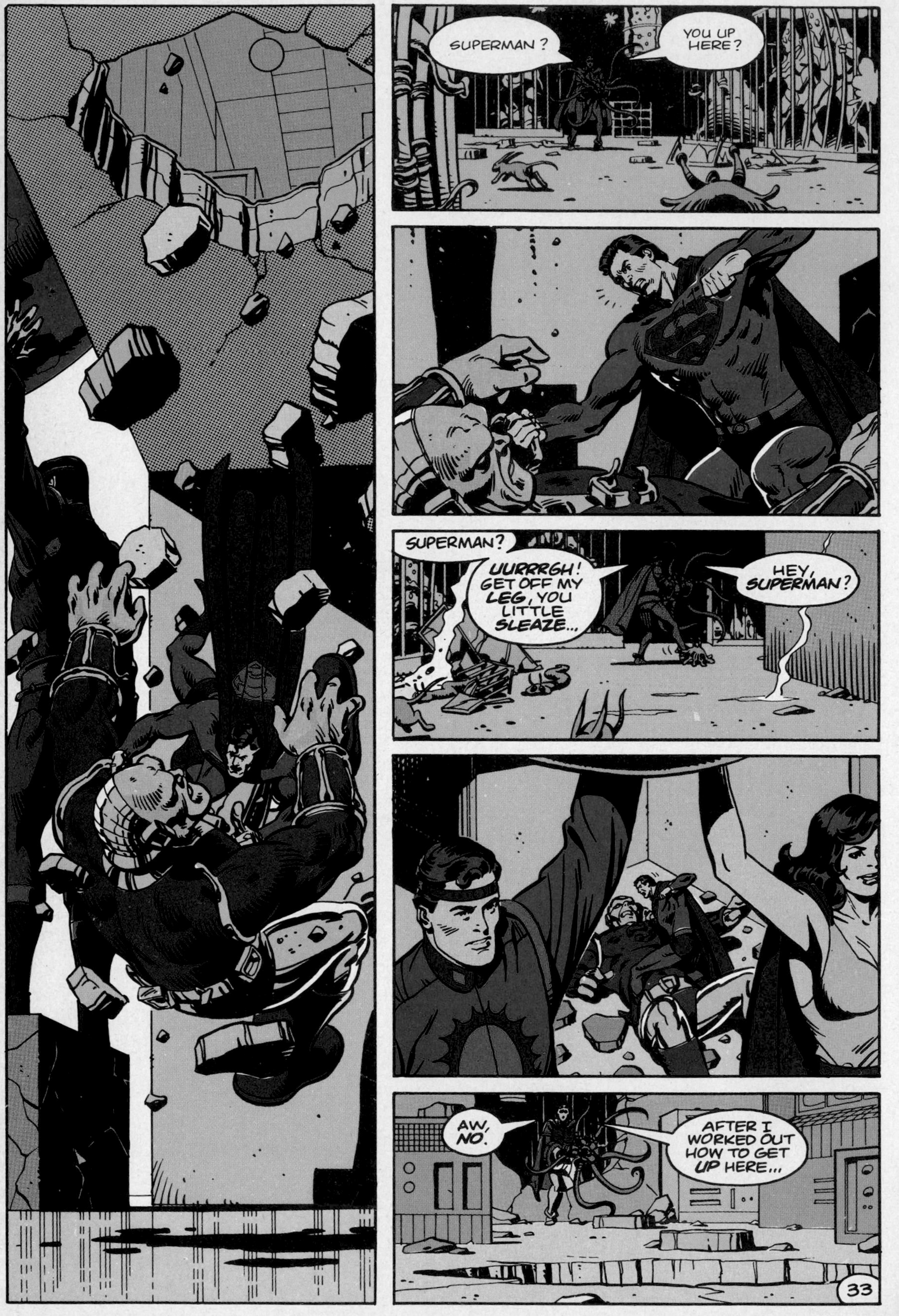
SUPERMAN ?
YOU UP HERE?
SUPERMAN?
UURRRGH! GET OFF MY LEG, YOU LITTLE SLEAZE...
HEY, SUPERMAN?
AW, NO.
AFTER I WORKED OUT HOW TO GET UP HERE...
33

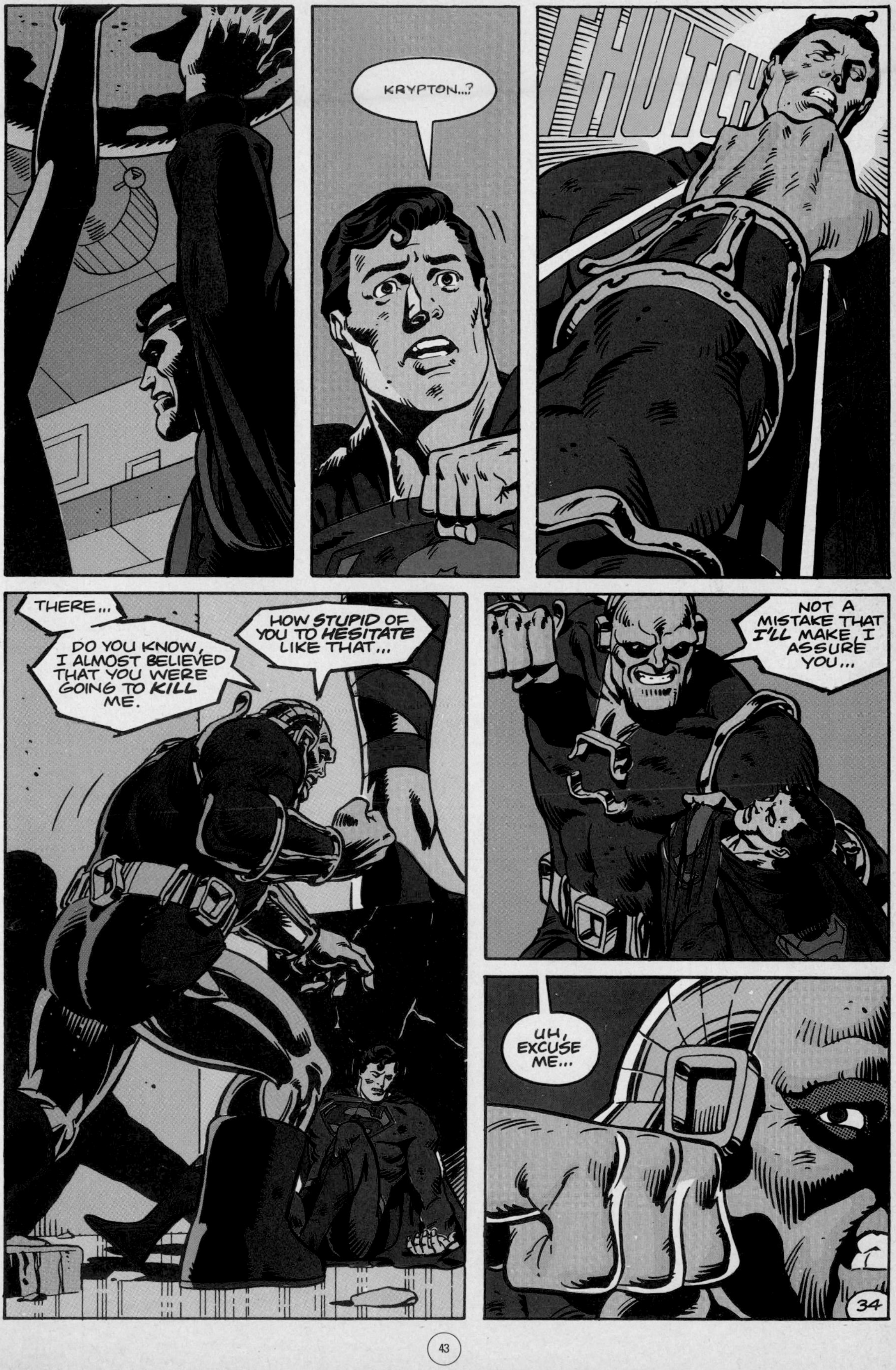
KRYPTON...?
THUTCH
THERE...
DO YOU KNOW, I ALMOST BELIEVED THAT YOU WERE GOING TO KILL ME.
HOW STUPID OF YOU TO HESITATE LIKE THAT...
NOT A MISTAKE THAT I'LL MAKE, I ASSURE YOU...
UH, EXCUSE ME...
34

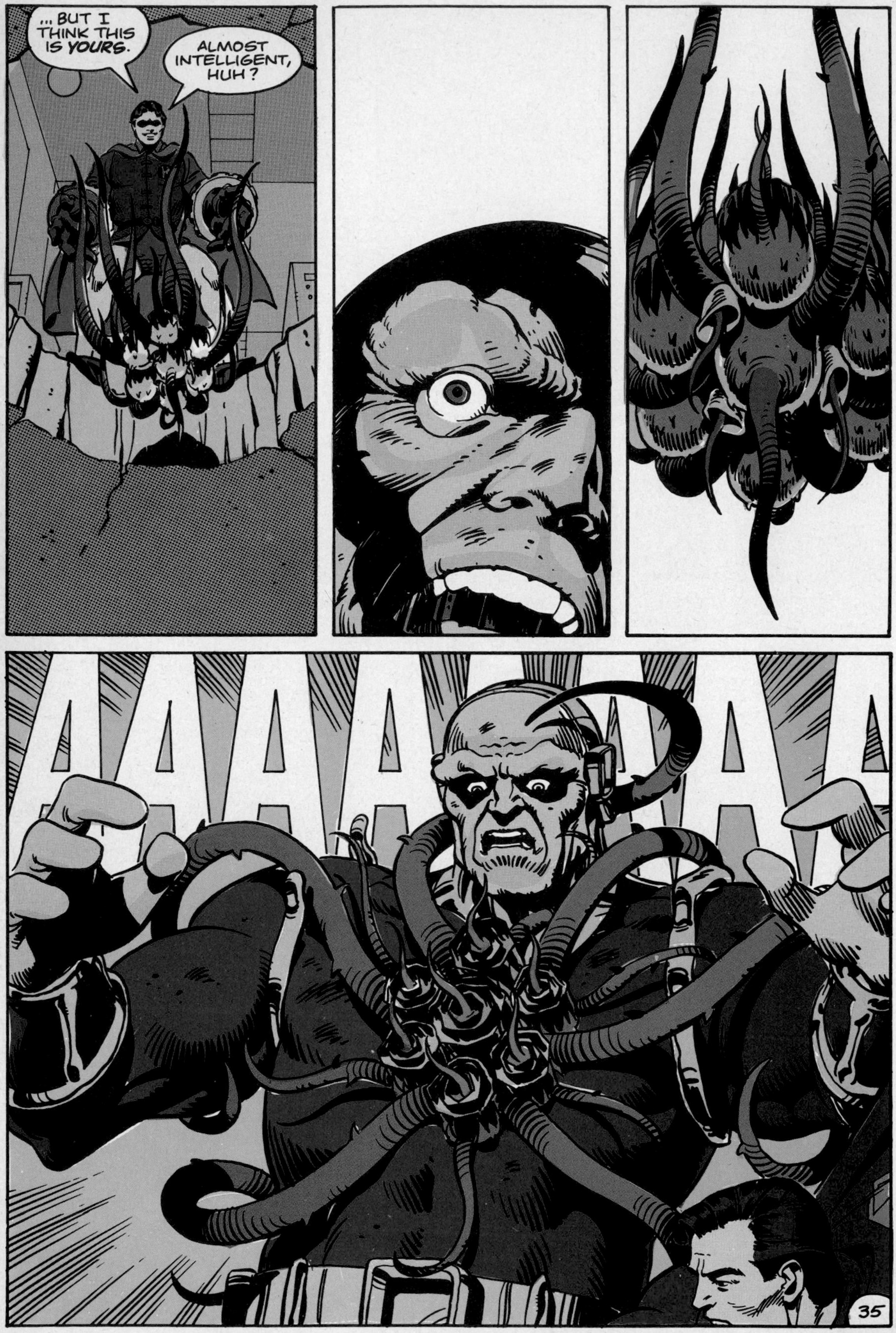
... BUT I THINK THIS IS YOURS.
ALMOST INTELLIGENT, HUH?
AAAAAAAAA
35

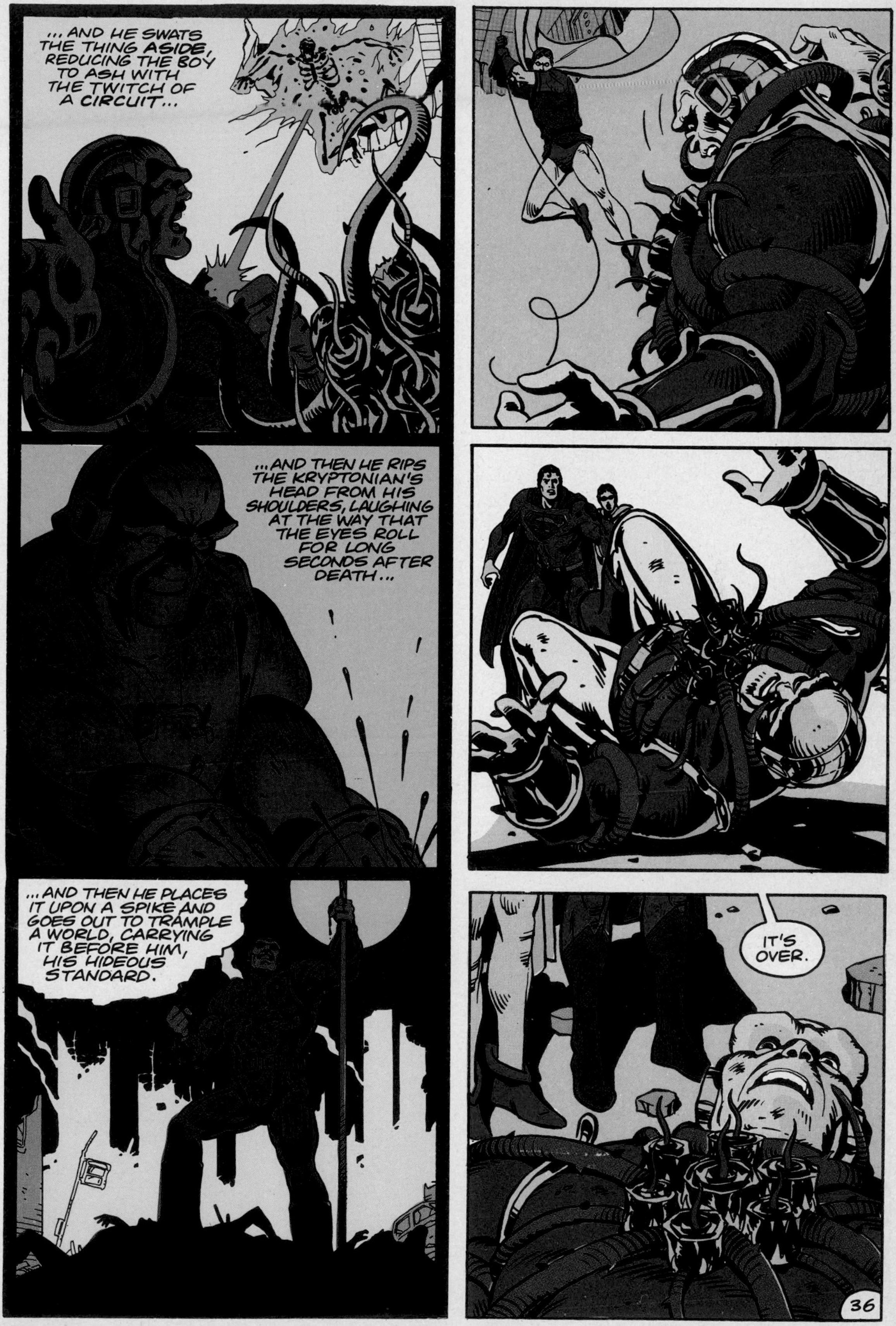
...AND HE SWATS THE THING ASIDE, REDUCING THE BOY TO ASH WITH THE TWITCH OF A CIRCUIT...
...AND THEN HE RIPS THE KRYPTONIAN'S HEAD FROM HIS SHOULDERS, LAUGHING AT THE WAY THAT THE EYES ROLL FOR LONG SECONDS AFTER DEATH...
...AND THEN HE PLACES IT UPON A SPIKE AND GOES OUT TO TRAMPLE A WORLD, CARRYING IT BEFORE HIM, HIS HIDEOUS STANDARD.
IT'S OVER.
36

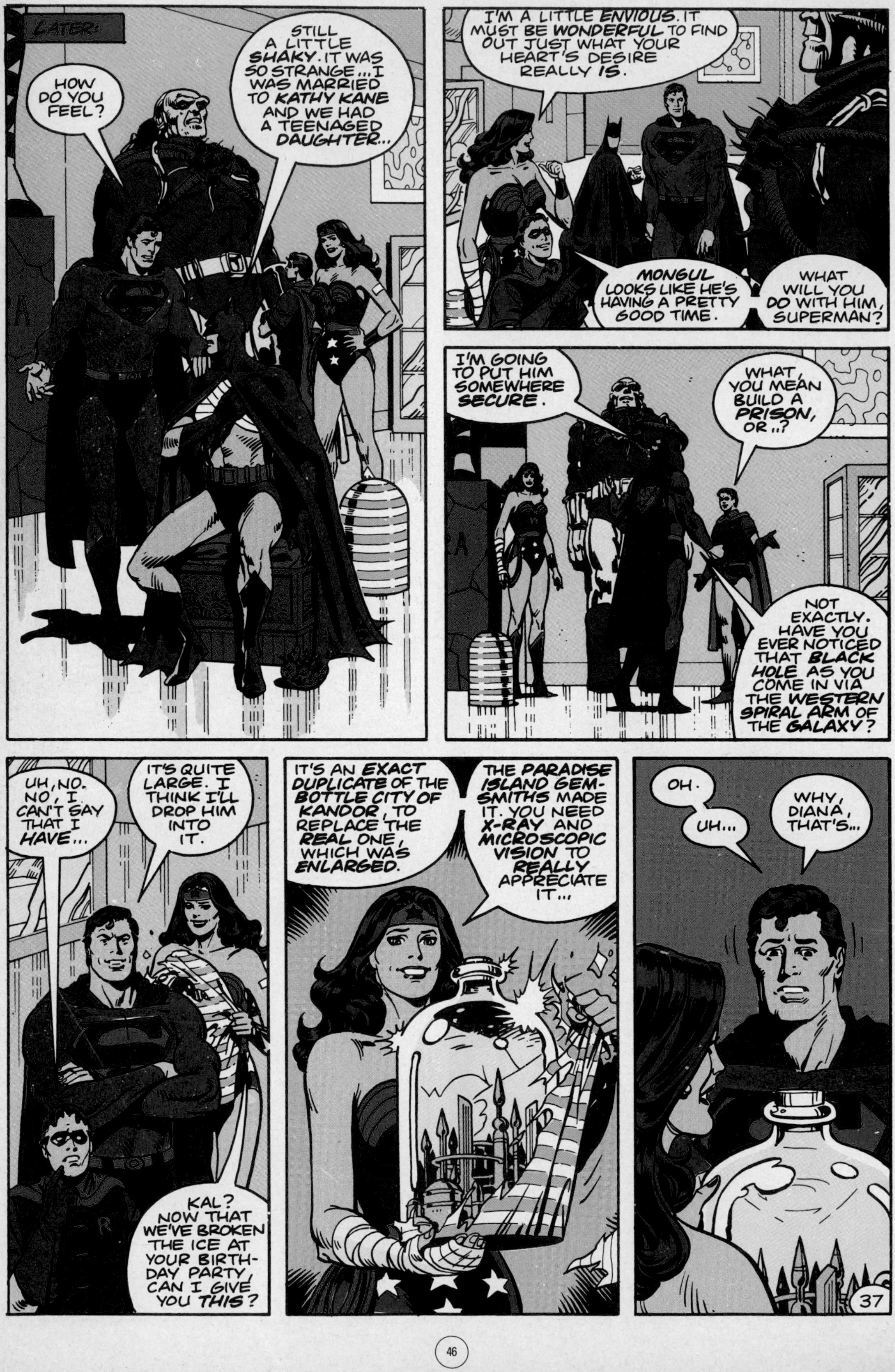
LATER:
HOW DO YOU FEEL?
STILL A LITTLE SHAKY. IT WAS SO STRANGE... I WAS MARRIED TO KATHY KANE AND WE HAD A TEENAGED DAUGHTER...
I'M A LITTLE ENVIOUS. IT MUST BE WONDERFUL TO FIND OUT JUST WHAT YOUR HEART'S DESIRE REALLY IS.
MONGUL LOOKS LIKE HE'S HAVING A PRETTY GOOD TIME.
WHAT WILL YOU DO WITH HIM, SUPERMAN?
I'M GOING TO PUT HIM SOMEWHERE SECURE.
WHAT, YOU MEAN BUILD A PRISON, OR..?
NOT EXACTLY. HAVE YOU EVER NOTICED THAT BLACK HOLE AS YOU COME IN VIA THE WESTERN SPIRAL ARM OF THE GALAXY?
UH, NO. NO, I CAN'T SAY THAT I HAVE...
IT'S QUITE LARGE. I THINK I'LL DROP HIM INTO IT.
KAL? NOW THAT WE'VE BROKEN THE ICE AT YOUR BIRTH-DAY PARTY, CAN I GIVE YOU THIS?
IT'S AN EXACT DUPLICATE OF THE BOTTLE CITY OF KANDOR, TO REPLACE THE REAL ONE, WHICH WAS ENLARGED.
THE PARADISE ISLAND GEM-SMITHS MADE IT. YOU NEED X-RAY AND MICROSCOPIC VISION TO REALLY APPRECIATE IT...
OH.
UH...
WHY, DIANA, THAT'S...
37

...JUST...

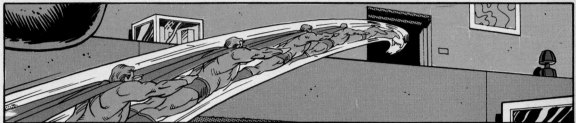

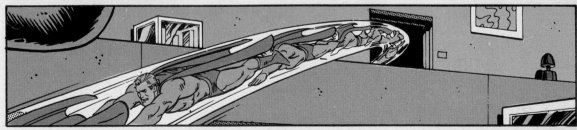

...JUST...

38

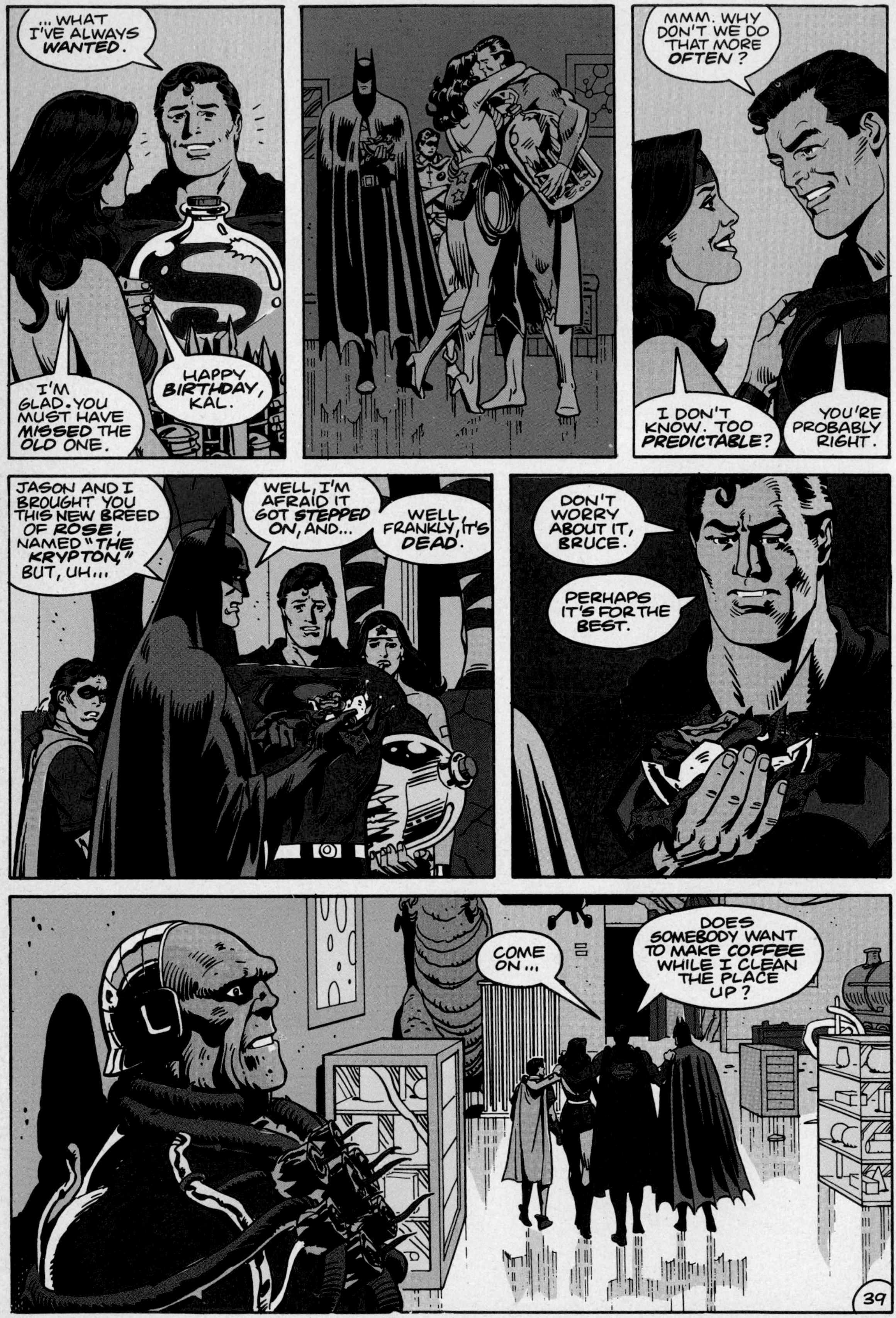

... WHAT I'VE ALWAYS WANTED.
I'M GLAD. YOU MUST HAVE MISSED THE OLD ONE.
HAPPY BIRTHDAY, KAL.
MMM. WHY DON'T WE DO THAT MORE OFTEN?
I DON'T KNOW. TOO PREDICTABLE?
YOU'RE PROBABLY RIGHT.
JASON AND I BROUGHT YOU THIS NEW BREED OF ROSE, NAMED "THE KRYPTON," BUT, UH...
WELL, I'M AFRAID IT GOT STEPPED ON, AND...
WELL, FRANKLY, IT'S DEAD.
DON'T WORRY ABOUT IT, BRUCE.
PERHAPS IT'S FOR THE BEST.
COME ON...
DOES SOMEBODY WANT TO MAKE COFFEE WHILE I CLEAN THE PLACE UP?
39

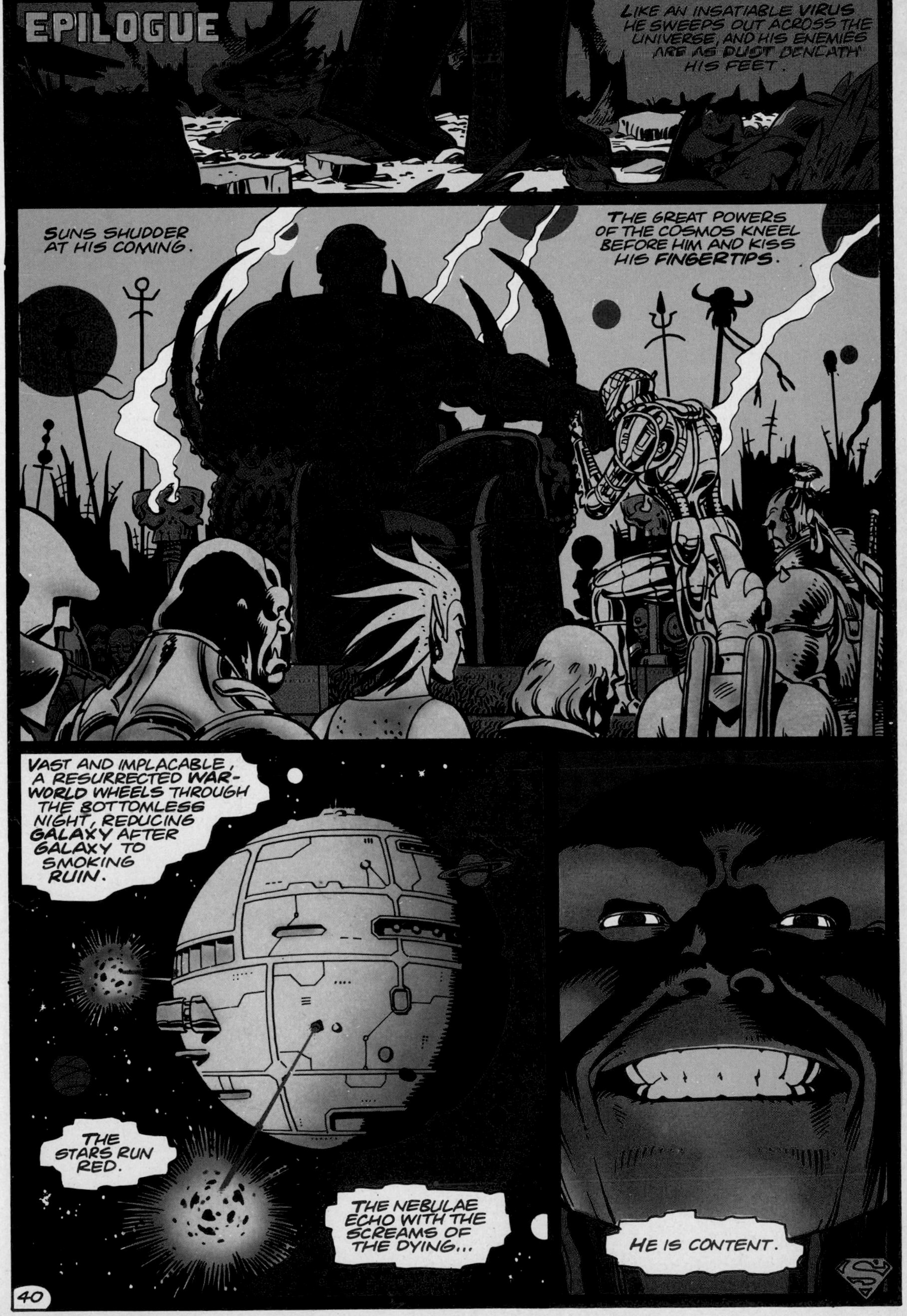
EPILOGUE
LIKE AN INSATIABLE VIRUS HE SWEEPS OUT ACROSS THE UNIVERSE, AND HIS ENEMIES ARE AS DUST BENEATH HIS FEET.
SUNS SHUDDER AT HIS COMING.
THE GREAT POWERS OF THE COSMOS KNEEL BEFORE HIM AND KISS HIS FINGERTIPS.
VAST AND IMPLACABLE, A RESURRECTED WARWORLD WHEELS THROUGH THE BOTTOMLESS NIGHT, REDUCING GALAXY AFTER GALAXY TO SMOKING RUIN.
THE STARS RUN RED.
THE NEBULAE ECHO WITH THE SCREAMS OF THE DYING...
HE IS CONTENT.
40

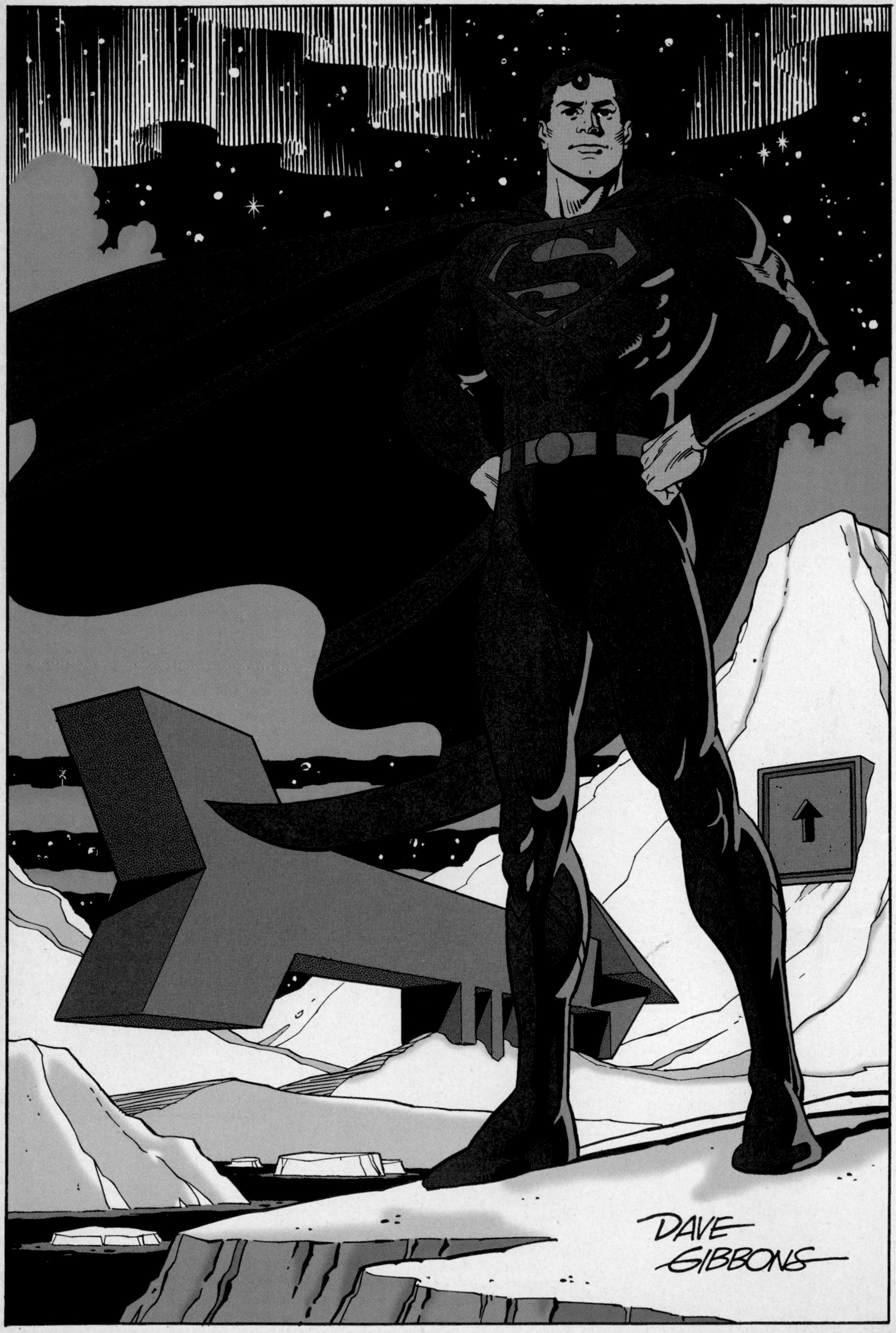
DAVE
GIBBONS

Almost immediately following SWAMP THING, Alan Moore was in demand. High demand, actually. As editors clamored for his time, Alan was being given many tempting offers, including just about every character DC was currently publishing. Len Wein, the editor who initially brought Alan's work to DC, found out he was in a bit of a jam on his Green Arrow feature. The seven-page backup in DETECTIVE COMICS was an opportunity to keep the character in the public eye until his popularity merited a mini-series or more.

At the time, it had been written by Joey Cavalieri, but the artists he had been paired with had proven slow or had taken on too much work and as a result, Wein found he needed a fill-in. In conversation with Moore, Wein inquired about a possible Green Arrow story. Moore mused on it some since, after all, he cut his teeth working in short incremental stories for Britain's *2000 A.D.* magazine. He came up with the notion that became "Night Olympics," but wanted to know who the artist would be since he preferred writing to the artist's strengths.

Klaus Janson was predominantly known as an inker back in the 1980s, but was seeking ways to get some practical experience as a penciller. Much of his schedule had been cleared so he would be able to ink Frank Miller on *The Dark Knight Returns* but there were gaps of time while he was awaiting pages. Wein saw Klaus in the hall and they got to talking and the next thing Janson knew, he was assigned to work with Alan Moore.

"I was in awe of his talent," Janson recalls. "The idea of working with him as a storyteller was not something that had occurred to me, but I was game if he was." Then the scripts arrived, filled with Moore's typical depth of description, rambling commentary and other details. Janson was stunned. "It was only two seven-page stories and felt like a phone book," he says with a laugh. Still, the detailed

script gave the artist everything he needed to know — and more — about the story.

"I was very comfortable with pencilling and inking something short but still hadn't gained that much confidence. Moore's script proved an excellent tutorial in pacing and scene-setting. Knowing my work, he kept things on rooftops and in the dark, letting me play with light and shadow. It was both daunting and exhilarating."

At the time, Janson was committed to photographing almost everything he drew. "The subway scenes were shot at 14th Street and 7th Avenue here in Manhattan," he reveals. "A lot of the rooftops were photos taken from the building I lived in at the time. Most of the figure work, which gave me a lot of trouble at that point, was a combination of friends posing for photos and swipes from the Neal Adams/Dick Giordano run on GREEN LANTERN/GREEN ARROW.

"Sometime after the story came out I found myself at dinner with Jenette Kahn, Frank Miller and Alan Moore in San Diego. It turned out to be the only time I ever got to spend with Alan and I remember him as being very *intense*. I think he vibrated at a different wavelength than the rest of us. He was quite humble for someone with as much skill and talent as he obviously has, and he acknowledged the work I put into the Green Arrow story. The most interesting part of that dinner was when we got into a 'can you top this' plotting session for Superman (I think a revamp was on the horizon). I couldn't keep up with Alan and Frank and sat back to watch what was probably the best show of the convention. Alan and Frank threw down their story ideas like poker players slapping their cards on the table, each one besting the last. I think it was Alan who got the final one in when he looked at all of us and said, 'Superman in Hell.'

"Now that was a good meal!"

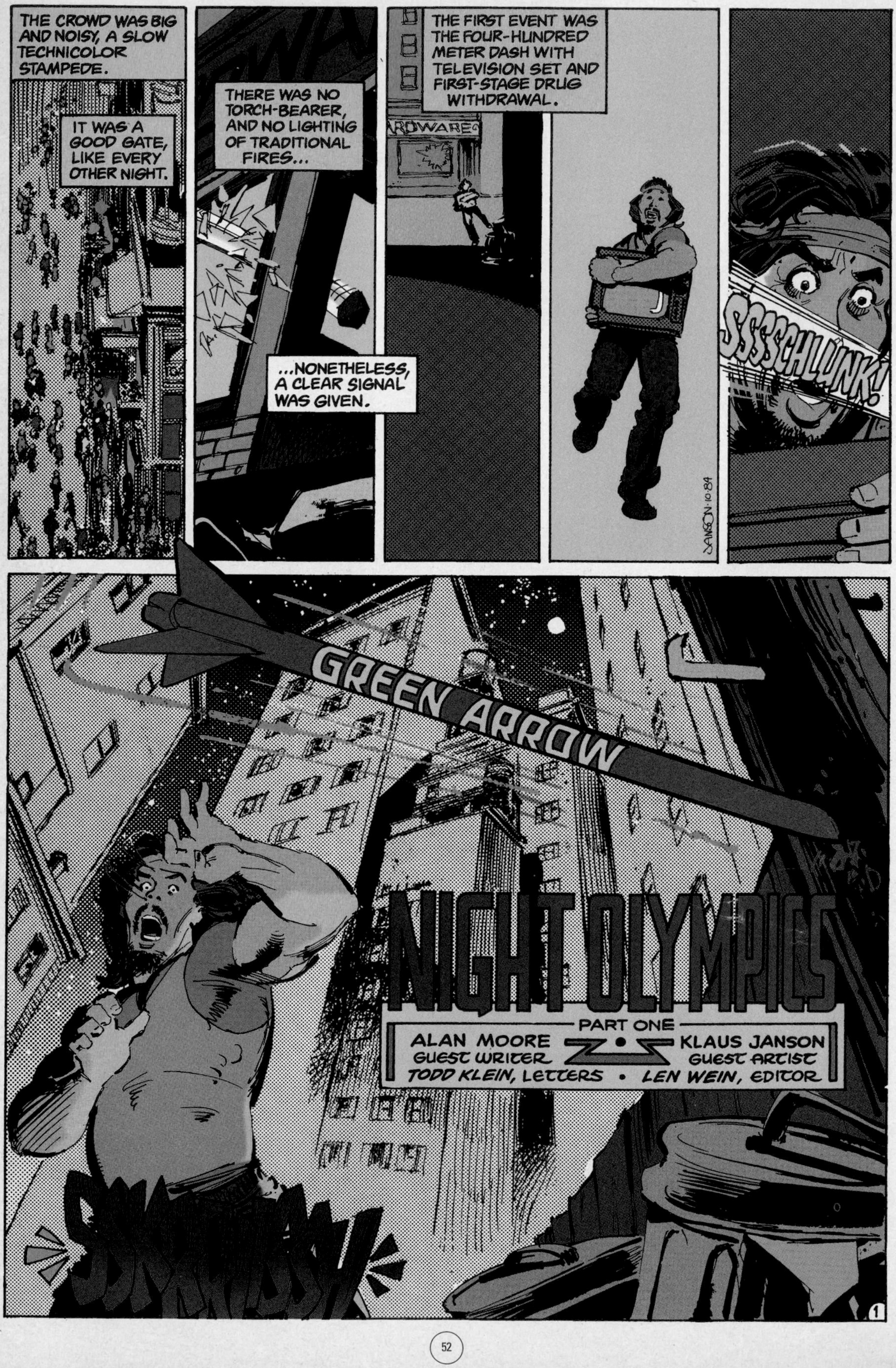
THE CROWD WAS BIG AND NOISY, A SLOW TECHNICOLOR STAMPEDE.
IT WAS A GOOD GATE, LIKE EVERY OTHER NIGHT.
THERE WAS NO TORCH-BEARER, AND NO LIGHTING OF TRADITIONAL FIRES...
...NONETHELESS, A CLEAR SIGNAL WAS GIVEN.
THE FIRST EVENT WAS THE FOUR-HUNDRED METER DASH WITH TELEVISION SET AND FIRST-STAGE DRUG WITHDRAWAL.
ARDWARE
JANSON 10.84
SSSSCHLUNK!
GREEN ARROW
NIGHT OLYMPICS
PART ONE
ALAN MOORE GUEST WRITER
KLAUS JANSON GUEST ARTIST
TODD KLEIN, LETTERS • LEN WEIN, EDITOR
1

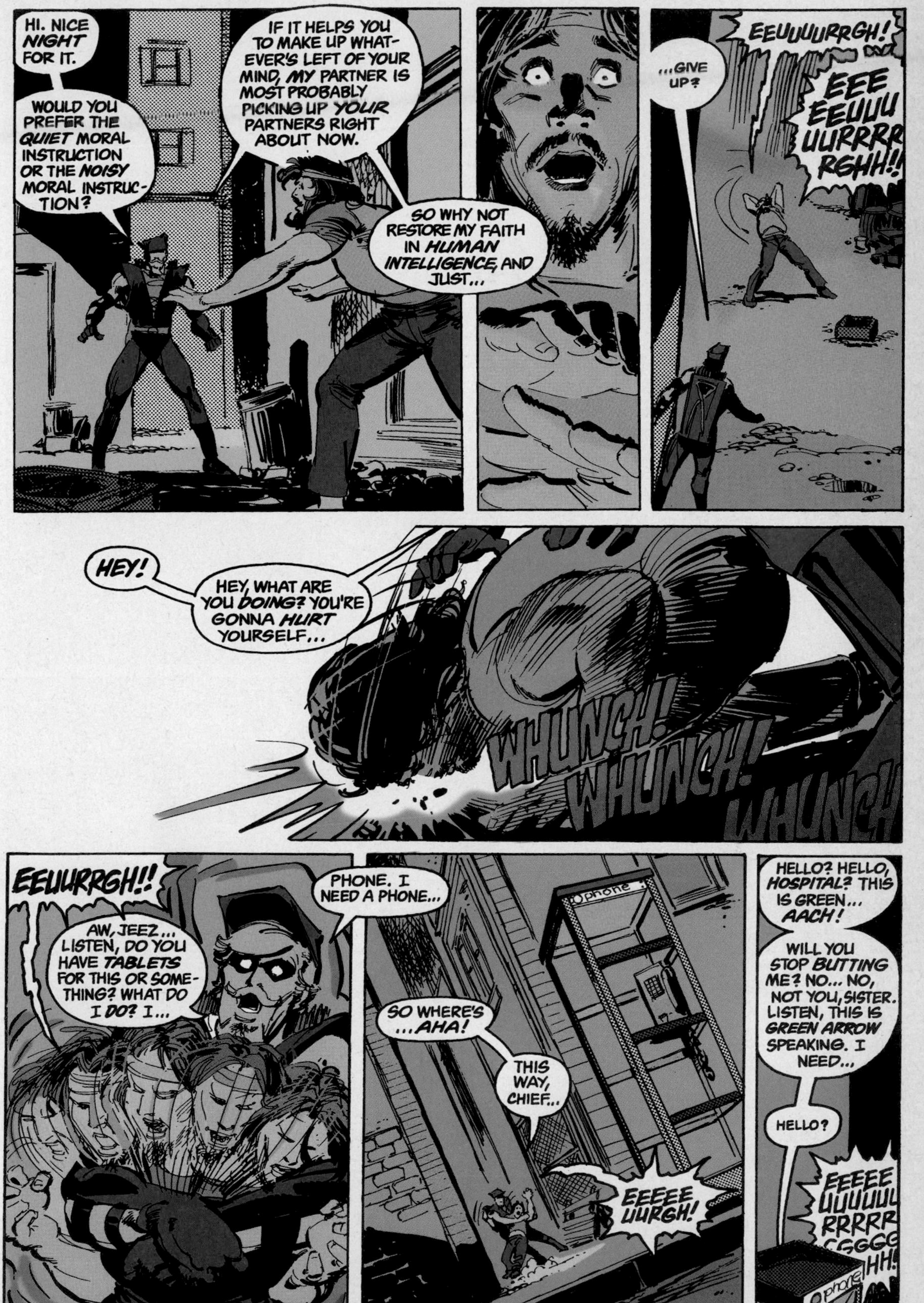

HI. NICE NIGHT FOR IT.
WOULD YOU PREFER THE QUIET MORAL INSTRUCTION OR THE NOISY MORAL INSTRUCTION?
IF IT HELPS YOU TO MAKE UP WHATEVER'S LEFT OF YOUR MIND, MY PARTNER IS MOST PROBABLY PICKING UP YOUR PARTNERS RIGHT ABOUT NOW.
SO WHY NOT RESTORE MY FAITH IN HUMAN INTELLIGENCE, AND JUST...
...GIVE UP?
EEUUUURRGH!
EEE EEUUU UURRRR RGHH!!
HEY!
HEY, WHAT ARE YOU DOING? YOU'RE GONNA HURT YOURSELF...
WHUNCH!
WHUNCH!
WHUNCH
EEUURRGH!!
AW, JEEZ... LISTEN, DO YOU HAVE TABLETS FOR THIS OR SOMETHING? WHAT DO I DO? I...
PHONE. I NEED A PHONE...
phone
SO WHERE'S ...AHA!
THIS WAY, CHIEF...
EEEEE UURGH!
HELLO? HELLO, HOSPITAL? THIS IS GREEN... AACH!
WILL YOU STOP BUTTING ME? NO... NO, NOT YOU, SISTER. LISTEN, THIS IS GREEN ARROW SPEAKING. I NEED...
HELLO?
EEEEE UUUUUU RRRRR GGGG HH!
phone
2

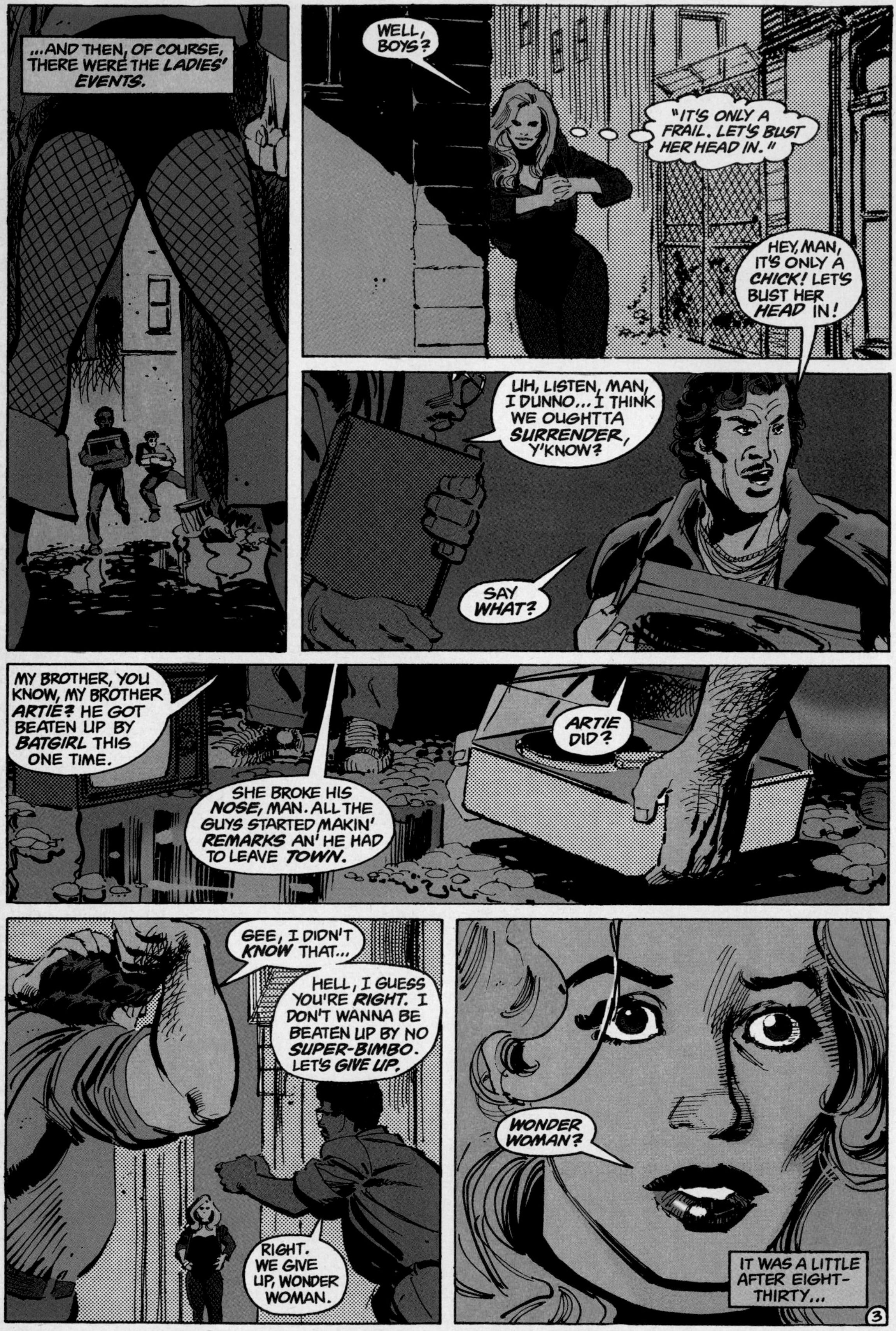
...AND THEN, OF COURSE, THERE WERE THE LADIES' EVENTS.
WELL, BOYS?
"IT'S ONLY A FRAIL. LET'S BUST HER HEAD IN."
HEY, MAN, IT'S ONLY A CHICK! LET'S BUST HER HEAD IN!
UH, LISTEN, MAN, I DUNNO... I THINK WE OUGHTTA SURRENDER, Y'KNOW?
SAY WHAT?
MY BROTHER, YOU KNOW, MY BROTHER ARTIE? HE GOT BEATEN UP BY BATGIRL THIS ONE TIME.
ARTIE DID?
SHE BROKE HIS NOSE, MAN. ALL THE GUYS STARTED MAKIN' REMARKS AN' HE HAD TO LEAVE TOWN.
GEE, I DIDN'T KNOW THAT...
HELL, I GUESS YOU'RE RIGHT. I DON'T WANNA BE BEATEN UP BY NO SUPER-BIMBO. LET'S GIVE UP.
RIGHT. WE GIVE UP, WONDER WOMAN.
WONDER WOMAN?
IT WAS A LITTLE AFTER EIGHT-THIRTY...
3

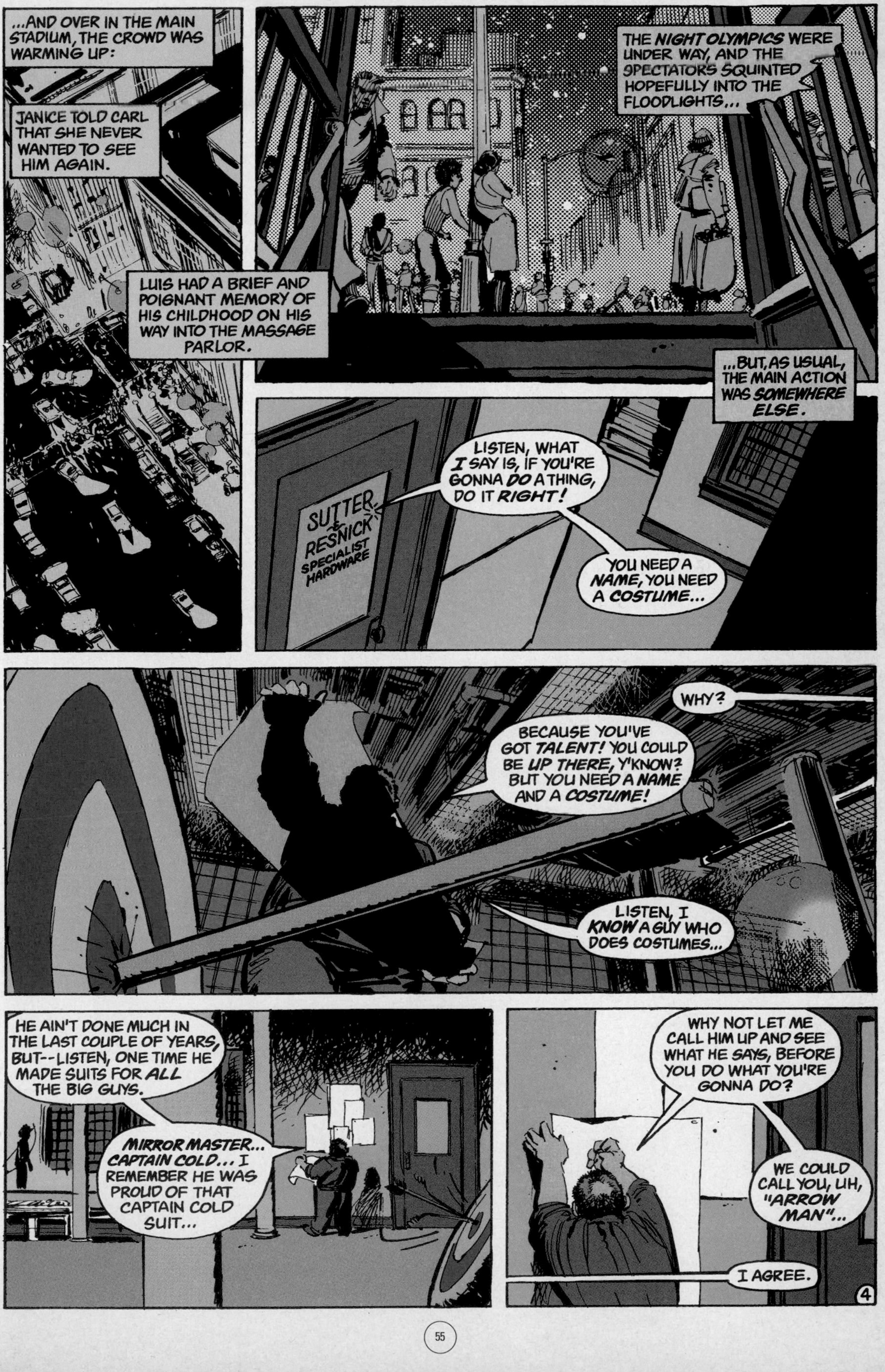
...AND OVER IN THE MAIN STADIUM, THE CROWD WAS WARMING UP:
JANICE TOLD CARL THAT SHE NEVER WANTED TO SEE HIM AGAIN.
LUIS HAD A BRIEF AND POIGNANT MEMORY OF HIS CHILDHOOD ON HIS WAY INTO THE MASSAGE PARLOR.
THE NIGHT OLYMPICS WERE UNDER WAY, AND THE SPECTATORS SQUINTED HOPEFULLY INTO THE FLOODLIGHTS...
...BUT, AS USUAL, THE MAIN ACTION WAS SOMEWHERE ELSE.
SUTTER & RESNICK SPECIALIST HARDWARE
LISTEN, WHAT I SAY IS, IF YOU'RE GONNA DO A THING, DO IT RIGHT!
YOU NEED A NAME, YOU NEED A COSTUME...
WHY?
BECAUSE YOU'VE GOT TALENT! YOU COULD BE UP THERE, Y'KNOW? BUT YOU NEED A NAME AND A COSTUME!
LISTEN, I KNOW A GUY WHO DOES COSTUMES...
HE AIN'T DONE MUCH IN THE LAST COUPLE OF YEARS, BUT--LISTEN, ONE TIME HE MADE SUITS FOR ALL THE BIG GUYS.
MIRROR MASTER... CAPTAIN COLD... I REMEMBER HE WAS PROUD OF THAT CAPTAIN COLD SUIT...
WHY NOT LET ME CALL HIM UP AND SEE WHAT HE SAYS, BEFORE YOU DO WHAT YOU'RE GONNA DO?
WE COULD CALL YOU, UH, "ARROW MAN"...
I AGREE.
4

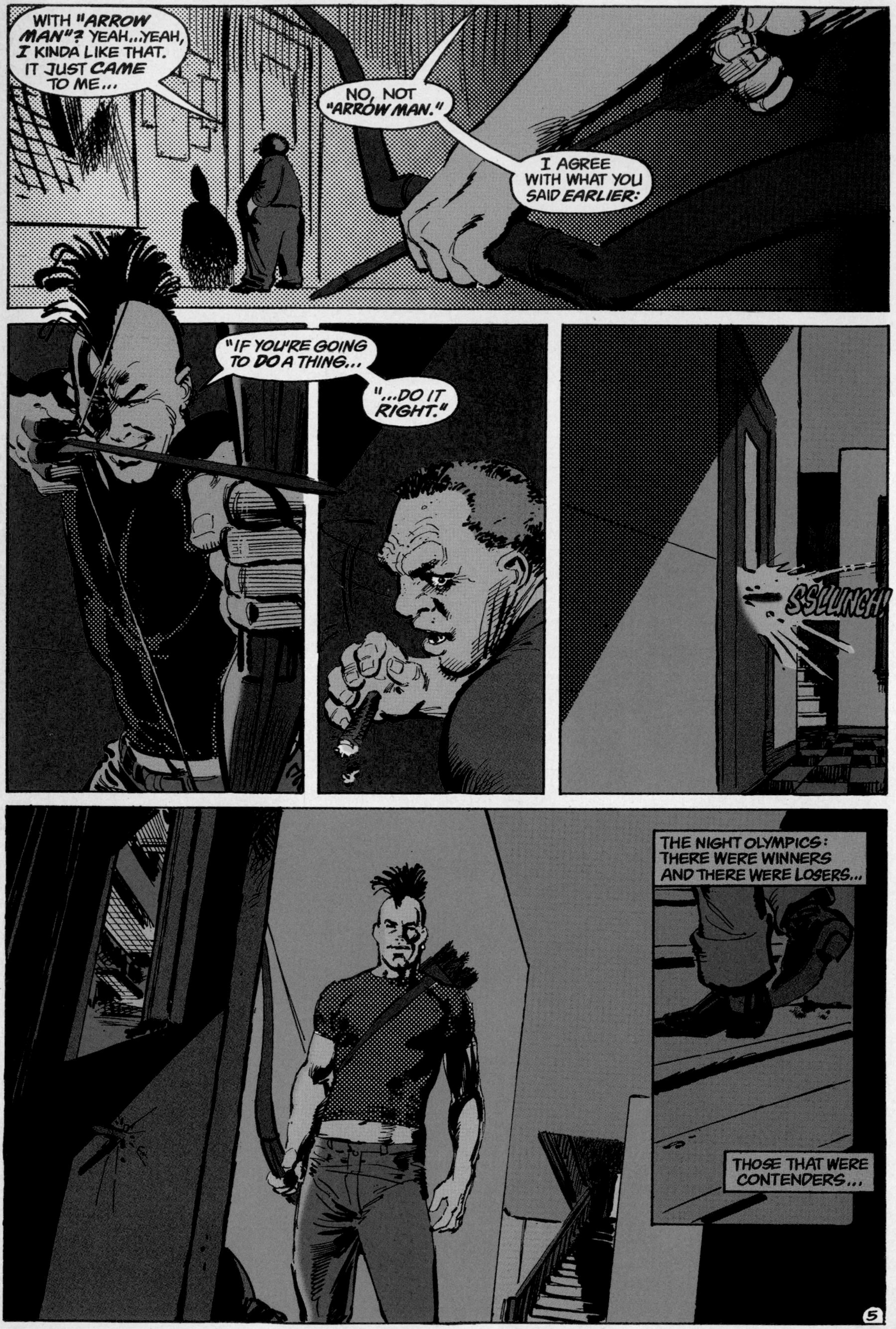
WITH "ARROW MAN"? YEAH...YEAH, I KINDA LIKE THAT. IT JUST CAME TO ME...
NO, NOT "ARROW MAN."
I AGREE WITH WHAT YOU SAID EARLIER:
"IF YOU'RE GOING TO DO A THING...
"...DO IT RIGHT."
SSLLUNCH!
THE NIGHT OLYMPICS: THERE WERE WINNERS AND THERE WERE LOSERS...
THOSE THAT WERE CONTENDERS...
5

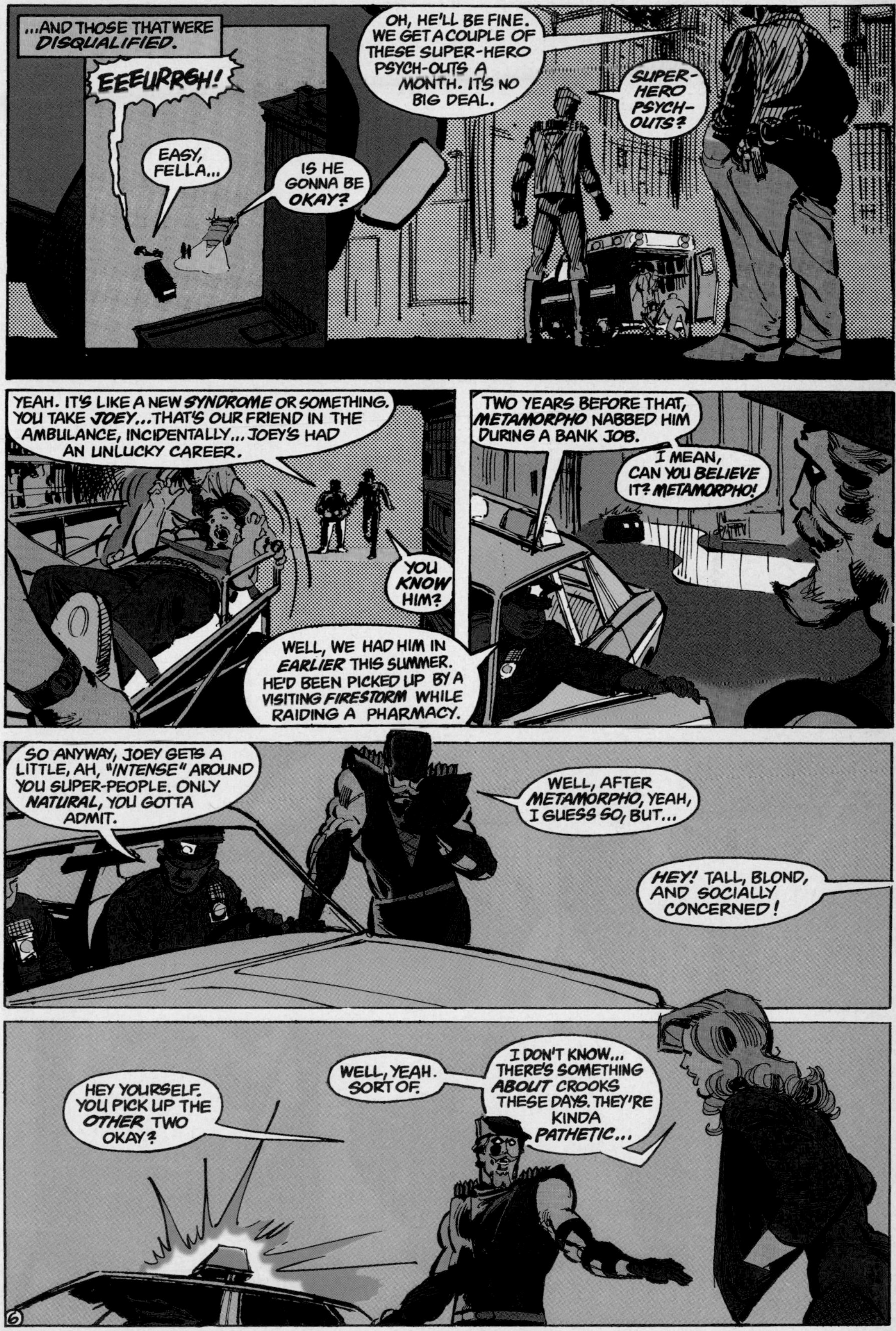
...AND THOSE THAT WERE DISQUALIFIED.
EEEURRGH!
EASY, FELLA...
IS HE GONNA BE OKAY?
OH, HE'LL BE FINE. WE GET A COUPLE OF THESE SUPER-HERO PSYCH-OUTS A MONTH. IT'S NO BIG DEAL.
SUPER-HERO PSYCH-OUTS?
YEAH. IT'S LIKE A NEW SYNDROME OR SOMETHING. YOU TAKE JOEY...THAT'S OUR FRIEND IN THE AMBULANCE, INCIDENTALLY... JOEY'S HAD AN UNLUCKY CAREER.
YOU KNOW HIM?
WELL, WE HAD HIM IN EARLIER THIS SUMMER. HE'D BEEN PICKED UP BY A VISITING FIRESTORM WHILE RAIDING A PHARMACY.
TWO YEARS BEFORE THAT, METAMORPHO NABBED HIM DURING A BANK JOB.
I MEAN, CAN YOU BELIEVE IT? METAMORPHO!
SO ANYWAY, JOEY GETS A LITTLE, AH, "INTENSE" AROUND YOU SUPER-PEOPLE. ONLY NATURAL, YOU GOTTA ADMIT.
WELL, AFTER METAMORPHO, YEAH, I GUESS SO, BUT...
HEY! TALL, BLOND, AND SOCIALLY CONCERNED!
HEY YOURSELF. YOU PICK UP THE OTHER TWO OKAY?
WELL, YEAH. SORT OF.
I DON'T KNOW... THERE'S SOMETHING ABOUT CROOKS THESE DAYS. THEY'RE KINDA PATHETIC...
6

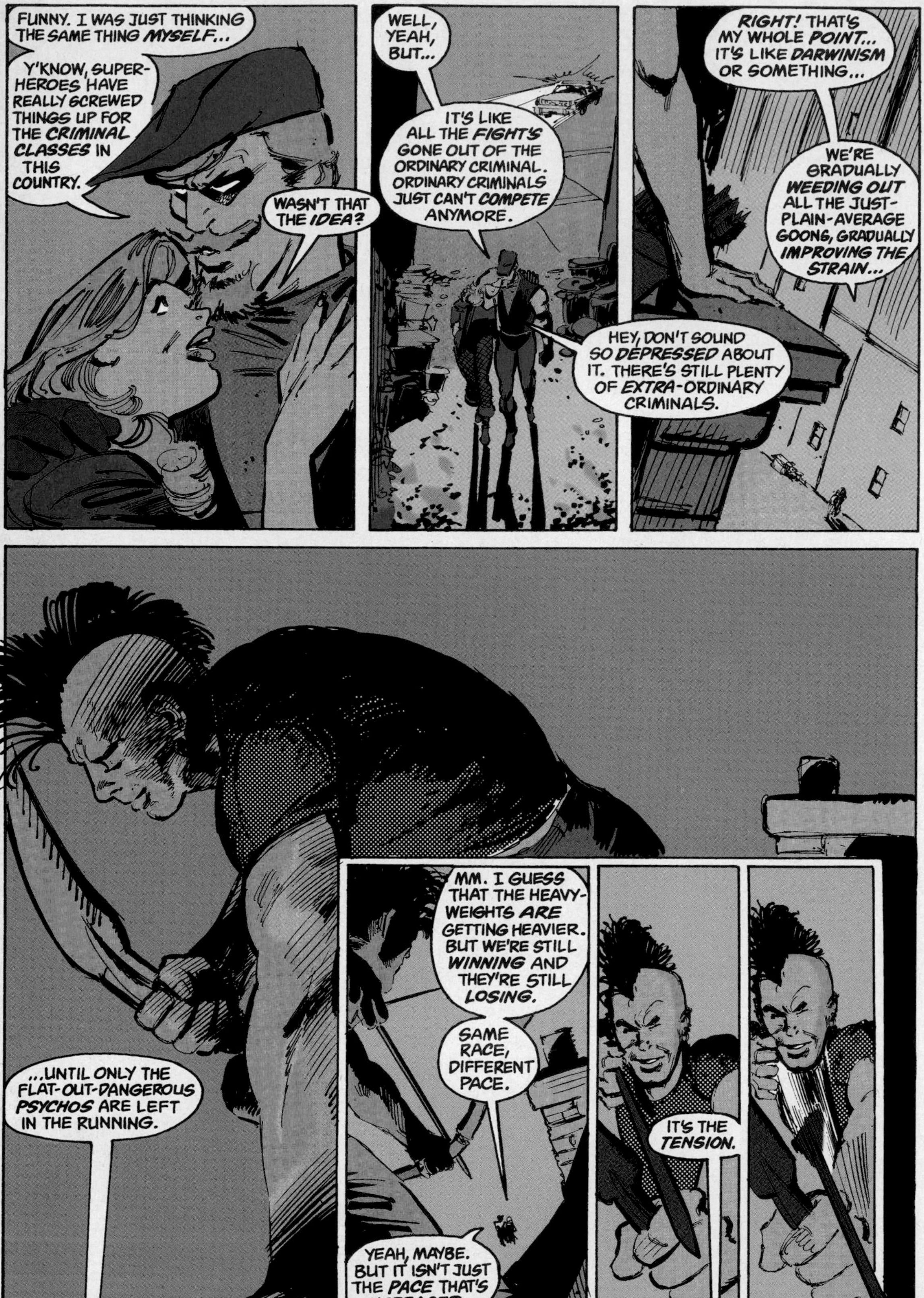
FUNNY. I WAS JUST THINKING THE SAME THING MYSELF...
Y'KNOW, SUPER-HEROES HAVE REALLY SCREWED THINGS UP FOR THE CRIMINAL CLASSES IN THIS COUNTRY.
WASN'T THAT THE IDEA?
WELL, YEAH, BUT...
IT'S LIKE ALL THE FIGHT'S GONE OUT OF THE ORDINARY CRIMINAL. ORDINARY CRIMINALS JUST CAN'T COMPETE ANYMORE.
HEY, DON'T SOUND SO DEPRESSED ABOUT IT. THERE'S STILL PLENTY OF EXTRA-ORDINARY CRIMINALS.
RIGHT! THAT'S MY WHOLE POINT... IT'S LIKE DARWINISM OR SOMETHING...
WE'RE GRADUALLY WEEDING OUT ALL THE JUST-PLAIN-AVERAGE GOONS, GRADUALLY IMPROVING THE STRAIN...
...UNTIL ONLY THE FLAT-OUT-DANGEROUS PSYCHOS ARE LEFT IN THE RUNNING.
MM. I GUESS THAT THE HEAVY-WEIGHTS ARE GETTING HEAVIER. BUT WE'RE STILL WINNING AND THEY'RE STILL LOSING.
SAME RACE, DIFFERENT PACE.
YEAH, MAYBE. BUT IT ISN'T JUST THE PACE THAT'S INCREASED...
IT'S THE TENSION.
TO BE CONTINUED...
7

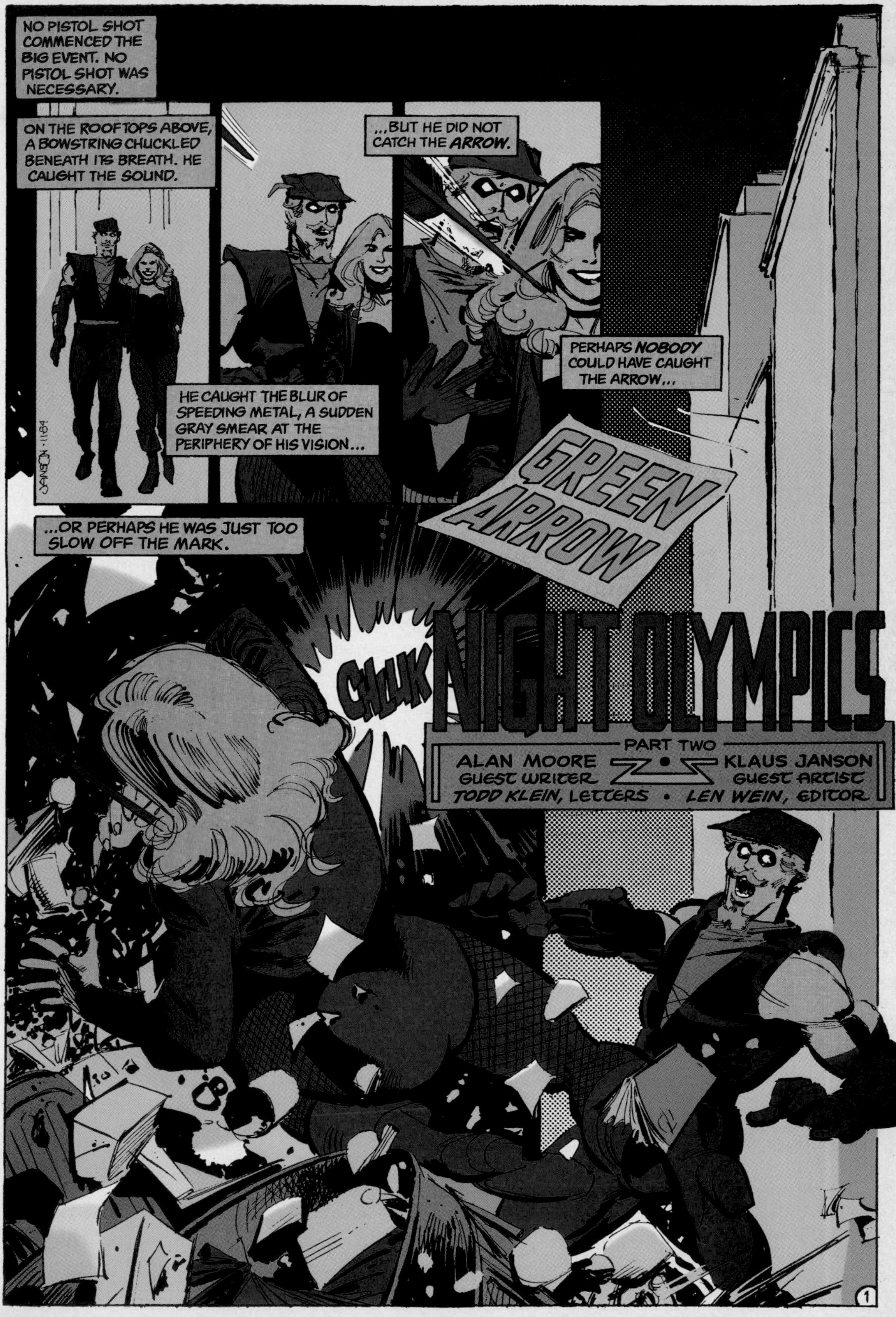

NO PISTOL SHOT COMMENCED THE BIG EVENT. NO PISTOL SHOT WAS NECESSARY.
ON THE ROOFTOPS ABOVE, A BOWSTRING CHUCKLED BENEATH ITS BREATH. HE CAUGHT THE SOUND.
HE CAUGHT THE BLUR OF SPEEDING METAL, A SUDDEN GRAY SMEAR AT THE PERIPHERY OF HIS VISION...
...BUT HE DID NOT CATCH THE ARROW.
PERHAPS NOBODY COULD HAVE CAUGHT THE ARROW...
...OR PERHAPS HE WAS JUST TOO SLOW OFF THE MARK.
GREEN ARROW
CHUK
NIGHT OLYMPICS
PART TWO
ALAN MOORE GUEST WRITER
KLAUS JANSON GUEST ARTIST
TODD KLEIN, LETTERS • LEN WEIN, EDITOR
JANSON 11.84
1

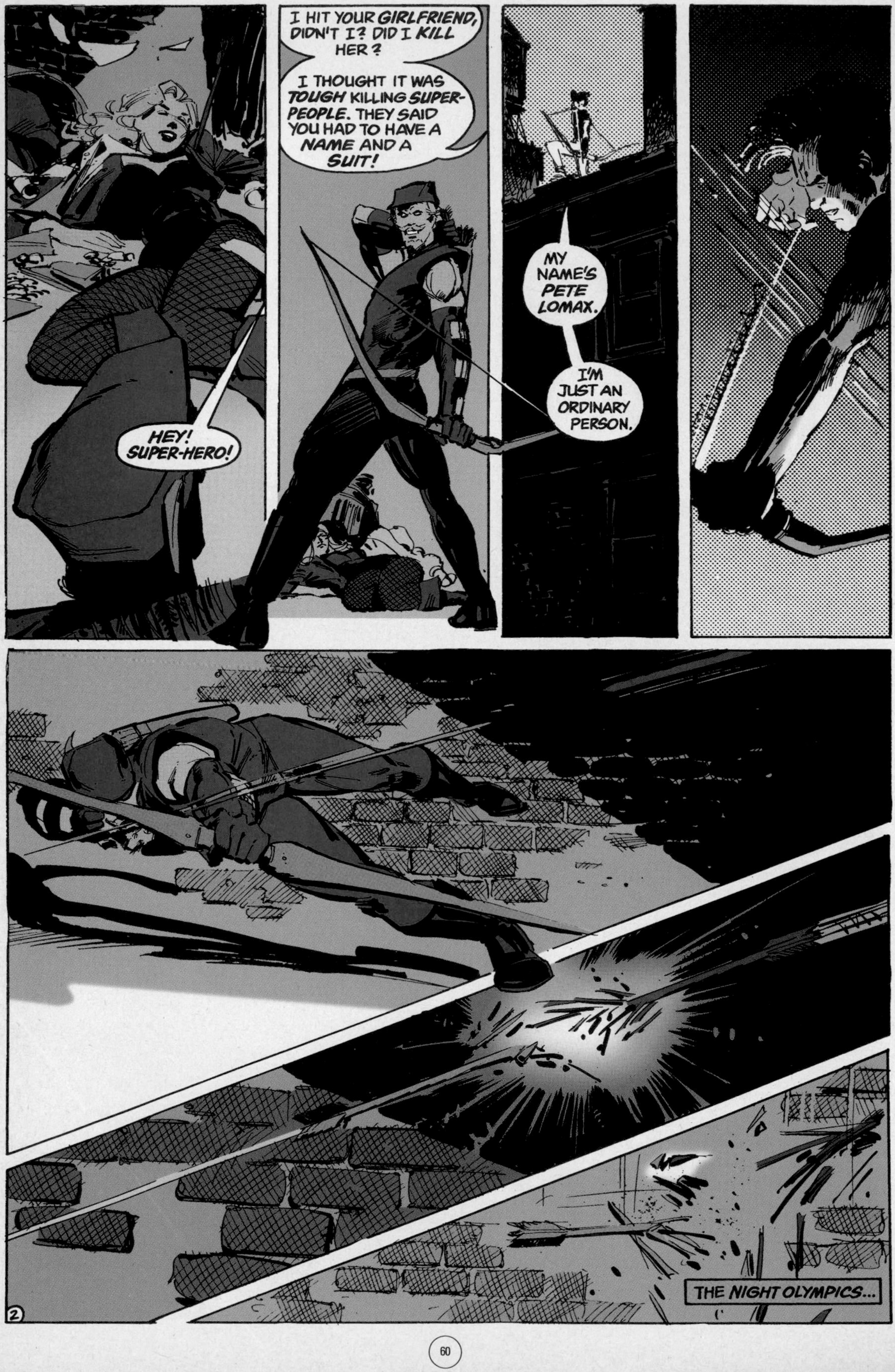
HEY! SUPER-HERO!
I HIT YOUR GIRLFRIEND, DIDN'T I? DID I KILL HER?
I THOUGHT IT WAS TOUGH KILLING SUPER-PEOPLE. THEY SAID YOU HAD TO HAVE A NAME AND A SUIT!
MY NAME'S PETE LOMAX.
I'M JUST AN ORDINARY PERSON.
THE NIGHT OLYMPICS...
2

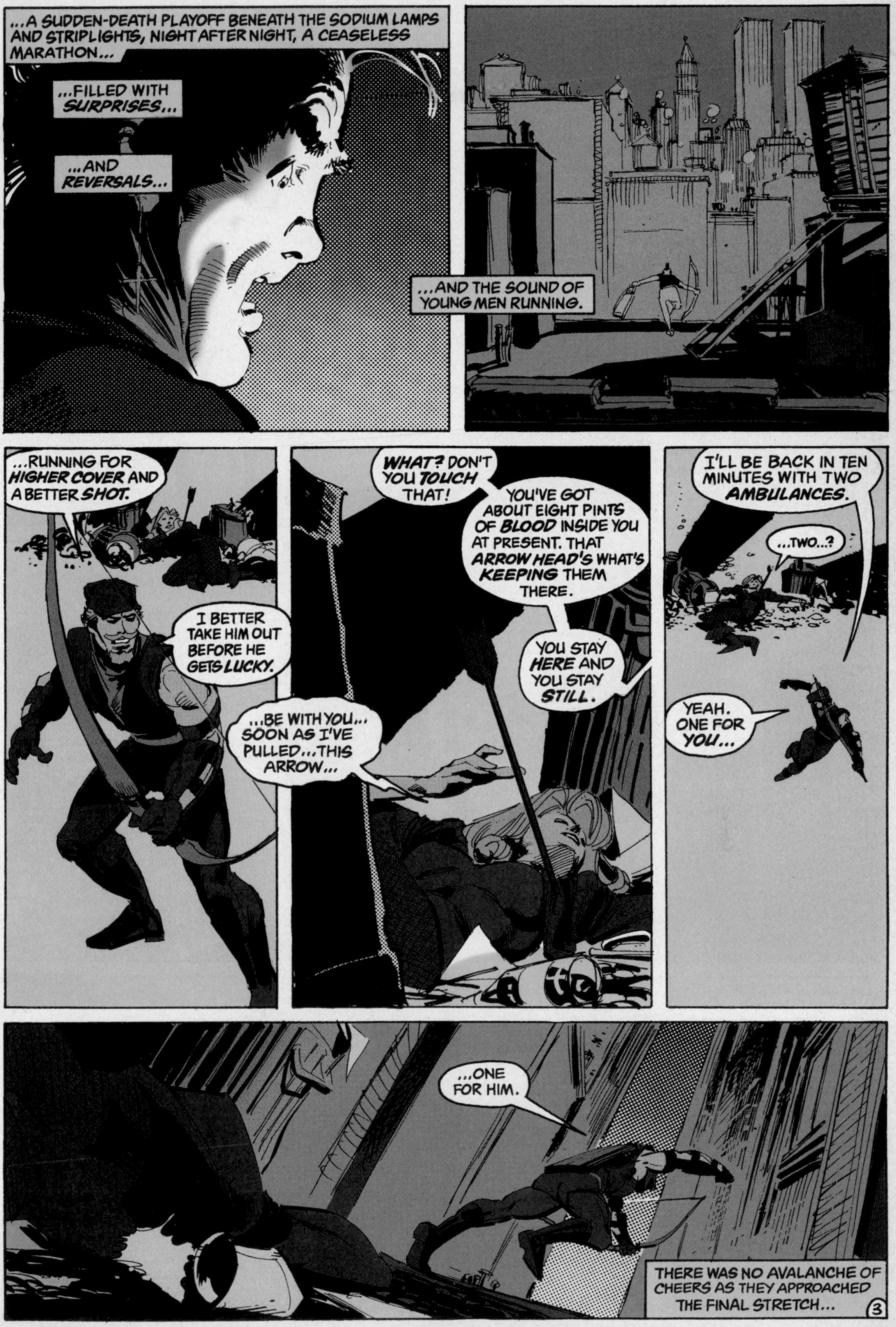

...A SUDDEN-DEATH PLAYOFF BENEATH THE SODIUM LAMPS AND STRIPLIGHTS, NIGHT AFTER NIGHT, A CEASELESS MARATHON...
...FILLED WITH SURPRISES...
...AND REVERSALS...
...AND THE SOUND OF YOUNG MEN RUNNING.
...RUNNING FOR HIGHER COVER AND A BETTER SHOT.
I BETTER TAKE HIM OUT BEFORE HE GETS LUCKY.
...BE WITH YOU... SOON AS I'VE PULLED...THIS ARROW...
WHAT? DON'T YOU TOUCH THAT!
YOU'VE GOT ABOUT EIGHT PINTS OF BLOOD INSIDE YOU AT PRESENT. THAT ARROW HEAD'S WHAT'S KEEPING THEM THERE.
YOU STAY HERE AND YOU STAY STILL.
I'LL BE BACK IN TEN MINUTES WITH TWO AMBULANCES.
...TWO...?
YEAH. ONE FOR YOU...
...ONE FOR HIM.
THERE WAS NO AVALANCHE OF CHEERS AS THEY APPROACHED THE FINAL STRETCH...
3

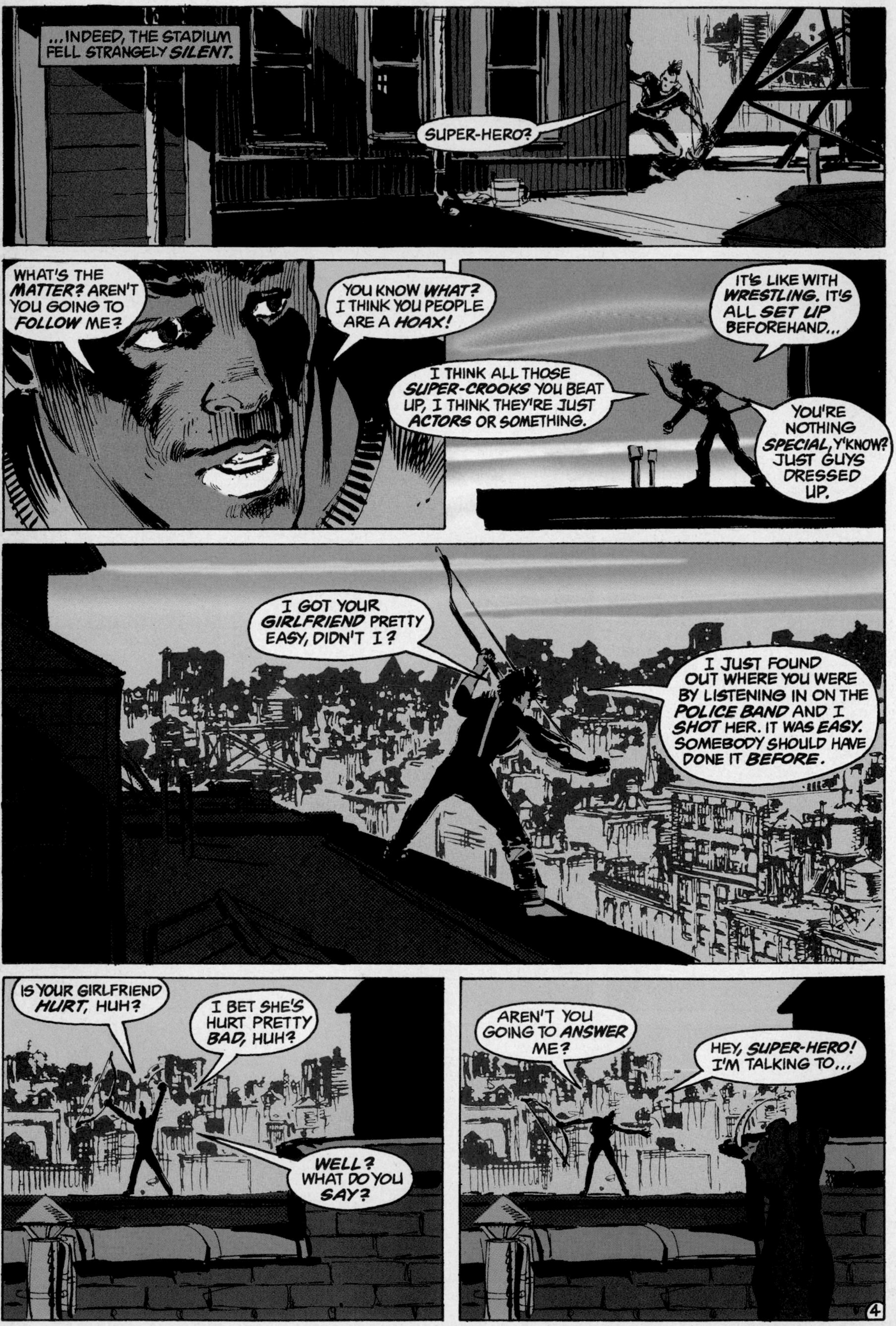
...INDEED, THE STADIUM FELL STRANGELY SILENT.
SUPER-HERO?
WHAT'S THE MATTER? AREN'T YOU GOING TO FOLLOW ME?
YOU KNOW WHAT? I THINK YOU PEOPLE ARE A HOAX!
IT'S LIKE WITH WRESTLING. IT'S ALL SET UP BEFOREHAND...
I THINK ALL THOSE SUPER-CROOKS YOU BEAT UP, I THINK THEY'RE JUST ACTORS OR SOMETHING.
YOU'RE NOTHING SPECIAL, Y'KNOW? JUST GUYS DRESSED UP.
I GOT YOUR GIRLFRIEND PRETTY EASY, DIDN'T I?
I JUST FOUND OUT WHERE YOU WERE BY LISTENING IN ON THE POLICE BAND AND I SHOT HER. IT WAS EASY. SOMEBODY SHOULD HAVE DONE IT BEFORE.
IS YOUR GIRLFRIEND HURT, HUH?
I BET SHE'S HURT PRETTY BAD, HUH?
WELL? WHAT DO YOU SAY?
AREN'T YOU GOING TO ANSWER ME?
HEY, SUPER-HERO! I'M TALKING TO...
4

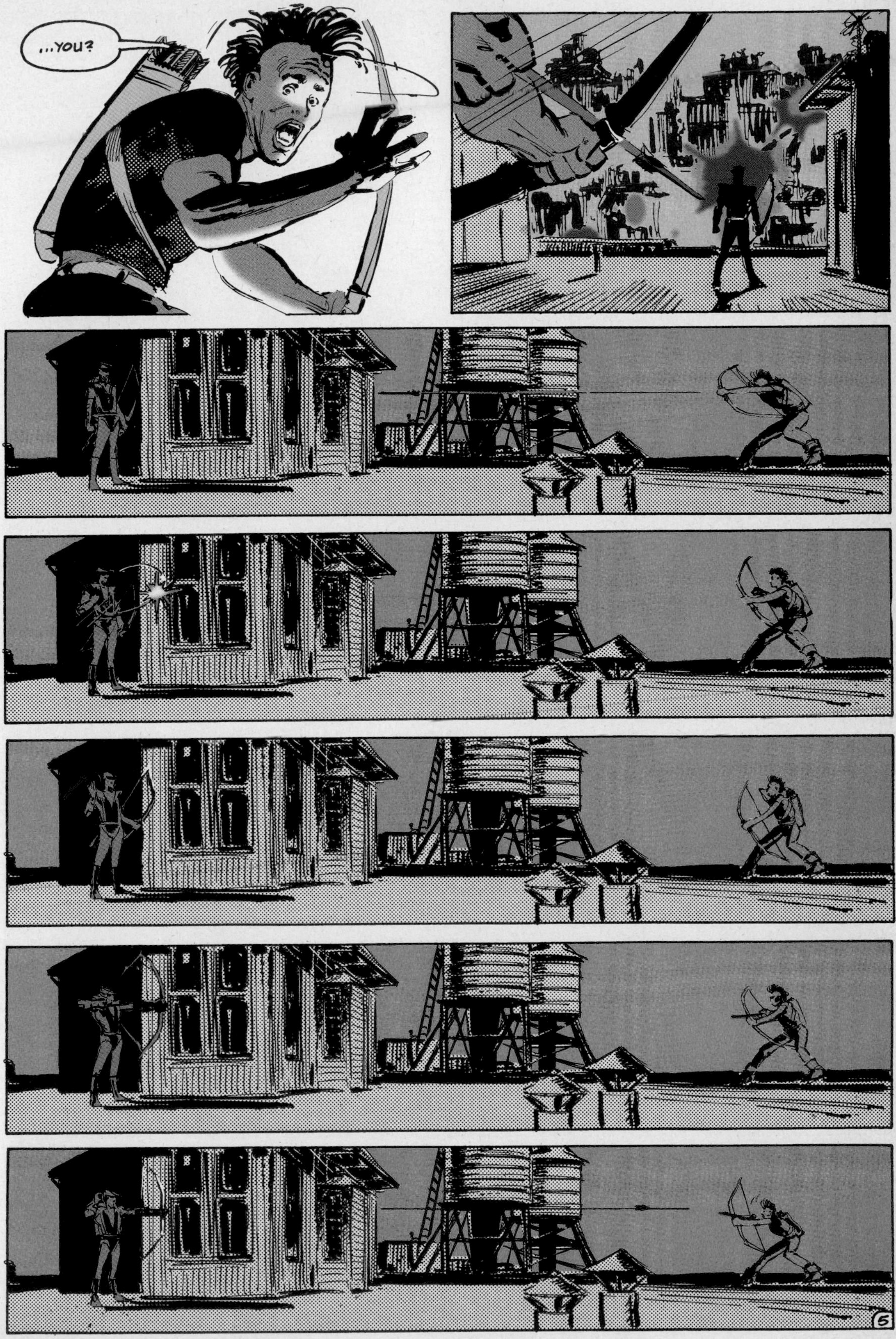
...YOU?
5

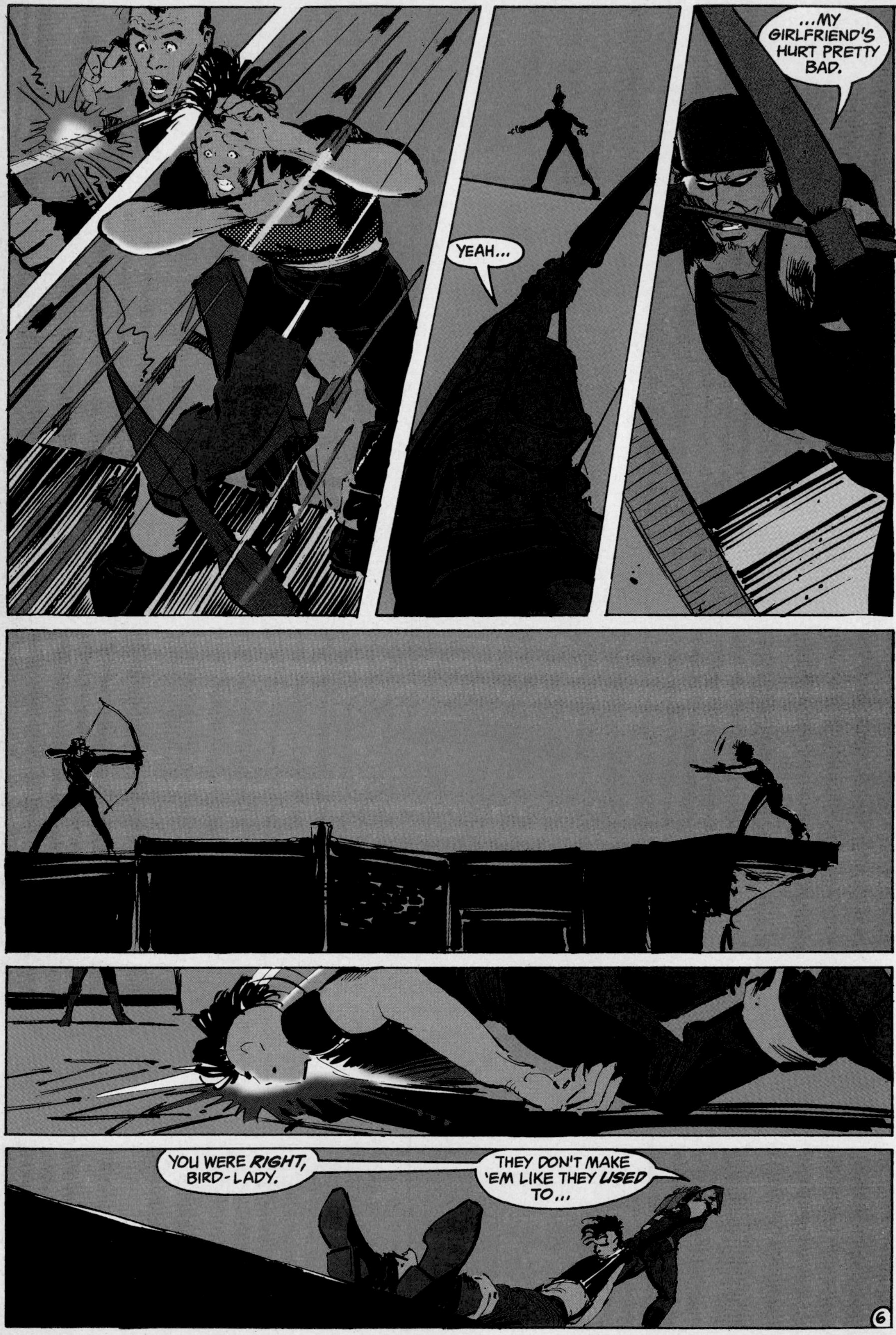
YEAH...
...MY GIRLFRIEND'S HURT PRETTY BAD.
YOU WERE RIGHT, BIRD-LADY.
THEY DON'T MAKE 'EM LIKE THEY USED TO...
6

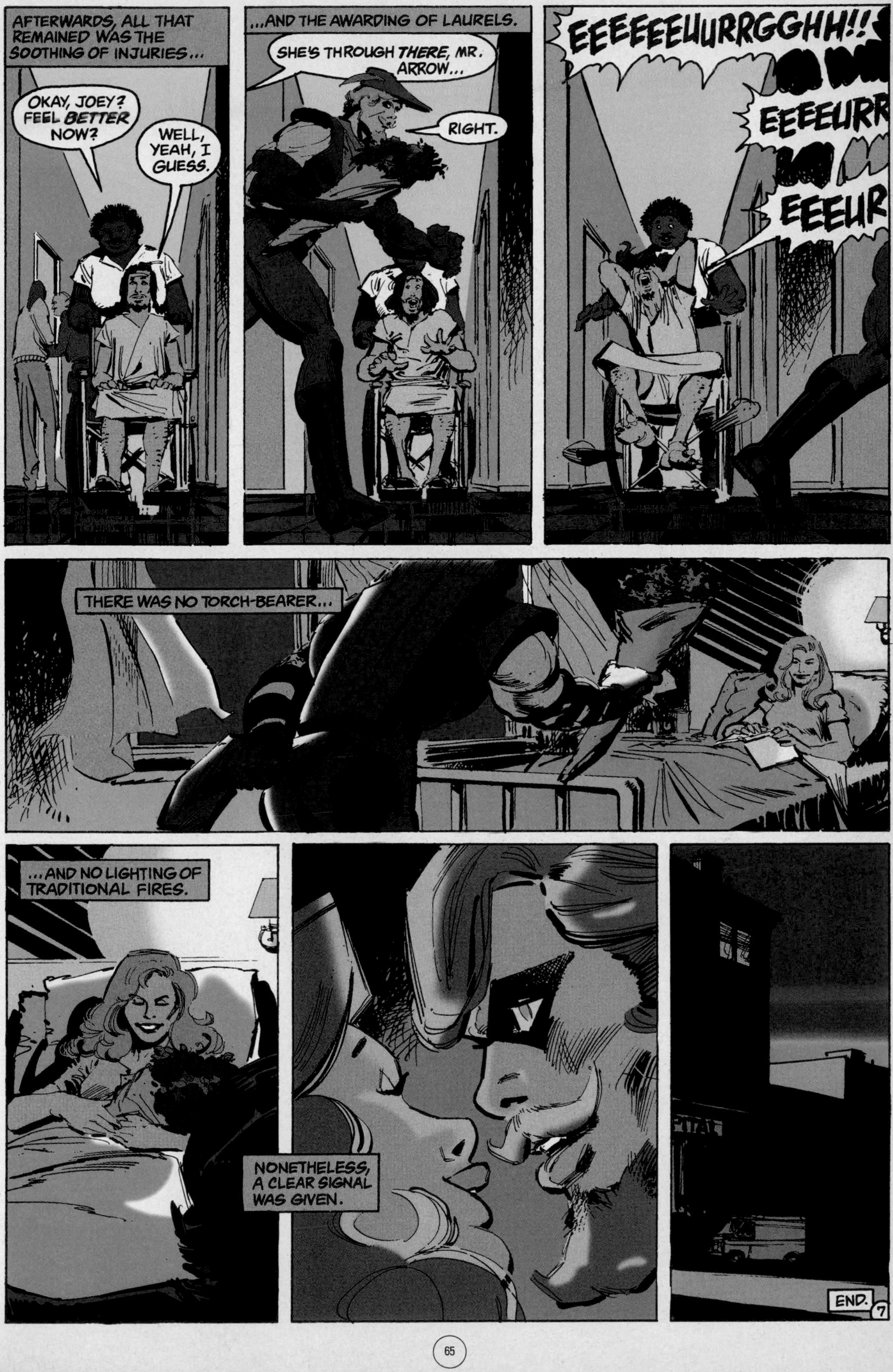
AFTERWARDS, ALL THAT REMAINED WAS THE SOOTHING OF INJURIES...
OKAY, JOEY? FEEL BETTER NOW?
WELL, YEAH, I GUESS.
...AND THE AWARDING OF LAURELS.
SHE'S THROUGH THERE, MR. ARROW...
RIGHT.
EEEEEEEUURRGGHH!!
EEEEURR
EEEUR
THERE WAS NO TORCH-BEARER...
...AND NO LIGHTING OF TRADITIONAL FIRES.
NONETHELESS, A CLEAR SIGNAL WAS GIVEN.
END.
7

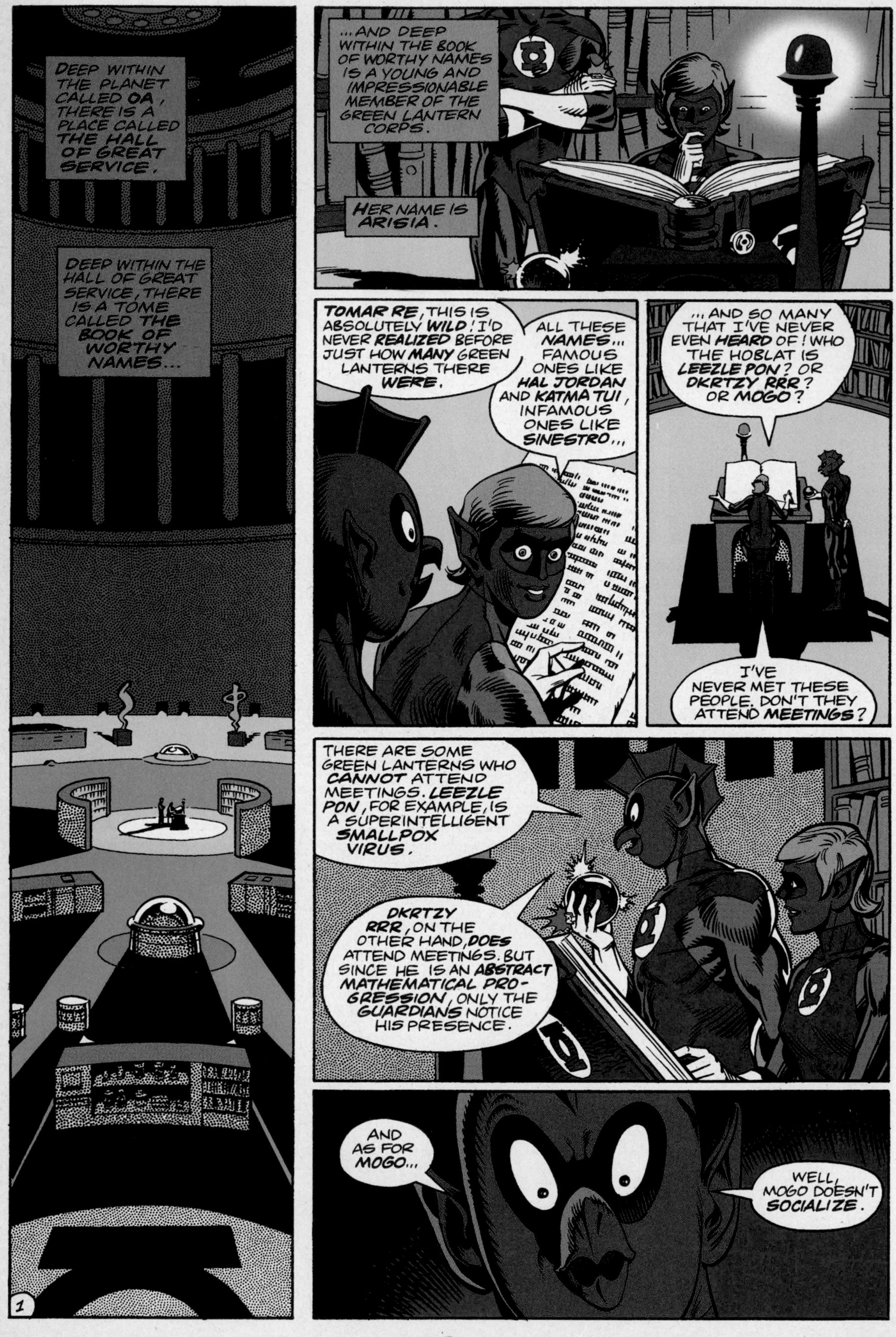
DEEP WITHIN THE PLANET CALLED OA, THERE IS A PLACE CALLED THE HALL OF GREAT SERVICE.
DEEP WITHIN THE HALL OF GREAT SERVICE, THERE IS A TOME CALLED THE BOOK OF WORTHY NAMES...
1
...AND DEEP WITHIN THE BOOK OF WORTHY NAMES IS A YOUNG AND IMPRESSIONABLE MEMBER OF THE GREEN LANTERN CORPS.
HER NAME IS ARISIA.
TOMAR RE, THIS IS ABSOLUTELY WILD! I'D NEVER REALIZED BEFORE JUST HOW MANY GREEN LANTERNS THERE WERE.
ALL THESE NAMES... FAMOUS ONES LIKE HAL JORDAN AND KATMA TUI, INFAMOUS ONES LIKE SINESTRO...
...AND SO MANY THAT I'VE NEVER EVEN HEARD OF! WHO THE HOBLAT IS LEEZLE PON? OR DKRTZY RRR? OR MOGO?
I'VE NEVER MET THESE PEOPLE. DON'T THEY ATTEND MEETINGS?
THERE ARE SOME GREEN LANTERNS WHO CANNOT ATTEND MEETINGS. LEEZLE PON, FOR EXAMPLE, IS A SUPERINTELLIGENT SMALLPOX VIRUS.
DKRTZY RRR, ON THE OTHER HAND, DOES ATTEND MEETINGS. BUT SINCE HE IS AN ABSTRACT MATHEMATICAL PRO-GRESSION, ONLY THE GUARDIANS NOTICE HIS PRESENCE.
AND AS FOR MOGO...
WELL, MOGO DOESN'T SOCIALIZE.

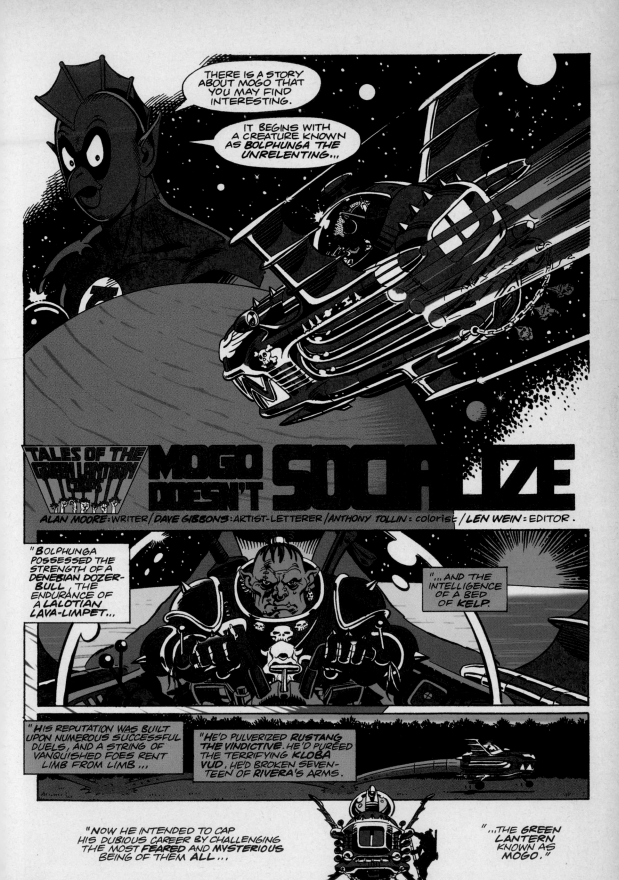

TALES OF THE GREEN LANTERN CORPS

MOGO DOESN'T SOCIALIZE

ALAN MOORE: WRITER / DAVE GIBBONS: ARTIST-LETTERER / ANTHONY TOLLIN: COLORIST / LEN WEIN: EDITOR.

THERE IS A STORY ABOUT MOGO THAT YOU MAY FIND INTERESTING.

IT BEGINS WITH A CREATURE KNOWN AS BOLPHUNGA THE UNRELENTING...

"BOLPHUNGA POSSESSED THE STRENGTH OF A DENEBIAN DOZER-BULL, THE ENDURANCE OF A LALOTIAN LAVA-LIMPET...

"...AND THE INTELLIGENCE OF A BED OF KELP.

"HIS REPUTATION WAS BUILT UPON NUMEROUS SUCCESSFUL DUELS, AND A STRING OF VANQUISHED FOES RENT LIMB FROM LIMB ...

"HE'D PULVERIZED RUSTANG THE VINDICTIVE. HE'D PURÉED THE TERRIFYING KLOBA VUD. HE'D BROKEN SEVEN-TEEN OF RIVERA'S ARMS.

"NOW HE INTENDED TO CAP HIS DUBIOUS CAREER BY CHALLENGING THE MOST FEARED AND MYSTERIOUS BEING OF THEM ALL ...

"...THE GREEN LANTERN KNOWN AS MOGO."

②

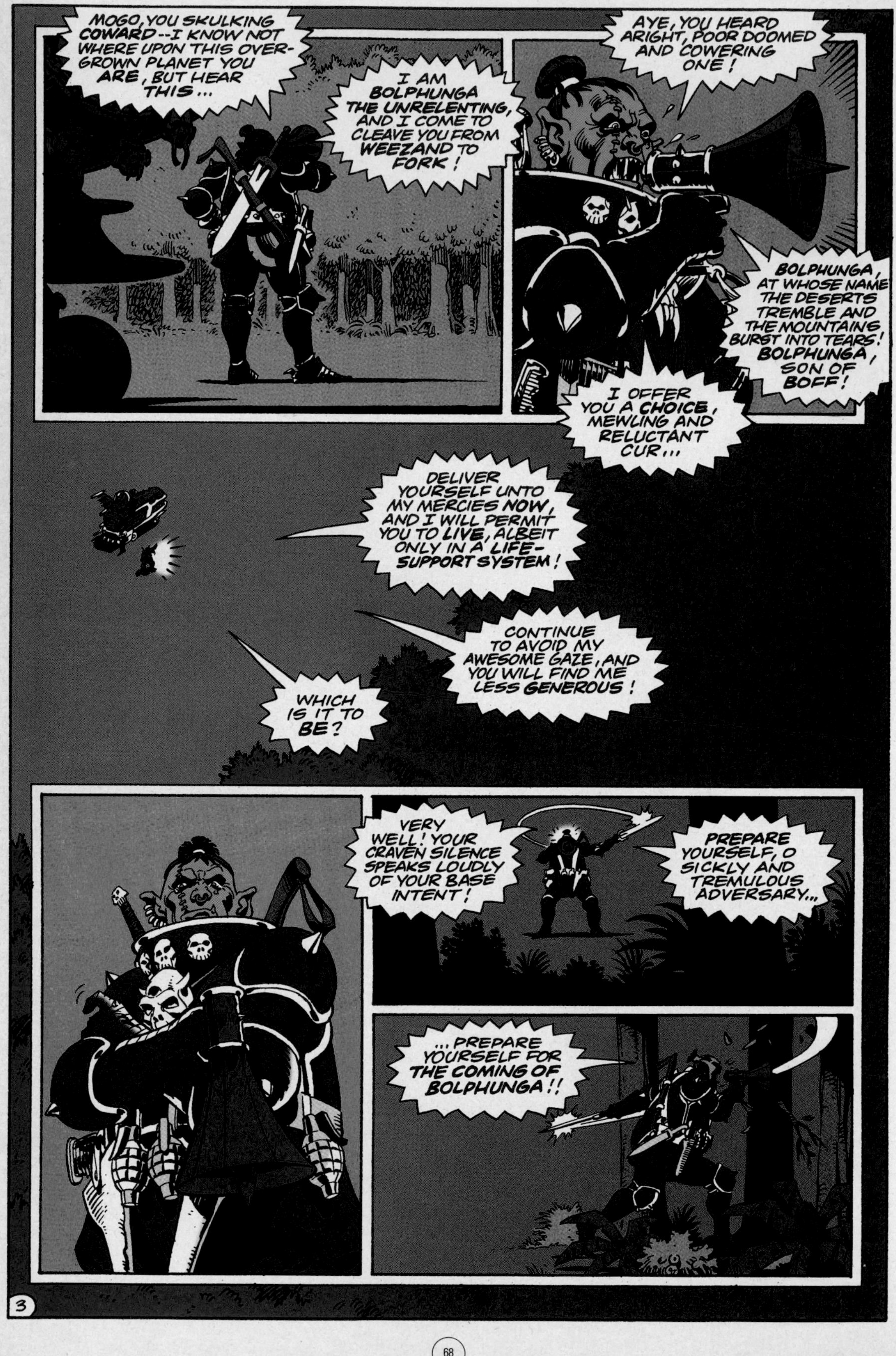
MOGO, YOU SKULKING COWARD--I KNOW NOT WHERE UPON THIS OVERGROWN PLANET YOU ARE, BUT HEAR THIS...
I AM BOLPHUNGA THE UNRELENTING, AND I COME TO CLEAVE YOU FROM WEEZAND TO FORK!
AYE, YOU HEARD ARIGHT, POOR DOOMED AND COWERING ONE!
BOLPHUNGA, AT WHOSE NAME THE DESERTS TREMBLE AND THE MOUNTAINS BURST INTO TEARS! BOLPHUNGA, SON OF BOFF!
I OFFER YOU A CHOICE, MEWLING AND RELUCTANT CUR...
DELIVER YOURSELF UNTO MY MERCIES NOW, AND I WILL PERMIT YOU TO LIVE, ALBEIT ONLY IN A LIFE-SUPPORT SYSTEM!
CONTINUE TO AVOID MY AWESOME GAZE, AND YOU WILL FIND ME LESS GENEROUS!
WHICH IS IT TO BE?
VERY WELL! YOUR CRAVEN SILENCE SPEAKS LOUDLY OF YOUR BASE INTENT!
PREPARE YOURSELF, O SICKLY AND TREMULOUS ADVERSARY...
...PREPARE YOURSELF FOR THE COMING OF BOLPHUNGA!!
3

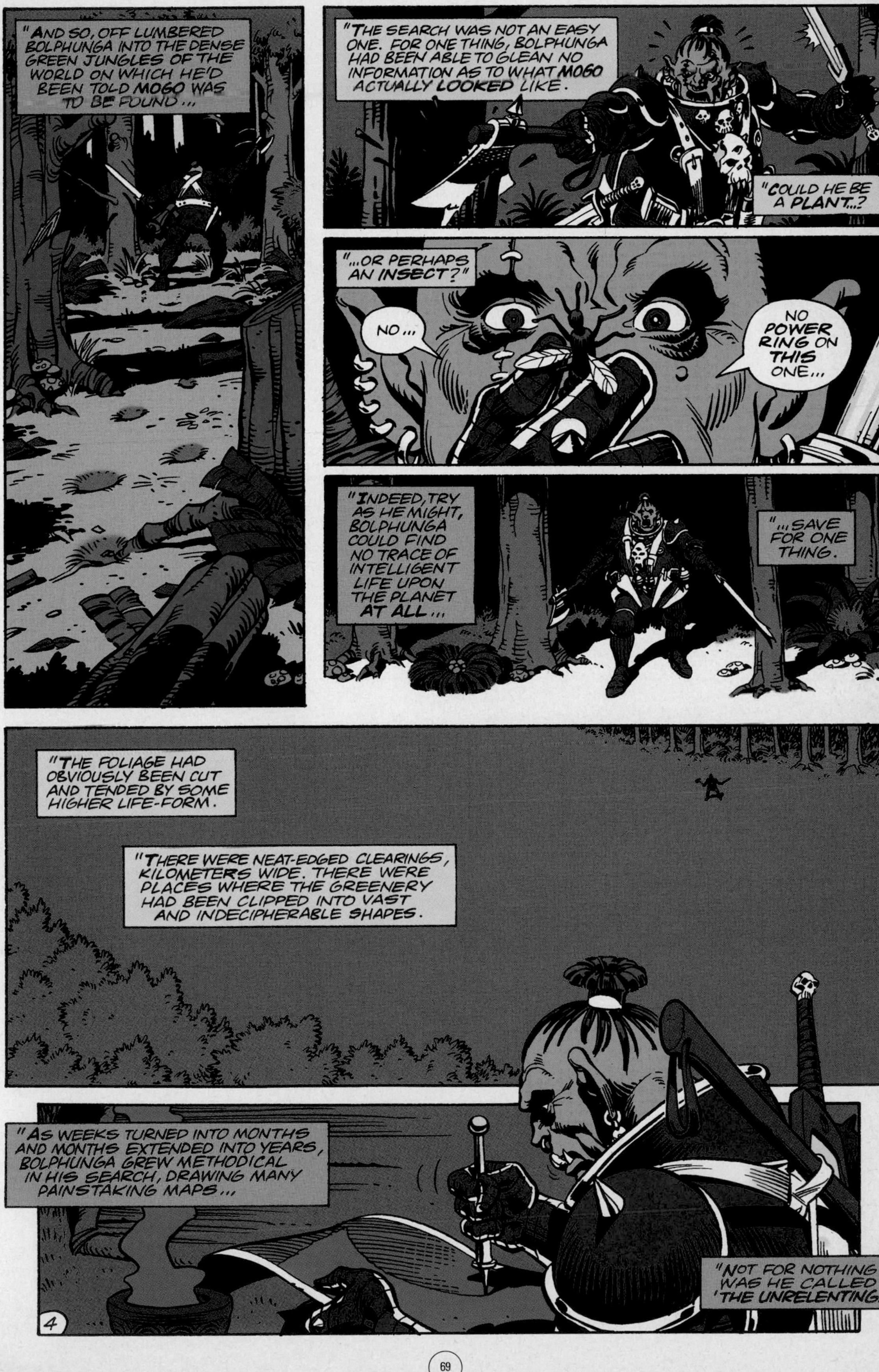
"AND SO, OFF LUMBERED BOLPHUNGA INTO THE DENSE GREEN JUNGLES OF THE WORLD ON WHICH HE'D BEEN TOLD MOGO WAS TO BE FOUND...
"THE SEARCH WAS NOT AN EASY ONE. FOR ONE THING, BOLPHUNGA HAD BEEN ABLE TO GLEAN NO INFORMATION AS TO WHAT MOGO ACTUALLY LOOKED LIKE.
"COULD HE BE A PLANT...?
"...OR PERHAPS AN INSECT?"
NO...
NO POWER RING ON THIS ONE...
"INDEED, TRY AS HE MIGHT, BOLPHUNGA COULD FIND NO TRACE OF INTELLIGENT LIFE UPON THE PLANET AT ALL...
"...SAVE FOR ONE THING.
"THE FOLIAGE HAD OBVIOUSLY BEEN CUT AND TENDED BY SOME HIGHER LIFE-FORM.
"THERE WERE NEAT-EDGED CLEARINGS, KILOMETERS WIDE. THERE WERE PLACES WHERE THE GREENERY HAD BEEN CLIPPED INTO VAST AND INDECIPHERABLE SHAPES.
"AS WEEKS TURNED INTO MONTHS AND MONTHS EXTENDED INTO YEARS, BOLPHUNGA GREW METHODICAL IN HIS SEARCH, DRAWING MANY PAINSTAKING MAPS...
"NOT FOR NOTHING WAS HE CALLED 'THE UNRELENTING.'
4

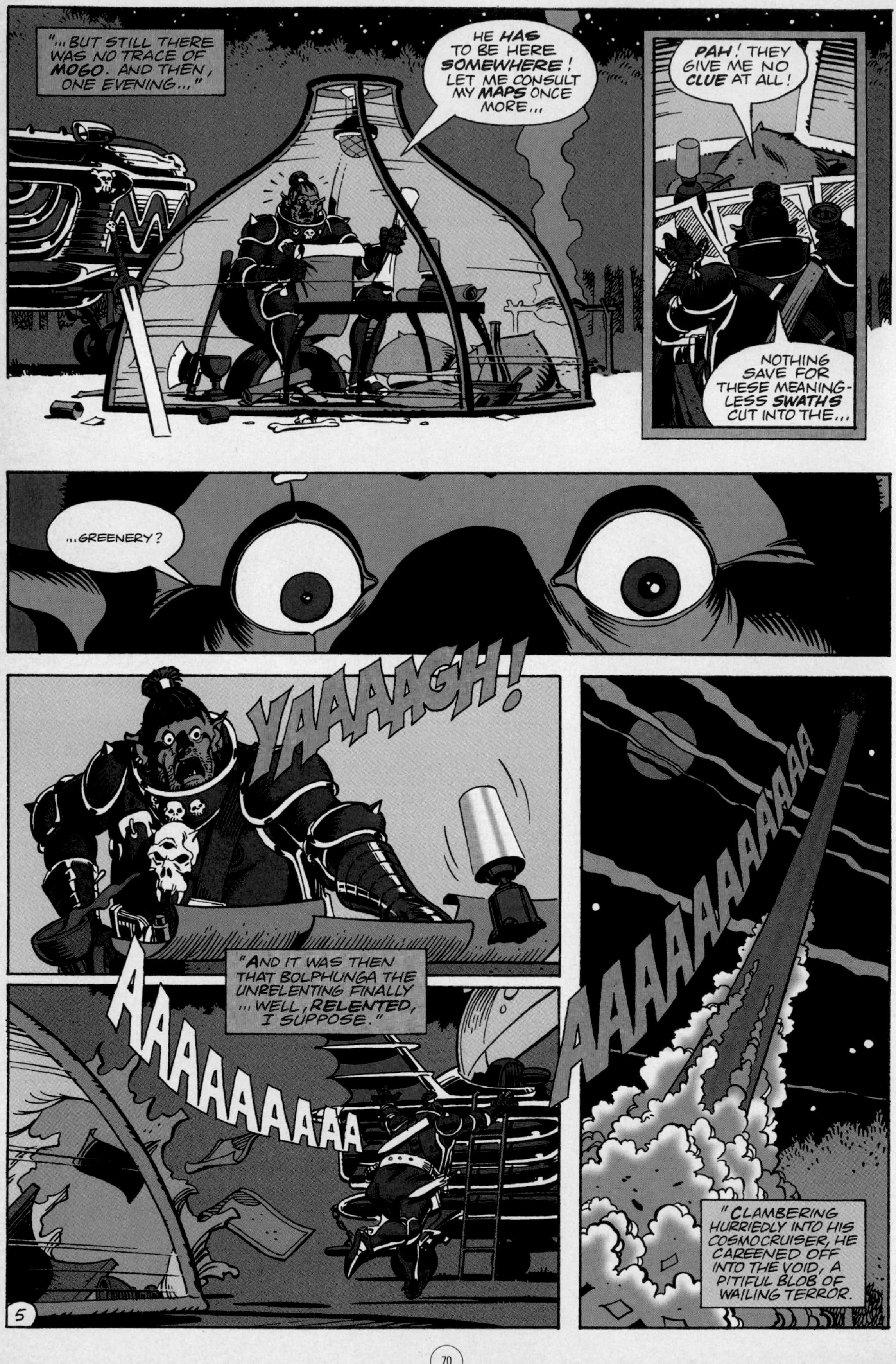
"...BUT STILL THERE WAS NO TRACE OF MOGO. AND THEN, ONE EVENING..."
HE HAS TO BE HERE SOMEWHERE! LET ME CONSULT MY MAPS ONCE MORE...
PAH! THEY GIVE ME NO CLUE AT ALL!
NOTHING SAVE FOR THESE MEANING-LESS SWATHS CUT INTO THE...
...GREENERY?
YAAAAGH!
"AND IT WAS THEN THAT BOLPHUNGA THE UNRELENTING FINALLY ...WELL, RELENTED, I SUPPOSE."
AAAAAAAAAAA
AAAAAAAAAAAAAAA
"CLAMBERING HURRIEDLY INTO HIS COSMOCRUISER, HE CAREENED OFF INTO THE VOID, A PITIFUL BLOB OF WAILING TERROR.
5

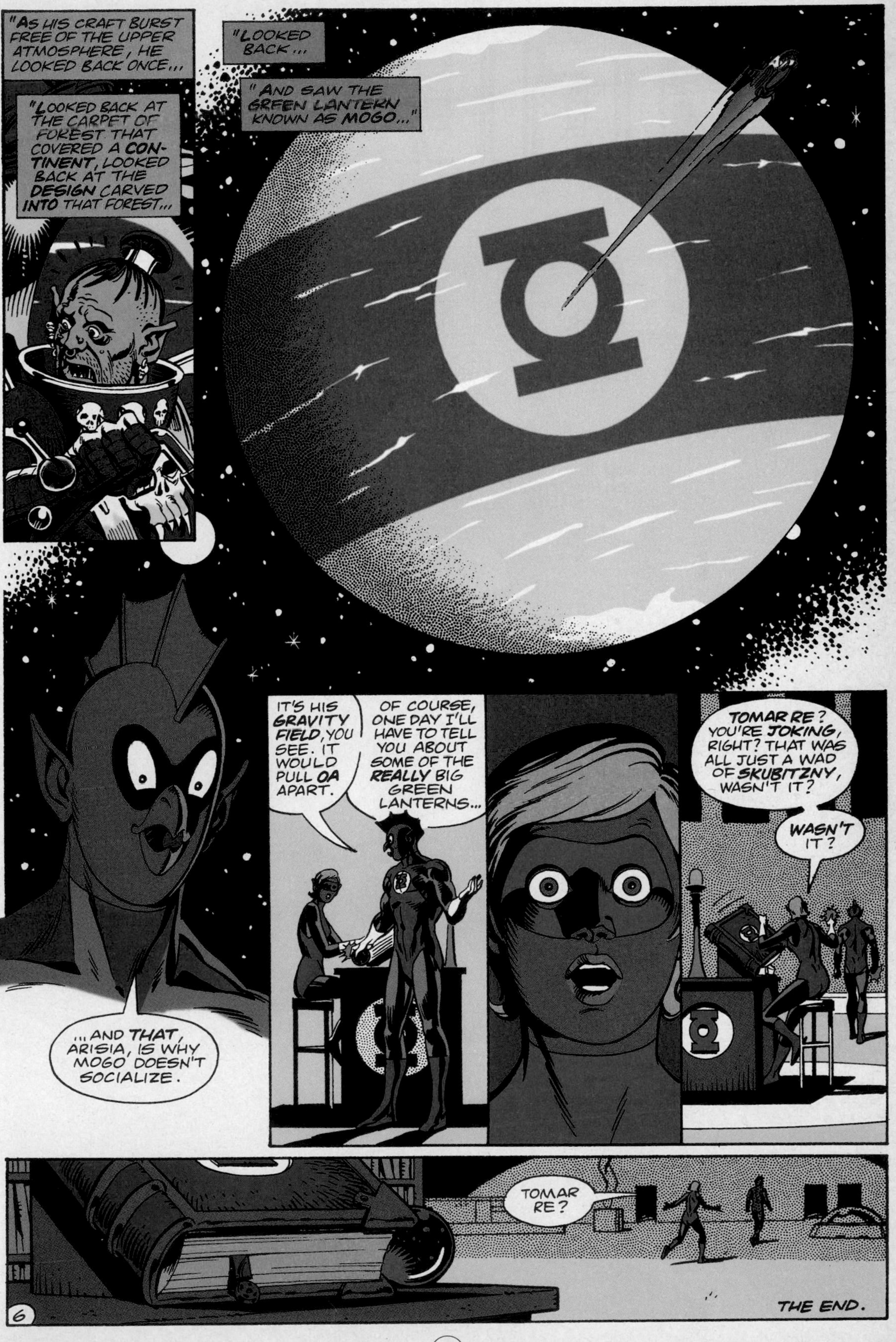

"AS HIS CRAFT BURST FREE OF THE UPPER ATMOSPHERE, HE LOOKED BACK ONCE...
"LOOKED BACK AT THE CARPET OF FOREST THAT COVERED A CON-TINENT, LOOKED BACK AT THE DESIGN CARVED INTO THAT FOREST...
"LOOKED BACK...
"AND SAW THE GREEN LANTERN KNOWN AS MOGO..."
...AND THAT, ARISIA, IS WHY MOGO DOESN'T SOCIALIZE.
IT'S HIS GRAVITY FIELD, YOU SEE. IT WOULD PULL OA APART.
OF COURSE, ONE DAY I'LL HAVE TO TELL YOU ABOUT SOME OF THE REALLY BIG GREEN LANTERNS...
TOMAR RE? YOU'RE JOKING, RIGHT? THAT WAS ALL JUST A WAD OF SKUBITZNY, WASN'T IT?
WASN'T IT?
6
TOMAR RE?
THE END.

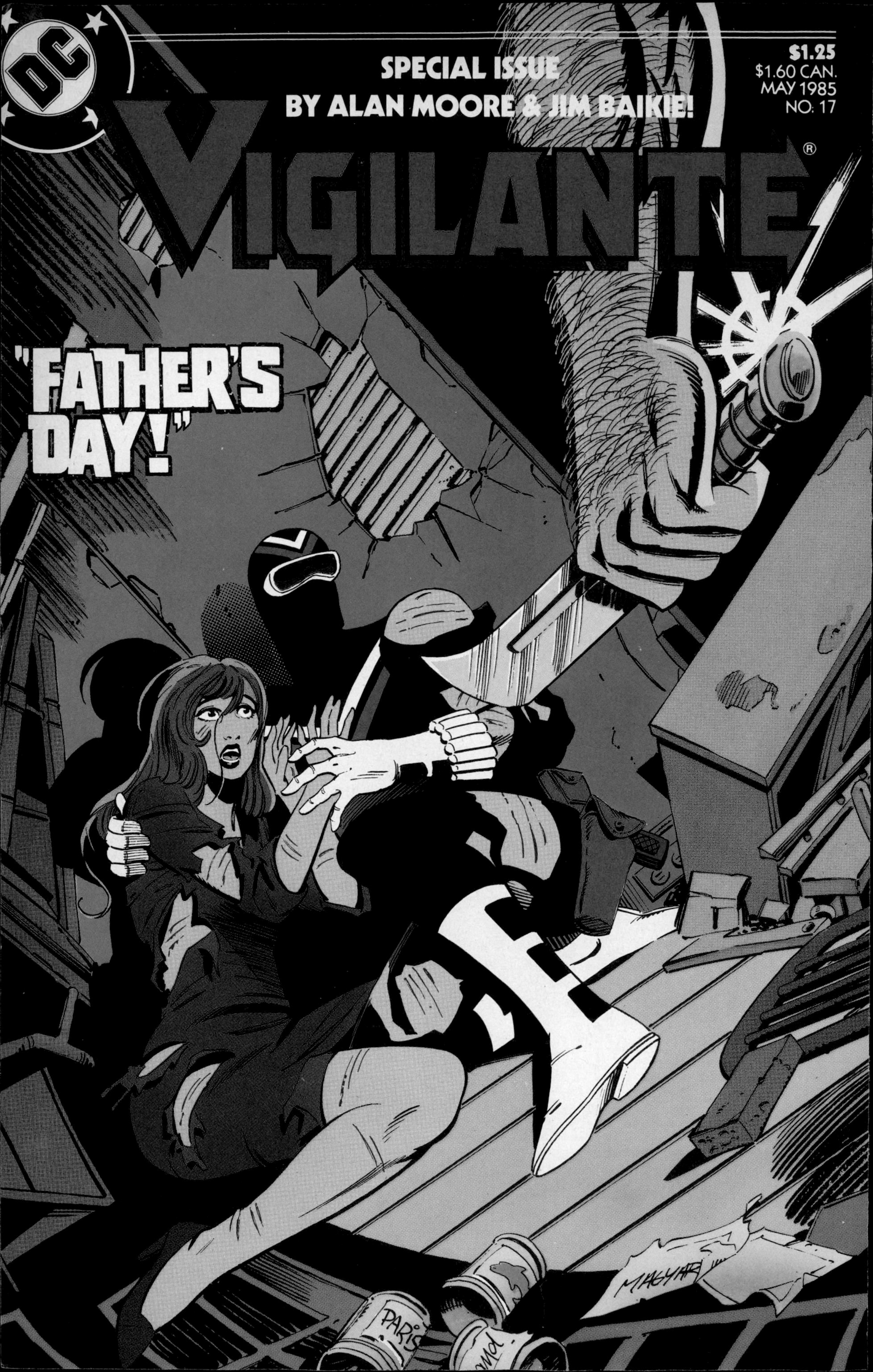
SPECIAL ISSUE
BY ALAN MOORE & JIM BAIKIE!
$1.25
$1.60 CAN.
MAY 1985
NO: 17
VIGILANTE®
"FATHER'S DAY!"
MAGYAR
PARIS

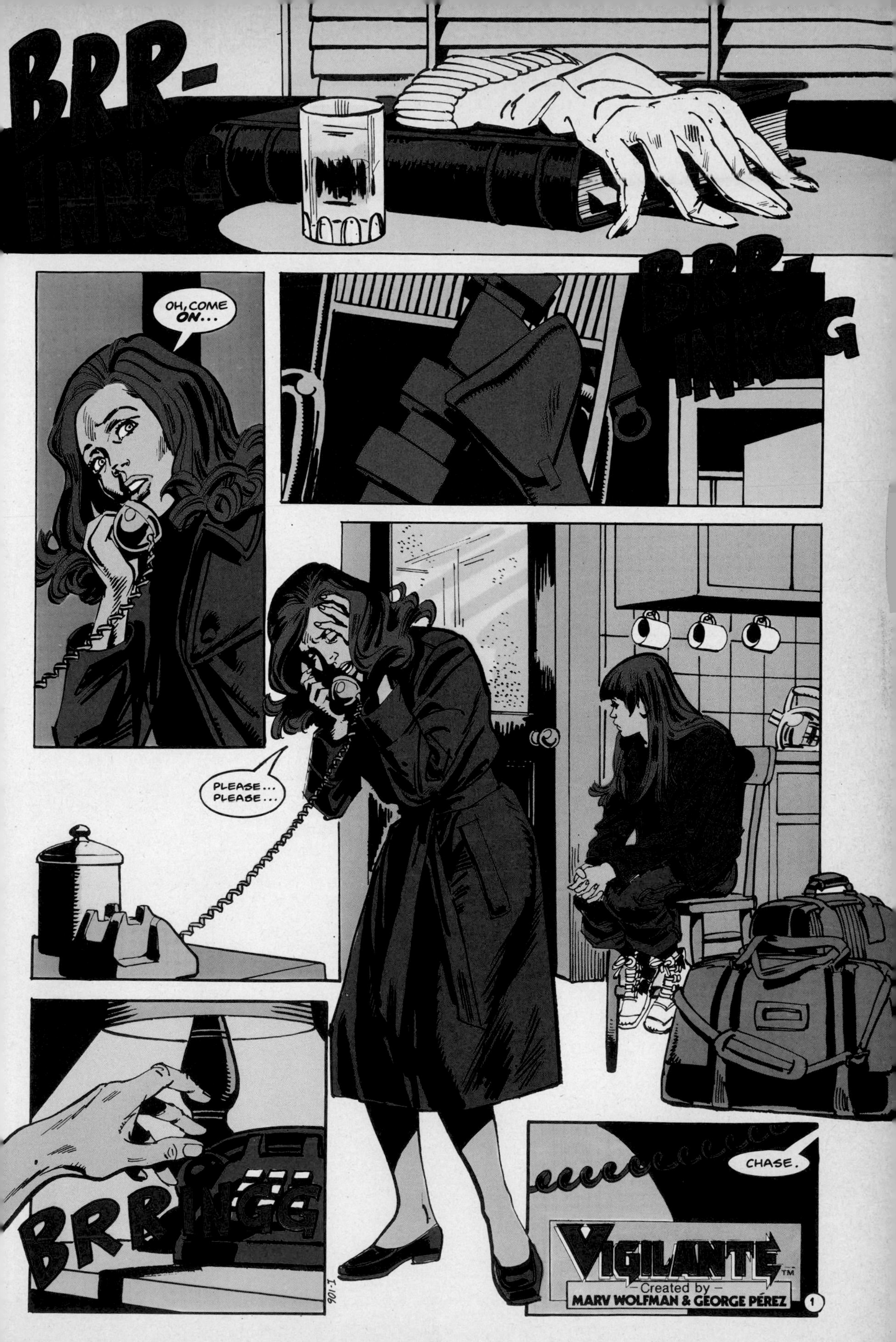
BRR-
INNGG
BRR-
INNGG
OH, COME ON...
PLEASE... PLEASE...
BRRINGG
CHASE.
VIGILANTE™
Created by
MARV WOLFMAN & GEORGE PÉREZ
1

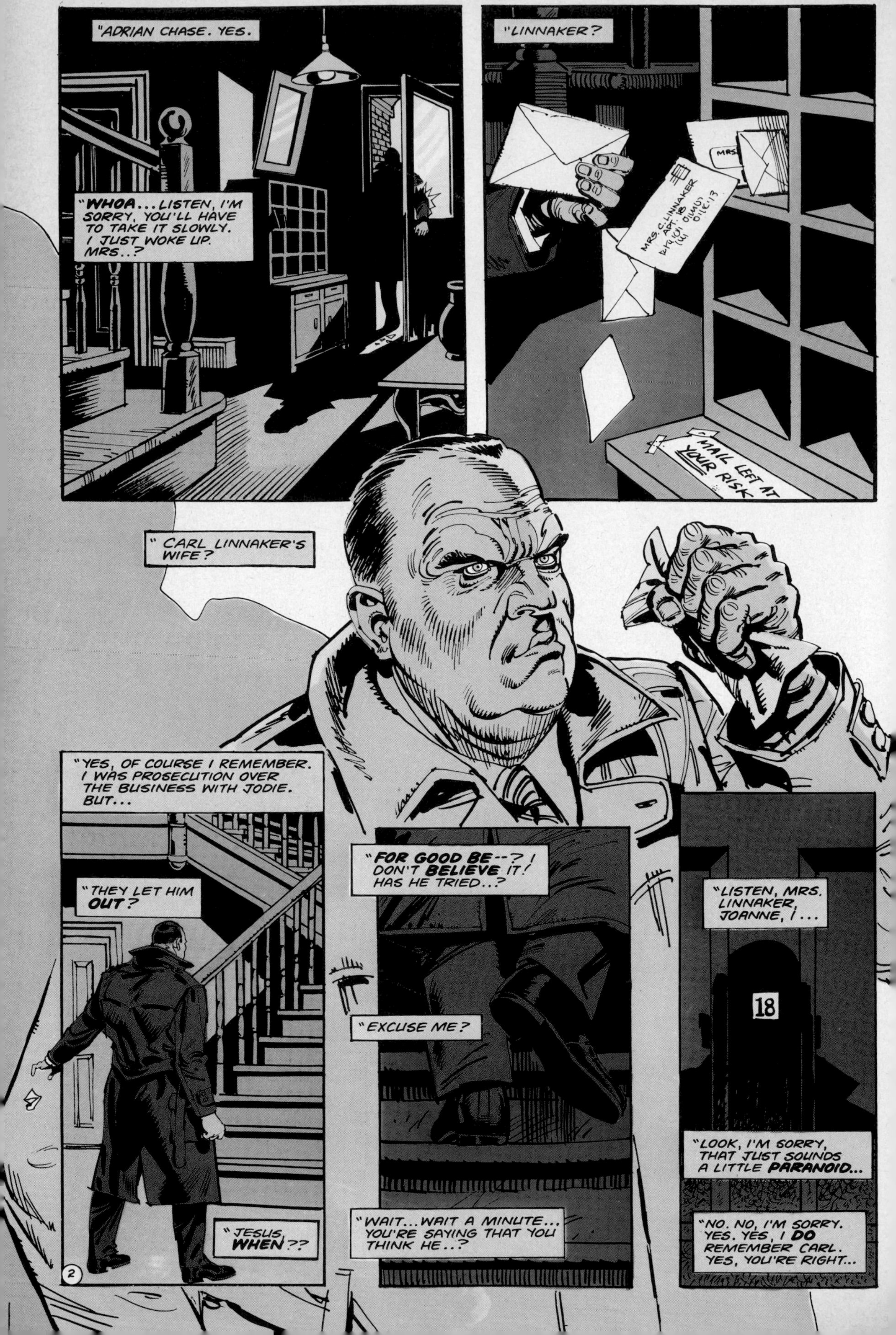

"ADRIAN CHASE. YES.
"WHOA... LISTEN, I'M SORRY, YOU'LL HAVE TO TAKE IT SLOWLY. I JUST WOKE UP. MRS..?
"LINNAKER?
MRS. C. LINNAKER APT. 18
MAIL LEFT AT YOUR RISK
" CARL LINNAKER'S WIFE?
"YES, OF COURSE I REMEMBER. I WAS PROSECUTION OVER THE BUSINESS WITH JODIE. BUT...
"THEY LET HIM OUT?
"JESUS, WHEN??
"FOR GOOD BE--? I DON'T BELIEVE IT! HAS HE TRIED..?
"EXCUSE ME?
"WAIT... WAIT A MINUTE... YOU'RE SAYING THAT YOU THINK HE..?
"LISTEN, MRS. LINNAKER, JOANNE, I...
18
"LOOK, I'M SORRY, THAT JUST SOUNDS A LITTLE PARANOID...
"NO. NO, I'M SORRY. YES. YES, I DO REMEMBER CARL. YES, YOU'RE RIGHT...

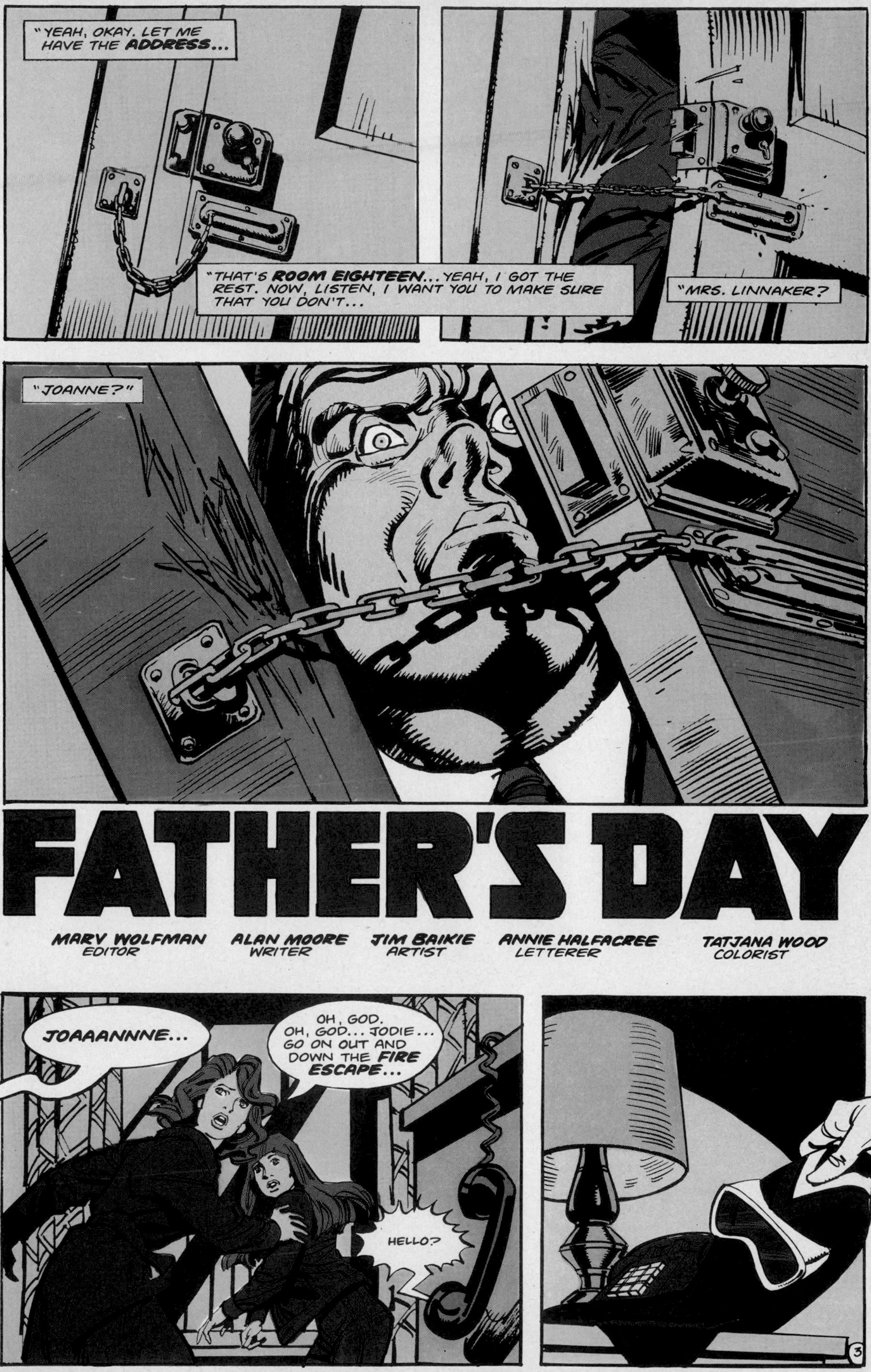
"YEAH, OKAY. LET ME HAVE THE ADDRESS...
"THAT'S ROOM EIGHTEEN... YEAH, I GOT THE REST. NOW, LISTEN, I WANT YOU TO MAKE SURE THAT YOU DON'T...
"MRS. LINNAKER?
"JOANNE?"
FATHER'S DAY
MARV WOLFMAN EDITOR
ALAN MOORE WRITER
JIM BAIKIE ARTIST
ANNIE HALFACREE LETTERER
TATJANA WOOD COLORIST
JOAAAANNNE...
OH, GOD. OH, GOD... JODIE... GO ON OUT AND DOWN THE FIRE ESCAPE...
HELLO?

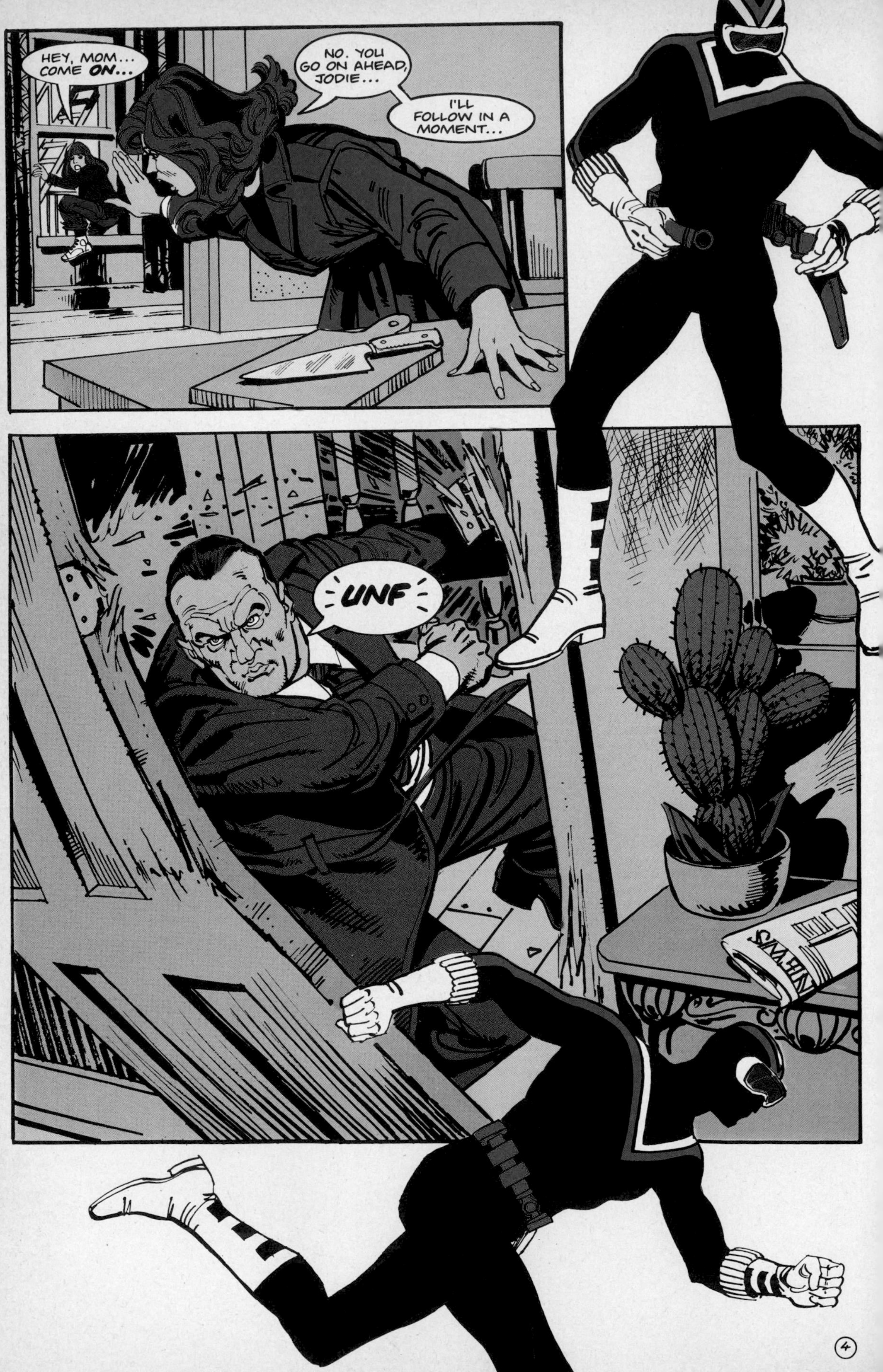
HEY, MOM... COME ON...
NO. YOU GO ON AHEAD, JODIE...
I'LL FOLLOW IN A MOMENT...
UNF
NEWS

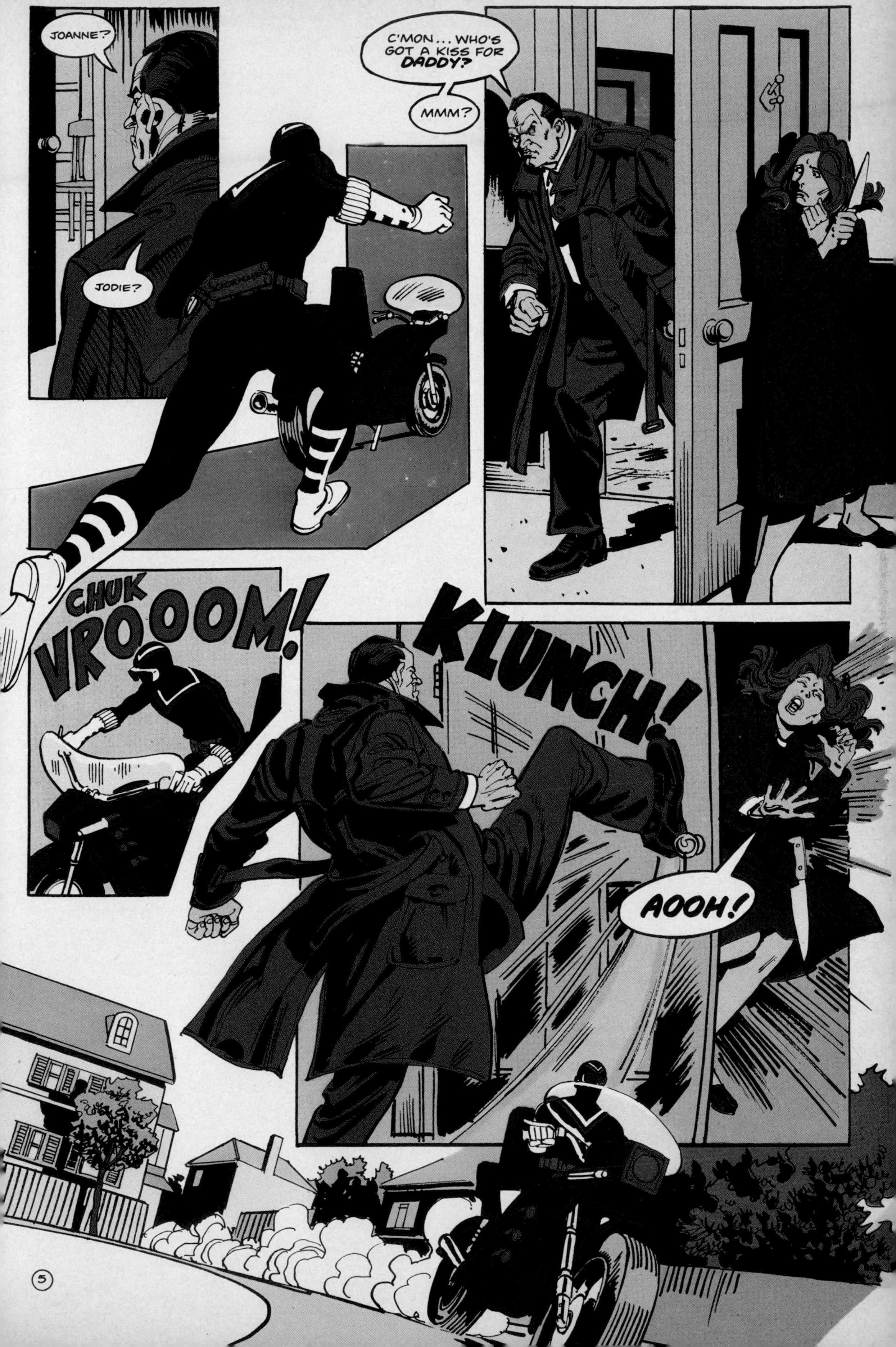
JOANNE?
JODIE?
C'MON... WHO'S GOT A KISS FOR DADDY?
MMM?
CHUK
VROOOM!
KLUNCH!
AOOH!

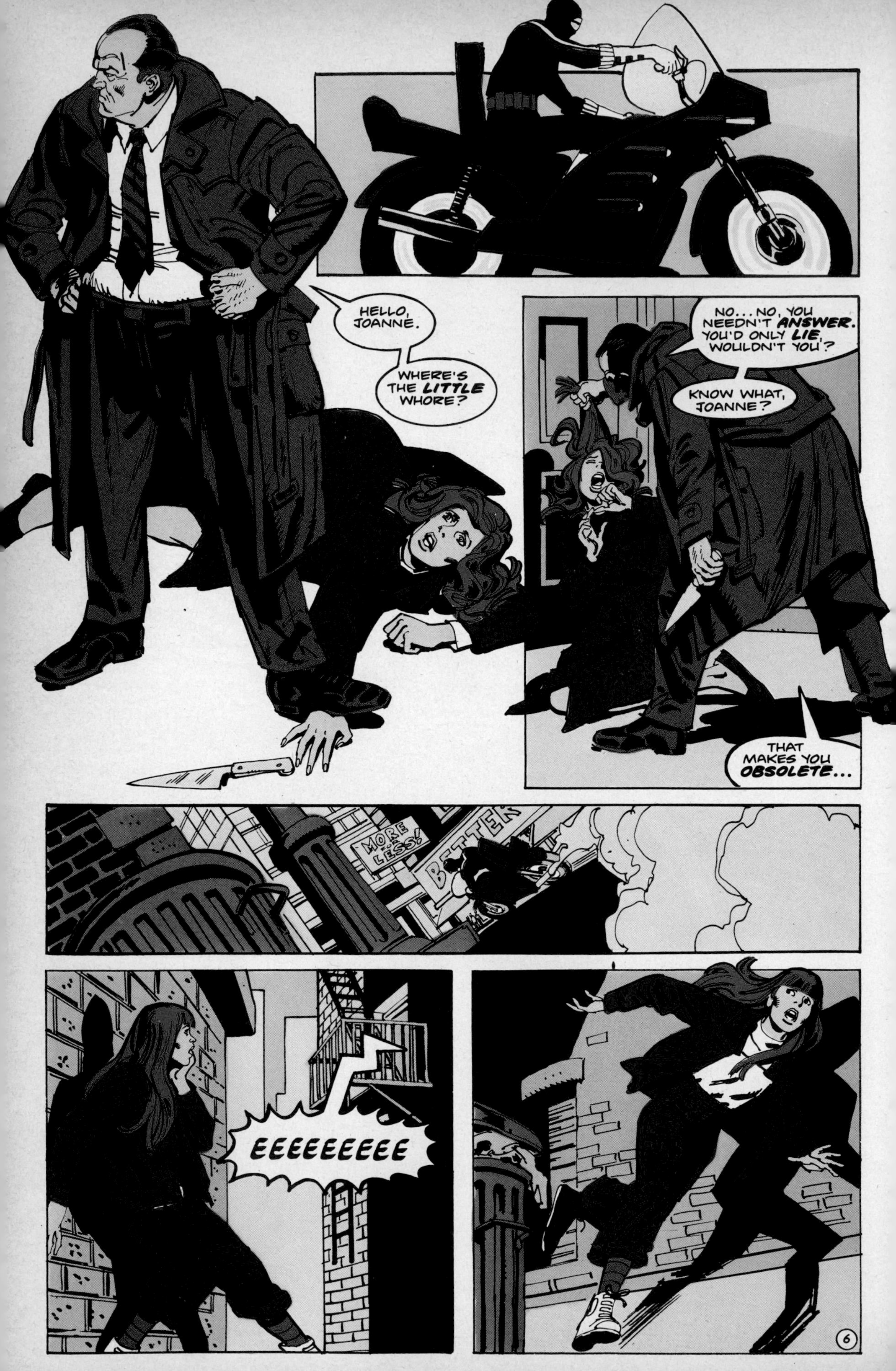
HELLO, JOANNE.
WHERE'S THE LITTLE WHORE?
NO... NO, YOU NEEDN'T ANSWER. YOU'D ONLY LIE, WOULDN'T YOU?
KNOW WHAT, JOANNE?
THAT MAKES YOU OBSOLETE...
MORE FOR LESS!
EEEEEEEEE

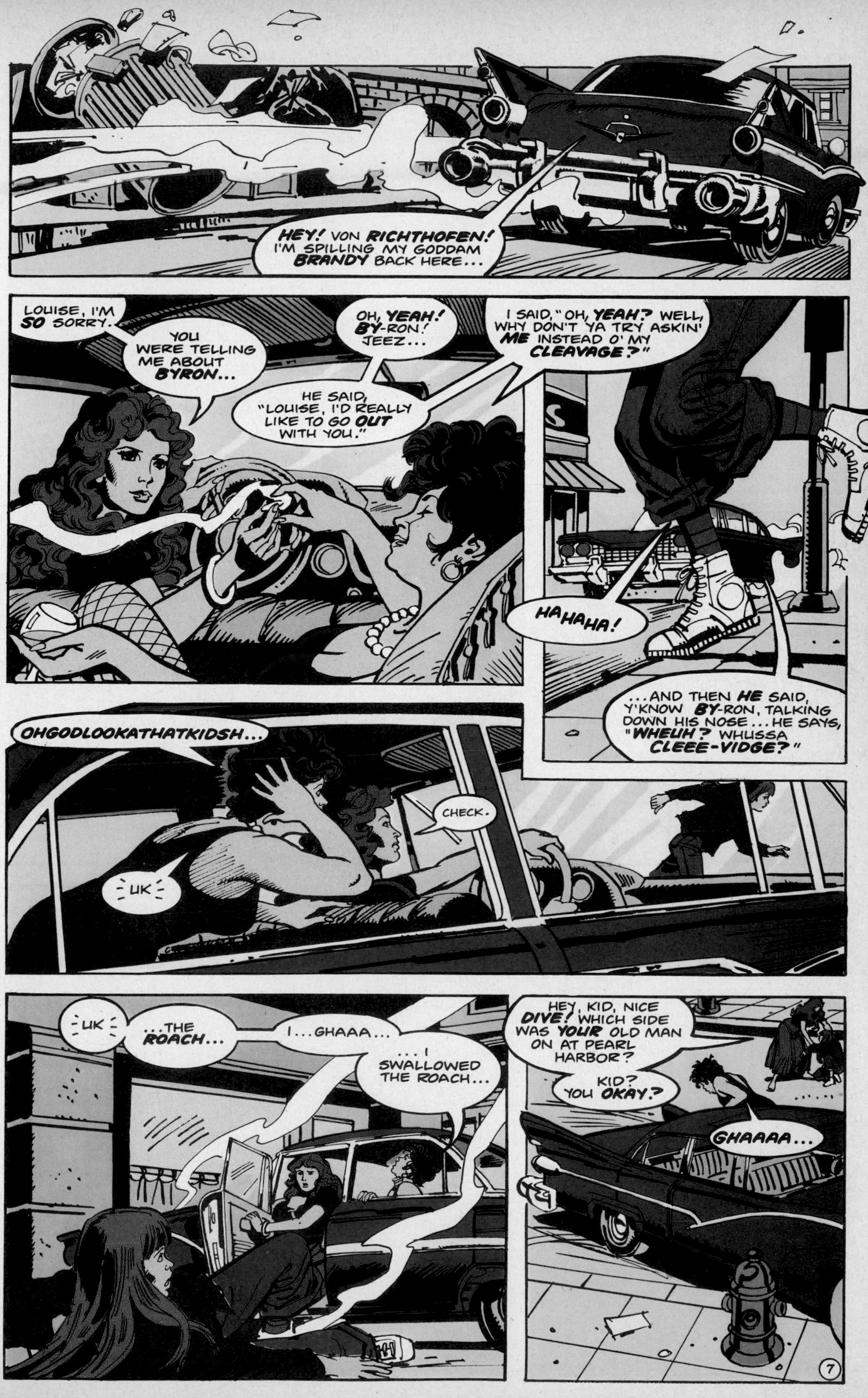
HEY! VON RICHTHOFEN! I'M SPILLING MY GODDAM BRANDY BACK HERE...
LOUISE, I'M SO SORRY.
YOU WERE TELLING ME ABOUT BYRON...
OH, YEAH! BY-RON! JEEZ...
HE SAID, "LOUISE, I'D REALLY LIKE TO GO OUT WITH YOU."
I SAID, "OH, YEAH? WELL, WHY DON'T YA TRY ASKIN' ME INSTEAD O' MY CLEAVAGE?"
HAHAHA!
...AND THEN HE SAID, Y'KNOW BY-RON, TALKING DOWN HIS NOSE... HE SAYS, "WHEUH? WHUSSA CLEEE-VIDGE?"
OHGODLOOKATHATKIDSH...
CHECK.
UK
UK
...THE ROACH...
I...GHAAA...
...I SWALLOWED THE ROACH...
HEY, KID, NICE DIVE! WHICH SIDE WAS YOUR OLD MAN ON AT PEARL HARBOR?
KID? YOU OKAY?
GHAAAA...

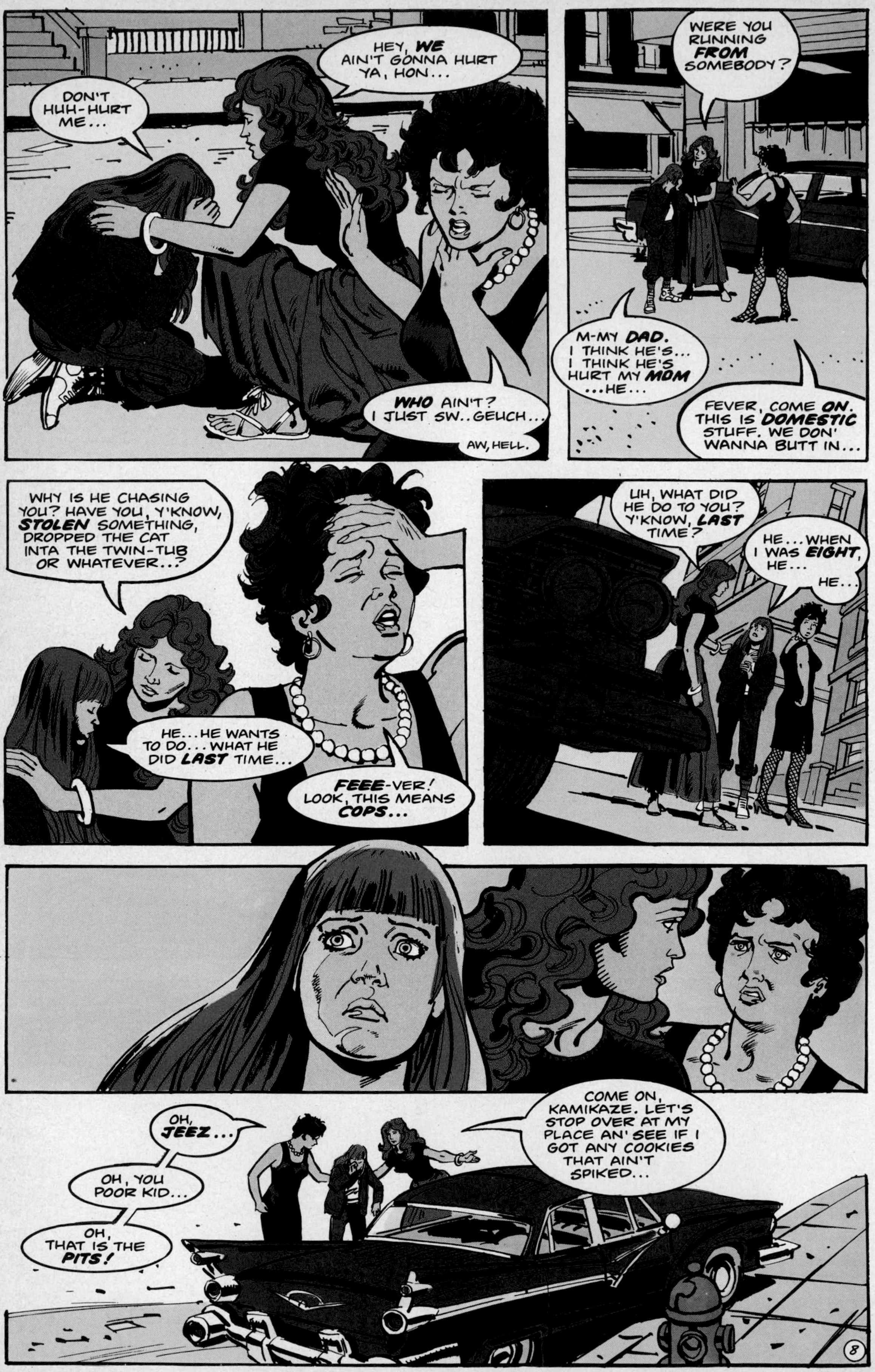
DON'T HUH-HURT ME...
HEY, WE AIN'T GONNA HURT YA, HON...
WHO AIN'T? I JUST SW..GEUCH...
AW, HELL.
WERE YOU RUNNING FROM SOMEBODY?
M-MY DAD. I THINK HE'S... I THINK HE'S HURT MY MOM ...HE...
FEVER, COME ON. THIS IS DOMESTIC STUFF. WE DON' WANNA BUTT IN...
WHY IS HE CHASING YOU? HAVE YOU, Y'KNOW, STOLEN SOMETHING, DROPPED THE CAT INTA THE TWIN-TUB OR WHATEVER..?
HE...HE WANTS TO DO...WHAT HE DID LAST TIME...
FEEE-VER! LOOK, THIS MEANS COPS...
UH, WHAT DID HE DO TO YOU? Y'KNOW, LAST TIME?
HE...WHEN I WAS EIGHT, HE...
HE...
OH, JEEZ...
OH, YOU POOR KID...
OH, THAT IS THE PITS!
COME ON, KAMIKAZE. LET'S STOP OVER AT MY PLACE AN' SEE IF I GOT ANY COOKIES THAT AIN'T SPIKED...
8

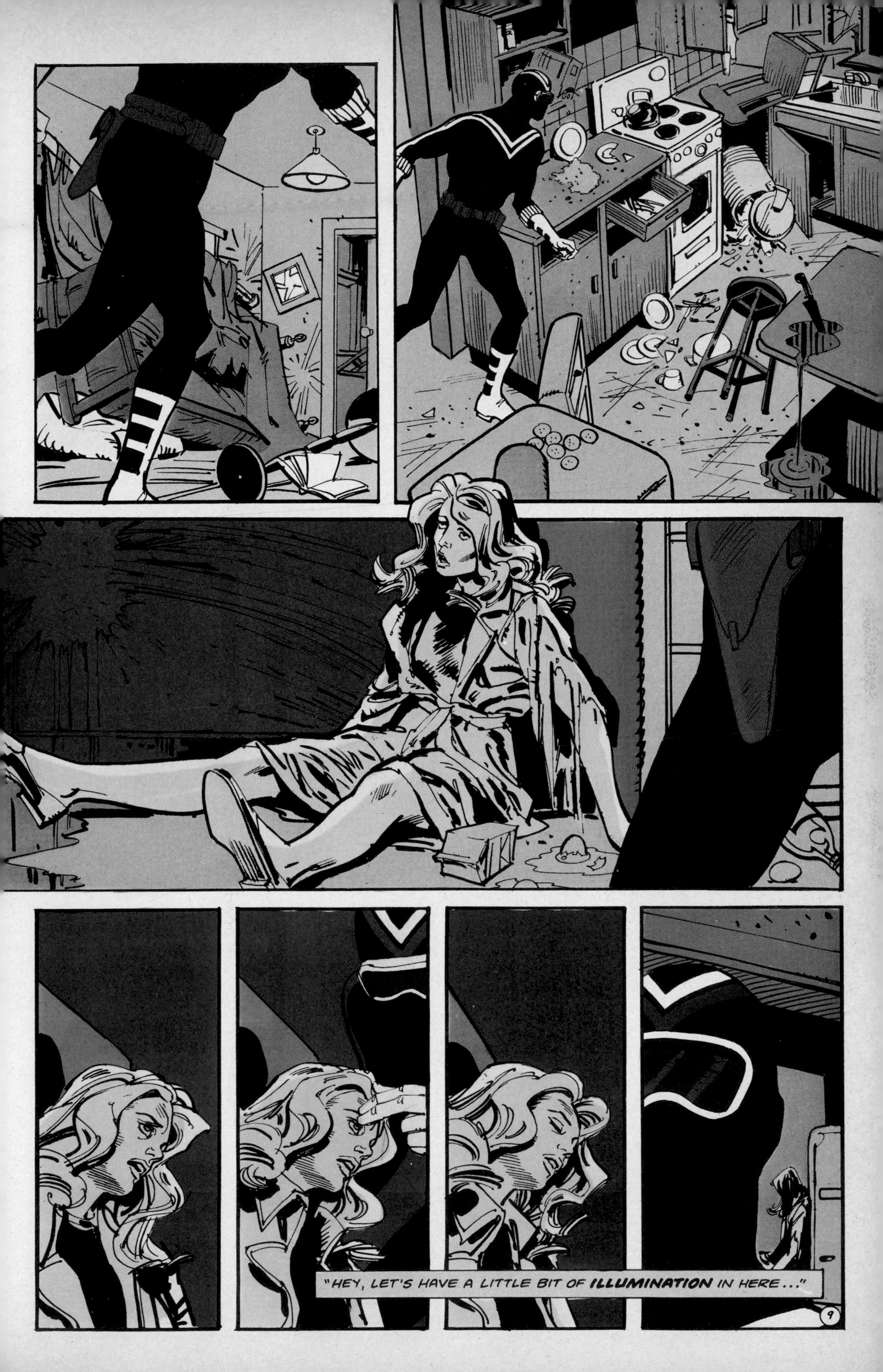
"HEY, LET'S HAVE A LITTLE BIT OF ILLUMINATION IN HERE..."

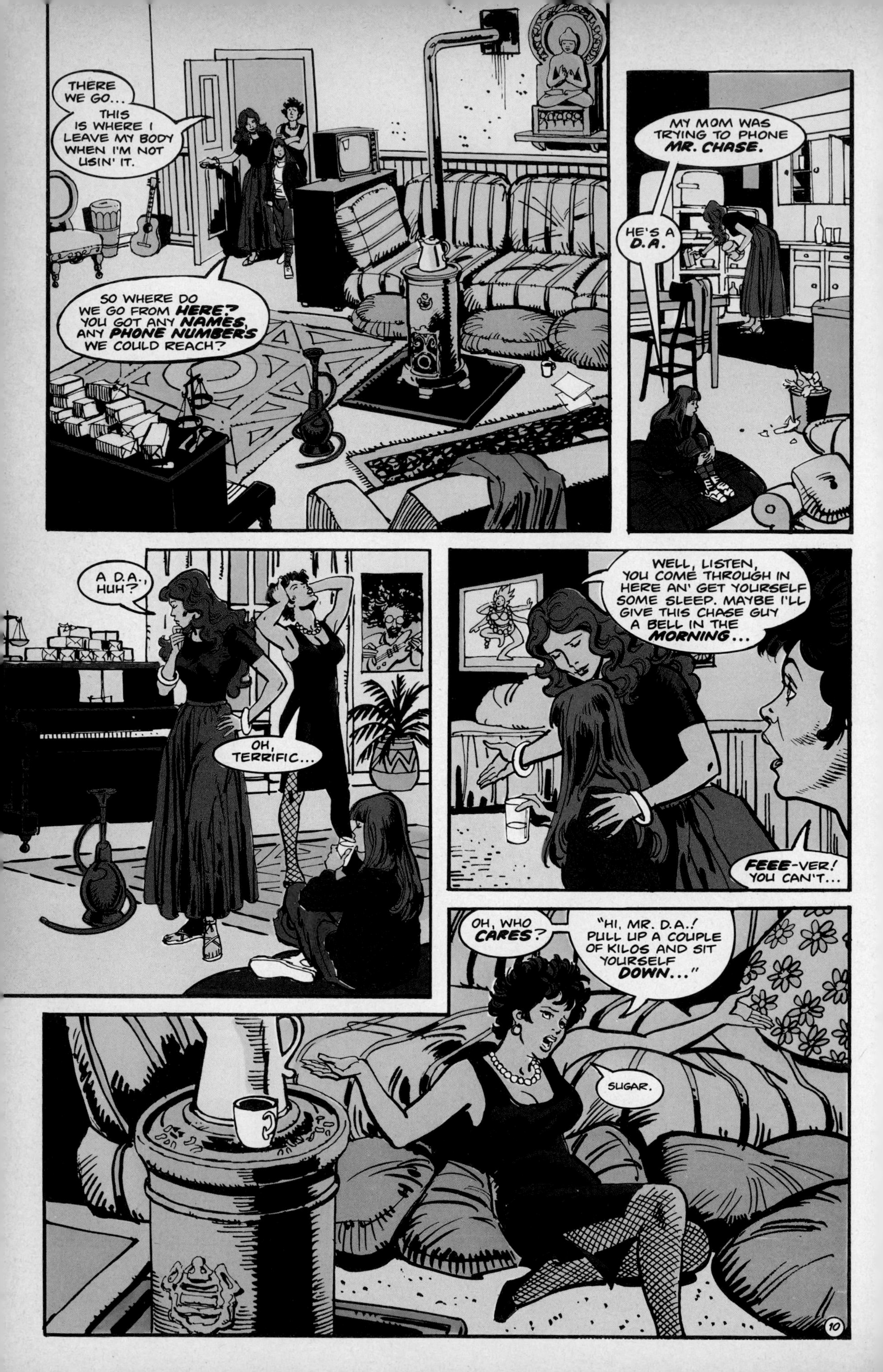
THERE WE GO... THIS IS WHERE I LEAVE MY BODY WHEN I'M NOT USIN' IT.
SO WHERE DO WE GO FROM HERE? YOU GOT ANY NAMES, ANY PHONE NUMBERS WE COULD REACH?
MY MOM WAS TRYING TO PHONE MR. CHASE.
HE'S A D.A.
A D.A., HUH?
OH, TERRIFIC...
WELL, LISTEN, YOU COME THROUGH IN HERE AN' GET YOURSELF SOME SLEEP. MAYBE I'LL GIVE THIS CHASE GUY A BELL IN THE MORNING...
FEEE-VER! YOU CAN'T...
OH, WHO CARES?
"HI, MR. D.A.! PULL UP A COUPLE OF KILOS AND SIT YOURSELF DOWN..."
SUGAR.

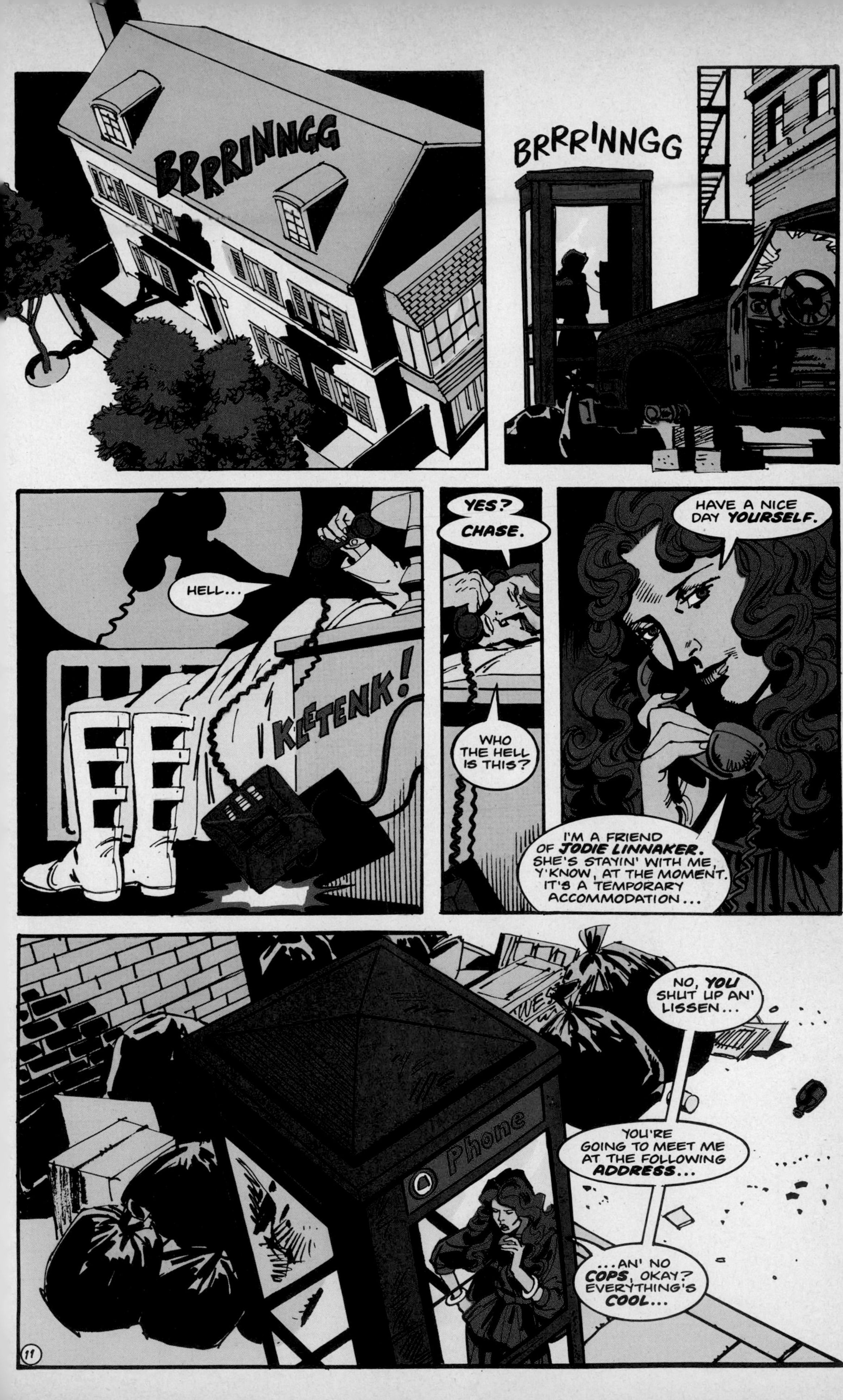
BRRRINNGG
BRRRINNGG
HELL...
KLETENK!
YES?
CHASE.
WHO THE HELL IS THIS?
HAVE A NICE DAY YOURSELF.
I'M A FRIEND OF JODIE LINNAKER. SHE'S STAYIN' WITH ME, Y'KNOW, AT THE MOMENT. IT'S A TEMPORARY ACCOMMODATION...
NO, YOU SHUT UP AN' LISSEN...
Phone
YOU'RE GOING TO MEET ME AT THE FOLLOWING ADDRESS...
...AN' NO COPS, OKAY? EVERYTHING'S COOL...

"OKAY... NOW, HERE'S WHAT I WANT YOU TO *DO*..."

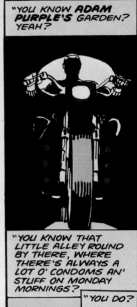

"YOU KNOW *ADAM PURPLE'S* GARDEN? YEAH?"

"YOU KNOW THAT LITTLE ALLEY ROUND BY THERE, WHERE THERE'S ALWAYS A LOT O' CONDOMS AN' STUFF ON MONDAY MORNINGS?"

"YOU DO?"

"OKAY. WELL, I'M GONNA BE THERE IN FIFTEEN MINUTES..."

"...AND I'M GONNA BE GONE IN *TWENTY*."

"SO, LIKE, I GUESS YOU OUGHTA *HURRY*, RIGHT?"

"WELL, IT'S BEEN REALLY NICE *TALKING* TO YOU AN' I HOPE I DIDN'T GET YOU OUTTA *BED* OR ANYTHING."

"BYE."

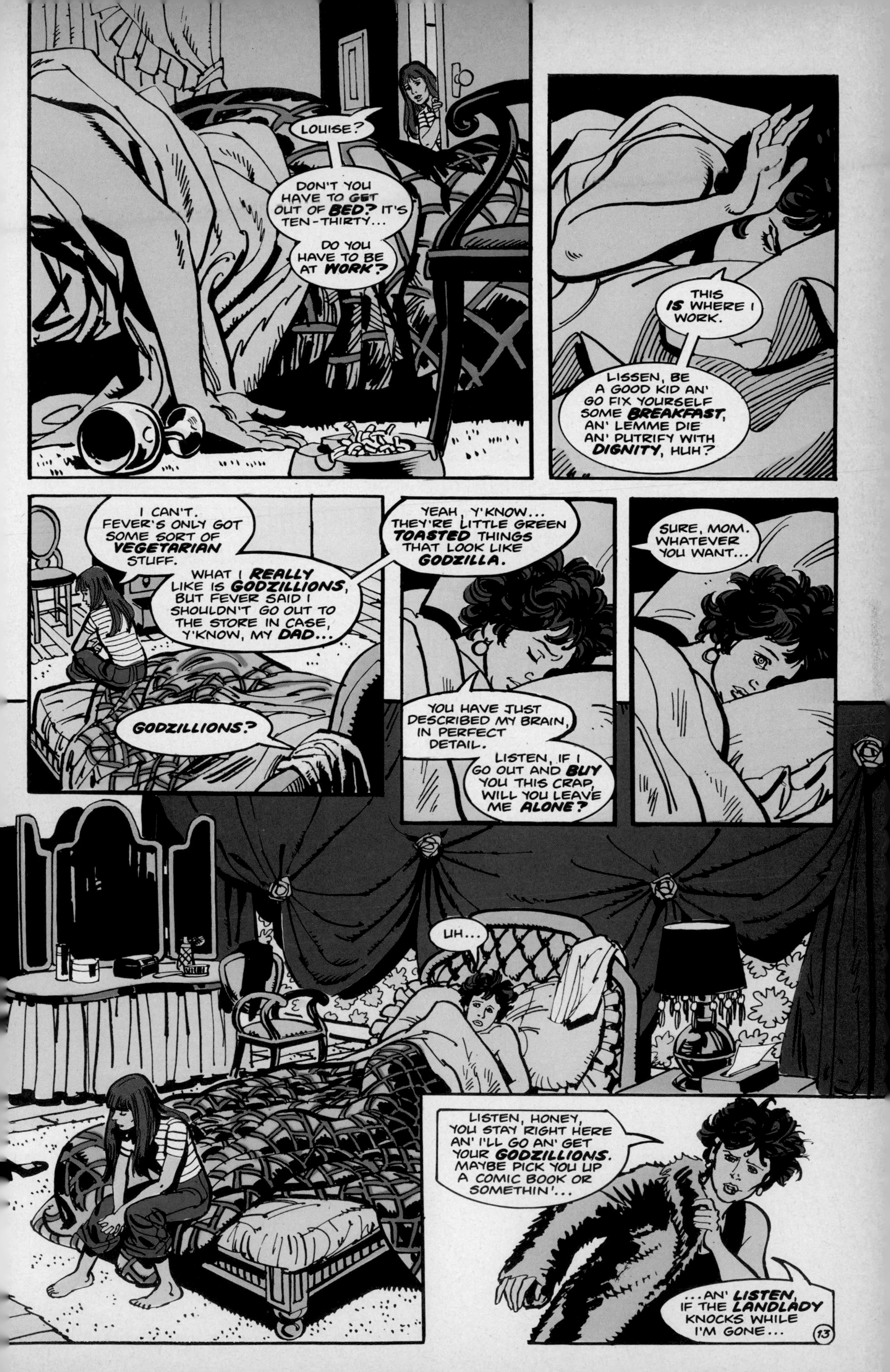

LOUISE?
DON'T YOU HAVE TO GET OUT OF BED? IT'S TEN-THIRTY...
DO YOU HAVE TO BE AT WORK?
THIS IS WHERE I WORK.
LISSEN, BE A GOOD KID AN' GO FIX YOURSELF SOME BREAKFAST, AN' LEMME DIE AN' PUTRIFY WITH DIGNITY, HUH?
I CAN'T. FEVER'S ONLY GOT SOME SORT OF VEGETARIAN STUFF.
WHAT I REALLY LIKE IS GODZILLIONS, BUT FEVER SAID I SHOULDN'T GO OUT TO THE STORE IN CASE, Y'KNOW, MY DAD...
GODZILLIONS?
YEAH, Y'KNOW... THEY'RE LITTLE GREEN TOASTED THINGS THAT LOOK LIKE GODZILLA.
YOU HAVE JUST DESCRIBED MY BRAIN, IN PERFECT DETAIL.
LISTEN, IF I GO OUT AND BUY YOU THIS CRAP, WILL YOU LEAVE ME ALONE?
SURE, MOM. WHATEVER YOU WANT...
UH...
LISTEN, HONEY, YOU STAY RIGHT HERE AN' I'LL GO AN' GET YOUR GODZILLIONS. MAYBE PICK YOU UP A COMIC BOOK OR SOMETHIN'...
...AN' LISTEN, IF THE LANDLADY KNOCKS WHILE I'M GONE...

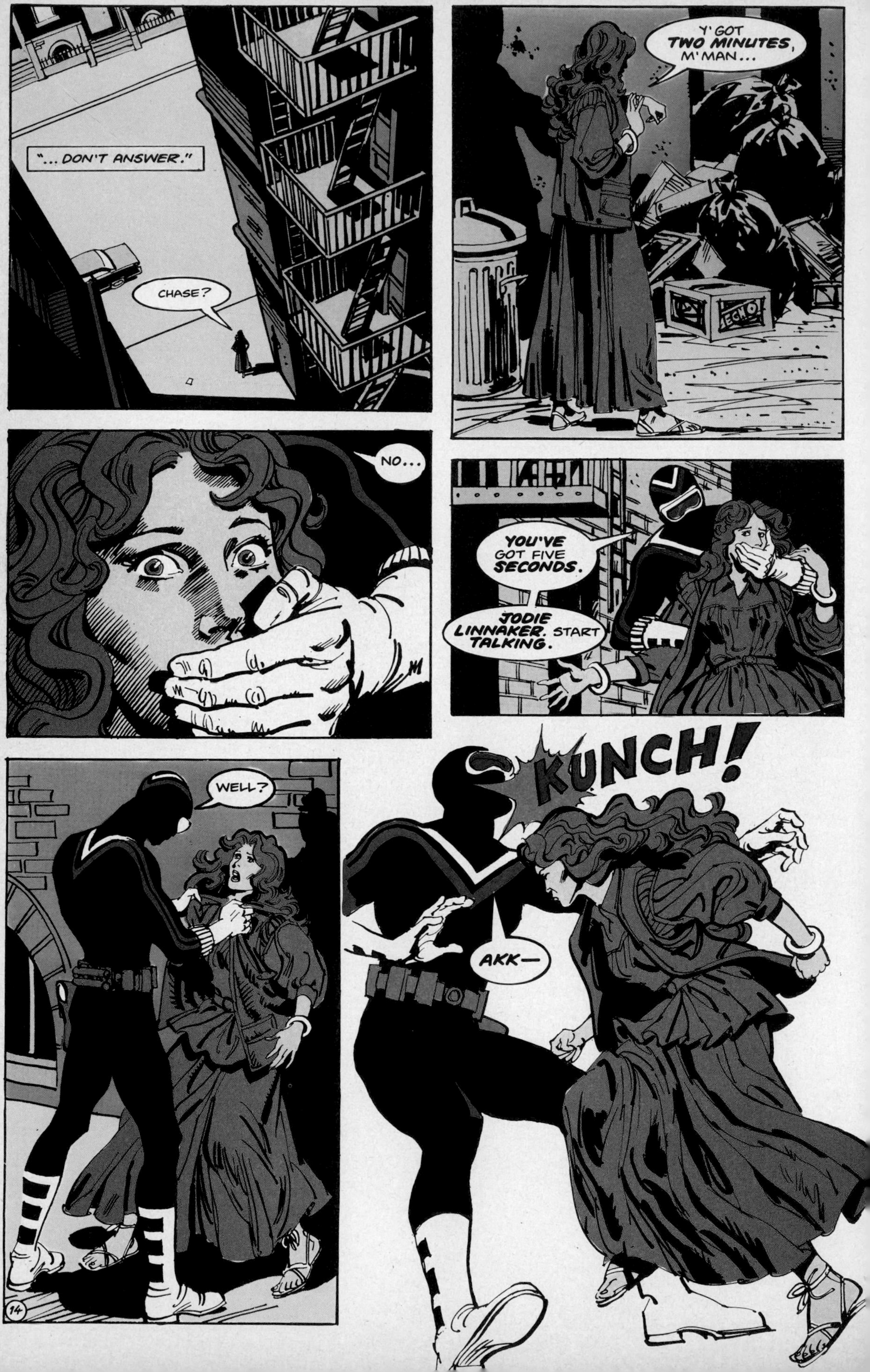
"... DON'T ANSWER."
CHASE?
Y' GOT TWO MINUTES, M'MAN...
NO...
YOU'VE GOT FIVE SECONDS.
JODIE LINNAKER. START TALKING.
WELL?
KUNCH!
AKK—
14

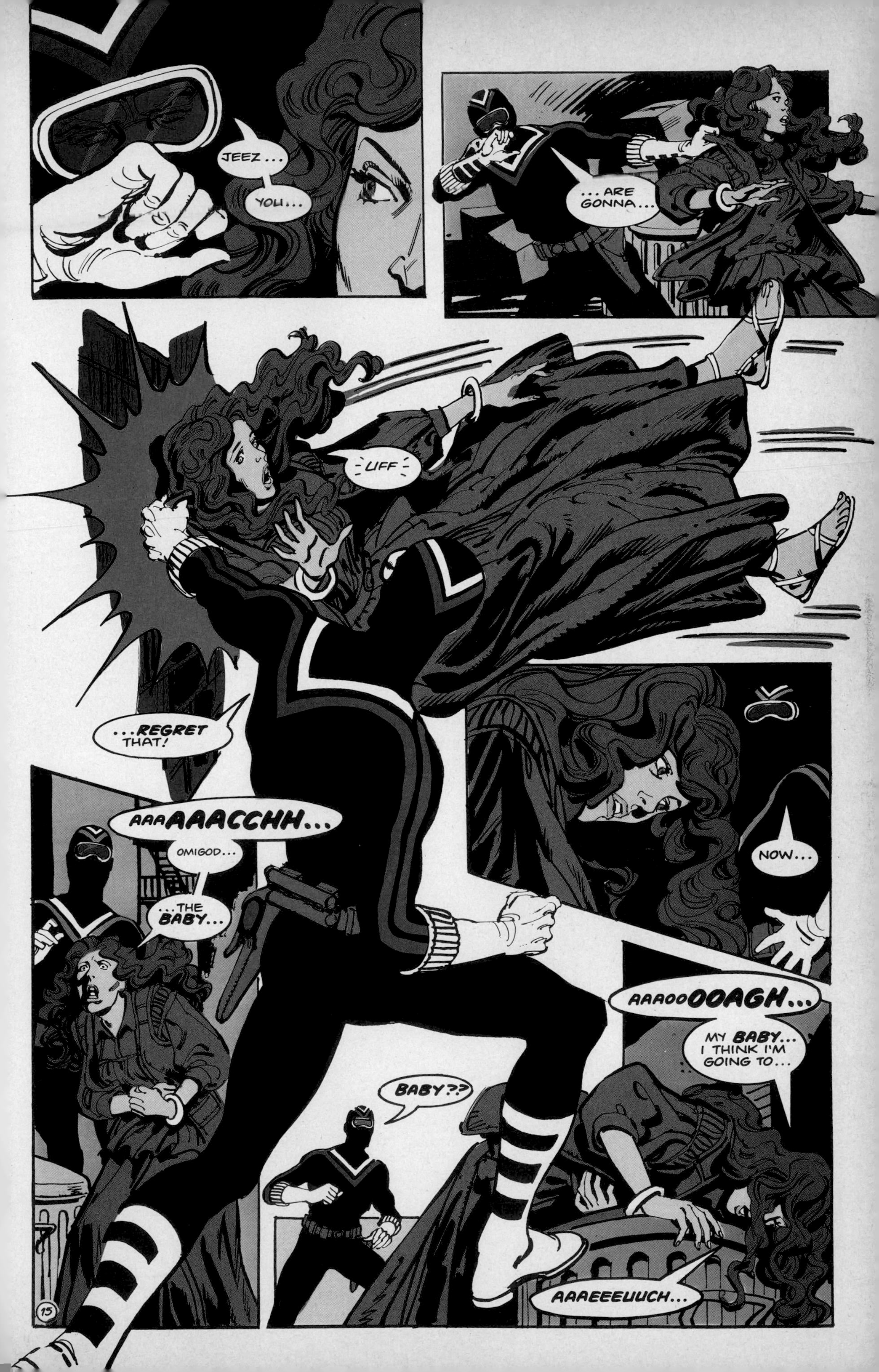
JEEZ...
YOU...
...ARE GONNA...
UFF
...REGRET THAT!
NOW...
AAAAAACCHH...
OMIGOD...
...THE BABY...
BABY??
AAAOOOOAGH...
MY BABY... I THINK I'M GOING TO...
AAAEEEUUCH...
15

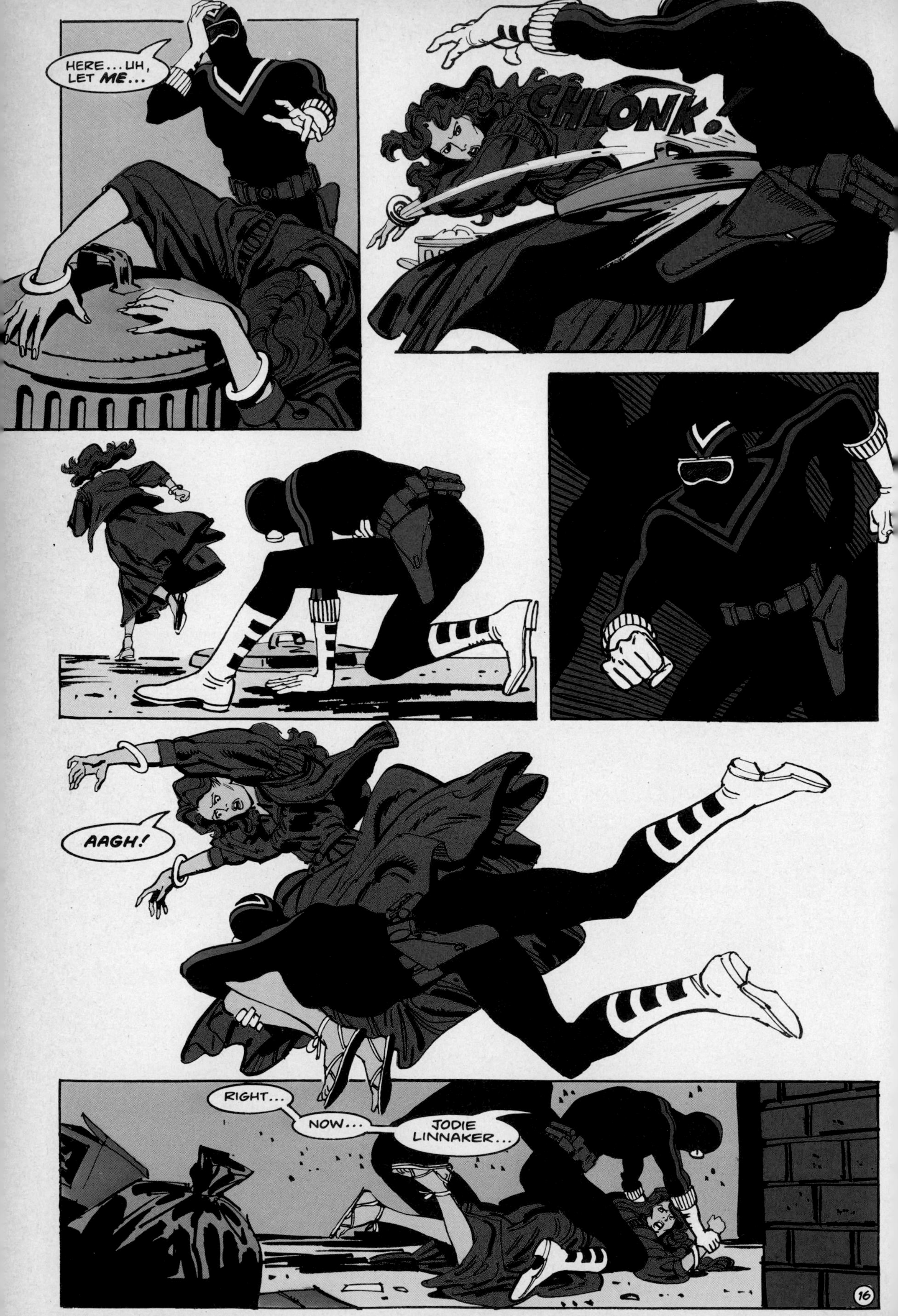
HERE... UH, LET ME...
CHLONK!
AAGH!
RIGHT...
NOW...
JODIE LINNAKER...
16

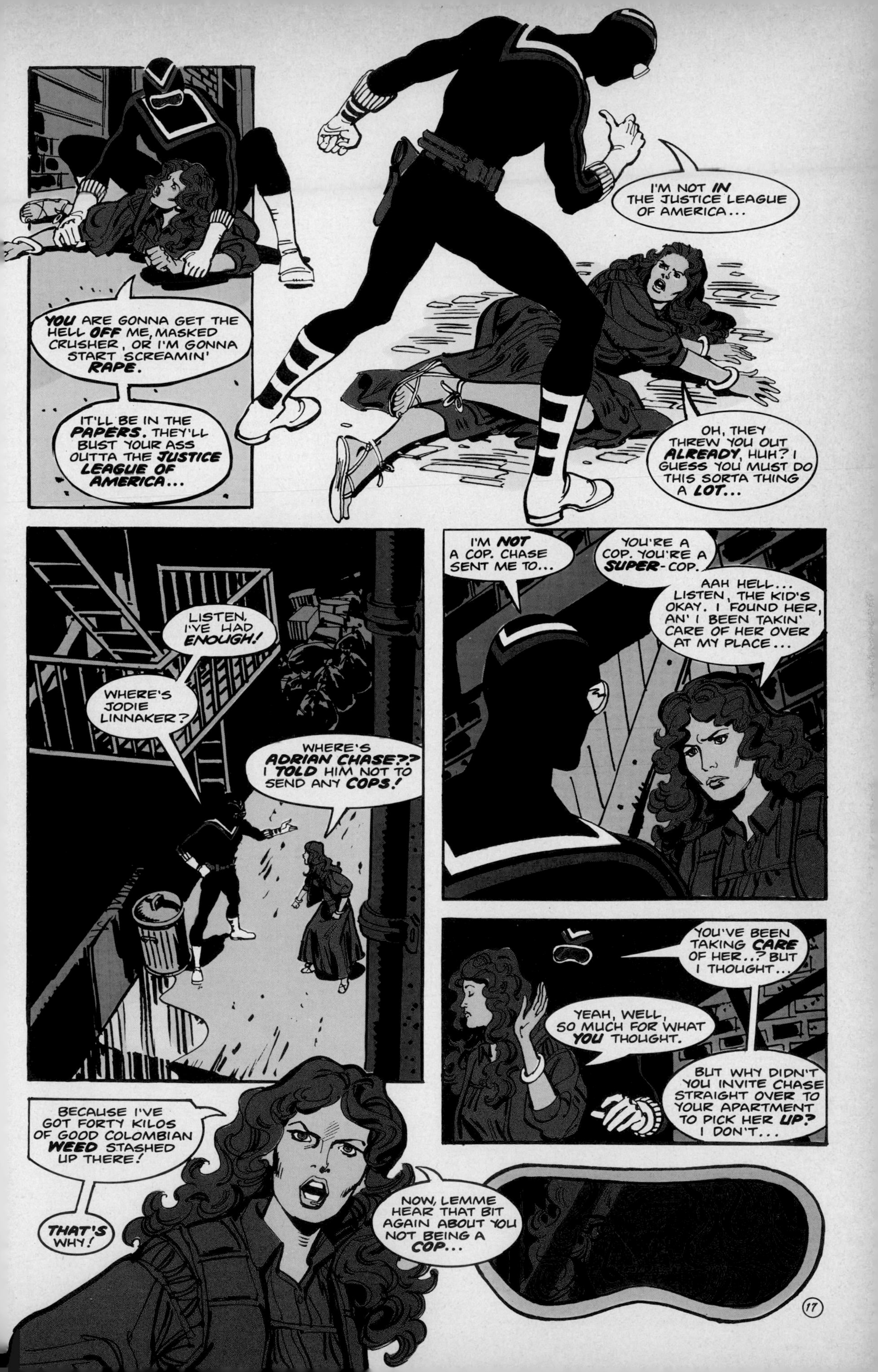
YOU ARE GONNA GET THE HELL OFF ME, MASKED CRUSHER, OR I'M GONNA START SCREAMIN' RAPE.
IT'LL BE IN THE PAPERS. THEY'LL BUST YOUR ASS OUTTA THE JUSTICE LEAGUE OF AMERICA...
I'M NOT IN THE JUSTICE LEAGUE OF AMERICA...
OH, THEY THREW YOU OUT ALREADY, HUH? I GUESS YOU MUST DO THIS SORTA THING A LOT...
LISTEN, I'VE HAD ENOUGH!
WHERE'S JODIE LINNAKER?
WHERE'S ADRIAN CHASE?? I TOLD HIM NOT TO SEND ANY COPS!
I'M NOT A COP. CHASE SENT ME TO...
YOU'RE A COP. YOU'RE A SUPER-COP.
AAH HELL... LISTEN, THE KID'S OKAY. I FOUND HER, AN' I BEEN TAKIN' CARE OF HER OVER AT MY PLACE...
YOU'VE BEEN TAKING CARE OF HER...? BUT I THOUGHT...
YEAH, WELL, SO MUCH FOR WHAT YOU THOUGHT.
BUT WHY DIDN'T YOU INVITE CHASE STRAIGHT OVER TO YOUR APARTMENT TO PICK HER UP? I DON'T...
BECAUSE I'VE GOT FORTY KILOS OF GOOD COLOMBIAN WEED STASHED UP THERE!
THAT'S WHY!
NOW, LEMME HEAR THAT BIT AGAIN ABOUT YOU NOT BEING A COP...

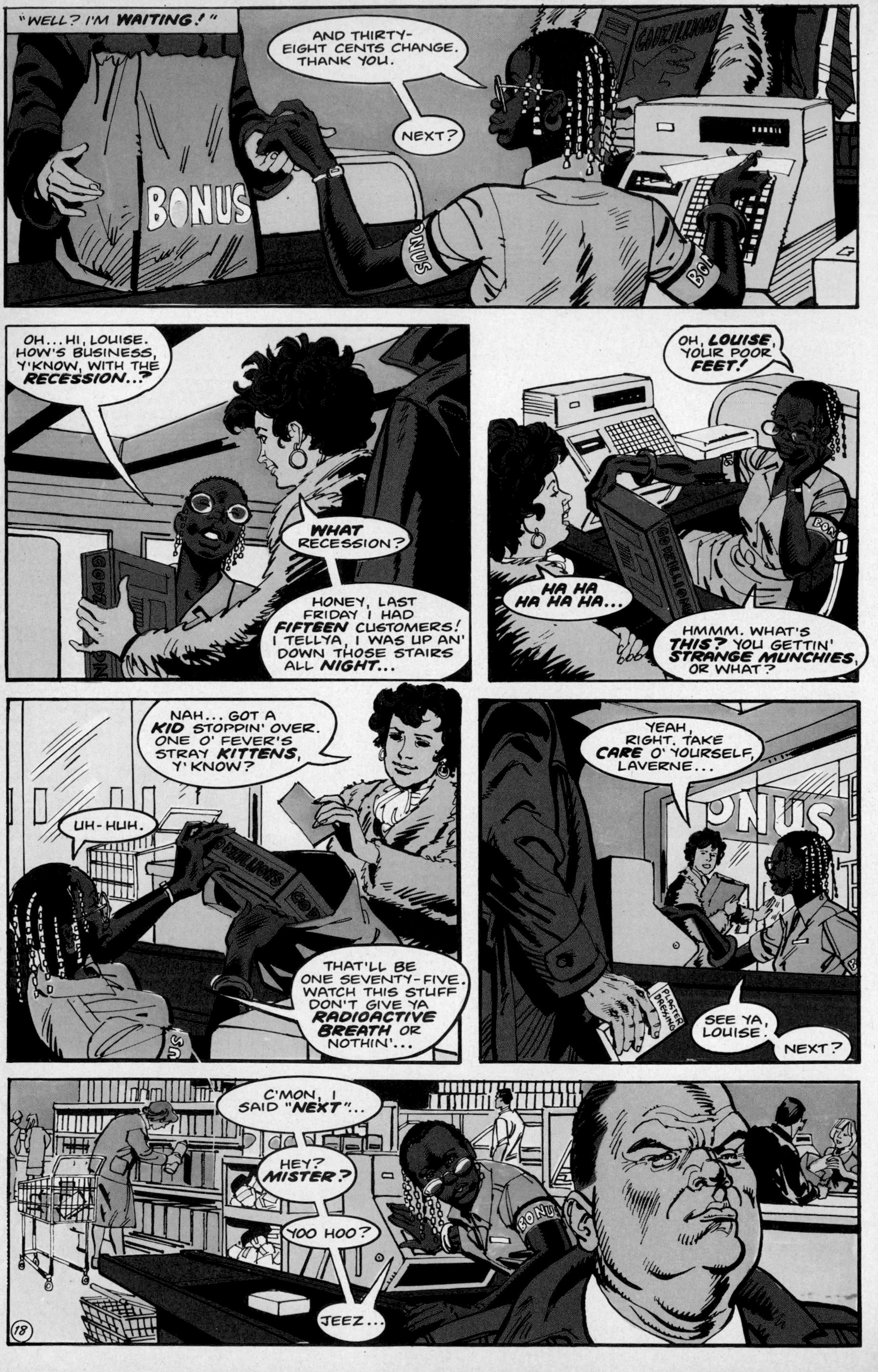
"WELL? I'M WAITING!"
AND THIRTY-EIGHT CENTS CHANGE. THANK YOU.
NEXT?
BONUS
OH... HI, LOUISE. HOW'S BUSINESS, Y'KNOW, WITH THE RECESSION...?
WHAT RECESSION?
HONEY, LAST FRIDAY I HAD FIFTEEN CUSTOMERS! I TELLYA, I WAS UP AN' DOWN THOSE STAIRS ALL NIGHT...
OH, LOUISE, YOUR POOR FEET!
HA HA HA HA HA...
HMMM. WHAT'S THIS? YOU GETTIN' STRANGE MUNCHIES, OR WHAT?
NAH... GOT A KID STOPPIN' OVER. ONE O' FEVER'S STRAY KITTENS, Y'KNOW?
UH-HUH.
THAT'LL BE ONE SEVENTY-FIVE. WATCH THIS STUFF DON'T GIVE YA RADIOACTIVE BREATH OR NOTHIN'...
YEAH, RIGHT. TAKE CARE O' YOURSELF, LAVERNE...
SEE YA, LOUISE.
NEXT?
PLASTER DRESSING
C'MON, I SAID "NEXT"...
HEY? MISTER?
YOO HOO?
JEEZ...

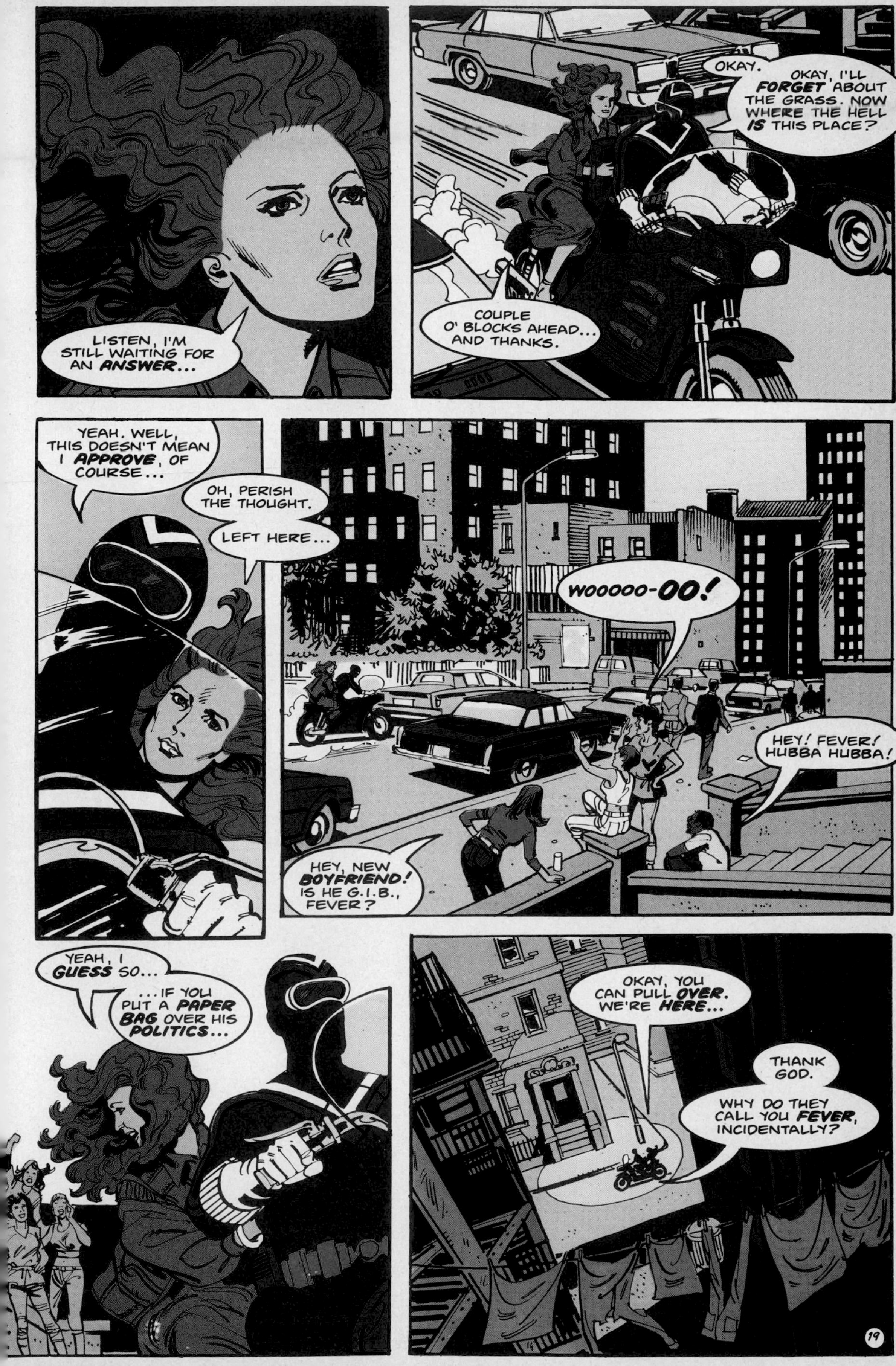

LISTEN, I'M STILL WAITING FOR AN ANSWER...
OKAY.
OKAY, I'LL FORGET ABOUT THE GRASS. NOW WHERE THE HELL IS THIS PLACE?
COUPLE O' BLOCKS AHEAD... AND THANKS.
YEAH. WELL, THIS DOESN'T MEAN I APPROVE, OF COURSE...
OH, PERISH THE THOUGHT.
LEFT HERE...
WOOOOO-OO!
HEY! FEVER! HUBBA HUBBA!
HEY, NEW BOYFRIEND! IS HE G.I.B., FEVER?
YEAH, I GUESS SO...
...IF YOU PUT A PAPER BAG OVER HIS POLITICS...
OKAY, YOU CAN PULL OVER. WE'RE HERE...
THANK GOD.
WHY DO THEY CALL YOU FEVER, INCIDENTALLY?

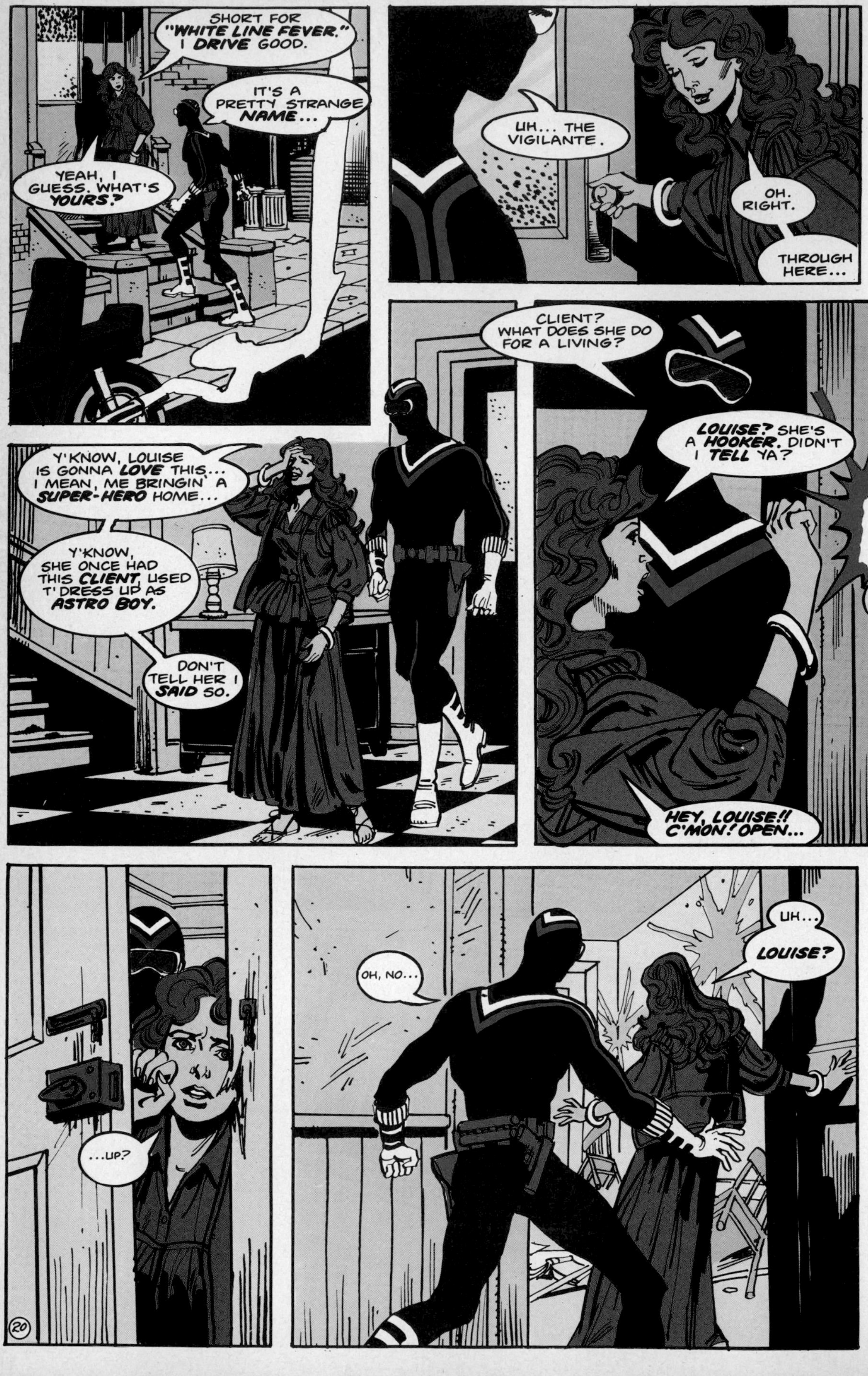
SHORT FOR "WHITE LINE FEVER." I DRIVE GOOD.
IT'S A PRETTY STRANGE NAME...
YEAH, I GUESS. WHAT'S YOURS?
UH... THE VIGILANTE.
OH. RIGHT.
THROUGH HERE...
Y'KNOW, LOUISE IS GONNA LOVE THIS... I MEAN, ME BRINGIN' A SUPER-HERO HOME...
Y'KNOW, SHE ONCE HAD THIS CLIENT, USED T' DRESS UP AS ASTRO BOY.
DON'T TELL HER I SAID SO.
CLIENT? WHAT DOES SHE DO FOR A LIVING?
LOUISE? SHE'S A HOOKER. DIDN'T I TELL YA?
HEY, LOUISE!! C'MON! OPEN...
...UP?
OH, NO...
UH...
LOUISE?

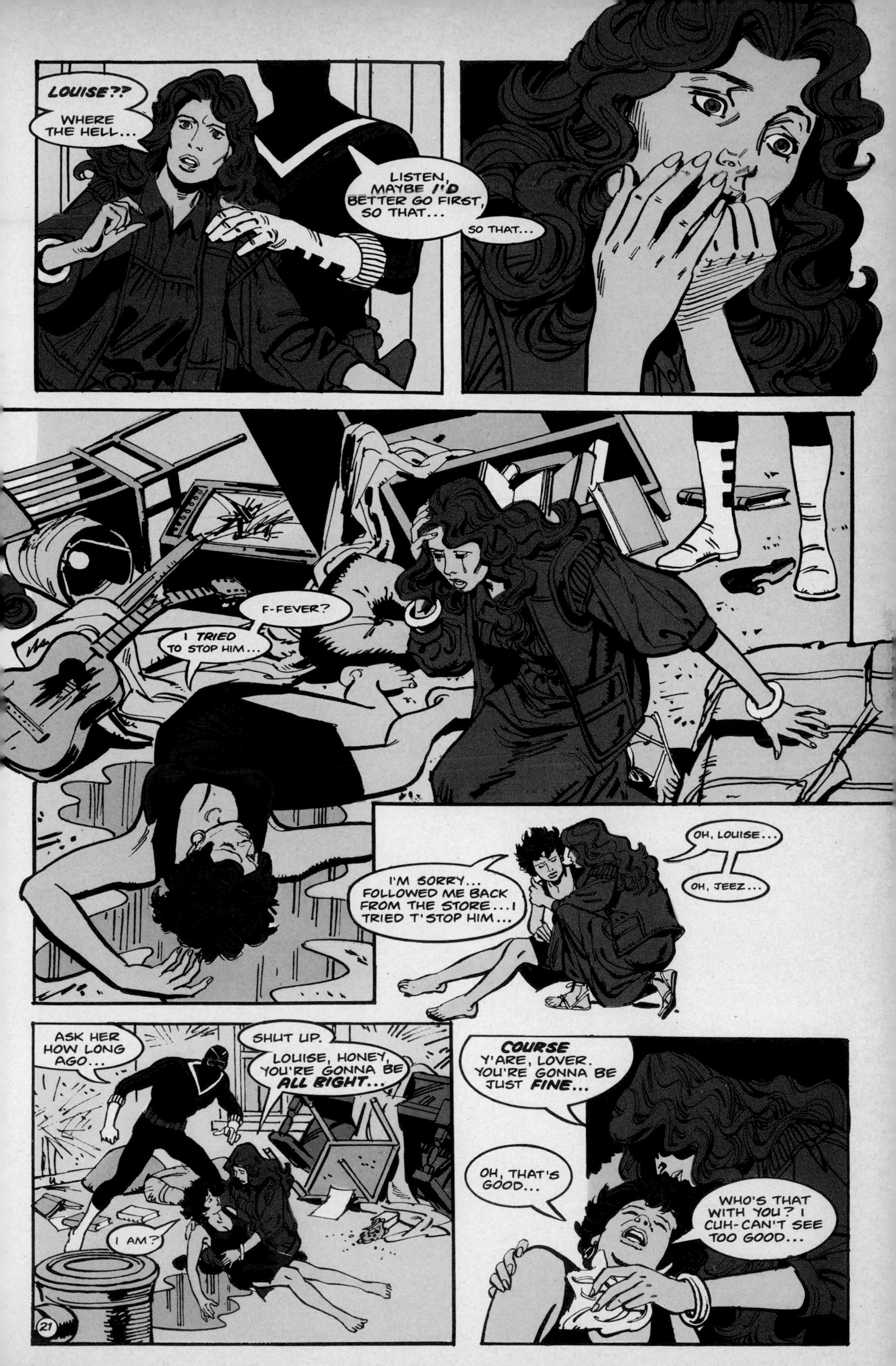
LOUISE?? WHERE THE HELL...
LISTEN, MAYBE I'D BETTER GO FIRST, SO THAT...
SO THAT...
F-FEVER?
I TRIED TO STOP HIM...
OH, LOUISE...
OH, JEEZ...
I'M SORRY... FOLLOWED ME BACK FROM THE STORE... I TRIED T'STOP HIM...
ASK HER HOW LONG AGO...
SHUT UP.
LOUISE, HONEY, YOU'RE GONNA BE ALL RIGHT...
I AM?
COURSE Y'ARE, LOVER. YOU'RE GONNA BE JUST FINE...
OH, THAT'S GOOD...
WHO'S THAT WITH YOU? I CUH-CAN'T SEE TOO GOOD...

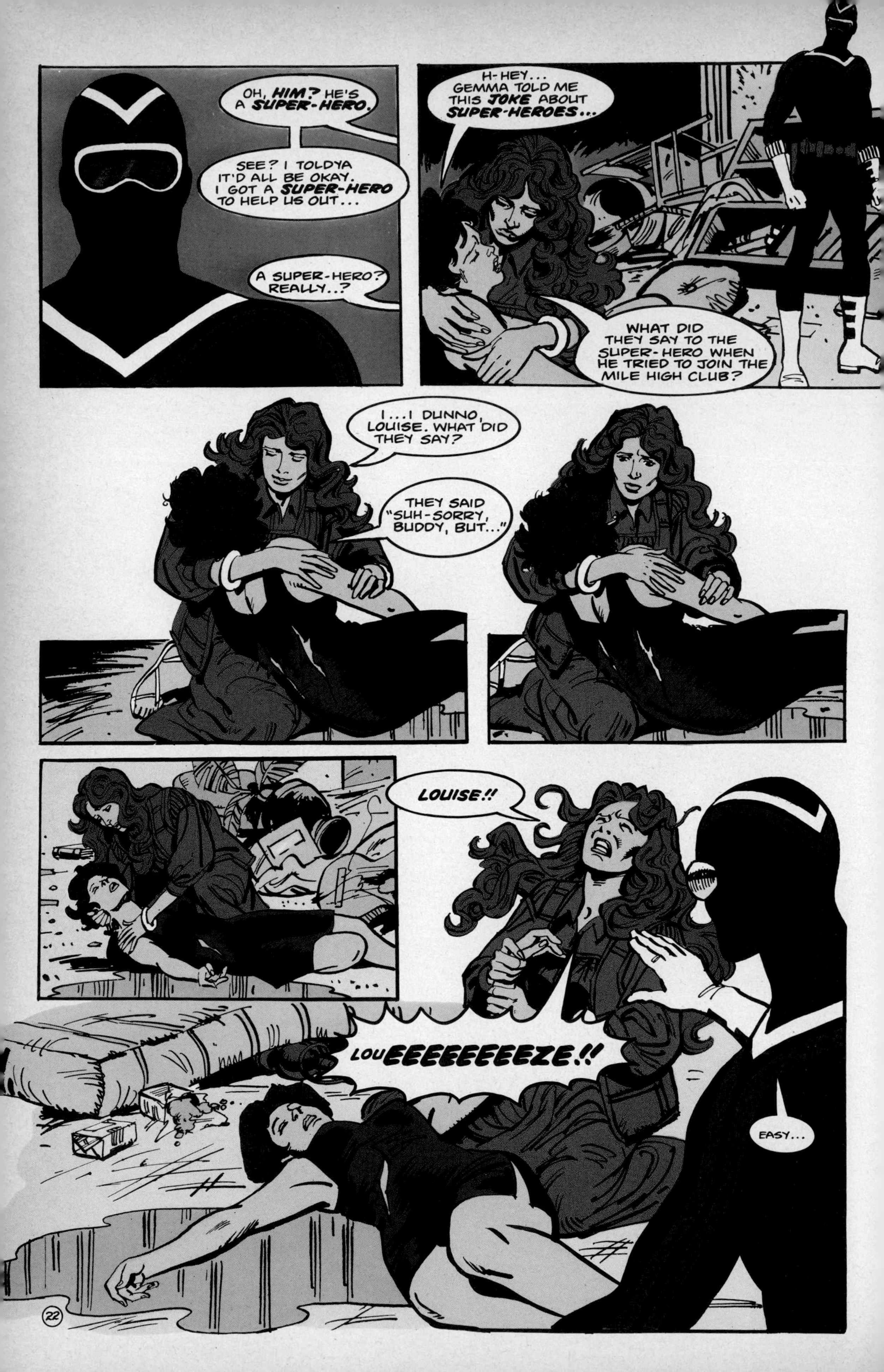
OH, HIM? HE'S A SUPER-HERO.
SEE? I TOLDYA IT'D ALL BE OKAY. I GOT A SUPER-HERO TO HELP US OUT...
A SUPER-HERO? REALLY..?
H-HEY... GEMMA TOLD ME THIS JOKE ABOUT SUPER-HEROES...
WHAT DID THEY SAY TO THE SUPER-HERO WHEN HE TRIED TO JOIN THE MILE HIGH CLUB?
I...I DUNNO, LOUISE. WHAT DID THEY SAY?
THEY SAID "SUH-SORRY, BUDDY, BUT..."
LOUISE!!
LOUEEEEEEEEEZE!!
EASY...

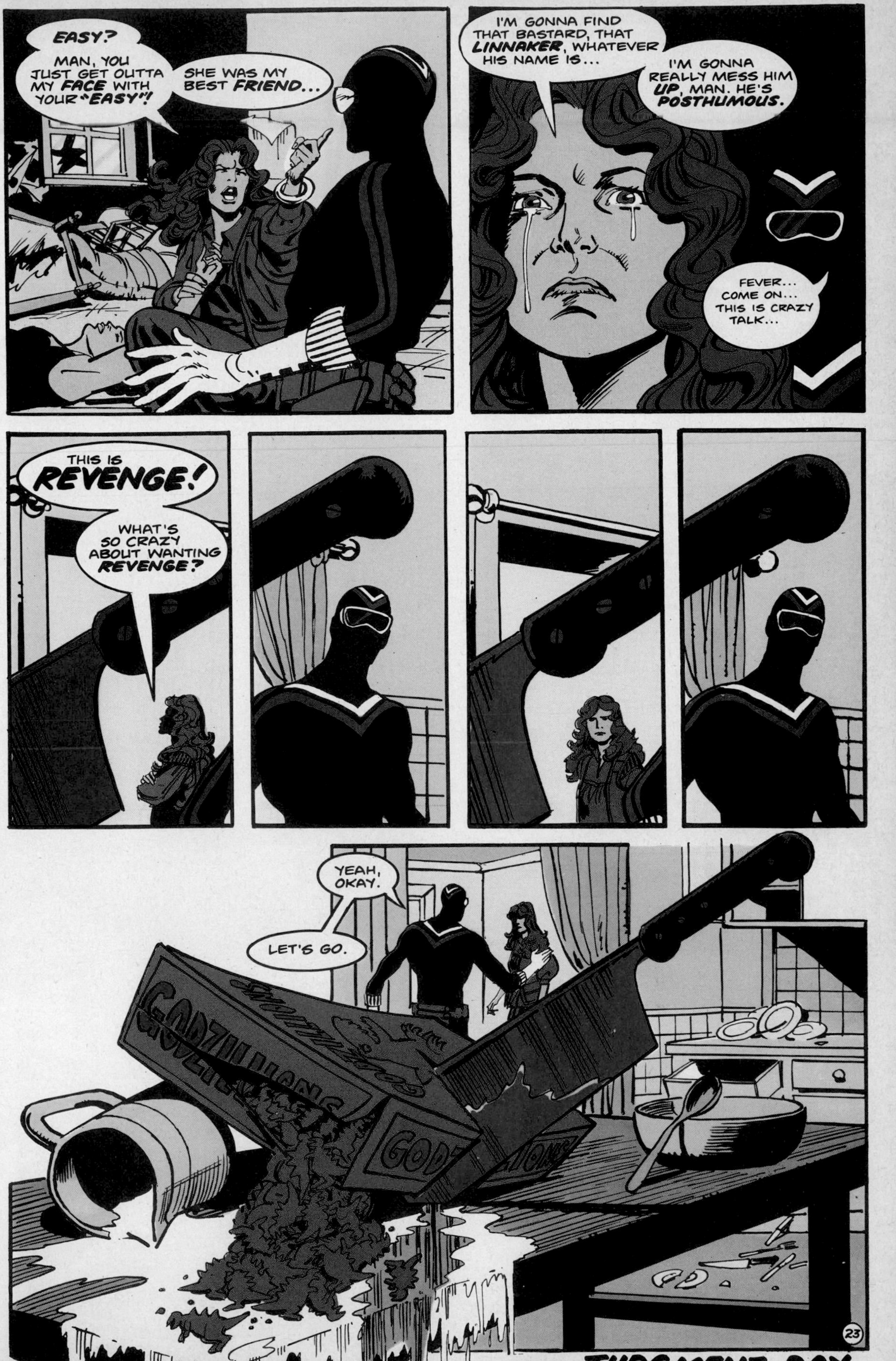
EASY? MAN, YOU JUST GET OUTTA MY FACE WITH YOUR "EASY"!
SHE WAS MY BEST FRIEND...
I'M GONNA FIND THAT BASTARD, THAT LINNAKER, WHATEVER HIS NAME IS...
I'M GONNA REALLY MESS HIM UP, MAN. HE'S POSTHUMOUS.
FEVER... COME ON... THIS IS CRAZY TALK...
THIS IS REVENGE!
WHAT'S SO CRAZY ABOUT WANTING REVENGE?
YEAH, OKAY.
LET'S GO.
GODZILLIONS
23
NEXT: JUDGMENT DAY.

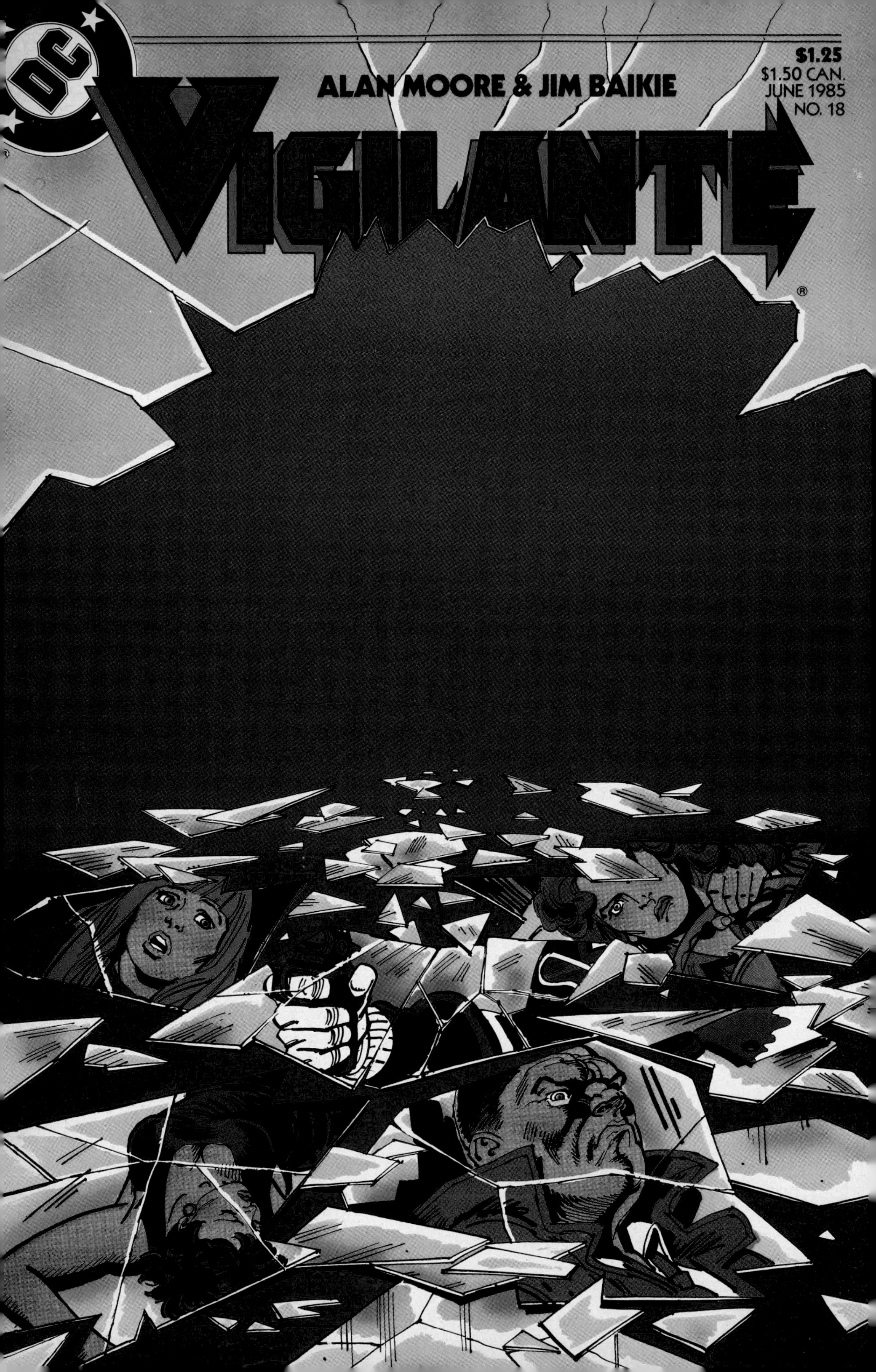
DC
ALAN MOORE & JIM BAIKIE
VIGILANTE
$1.25
$1.50 CAN.
JUNE 1985
NO. 18
®

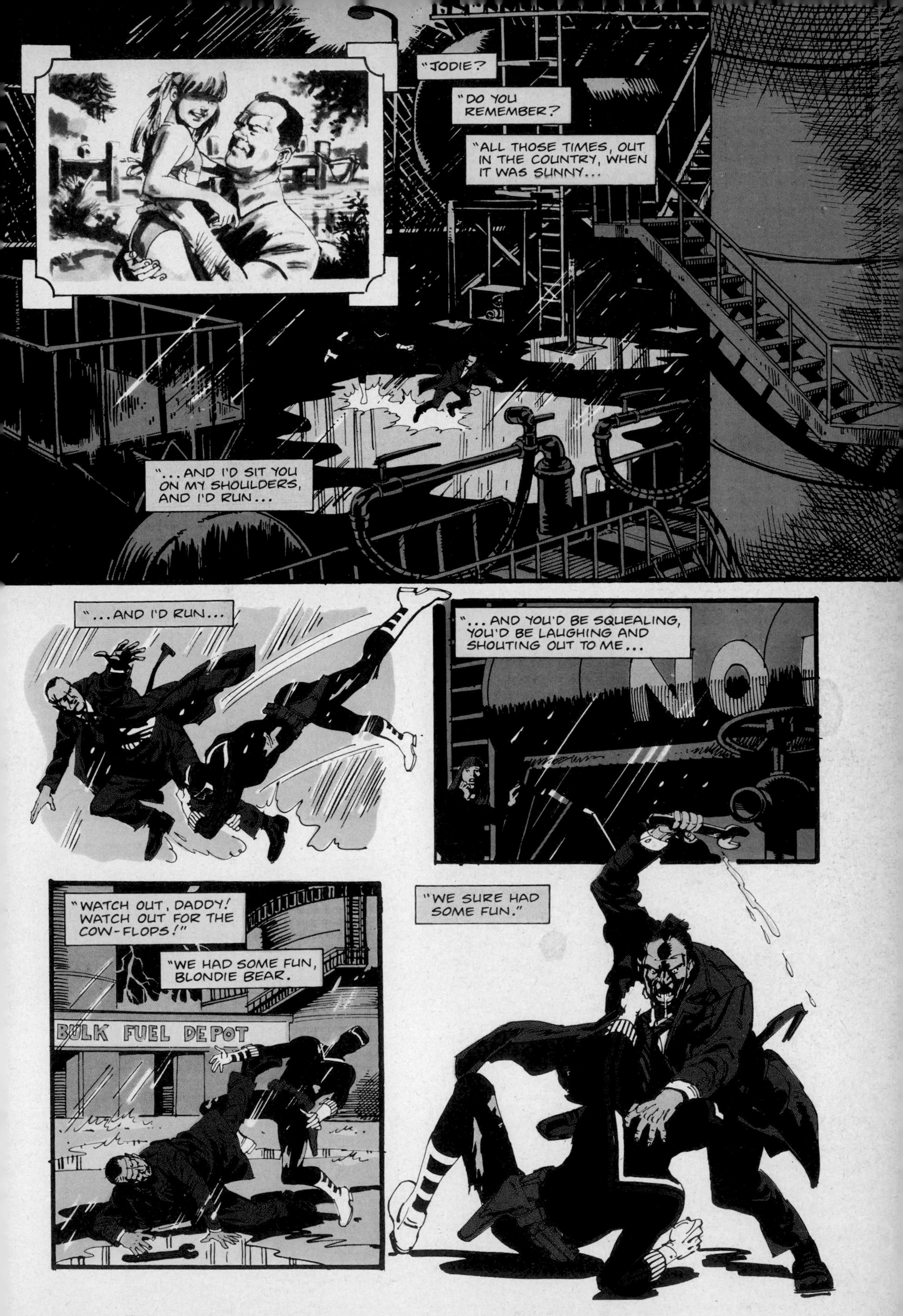
"JODIE?
"DO YOU REMEMBER?
"ALL THOSE TIMES, OUT IN THE COUNTRY, WHEN IT WAS SUNNY...
"...AND I'D SIT YOU ON MY SHOULDERS, AND I'D RUN...
"...AND I'D RUN...
"...AND YOU'D BE SQUEALING, YOU'D BE LAUGHING AND SHOUTING OUT TO ME...
"WATCH OUT, DADDY! WATCH OUT FOR THE COW-FLOPS!"
"WE HAD SOME FUN, BLONDIE BEAR.
BULK FUEL DEPOT
"WE SURE HAD SOME FUN."

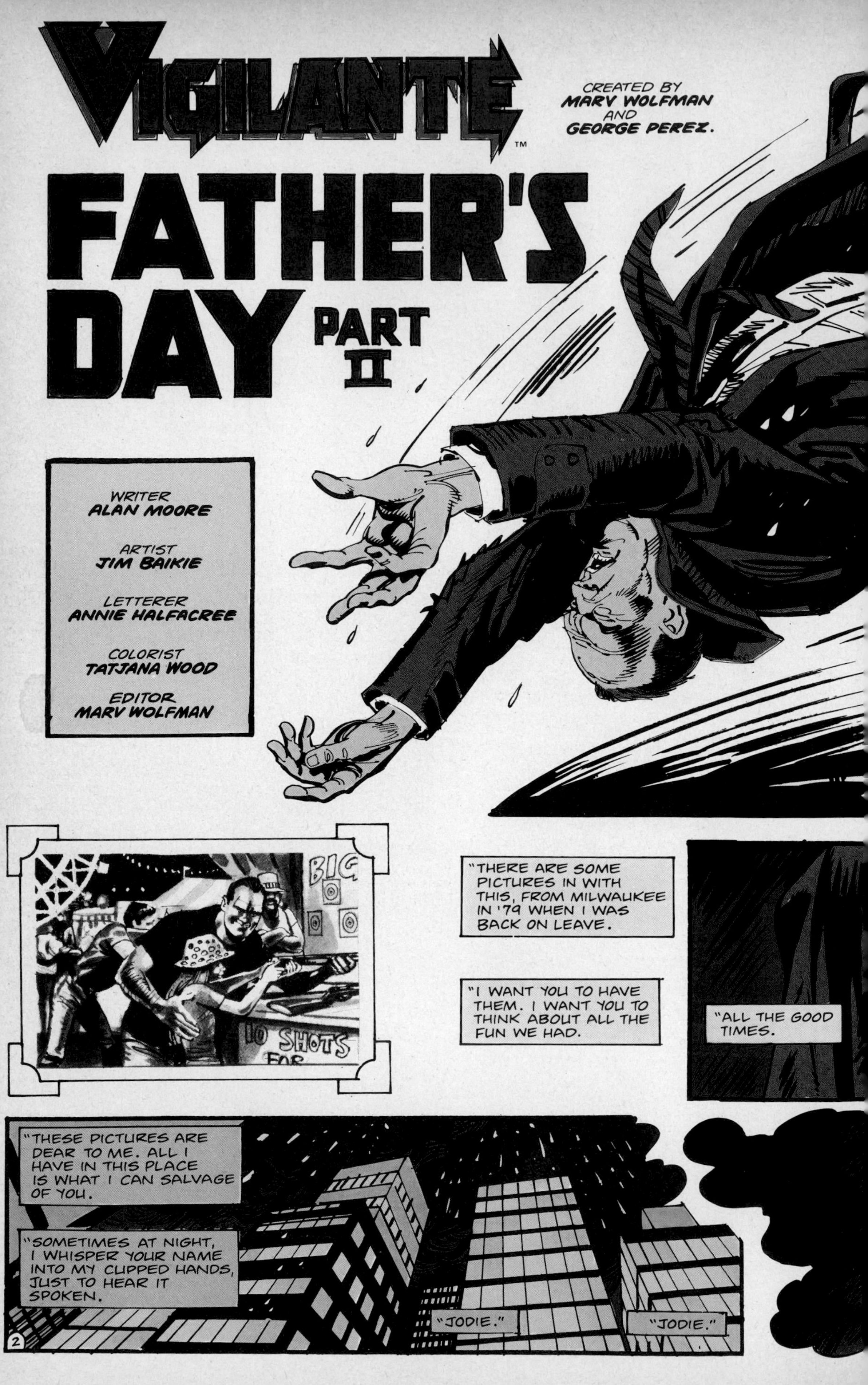
VIGILANTE™
CREATED BY MARV WOLFMAN AND GEORGE PEREZ.
FATHER'S DAY PART II
WRITER ALAN MOORE
ARTIST JIM BAIKIE
LETTERER ANNIE HALFACREE
COLORIST TATJANA WOOD
EDITOR MARV WOLFMAN
BIG
10 SHOTS FOR
"THERE ARE SOME PICTURES IN WITH THIS, FROM MILWAUKEE IN '79 WHEN I WAS BACK ON LEAVE.
"I WANT YOU TO HAVE THEM. I WANT YOU TO THINK ABOUT ALL THE FUN WE HAD.
"ALL THE GOOD TIMES.
"THESE PICTURES ARE DEAR TO ME. ALL I HAVE IN THIS PLACE IS WHAT I CAN SALVAGE OF YOU.
"SOMETIMES AT NIGHT, I WHISPER YOUR NAME INTO MY CUPPED HANDS, JUST TO HEAR IT SPOKEN.
"JODIE."
"JODIE."
2

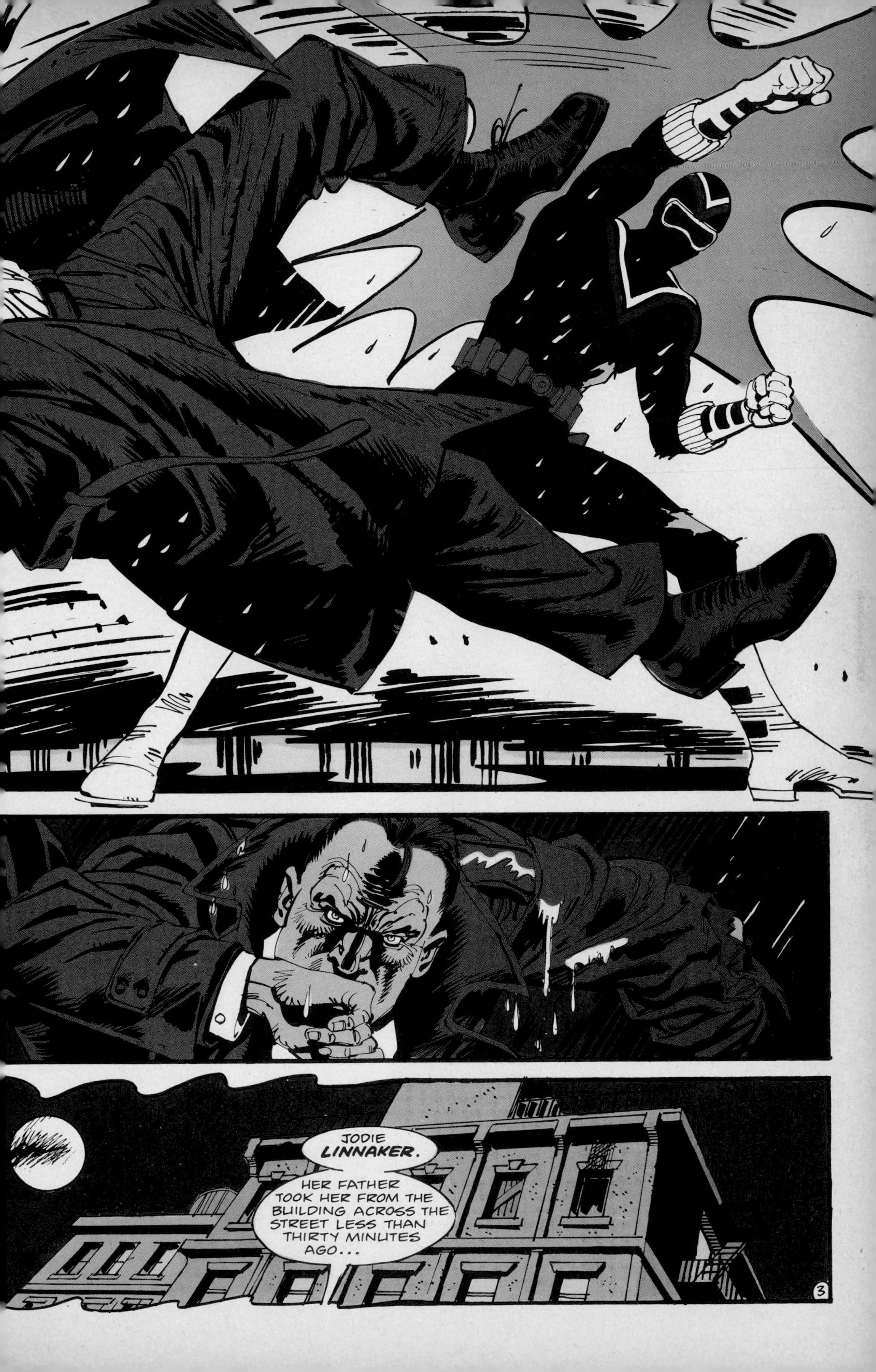
JODIE LINNAKER.
HER FATHER TOOK HER FROM THE BUILDING ACROSS THE STREET LESS THAN THIRTY MINUTES AGO...
3

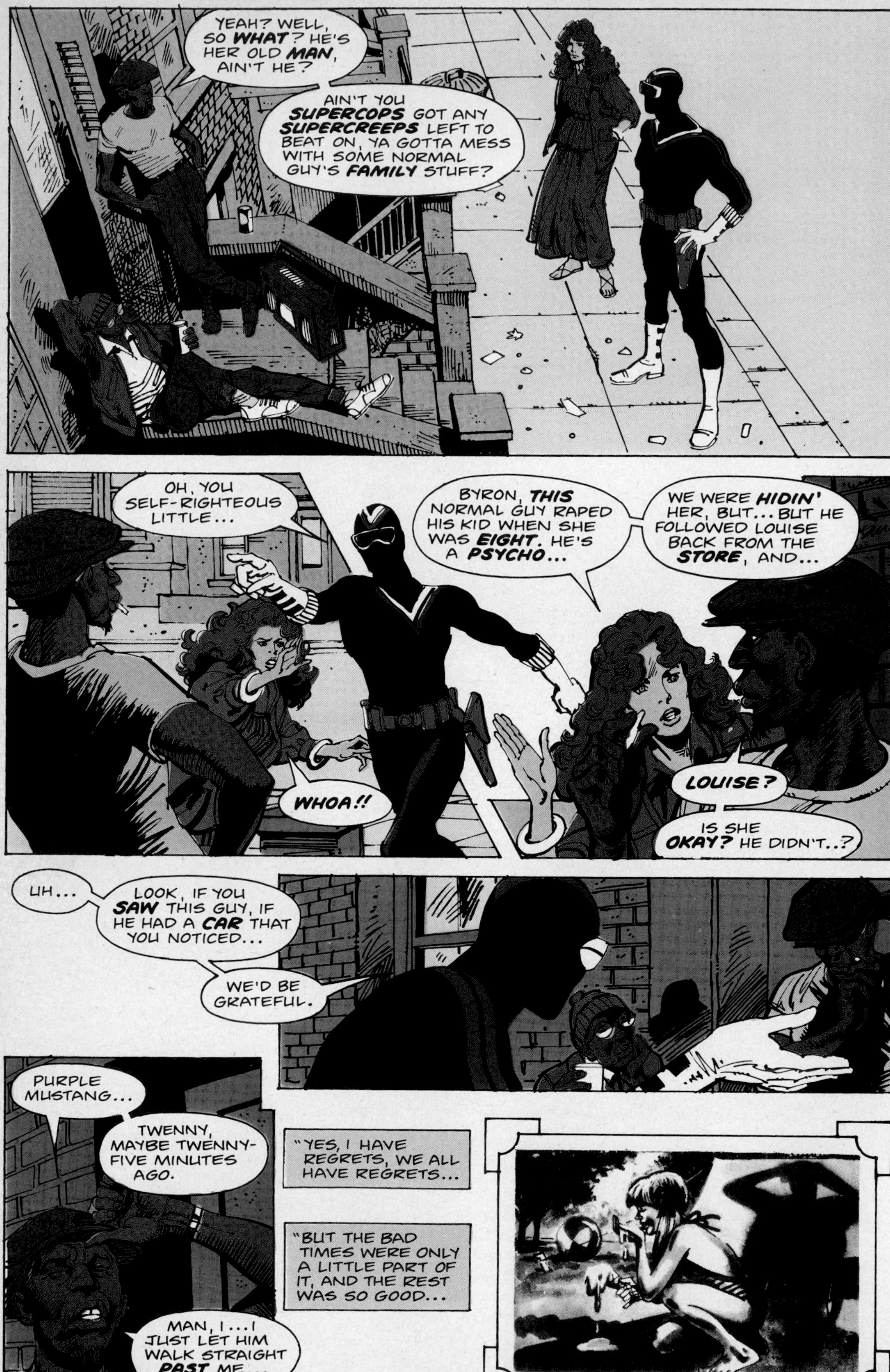
YEAH? WELL, SO WHAT? HE'S HER OLD MAN, AIN'T HE?
AIN'T YOU SUPERCOPS GOT ANY SUPERCREEPS LEFT TO BEAT ON, YA GOTTA MESS WITH SOME NORMAL GUY'S FAMILY STUFF?
OH, YOU SELF-RIGHTEOUS LITTLE...
BYRON, THIS NORMAL GUY RAPED HIS KID WHEN SHE WAS EIGHT. HE'S A PSYCHO...
WE WERE HIDIN' HER, BUT... BUT HE FOLLOWED LOUISE BACK FROM THE STORE, AND...
WHOA!!
LOUISE?
IS SHE OKAY? HE DIDN'T..?
UH...
LOOK, IF YOU SAW THIS GUY, IF HE HAD A CAR THAT YOU NOTICED...
WE'D BE GRATEFUL.
PURPLE MUSTANG...
TWENNY, MAYBE TWENNY-FIVE MINUTES AGO.
MAN, I...I JUST LET HIM WALK STRAIGHT PAST ME...
"YES, I HAVE REGRETS, WE ALL HAVE REGRETS...
"BUT THE BAD TIMES WERE ONLY A LITTLE PART OF IT, AND THE REST WAS SO GOOD...
4

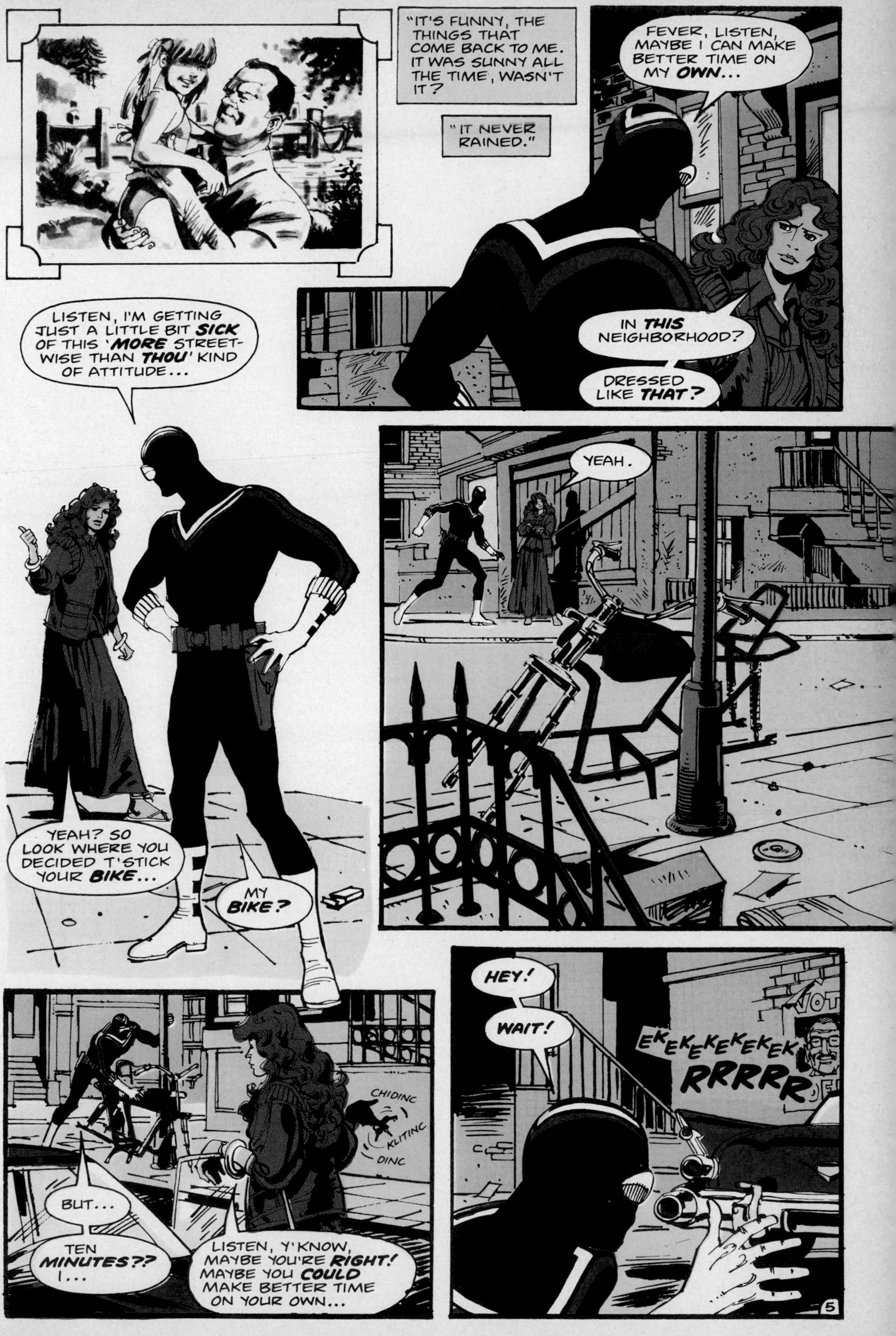

"IT'S FUNNY, THE THINGS THAT COME BACK TO ME. IT WAS SUNNY ALL THE TIME, WASN'T IT?
"IT NEVER RAINED."
FEVER, LISTEN, MAYBE I CAN MAKE BETTER TIME ON MY OWN...
IN THIS NEIGHBORHOOD?
DRESSED LIKE THAT?
LISTEN, I'M GETTING JUST A LITTLE BIT SICK OF THIS 'MORE STREET-WISE THAN THOU' KIND OF ATTITUDE...
YEAH? SO LOOK WHERE YOU DECIDED T'STICK YOUR BIKE...
MY BIKE?
YEAH.
CHIDINC
KLITINC
DINC
BUT...
TEN MINUTES?? I...
LISTEN, Y'KNOW, MAYBE YOU'RE RIGHT! MAYBE YOU COULD MAKE BETTER TIME ON YOUR OWN...
HEY!
WAIT!
EKEKEKEKEKEKEK RRRRR
5

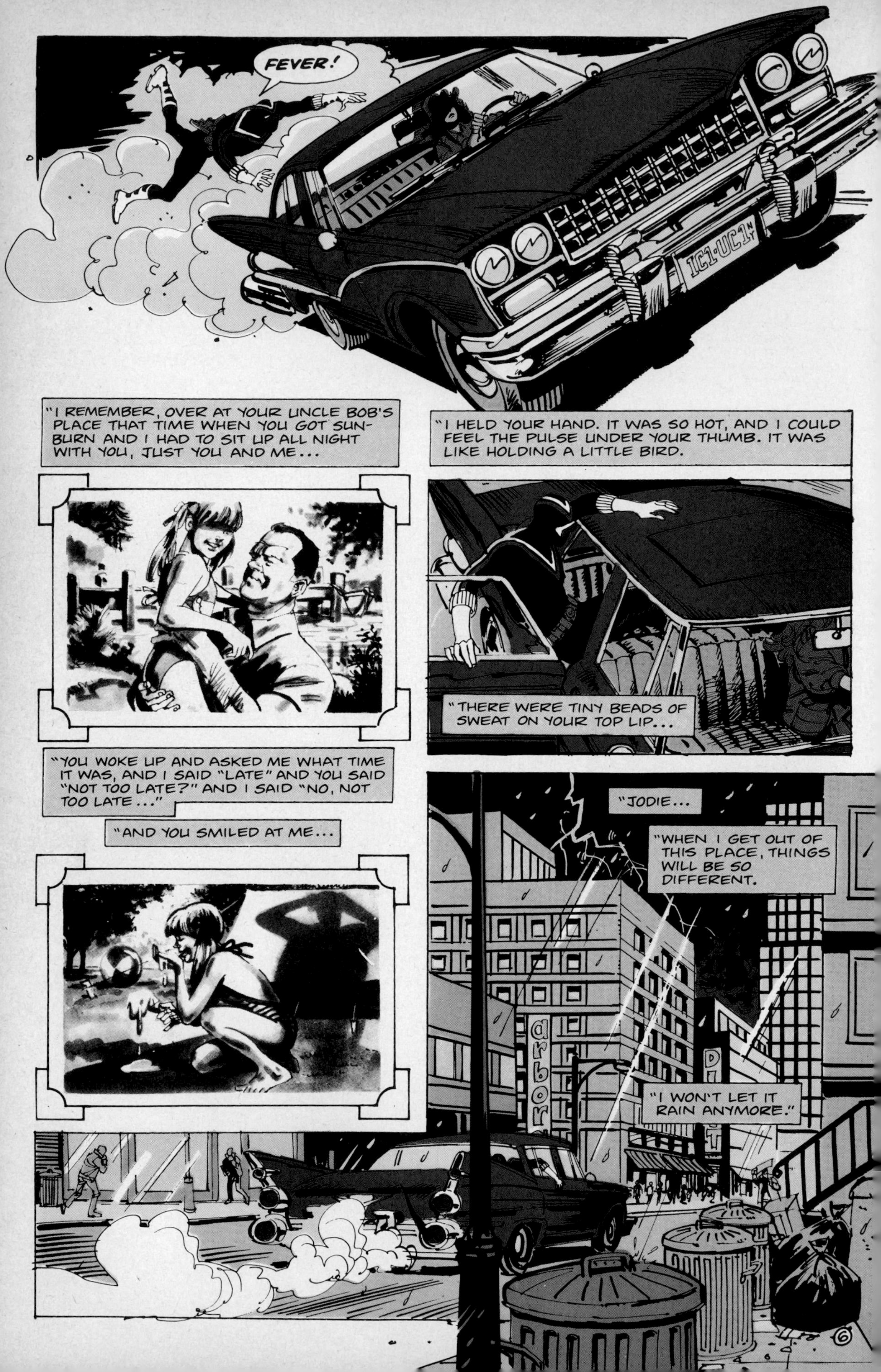
FEVER!
IC1·UC1 NY
"I REMEMBER, OVER AT YOUR UNCLE BOB'S PLACE THAT TIME WHEN YOU GOT SUN-BURN AND I HAD TO SIT UP ALL NIGHT WITH YOU, JUST YOU AND ME...
"I HELD YOUR HAND. IT WAS SO HOT, AND I COULD FEEL THE PULSE UNDER YOUR THUMB. IT WAS LIKE HOLDING A LITTLE BIRD.
"THERE WERE TINY BEADS OF SWEAT ON YOUR TOP LIP...
"YOU WOKE UP AND ASKED ME WHAT TIME IT WAS, AND I SAID "LATE" AND YOU SAID "NOT TOO LATE?" AND I SAID "NO, NOT TOO LATE..."
"AND YOU SMILED AT ME...
"JODIE...
"WHEN I GET OUT OF THIS PLACE, THINGS WILL BE SO DIFFERENT.
arbor
"I WON'T LET IT RAIN ANYMORE."

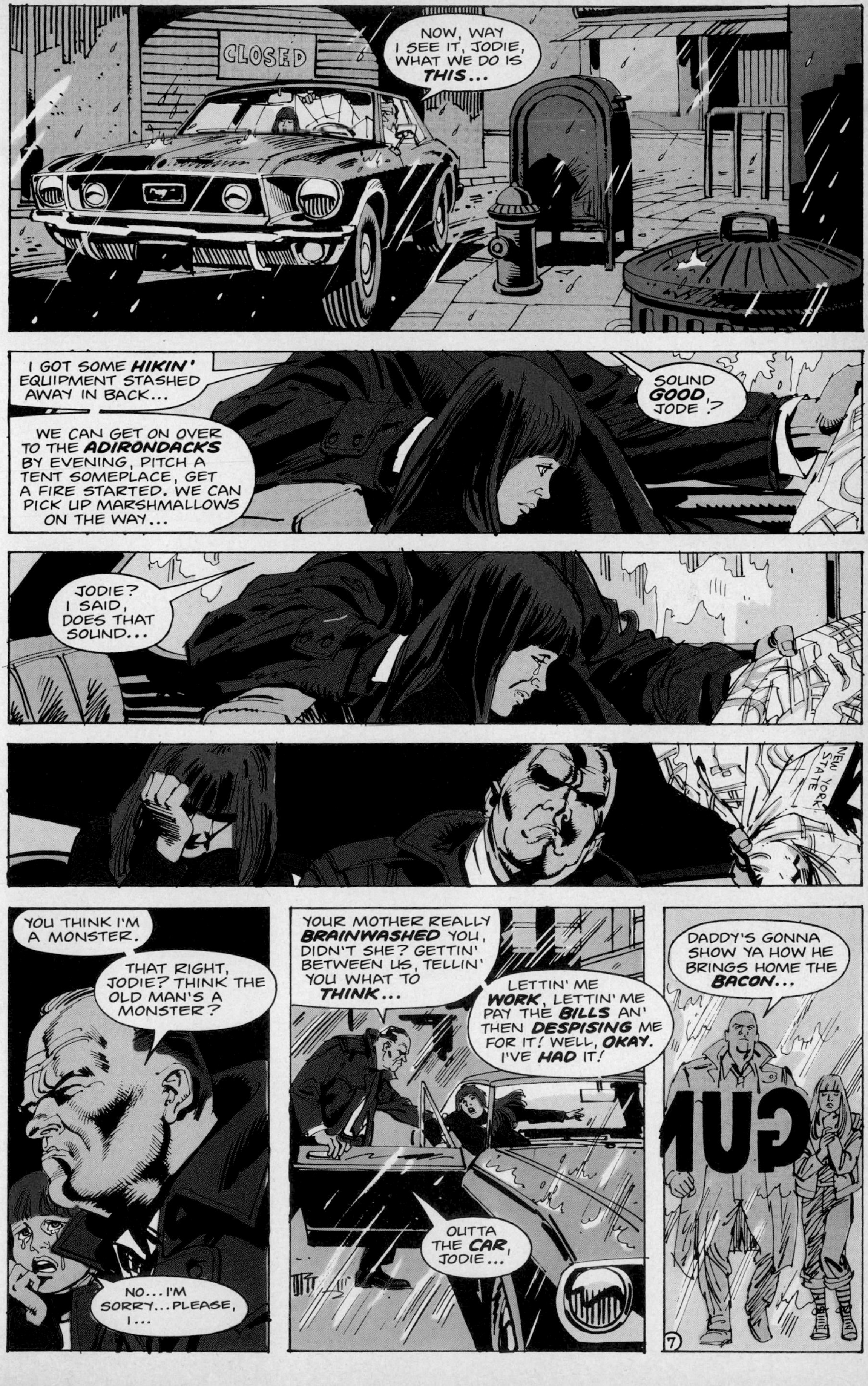
CLOSED
NOW, WAY I SEE IT, JODIE, WHAT WE DO IS THIS...
I GOT SOME HIKIN' EQUIPMENT STASHED AWAY IN BACK...
WE CAN GET ON OVER TO THE ADIRONDACKS BY EVENING, PITCH A TENT SOMEPLACE, GET A FIRE STARTED. WE CAN PICK UP MARSHMALLOWS ON THE WAY...
SOUND GOOD, JODE?
JODIE? I SAID, DOES THAT SOUND...
NEW YORK STATE
YOU THINK I'M A MONSTER.
THAT RIGHT, JODIE? THINK THE OLD MAN'S A MONSTER?
NO... I'M SORRY... PLEASE, I...
YOUR MOTHER REALLY BRAINWASHED YOU, DIDN'T SHE? GETTIN' BETWEEN US, TELLIN' YOU WHAT TO THINK...
LETTIN' ME WORK, LETTIN' ME PAY THE BILLS AN' THEN DESPISING ME FOR IT! WELL, OKAY. I'VE HAD IT!
OUTTA THE CAR, JODIE...
DADDY'S GONNA SHOW YA HOW HE BRINGS HOME THE BACON...
GUN
7

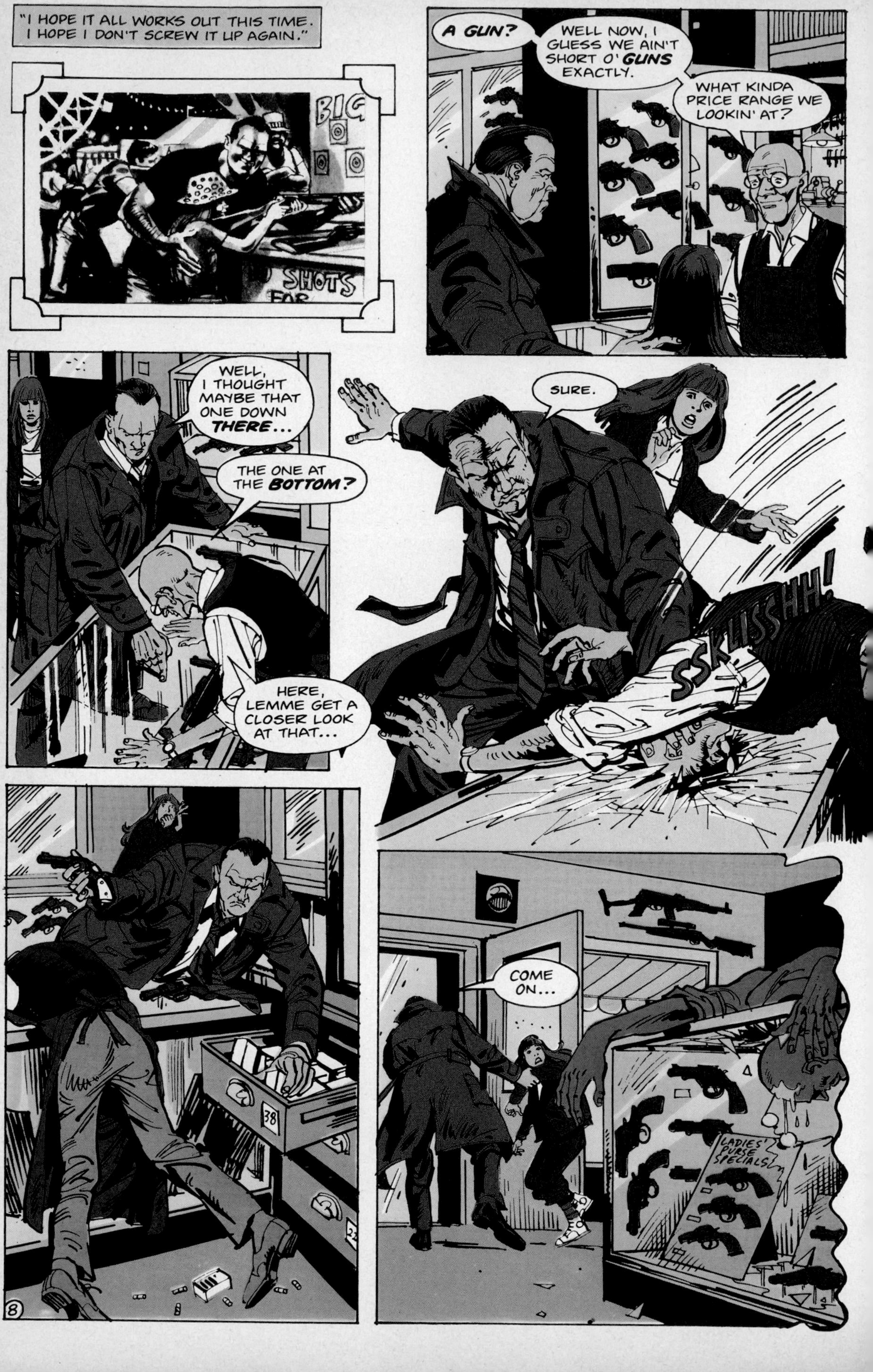
"I HOPE IT ALL WORKS OUT THIS TIME. I HOPE I DON'T SCREW IT UP AGAIN."
BIG
SHOTS
A GUN?
WELL NOW, I GUESS WE AIN'T SHORT O' GUNS EXACTLY.
WHAT KINDA PRICE RANGE WE LOOKIN' AT?
WELL, I THOUGHT MAYBE THAT ONE DOWN THERE...
THE ONE AT THE BOTTOM?
HERE, LEMME GET A CLOSER LOOK AT THAT...
SURE.
SSKLISSHH!
38
COME ON...
LADIES' PURSE SPECIALS
8

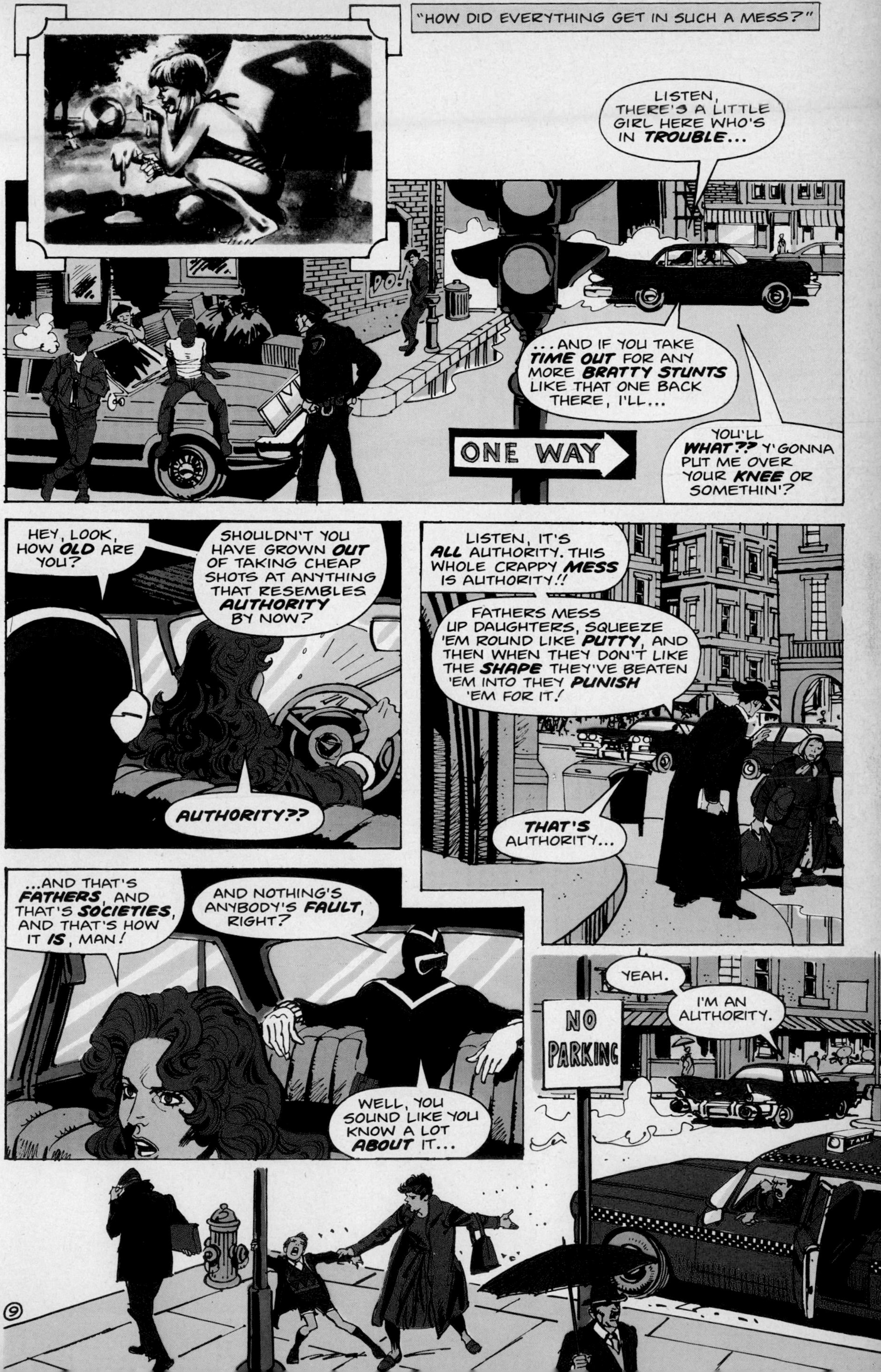
"HOW DID EVERYTHING GET IN SUCH A MESS?"
LISTEN, THERE'S A LITTLE GIRL HERE WHO'S IN TROUBLE...
...AND IF YOU TAKE TIME OUT FOR ANY MORE BRATTY STUNTS LIKE THAT ONE BACK THERE, I'LL...
ONE WAY
YOU'LL WHAT?? Y'GONNA PUT ME OVER YOUR KNEE OR SOMETHIN'?
HEY, LOOK, HOW OLD ARE YOU?
SHOULDN'T YOU HAVE GROWN OUT OF TAKING CHEAP SHOTS AT ANYTHING THAT RESEMBLES AUTHORITY BY NOW?
AUTHORITY??
LISTEN, IT'S ALL AUTHORITY. THIS WHOLE CRAPPY MESS IS AUTHORITY!!
FATHERS MESS UP DAUGHTERS, SQUEEZE 'EM ROUND LIKE PUTTY, AND THEN WHEN THEY DON'T LIKE THE SHAPE THEY'VE BEATEN 'EM INTO THEY PUNISH 'EM FOR IT!
THAT'S AUTHORITY...
...AND THAT'S FATHERS, AND THAT'S SOCIETIES, AND THAT'S HOW IT IS, MAN!
AND NOTHING'S ANYBODY'S FAULT, RIGHT?
WELL, YOU SOUND LIKE YOU KNOW A LOT ABOUT IT...
YEAH.
I'M AN AUTHORITY.
NO PARKING

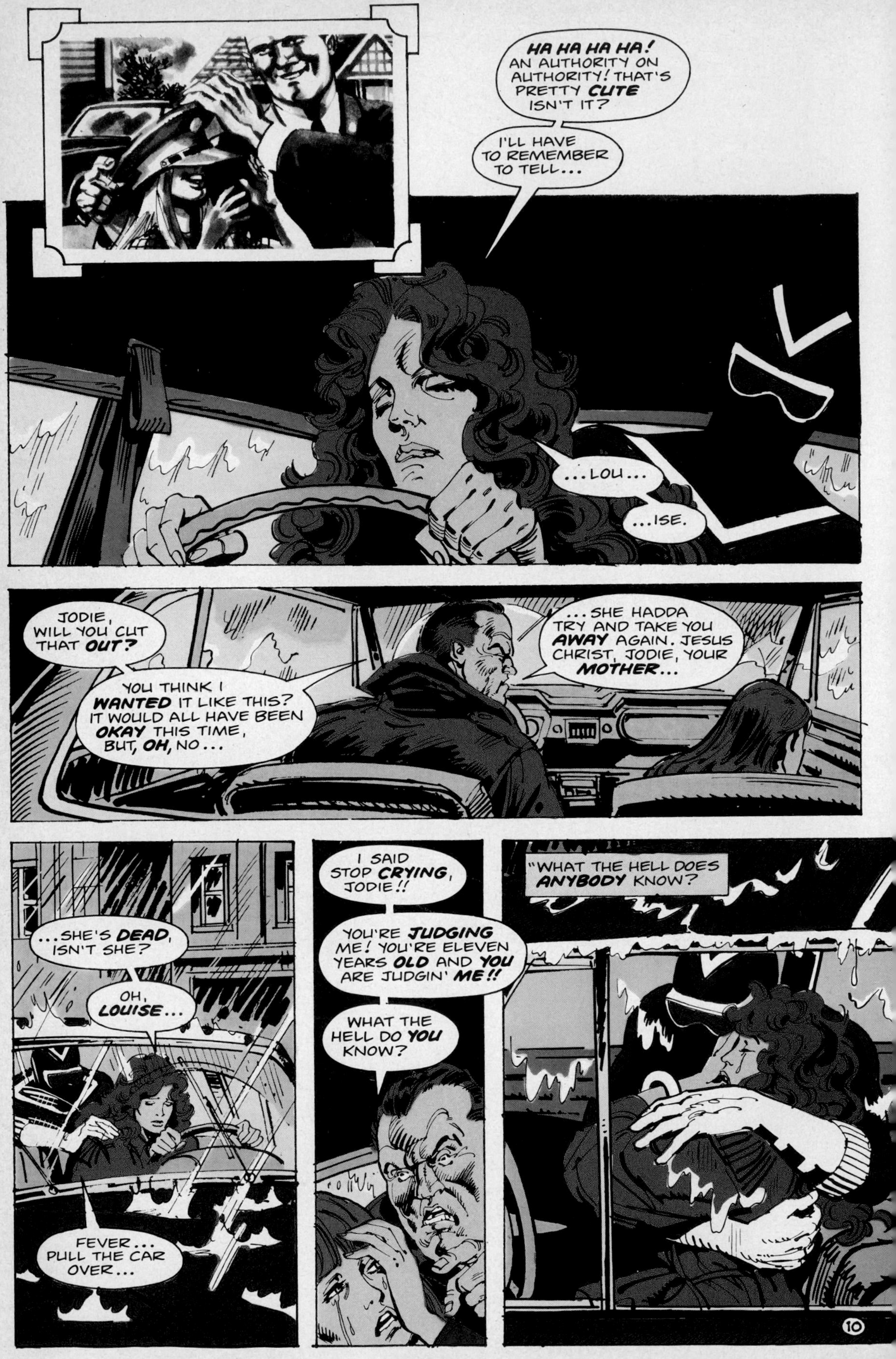

HA HA HA HA! AN AUTHORITY ON AUTHORITY! THAT'S PRETTY CUTE ISN'T IT?
I'LL HAVE TO REMEMBER TO TELL...
...LOU...
...ISE.
JODIE, WILL YOU CUT THAT OUT?
YOU THINK I WANTED IT LIKE THIS? IT WOULD ALL HAVE BEEN OKAY THIS TIME, BUT, OH, NO...
...SHE HADDA TRY AND TAKE YOU AWAY AGAIN. JESUS CHRIST, JODIE, YOUR MOTHER...
...SHE'S DEAD, ISN'T SHE?
OH, LOUISE...
FEVER... PULL THE CAR OVER...
I SAID STOP CRYING, JODIE!!
YOU'RE JUDGING ME! YOU'RE ELEVEN YEARS OLD AND YOU ARE JUDGIN' ME!!
WHAT THE HELL DO YOU KNOW?
"WHAT THE HELL DOES ANYBODY KNOW?
10

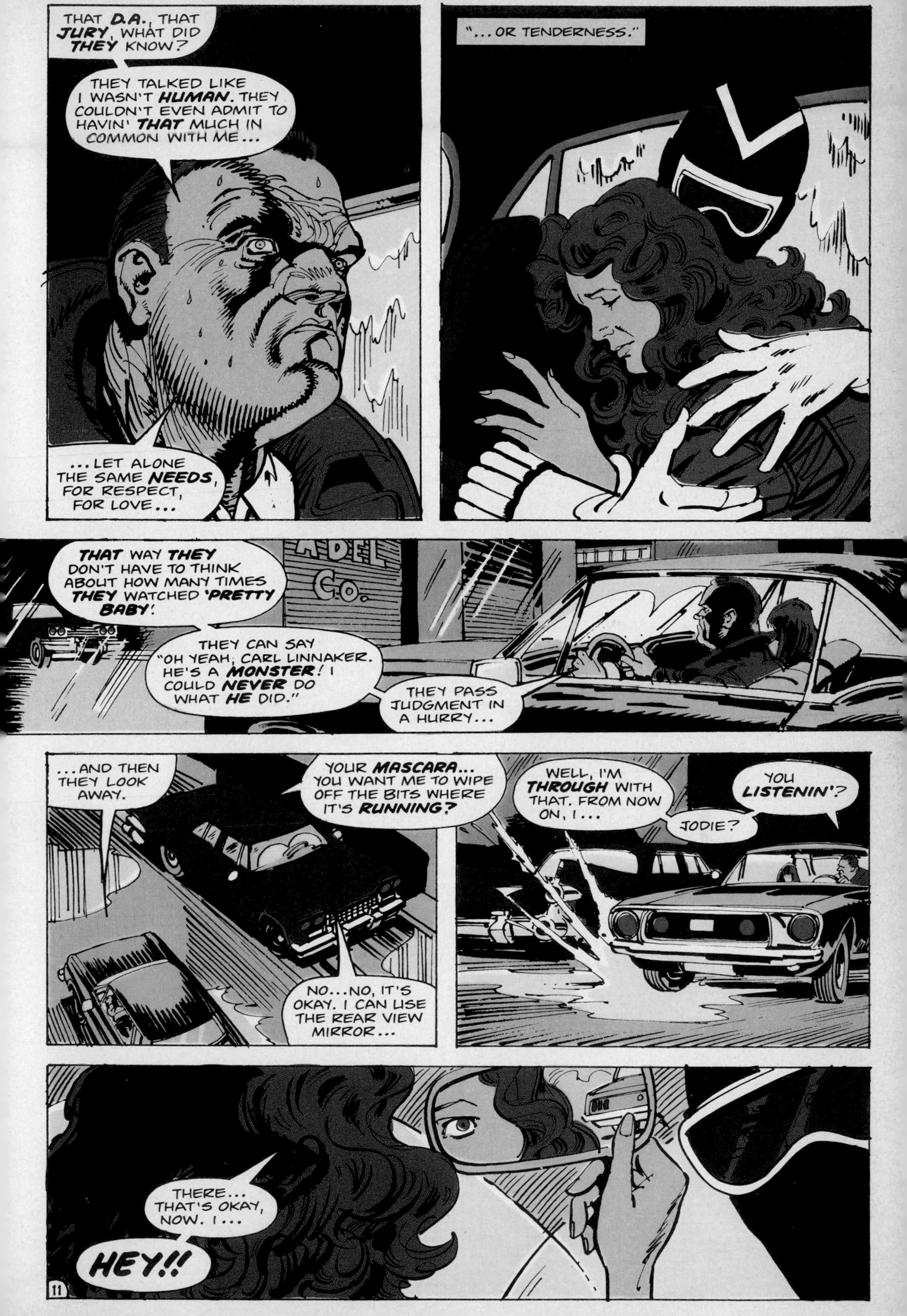
THAT D.A., THAT JURY, WHAT DID THEY KNOW?
THEY TALKED LIKE I WASN'T HUMAN. THEY COULDN'T EVEN ADMIT TO HAVIN' THAT MUCH IN COMMON WITH ME...
...LET ALONE THE SAME NEEDS, FOR RESPECT, FOR LOVE...
"...OR TENDERNESS."
THAT WAY THEY DON'T HAVE TO THINK ABOUT HOW MANY TIMES THEY WATCHED 'PRETTY BABY'.
THEY CAN SAY "OH YEAH, CARL LINNAKER. HE'S A MONSTER! I COULD NEVER DO WHAT HE DID."
THEY PASS JUDGMENT IN A HURRY...
...AND THEN THEY LOOK AWAY.
YOUR MASCARA... YOU WANT ME TO WIPE OFF THE BITS WHERE IT'S RUNNING?
NO...NO, IT'S OKAY. I CAN USE THE REAR VIEW MIRROR...
WELL, I'M THROUGH WITH THAT. FROM NOW ON, I...
JODIE?
YOU LISTENIN'?
THERE... THAT'S OKAY, NOW. I...
HEY!!

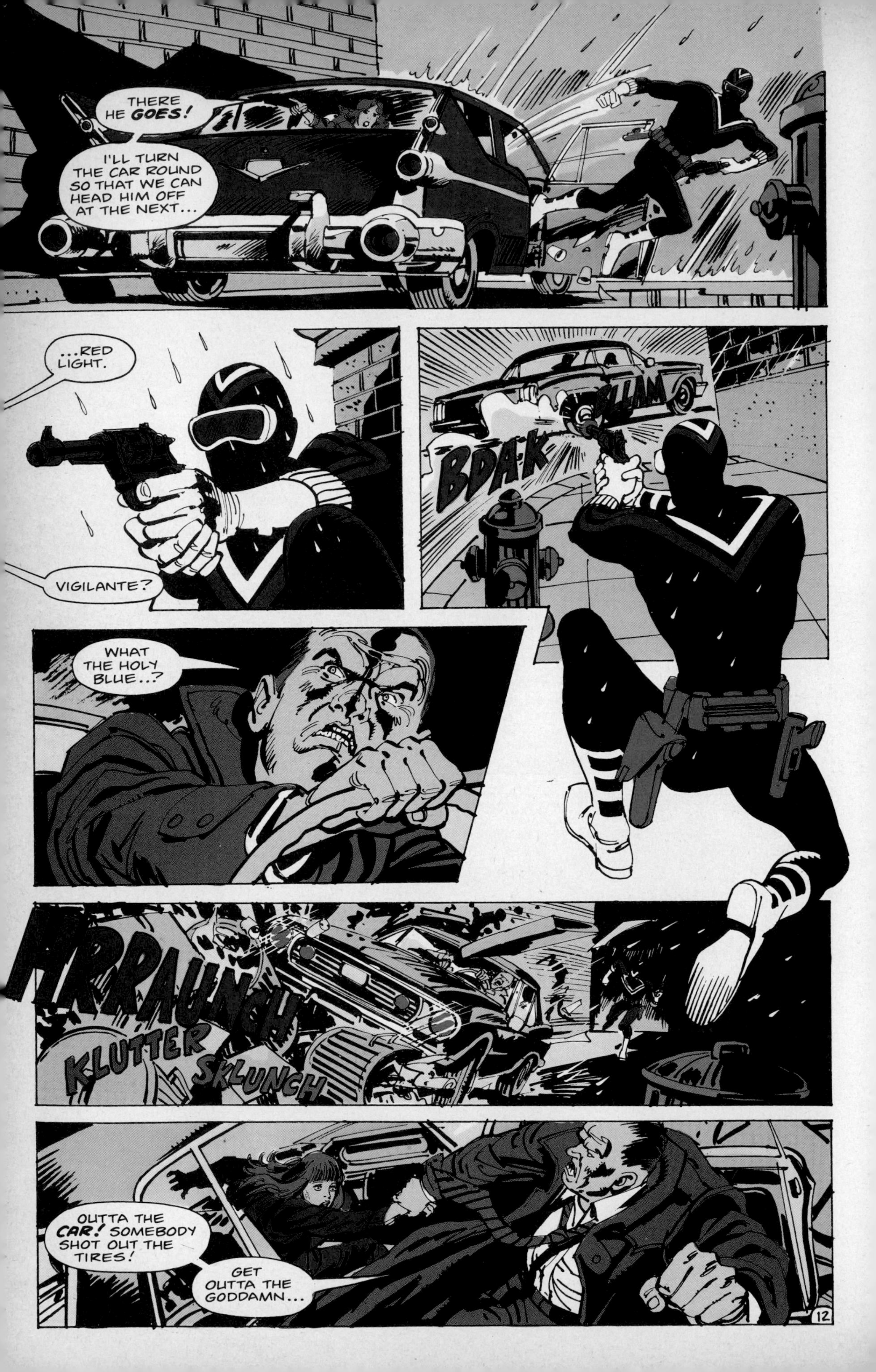
THERE HE GOES!
I'LL TURN THE CAR ROUND SO THAT WE CAN HEAD HIM OFF AT THE NEXT...
...RED LIGHT.
VIGILANTE?
BDAK
BLAM
WHAT THE HOLY BLUE...?
RRRAUNCH
KLUTTER
SKLUNCH
OUTTA THE CAR! SOMEBODY SHOT OUT THE TIRES!
GET OUTTA THE GODDAMN...

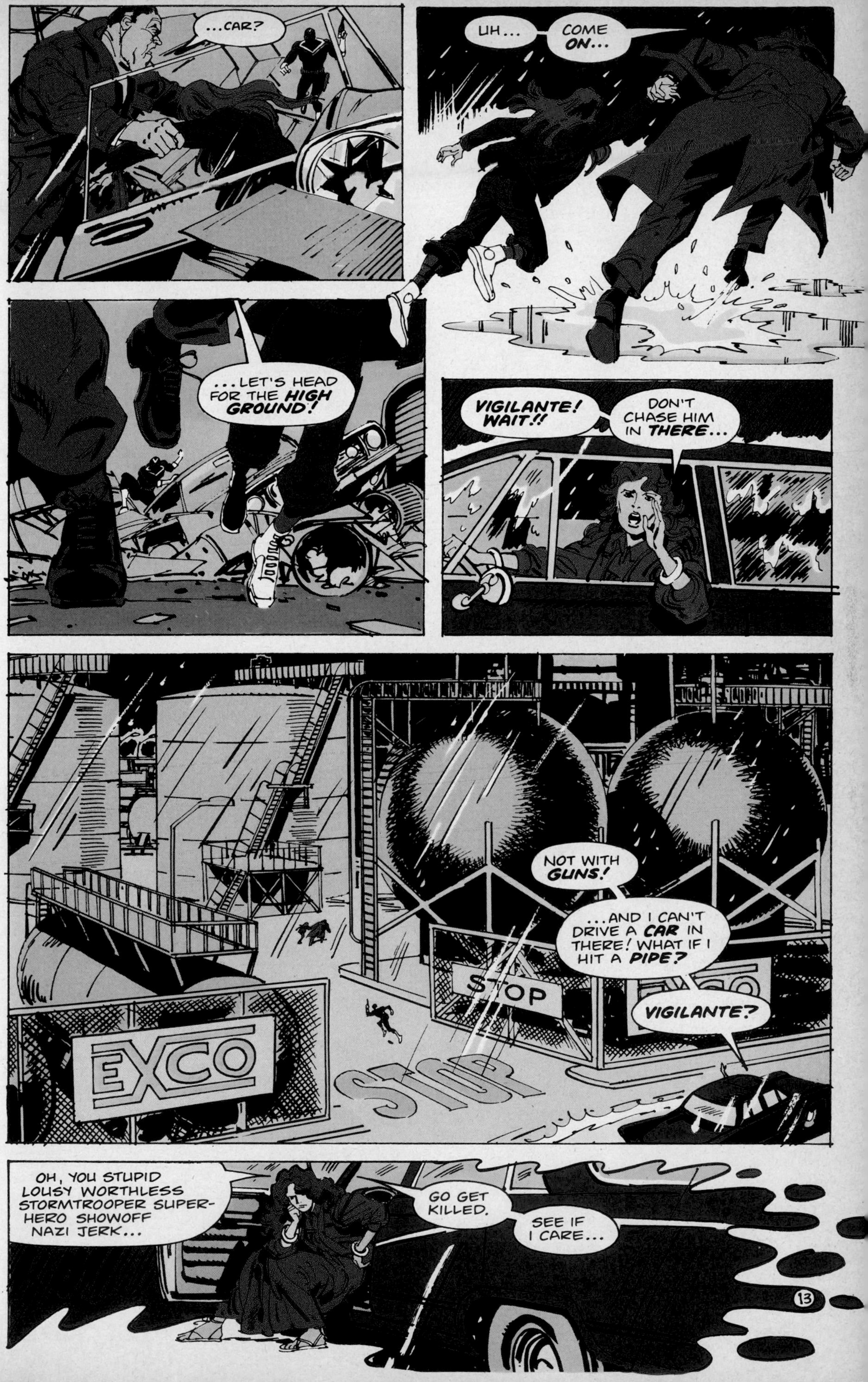
...CAR?
UH...
COME ON...
...LET'S HEAD FOR THE HIGH GROUND!
VIGILANTE! WAIT!!
DON'T CHASE HIM IN THERE...
NOT WITH GUNS!
...AND I CAN'T DRIVE A CAR IN THERE! WHAT IF I HIT A PIPE?
VIGILANTE?
EXCO
STOP
STOP
OH, YOU STUPID LOUSY WORTHLESS STORMTROOPER SUPER-HERO SHOWOFF NAZI JERK...
GO GET KILLED.
SEE IF I CARE...

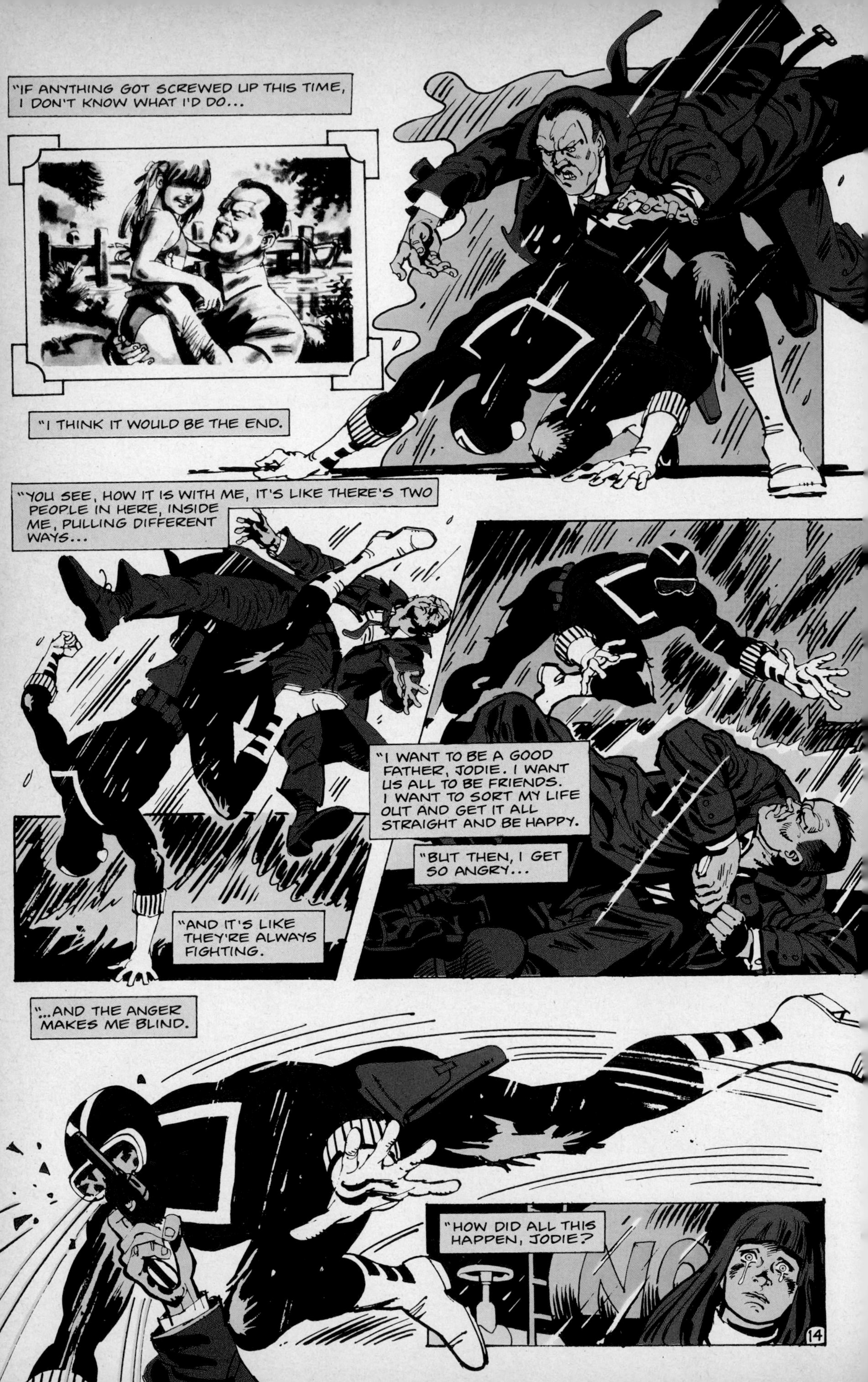
"IF ANYTHING GOT SCREWED UP THIS TIME, I DON'T KNOW WHAT I'D DO...
"I THINK IT WOULD BE THE END.
"YOU SEE, HOW IT IS WITH ME, IT'S LIKE THERE'S TWO PEOPLE IN HERE, INSIDE ME, PULLING DIFFERENT WAYS...
"AND IT'S LIKE THEY'RE ALWAYS FIGHTING.
"I WANT TO BE A GOOD FATHER, JODIE. I WANT US ALL TO BE FRIENDS. I WANT TO SORT MY LIFE OUT AND GET IT ALL STRAIGHT AND BE HAPPY.
"BUT THEN, I GET SO ANGRY...
"...AND THE ANGER MAKES ME BLIND.
"HOW DID ALL THIS HAPPEN, JODIE?
14

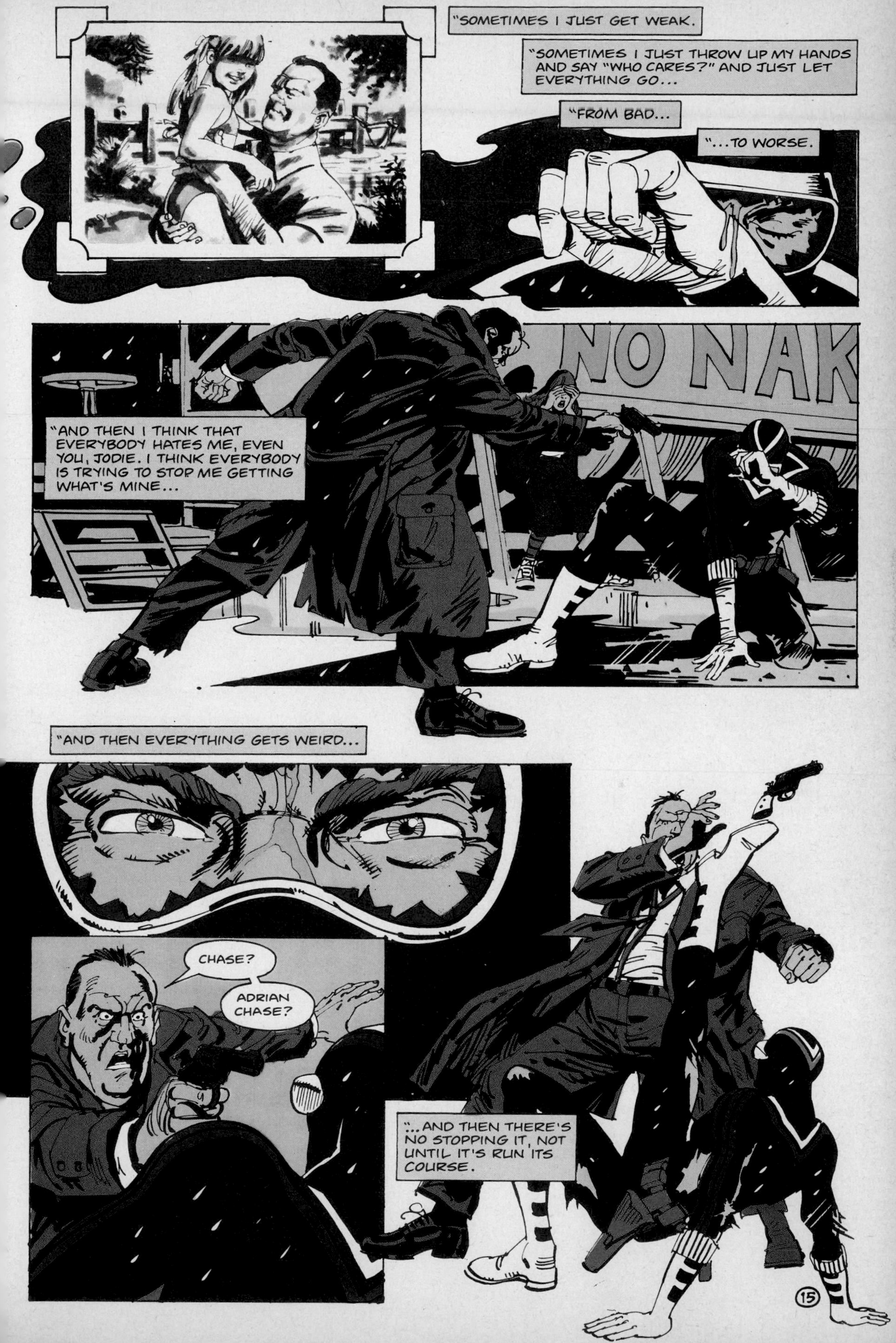
"SOMETIMES I JUST GET WEAK.
"SOMETIMES I JUST THROW UP MY HANDS AND SAY "WHO CARES?" AND JUST LET EVERYTHING GO...
"FROM BAD...
"...TO WORSE.
NO NAK
"AND THEN I THINK THAT EVERYBODY HATES ME, EVEN YOU, JODIE. I THINK EVERYBODY IS TRYING TO STOP ME GETTING WHAT'S MINE...
"AND THEN EVERYTHING GETS WEIRD...
CHASE?
ADRIAN CHASE?
"...AND THEN THERE'S NO STOPPING IT, NOT UNTIL IT'S RUN ITS COURSE.

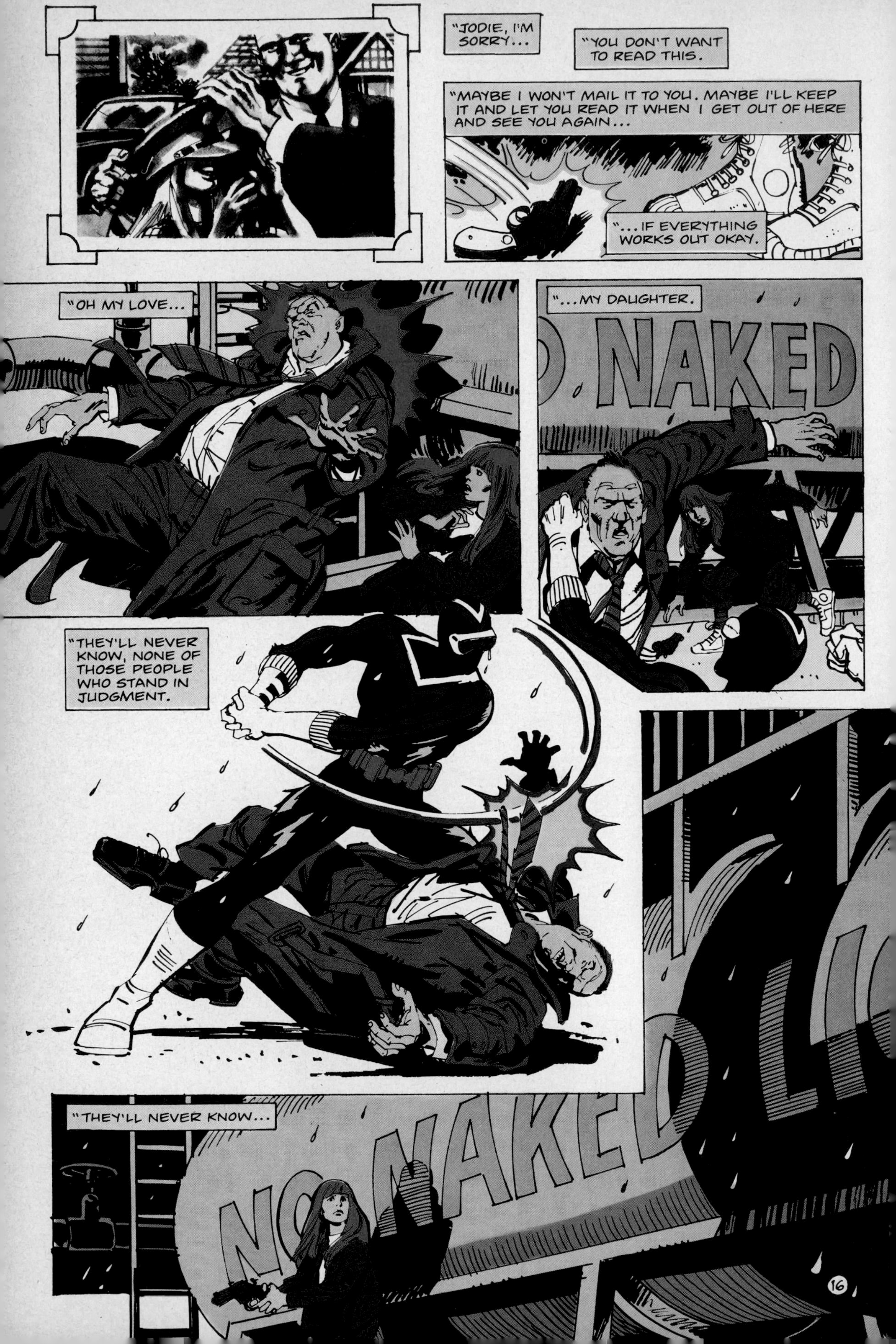
"JODIE, I'M SORRY...
"YOU DON'T WANT TO READ THIS.
"MAYBE I WON'T MAIL IT TO YOU. MAYBE I'LL KEEP IT AND LET YOU READ IT WHEN I GET OUT OF HERE AND SEE YOU AGAIN...
"...IF EVERYTHING WORKS OUT OKAY.
"OH MY LOVE...
"...MY DAUGHTER.
NAKED
"THEY'LL NEVER KNOW, NONE OF THOSE PEOPLE WHO STAND IN JUDGMENT.
"THEY'LL NEVER KNOW...
NO NAKED

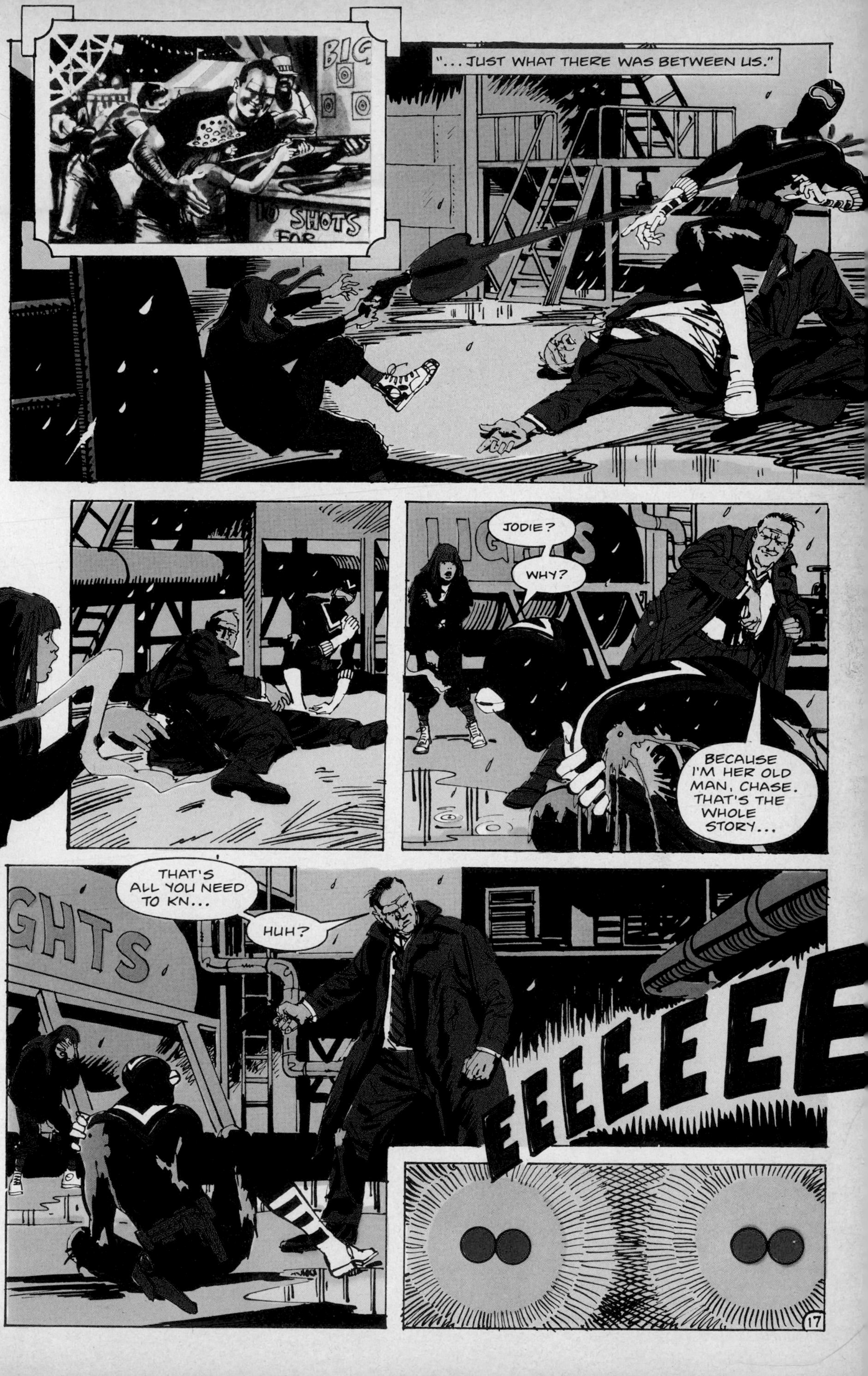

BIG
10 SHOTS FOR
"...JUST WHAT THERE WAS BETWEEN US."
JODIE?
WHY?
LIGHTS
BECAUSE I'M HER OLD MAN, CHASE. THAT'S THE WHOLE STORY...
THAT'S ALL YOU NEED TO KN...
HUH?
GHTS
EEEEEEE

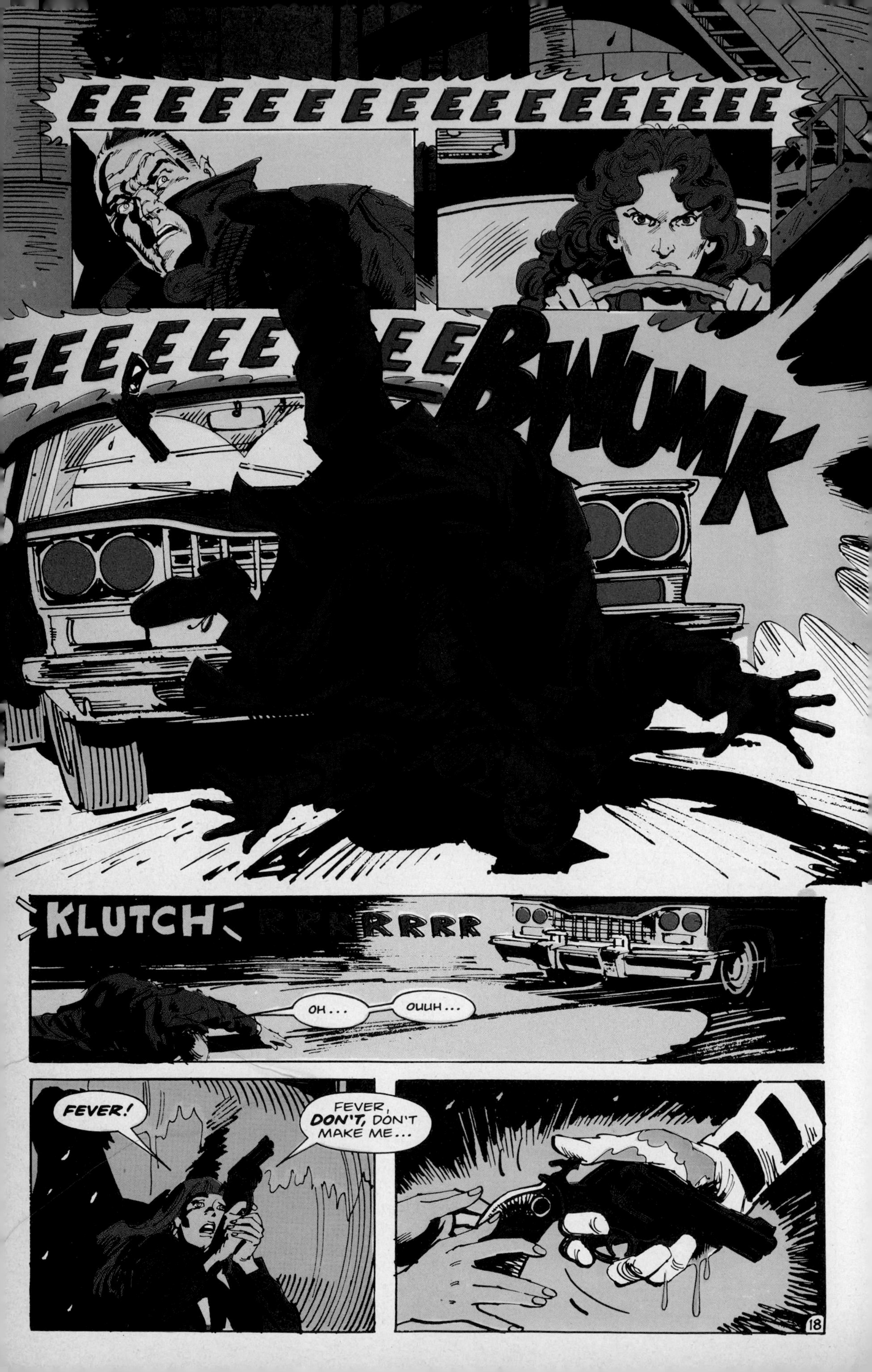
EEEEEEEEEEEEEEE
EEEEEEEEE
BWUMK
KLUTCH
RRRRRRRR
OH...
OUUH...
FEVER!
FEVER, DON'T, DON'T MAKE ME...

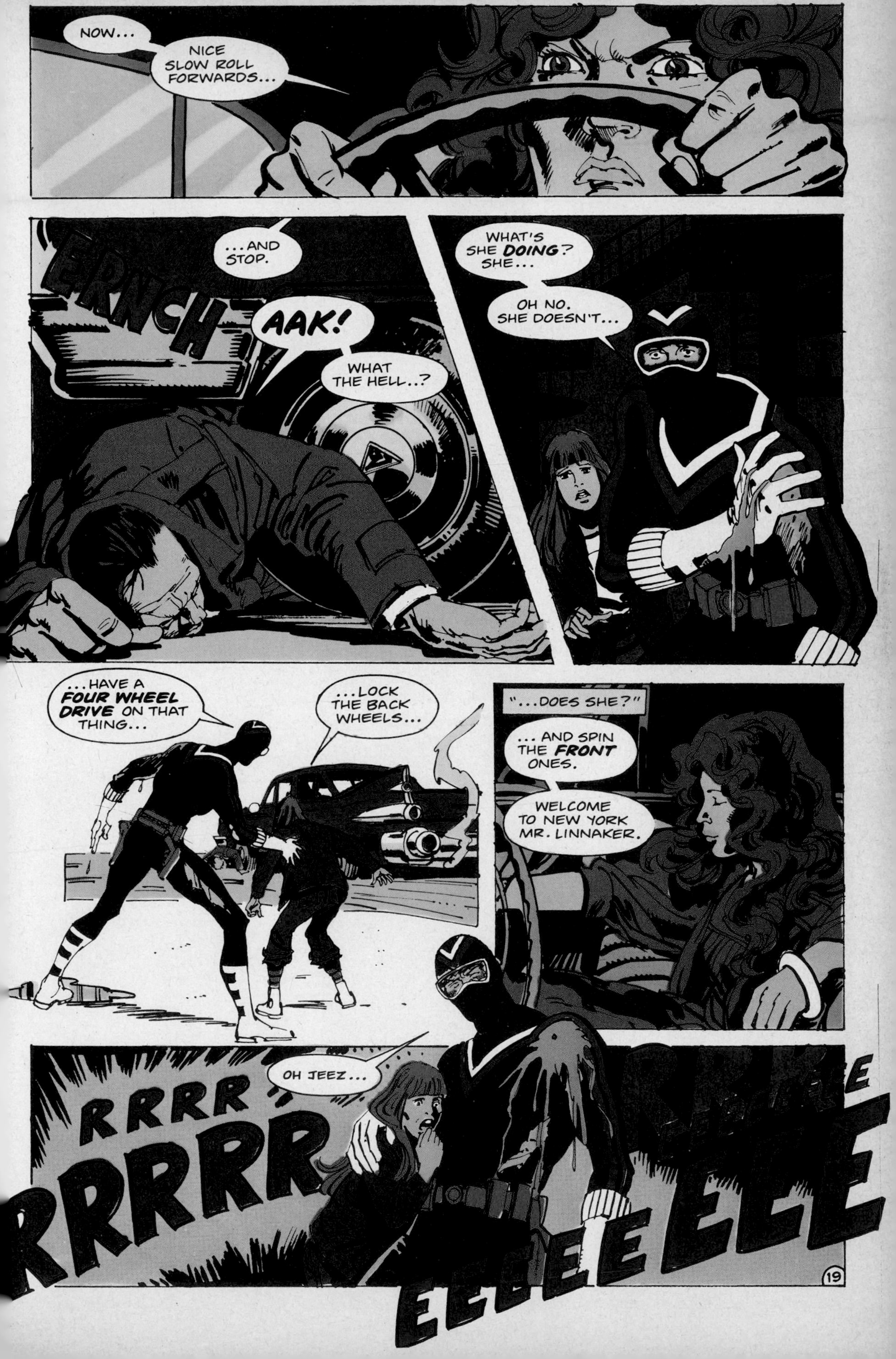
NOW...
NICE SLOW ROLL FORWARDS...
ERNCH
...AND STOP.
AAK!
WHAT THE HELL..?
WHAT'S SHE **DOING**? SHE...
OH NO. SHE DOESN'T...
...HAVE A **FOUR WHEEL DRIVE** ON THAT THING...
...LOCK THE BACK WHEELS...
"...DOES SHE?"
...AND SPIN THE **FRONT** ONES.
WELCOME TO NEW YORK MR. LINNAKER.
OH JEEZ...
RRRR
RRRRR
EEEEEEE
EEEEE

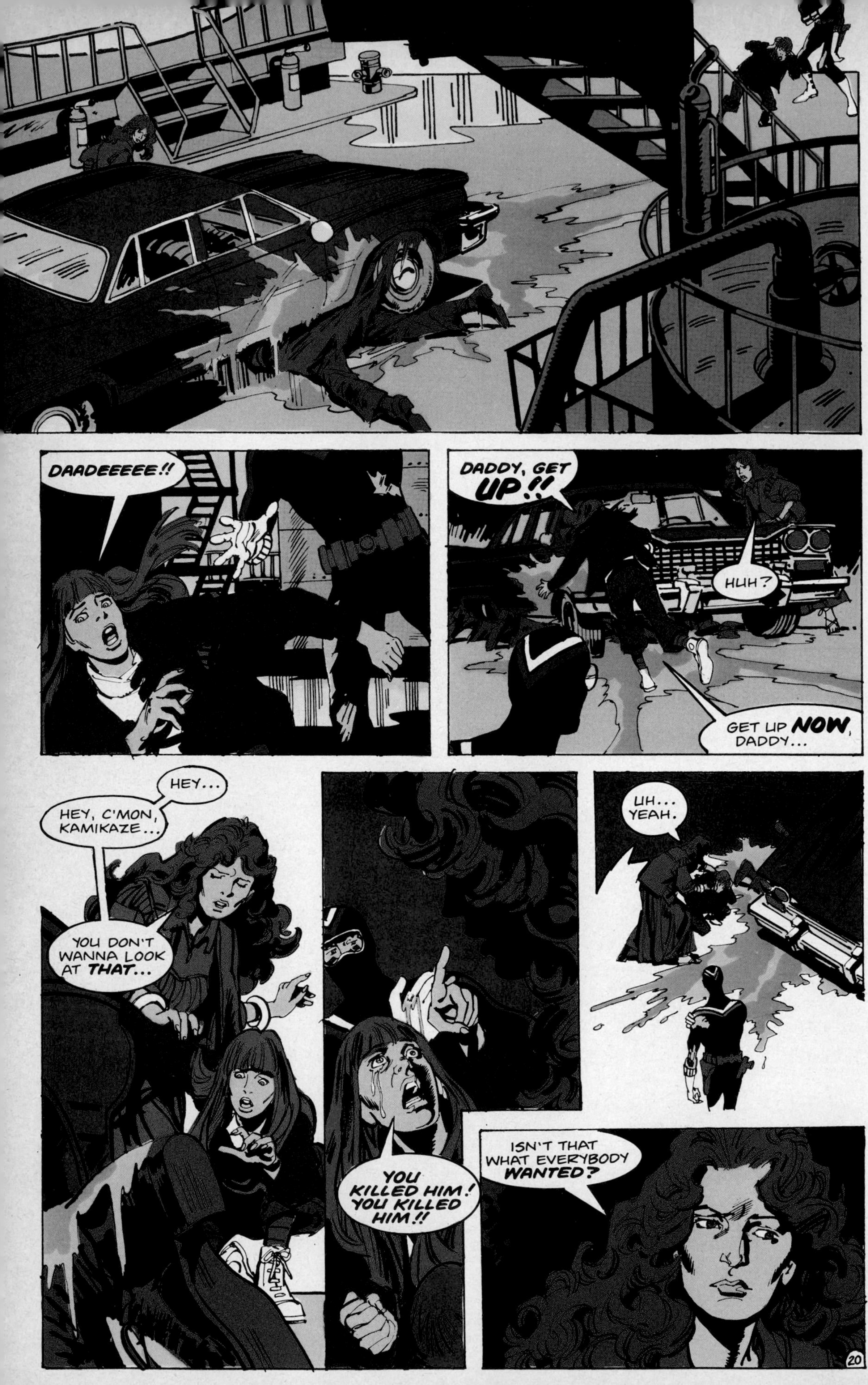
DAADEEEEE!!
DADDY, GET UP!!
HUH?
GET UP NOW, DADDY...
HEY...
HEY, C'MON, KAMIKAZE...
YOU DON'T WANNA LOOK AT THAT...
YOU KILLED HIM! YOU KILLED HIM!!
UH... YEAH.
ISN'T THAT WHAT EVERYBODY WANTED?
20

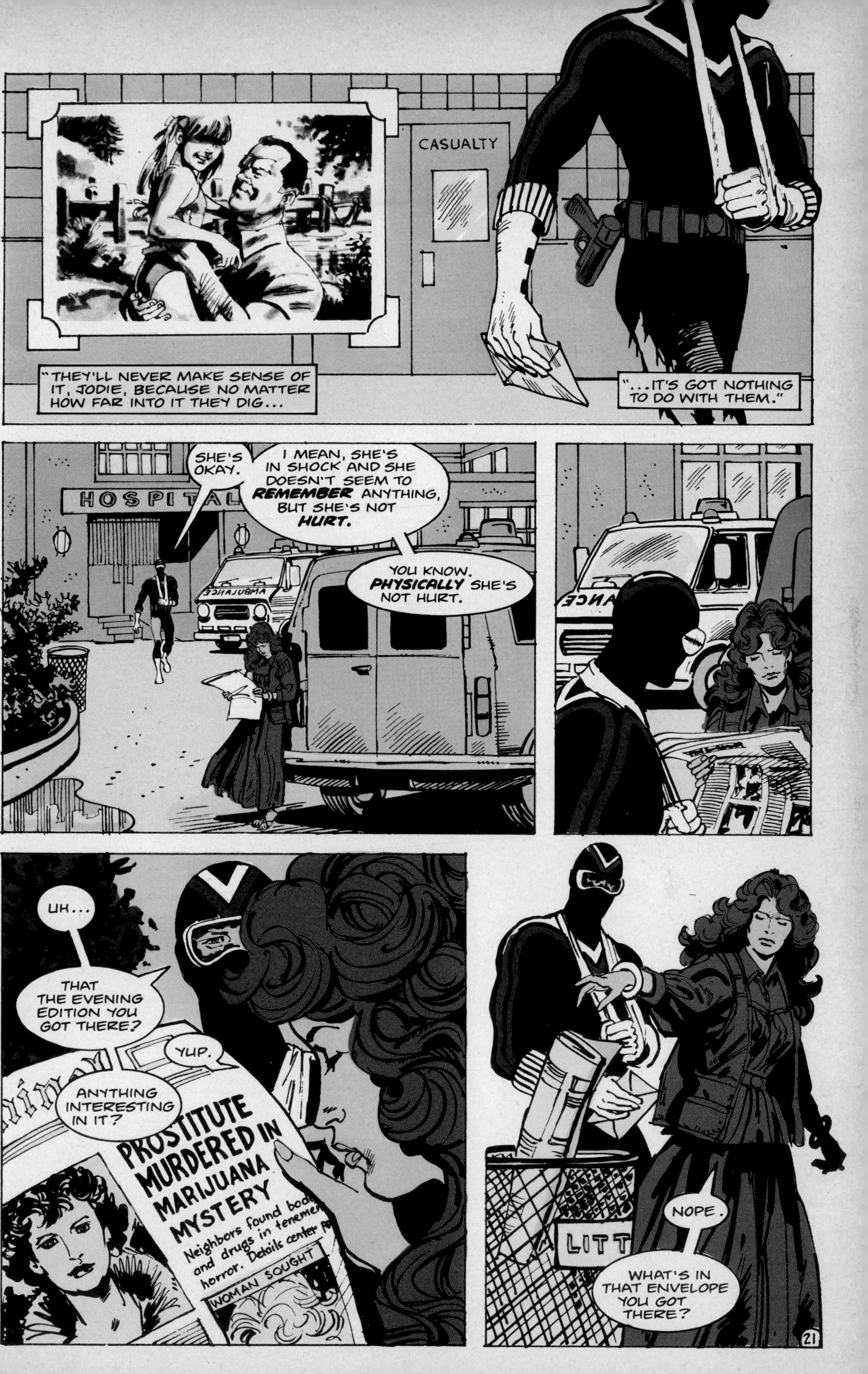
CASUALTY
"THEY'LL NEVER MAKE SENSE OF IT, JODIE, BECAUSE NO MATTER HOW FAR INTO IT THEY DIG...
"...IT'S GOT NOTHING TO DO WITH THEM."
HOSPITAL
SHE'S OKAY.
I MEAN, SHE'S IN SHOCK AND SHE DOESN'T SEEM TO **REMEMBER** ANYTHING, BUT SHE'S NOT **HURT.**
YOU KNOW. **PHYSICALLY** SHE'S NOT HURT.
UH...
THAT THE EVENING EDITION YOU GOT THERE?
YUP.
ANYTHING INTERESTING IN IT?
PROSTITUTE MURDERED IN MARIJUANA MYSTERY
Neighbors found body and drugs in tenement horror. Details center page
WOMAN SOUGHT
LITT
NOPE.
WHAT'S IN THAT ENVELOPE YOU GOT THERE?

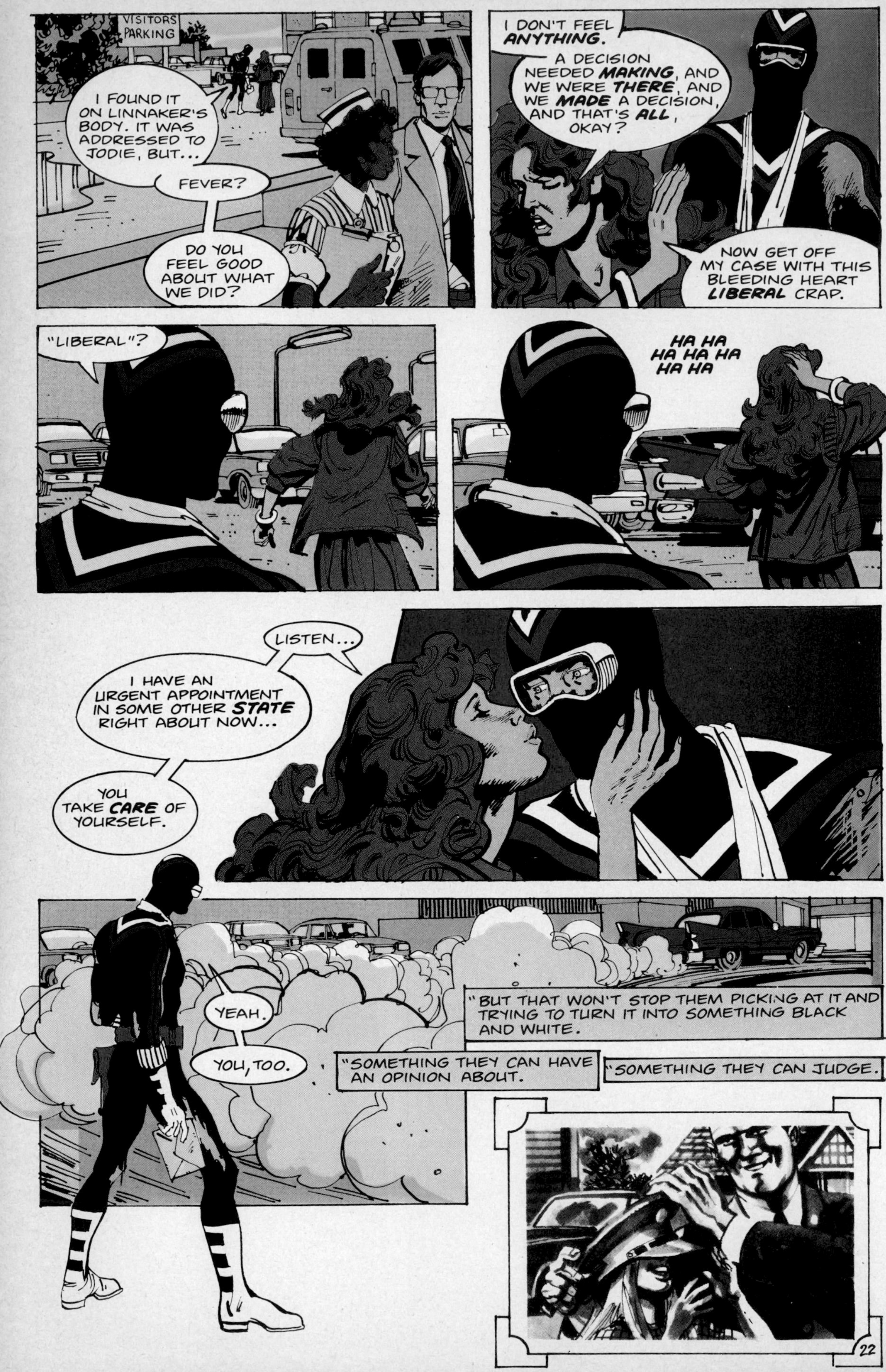
VISITORS PARKING
I FOUND IT ON LINNAKER'S BODY. IT WAS ADDRESSED TO JODIE, BUT...
FEVER?
DO YOU FEEL GOOD ABOUT WHAT WE DID?
I DON'T FEEL ANYTHING.
A DECISION NEEDED MAKING, AND WE WERE THERE, AND WE MADE A DECISION, AND THAT'S ALL, OKAY?
NOW GET OFF MY CASE WITH THIS BLEEDING HEART LIBERAL CRAP.
"LIBERAL"?
HA HA HA HA HA HA HA
LISTEN...
I HAVE AN URGENT APPOINTMENT IN SOME OTHER STATE RIGHT ABOUT NOW...
YOU TAKE CARE OF YOURSELF.
YEAH.
YOU, TOO.
"BUT THAT WON'T STOP THEM PICKING AT IT AND TRYING TO TURN IT INTO SOMETHING BLACK AND WHITE.
"SOMETHING THEY CAN HAVE AN OPINION ABOUT.
"SOMETHING THEY CAN JUDGE.

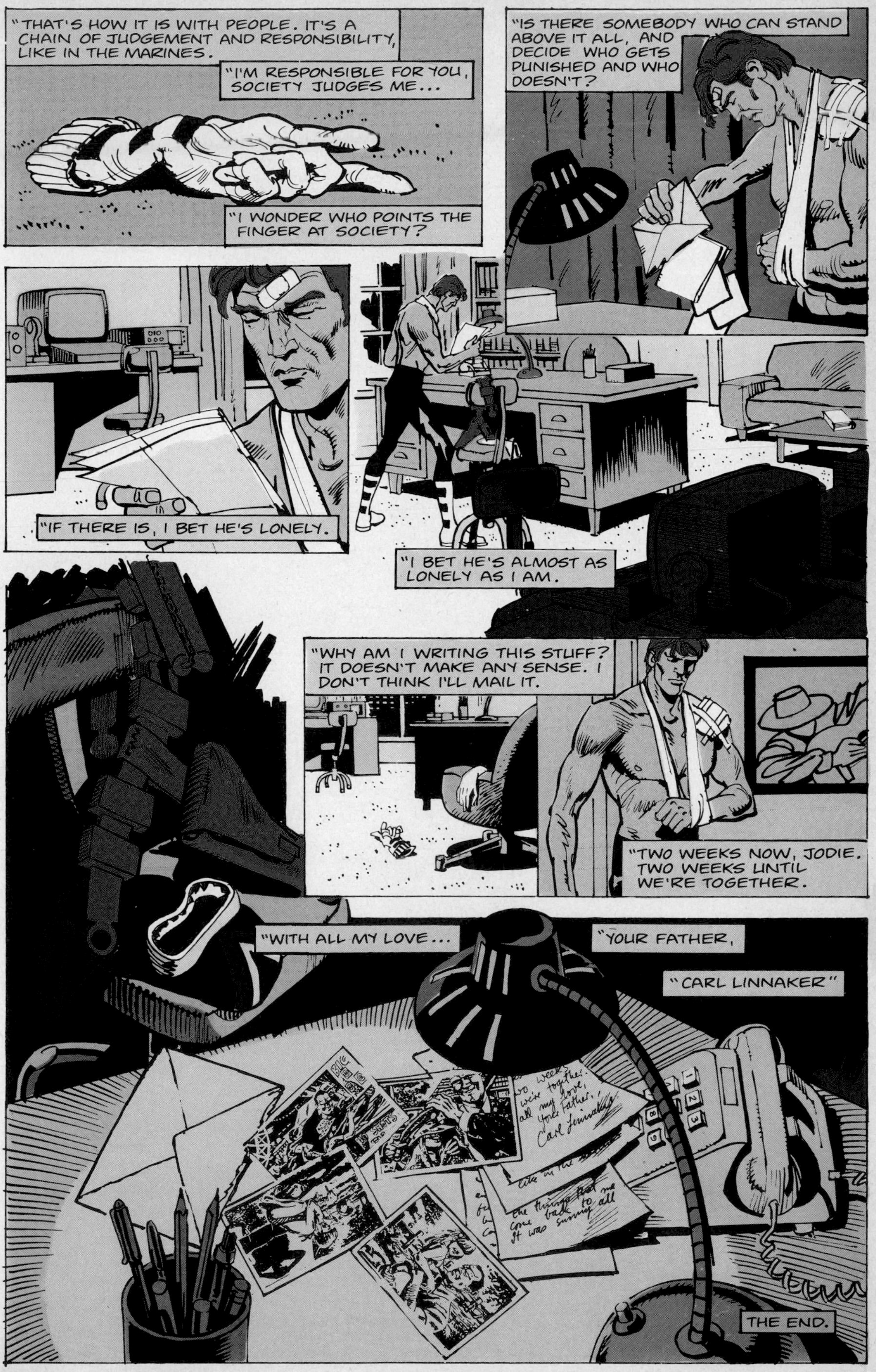
"THAT'S HOW IT IS WITH PEOPLE. IT'S A CHAIN OF JUDGEMENT AND RESPONSIBILITY, LIKE IN THE MARINES.
"I'M RESPONSIBLE FOR YOU, SOCIETY JUDGES ME...
"I WONDER WHO POINTS THE FINGER AT SOCIETY?
"IS THERE SOMEBODY WHO CAN STAND ABOVE IT ALL, AND DECIDE WHO GETS PUNISHED AND WHO DOESN'T?
"IF THERE IS, I BET HE'S LONELY.
"I BET HE'S ALMOST AS LONELY AS I AM.
"WHY AM I WRITING THIS STUFF? IT DOESN'T MAKE ANY SENSE. I DON'T THINK I'LL MAIL IT.
"TWO WEEKS NOW, JODIE. TWO WEEKS UNTIL WE'RE TOGETHER.
"WITH ALL MY LOVE...
"YOUR FATHER,
"CARL LINNAKER"
THE END.

DEAREST *GUILDMASTERS*...

...DEAREST *FLYBLOATED*, *ROT-WEBBED* GUILDMASTERS, *INEDIBLE* EVEN TO YOUR OWN *MATES*...

...AS YOU MAY HAVE *DEDUCED*, MY FIBERS ARE SATURATED WITH VINTAGE *ACIDS*, I'M *DRUNK*, AND THIS IS MY *LAST MESSAGE* TO YOU.

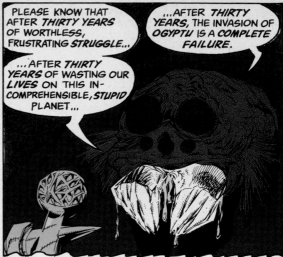

PLEASE KNOW THAT AFTER *THIRTY YEARS* OF WORTHLESS, FRUSTRATING *STRUGGLE*...

...AFTER *THIRTY YEARS* OF WASTING OUR *LIVES* ON THIS IN- COMPREHENSIBLE, *STUPID* PLANET...

...AFTER *THIRTY YEARS*, THE INVASION OF *OGYPTU* IS A *COMPLETE FAILURE*.

"I SHOULD HAVE *KNOWN*, FROM THE MOMENT I FIRST SAW THE TWO MOTIONLESS *GIANTS*...

"...ALL THOSE *BITTER* YEARS AGO..."

VEGA
'BRIEF LIVES'

ALAN MOORE, WRITER —O— *KEVIN O'NEILL*, ARTIST

CARL GAFFORD, COLORIST • *T. KLEIN*, LETTERS • *ALAN GOLD*, EDITOR

1

"IT TOOK TWENTY LUNAR RIPENINGS BEFORE WE REALIZED THAT WE WERE LOOKING AT AN ACTUAL LIFE-FORM..."

LAST SNOWCYCLE, THE STATUE ON THE *LEFT* HAD ITS EYES *FULLY* OPEN. NOW THEY'RE HALF *CLOSED*...

"...AND ANOTHER *TEN* BEFORE WE BEGAN TO *UNDERSTAND* THEM."

I BELIEVE THE GIANTS OPERATE IN A *DIFFERENT TIME FRAME*, FAR *SLOWER* THAN OUR OWN, WHERE THE BLINKING OF AN *EYE* LASTS TEN OF OUR *YEARS*...

"BUT I WAS MORE *HEADSTRONG* THEN, AND UNAWARE OF THE PROBLEM'S *MAGNITUDE*..."

I DON'T CARE *WHAT* SPEED THEY LIVE AT!

THEY HAVE BEEN INVADED BY THE *SPIDER GUILD* AND THEY SHALL LEARN TO *FEAR* US!

"THE DIFFICULTY WAS IN MAKING THE GIANTS *AWARE* THAT THEY HAD BEEN *CONQUERED*."

WE CAN'T COMMUNICATE... FOR *THEM*, WE'RE MOVING TOO FAST TO *SEE*.

WE'D HAVE TO STAND STILL FOR *DECADES* BEFORE THEY'D *NOTICE* US.

"BUT I DID NOT GIVE IN. AHH...HOW *FIERCE* I WAS IN MY YOUTH. HOW *RESOLUTE*..."

THEN THEY SHALL *FEEL* OUR PRESENCE. *PAIN* IS THE ONLY *UNIVERSAL LANGUAGE*!

GIVE ME THAT *GEMBURNER*...

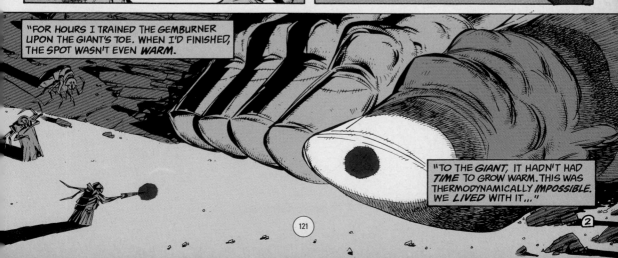

"FOR HOURS I TRAINED THE GEMBURNER UPON THE GIANT'S TOE. WHEN I'D FINISHED, THE SPOT WASN'T EVEN *WARM*.

"TO THE *GIANT*, IT HADN'T HAD *TIME* TO GROW WARM. THIS WAS THERMODYNAMICALLY *IMPOSSIBLE*. WE *LIVED* WITH IT..."

2

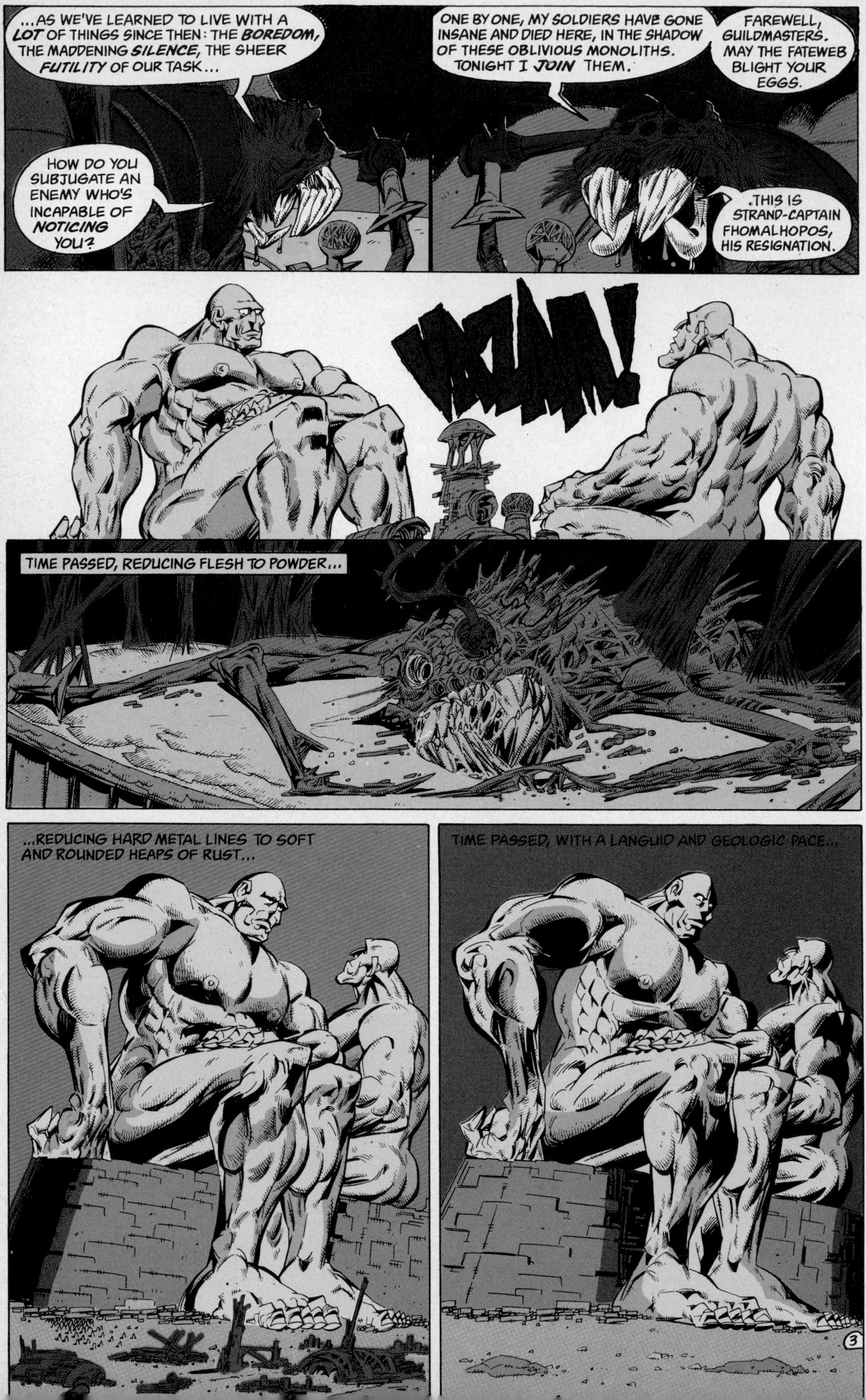

...AS WE'VE LEARNED TO LIVE WITH A LOT OF THINGS SINCE THEN: THE BOREDOM, THE MADDENING SILENCE, THE SHEER FUTILITY OF OUR TASK...
HOW DO YOU SUBJUGATE AN ENEMY WHO'S INCAPABLE OF NOTICING YOU?
ONE BY ONE, MY SOLDIERS HAVE GONE INSANE AND DIED HERE, IN THE SHADOW OF THESE OBLIVIOUS MONOLITHS. TONIGHT I JOIN THEM.
FAREWELL, GUILDMASTERS. MAY THE FATEWEB BLIGHT YOUR EGGS.
.THIS IS STRAND-CAPTAIN FHOMALHOPOS, HIS RESIGNATION.
VRZAM!
TIME PASSED, REDUCING FLESH TO POWDER...
...REDUCING HARD METAL LINES TO SOFT AND ROUNDED HEAPS OF RUST...
TIME PASSED, WITH A LANGUID AND GEOLOGIC PACE...
3

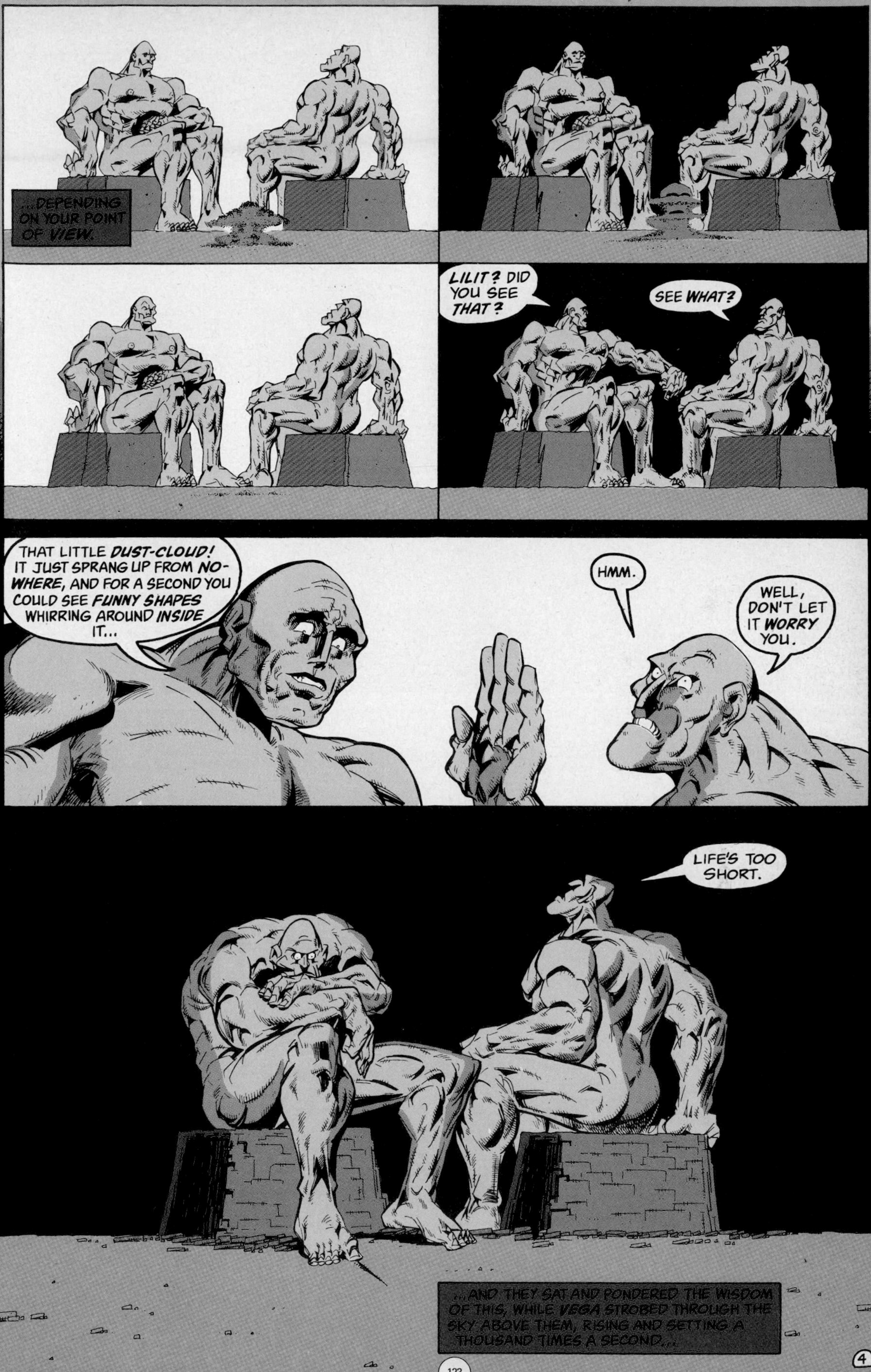
...DEPENDING ON YOUR POINT OF VIEW.
LILIT? DID YOU SEE THAT?
SEE WHAT?
THAT LITTLE DUST-CLOUD! IT JUST SPRANG UP FROM NO-WHERE, AND FOR A SECOND YOU COULD SEE FUNNY SHAPES WHIRRING AROUND INSIDE IT...
HMM.
WELL, DON'T LET IT WORRY YOU.
LIFE'S TOO SHORT.
...AND THEY SAT AND PONDERED THE WISDOM OF THIS, WHILE VEGA STROBED THROUGH THE SKY ABOVE THEM, RISING AND SETTING A THOUSAND TIMES A SECOND...
4

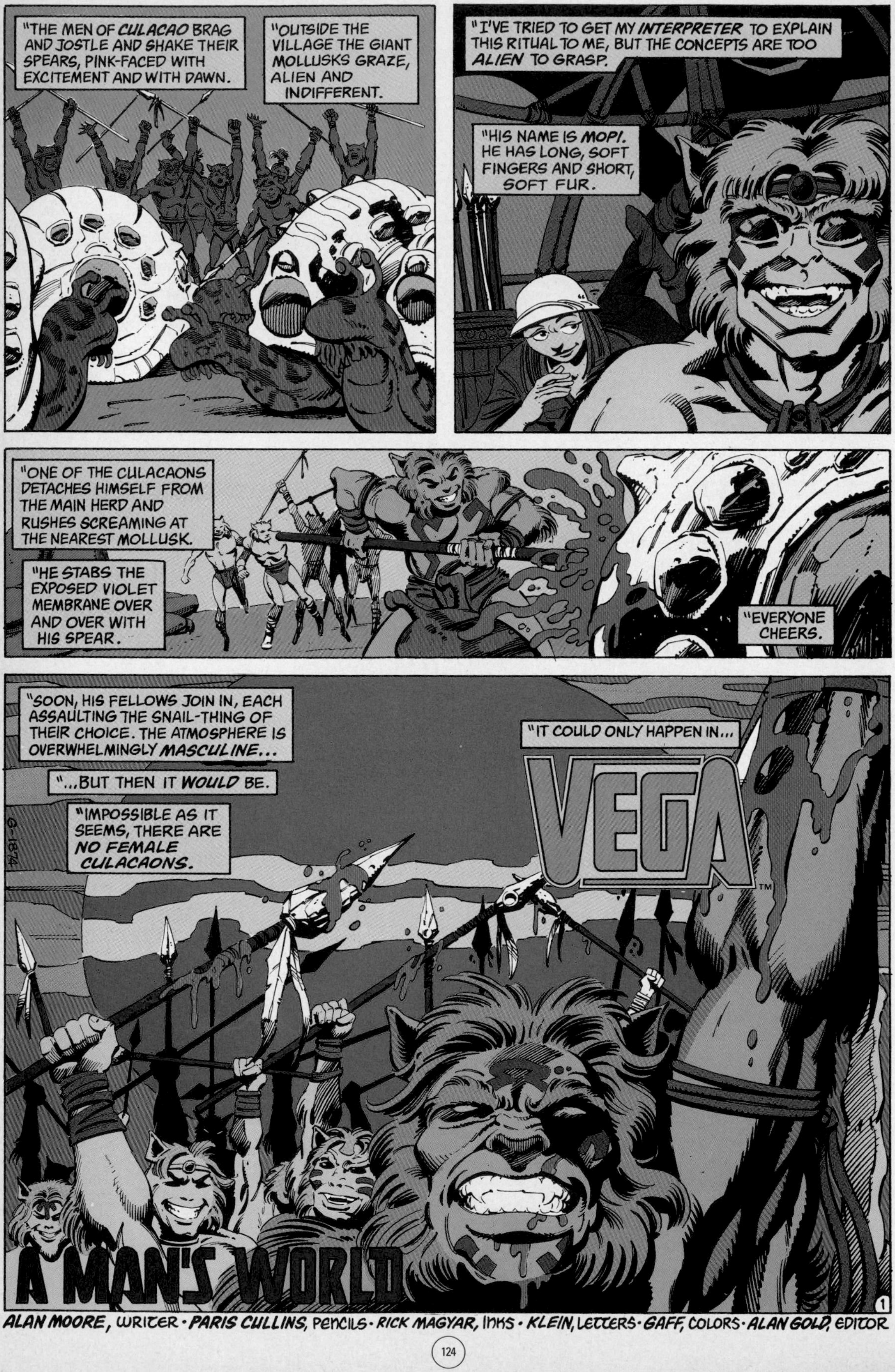
"THE MEN OF CULACAO BRAG AND JOSTLE AND SHAKE THEIR SPEARS, PINK-FACED WITH EXCITEMENT AND WITH DAWN.
"OUTSIDE THE VILLAGE THE GIANT MOLLUSKS GRAZE, ALIEN AND INDIFFERENT.
"I'VE TRIED TO GET MY INTERPRETER TO EXPLAIN THIS RITUAL TO ME, BUT THE CONCEPTS ARE TOO ALIEN TO GRASP.
"HIS NAME IS MOPI. HE HAS LONG, SOFT FINGERS AND SHORT, SOFT FUR.
"ONE OF THE CULACAONS DETACHES HIMSELF FROM THE MAIN HERD AND RUSHES SCREAMING AT THE NEAREST MOLLUSK.
"HE STABS THE EXPOSED VIOLET MEMBRANE OVER AND OVER WITH HIS SPEAR.
"EVERYONE CHEERS.
"SOON, HIS FELLOWS JOIN IN, EACH ASSAULTING THE SNAIL-THING OF THEIR CHOICE. THE ATMOSPHERE IS OVERWHELMINGLY MASCULINE...
"...BUT THEN IT WOULD BE.
"IMPOSSIBLE AS IT SEEMS, THERE ARE NO FEMALE CULACAONS.
"IT COULD ONLY HAPPEN IN...
VEGA™
G-1874
A MAN'S WORLD
1
ALAN MOORE, WRITER · PARIS CULLINS, PENCILS · RICK MAGYAR, INKS · KLEIN, LETTERS · GAFF, COLORS · ALAN GOLD, EDITOR

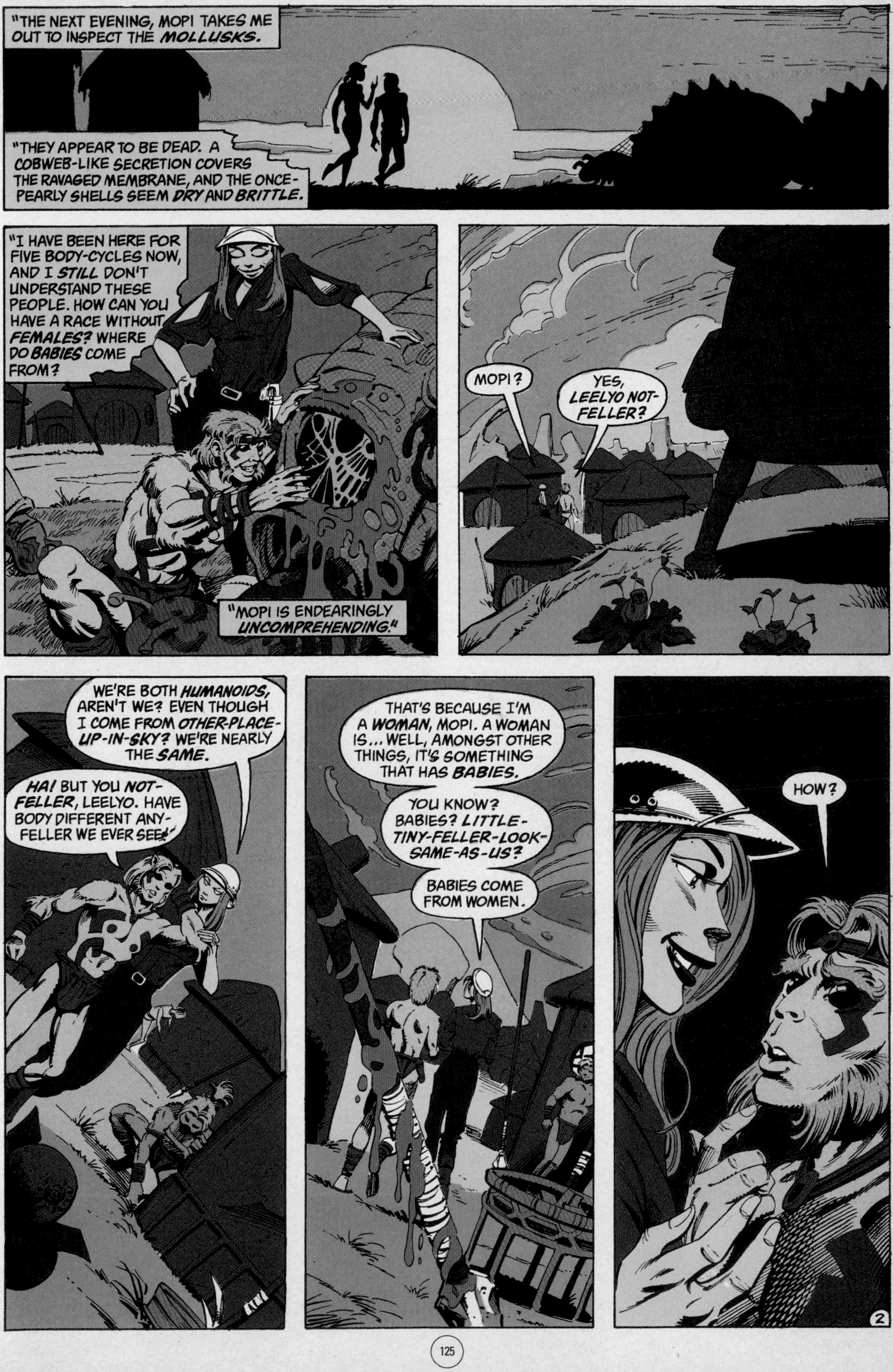
"THE NEXT EVENING, MOPI TAKES ME OUT TO INSPECT THE MOLLUSKS.
"THEY APPEAR TO BE DEAD. A COBWEB-LIKE SECRETION COVERS THE RAVAGED MEMBRANE, AND THE ONCE-PEARLY SHELLS SEEM DRY AND BRITTLE.
"I HAVE BEEN HERE FOR FIVE BODY-CYCLES NOW, AND I STILL DON'T UNDERSTAND THESE PEOPLE. HOW CAN YOU HAVE A RACE WITHOUT FEMALES? WHERE DO BABIES COME FROM?
"MOPI IS ENDEARINGLY UNCOMPREHENDING."
MOPI?
YES, LEELYO NOT-FELLER?
WE'RE BOTH HUMANOIDS, AREN'T WE? EVEN THOUGH I COME FROM OTHER-PLACE-UP-IN-SKY? WE'RE NEARLY THE SAME.
HA! BUT YOU NOT-FELLER, LEELYO. HAVE BODY DIFFERENT ANY-FELLER WE EVER SEE!
THAT'S BECAUSE I'M A WOMAN, MOPI. A WOMAN IS... WELL, AMONGST OTHER THINGS, IT'S SOMETHING THAT HAS BABIES.
YOU KNOW? BABIES? LITTLE-TINY-FELLER-LOOK-SAME-AS-US?
BABIES COME FROM WOMEN.
HOW?
2

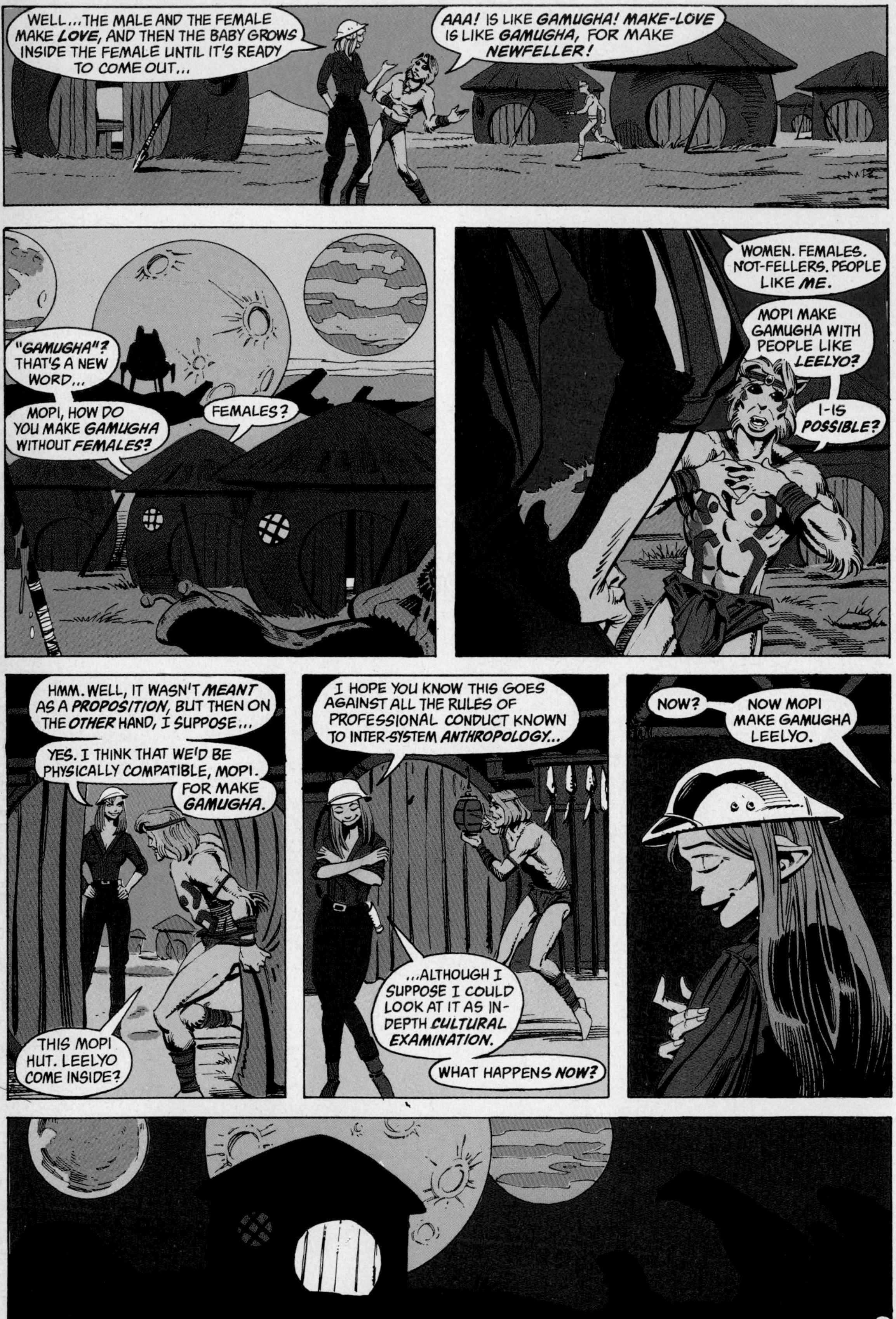
WELL...THE MALE AND THE FEMALE MAKE LOVE, AND THEN THE BABY GROWS INSIDE THE FEMALE UNTIL IT'S READY TO COME OUT...
AAA! IS LIKE GAMUGHA! MAKE-LOVE IS LIKE GAMUGHA, FOR MAKE NEWFELLER!
"GAMUGHA"? THAT'S A NEW WORD...
MOPI, HOW DO YOU MAKE GAMUGHA WITHOUT FEMALES?
FEMALES?
WOMEN. FEMALES. NOT-FELLERS. PEOPLE LIKE ME.
MOPI MAKE GAMUGHA WITH PEOPLE LIKE LEELYO?
I-IS POSSIBLE?
HMM. WELL, IT WASN'T MEANT AS A PROPOSITION, BUT THEN ON THE OTHER HAND, I SUPPOSE...
YES. I THINK THAT WE'D BE PHYSICALLY COMPATIBLE, MOPI.
FOR MAKE GAMUGHA.
THIS MOPI HUT. LEELYO COME INSIDE?
I HOPE YOU KNOW THIS GOES AGAINST ALL THE RULES OF PROFESSIONAL CONDUCT KNOWN TO INTER-SYSTEM ANTHROPOLOGY...
...ALTHOUGH I SUPPOSE I COULD LOOK AT IT AS IN-DEPTH CULTURAL EXAMINATION.
WHAT HAPPENS NOW?
NOW?
NOW MOPI MAKE GAMUGHA LEELYO.
3

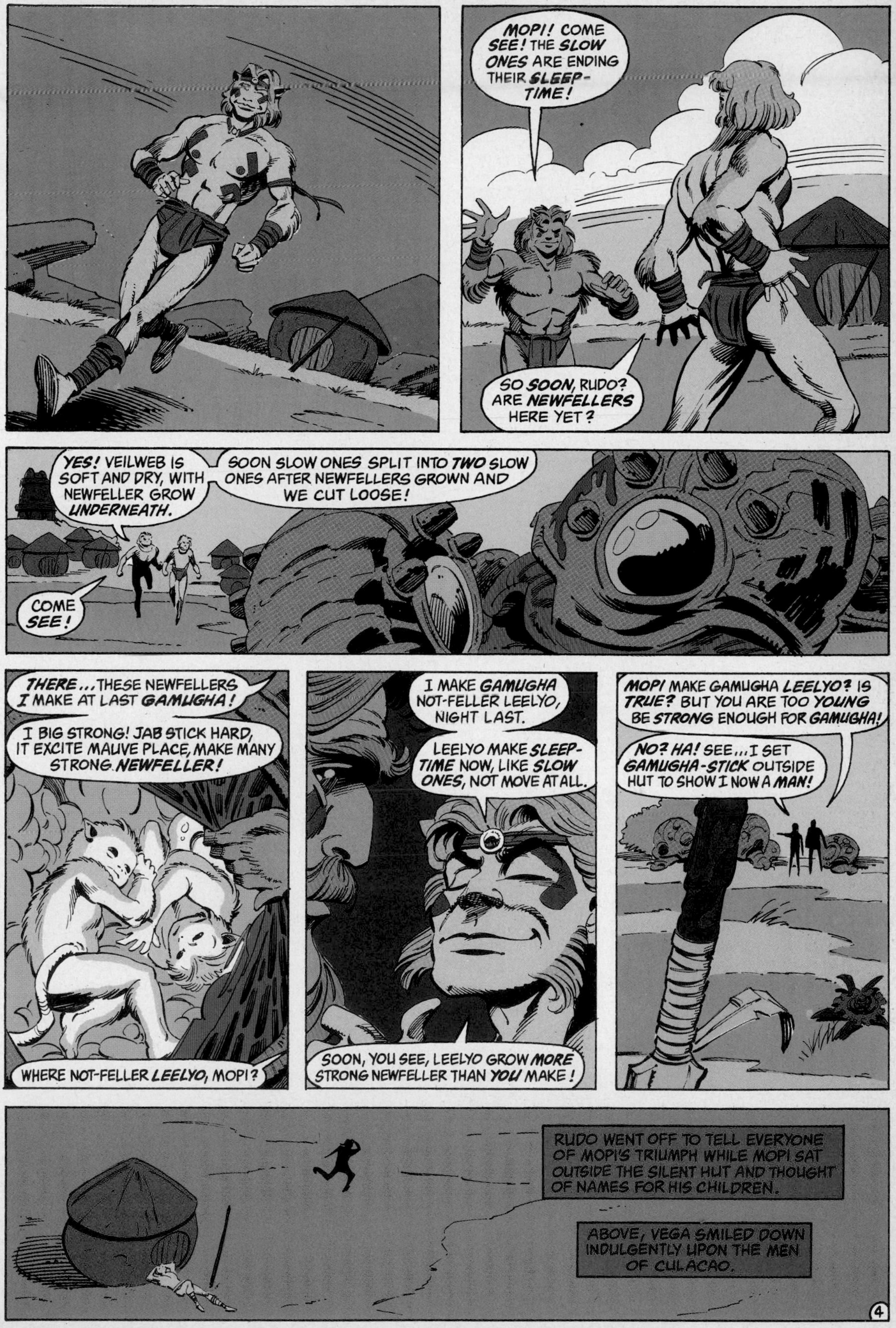
MOPI! COME SEE! THE SLOW ONES ARE ENDING THEIR SLEEP-TIME!
SO SOON, RUDO? ARE NEWFELLERS HERE YET?
YES! VEILWEB IS SOFT AND DRY, WITH NEWFELLER GROW UNDERNEATH.
SOON SLOW ONES SPLIT INTO TWO SLOW ONES AFTER NEWFELLERS GROWN AND WE CUT LOOSE!
COME SEE!
THERE... THESE NEWFELLERS I MAKE AT LAST GAMUGHA!
I BIG STRONG! JAB STICK HARD, IT EXCITE MAUVE PLACE, MAKE MANY STRONG NEWFELLER!
WHERE NOT-FELLER LEELYO, MOPI?
I MAKE GAMUGHA NOT-FELLER LEELYO, NIGHT LAST.
LEELYO MAKE SLEEP-TIME NOW, LIKE SLOW ONES, NOT MOVE AT ALL.
SOON, YOU SEE, LEELYO GROW MORE STRONG NEWFELLER THAN YOU MAKE!
MOPI MAKE GAMUGHA LEELYO? IS TRUE? BUT YOU ARE TOO YOUNG BE STRONG ENOUGH FOR GAMUGHA!
NO? HA! SEE... I SET GAMUGHA-STICK OUTSIDE HUT TO SHOW I NOW A MAN!
RUDO WENT OFF TO TELL EVERYONE OF MOPI'S TRIUMPH WHILE MOPI SAT OUTSIDE THE SILENT HUT AND THOUGHT OF NAMES FOR HIS CHILDREN.
ABOVE, VEGA SMILED DOWN INDULGENTLY UPON THE MEN OF CULACAO.
4

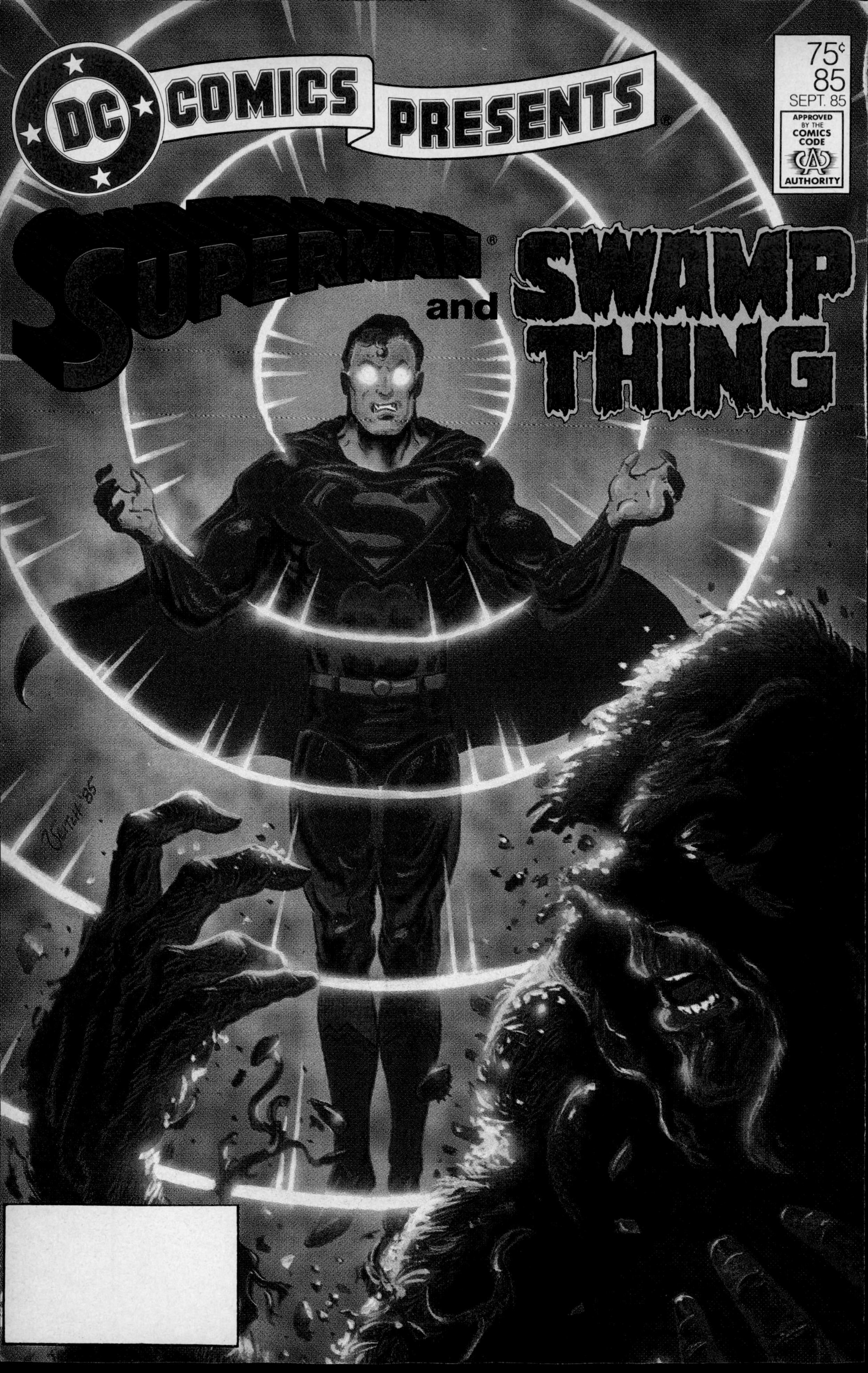
DC
COMICS PRESENTS
75¢
85
SEPT. 85
APPROVED BY THE COMICS CODE AUTHORITY
SUPERMAN
and
SWAMP THING

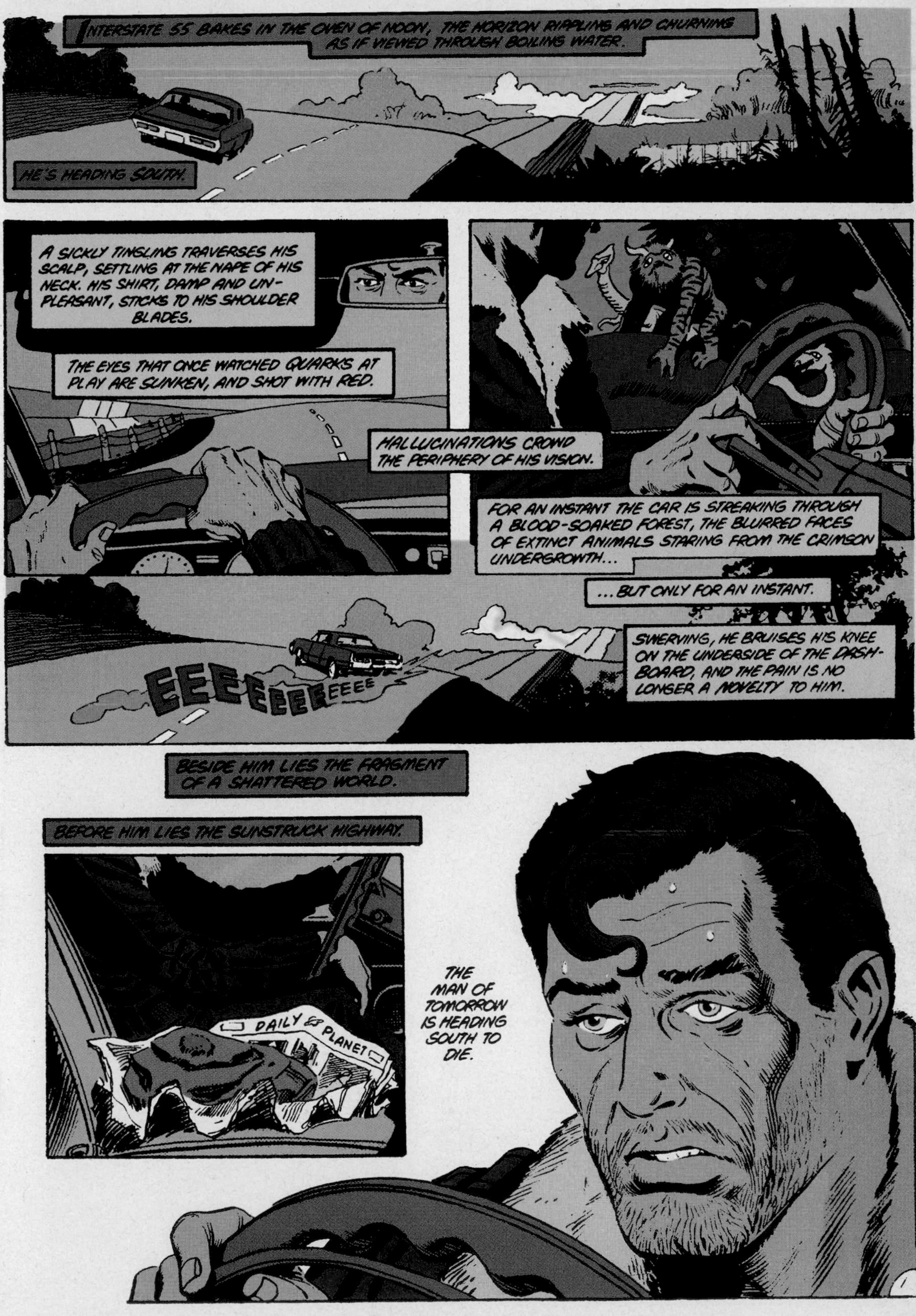
INTERSTATE 55 BAKES IN THE OVEN OF NOON, THE HORIZON RIPPLING AND CHURNING AS IF VIEWED THROUGH BOILING WATER.
HE'S HEADING SOUTH.
A SICKLY TINGLING TRAVERSES HIS SCALP, SETTLING AT THE NAPE OF HIS NECK. HIS SHIRT, DAMP AND UNPLEASANT, STICKS TO HIS SHOULDER BLADES.
THE EYES THAT ONCE WATCHED QUARKS AT PLAY ARE SUNKEN, AND SHOT WITH RED.
HALLUCINATIONS CROWD THE PERIPHERY OF HIS VISION.
FOR AN INSTANT THE CAR IS STREAKING THROUGH A BLOOD-SOAKED FOREST, THE BLURRED FACES OF EXTINCT ANIMALS STARING FROM THE CRIMSON UNDERGROWTH...
...BUT ONLY FOR AN INSTANT.
EEEEEEEEEEEE
SWERVING, HE BRUISES HIS KNEE ON THE UNDERSIDE OF THE DASHBOARD, AND THE PAIN IS NO LONGER A NOVELTY TO HIM.
BESIDE HIM LIES THE FRAGMENT OF A SHATTERED WORLD.
BEFORE HIM LIES THE SUNSTRUCK HIGHWAY.
DAILY PLANET
THE MAN OF TOMORROW IS HEADING SOUTH TO DIE.

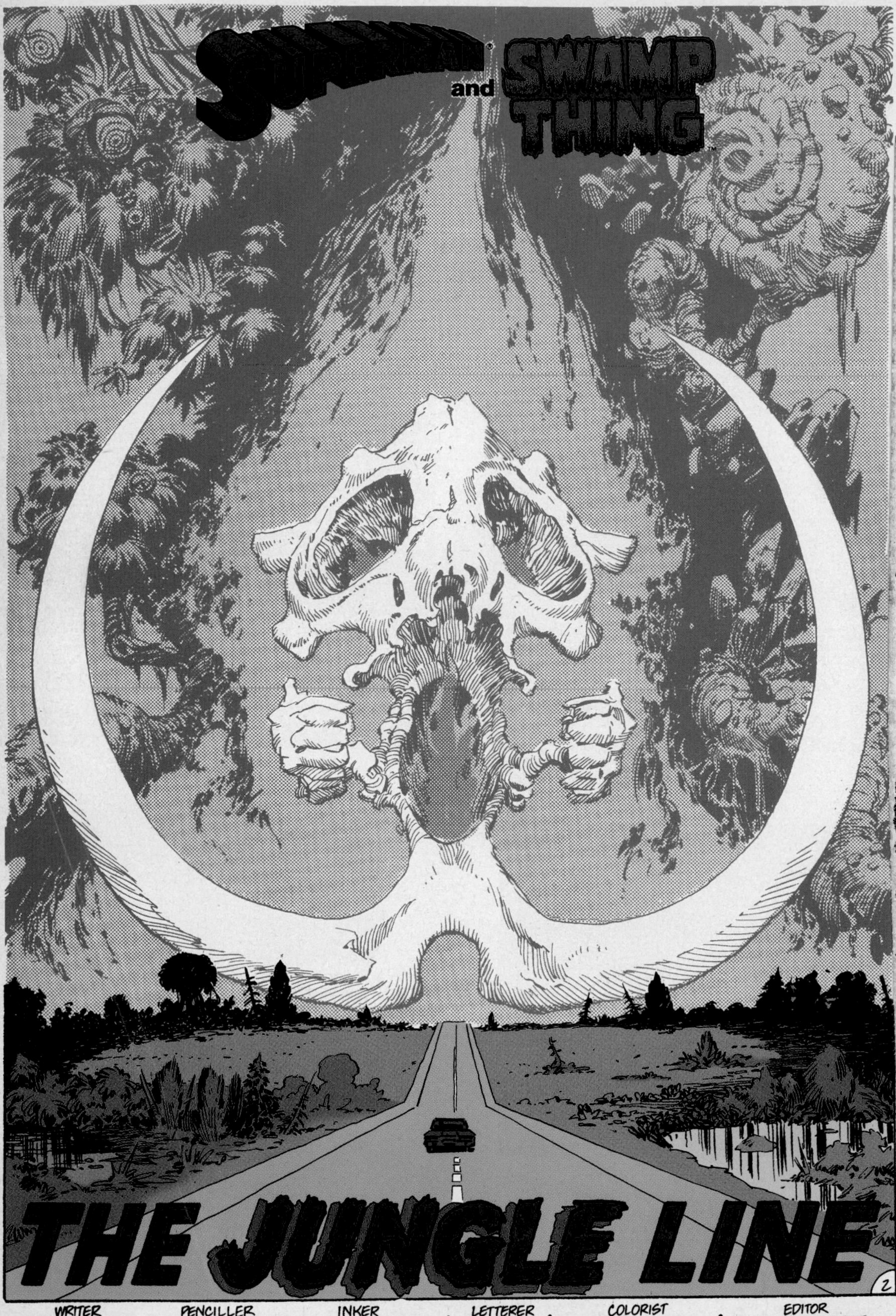
SUPERMAN and SWAMP THING
THE JUNGLE LINE
2

WRITER ALAN MOORE • PENCILLER RICK VEITCH • INKER AL WILLIAMSON • LETTERER COSTANZA • COLORIST TATJANA WOOD • EDITOR JULIUS SCHWARTZ

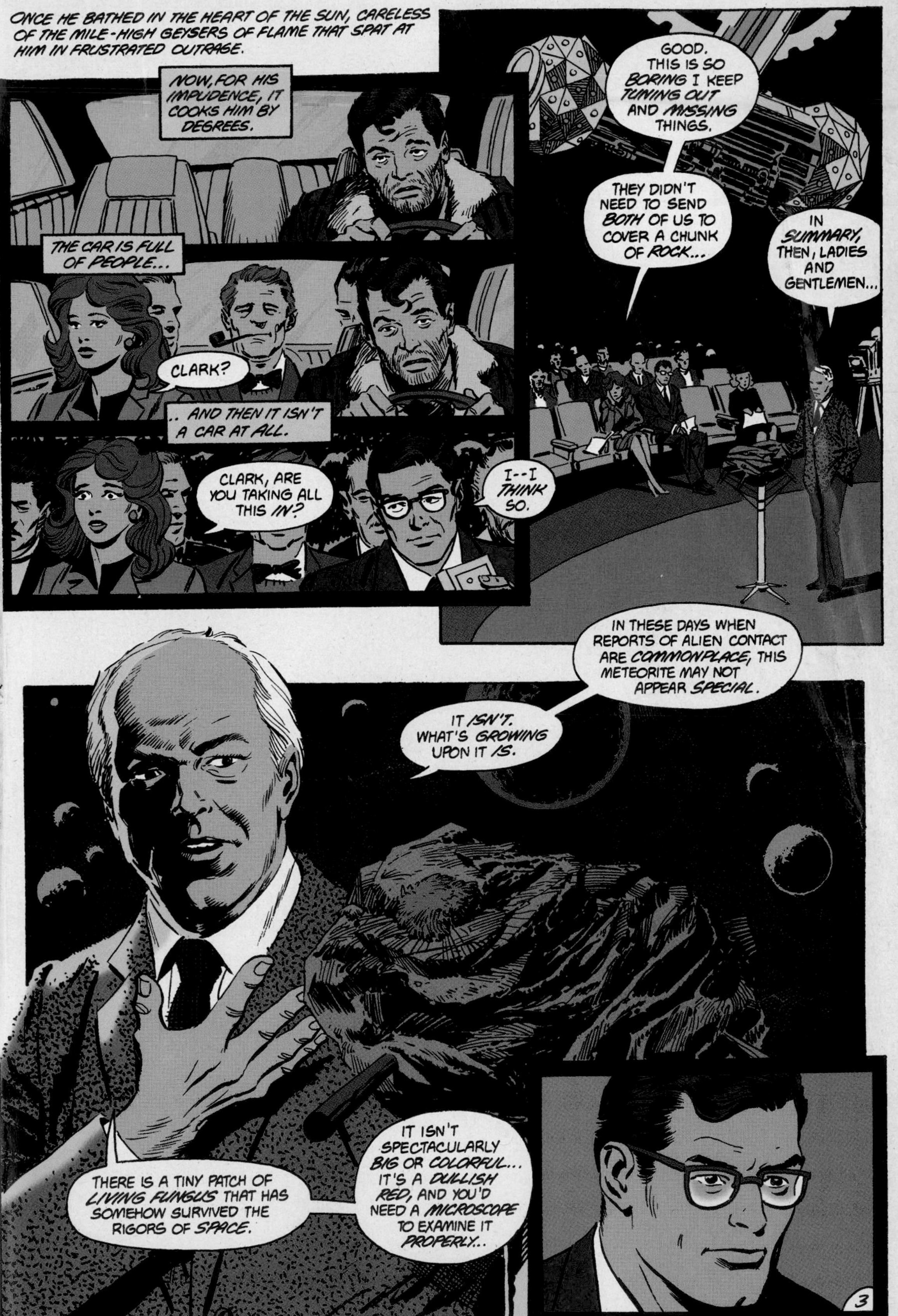
ONCE HE BATHED IN THE HEART OF THE SUN, CARELESS OF THE MILE-HIGH GEYSERS OF FLAME THAT SPAT AT HIM IN FRUSTRATED OUTRAGE.
NOW, FOR HIS IMPUDENCE, IT COOKS HIM BY DEGREES.
THE CAR IS FULL OF PEOPLE...
CLARK?
.. AND THEN IT ISN'T A CAR AT ALL.
CLARK, ARE YOU TAKING ALL THIS IN?
I--I THINK SO.
GOOD. THIS IS SO BORING I KEEP TUNING OUT AND MISSING THINGS.
THEY DIDN'T NEED TO SEND BOTH OF US TO COVER A CHUNK OF ROCK...
IN SUMMARY, THEN, LADIES AND GENTLEMEN...
IN THESE DAYS WHEN REPORTS OF ALIEN CONTACT ARE COMMONPLACE, THIS METEORITE MAY NOT APPEAR SPECIAL.
IT ISN'T. WHAT'S GROWING UPON IT IS.
THERE IS A TINY PATCH OF LIVING FUNGUS THAT HAS SOMEHOW SURVIVED THE RIGORS OF SPACE.
IT ISN'T SPECTACULARLY BIG OR COLORFUL... IT'S A DULLISH RED, AND YOU'D NEED A MICROSCOPE TO EXAMINE IT PROPERLY...
3

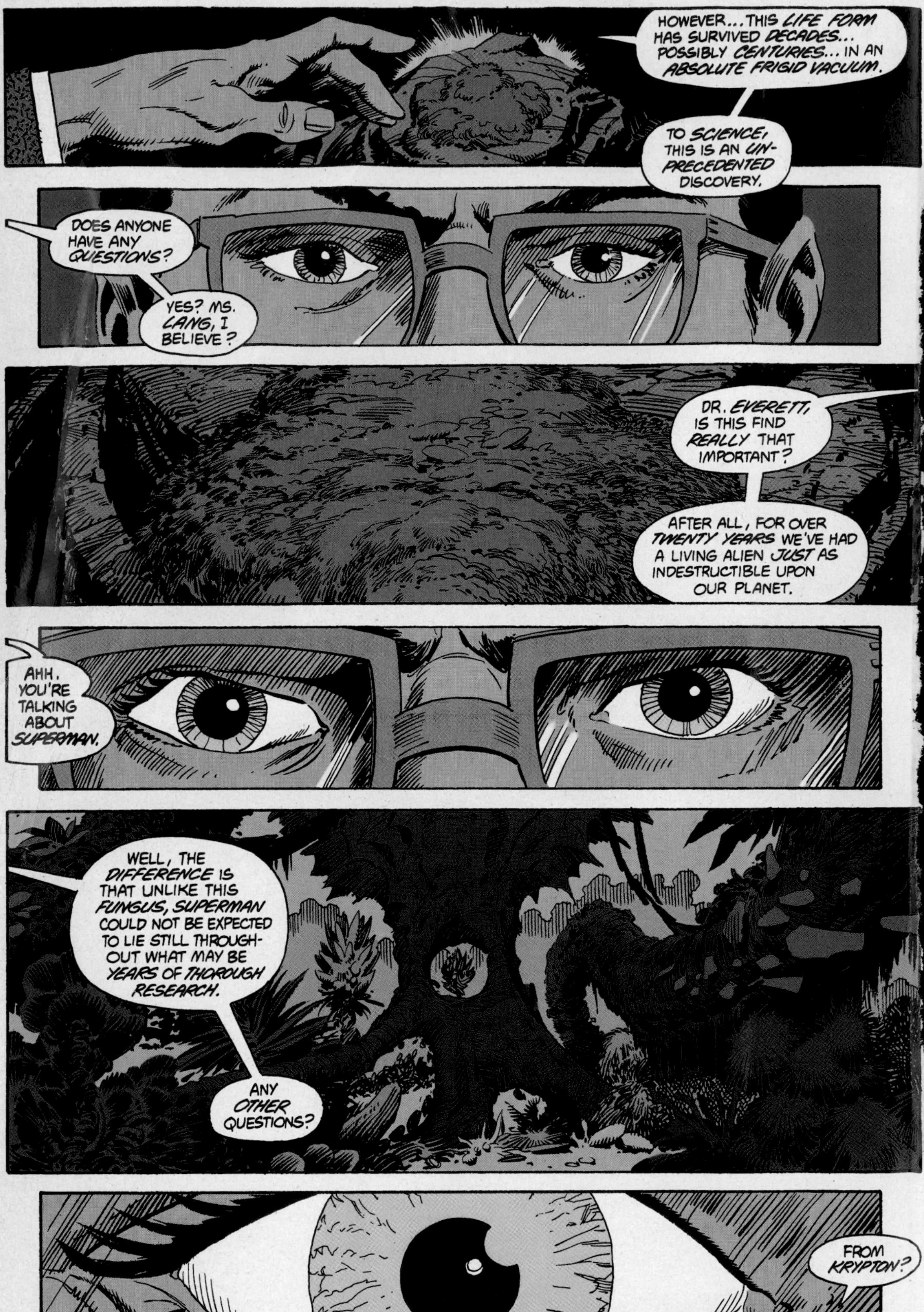
HOWEVER... THIS LIFE FORM HAS SURVIVED DECADES... POSSIBLY CENTURIES... IN AN ABSOLUTE FRIGID VACUUM.
TO SCIENCE, THIS IS AN UN-PRECEDENTED DISCOVERY.
DOES ANYONE HAVE ANY QUESTIONS?
YES? MS. LANG, I BELIEVE?
DR. EVERETT, IS THIS FIND REALLY THAT IMPORTANT?
AFTER ALL, FOR OVER TWENTY YEARS WE'VE HAD A LIVING ALIEN JUST AS INDESTRUCTIBLE UPON OUR PLANET.
AHH. YOU'RE TALKING ABOUT SUPERMAN.
WELL, THE DIFFERENCE IS THAT UNLIKE THIS FUNGUS, SUPERMAN COULD NOT BE EXPECTED TO LIE STILL THROUGH-OUT WHAT MAY BE YEARS OF THOROUGH RESEARCH.
ANY OTHER QUESTIONS?
FROM KRYPTON?
4

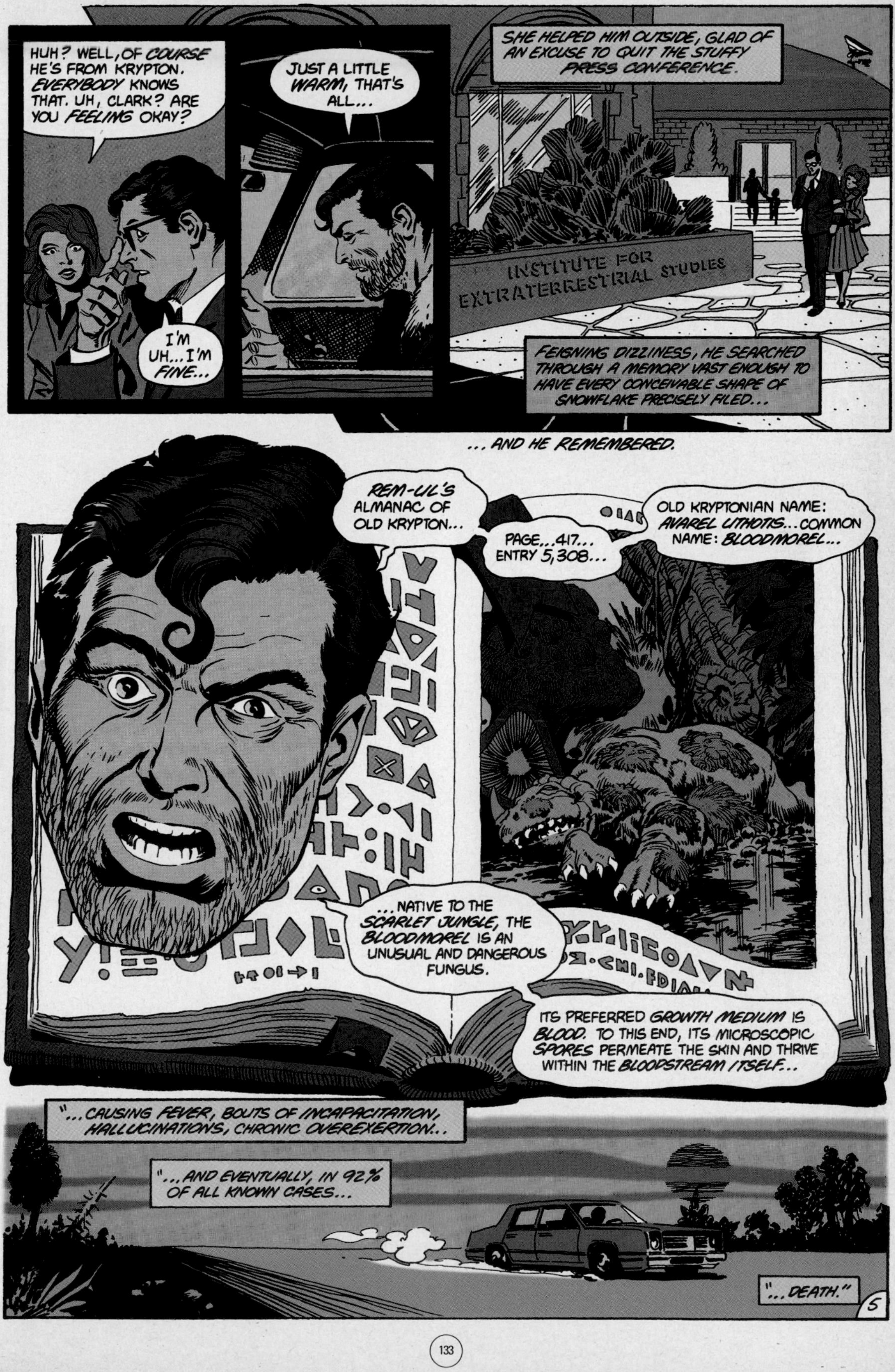

HUH? WELL, OF COURSE HE'S FROM KRYPTON. EVERYBODY KNOWS THAT. UH, CLARK? ARE YOU FEELING OKAY?
I'M UH...I'M FINE...
JUST A LITTLE WARM, THAT'S ALL...
SHE HELPED HIM OUTSIDE, GLAD OF AN EXCUSE TO QUIT THE STUFFY PRESS CONFERENCE.
INSTITUTE FOR EXTRATERRESTRIAL STUDIES
FEIGNING DIZZINESS, HE SEARCHED THROUGH A MEMORY VAST ENOUGH TO HAVE EVERY CONCEIVABLE SHAPE OF SNOWFLAKE PRECISELY FILED...
... AND HE REMEMBERED.
REM-UL'S ALMANAC OF OLD KRYPTON...
PAGE...417... ENTRY 5,308...
OLD KRYPTONIAN NAME: AVAREL UTHOTIS...COMMON NAME: BLOODMOREL...
...NATIVE TO THE SCARLET JUNGLE, THE BLOODMOREL IS AN UNUSUAL AND DANGEROUS FUNGUS.
ITS PREFERRED GROWTH MEDIUM IS BLOOD. TO THIS END, ITS MICROSCOPIC SPORES PERMEATE THE SKIN AND THRIVE WITHIN THE BLOODSTREAM ITSELF...
"...CAUSING FEVER, BOUTS OF INCAPACITATION, HALLUCINATIONS, CHRONIC OVEREXERTION...
"...AND EVENTUALLY, IN 92% OF ALL KNOWN CASES...
"...DEATH."
5

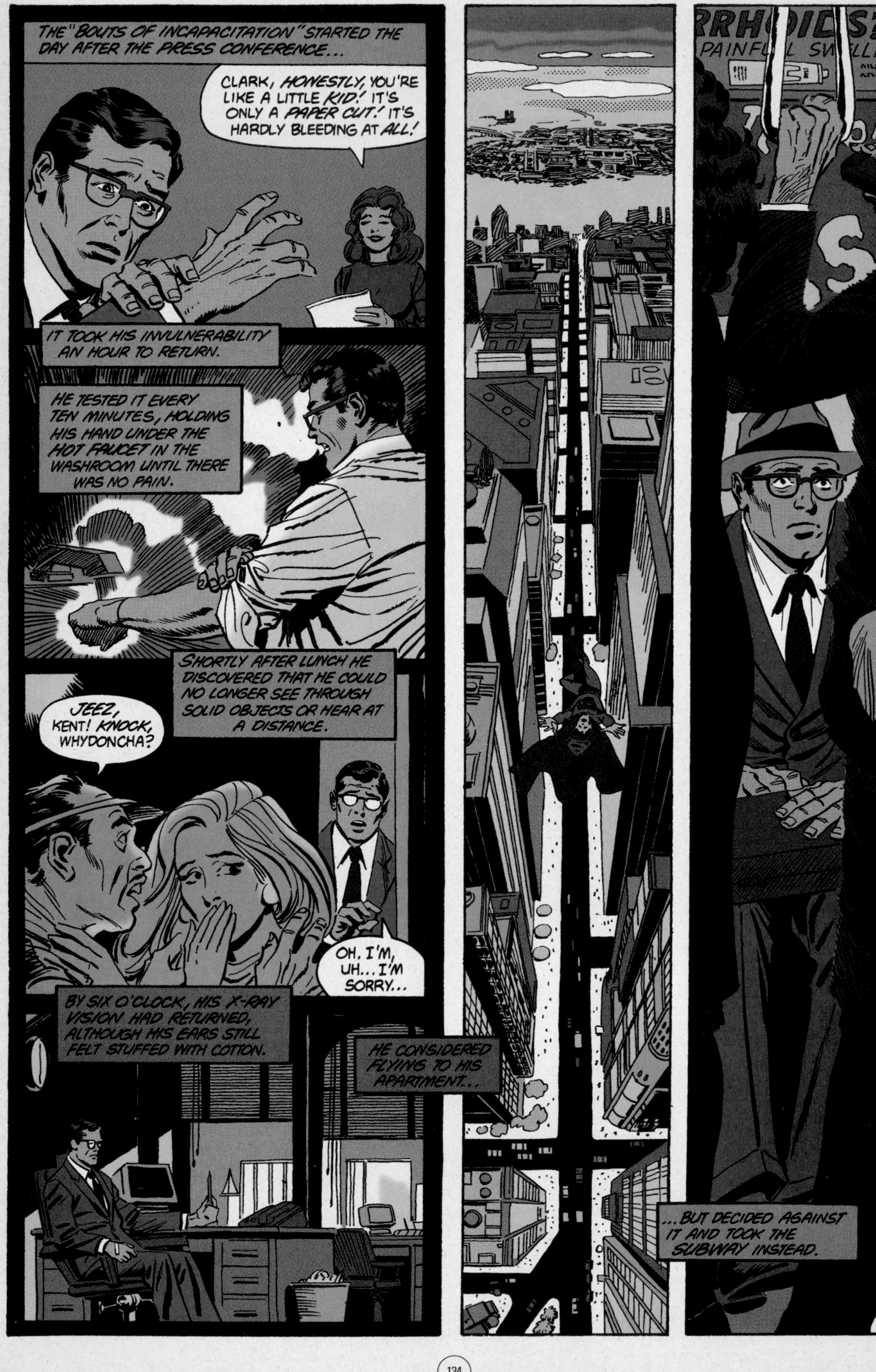

THE "BOUTS OF INCAPACITATION" STARTED THE DAY AFTER THE PRESS CONFERENCE...
CLARK, HONESTLY, YOU'RE LIKE A LITTLE KID! IT'S ONLY A PAPER CUT! IT'S HARDLY BLEEDING AT ALL!
IT TOOK HIS INVULNERABILITY AN HOUR TO RETURN.
HE TESTED IT EVERY TEN MINUTES, HOLDING HIS HAND UNDER THE HOT FAUCET IN THE WASHROOM UNTIL THERE WAS NO PAIN.
SHORTLY AFTER LUNCH HE DISCOVERED THAT HE COULD NO LONGER SEE THROUGH SOLID OBJECTS OR HEAR AT A DISTANCE.
JEEZ, KENT! KNOCK, WHYDONCHA?
OH. I'M, UH... I'M SORRY...
BY SIX O'CLOCK, HIS X-RAY VISION HAD RETURNED, ALTHOUGH HIS EARS STILL FELT STUFFED WITH COTTON.
HE CONSIDERED FLYING TO HIS APARTMENT...
RRHOIDS?
PAINFUL SWELLING
...BUT DECIDED AGAINST IT AND TOOK THE SUBWAY INSTEAD.
6

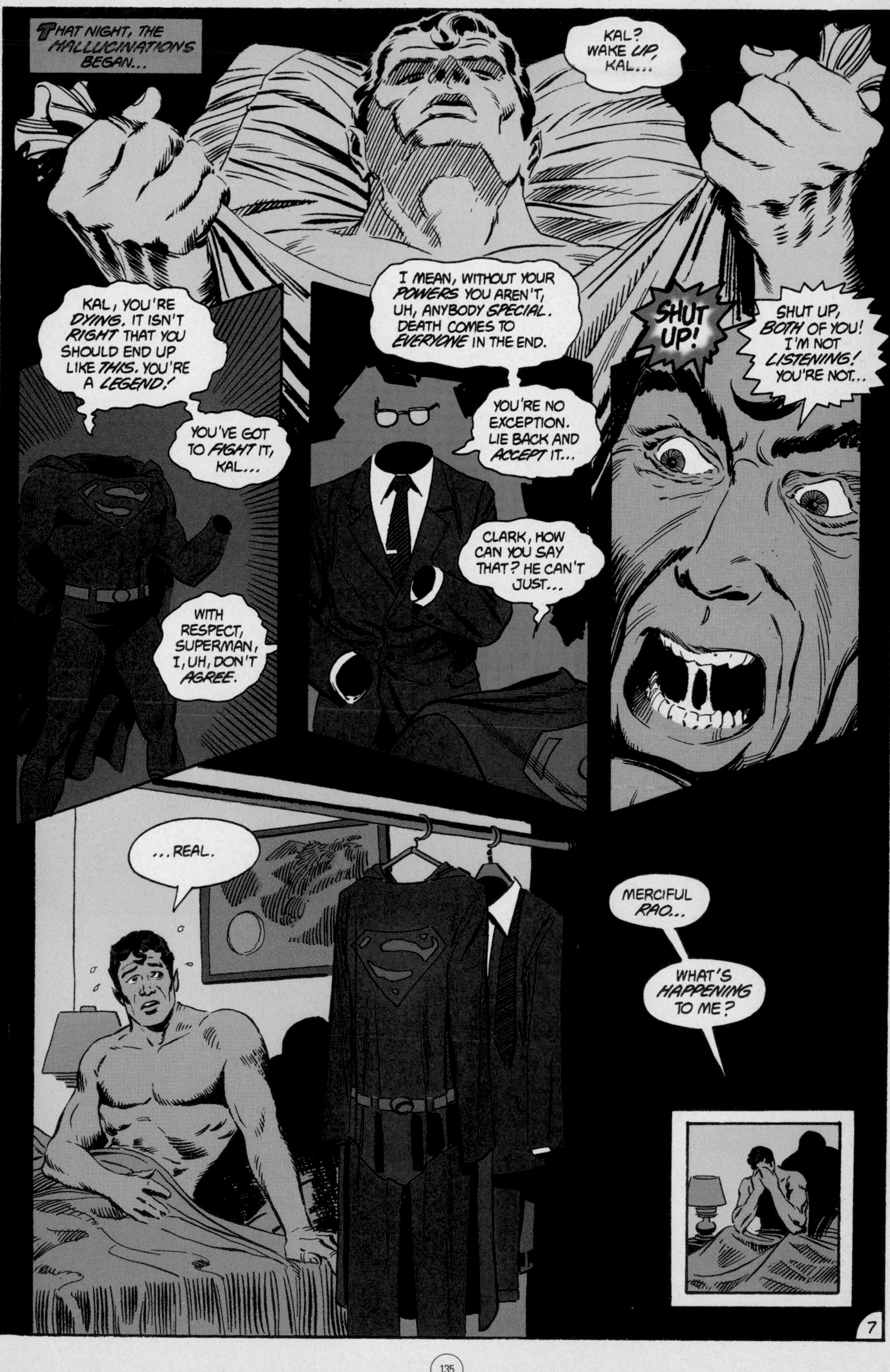
THAT NIGHT, THE HALLUCINATIONS BEGAN...
KAL? WAKE UP, KAL...
KAL, YOU'RE DYING. IT ISN'T RIGHT THAT YOU SHOULD END UP LIKE THIS. YOU'RE A LEGEND!
YOU'VE GOT TO FIGHT IT, KAL...
WITH RESPECT, SUPERMAN, I, UH, DON'T AGREE.
I MEAN, WITHOUT YOUR POWERS YOU AREN'T, UH, ANYBODY SPECIAL. DEATH COMES TO EVERYONE IN THE END.
YOU'RE NO EXCEPTION. LIE BACK AND ACCEPT IT...
CLARK, HOW CAN YOU SAY THAT? HE CAN'T JUST...
SHUT UP!
SHUT UP, BOTH OF YOU! I'M NOT LISTENING! YOU'RE NOT...
...REAL.
MERCIFUL RAO...
WHAT'S HAPPENING TO ME?
7

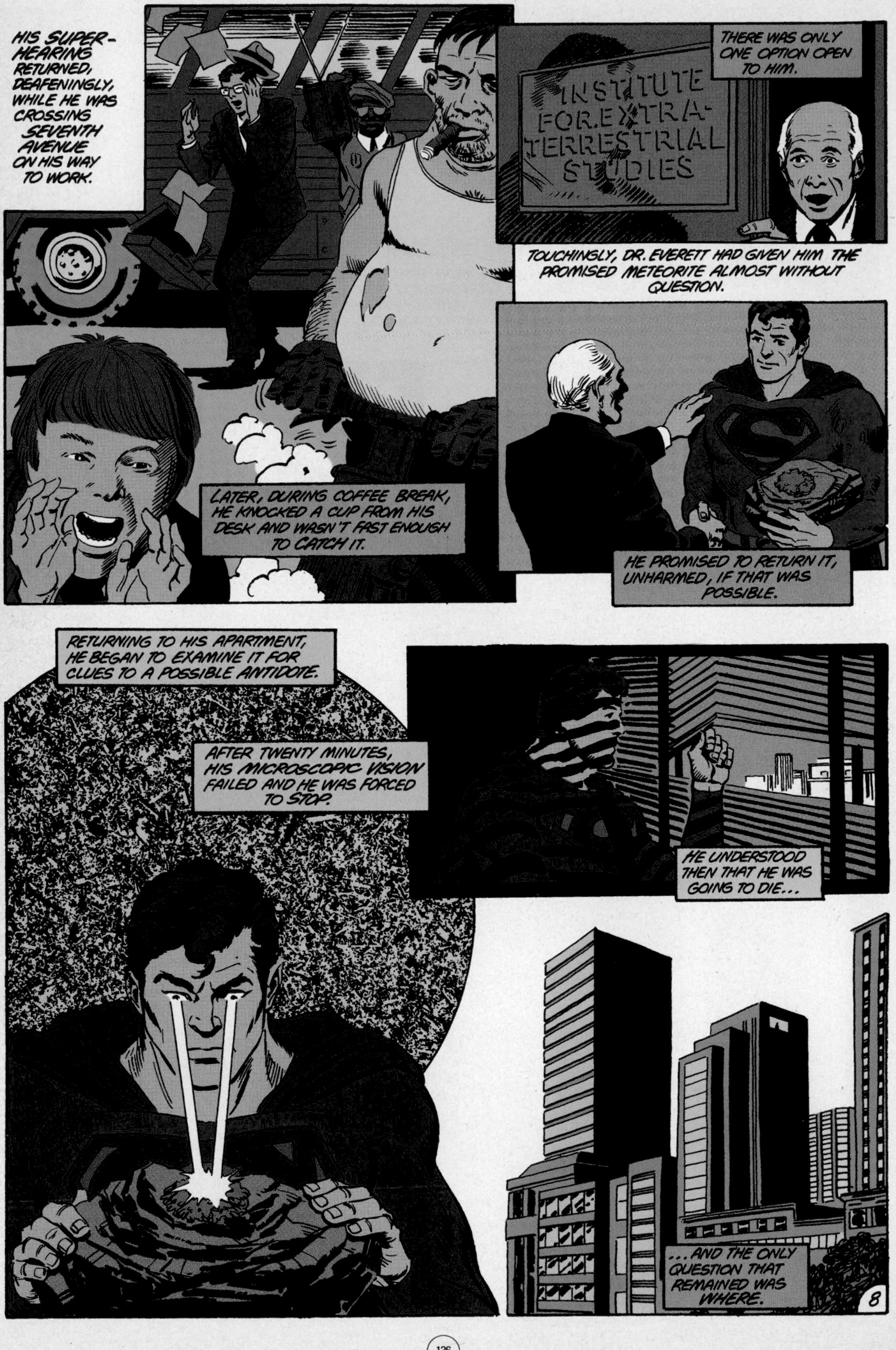
HIS SUPER-HEARING RETURNED, DEAFENINGLY, WHILE HE WAS CROSSING SEVENTH AVENUE ON HIS WAY TO WORK.
LATER, DURING COFFEE BREAK, HE KNOCKED A CUP FROM HIS DESK AND WASN'T FAST ENOUGH TO CATCH IT.
THERE WAS ONLY ONE OPTION OPEN TO HIM.
INSTITUTE FOR EXTRA-TERRESTRIAL STUDIES
TOUCHINGLY, DR. EVERETT HAD GIVEN HIM THE PROMISED METEORITE ALMOST WITHOUT QUESTION.
HE PROMISED TO RETURN IT, UNHARMED, IF THAT WAS POSSIBLE.
RETURNING TO HIS APARTMENT, HE BEGAN TO EXAMINE IT FOR CLUES TO A POSSIBLE ANTIDOTE.
AFTER TWENTY MINUTES, HIS MICROSCOPIC VISION FAILED AND HE WAS FORCED TO STOP.
HE UNDERSTOOD THEN THAT HE WAS GOING TO DIE...
...AND THE ONLY QUESTION THAT REMAINED WAS WHERE.
8

HE WANTED TO BE *ALONE* WHEN IT HAPPENED, BUT HIS *FORTRESS* WAS TOO DISTANT, AND FLYING WAS *UNTHINKABLE.*

COAST CITY

CENTRAL CITY

STAR CITY

HE ALSO ELIMINATED GOTHAM, NEW YORK, WASHINGTON, AND ALL OTHER CITIES FREQUENTED BY THE SUPER-HERO COMMUNITY.

*F*INALLY, HE BOUGHT A *SECONDHAND CAR* IN A CASH TRANSACTION UNDER THE NAME OF *CAL ELLIS.*

SUPER DEALS

AL'S USED CARS

TAKING THE *METEORITE,* JUST IN CASE, HE MADE FOR THE ONE PLACE IN AMERICA WITH *NO INDIGENOUS SUPERHUMANS...*

HE HEADED SOUTH.

BLAAAAAAAA

HHROOM

9

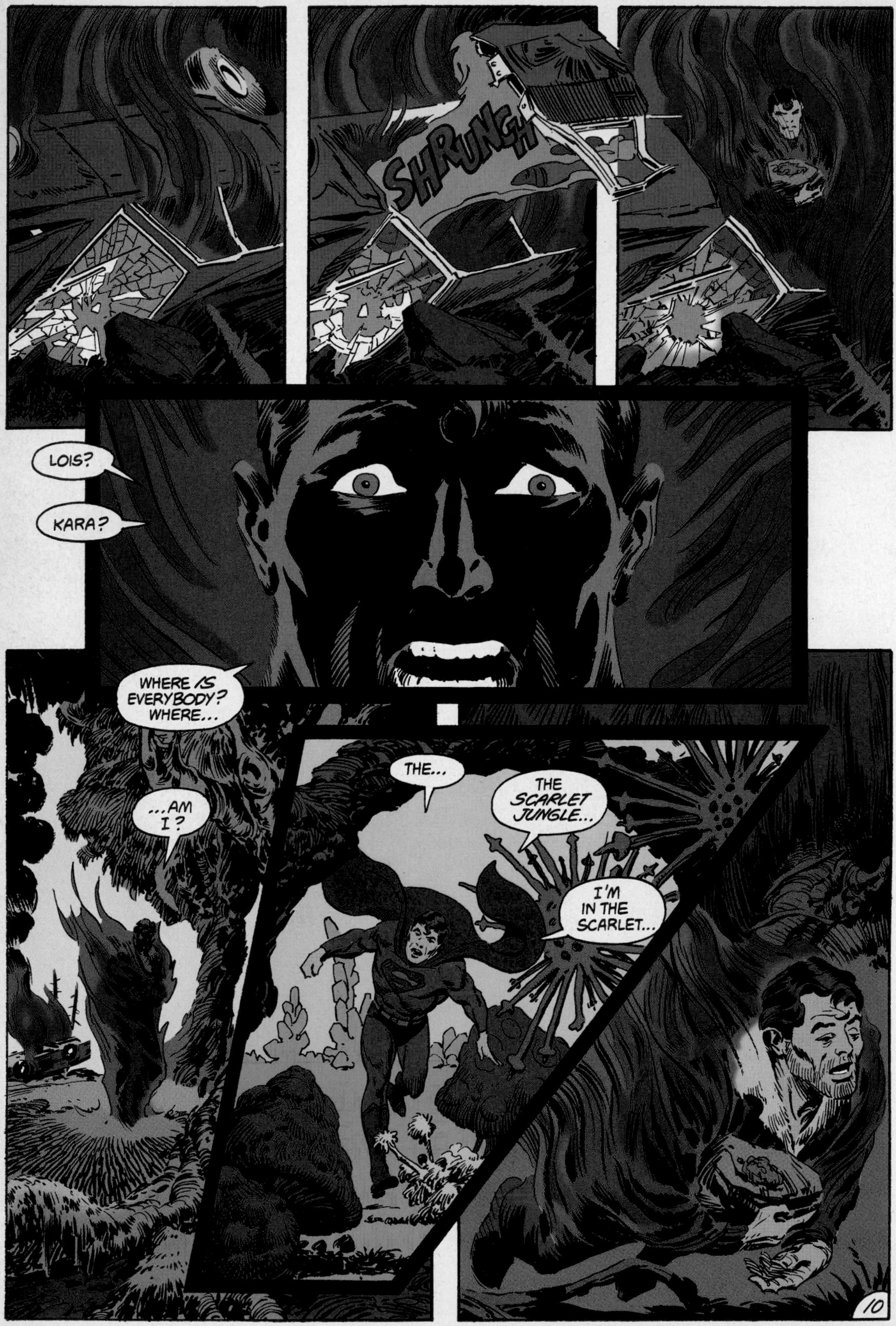
SHRUNCH
LOIS?
KARA?
WHERE IS EVERYBODY? WHERE...
...AM I?
THE...
THE SCARLET JUNGLE...
I'M IN THE SCARLET...
10

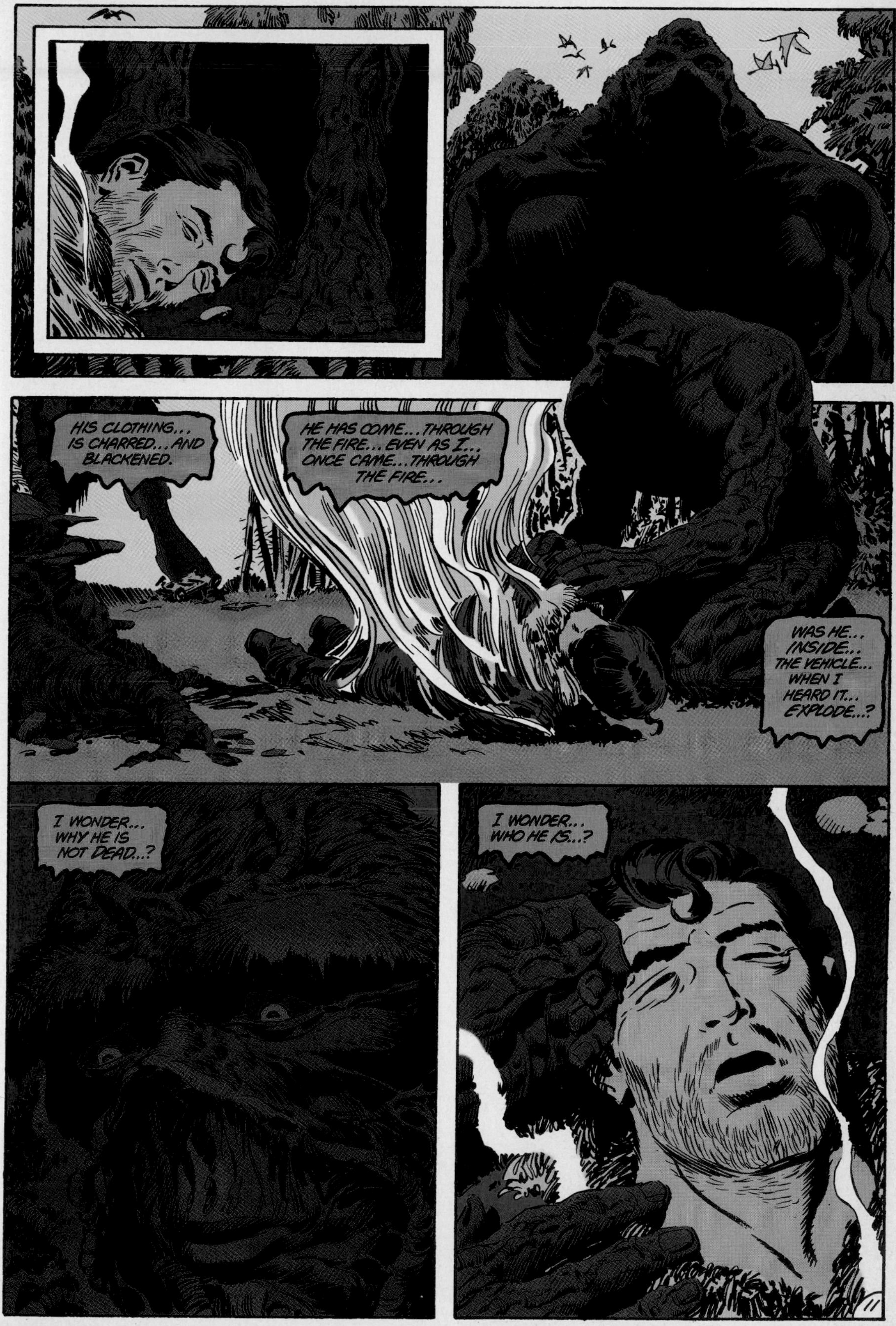
HIS CLOTHING... IS CHARRED...AND BLACKENED.
HE HAS COME...THROUGH THE FIRE... EVEN AS I... ONCE CAME...THROUGH THE FIRE...
WAS HE... INSIDE... THE VEHICLE... WHEN I HEARD IT... EXPLODE...?
I WONDER... WHY HE IS NOT DEAD...?
I WONDER... WHO HE IS...?

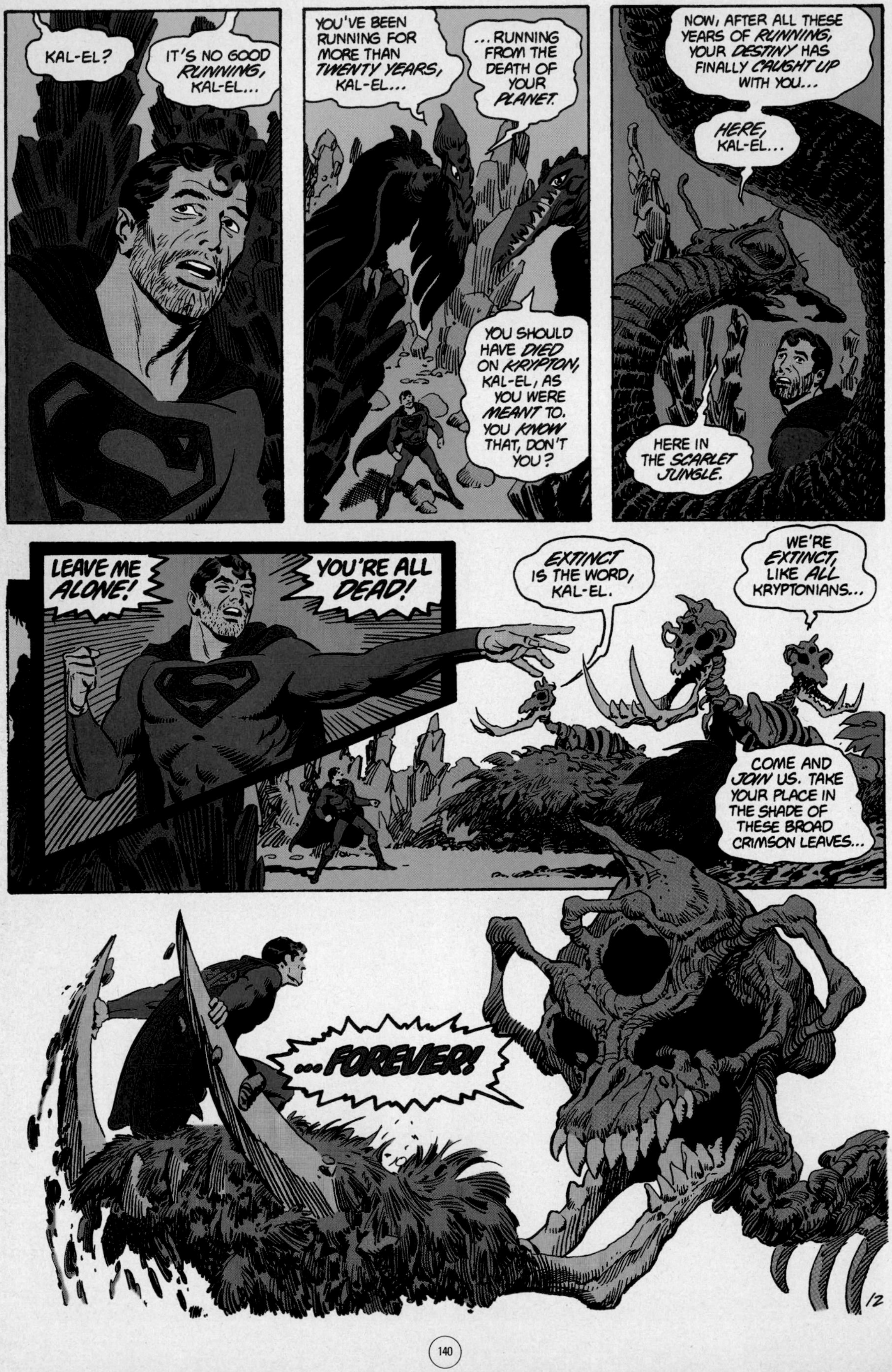
KAL-EL?
IT'S NO GOOD RUNNING, KAL-EL...
YOU'VE BEEN RUNNING FOR MORE THAN TWENTY YEARS, KAL-EL...
...RUNNING FROM THE DEATH OF YOUR PLANET.
YOU SHOULD HAVE DIED ON KRYPTON, KAL-EL, AS YOU WERE MEANT TO. YOU KNOW THAT, DON'T YOU?
NOW, AFTER ALL THESE YEARS OF RUNNING, YOUR DESTINY HAS FINALLY CAUGHT UP WITH YOU...
HERE, KAL-EL...
HERE IN THE SCARLET JUNGLE.
LEAVE ME ALONE!
YOU'RE ALL DEAD!
EXTINCT IS THE WORD, KAL-EL.
WE'RE EXTINCT, LIKE ALL KRYPTONIANS...
COME AND JOIN US. TAKE YOUR PLACE IN THE SHADE OF THESE BROAD CRIMSON LEAVES...
...FOREVER!
12

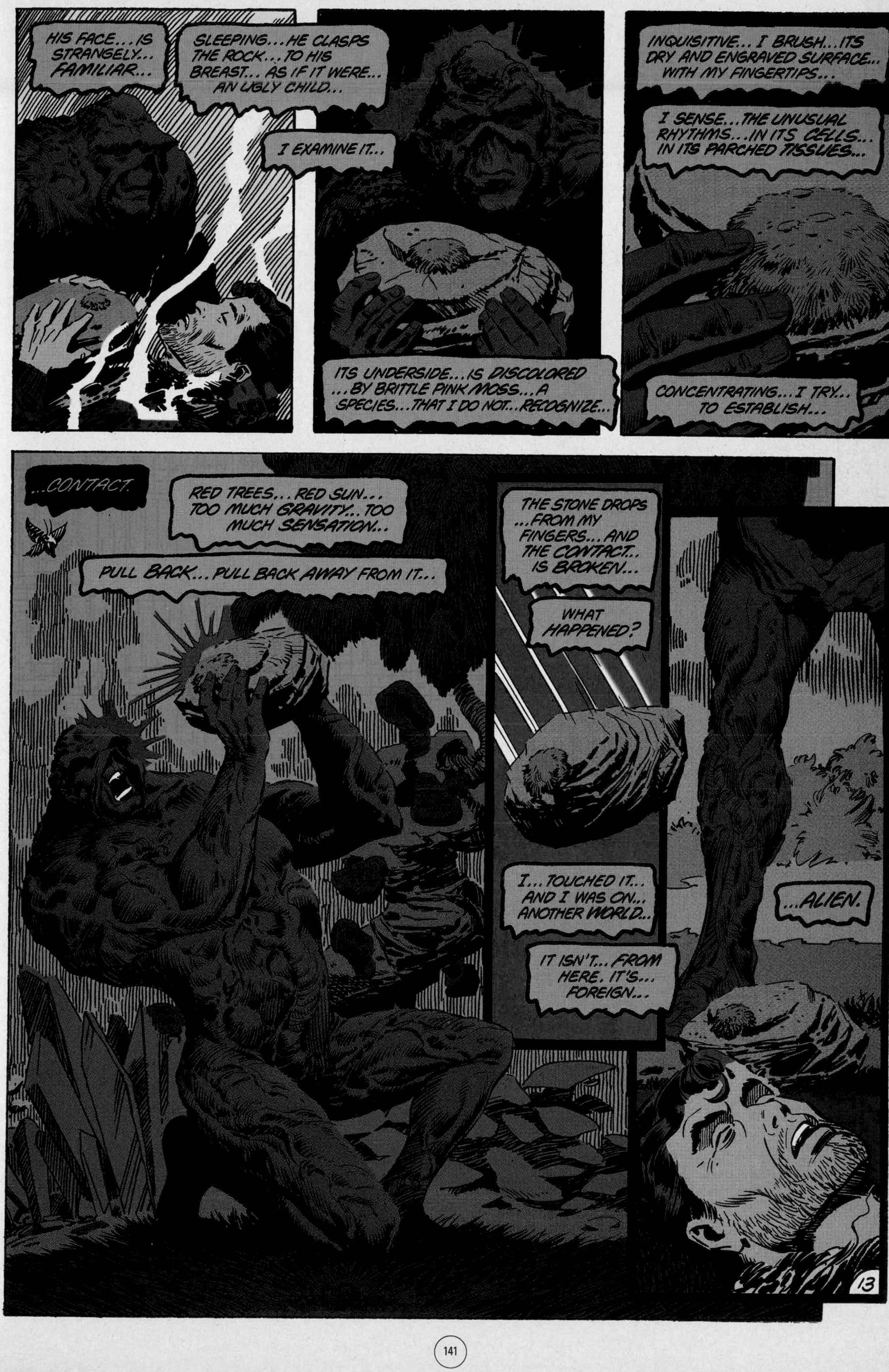
HIS FACE... IS STRANGELY... FAMILIAR...
SLEEPING... HE CLASPS THE ROCK... TO HIS BREAST... AS IF IT WERE... AN UGLY CHILD...
I EXAMINE IT...
ITS UNDERSIDE... IS DISCOLORED ...BY BRITTLE PINK MOSS... A SPECIES... THAT I DO NOT... RECOGNIZE...
INQUISITIVE... I BRUSH... ITS DRY AND ENGRAVED SURFACE... WITH MY FINGERTIPS...
I SENSE... THE UNUSUAL RHYTHMS... IN ITS CELLS... IN ITS PARCHED TISSUES...
CONCENTRATING... I TRY... TO ESTABLISH...
...CONTACT.
RED TREES... RED SUN... TOO MUCH GRAVITY... TOO MUCH SENSATION...
PULL BACK... PULL BACK AWAY FROM IT...
THE STONE DROPS ...FROM MY FINGERS... AND THE CONTACT.. IS BROKEN...
WHAT HAPPENED?
I... TOUCHED IT... AND I WAS ON... ANOTHER WORLD...
IT ISN'T... FROM HERE. IT'S... FOREIGN...
...ALIEN.
13

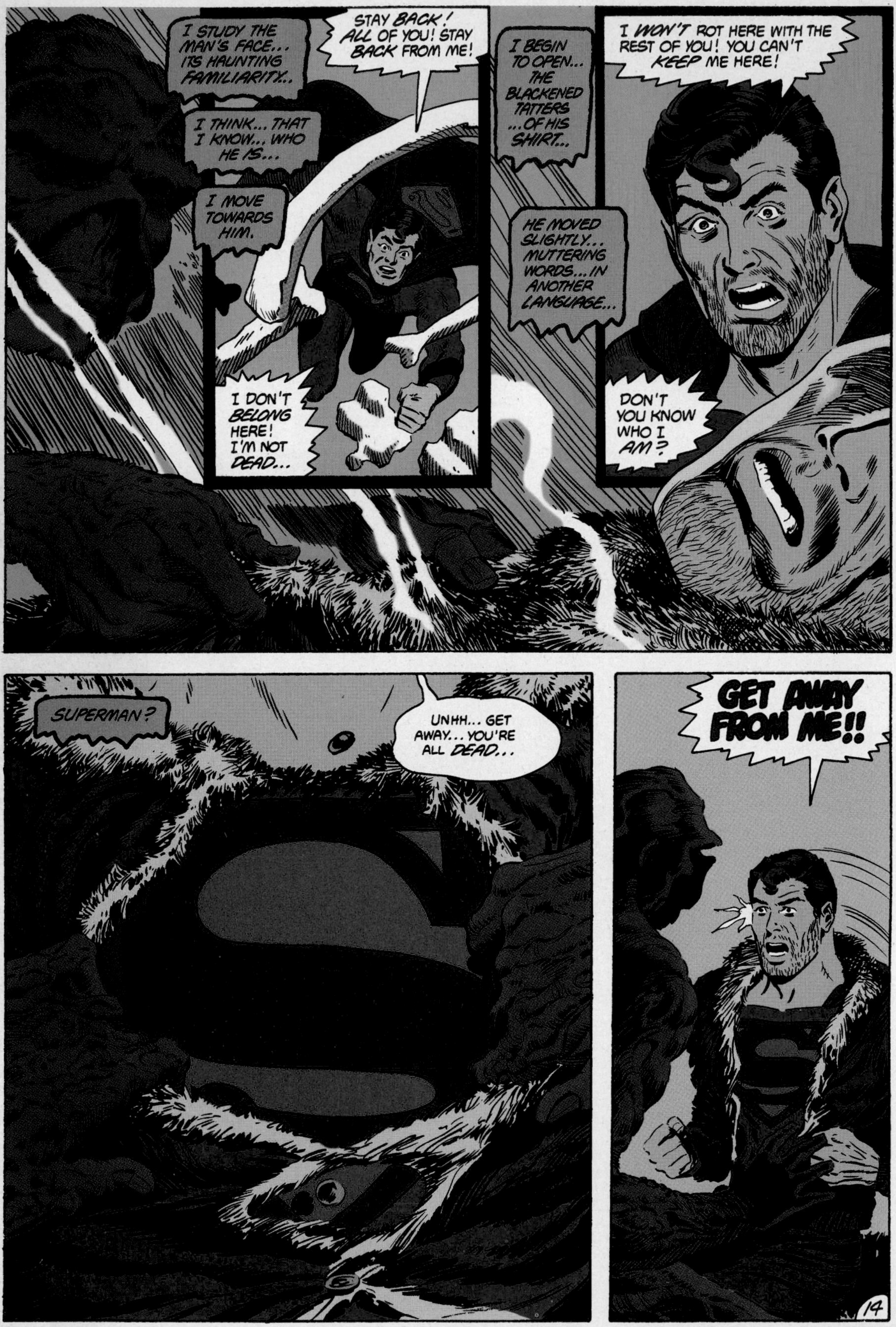

I STUDY THE MAN'S FACE... ITS HAUNTING FAMILIARITY...
I THINK... THAT I KNOW... WHO HE IS...
I MOVE TOWARDS HIM.
STAY BACK! ALL OF YOU! STAY BACK FROM ME!
I DON'T BELONG HERE! I'M NOT DEAD...
I BEGIN TO OPEN... THE BLACKENED TATTERS ...OF HIS SHIRT...
HE MOVED SLIGHTLY... MUTTERING WORDS... IN ANOTHER LANGUAGE...
I WON'T ROT HERE WITH THE REST OF YOU! YOU CAN'T KEEP ME HERE!
DON'T YOU KNOW WHO I AM?
SUPERMAN?
UNHH... GET AWAY... YOU'RE ALL DEAD...
GET AWAY FROM ME!!
14

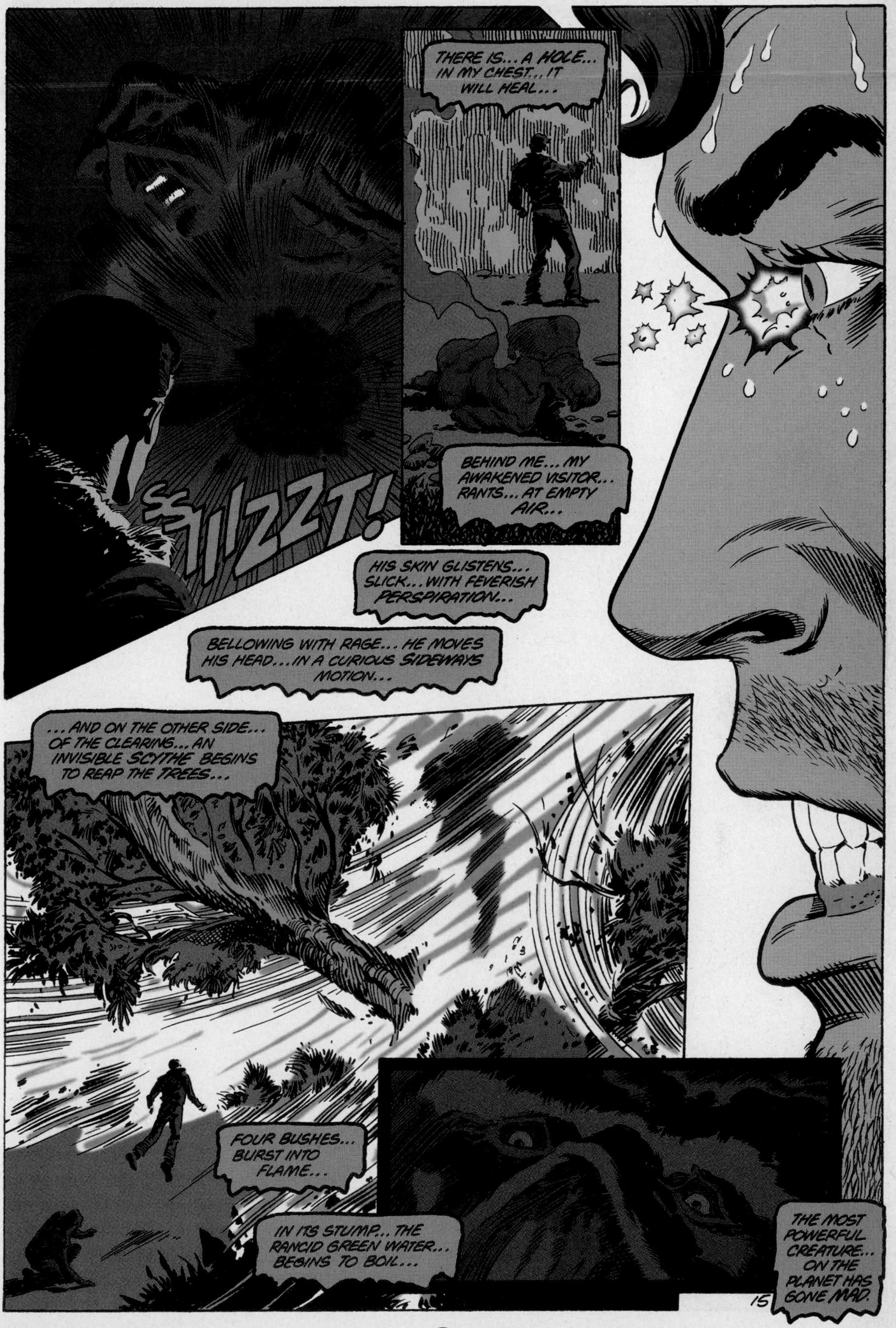
THERE IS... A HOLE... IN MY CHEST... IT WILL HEAL...
BEHIND ME... MY AWAKENED VISITOR... RANTS... AT EMPTY AIR...
SSIZZZT!
HIS SKIN GLISTENS... SLICK... WITH FEVERISH PERSPIRATION...
BELLOWING WITH RAGE... HE MOVES HIS HEAD... IN A CURIOUS SIDEWAYS MOTION...
...AND ON THE OTHER SIDE... OF THE CLEARING... AN INVISIBLE SCYTHE BEGINS TO REAP THE TREES...
FOUR BUSHES... BURST INTO FLAME...
IN ITS STUMP... THE RANCID GREEN WATER... BEGINS TO BOIL...
THE MOST POWERFUL CREATURE... ON THE PLANET HAS GONE MAD.
15

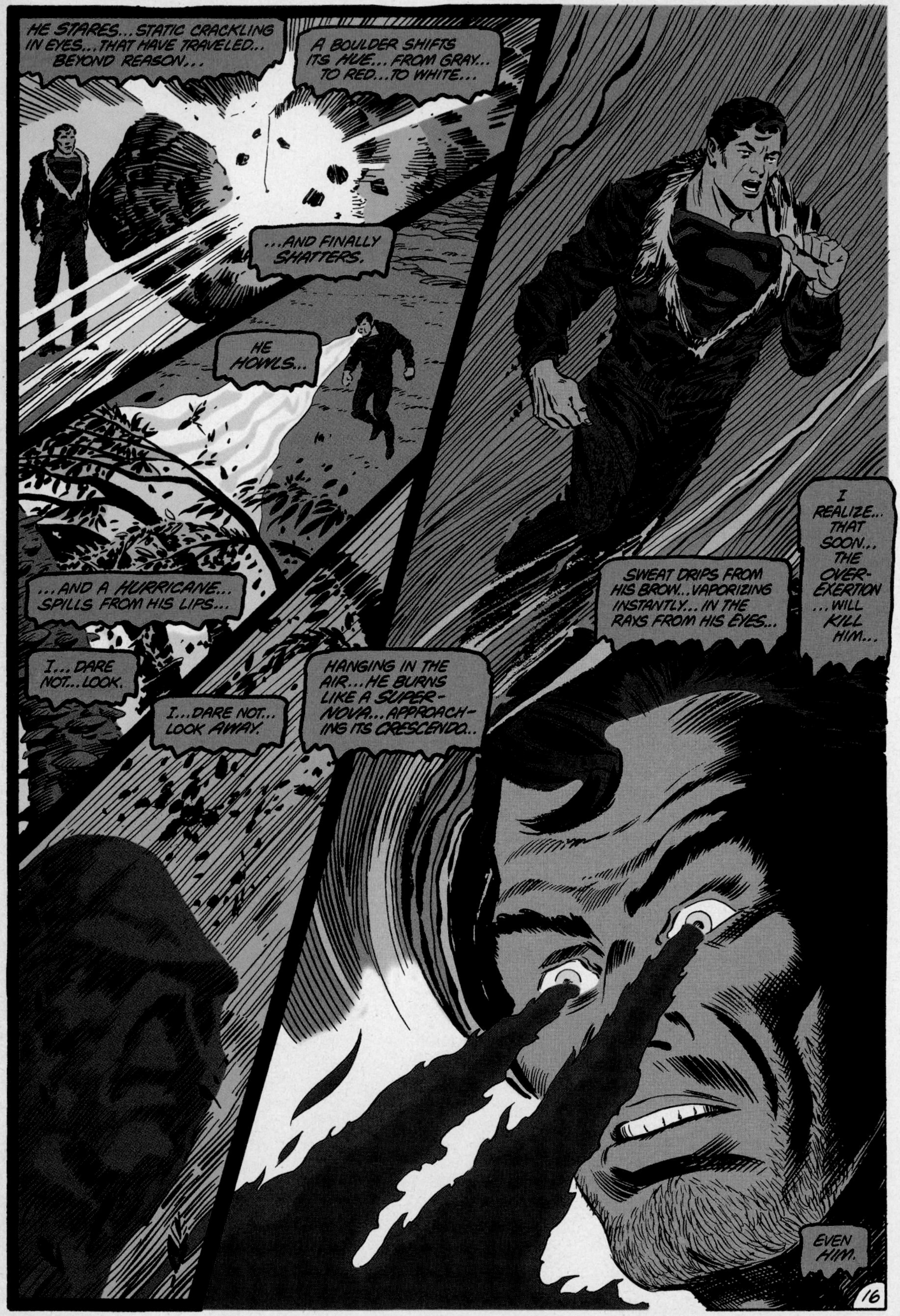
HE STARES... STATIC CRACKLING IN EYES... THAT HAVE TRAVELED... BEYOND REASON...
A BOULDER SHIFTS ITS HUE... FROM GRAY... TO RED... TO WHITE...
...AND FINALLY SHATTERS.
HE HOWLS...
...AND A HURRICANE... SPILLS FROM HIS LIPS...
I... DARE NOT... LOOK.
I... DARE NOT... LOOK AWAY.
SWEAT DRIPS FROM HIS BROW... VAPORIZING INSTANTLY... IN THE RAYS FROM HIS EYES...
I REALIZE... THAT SOON... THE OVER-EXERTION ...WILL KILL HIM...
HANGING IN THE AIR... HE BURNS LIKE A SUPER-NOVA... APPROACHING ITS CRESCENDO...
EVEN HIM.
16

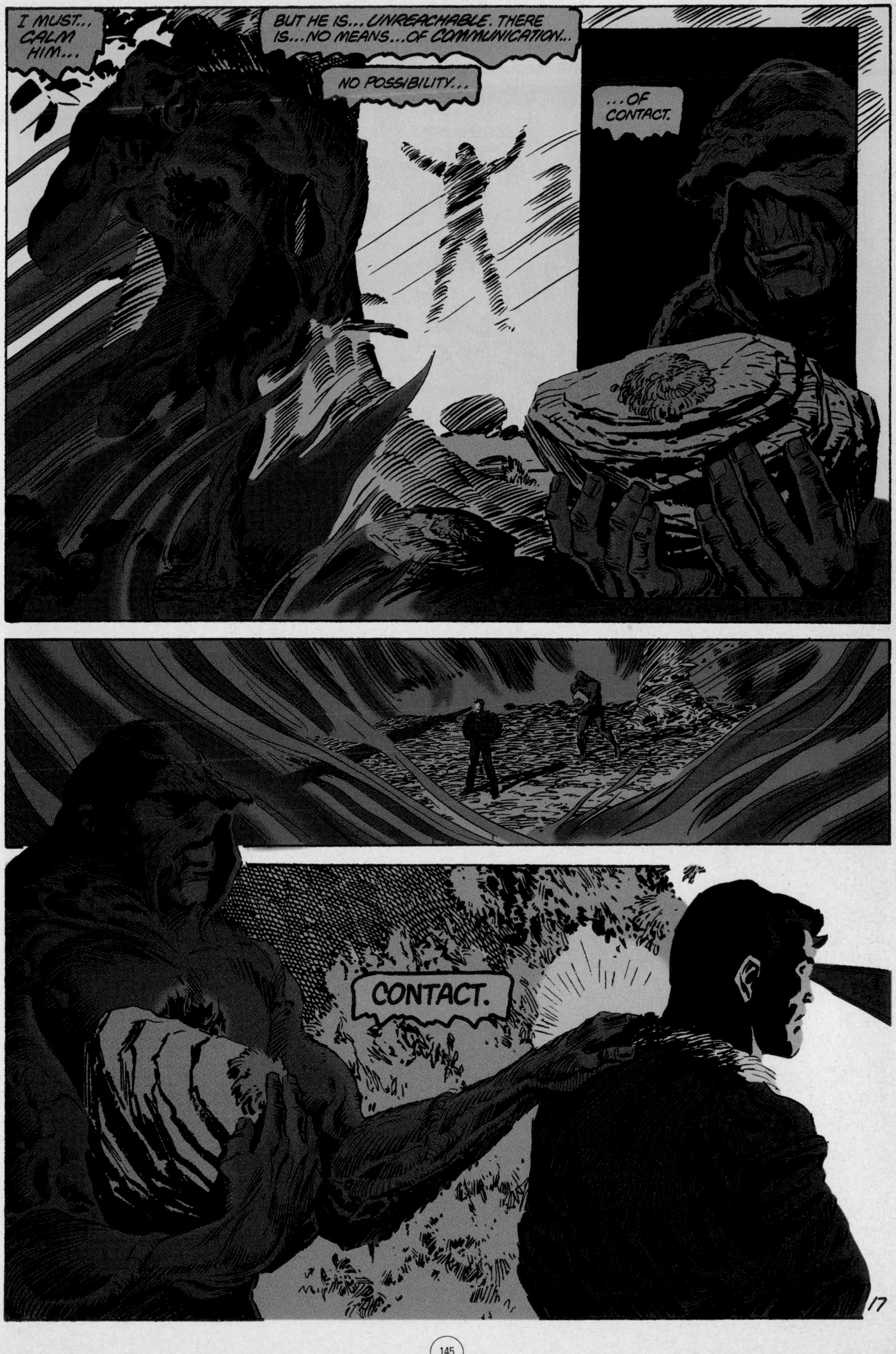
I MUST... CALM HIM...
BUT HE IS... UNREACHABLE. THERE IS... NO MEANS... OF COMMUNICATION...
NO POSSIBILITY...
...OF CONTACT.
CONTACT.
17

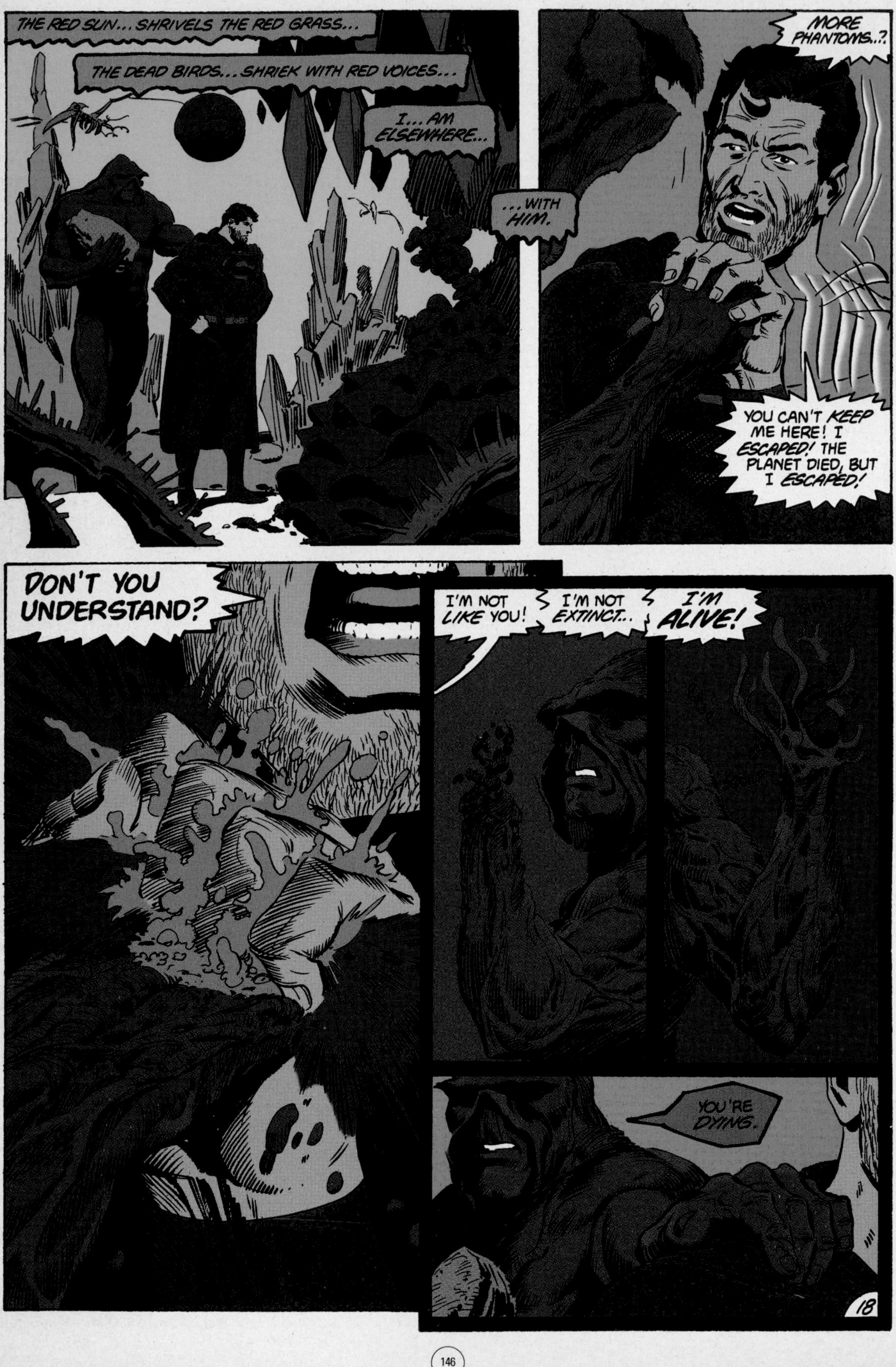

THE RED SUN... SHRIVELS THE RED GRASS...
THE DEAD BIRDS... SHRIEK WITH RED VOICES...
I... AM ELSEWHERE...
...WITH HIM.
MORE PHANTOMS..?
YOU CAN'T KEEP ME HERE! I ESCAPED! THE PLANET DIED, BUT I ESCAPED!
DON'T YOU UNDERSTAND?
I'M NOT LIKE YOU!
I'M NOT EXTINCT...
I'M ALIVE!
YOU'RE DYING.
18

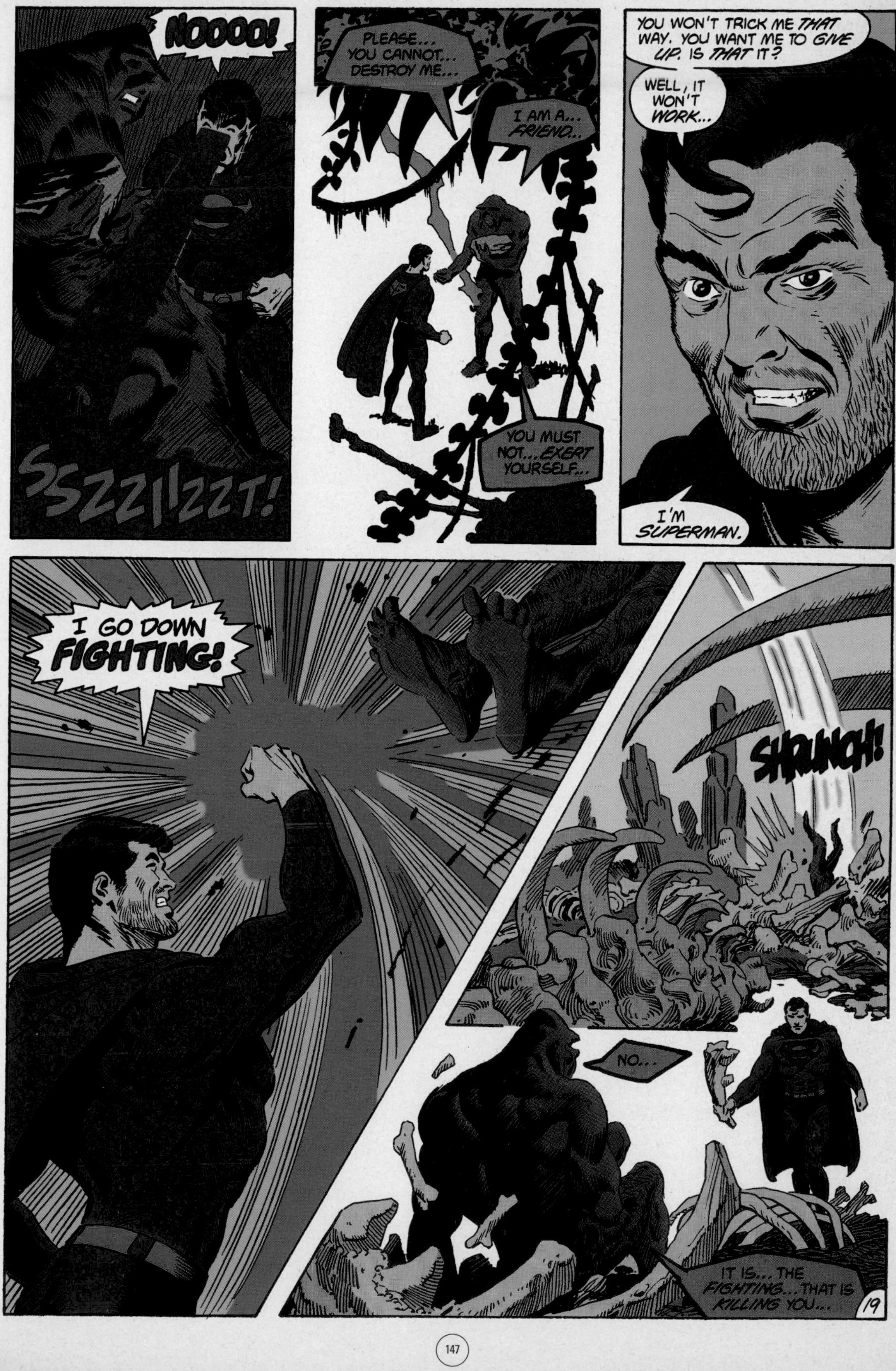
NOOOO!
SSZZIIZZT!
PLEASE... YOU CANNOT... DESTROY ME...
I AM A... FRIEND...
YOU MUST NOT... EXERT YOURSELF...
YOU WON'T TRICK ME THAT WAY. YOU WANT ME TO GIVE UP. IS THAT IT?
WELL, IT WON'T WORK...
I'M SUPERMAN.
I GO DOWN FIGHTING!
SHRUNCH!
NO...
IT IS... THE FIGHTING... THAT IS KILLING YOU...
19

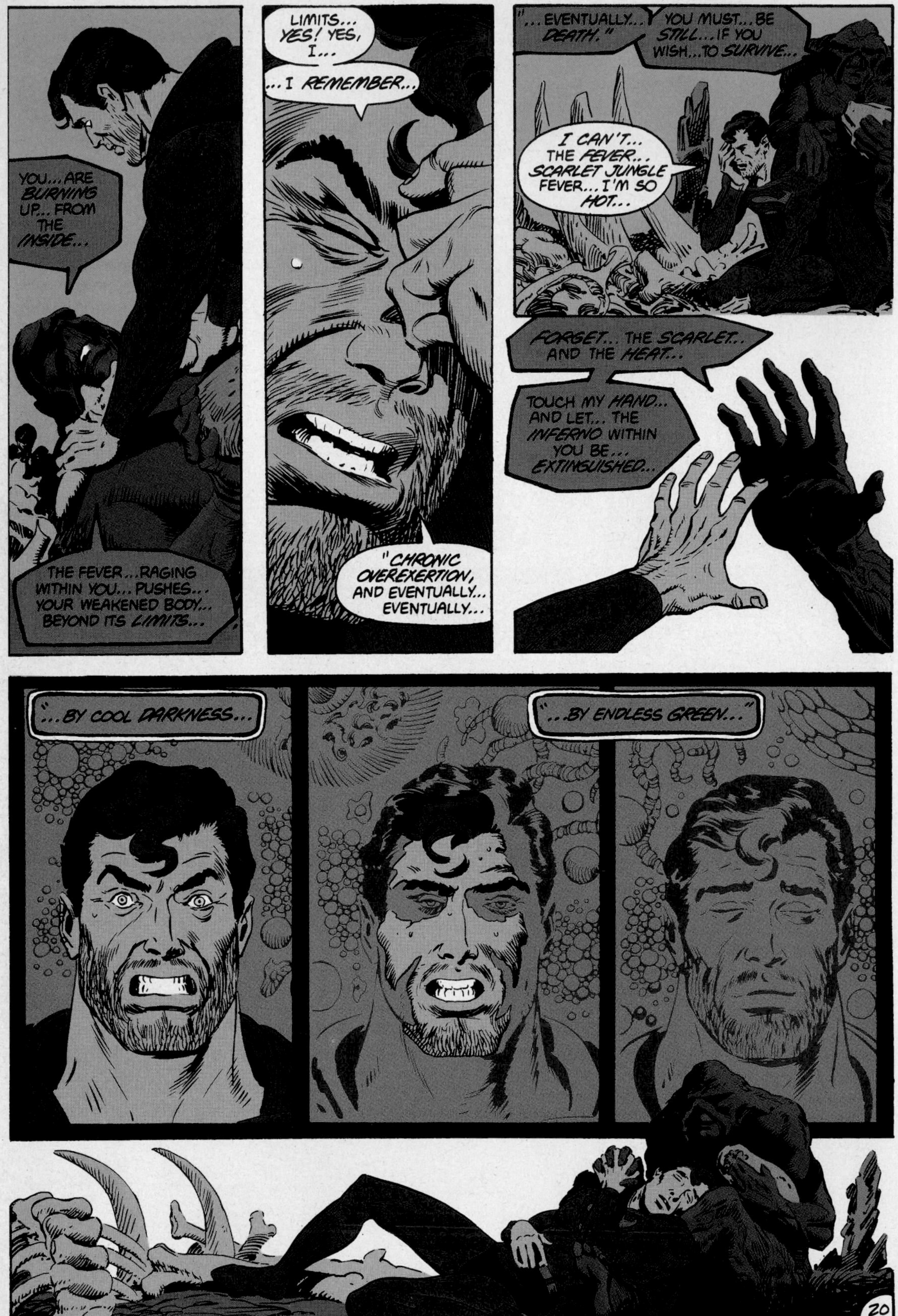
YOU... ARE BURNING UP... FROM THE INSIDE...
THE FEVER... RAGING WITHIN YOU... PUSHES... YOUR WEAKENED BODY... BEYOND ITS LIMITS...
LIMITS... YES! YES, I...
...I REMEMBER...
"CHRONIC OVEREXERTION, AND EVENTUALLY... EVENTUALLY...
"...EVENTUALLY... DEATH."
YOU MUST... BE STILL... IF YOU WISH... TO SURVIVE...
I CAN'T... THE FEVER... SCARLET JUNGLE FEVER... I'M SO HOT...
FORGET... THE SCARLET... AND THE HEAT...
TOUCH MY HAND... AND LET... THE INFERNO WITHIN YOU BE... EXTINGUISHED...
"...BY COOL DARKNESS...
"...BY ENDLESS GREEN..."
20

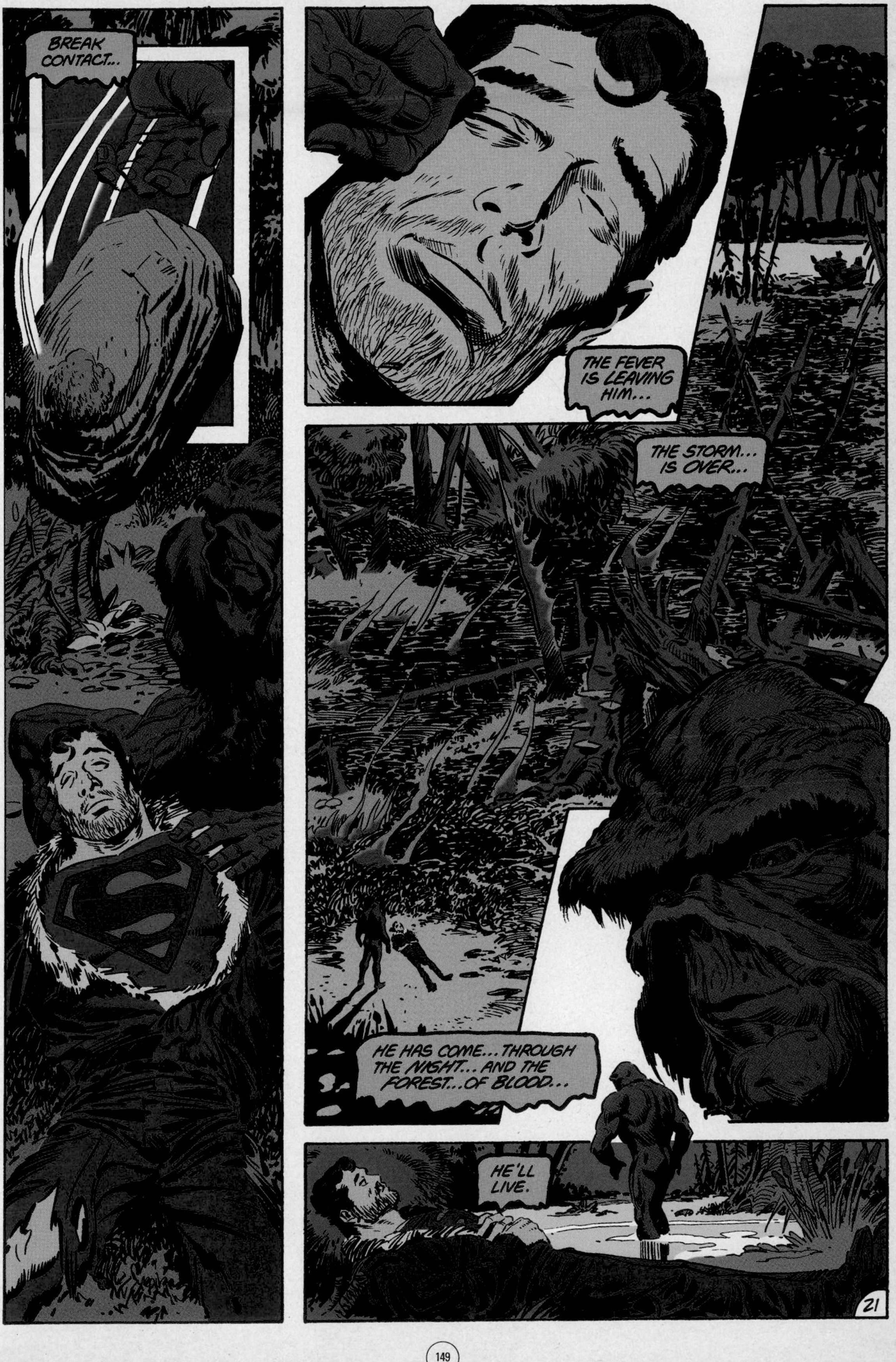
BREAK CONTACT...
THE FEVER IS LEAVING HIM...
THE STORM... IS OVER...
HE HAS COME... THROUGH THE NIGHT... AND THE FOREST... OF BLOOD...
HE'LL LIVE.
21

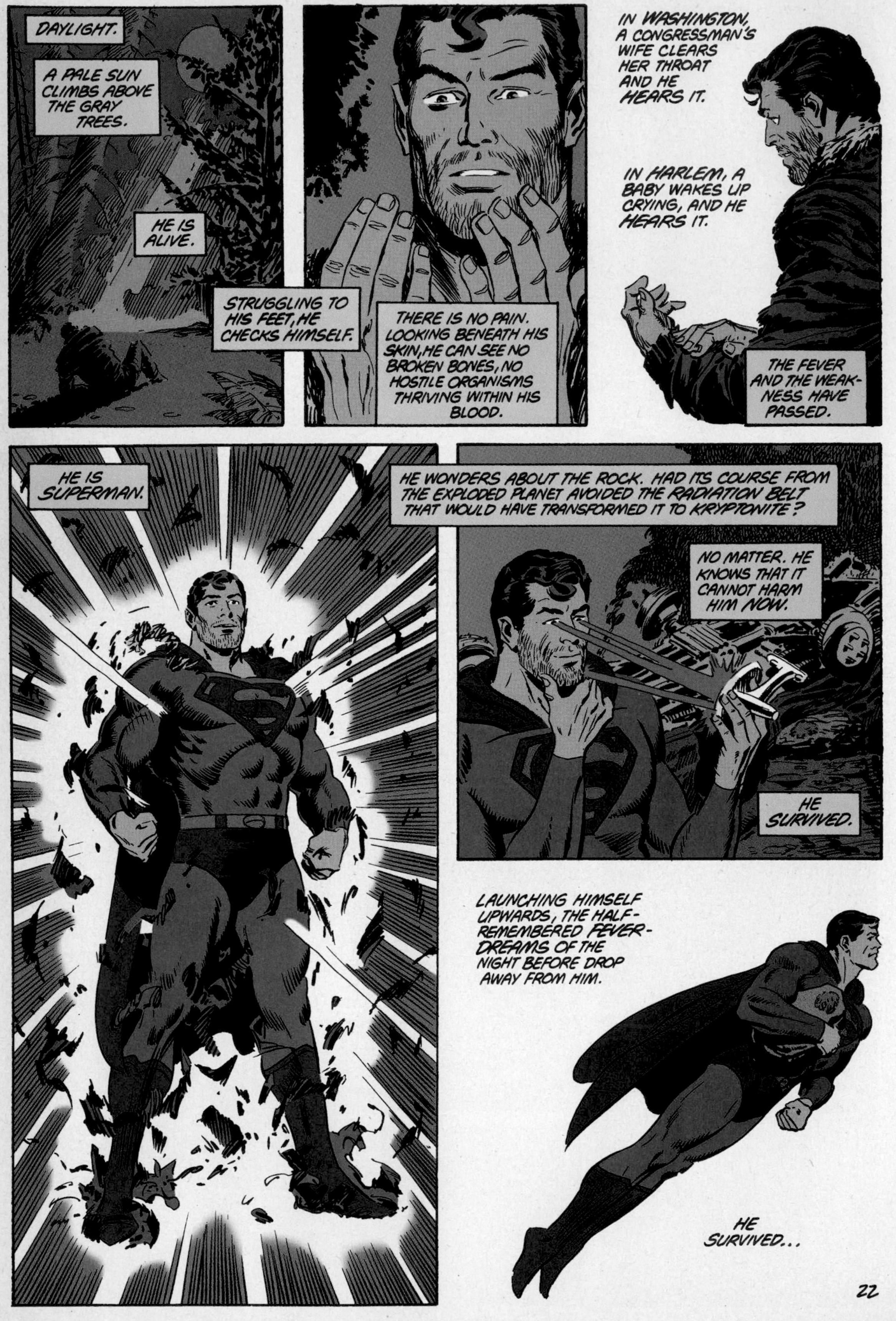
DAYLIGHT.
A PALE SUN CLIMBS ABOVE THE GRAY TREES.
HE IS ALIVE.
STRUGGLING TO HIS FEET, HE CHECKS HIMSELF.
THERE IS NO PAIN. LOOKING BENEATH HIS SKIN, HE CAN SEE NO BROKEN BONES, NO HOSTILE ORGANISMS THRIVING WITHIN HIS BLOOD.
IN WASHINGTON, A CONGRESSMAN'S WIFE CLEARS HER THROAT AND HE HEARS IT.
IN HARLEM, A BABY WAKES UP CRYING, AND HE HEARS IT.
THE FEVER AND THE WEAKNESS HAVE PASSED.
HE IS SUPERMAN.
HE WONDERS ABOUT THE ROCK. HAD ITS COURSE FROM THE EXPLODED PLANET AVOIDED THE RADIATION BELT THAT WOULD HAVE TRANSFORMED IT TO KRYPTONITE?
NO MATTER. HE KNOWS THAT IT CANNOT HARM HIM NOW.
HE SURVIVED.
LAUNCHING HIMSELF UPWARDS, THE HALF-REMEMBERED FEVER-DREAMS OF THE NIGHT BEFORE DROP AWAY FROM HIM.
HE SURVIVED...
22

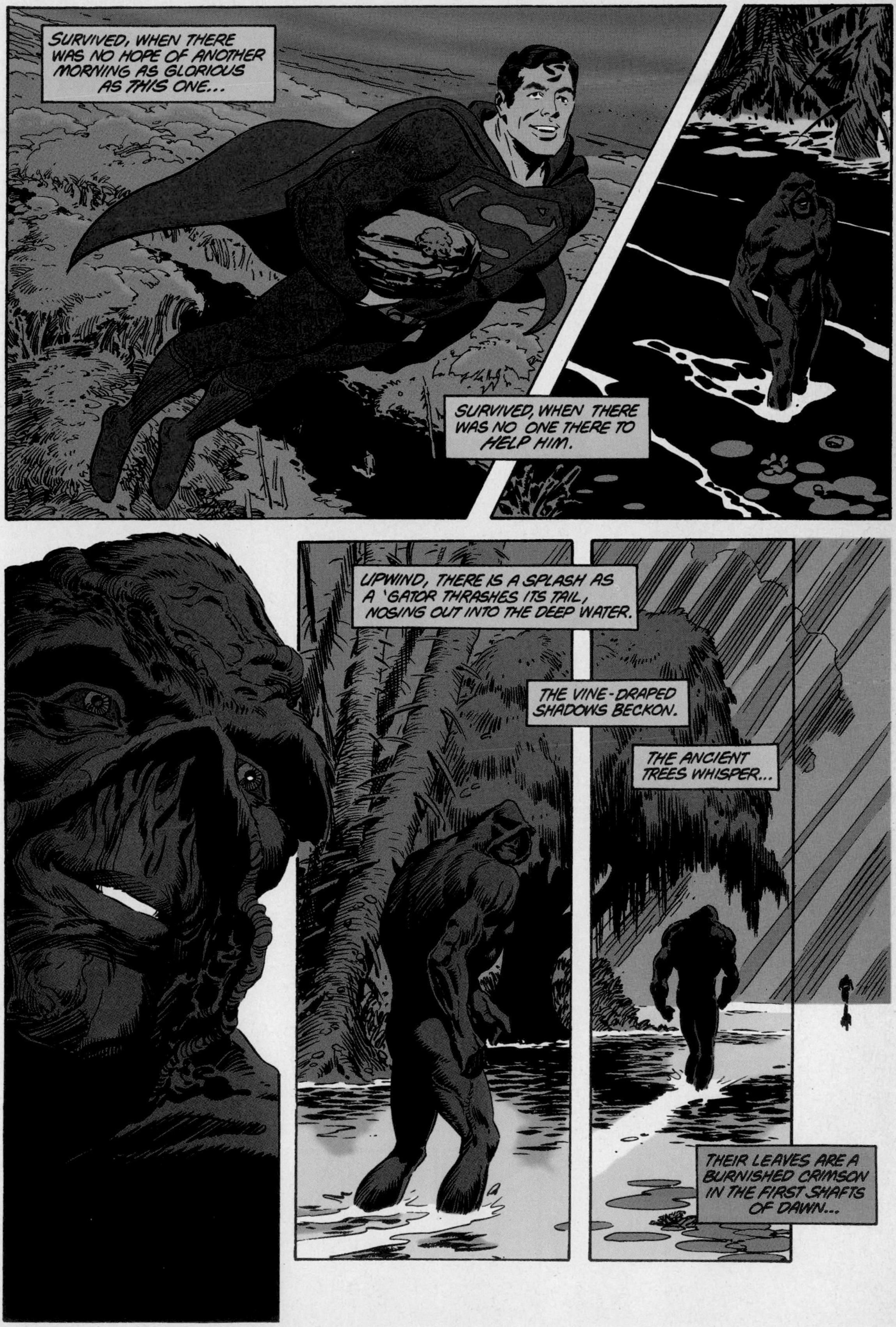

SURVIVED, WHEN THERE WAS NO HOPE OF ANOTHER MORNING AS GLORIOUS AS THIS ONE...
SURVIVED, WHEN THERE WAS NO ONE THERE TO HELP HIM.
UPWIND, THERE IS A SPLASH AS A 'GATOR THRASHES ITS TAIL, NOSING OUT INTO THE DEEP WATER.
THE VINE-DRAPED SHADOWS BECKON.
THE ANCIENT TREES WHISPER...
THEIR LEAVES ARE A BURNISHED CRIMSON IN THE FIRST SHAFTS OF DAWN...

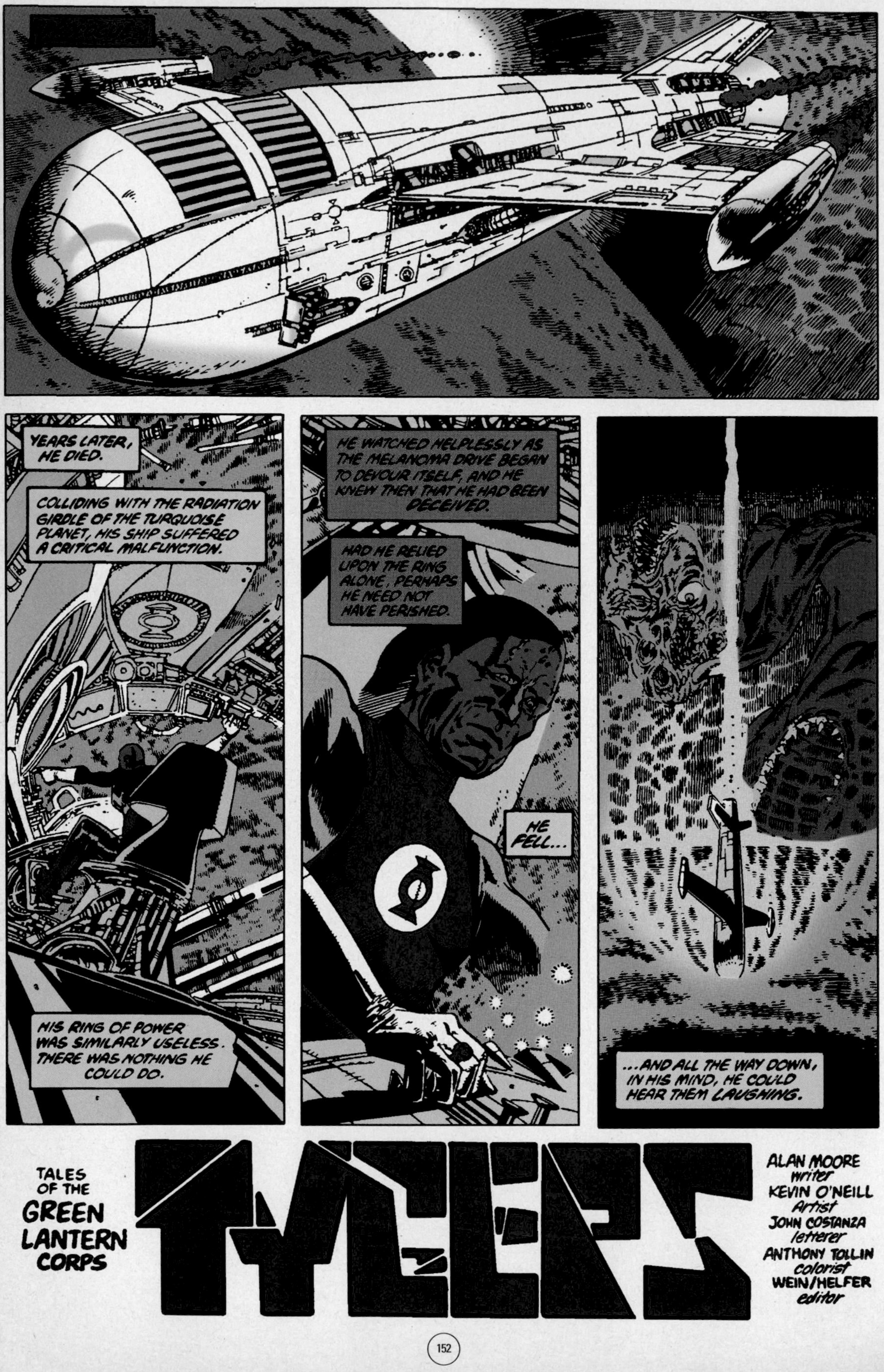
YEARS LATER, HE DIED.
COLLIDING WITH THE RADIATION GIRDLE OF THE TURQUOISE PLANET, HIS SHIP SUFFERED A CRITICAL MALFUNCTION.
HIS RING OF POWER WAS SIMILARLY USELESS. THERE WAS NOTHING HE COULD DO.
HE WATCHED HELPLESSLY AS THE MELANOMA DRIVE BEGAN TO DEVOUR ITSELF, AND HE KNEW THEN THAT HE HAD BEEN DECEIVED.
HAD HE RELIED UPON THE RING ALONE, PERHAPS HE NEED NOT HAVE PERISHED.
HE FELL...
...AND ALL THE WAY DOWN, IN HIS MIND, HE COULD HEAR THEM LAUGHING.

TALES OF THE GREEN LANTERN CORPS

TYGERS

ALAN MOORE *writer*
KEVIN O'NEILL *Artist*
JOHN COSTANZA *letterer*
ANTHONY TOLLIN *colorist*
WEIN/HELFER *editor*

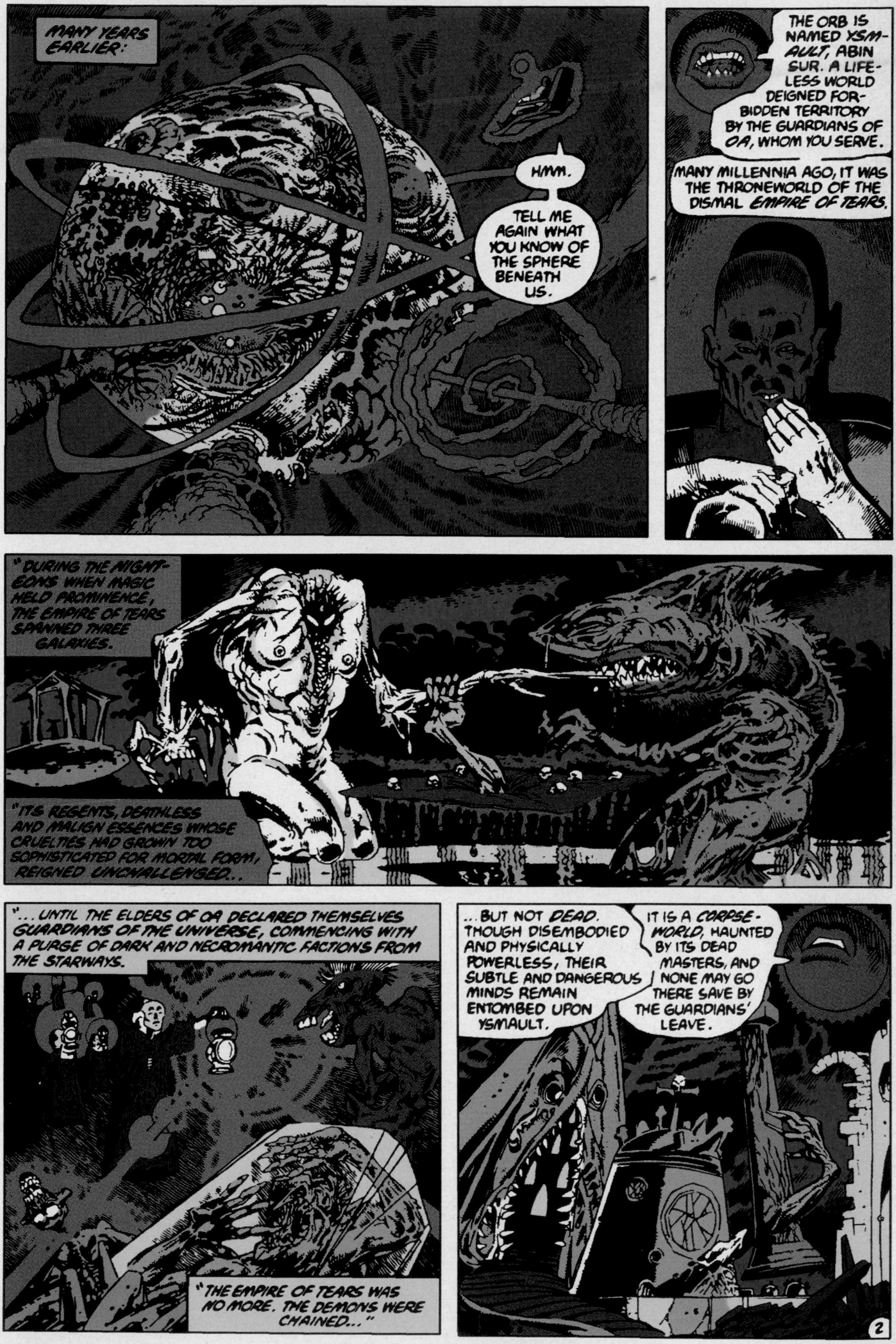
MANY YEARS EARLIER:
HMM.
TELL ME AGAIN WHAT YOU KNOW OF THE SPHERE BENEATH US.
THE ORB IS NAMED YSMAULT, ABIN SUR. A LIFELESS WORLD DEIGNED FORBIDDEN TERRITORY BY THE GUARDIANS OF OA, WHOM YOU SERVE.
MANY MILLENNIA AGO, IT WAS THE THRONEWORLD OF THE DISMAL EMPIRE OF TEARS.
"DURING THE NIGHT-EONS WHEN MAGIC HELD PROMINENCE, THE EMPIRE OF TEARS SPANNED THREE GALAXIES.
"ITS REGENTS, DEATHLESS AND MALIGN ESSENCES WHOSE CRUELTIES HAD GROWN TOO SOPHISTICATED FOR MORTAL FORM, REIGNED UNCHALLENGED...
"...UNTIL THE ELDERS OF OA DECLARED THEMSELVES GUARDIANS OF THE UNIVERSE, COMMENCING WITH A PURGE OF DARK AND NECROMANTIC FACTIONS FROM THE STARWAYS.
"THE EMPIRE OF TEARS WAS NO MORE. THE DEMONS WERE CHAINED..."
...BUT NOT DEAD. THOUGH DISEMBODIED AND PHYSICALLY POWERLESS, THEIR SUBTLE AND DANGEROUS MINDS REMAIN ENTOMBED UPON YSMAULT.
IT IS A CORPSE-WORLD, HAUNTED BY ITS DEAD MASTERS, AND NONE MAY GO THERE SAVE BY THE GUARDIANS' LEAVE.
2

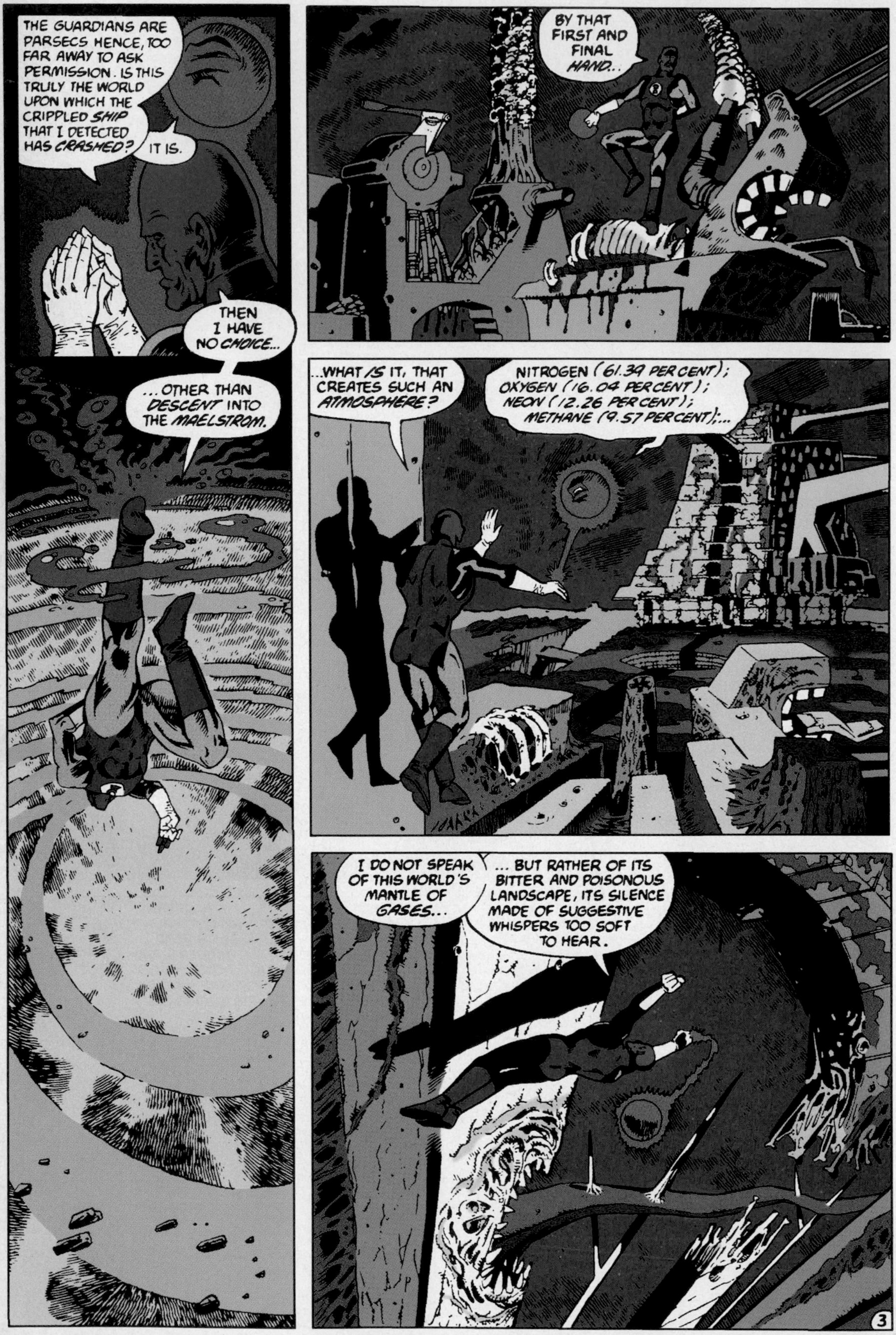
THE GUARDIANS ARE PARSECS HENCE, TOO FAR AWAY TO ASK PERMISSION. IS THIS TRULY THE WORLD UPON WHICH THE CRIPPLED SHIP THAT I DETECTED HAS CRASHED?
IT IS.
THEN I HAVE NO CHOICE...
BY THAT FIRST AND FINAL HAND...
...OTHER THAN DESCENT INTO THE MAELSTROM.
...WHAT IS IT, THAT CREATES SUCH AN ATMOSPHERE?
NITROGEN (61.39 PERCENT); OXYGEN (16.04 PERCENT); NEON (12.26 PERCENT); METHANE (9.57 PERCENT);...
I DO NOT SPEAK OF THIS WORLD'S MANTLE OF GASES...
... BUT RATHER OF ITS BITTER AND POISONOUS LANDSCAPE, ITS SILENCE MADE OF SUGGESTIVE WHISPERS TOO SOFT TO HEAR.
3

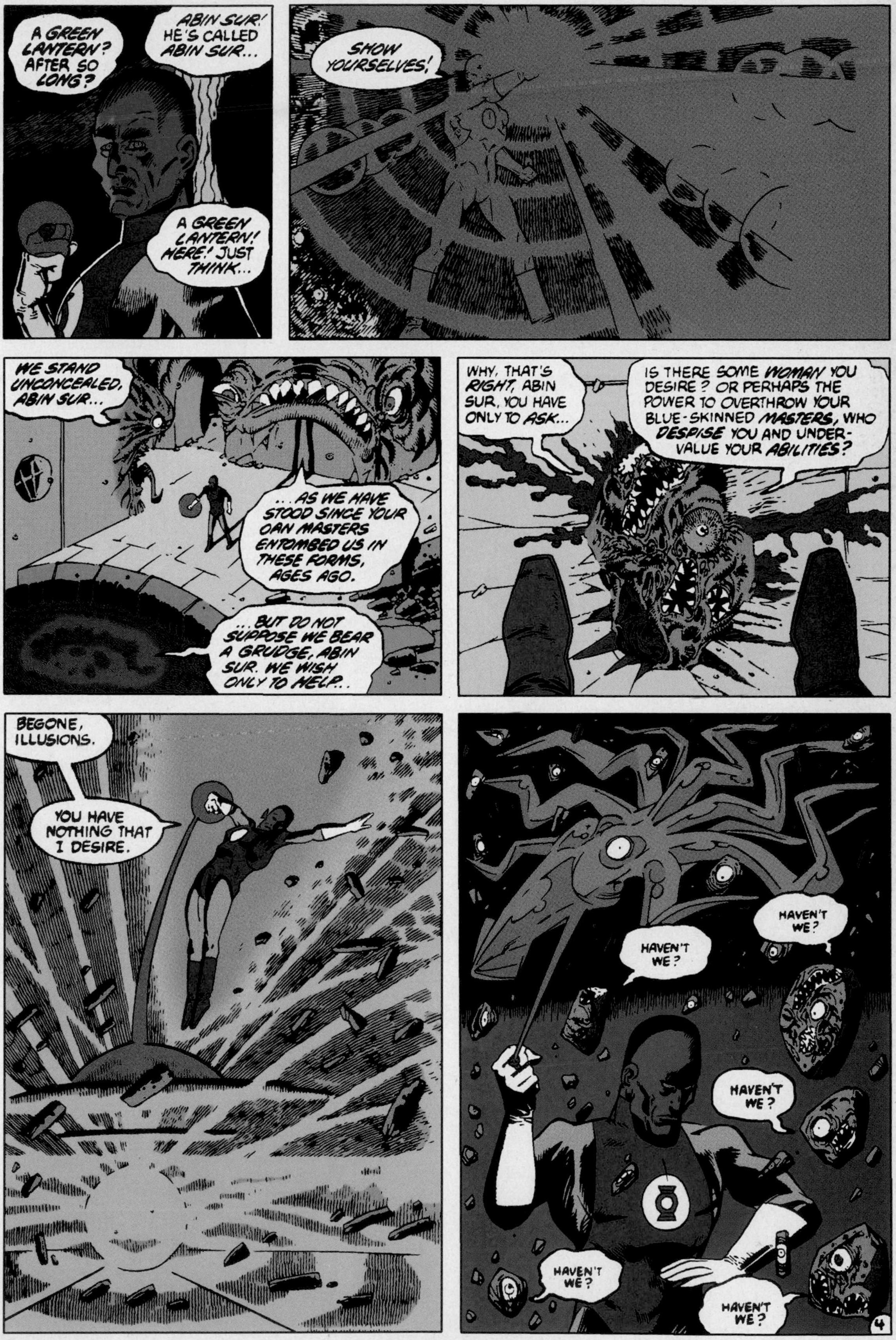
A GREEN LANTERN? AFTER SO LONG?
ABIN SUR! HE'S CALLED ABIN SUR...
A GREEN LANTERN! HERE! JUST THINK...
SHOW YOURSELVES!
WE STAND UNCONCEALED, ABIN SUR...
...AS WE HAVE STOOD SINCE YOUR OAN MASTERS ENTOMBED US IN THESE FORMS, AGES AGO.
...BUT DO NOT SUPPOSE WE BEAR A GRUDGE, ABIN SUR. WE WISH ONLY TO HELP...
WHY, THAT'S RIGHT, ABIN SUR, YOU HAVE ONLY TO ASK...
IS THERE SOME WOMAN YOU DESIRE? OR PERHAPS THE POWER TO OVERTHROW YOUR BLUE-SKINNED MASTERS, WHO DESPISE YOU AND UNDERVALUE YOUR ABILITIES?
BEGONE, ILLUSIONS.
YOU HAVE NOTHING THAT I DESIRE.
HAVEN'T WE?
HAVEN'T WE?
HAVEN'T WE?
HAVEN'T WE?
HAVEN'T WE?
4

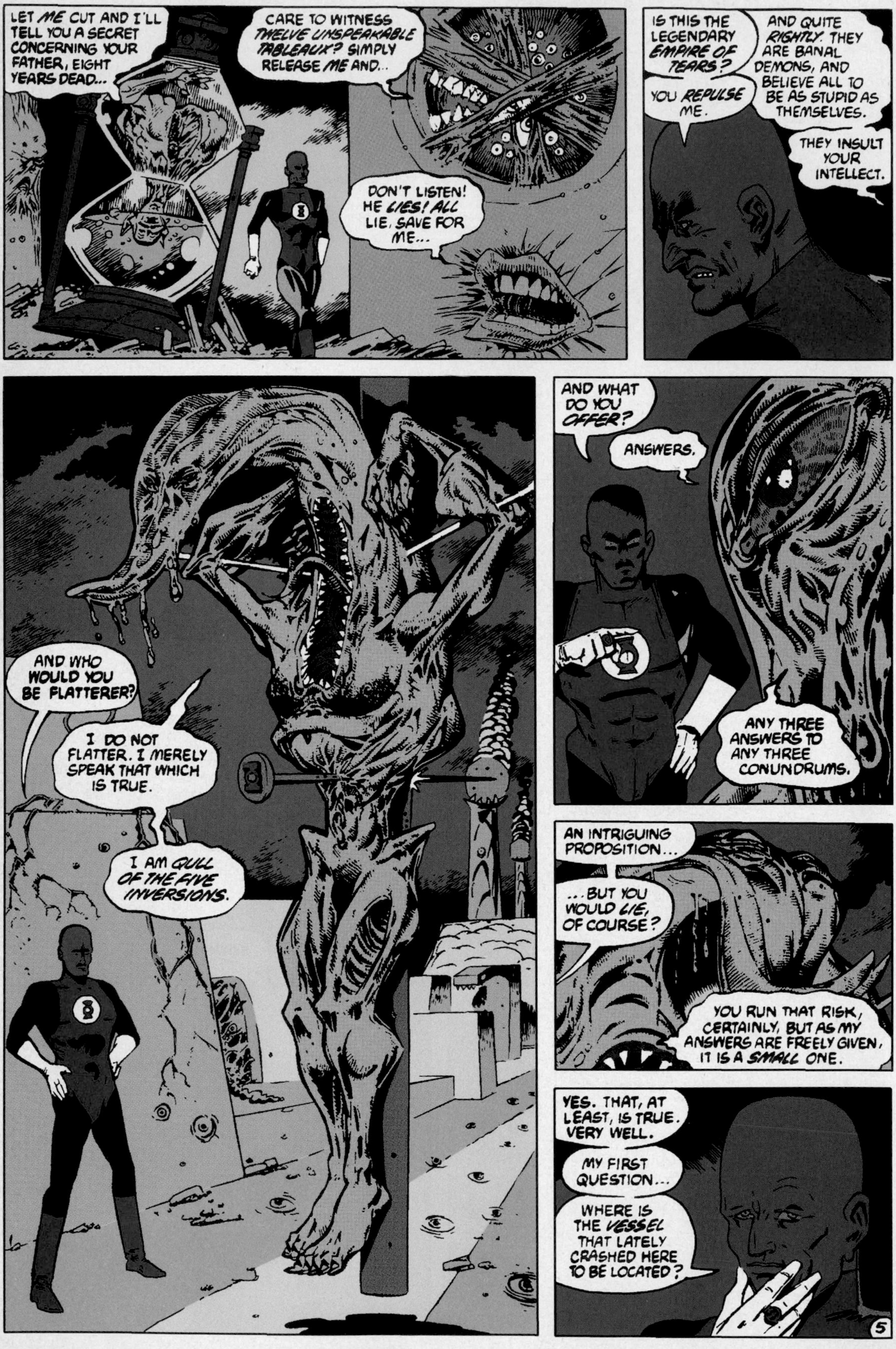

LET *ME* CUT AND I'LL TELL YOU A SECRET CONCERNING YOUR FATHER, EIGHT YEARS DEAD...
CARE TO WITNESS *TWELVE UNSPEAKABLE TABLEAUX*? SIMPLY RELEASE *ME* AND...
DON'T LISTEN! HE *LIES! ALL* LIE, SAVE FOR *ME*...
IS THIS THE LEGENDARY *EMPIRE OF TEARS*?
YOU *REPULSE* ME.
AND QUITE *RIGHTLY*. THEY ARE BANAL DEMONS, AND BELIEVE ALL TO BE AS STUPID AS THEMSELVES.
THEY INSULT YOUR INTELLECT.
AND WHO WOULD YOU BE FLATTERER?
I DO NOT FLATTER. I MERELY SPEAK THAT WHICH IS TRUE.
I AM *QULL OF THE FIVE INVERSIONS*.
AND WHAT DO YOU *OFFER*?
ANSWERS.
ANY THREE ANSWERS TO ANY THREE CONUNDRUMS.
AN INTRIGUING PROPOSITION...
...BUT YOU WOULD *LIE*, OF COURSE?
YOU RUN THAT RISK, CERTAINLY, BUT AS MY ANSWERS ARE FREELY GIVEN, IT IS A *SMALL* ONE.
YES. THAT, AT LEAST, IS TRUE. VERY WELL.
MY FIRST QUESTION...
WHERE IS THE *VESSEL* THAT LATELY CRASHED HERE TO BE LOCATED?
5

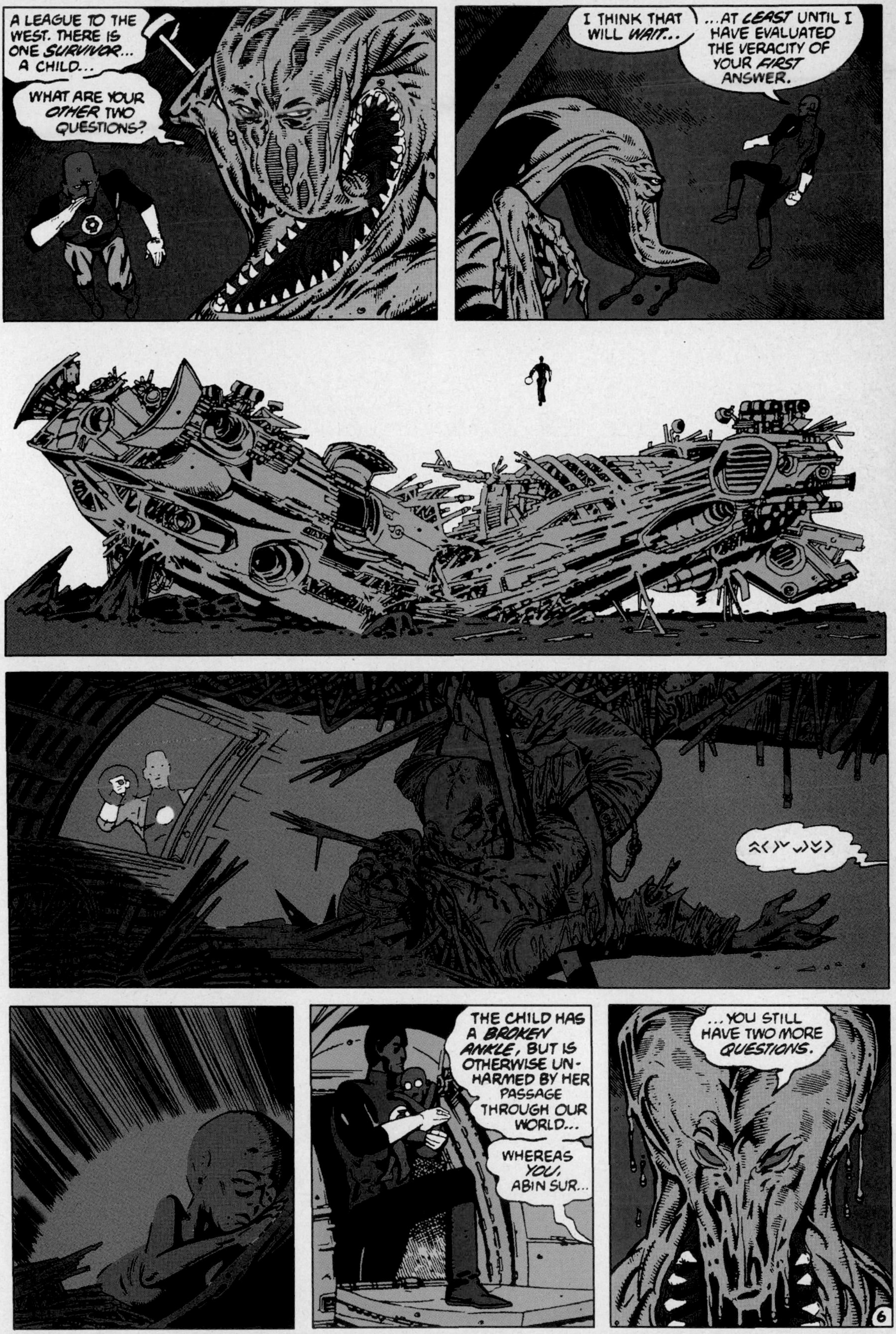
A LEAGUE TO THE WEST. THERE IS ONE SURVIVOR... A CHILD...
WHAT ARE YOUR OTHER TWO QUESTIONS?
I THINK THAT WILL WAIT...
...AT LEAST UNTIL I HAVE EVALUATED THE VERACITY OF YOUR FIRST ANSWER.
THE CHILD HAS A BROKEN ANKLE, BUT IS OTHERWISE UN-HARMED BY HER PASSAGE THROUGH OUR WORLD...
WHEREAS YOU, ABIN SUR...
...YOU STILL HAVE TWO MORE QUESTIONS.
6

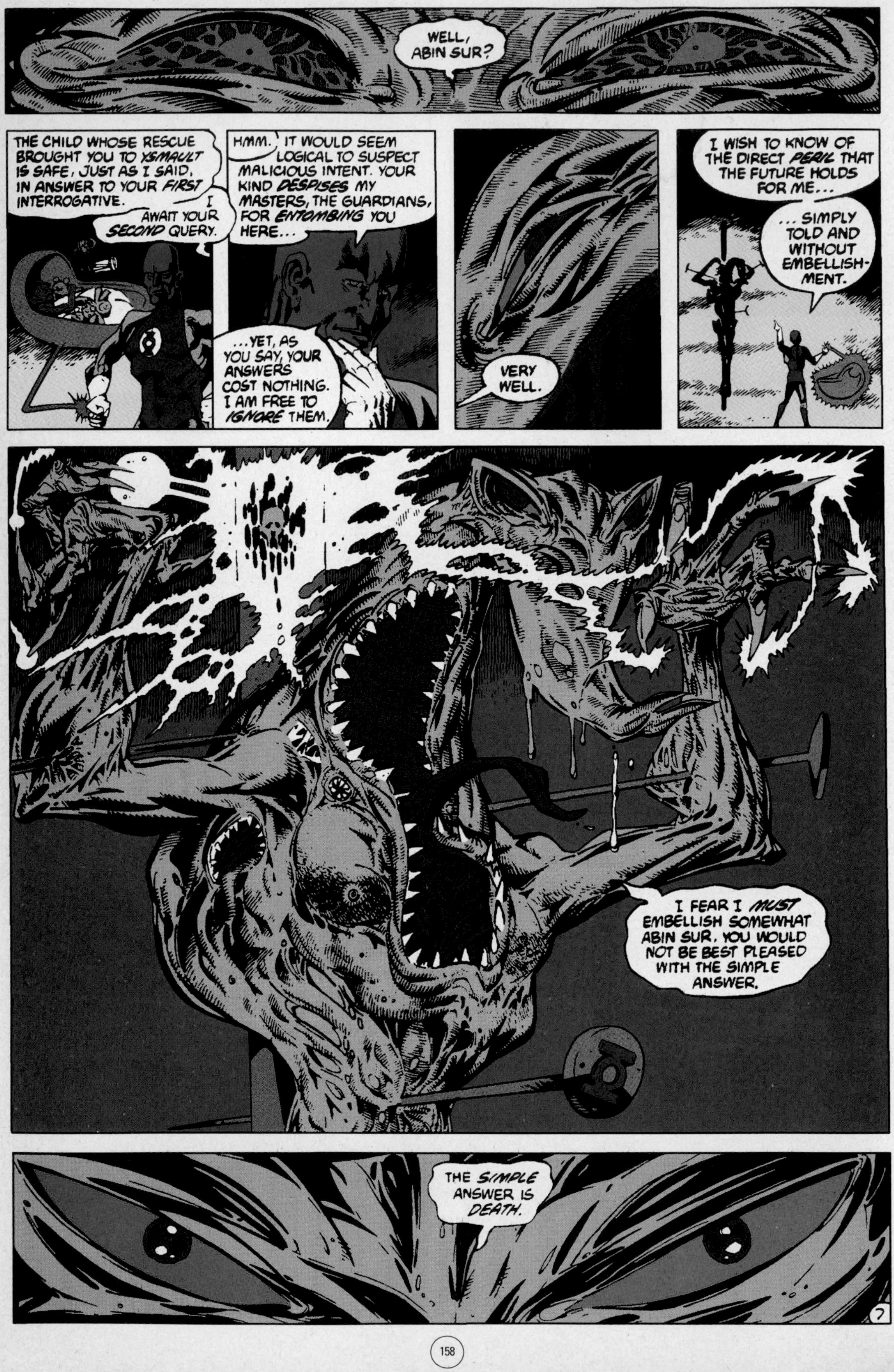
WELL, ABIN SUR?
THE CHILD WHOSE RESCUE BROUGHT YOU TO YSMAULT IS SAFE, JUST AS I SAID, IN ANSWER TO YOUR FIRST INTERROGATIVE.
I AWAIT YOUR SECOND QUERY.
HMM. IT WOULD SEEM LOGICAL TO SUSPECT MALICIOUS INTENT. YOUR KIND DESPISES MY MASTERS, THE GUARDIANS, FOR ENTOMBING YOU HERE...
...YET, AS YOU SAY, YOUR ANSWERS COST NOTHING. I AM FREE TO IGNORE THEM.
VERY WELL.
I WISH TO KNOW OF THE DIRECT PERIL THAT THE FUTURE HOLDS FOR ME...
...SIMPLY TOLD AND WITHOUT EMBELLISHMENT.
I FEAR I MUST EMBELLISH SOMEWHAT ABIN SUR. YOU WOULD NOT BE BEST PLEASED WITH THE SIMPLE ANSWER.
THE SIMPLE ANSWER IS DEATH.
7

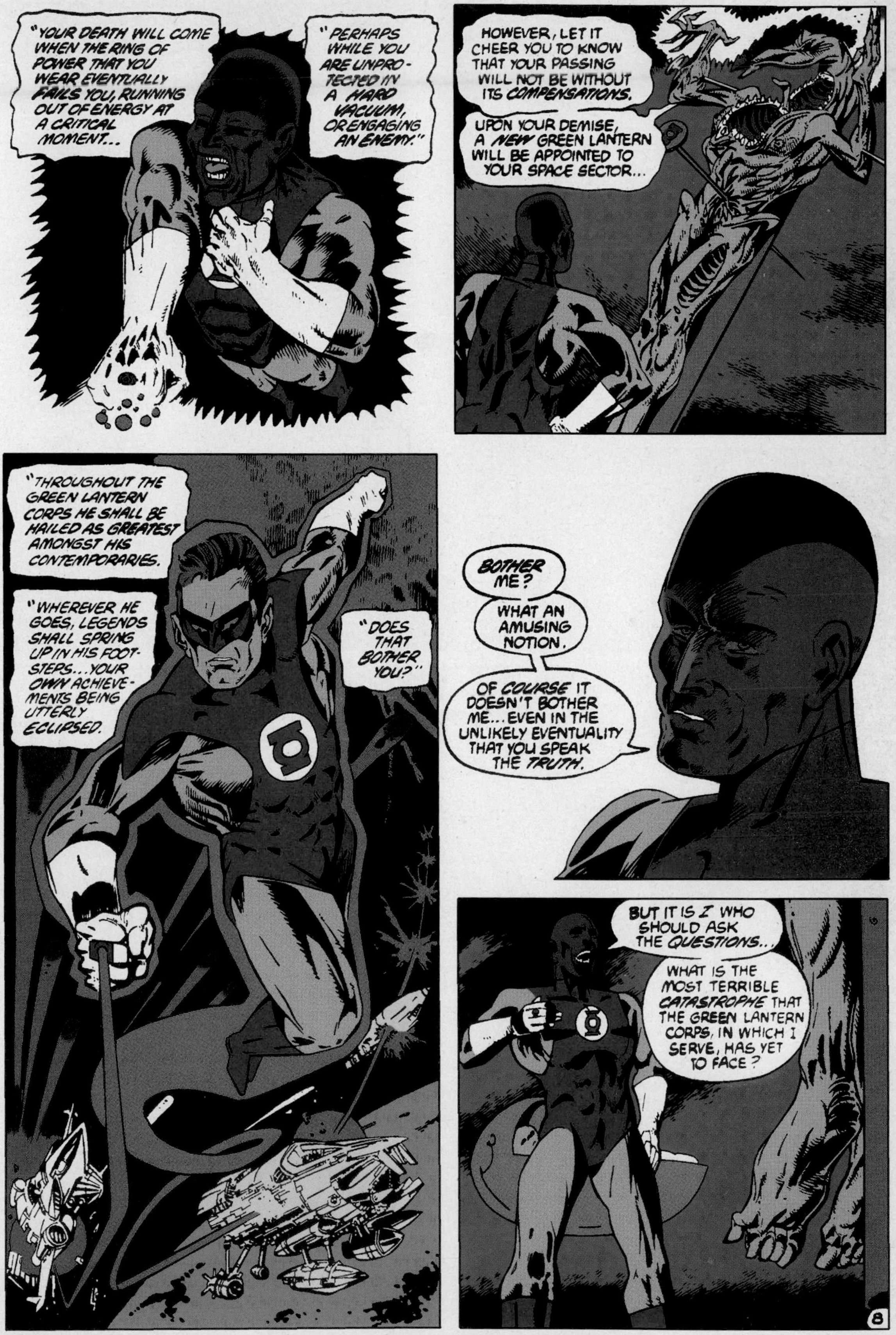
"YOUR DEATH WILL COME WHEN THE RING OF POWER THAT YOU WEAR EVENTUALLY FAILS YOU, RUNNING OUT OF ENERGY AT A CRITICAL MOMENT...
"PERHAPS WHILE YOU ARE UNPRO-TECTED IN A HARD VACUUM, OR ENGAGING AN ENEMY."
HOWEVER, LET IT CHEER YOU TO KNOW THAT YOUR PASSING WILL NOT BE WITHOUT ITS COMPENSATIONS.
UPON YOUR DEMISE, A NEW GREEN LANTERN WILL BE APPOINTED TO YOUR SPACE SECTOR...
"THROUGHOUT THE GREEN LANTERN CORPS HE SHALL BE HAILED AS GREATEST AMONGST HIS CONTEMPORARIES.
"WHEREVER HE GOES, LEGENDS SHALL SPRING UP IN HIS FOOT-STEPS... YOUR OWN ACHIEVE-MENTS BEING UTTERLY ECLIPSED.
"DOES THAT BOTHER YOU?"
BOTHER ME?
WHAT AN AMUSING NOTION.
OF COURSE IT DOESN'T BOTHER ME... EVEN IN THE UNLIKELY EVENTUALITY THAT YOU SPEAK THE TRUTH.
BUT IT IS I WHO SHOULD ASK THE QUESTIONS...
WHAT IS THE MOST TERRIBLE CATASTROPHE THAT THE GREEN LANTERN CORPS, IN WHICH I SERVE, HAS YET TO FACE?
8

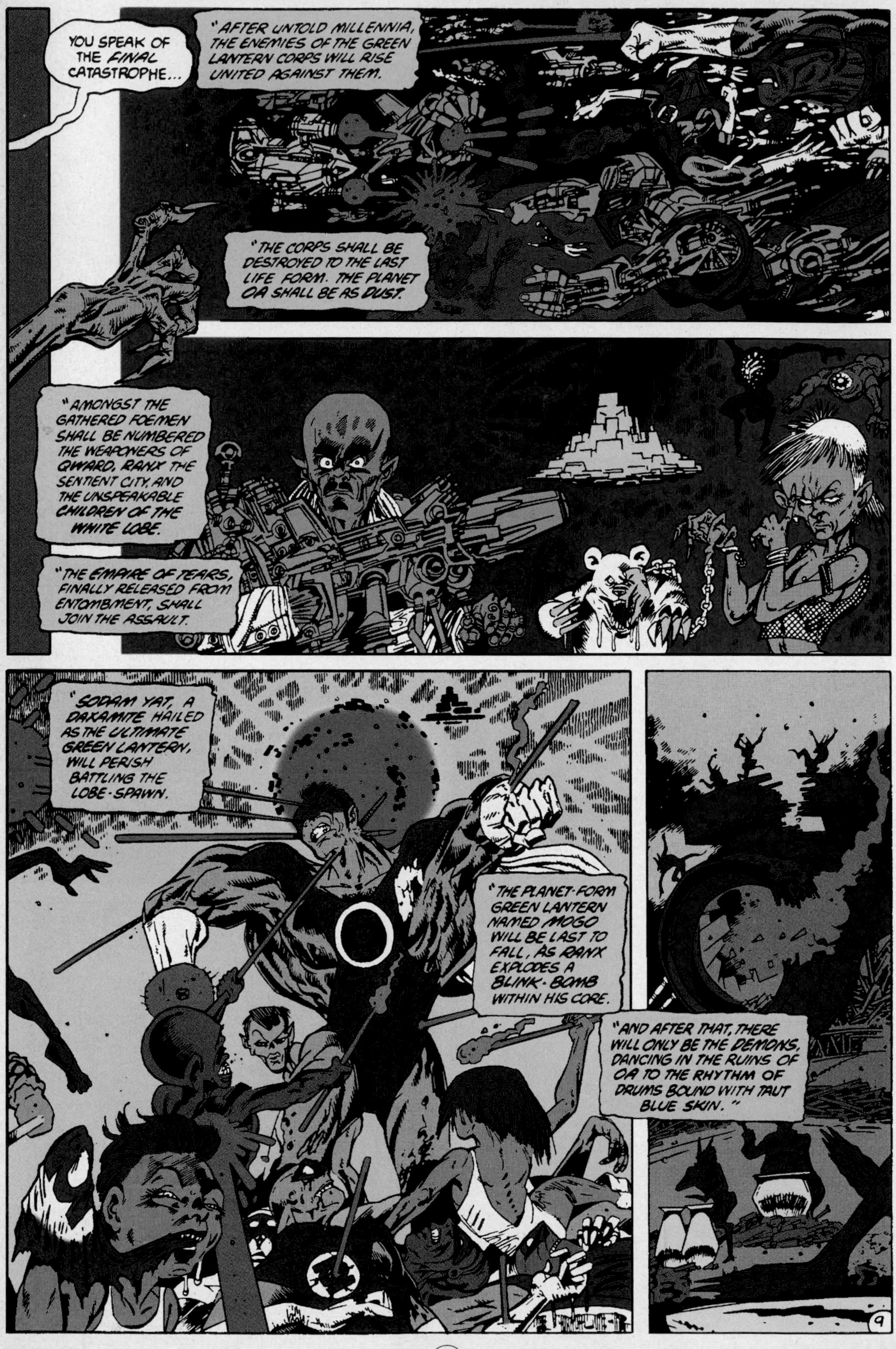

YOU SPEAK OF THE FINAL CATASTROPHE...
"AFTER UNTOLD MILLENNIA, THE ENEMIES OF THE GREEN LANTERN CORPS WILL RISE UNITED AGAINST THEM.
"THE CORPS SHALL BE DESTROYED TO THE LAST LIFE FORM. THE PLANET OA SHALL BE AS DUST.
"AMONGST THE GATHERED FOEMEN SHALL BE NUMBERED THE WEAPONERS OF QWARD, RANX THE SENTIENT CITY, AND THE UNSPEAKABLE CHILDREN OF THE WHITE LOBE.
"THE EMPIRE OF TEARS, FINALLY RELEASED FROM ENTOMBMENT, SHALL JOIN THE ASSAULT.
"SODAM YAT, A DAXAMITE HAILED AS THE ULTIMATE GREEN LANTERN, WILL PERISH BATTLING THE LOBE-SPAWN.
"THE PLANET-FORM GREEN LANTERN NAMED MOGO WILL BE LAST TO FALL, AS RANX EXPLODES A BLINK-BOMB WITHIN HIS CORE.
"AND AFTER THAT, THERE WILL ONLY BE THE DEMONS, DANCING IN THE RUINS OF OA TO THE RHYTHM OF DRUMS BOUND WITH TAUT BLUE SKIN."
9

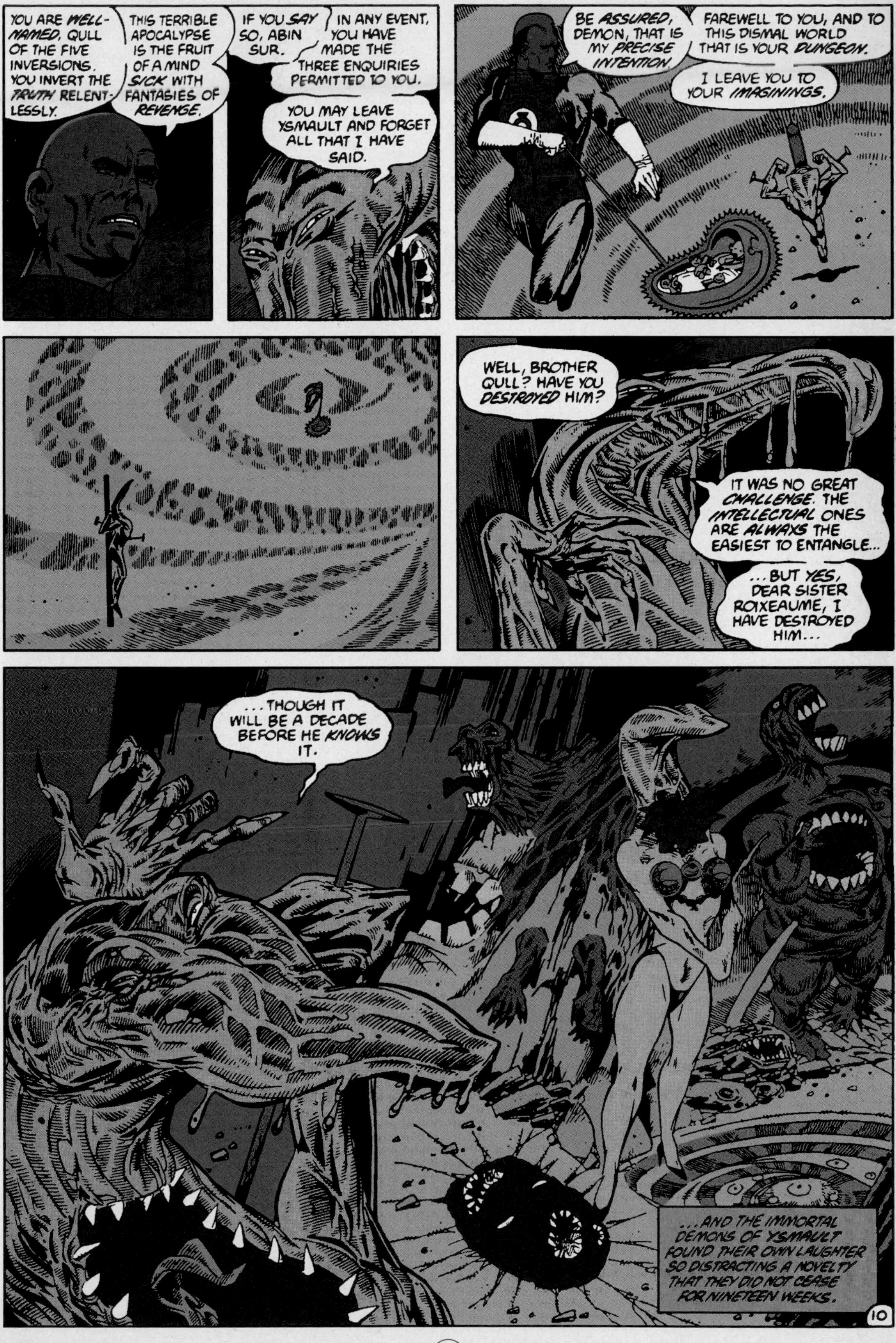
YOU ARE WELL-NAMED, QULL OF THE FIVE INVERSIONS. YOU INVERT THE TRUTH RELENTLESSLY.
THIS TERRIBLE APOCALYPSE IS THE FRUIT OF A MIND SICK WITH FANTASIES OF REVENGE.
IF YOU SAY SO, ABIN SUR.
IN ANY EVENT, YOU HAVE MADE THE THREE ENQUIRIES PERMITTED TO YOU.
YOU MAY LEAVE YSMAULT AND FORGET ALL THAT I HAVE SAID.
BE ASSURED, DEMON, THAT IS MY PRECISE INTENTION.
FAREWELL TO YOU, AND TO THIS DISMAL WORLD THAT IS YOUR DUNGEON.
I LEAVE YOU TO YOUR IMAGININGS.
WELL, BROTHER QULL? HAVE YOU DESTROYED HIM?
IT WAS NO GREAT CHALLENGE. THE INTELLECTUAL ONES ARE ALWAYS THE EASIEST TO ENTANGLE...
...BUT YES, DEAR SISTER ROIXEAUME, I HAVE DESTROYED HIM...
...THOUGH IT WILL BE A DECADE BEFORE HE KNOWS IT.
...AND THE IMMORTAL DEMONS OF YSMAULT FOUND THEIR OWN LAUGHTER SO DISTRACTING A NOVELTY THAT THEY DID NOT CEASE FOR NINETEEN WEEKS.
10

ABIN SUR'S RUMINATIONS UPON THE MATTER ENDURED FAR LONGER...

HMM.

SO TELL ME... IS THERE A CHANCE THAT YOU MIGHT RUN OUT OF ENERGIES AT SOME VITAL INSTANT, IRRESPECTIVE OF WHETHER QULL LIED?

A REMOTE CHANCE, BUT YES... IT IS POSSIBLE.

THEN I CAN SEE NO HARM IN OBSERVING PRECAUTIONS. PERHAPS ON LONGER MISSIONS I SHOULD TRAVEL BY STARSHIP, CONSERVING YOUR ENERGIES?

I HAVE NO OBJECTION TO THIS PROPOSAL.

GOOD.

THEN I MAY PUT THE EMPIRE OF TEARS AND THEIR MORBID SPECULATIONS ENTIRELY FROM MY MIND.

INCIDENTALLY, IS IT NOT TIME THAT I RECHARGED YOU? YOU MUST BE LOW ON POWER...

YOU RECHARGED ME BUT AN HOUR AGO, ABIN SUR.

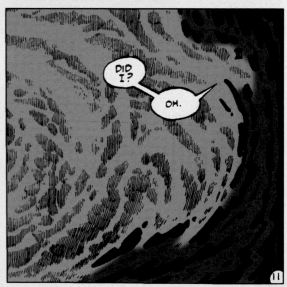

DID I?

OH.

11

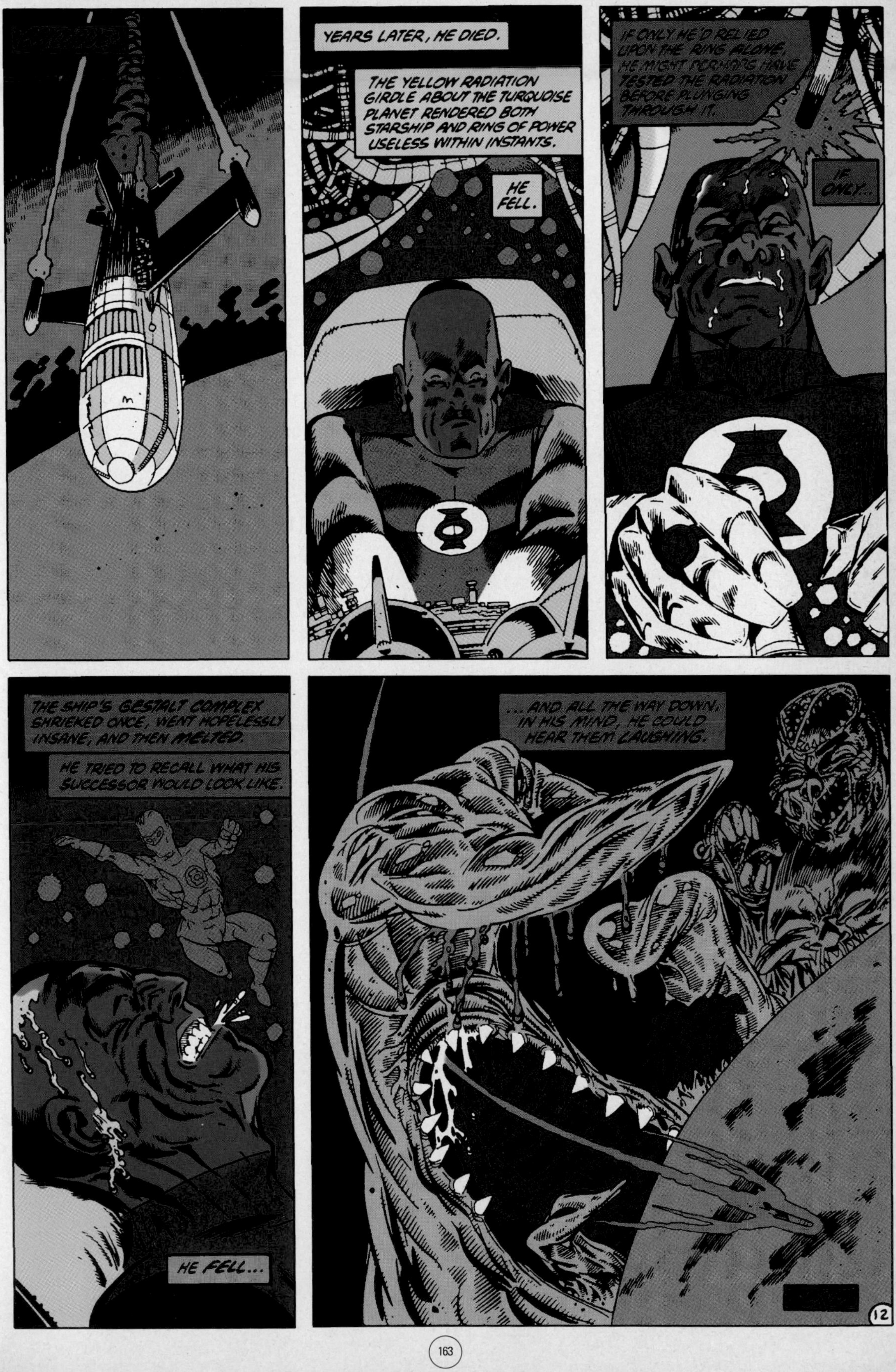
YEARS LATER, HE DIED.
THE YELLOW RADIATION GIRDLE ABOUT THE TURQUOISE PLANET RENDERED BOTH STARSHIP AND RING OF POWER USELESS WITHIN INSTANTS.
HE FELL.
IF ONLY HE'D RELIED UPON THE RING ALONE, HE MIGHT PERHAPS HAVE TESTED THE RADIATION BEFORE PLUNGING THROUGH IT.
IF ONLY...
THE SHIP'S GESTALT COMPLEX SHRIEKED ONCE, WENT HOPELESSLY INSANE, AND THEN MELTED.
HE TRIED TO RECALL WHAT HIS SUCCESSOR WOULD LOOK LIKE.
HE FELL...
...AND ALL THE WAY DOWN, IN HIS MIND, HE COULD HEAR THEM LAUGHING.

ON "WHATEVER HAPPENED TO THE MAN OF TOMORROW"?

BY PAUL **KUPPERBERG**

John Byrne had signed on to write and pencil the relaunched Superman, beginning with THE MAN OF STEEL miniseries that went on sale in July, 1986. That left Superman editor Julius Schwartz with the opportunity to do a grand finale for his stewardship of SUPERMAN and ACTION COMICS. "I started to think, what am I going to put in my last two issues. And in the middle of the night it came to me: I would make believe that my last issues of SUPERMAN and ACTION COMICS were *actually* going to be the last issues," Schwartz recalled.

"Therefore it was incumbent upon me to clean up, to explain all the things that had been going on in the previous years. For example, did Lois Lane ever find out that Clark Kent was Superman? Did they ever get married? What happened to Jimmy Olsen, to Perry White, to all the villains? I had to clear it up." With a definitive story direction in mind, Julie set out to find a writer to handle the scripting.

"The next morning, still wondering what to do about it, I happened to be having breakfast with Alan Moore. So I told him about my difficulties. At that point, he literally rose out of his chair, put his hands around my neck, and said, 'If you let anybody but me write that story, I'll kill you.' Since I didn't want to be an accessory to my own murder, I agreed."

So, in a letter to Moore dated September 19, 1985, Julie proclaimed, "The time has come! Meaning that I've just been informed that the September cover-dated issues of SUPERMAN and ACTION will be my last before John Byrne and Co. take over.

"What I'm getting at is: the time has come for you to type up the story your 'mouth' agreed to do — that is an 'imaginary' Superman story that would serve as the 'last' Superman story if the magazines were discontinued — what would happen to Superman, Clark Kent, Lois Lane, Lana Lang, Jimmy Olsen, Perry White, Luthor, Brainiac, Mr. Mxyzptlk, and all the *et cetera* you can deal with."

The matter of an artist for the 'last' Superman story was never in question. In the preceding thirty years or so, Curt Swan had become, in the minds of generations of readers, the definitive Superman artist, responsible for a staggering number of stories starring the last son of Krypton. Certainly if anyone deserved to do the honors on what was sure to become one of the most memorable Superman stories of all time, it was Curt.

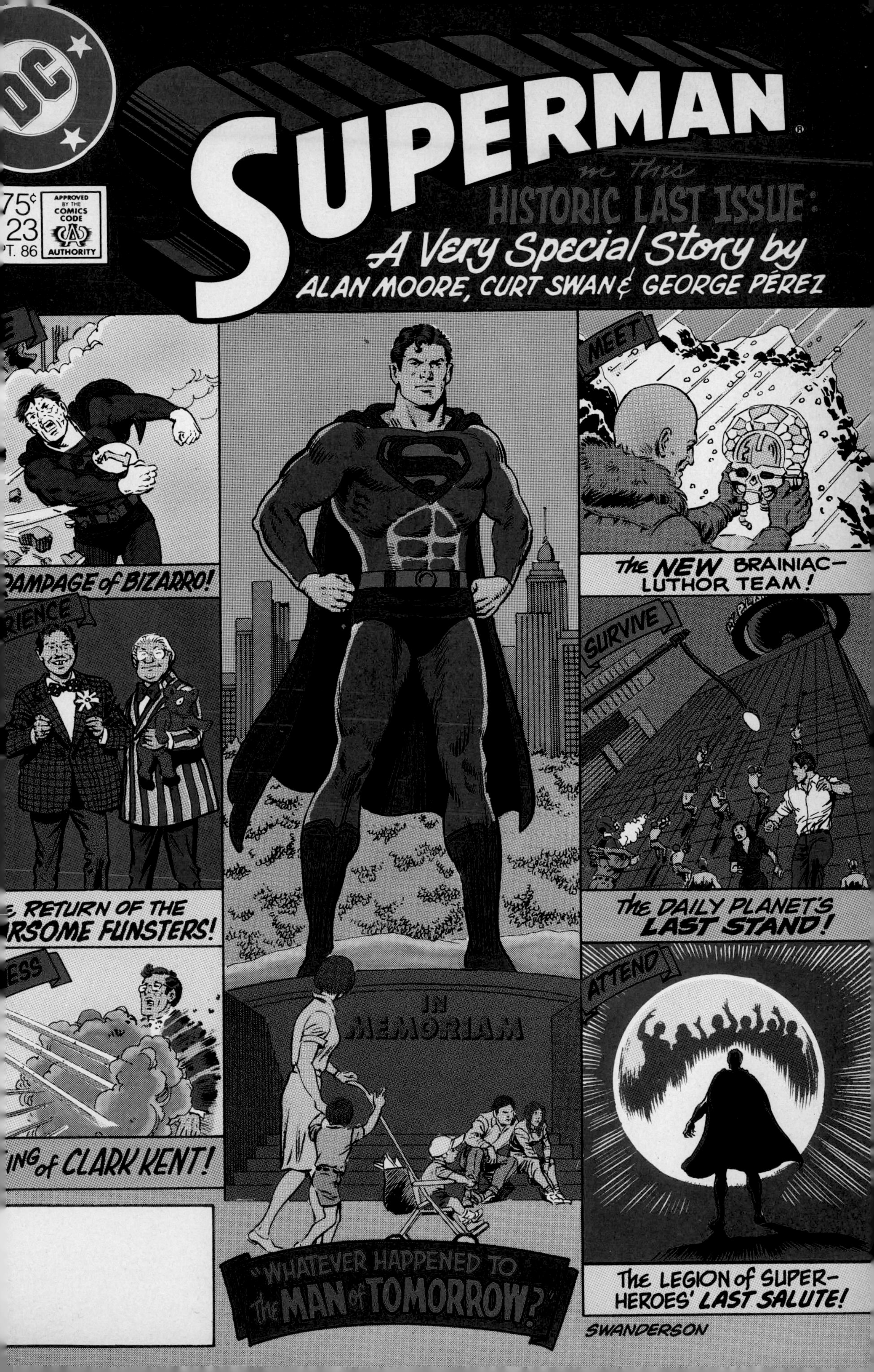

DC
SUPERMAN
75¢
23
PT. 86
APPROVED BY THE COMICS CODE AUTHORITY
in this
HISTORIC LAST ISSUE:
A Very Special Story by
ALAN MOORE, CURT SWAN & GEORGE PÉREZ
RAMPAGE of BIZARRO!
MEET
The NEW BRAINIAC-LUTHOR TEAM!
RIENCE
SURVIVE
E RETURN OF THE
RSOME FUNSTERS!
The DAILY PLANET'S LAST STAND!
ESS
ATTEND
IN MEMORIAM
ING of CLARK KENT!
"WHATEVER HAPPENED TO The MAN of TOMORROW?"
The LEGION of SUPER-HEROES' LAST SALUTE!
SWANDERSON

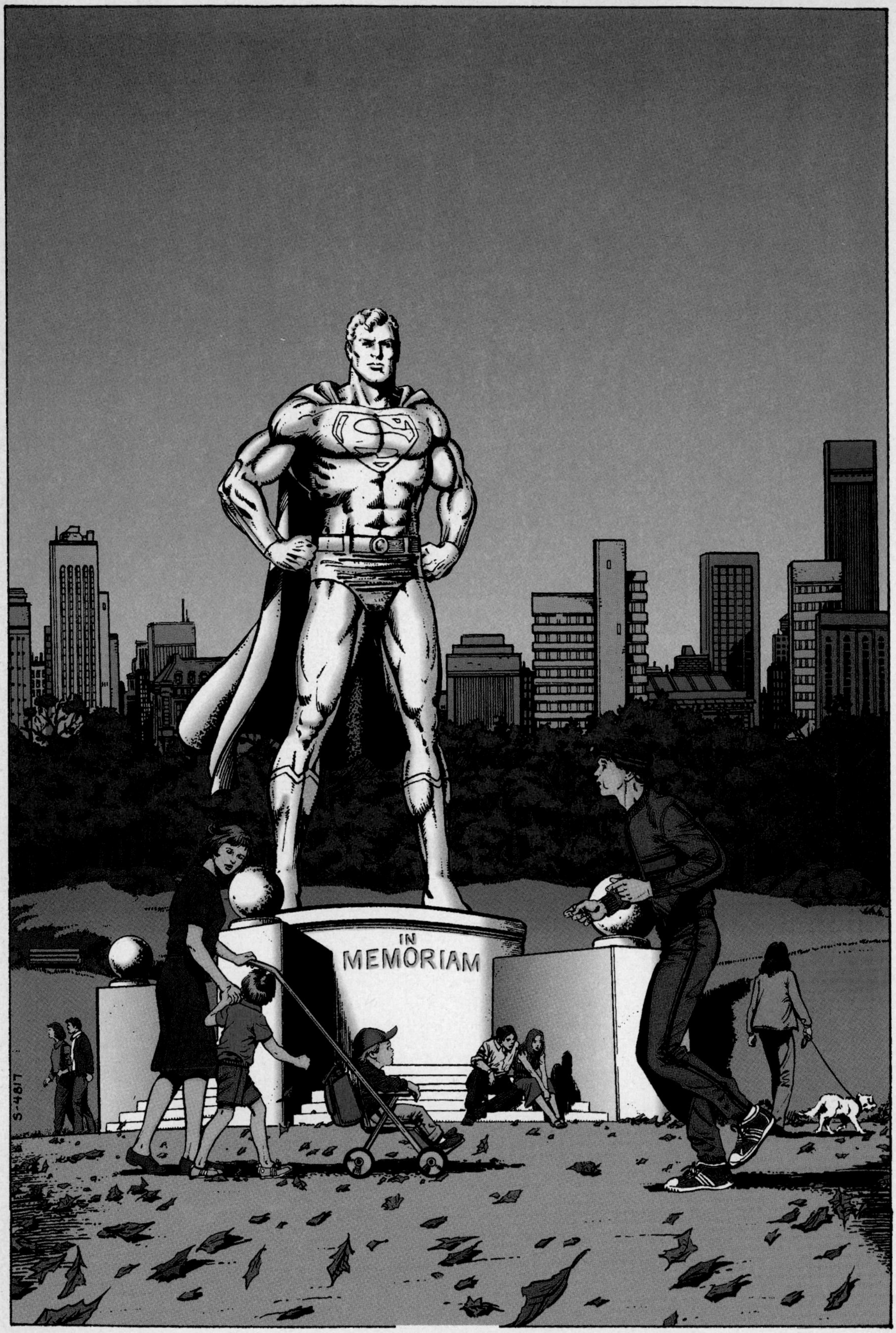
IN
MEMORIAM

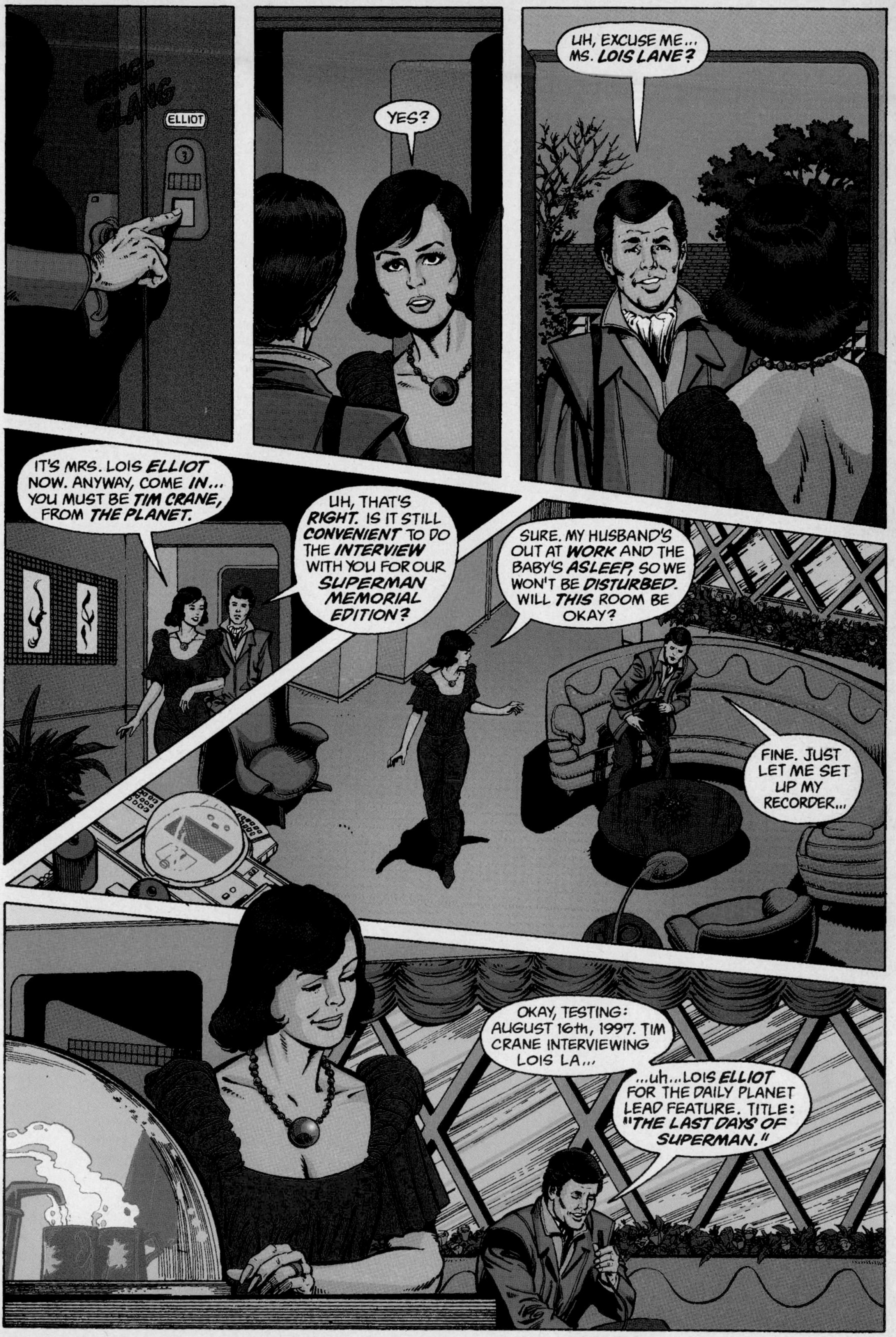
ELLIOT
YES?
UH, EXCUSE ME... MS. LOIS LANE?
IT'S MRS. LOIS ELLIOT NOW. ANYWAY, COME IN... YOU MUST BE TIM CRANE, FROM THE PLANET.
UH, THAT'S RIGHT. IS IT STILL CONVENIENT TO DO THE INTERVIEW WITH YOU FOR OUR SUPERMAN MEMORIAL EDITION?
SURE. MY HUSBAND'S OUT AT WORK AND THE BABY'S ASLEEP, SO WE WON'T BE DISTURBED. WILL THIS ROOM BE OKAY?
FINE. JUST LET ME SET UP MY RECORDER...
OKAY, TESTING: AUGUST 16th, 1997. TIM CRANE INTERVIEWING LOIS LA...
...uh...LOIS ELLIOT FOR THE DAILY PLANET LEAD FEATURE. TITLE: "THE LAST DAYS OF SUPERMAN."

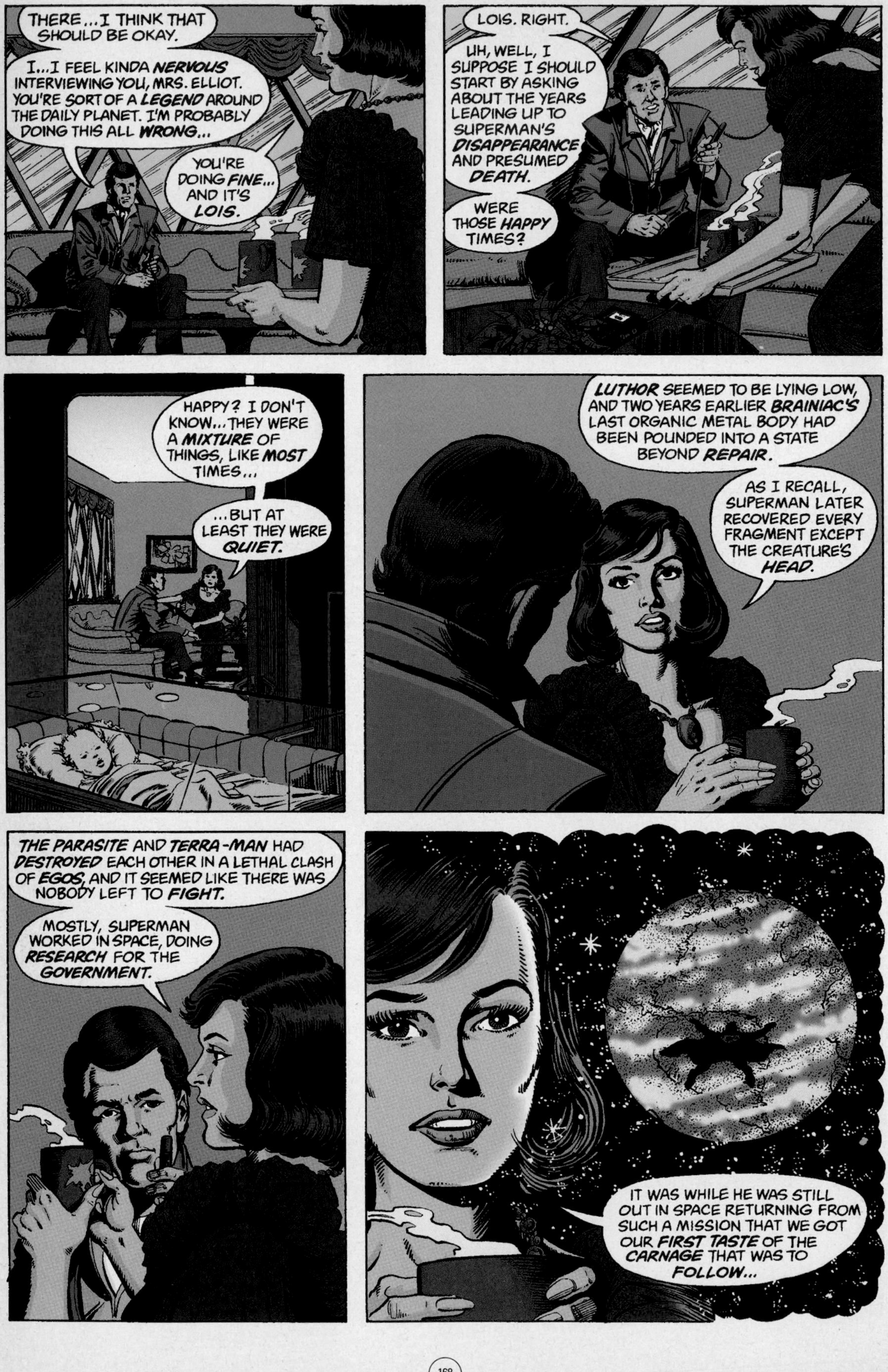
THERE... I THINK THAT SHOULD BE OKAY.
I... I FEEL KINDA NERVOUS INTERVIEWING YOU, MRS. ELLIOT. YOU'RE SORT OF A LEGEND AROUND THE DAILY PLANET. I'M PROBABLY DOING THIS ALL WRONG...
YOU'RE DOING FINE... AND IT'S LOIS.
LOIS. RIGHT.
UH, WELL, I SUPPOSE I SHOULD START BY ASKING ABOUT THE YEARS LEADING UP TO SUPERMAN'S DISAPPEARANCE AND PRESUMED DEATH.
WERE THOSE HAPPY TIMES?
HAPPY? I DON'T KNOW... THEY WERE A MIXTURE OF THINGS, LIKE MOST TIMES...
...BUT AT LEAST THEY WERE QUIET.
LUTHOR SEEMED TO BE LYING LOW, AND TWO YEARS EARLIER BRAINIAC'S LAST ORGANIC METAL BODY HAD BEEN POUNDED INTO A STATE BEYOND REPAIR.
AS I RECALL, SUPERMAN LATER RECOVERED EVERY FRAGMENT EXCEPT THE CREATURE'S HEAD.
THE PARASITE AND TERRA-MAN HAD DESTROYED EACH OTHER IN A LETHAL CLASH OF EGOS, AND IT SEEMED LIKE THERE WAS NOBODY LEFT TO FIGHT.
MOSTLY, SUPERMAN WORKED IN SPACE, DOING RESEARCH FOR THE GOVERNMENT.
IT WAS WHILE HE WAS STILL OUT IN SPACE RETURNING FROM SUCH A MISSION THAT WE GOT OUR FIRST TASTE OF THE CARNAGE THAT WAS TO FOLLOW...

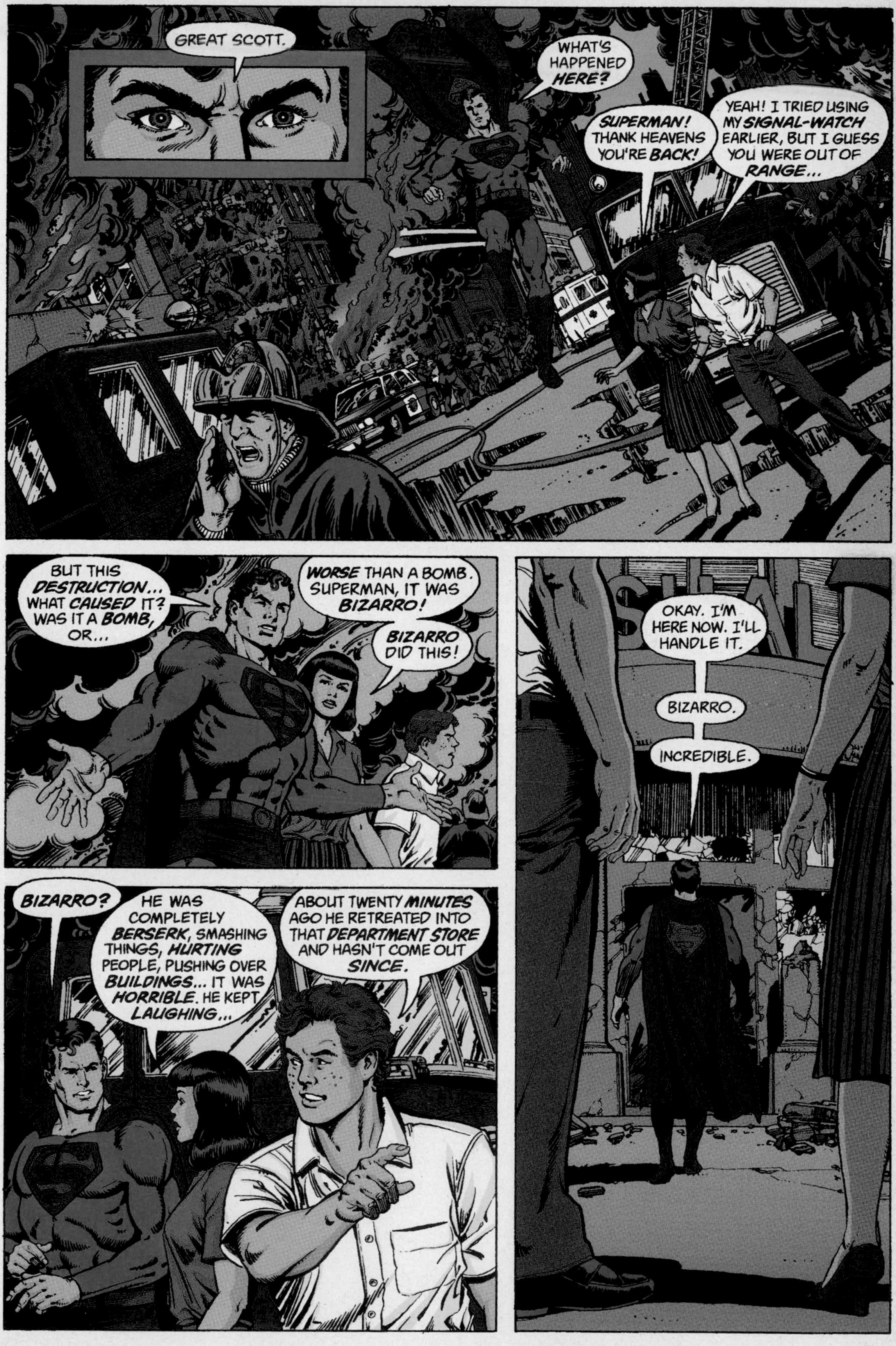
GREAT SCOTT.
WHAT'S HAPPENED HERE?
SUPERMAN! THANK HEAVENS YOU'RE BACK!
YEAH! I TRIED USING MY SIGNAL-WATCH EARLIER, BUT I GUESS YOU WERE OUT OF RANGE...
BUT THIS DESTRUCTION... WHAT CAUSED IT? WAS IT A BOMB, OR...
WORSE THAN A BOMB. SUPERMAN, IT WAS BIZARRO!
BIZARRO DID THIS!
BIZARRO?
HE WAS COMPLETELY BERSERK, SMASHING THINGS, HURTING PEOPLE, PUSHING OVER BUILDINGS... IT WAS HORRIBLE. HE KEPT LAUGHING...
ABOUT TWENTY MINUTES AGO HE RETREATED INTO THAT DEPARTMENT STORE AND HASN'T COME OUT SINCE.
OKAY. I'M HERE NOW. I'LL HANDLE IT.
BIZARRO.
INCREDIBLE.

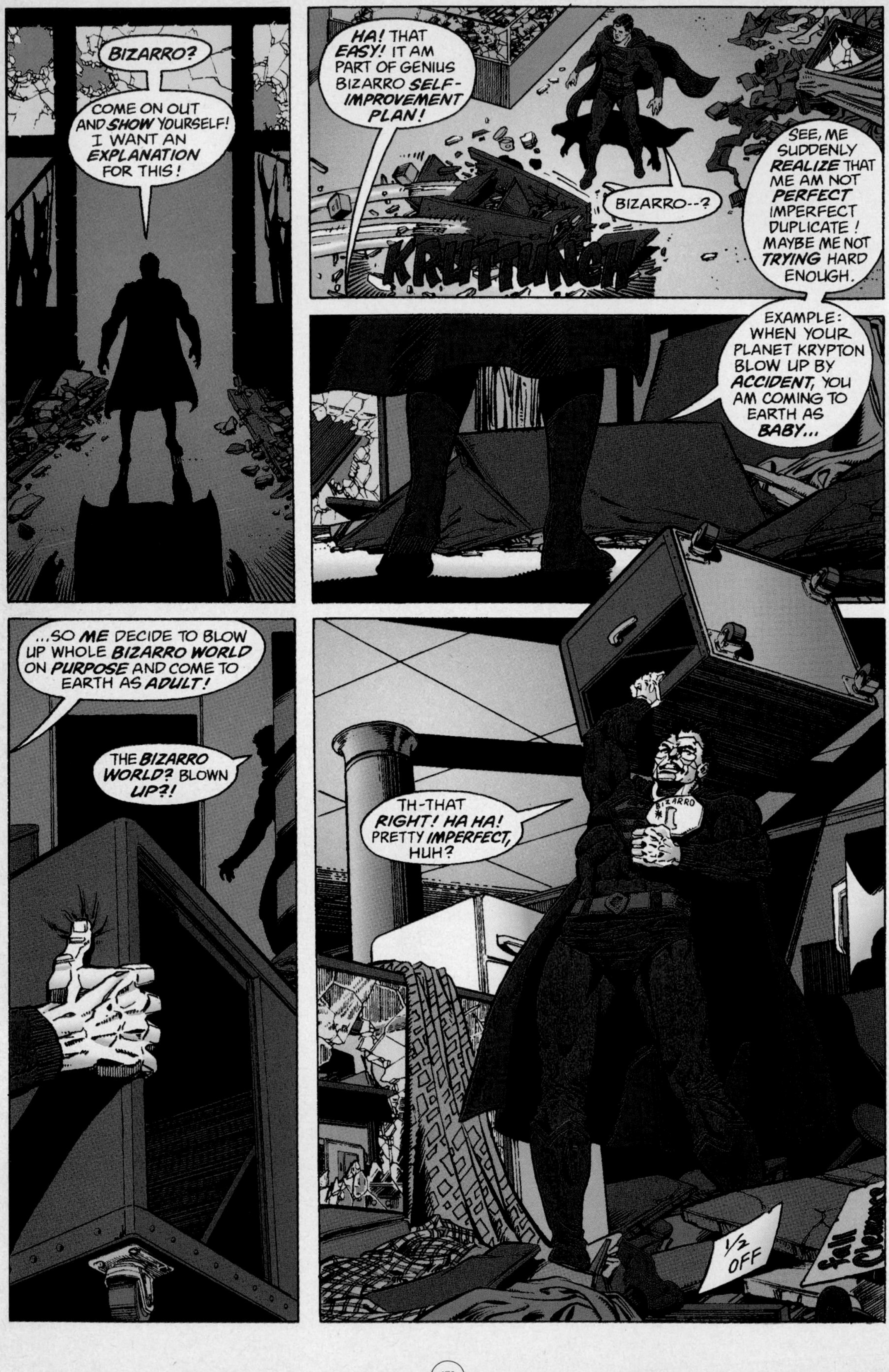
BIZARRO?
COME ON OUT AND SHOW YOURSELF! I WANT AN EXPLANATION FOR THIS!
HA! THAT EASY! IT AM PART OF GENIUS BIZARRO SELF-IMPROVEMENT PLAN!
KRUNNCH
BIZARRO--?
SEE, ME SUDDENLY REALIZE THAT ME AM NOT PERFECT IMPERFECT DUPLICATE! MAYBE ME NOT TRYING HARD ENOUGH.
EXAMPLE: WHEN YOUR PLANET KRYPTON BLOW UP BY ACCIDENT, YOU AM COMING TO EARTH AS BABY...
...SO ME DECIDE TO BLOW UP WHOLE BIZARRO WORLD ON PURPOSE AND COME TO EARTH AS ADULT!
THE BIZARRO WORLD? BLOWN UP?!
TH-THAT RIGHT! HA HA! PRETTY IMPERFECT, HUH?
BIZARRO
1/2 OFF

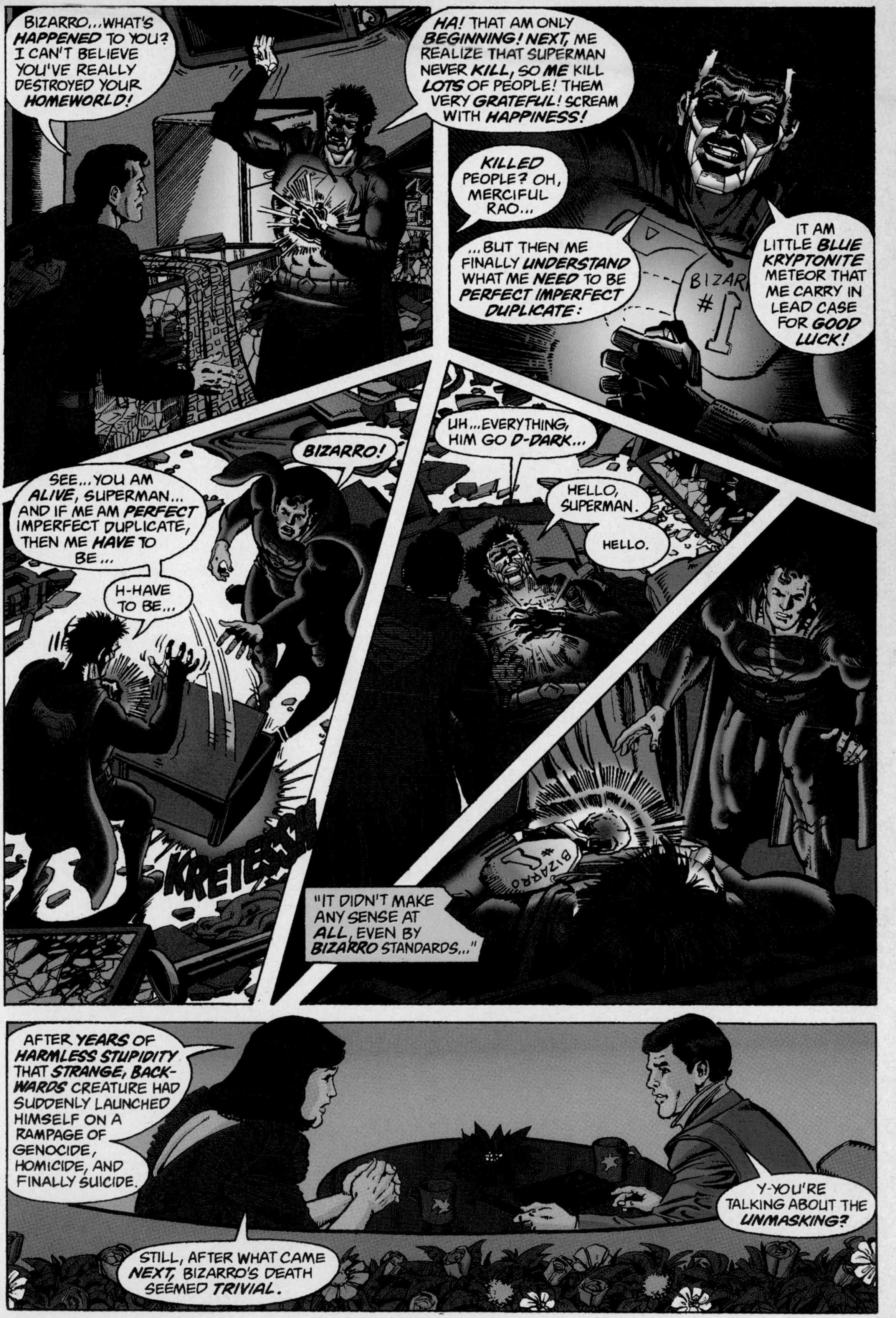
BIZARRO...WHAT'S HAPPENED TO YOU? I CAN'T BELIEVE YOU'VE REALLY DESTROYED YOUR HOMEWORLD!
HA! THAT AM ONLY BEGINNING! NEXT, ME REALIZE THAT SUPERMAN NEVER KILL, SO ME KILL LOTS OF PEOPLE! THEM VERY GRATEFUL! SCREAM WITH HAPPINESS!
KILLED PEOPLE? OH, MERCIFUL RAO...
...BUT THEN ME FINALLY UNDERSTAND WHAT ME NEED TO BE PERFECT IMPERFECT DUPLICATE:
IT AM LITTLE BLUE KRYPTONITE METEOR THAT ME CARRY IN LEAD CASE FOR GOOD LUCK!
BIZARRO!
SEE...YOU AM ALIVE, SUPERMAN... AND IF ME AM PERFECT IMPERFECT DUPLICATE, THEN ME HAVE TO BE...
H-HAVE TO BE...
KRETESSH
UH...EVERYTHING, HIM GO D-DARK...
HELLO, SUPERMAN.
HELLO.
"IT DIDN'T MAKE ANY SENSE AT ALL, EVEN BY BIZARRO STANDARDS..."
AFTER YEARS OF HARMLESS STUPIDITY THAT STRANGE, BACKWARDS CREATURE HAD SUDDENLY LAUNCHED HIMSELF ON A RAMPAGE OF GENOCIDE, HOMICIDE, AND FINALLY SUICIDE.
Y-YOU'RE TALKING ABOUT THE UNMASKING?
STILL, AFTER WHAT CAME NEXT, BIZARRO'S DEATH SEEMED TRIVIAL.

"YES. I'M TALKING ABOUT THE *UNMASKING.*"

DELIVERY FOR MR. *KENT...*

UH, *I'M* CLARK KENT. WHAT *IS* IT?

TWO *PARCELS,* DELIVERED OUTSIDE JUST NOW. THE *BIG* ONE'S REAL *HEAVY.*

CLARK, WE'RE ON THE *AIR* IN THREE MINUTES!

OH, THIS WON'T TAKE A SECOND, LANA. I'LL JUST OPEN THE *LITTLE* ONE, AND...

HMM. THAT'S ODD.

WHAT *IS* IT?

IT'S A LOT OF LITTLE *SUPERMAN ACTION FIGURES...*

OH! I'VE SEEN THOSE *AROUND!* THEY'RE *GREAT!*

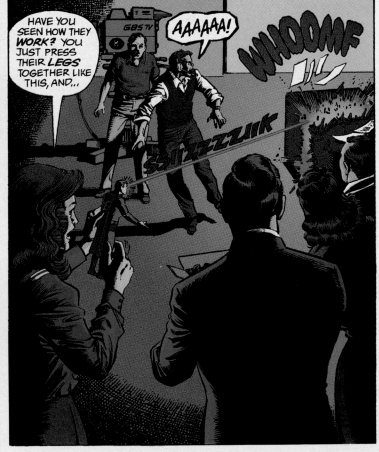

HAVE YOU SEEN HOW THEY *WORK?* YOU JUST PRESS THEIR *LEGS* TOGETHER LIKE THIS, AND...

AAAAAA!

WHOOMF

SSHZZZZIIK

172

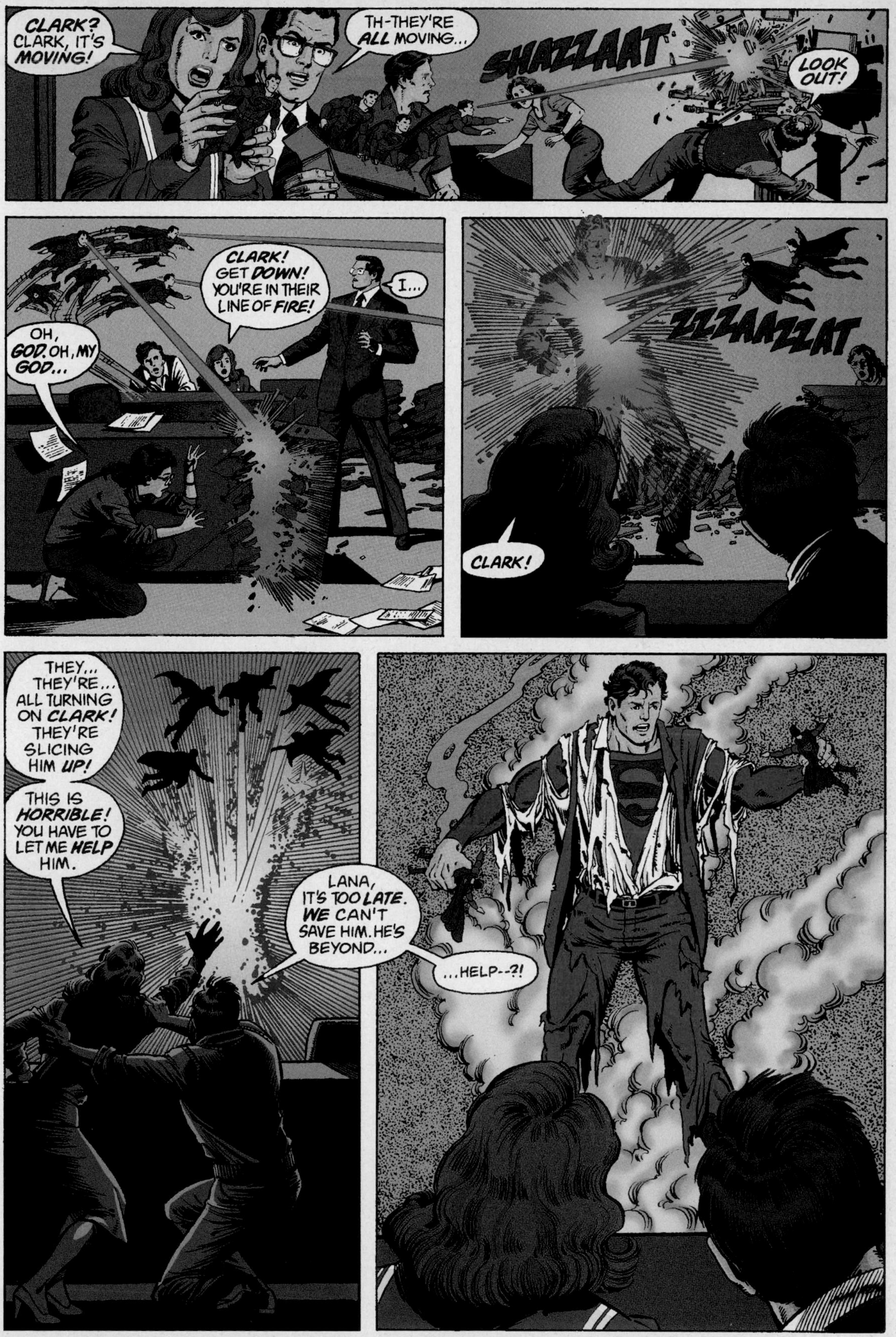
CLARK? CLARK, IT'S MOVING!
TH-THEY'RE ALL MOVING...
SHAZZAAT
LOOK OUT!
CLARK! GET DOWN! YOU'RE IN THEIR LINE OF FIRE!
I...
OH, GOD. OH, MY GOD...
ZZZAAZZAT
CLARK!
THEY... THEY'RE... ALL TURNING ON CLARK! THEY'RE SLICING HIM UP!
THIS IS HORRIBLE! YOU HAVE TO LET ME HELP HIM.
LANA, IT'S TOO LATE. WE CAN'T SAVE HIM. HE'S BEYOND...
...HELP--?!

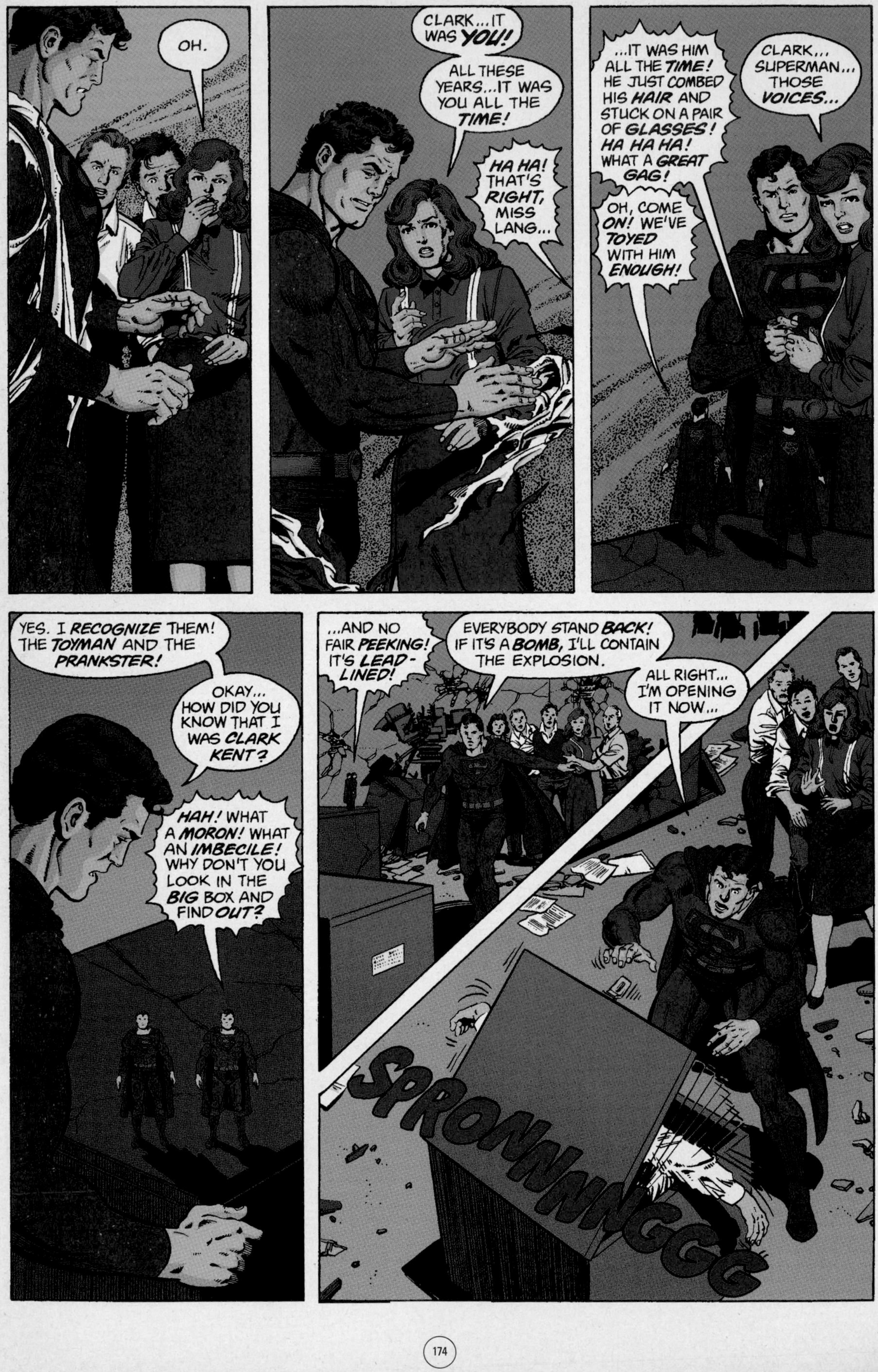
OH.
CLARK...IT WAS YOU!
ALL THESE YEARS...IT WAS YOU ALL THE TIME!
HA HA! THAT'S RIGHT, MISS LANG...
...IT WAS HIM ALL THE TIME! HE JUST COMBED HIS HAIR AND STUCK ON A PAIR OF GLASSES! HA HA HA! WHAT A GREAT GAG!
OH, COME ON! WE'VE TOYED WITH HIM ENOUGH!
CLARK... SUPERMAN... THOSE VOICES...
YES. I RECOGNIZE THEM! THE TOYMAN AND THE PRANKSTER!
OKAY... HOW DID YOU KNOW THAT I WAS CLARK KENT?
HAH! WHAT A MORON! WHAT AN IMBECILE! WHY DON'T YOU LOOK IN THE BIG BOX AND FIND OUT?
...AND NO FAIR PEEKING! IT'S LEAD-LINED!
EVERYBODY STAND BACK! IF IT'S A BOMB, I'LL CONTAIN THE EXPLOSION.
ALL RIGHT... I'M OPENING IT NOW...
SPRONNNNNGGG

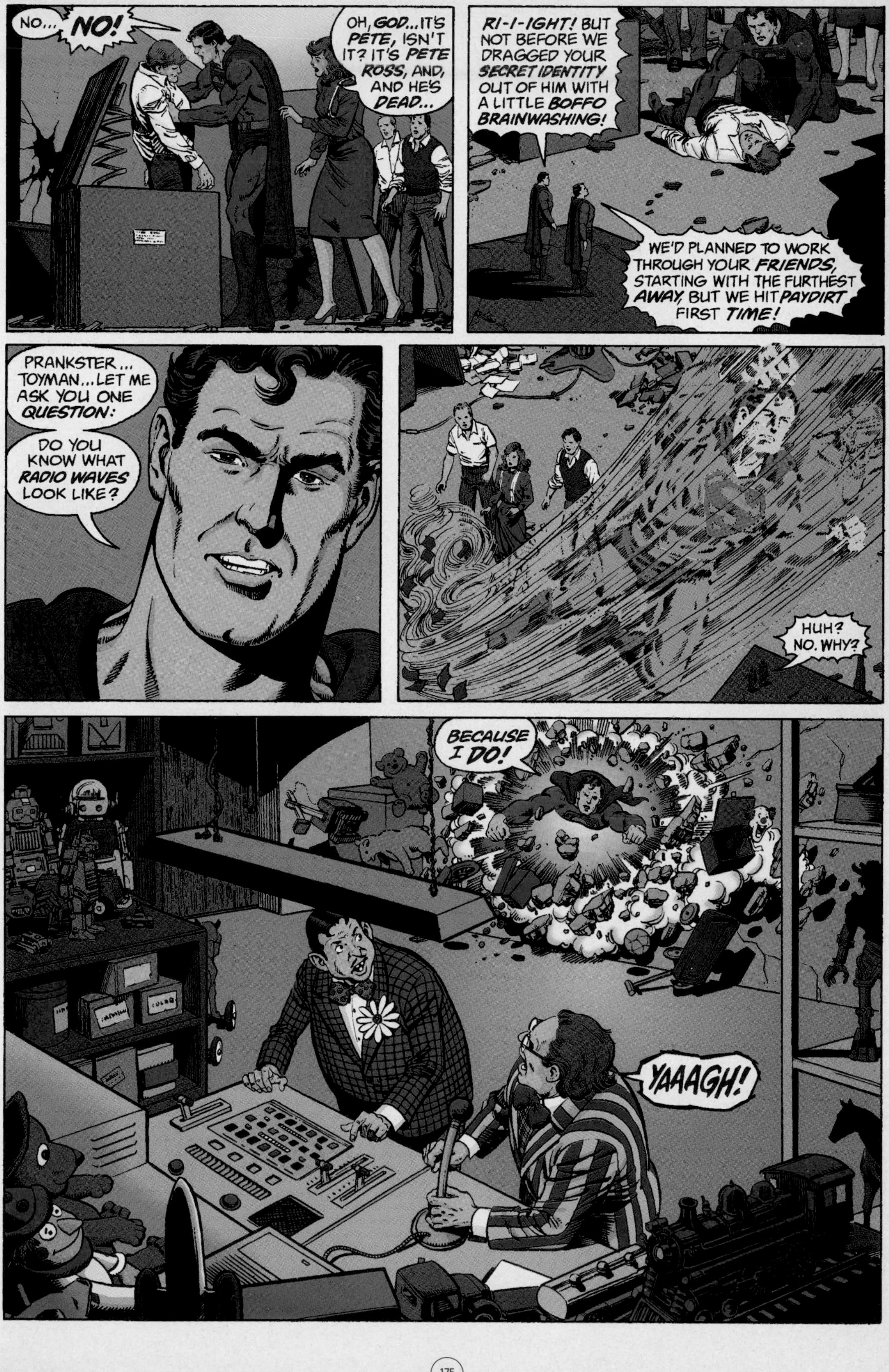
NO... NO!
OH, GOD... IT'S PETE, ISN'T IT? IT'S PETE ROSS, AND, AND HE'S DEAD...
RI-I-IGHT! BUT NOT BEFORE WE DRAGGED YOUR SECRET IDENTITY OUT OF HIM WITH A LITTLE BOFFO BRAINWASHING!
WE'D PLANNED TO WORK THROUGH YOUR FRIENDS, STARTING WITH THE FURTHEST AWAY, BUT WE HIT PAYDIRT FIRST TIME!
PRANKSTER... TOYMAN... LET ME ASK YOU ONE QUESTION:
DO YOU KNOW WHAT RADIO WAVES LOOK LIKE?
HUH? NO. WHY?
BECAUSE I DO!
YAAAGH!

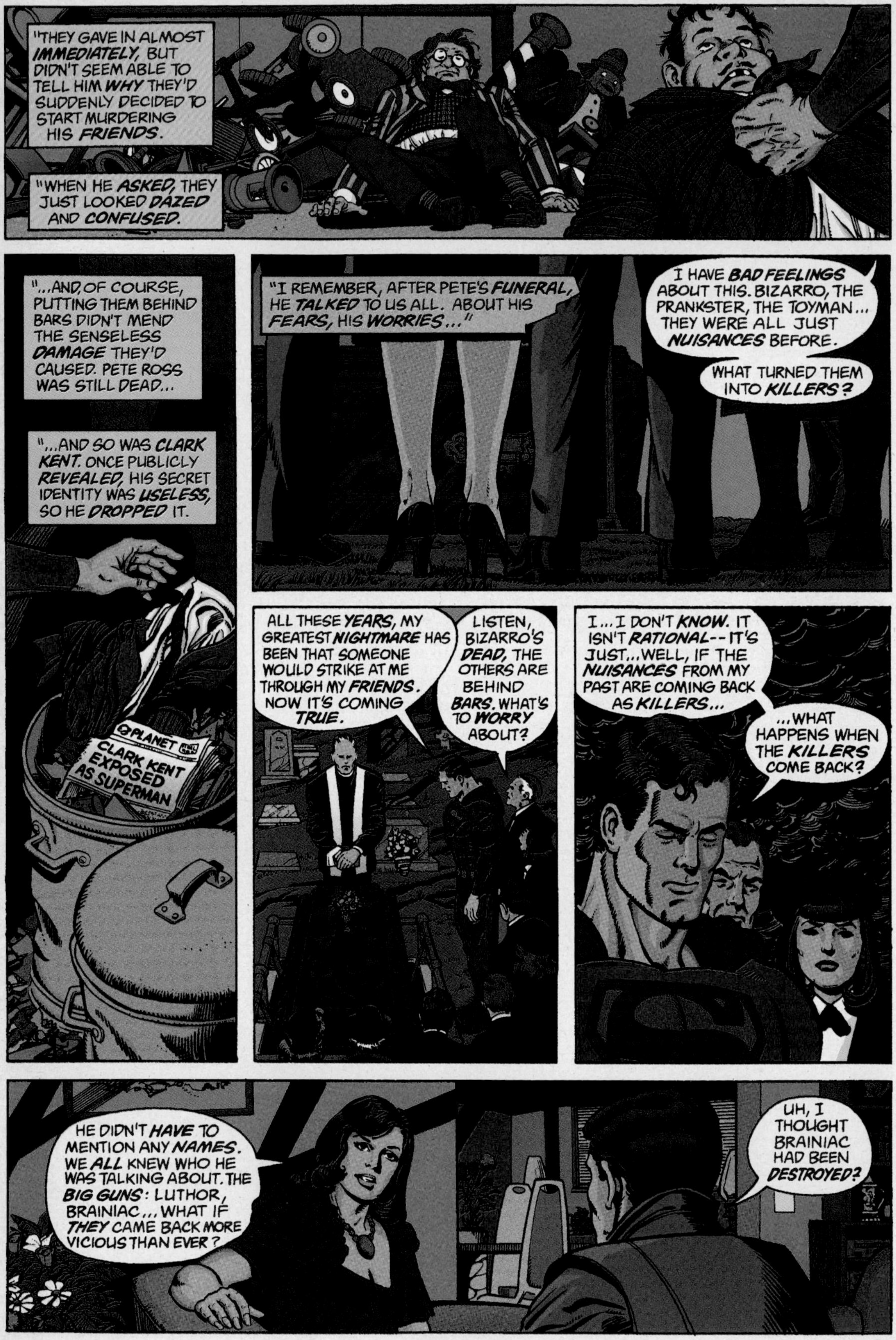
"THEY GAVE IN ALMOST IMMEDIATELY, BUT DIDN'T SEEM ABLE TO TELL HIM WHY THEY'D SUDDENLY DECIDED TO START MURDERING HIS FRIENDS.
"WHEN HE ASKED, THEY JUST LOOKED DAZED AND CONFUSED.
"...AND, OF COURSE, PUTTING THEM BEHIND BARS DIDN'T MEND THE SENSELESS DAMAGE THEY'D CAUSED. PETE ROSS WAS STILL DEAD...
"...AND SO WAS CLARK KENT. ONCE PUBLICLY REVEALED, HIS SECRET IDENTITY WAS USELESS, SO HE DROPPED IT.
PLANET
CLARK KENT EXPOSED AS SUPERMAN
"I REMEMBER, AFTER PETE'S FUNERAL, HE TALKED TO US ALL. ABOUT HIS FEARS, HIS WORRIES..."
I HAVE BAD FEELINGS ABOUT THIS. BIZARRO, THE PRANKSTER, THE TOYMAN... THEY WERE ALL JUST NUISANCES BEFORE.
WHAT TURNED THEM INTO KILLERS?
ALL THESE YEARS, MY GREATEST NIGHTMARE HAS BEEN THAT SOMEONE WOULD STRIKE AT ME THROUGH MY FRIENDS. NOW IT'S COMING TRUE.
LISTEN, BIZARRO'S DEAD, THE OTHERS ARE BEHIND BARS. WHAT'S TO WORRY ABOUT?
I... I DON'T KNOW. IT ISN'T RATIONAL-- IT'S JUST... WELL, IF THE NUISANCES FROM MY PAST ARE COMING BACK AS KILLERS...
...WHAT HAPPENS WHEN THE KILLERS COME BACK?
HE DIDN'T HAVE TO MENTION ANY NAMES. WE ALL KNEW WHO HE WAS TALKING ABOUT. THE BIG GUNS: LUTHOR, BRAINIAC... WHAT IF THEY CAME BACK MORE VICIOUS THAN EVER?
UH, I THOUGHT BRAINIAC HAD BEEN DESTROYED?

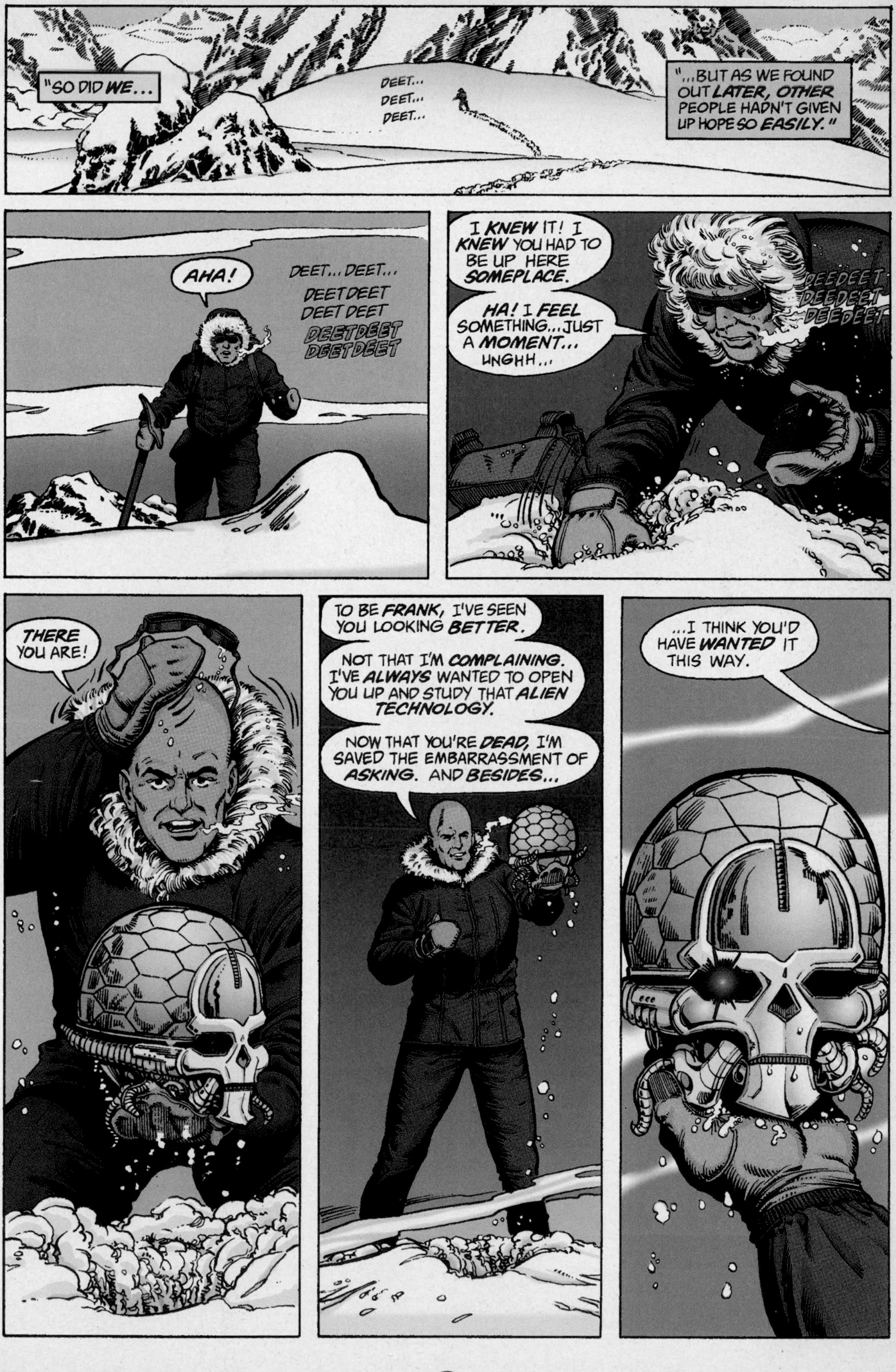
"SO DID WE...
DEET... DEET... DEET...
"...BUT AS WE FOUND OUT LATER, OTHER PEOPLE HADN'T GIVEN UP HOPE SO EASILY."
AHA!
DEET... DEET... DEET DEET DEET DEET DEETDEET DEETDEET
I KNEW IT! I KNEW YOU HAD TO BE UP HERE SOMEPLACE.
HA! I FEEL SOMETHING... JUST A MOMENT... UNGHH...
DEEDEET DEEDEET DEEDEET
THERE YOU ARE!
TO BE FRANK, I'VE SEEN YOU LOOKING BETTER.
NOT THAT I'M COMPLAINING. I'VE ALWAYS WANTED TO OPEN YOU UP AND STUDY THAT ALIEN TECHNOLOGY.
NOW THAT YOU'RE DEAD, I'M SAVED THE EMBARRASSMENT OF ASKING. AND BESIDES...
...I THINK YOU'D HAVE WANTED IT THIS WAY.

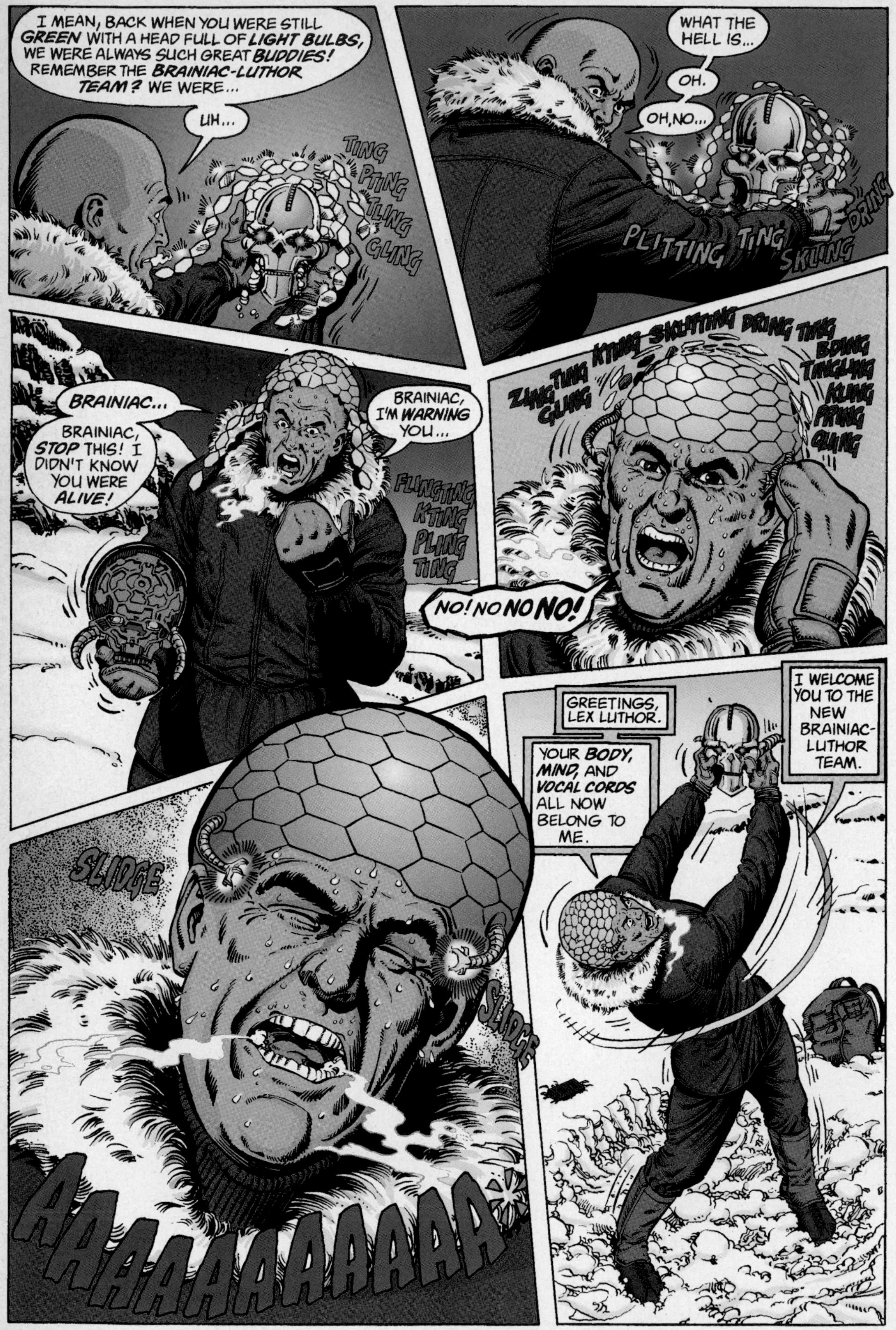
I MEAN, BACK WHEN YOU WERE STILL GREEN WITH A HEAD FULL OF LIGHT BULBS, WE WERE ALWAYS SUCH GREAT BUDDIES! REMEMBER THE BRAINIAC-LUTHOR TEAM? WE WERE...
UH...
TING PTING TLING GLING
WHAT THE HELL IS...
OH.
OH, NO...
PLITTING TING SKLING DRING
BRAINIAC...
BRAINIAC, STOP THIS! I DIDN'T KNOW YOU WERE ALIVE!
BRAINIAC, I'M WARNING YOU...
FLINGTING KTING PLING TING
ZING TING GLING KTING SKLITTING DRING TING BDING TINGLING KLING PRING GLING
NO! NO NO NO!
SLIDGE
SLIDGE
AAAAAAAAAAAA
GREETINGS, LEX LUTHOR.
YOUR BODY, MIND, AND VOCAL CORDS ALL NOW BELONG TO ME.
I WELCOME YOU TO THE NEW BRAINIAC-LUTHOR TEAM.

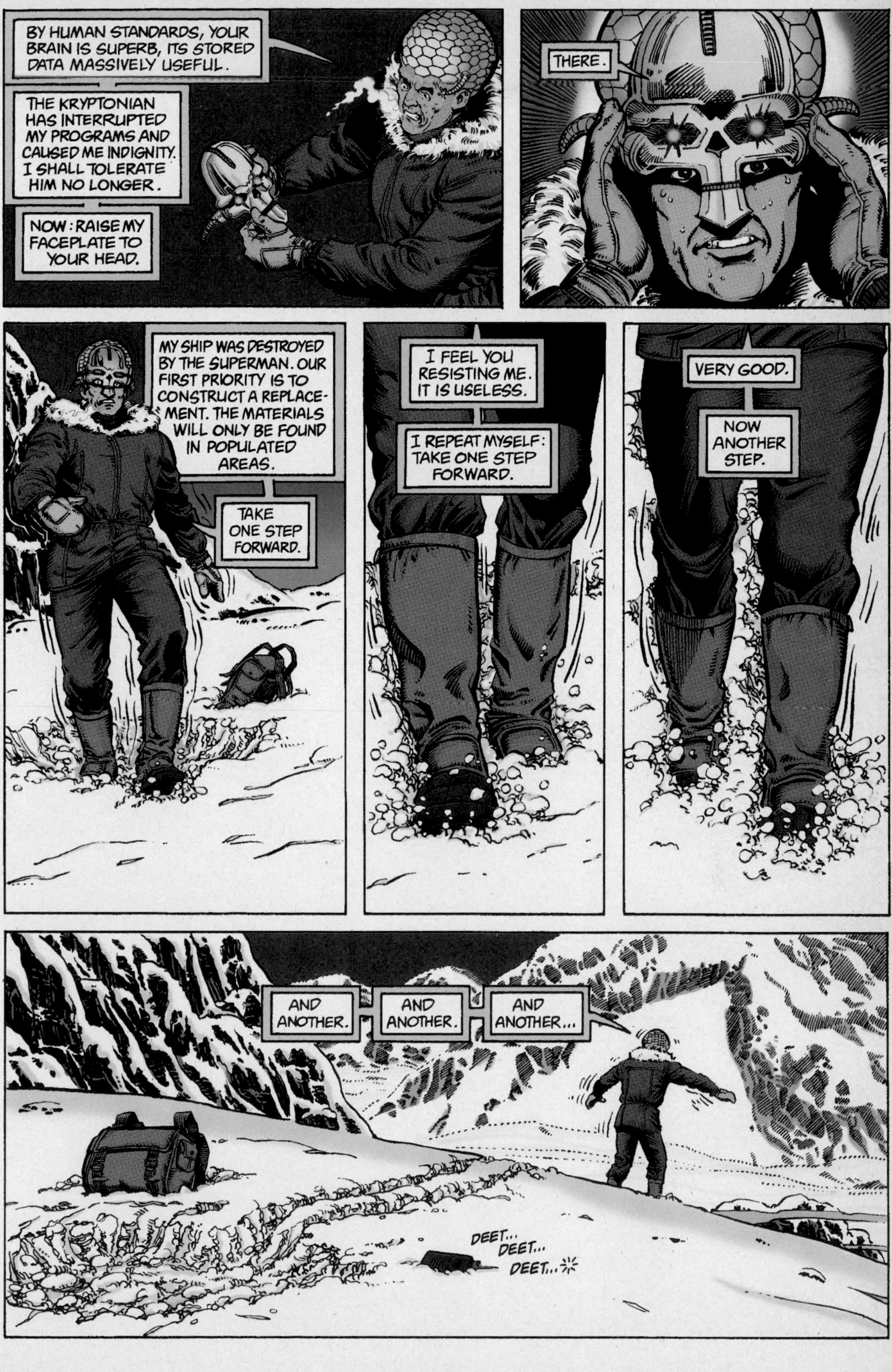
BY HUMAN STANDARDS, YOUR BRAIN IS SUPERB, ITS STORED DATA MASSIVELY USEFUL.
THE KRYPTONIAN HAS INTERRUPTED MY PROGRAMS AND CAUSED ME INDIGNITY. I SHALL TOLERATE HIM NO LONGER.
NOW: RAISE MY FACEPLATE TO YOUR HEAD.
THERE.
MY SHIP WAS DESTROYED BY THE SUPERMAN. OUR FIRST PRIORITY IS TO CONSTRUCT A REPLACEMENT. THE MATERIALS WILL ONLY BE FOUND IN POPULATED AREAS.
TAKE ONE STEP FORWARD.
I FEEL YOU RESISTING ME. IT IS USELESS.
I REPEAT MYSELF: TAKE ONE STEP FORWARD.
VERY GOOD.
NOW ANOTHER STEP.
AND ANOTHER.
AND ANOTHER.
AND ANOTHER...
DEET... DEET... DEET...

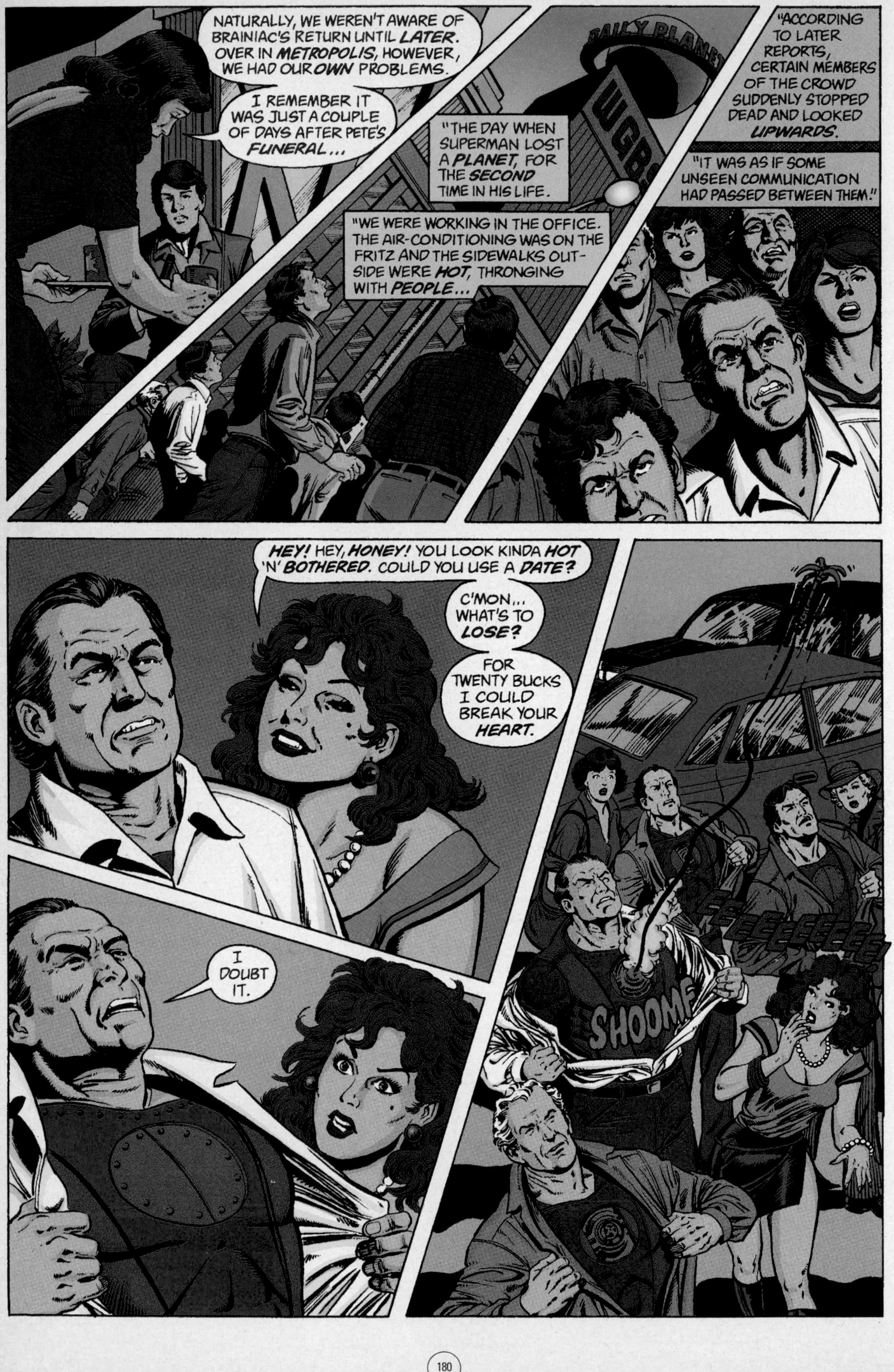
NATURALLY, WE WEREN'T AWARE OF BRAINIAC'S RETURN UNTIL LATER. OVER IN METROPOLIS, HOWEVER, WE HAD OUR OWN PROBLEMS.
I REMEMBER IT WAS JUST A COUPLE OF DAYS AFTER PETE'S FUNERAL...
DAILY PLANET
WGBS
"THE DAY WHEN SUPERMAN LOST A PLANET, FOR THE SECOND TIME IN HIS LIFE.
"WE WERE WORKING IN THE OFFICE. THE AIR-CONDITIONING WAS ON THE FRITZ AND THE SIDEWALKS OUTSIDE WERE HOT, THRONGING WITH PEOPLE...
"ACCORDING TO LATER REPORTS, CERTAIN MEMBERS OF THE CROWD SUDDENLY STOPPED DEAD AND LOOKED UPWARDS.
"IT WAS AS IF SOME UNSEEN COMMUNICATION HAD PASSED BETWEEN THEM."
HEY! HEY, HONEY! YOU LOOK KINDA HOT 'N' BOTHERED. COULD YOU USE A DATE?
C'MON... WHAT'S TO LOSE?
FOR TWENTY BUCKS I COULD BREAK YOUR HEART.
I DOUBT IT.
SHOOMF
EEEEEEEEE

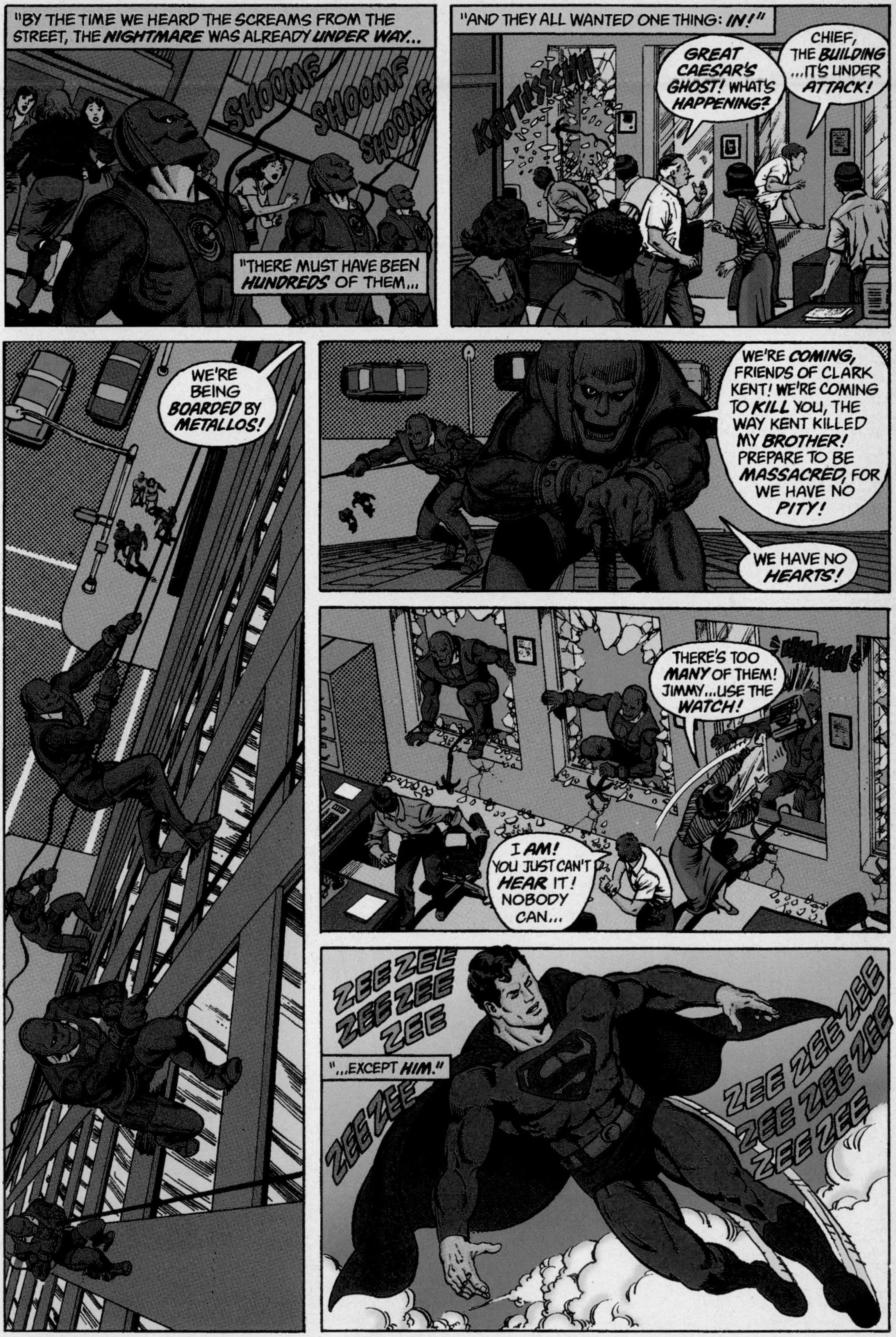
"BY THE TIME WE HEARD THE SCREAMS FROM THE STREET, THE NIGHTMARE WAS ALREADY UNDER WAY...
SHOOMF SHOOMF SHOOMF
"THERE MUST HAVE BEEN HUNDREDS OF THEM...
"AND THEY ALL WANTED ONE THING: IN!"
KRITTSSSHH
GREAT CAESAR'S GHOST! WHAT'S HAPPENING?
CHIEF, THE BUILDING ...IT'S UNDER ATTACK!
WE'RE BEING BOARDED BY METALLOS!
WE'RE COMING, FRIENDS OF CLARK KENT! WE'RE COMING TO KILL YOU, THE WAY KENT KILLED MY BROTHER! PREPARE TO BE MASSACRED, FOR WE HAVE NO PITY!
WE HAVE NO HEARTS!
THERE'S TOO MANY OF THEM! JIMMY...USE THE WATCH!
I AM! YOU JUST CAN'T HEAR IT! NOBODY CAN...
ZEE ZEE ZEE ZEE ZEE
"...EXCEPT HIM."
ZEE ZEE
ZEE ZEE ZEE ZEE ZEE ZEE ZEE ZEE

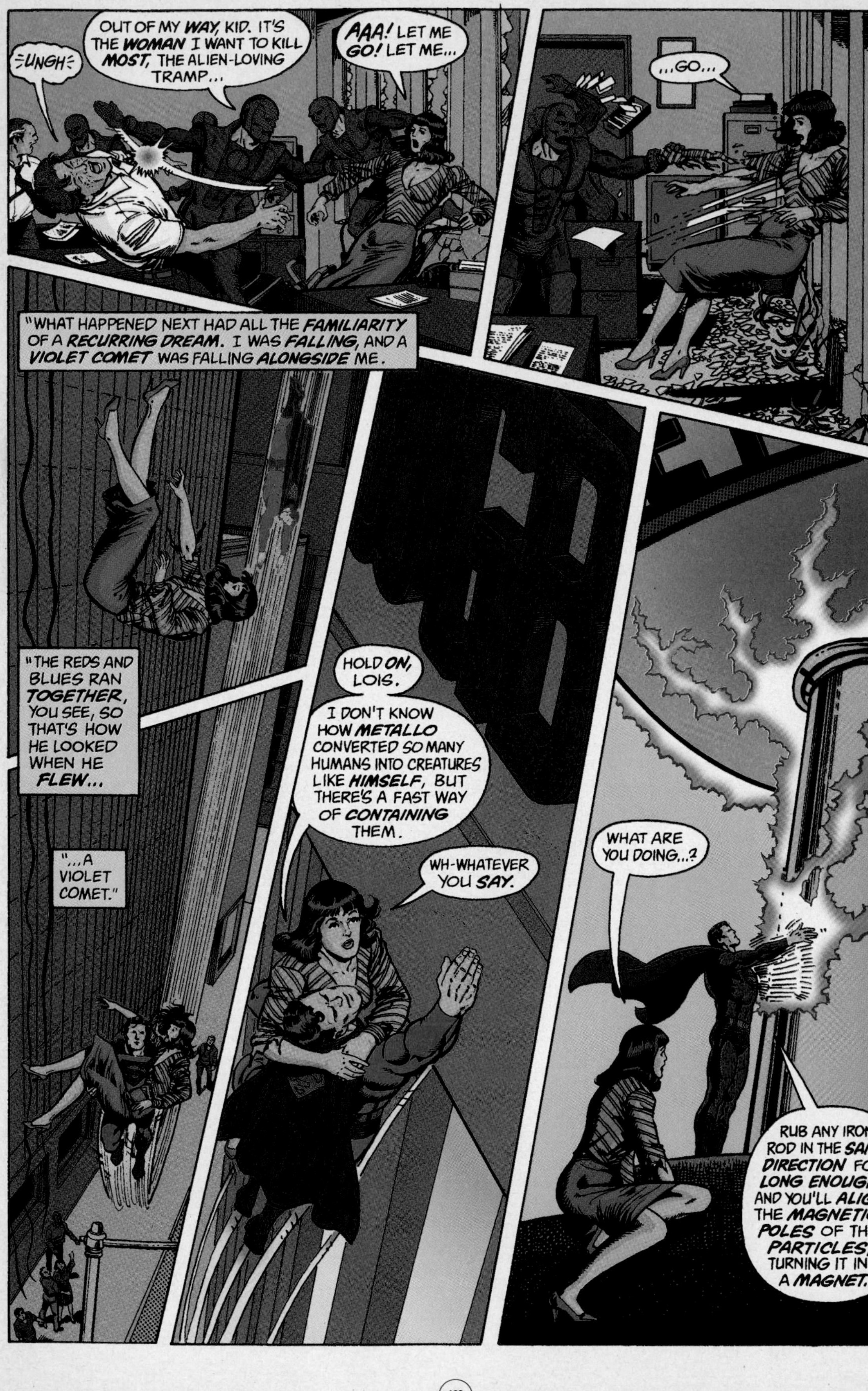
UNGH
OUT OF MY WAY, KID. IT'S THE WOMAN I WANT TO KILL MOST, THE ALIEN-LOVING TRAMP...
AAA! LET ME GO! LET ME...
...GO...
"WHAT HAPPENED NEXT HAD ALL THE FAMILIARITY OF A RECURRING DREAM. I WAS FALLING, AND A VIOLET COMET WAS FALLING ALONGSIDE ME.
"THE REDS AND BLUES RAN TOGETHER, YOU SEE, SO THAT'S HOW HE LOOKED WHEN HE FLEW...
"...A VIOLET COMET."
HOLD ON, LOIS.
I DON'T KNOW HOW METALLO CONVERTED SO MANY HUMANS INTO CREATURES LIKE HIMSELF, BUT THERE'S A FAST WAY OF CONTAINING THEM.
WH-WHATEVER YOU SAY.
WHAT ARE YOU DOING...?
RUB ANY IRON ROD IN THE SAME DIRECTION FOR LONG ENOUGH AND YOU'LL ALIGN THE MAGNETIC POLES OF THE PARTICLES, TURNING IT INTO A MAGNET...

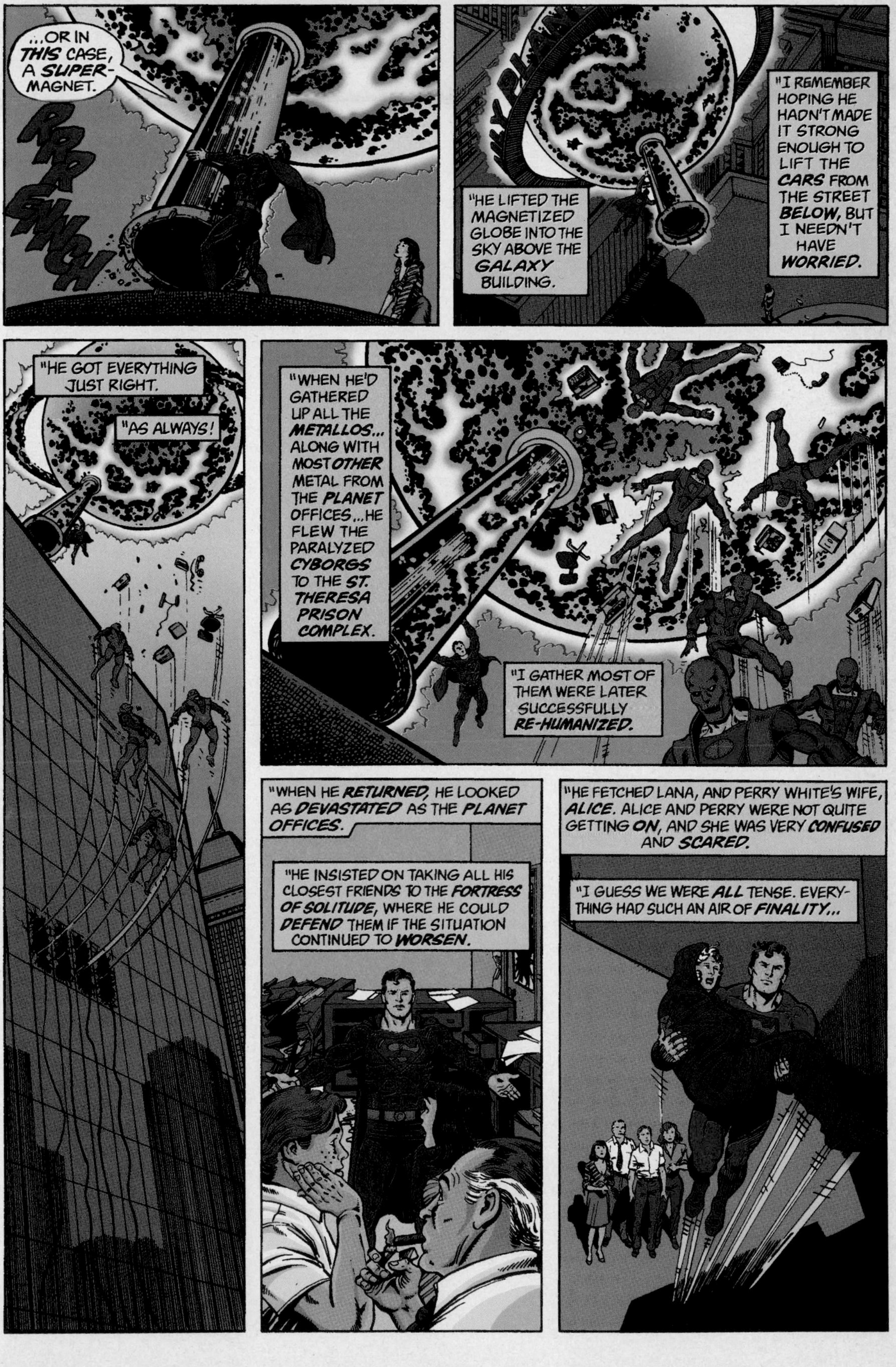
...OR IN THIS CASE, A SUPER-MAGNET.
RRRGNNCH
"HE LIFTED THE MAGNETIZED GLOBE INTO THE SKY ABOVE THE GALAXY BUILDING.
"I REMEMBER HOPING HE HADN'T MADE IT STRONG ENOUGH TO LIFT THE CARS FROM THE STREET BELOW, BUT I NEEDN'T HAVE WORRIED.
"HE GOT EVERYTHING JUST RIGHT.
"AS ALWAYS!
"WHEN HE'D GATHERED UP ALL THE METALLOS... ALONG WITH MOST OTHER METAL FROM THE PLANET OFFICES...HE FLEW THE PARALYZED CYBORGS TO THE ST. THERESA PRISON COMPLEX.
"I GATHER MOST OF THEM WERE LATER SUCCESSFULLY RE-HUMANIZED.
"WHEN HE RETURNED, HE LOOKED AS DEVASTATED AS THE PLANET OFFICES.
"HE INSISTED ON TAKING ALL HIS CLOSEST FRIENDS TO THE FORTRESS OF SOLITUDE, WHERE HE COULD DEFEND THEM IF THE SITUATION CONTINUED TO WORSEN.
"HE FETCHED LANA, AND PERRY WHITE'S WIFE, ALICE. ALICE AND PERRY WERE NOT QUITE GETTING ON, AND SHE WAS VERY CONFUSED AND SCARED.
"I GUESS WE WERE ALL TENSE. EVERY-THING HAD SUCH AN AIR OF FINALITY...

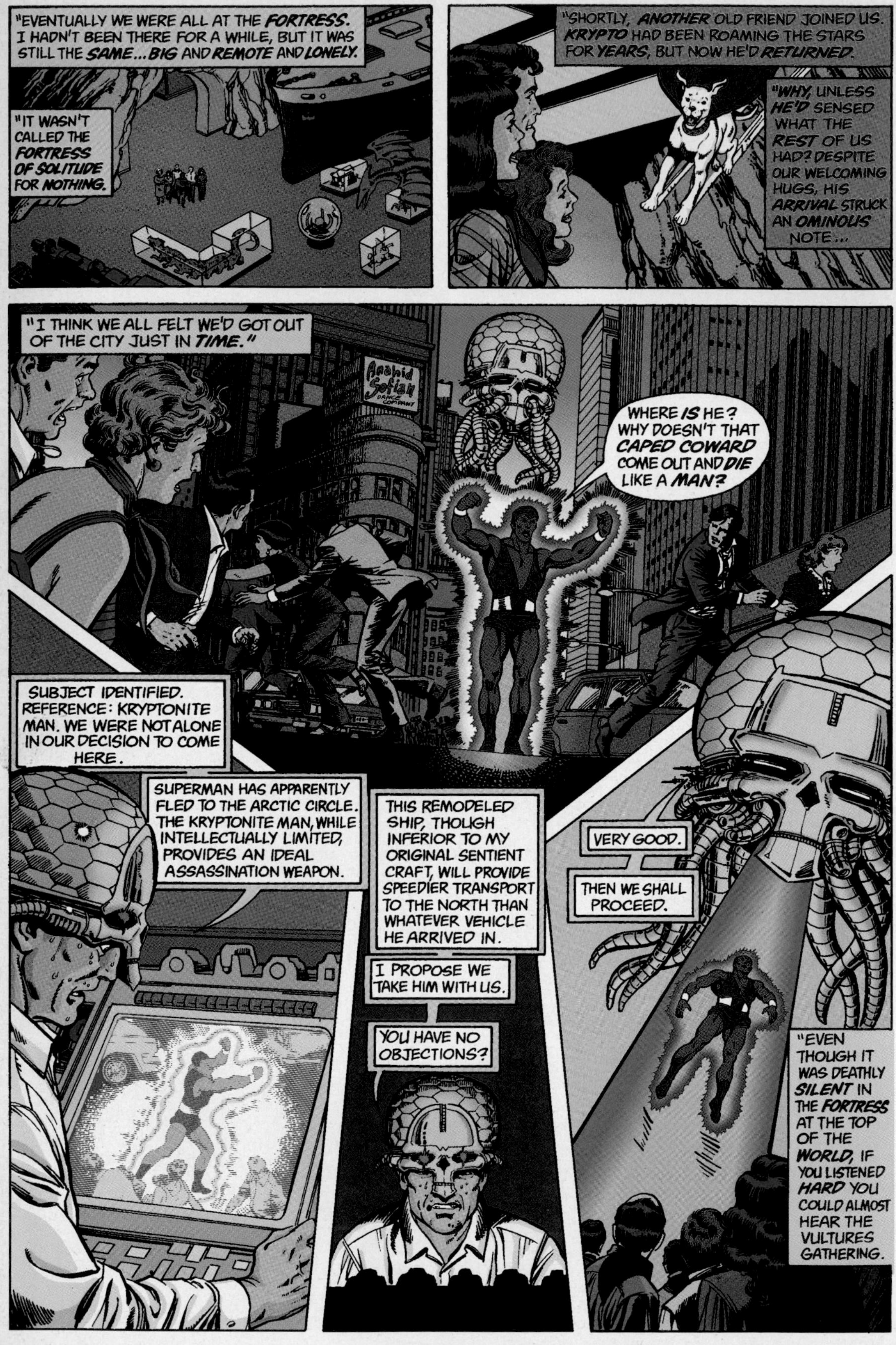
"EVENTUALLY WE WERE ALL AT THE FORTRESS. I HADN'T BEEN THERE FOR A WHILE, BUT IT WAS STILL THE SAME... BIG AND REMOTE AND LONELY.
"IT WASN'T CALLED THE FORTRESS OF SOLITUDE FOR NOTHING.
"SHORTLY, ANOTHER OLD FRIEND JOINED US. KRYPTO HAD BEEN ROAMING THE STARS FOR YEARS, BUT NOW HE'D RETURNED.
"WHY, UNLESS HE'D SENSED WHAT THE REST OF US HAD? DESPITE OUR WELCOMING HUGS, HIS ARRIVAL STRUCK AN OMINOUS NOTE...
"I THINK WE ALL FELT WE'D GOT OUT OF THE CITY JUST IN TIME."
WHERE IS HE? WHY DOESN'T THAT CAPED COWARD COME OUT AND DIE LIKE A MAN?
SUBJECT IDENTIFIED. REFERENCE: KRYPTONITE MAN. WE WERE NOT ALONE IN OUR DECISION TO COME HERE.
SUPERMAN HAS APPARENTLY FLED TO THE ARCTIC CIRCLE. THE KRYPTONITE MAN, WHILE INTELLECTUALLY LIMITED, PROVIDES AN IDEAL ASSASSINATION WEAPON.
THIS REMODELED SHIP, THOUGH INFERIOR TO MY ORIGINAL SENTIENT CRAFT, WILL PROVIDE SPEEDIER TRANSPORT TO THE NORTH THAN WHATEVER VEHICLE HE ARRIVED IN.
I PROPOSE WE TAKE HIM WITH US.
YOU HAVE NO OBJECTIONS?
VERY GOOD.
THEN WE SHALL PROCEED.
"EVEN THOUGH IT WAS DEATHLY SILENT IN THE FORTRESS AT THE TOP OF THE WORLD, IF YOU LISTENED HARD YOU COULD ALMOST HEAR THE VULTURES GATHERING.

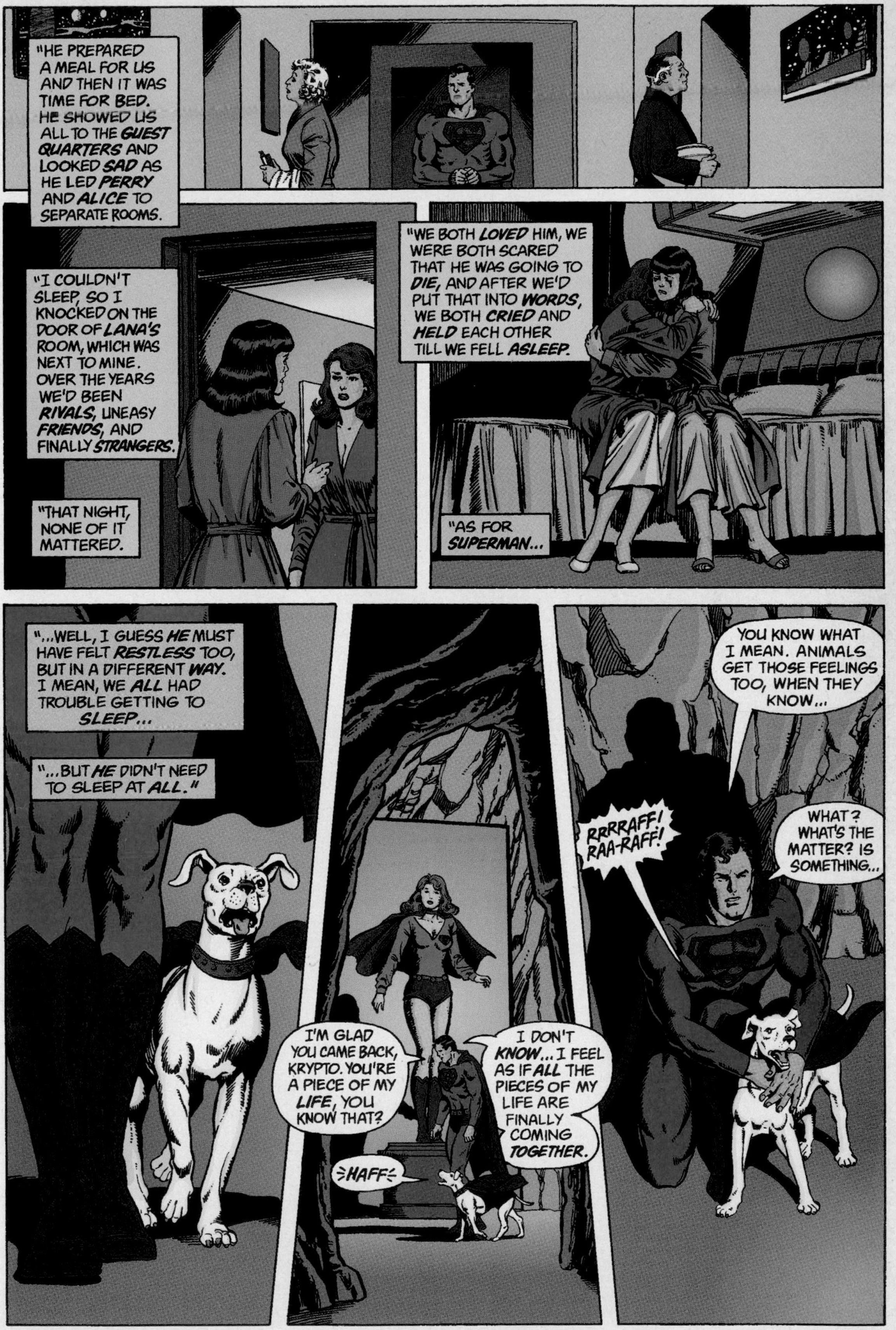
"HE PREPARED A MEAL FOR US AND THEN IT WAS TIME FOR BED. HE SHOWED US ALL TO THE GUEST QUARTERS AND LOOKED SAD AS HE LED PERRY AND ALICE TO SEPARATE ROOMS.
"I COULDN'T SLEEP, SO I KNOCKED ON THE DOOR OF LANA'S ROOM, WHICH WAS NEXT TO MINE. OVER THE YEARS WE'D BEEN RIVALS, UNEASY FRIENDS, AND FINALLY STRANGERS.
"THAT NIGHT, NONE OF IT MATTERED.
"WE BOTH LOVED HIM, WE WERE BOTH SCARED THAT HE WAS GOING TO DIE, AND AFTER WE'D PUT THAT INTO WORDS, WE BOTH CRIED AND HELD EACH OTHER TILL WE FELL ASLEEP.
"AS FOR SUPERMAN...
"...WELL, I GUESS HE MUST HAVE FELT RESTLESS TOO, BUT IN A DIFFERENT WAY. I MEAN, WE ALL HAD TROUBLE GETTING TO SLEEP...
"...BUT HE DIDN'T NEED TO SLEEP AT ALL."
I'M GLAD YOU CAME BACK, KRYPTO. YOU'RE A PIECE OF MY LIFE, YOU KNOW THAT?
HAFF
I DON'T KNOW... I FEEL AS IF ALL THE PIECES OF MY LIFE ARE FINALLY COMING TOGETHER.
RRRRAFF! RAA-RAFF!
YOU KNOW WHAT I MEAN. ANIMALS GET THOSE FEELINGS TOO, WHEN THEY KNOW...
WHAT? WHAT'S THE MATTER? IS SOMETHING...

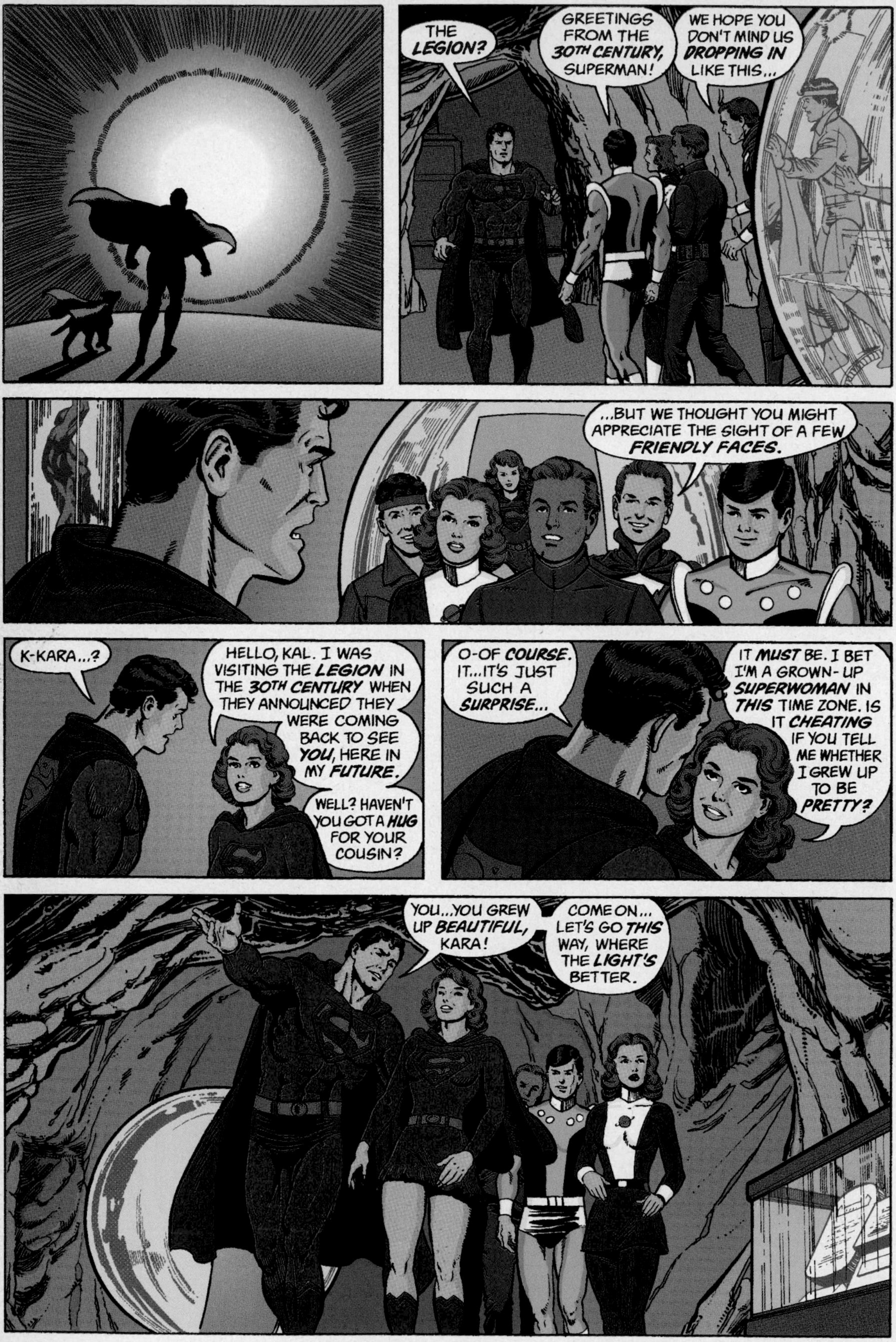
THE LEGION?
GREETINGS FROM THE 30TH CENTURY, SUPERMAN!
WE HOPE YOU DON'T MIND US DROPPING IN LIKE THIS...
...BUT WE THOUGHT YOU MIGHT APPRECIATE THE SIGHT OF A FEW FRIENDLY FACES.
K-KARA...?
HELLO, KAL. I WAS VISITING THE LEGION IN THE 30TH CENTURY WHEN THEY ANNOUNCED THEY WERE COMING BACK TO SEE YOU, HERE IN MY FUTURE.
WELL? HAVEN'T YOU GOT A HUG FOR YOUR COUSIN?
O-OF COURSE. IT...IT'S JUST SUCH A SURPRISE...
IT MUST BE. I BET I'M A GROWN-UP SUPERWOMAN IN THIS TIME ZONE. IS IT CHEATING IF YOU TELL ME WHETHER I GREW UP TO BE PRETTY?
YOU...YOU GREW UP BEAUTIFUL, KARA!
COME ON... LET'S GO THIS WAY, WHERE THE LIGHT'S BETTER.

HELLO, KRYPTO! HELLO, BOY! I HOPE YOU AND *STREAKY* AREN'T STILL *SCRAPPING* ALL THE TIME!

SUPERMAN? COULD I HAVE A WORD?

YES. YES, OF COURSE, BRAINIAC.

SUPERMAN, WE WANTED TO PRESENT YOU WITH *THIS*, ON BEHALF OF...

BRAINIAC, WHAT'S THE *MEANING* OF THIS?

YOU *KNOW* SUPERGIRL IS *DEAD* IN THIS ERA. YOU'RE FROM THE *FUTURE*! IT'S *HISTORY* TO YOU!

I--I'M *SORRY*. SHE *INSISTED* ON COMING. I REALIZE HOW *DISTRESSING* IT MUST BE...

I *DOUBT* IT! YOU TALK *CALMLY* TO US, ALL THE WHILE KNOWING OUR *DEATH DATES* AS ANCIENT HISTORY. HOW CAN YOU *DO* IT?

SUPERMAN, YOU ARE BEING *UNFAIR*.

IN *YOUR* PAST, AS *SUPERBOY*, YOU HAVE SEEN SOME OF *OUR* FUTURE. WOULD *YOU* TELL *US* IF YOU KNEW OF SOME *UNAVOIDABLE DOOM* AWAITING US?

NO. NO, YOU'RE *RIGHT*.

FORGIVE ME, BRAINIAC. I'M JUST UNDER *PRESSURE* AT THE MOMENT.

OF COURSE.

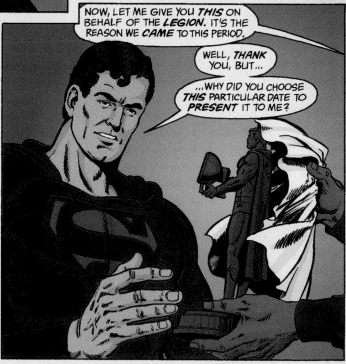

NOW, LET ME GIVE YOU *THIS* ON BEHALF OF THE *LEGION*. IT'S THE REASON WE *CAME* TO THIS PERIOD.

WELL, *THANK* YOU, BUT...

...WHY DID YOU CHOOSE *THIS* PARTICULAR DATE TO *PRESENT* IT TO ME?

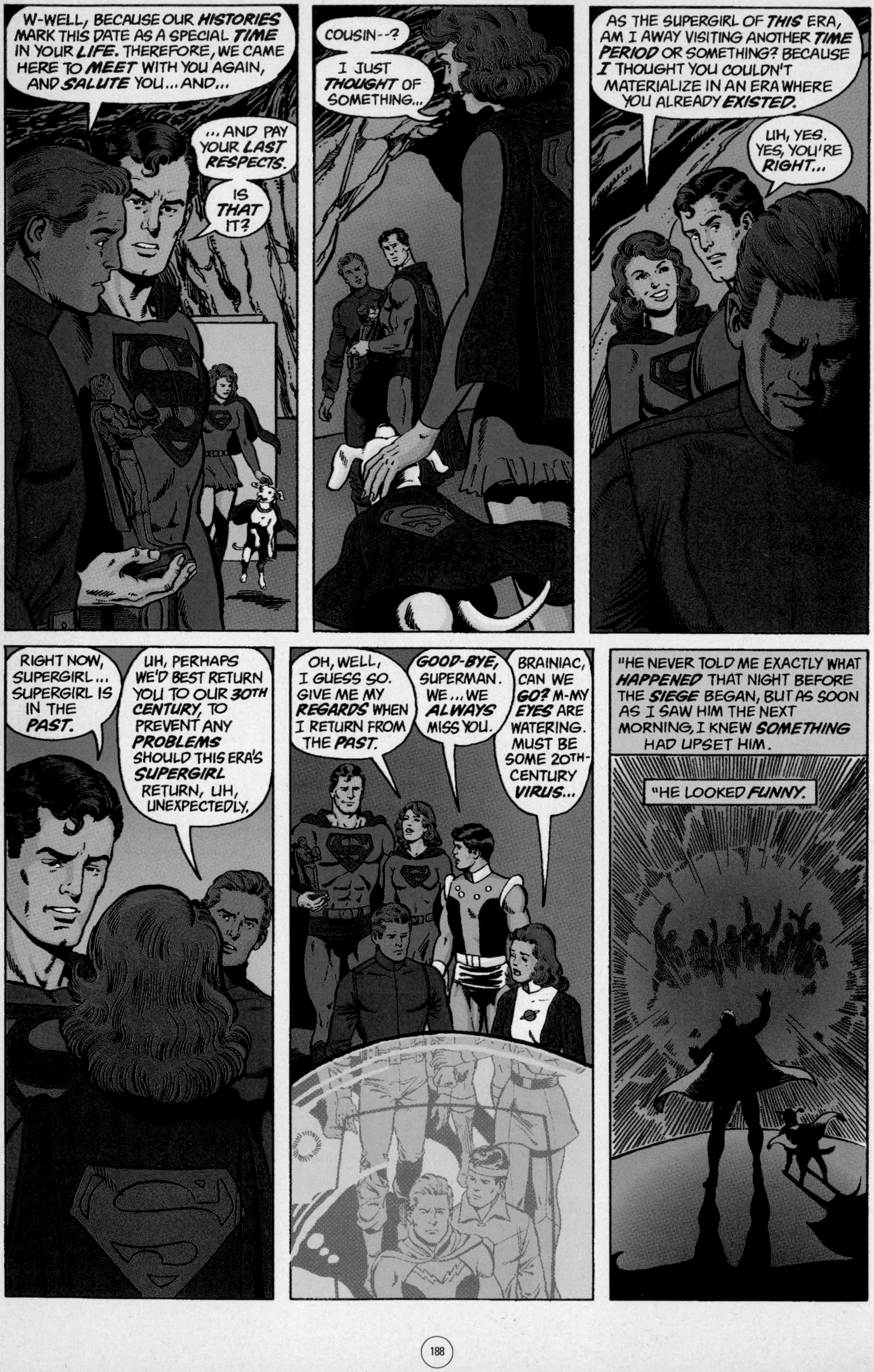
W-WELL, BECAUSE OUR HISTORIES MARK THIS DATE AS A SPECIAL TIME IN YOUR LIFE. THEREFORE, WE CAME HERE TO MEET WITH YOU AGAIN, AND SALUTE YOU... AND...
...AND PAY YOUR LAST RESPECTS.
IS THAT IT?
COUSIN--?
I JUST THOUGHT OF SOMETHING...
AS THE SUPERGIRL OF THIS ERA, AM I AWAY VISITING ANOTHER TIME PERIOD OR SOMETHING? BECAUSE I THOUGHT YOU COULDN'T MATERIALIZE IN AN ERA WHERE YOU ALREADY EXISTED.
UH, YES. YES, YOU'RE RIGHT...
RIGHT NOW, SUPERGIRL... SUPERGIRL IS IN THE PAST.
UH, PERHAPS WE'D BEST RETURN YOU TO OUR 30TH CENTURY, TO PREVENT ANY PROBLEMS SHOULD THIS ERA'S SUPERGIRL RETURN, UH, UNEXPECTEDLY.
OH, WELL, I GUESS SO. GIVE ME MY REGARDS WHEN I RETURN FROM THE PAST.
GOOD-BYE, SUPERMAN. WE... WE ALWAYS MISS YOU.
BRAINIAC, CAN WE GO? M-MY EYES ARE WATERING. MUST BE SOME 20TH-CENTURY VIRUS...
"HE NEVER TOLD ME EXACTLY WHAT HAPPENED THAT NIGHT BEFORE THE SIEGE BEGAN, BUT AS SOON AS I SAW HIM THE NEXT MORNING, I KNEW SOMETHING HAD UPSET HIM.
"HE LOOKED FUNNY.

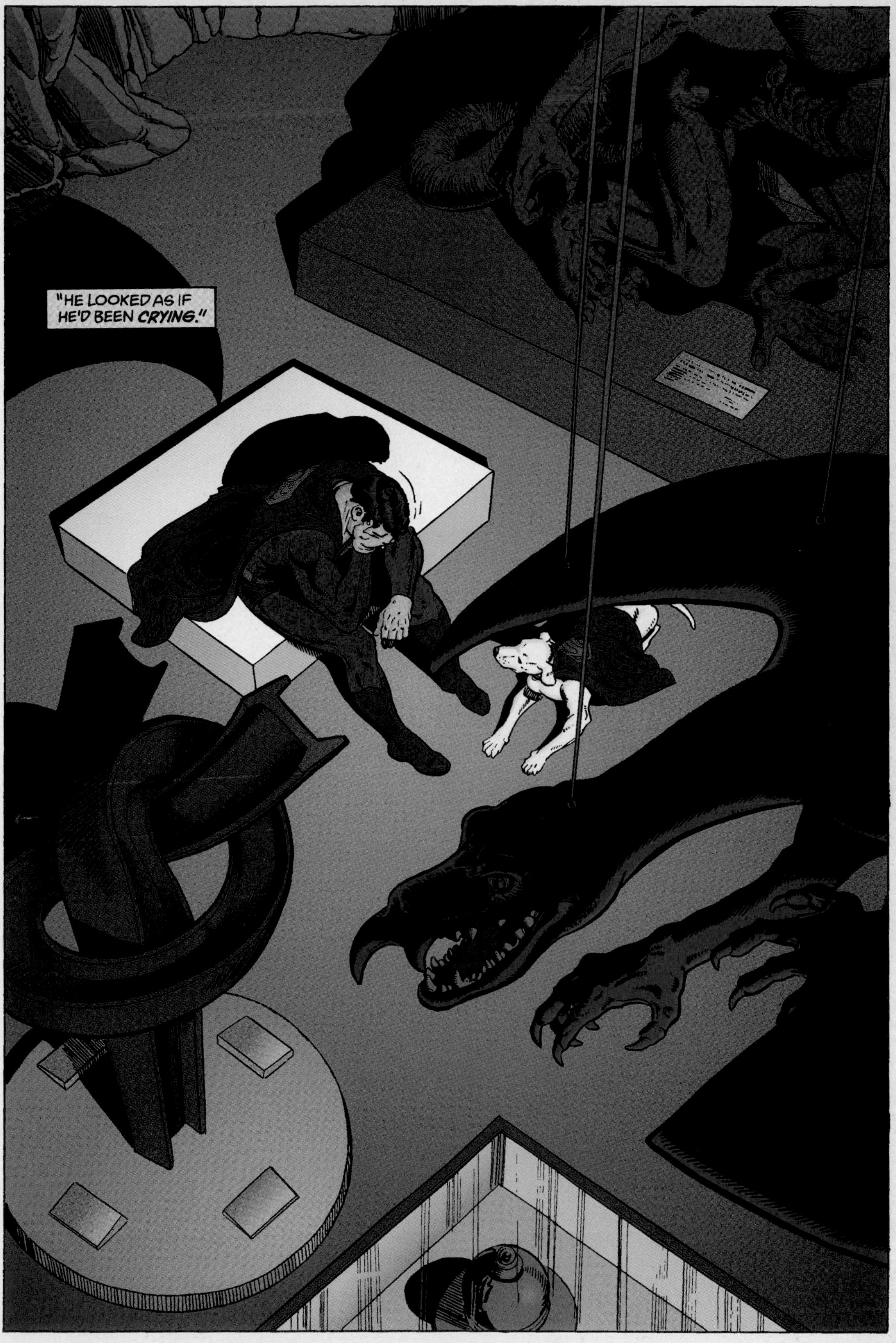
"HE LOOKED AS IF HE'D BEEN CRYING."

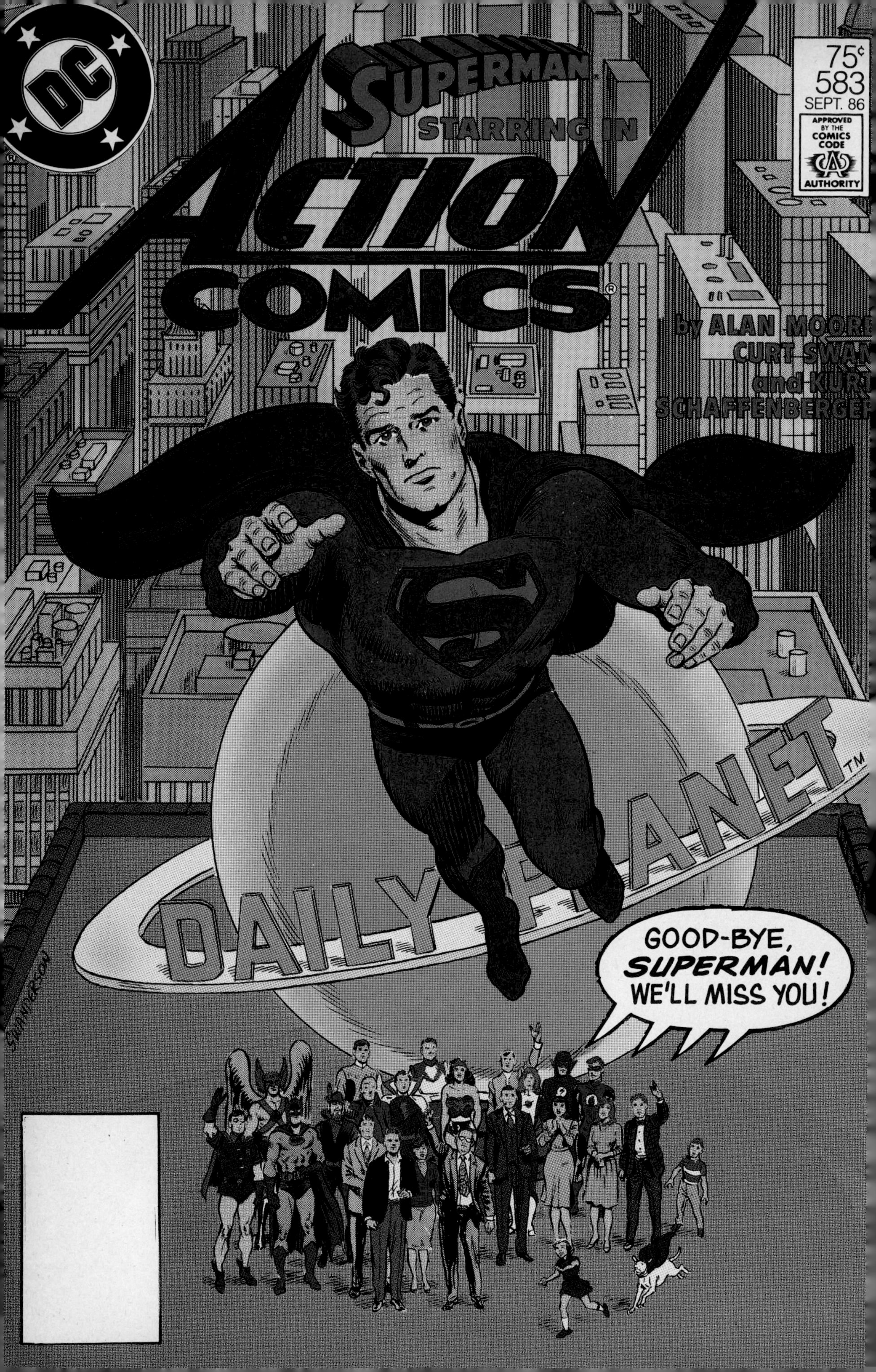
Superman
starring in
Action Comics
75¢
583
SEPT. 86
APPROVED BY THE COMICS CODE AUTHORITY
by ALAN MOORE
CURT SWAN
and KURT SCHAFFENBERGER
DAILY PLANET
GOOD-BYE, SUPERMAN! WE'LL MISS YOU!

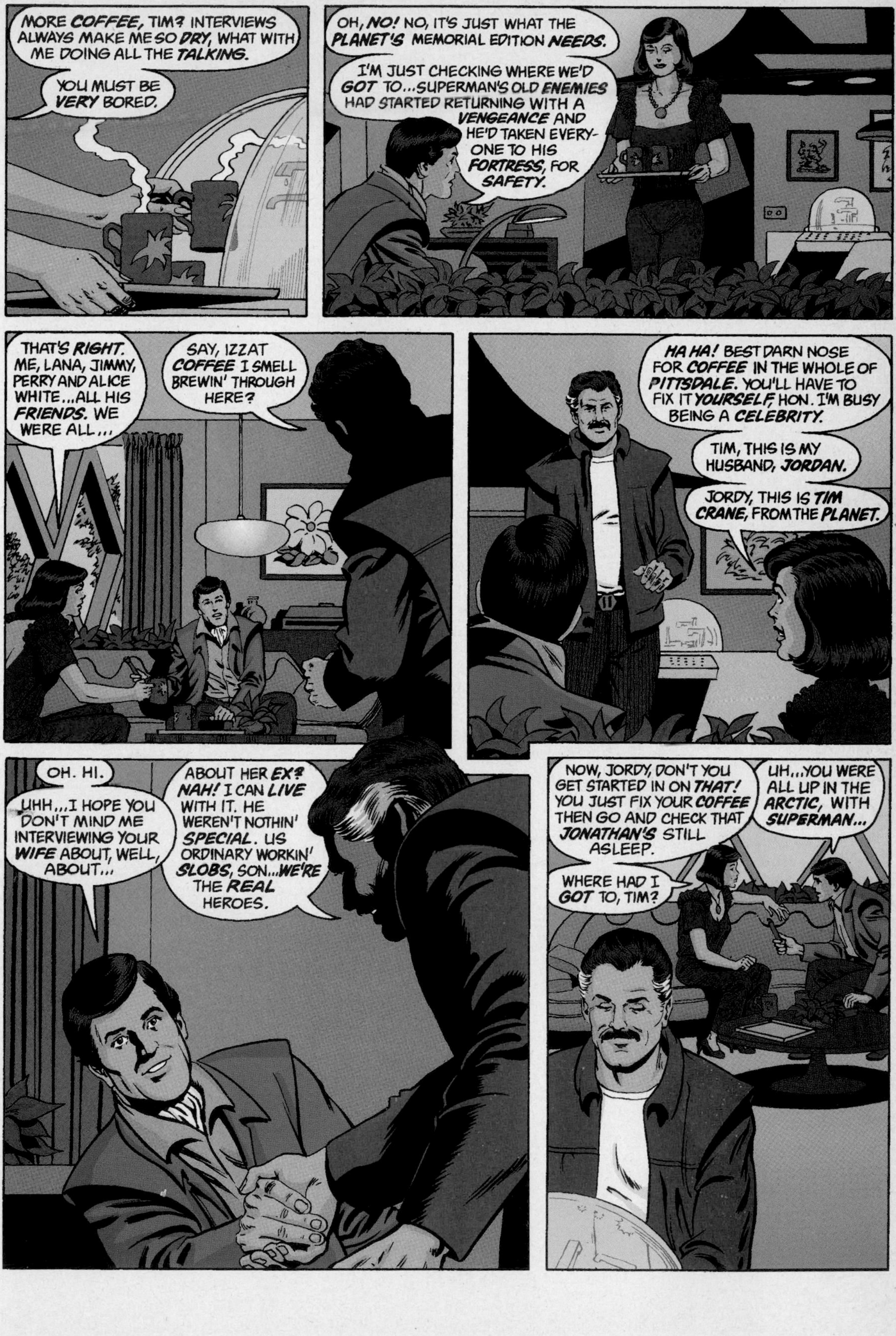
MORE COFFEE, TIM? INTERVIEWS ALWAYS MAKE ME SO DRY, WHAT WITH ME DOING ALL THE TALKING.
YOU MUST BE VERY BORED.
OH, NO! NO, IT'S JUST WHAT THE PLANET'S MEMORIAL EDITION NEEDS.
I'M JUST CHECKING WHERE WE'D GOT TO... SUPERMAN'S OLD ENEMIES HAD STARTED RETURNING WITH A VENGEANCE AND HE'D TAKEN EVERYONE TO HIS FORTRESS, FOR SAFETY.
THAT'S RIGHT. ME, LANA, JIMMY, PERRY AND ALICE WHITE... ALL HIS FRIENDS. WE WERE ALL...
SAY, IZZAT COFFEE I SMELL BREWIN' THROUGH HERE?
HA HA! BEST DARN NOSE FOR COFFEE IN THE WHOLE OF PITTSDALE. YOU'LL HAVE TO FIX IT YOURSELF, HON. I'M BUSY BEING A CELEBRITY.
TIM, THIS IS MY HUSBAND, JORDAN.
JORDY, THIS IS TIM CRANE, FROM THE PLANET.
OH. HI.
UHH... I HOPE YOU DON'T MIND ME INTERVIEWING YOUR WIFE ABOUT, WELL, ABOUT...
ABOUT HER EX? NAH! I CAN LIVE WITH IT. HE WEREN'T NOTHIN' SPECIAL. US ORDINARY WORKIN' SLOBS, SON... WE'RE THE REAL HEROES.
NOW, JORDY, DON'T YOU GET STARTED IN ON THAT! YOU JUST FIX YOUR COFFEE THEN GO AND CHECK THAT JONATHAN'S STILL ASLEEP.
WHERE HAD I GOT TO, TIM?
UH... YOU WERE ALL UP IN THE ARCTIC, WITH SUPERMAN...

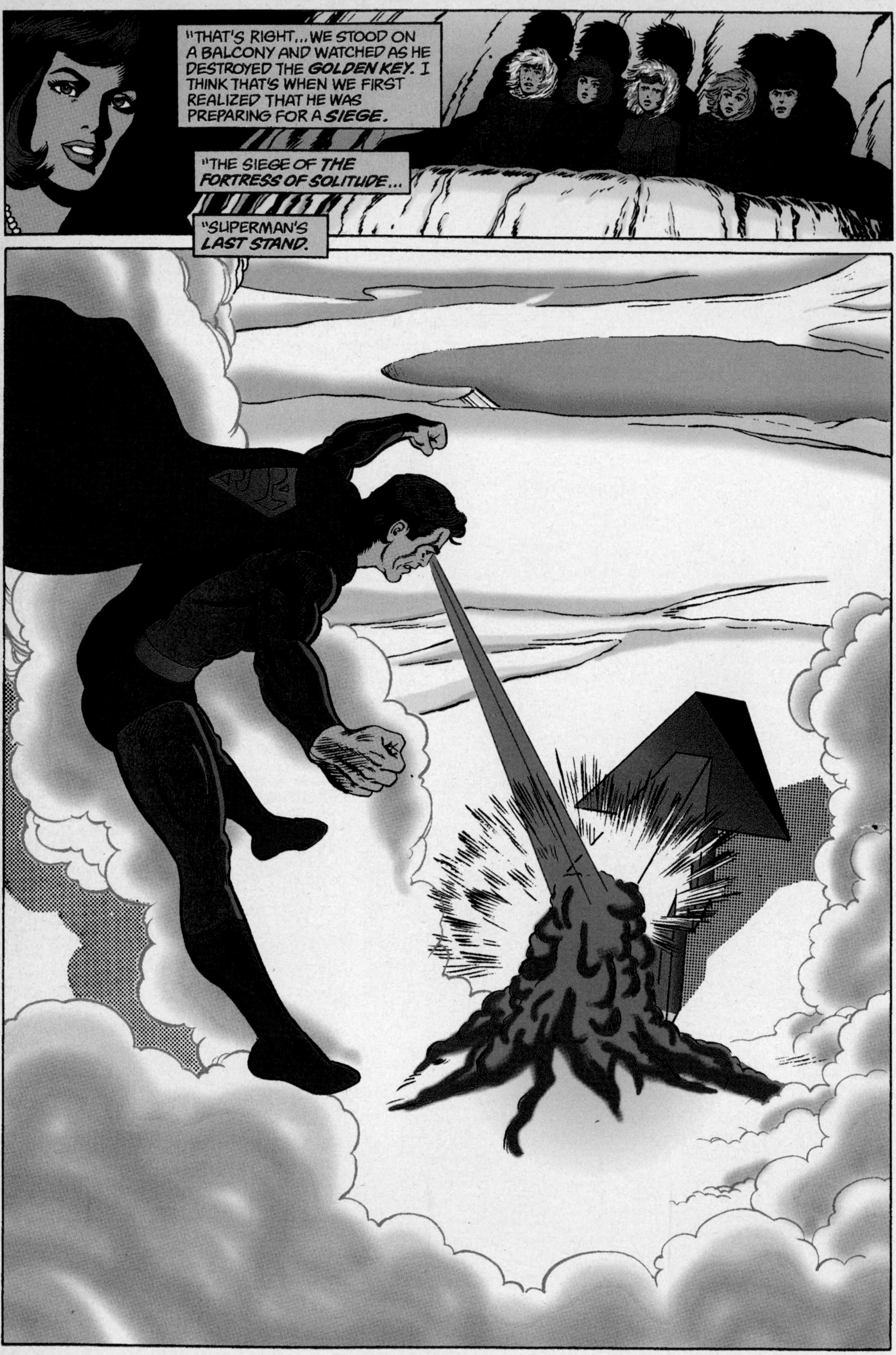
"THAT'S RIGHT... WE STOOD ON A BALCONY AND WATCHED AS HE DESTROYED THE GOLDEN KEY. I THINK THAT'S WHEN WE FIRST REALIZED THAT HE WAS PREPARING FOR A SIEGE.
"THE SIEGE OF THE FORTRESS OF SOLITUDE...
"SUPERMAN'S LAST STAND.

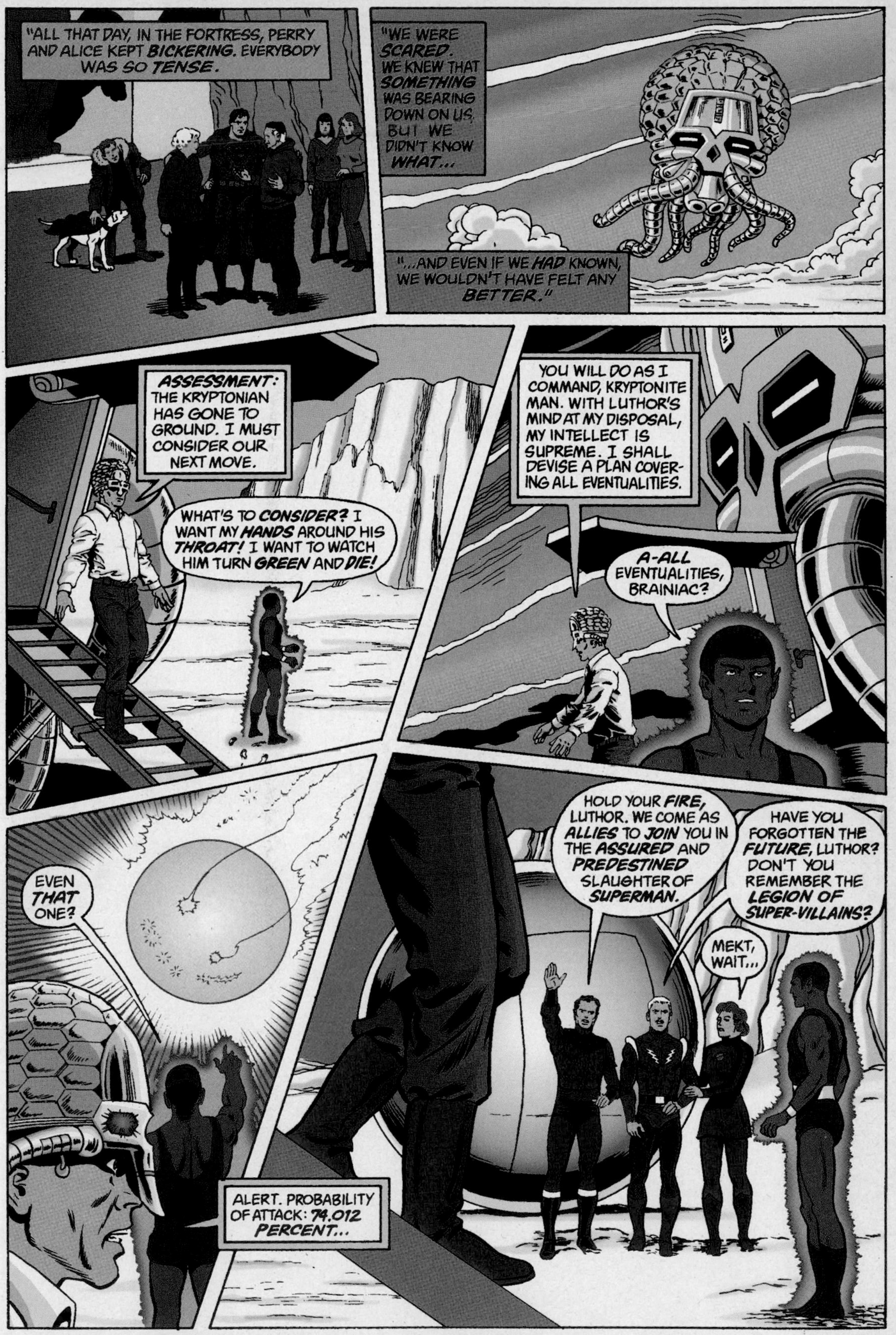
"ALL THAT DAY, IN THE FORTRESS, PERRY AND ALICE KEPT BICKERING. EVERYBODY WAS SO TENSE.
"WE WERE SCARED. WE KNEW THAT SOMETHING WAS BEARING DOWN ON US. BUT WE DIDN'T KNOW WHAT...
"...AND EVEN IF WE HAD KNOWN, WE WOULDN'T HAVE FELT ANY BETTER."
ASSESSMENT: THE KRYPTONIAN HAS GONE TO GROUND. I MUST CONSIDER OUR NEXT MOVE.
WHAT'S TO CONSIDER? I WANT MY HANDS AROUND HIS THROAT! I WANT TO WATCH HIM TURN GREEN AND DIE!
YOU WILL DO AS I COMMAND, KRYPTONITE MAN. WITH LUTHOR'S MIND AT MY DISPOSAL, MY INTELLECT IS SUPREME. I SHALL DEVISE A PLAN COVERING ALL EVENTUALITIES.
A-ALL EVENTUALITIES, BRAINIAC?
EVEN THAT ONE?
ALERT. PROBABILITY OF ATTACK: 74.012 PERCENT...
HOLD YOUR FIRE, LUTHOR. WE COME AS ALLIES TO JOIN YOU IN THE ASSURED AND PREDESTINED SLAUGHTER OF SUPERMAN.
HAVE YOU FORGOTTEN THE FUTURE, LUTHOR? DON'T YOU REMEMBER THE LEGION OF SUPER-VILLAINS?
MEKT, WAIT...

I--I'M SCANNING LUTHOR'S *MIND*... IT'S BEING *DOMINATED* BY SOMETHING *COLD, EMOTIONLESS*...

ON HIS *HEAD*...IS THAT SOME SORT OF *HELMET*, OR...?

LEX LUTHOR IS NOW MERELY THE VESSEL OF BRAINIAC.

QUERY: WHAT MANNER OF BEINGS ARE YOU?

W-WE ARE *SATURN WOMAN, LIGHTNING LORD,* AND *COSMIC KING,* FROM THE *30TH* CENTURY...

ACCORDING TO *LEGEND,* DURING THESE DAYS, SUPERMAN MET HIS *GREATEST FOE* IN BATTLE AND WAS *NO MORE.*

CERTAIN OF *VICTORY,* WE'VE COME TO *PARTIC-IPATE.*

HIS GREATEST *FOE?* OF COURSE. I SHRUNK KANDOR. I WAS ALWAYS HIS GREATEST FOE.

QUERY: WHY SHOULD I PERMIT YOU TO SHARE MY *VICTORY?*

BECAUSE WE'RE FROM THE *FUTURE.* WE *KNOW* THINGS.

FOR *EXAMPLE,* IT'S *SAID* THAT DURING SUPERMAN'S *LAST DAYS,* ALL OF EARTH'S *CHAMPIONS* FLOCKED TO *HELP* HIM...

THAT IS LOGICAL. THIS WORLD'S OTHER SUPER-HUMANS ARE CERTAIN TO INTERFERE.

I SHALL ERECT AN IMPENETRABLE FORCE-SCREEN IMMEDIATELY.

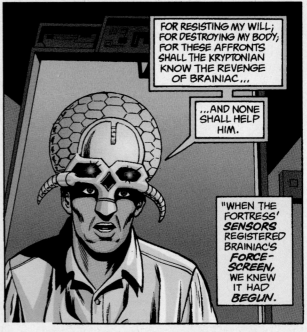

FOR RESISTING MY WILL; FOR DESTROYING MY BODY; FOR THESE AFFRONTS SHALL THE KRYPTONIAN KNOW THE REVENGE OF BRAINIAC...

...AND NONE SHALL HELP HIM.

"WHEN THE FORTRESS' *SENSORS* REGISTERED BRAINIAC'S *FORCE-SCREEN,* WE KNEW IT HAD *BEGUN.*"

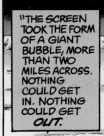

"THE SCREEN TOOK THE FORM OF A GIANT BUBBLE, MORE THAN TWO MILES ACROSS. NOTHING COULD GET IN. NOTHING COULD GET **OUT**.

"AROUND **NOON**, THE VILLAINS BEGAN FIRING ON THE **FORTRESS** USING WEAPONS FROM BRAINIAC'S **SHIP**.

"SUPERMAN **DESTROYED** MOST OF THE DEVICES FROM **LONG RANGE**, USING **HEAT VISION**, BUT THE **FORCE-SCREEN GENERATOR** WAS TOO WELL **SHIELDED**.

"DURING THE AFTERNOON, HE TOOK **KRYPTO** AND ATTEMPTED A **FRONTAL ASSAULT**, BUT THEY WERE DRIVEN **BACK** BY THE **KRYPTONITE MAN**.

"HIS **POWERS** SEEMED TO HAVE INCREASED **TENFOLD**. THEY COULDN'T EVEN GET **NEAR** HIM.

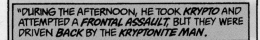

"WITH **TWILIGHT**, **OTHER** HEROES BEGAN ARRIVING OUTSIDE THE **BARRIER**. THOSE THAT WERE HIS **FRIENDS**...

"THOSE THAT WERE ALMOST HIS **RIVALS**...

"...THOSE THAT MIGHT HAVE BEEN HIS **LOVERS**. IT DIDN'T MATTER. **NONE** OF THEM COULD **PENETRATE** IT.

"AS NIGHT FELL, IT SEEMED THAT A **STANDOFF** HAD BEEN DECLARED, AND THERE WAS A **LULL** IN THE **BATTLE**. WE **ALL** KNEW IT WOULDN'T LAST LONG.

"WE FIGURED WE HAD AT LEAST UNTIL **MORNING**, SO WE DECIDED TO GET SOME **SLEEP**...

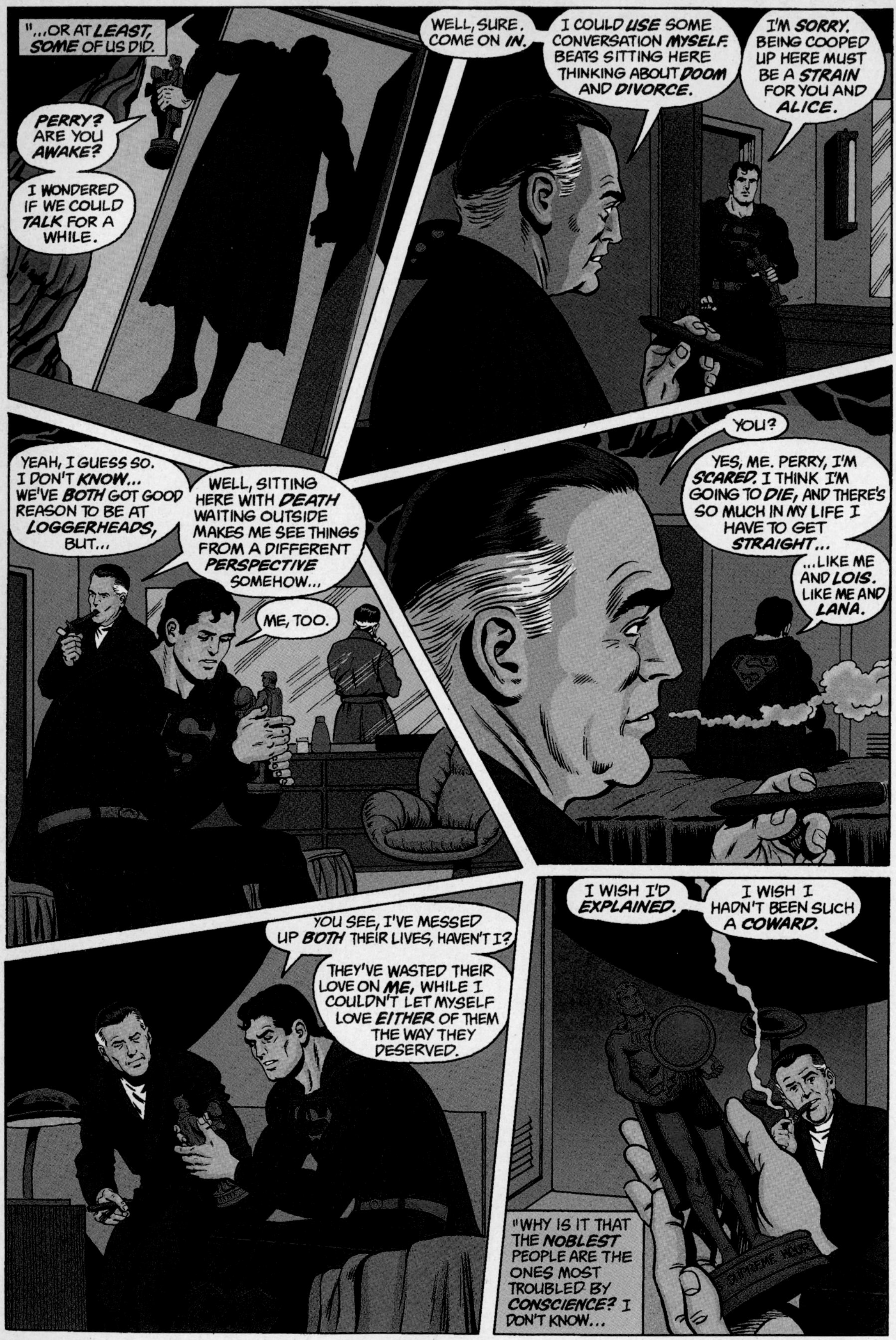

"...OR AT LEAST, SOME OF US DID.
PERRY? ARE YOU AWAKE?
I WONDERED IF WE COULD TALK FOR A WHILE.
WELL, SURE. COME ON IN.
I COULD USE SOME CONVERSATION MYSELF. BEATS SITTING HERE THINKING ABOUT DOOM AND DIVORCE.
I'M SORRY. BEING COOPED UP HERE MUST BE A STRAIN FOR YOU AND ALICE.
YEAH, I GUESS SO. I DON'T KNOW... WE'VE BOTH GOT GOOD REASON TO BE AT LOGGERHEADS, BUT...
WELL, SITTING HERE WITH DEATH WAITING OUTSIDE MAKES ME SEE THINGS FROM A DIFFERENT PERSPECTIVE SOMEHOW...
ME, TOO.
YOU?
YES, ME. PERRY, I'M SCARED. I THINK I'M GOING TO DIE, AND THERE'S SO MUCH IN MY LIFE I HAVE TO GET STRAIGHT...
...LIKE ME AND LOIS. LIKE ME AND LANA.
YOU SEE, I'VE MESSED UP BOTH THEIR LIVES, HAVEN'T I?
THEY'VE WASTED THEIR LOVE ON ME, WHILE I COULDN'T LET MYSELF LOVE EITHER OF THEM THE WAY THEY DESERVED.
I WISH I'D EXPLAINED.
I WISH I HADN'T BEEN SUCH A COWARD.
"WHY IS IT THAT THE NOBLEST PEOPLE ARE THE ONES MOST TROUBLED BY CONSCIENCE? I DON'T KNOW...

"...BUT SUPERMAN AND PERRY WEREN'T THE *ONLY* ONES WHO COULDN'T SLEEP THAT NIGHT."

LANA? WHAT ARE *YOU* DOING UP HERE?

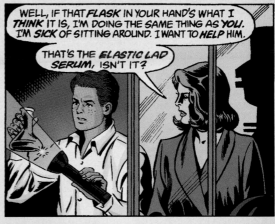

WELL, IF THAT *FLASK* IN YOUR HAND'S WHAT I *THINK* IT IS, I'M DOING THE SAME THING AS *YOU.* I'M *SICK* OF SITTING AROUND. I WANT TO *HELP* HIM.

THAT'S THE *ELASTIC LAD SERUM,* ISN'T IT?

YES. I *KNEW* HE KEPT A SAMPLE IN HIS *TROPHY ROOM ANNEX,* SO I CAME TO *FIND* IT.

ALL THESE YEARS, THEY'VE CALLED ME *"SUPERMAN'S FRIEND."* I FIGURE HERE'S WHERE I START *PAYING* FOR THE PRIVILEGE.

HOW ABOUT YOU?

ELASTIC LAD SERUM

I HAD THE SAME *IDEA.* I REMEMBER YEARS AGO, THERE WERE TIMES WE GAINED *SUPER-POWERS* TEMPORARILY. I REMEMBER THERE WAS THIS *LAKE* THAT *LOIS* AND I BATHED IN...

"MAGIC" LAKE WATER (PROBABLE UNIDENTIFIED RADIATION SOURCE.)

HEY...LOOK! HERE'S A CASE OF SOUVENIR *COSTUMES!*

THEN WE'RE IN *LUCK!*

TURN YOUR BACK, RED, WHILE I' TAKE A QUICK *DIP.*

OH.

OH, THE *FEELING.* I *REMEMBER* NOW... MY SKIN, TINGLING AS IT GETS *HARDER...*MY SENSES *EXPANDING...* X-RAY VISION... *MICROSCOPIC VISION...*

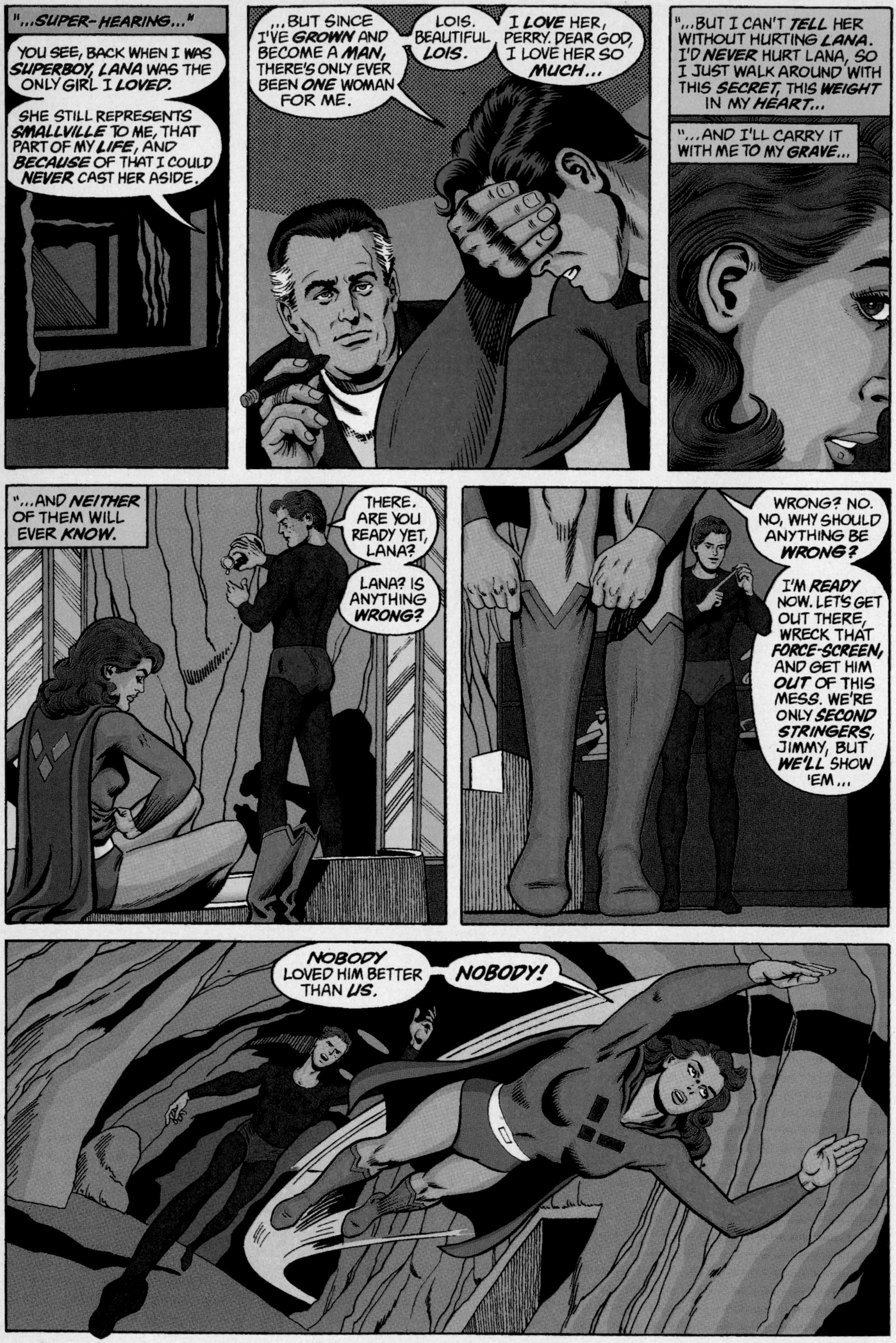
"...SUPER-HEARING..."
YOU SEE, BACK WHEN I WAS SUPERBOY, LANA WAS THE ONLY GIRL I LOVED.
SHE STILL REPRESENTS SMALLVILLE TO ME, THAT PART OF MY LIFE, AND BECAUSE OF THAT I COULD NEVER CAST HER ASIDE.
...BUT SINCE I'VE GROWN AND BECOME A MAN, THERE'S ONLY EVER BEEN ONE WOMAN FOR ME.
LOIS. BEAUTIFUL LOIS.
I LOVE HER, PERRY. DEAR GOD, I LOVE HER SO MUCH...
"...BUT I CAN'T TELL HER WITHOUT HURTING LANA. I'D NEVER HURT LANA, SO I JUST WALK AROUND WITH THIS SECRET, THIS WEIGHT IN MY HEART...
"...AND I'LL CARRY IT WITH ME TO MY GRAVE...
"...AND NEITHER OF THEM WILL EVER KNOW.
THERE. ARE YOU READY YET, LANA?
LANA? IS ANYTHING WRONG?
WRONG? NO. NO, WHY SHOULD ANYTHING BE WRONG?
I'M READY NOW. LET'S GET OUT THERE, WRECK THAT FORCE-SCREEN, AND GET HIM OUT OF THIS MESS. WE'RE ONLY SECOND STRINGERS, JIMMY, BUT WE'LL SHOW 'EM...
NOBODY LOVED HIM BETTER THAN US.
NOBODY!

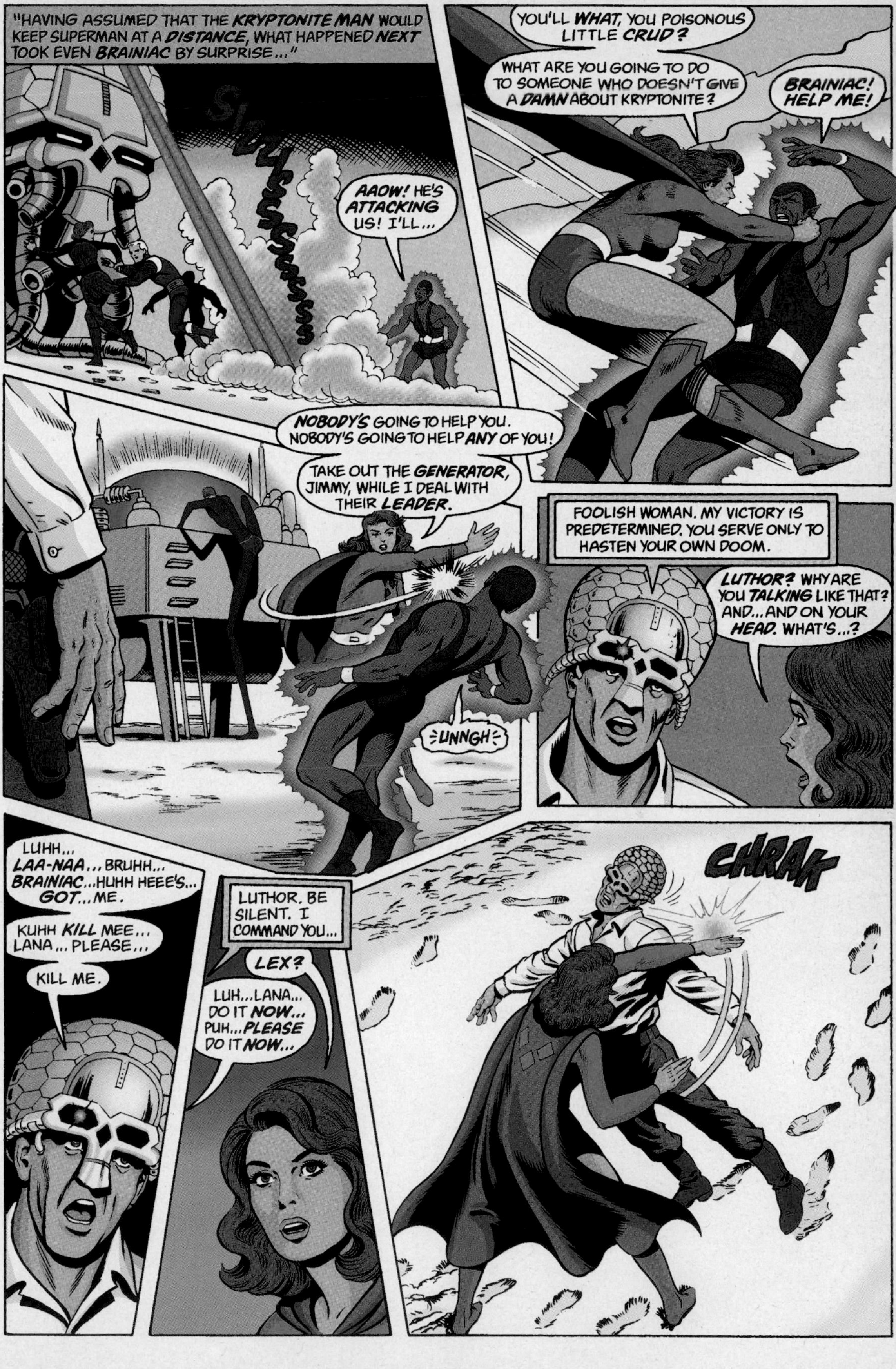
"HAVING ASSUMED THAT THE KRYPTONITE MAN WOULD KEEP SUPERMAN AT A DISTANCE, WHAT HAPPENED NEXT TOOK EVEN BRAINIAC BY SURPRISE..."
SSSSSSSSSS
AAOW! HE'S ATTACKING US! I'LL...
YOU'LL WHAT, YOU POISONOUS LITTLE CRUD?
WHAT ARE YOU GOING TO DO TO SOMEONE WHO DOESN'T GIVE A DAMN ABOUT KRYPTONITE?
BRAINIAC! HELP ME!
NOBODY'S GOING TO HELP YOU. NOBODY'S GOING TO HELP ANY OF YOU!
TAKE OUT THE GENERATOR, JIMMY, WHILE I DEAL WITH THEIR LEADER.
UNNGH
FOOLISH WOMAN. MY VICTORY IS PREDETERMINED. YOU SERVE ONLY TO HASTEN YOUR OWN DOOM.
LUTHOR? WHY ARE YOU TALKING LIKE THAT? AND... AND ON YOUR HEAD. WHAT'S...?
LUHH... LAA-NAA... BRUHH... BRAINIAC...HUHH HEEE'S... GOT...ME.
KUHH KILL MEE... LANA... PLEASE...
KILL ME.
LUTHOR. BE SILENT. I COMMAND YOU...
LEX?
LUH...LANA... DO IT NOW... PUH...PLEASE DO IT NOW...
CHRAK

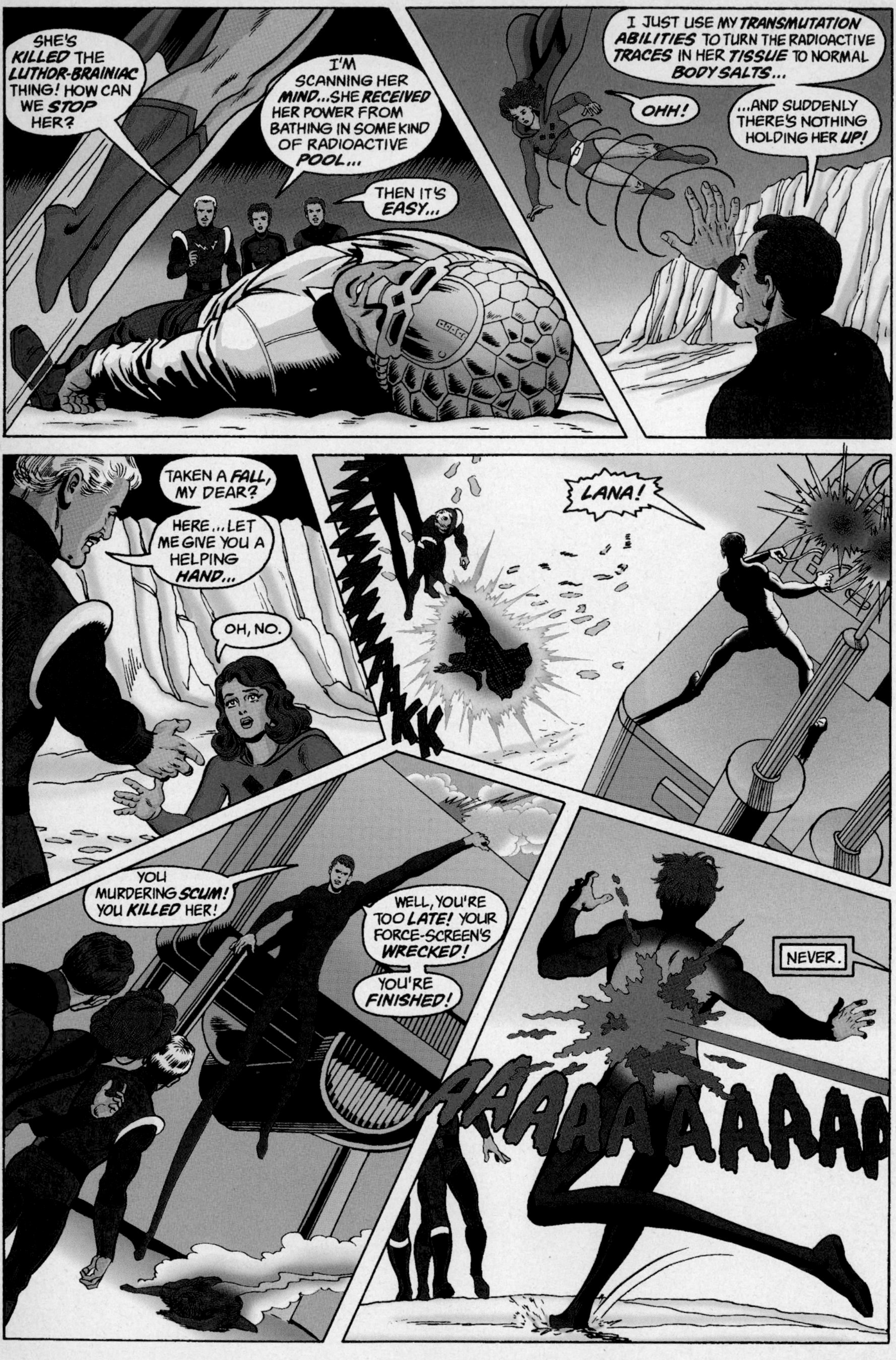
SHE'S KILLED THE LUTHOR-BRAINIAC THING! HOW CAN WE STOP HER?
I'M SCANNING HER MIND...SHE RECEIVED HER POWER FROM BATHING IN SOME KIND OF RADIOACTIVE POOL...
THEN IT'S EASY...
I JUST USE MY TRANSMUTATION ABILITIES TO TURN THE RADIOACTIVE TRACES IN HER TISSUE TO NORMAL BODY SALTS...
OHH!
...AND SUDDENLY THERE'S NOTHING HOLDING HER UP!
TAKEN A FALL, MY DEAR?
HERE...LET ME GIVE YOU A HELPING HAND...
OH, NO.
KRAKK
LANA!
YOU MURDERING SCUM! YOU KILLED HER!
WELL, YOU'RE TOO LATE! YOUR FORCE-SCREEN'S WRECKED!
YOU'RE FINISHED!
NEVER.
AAAAAAAAAAP

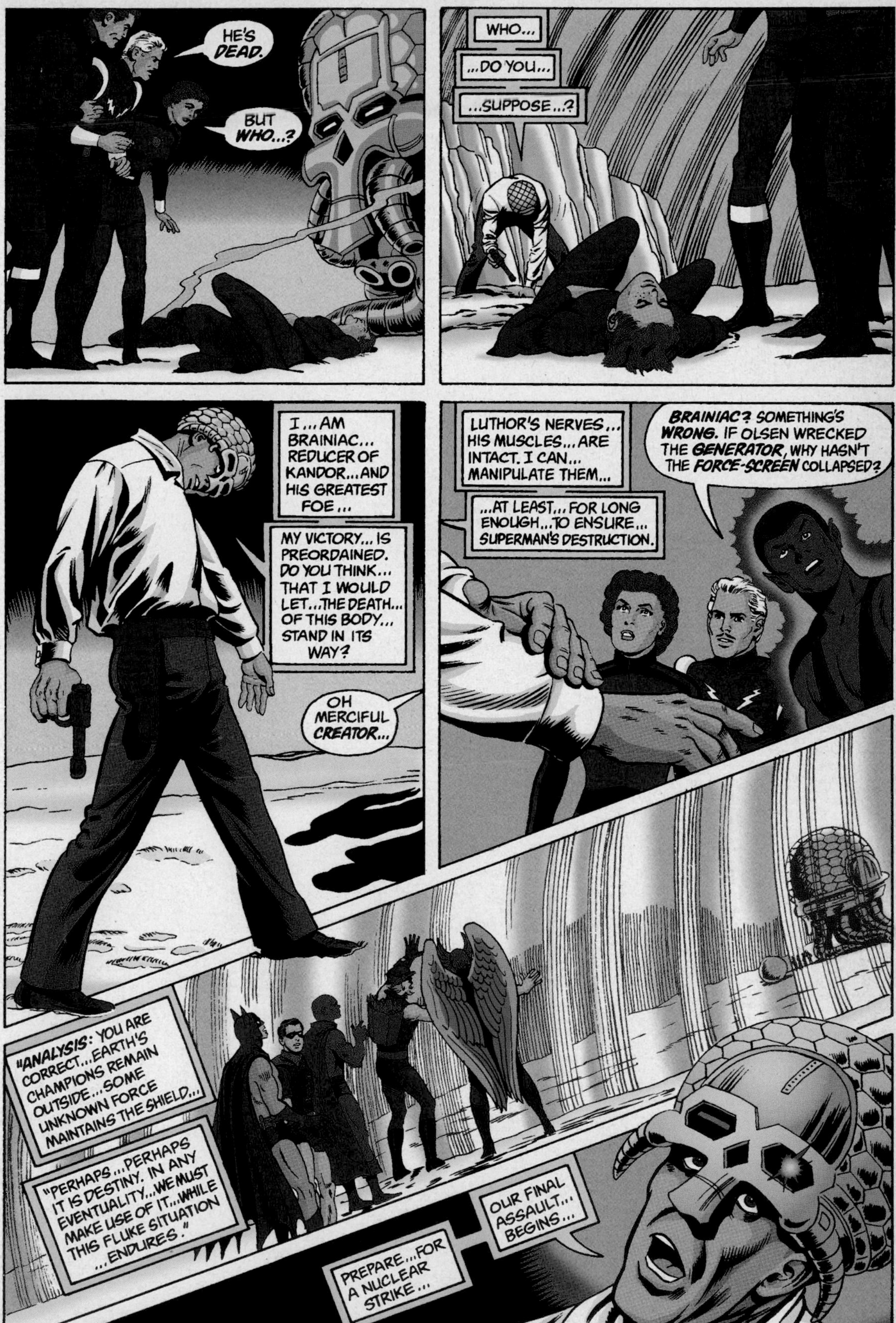
HE'S DEAD.
BUT WHO...?
WHO...
...DO YOU...
...SUPPOSE...?
I...AM BRAINIAC... REDUCER OF KANDOR...AND HIS GREATEST FOE...
MY VICTORY... IS PREORDAINED. DO YOU THINK... THAT I WOULD LET...THE DEATH... OF THIS BODY... STAND IN ITS WAY?
OH MERCIFUL CREATOR...
LUTHOR'S NERVES... HIS MUSCLES...ARE INTACT. I CAN... MANIPULATE THEM...
...AT LEAST...FOR LONG ENOUGH...TO ENSURE... SUPERMAN'S DESTRUCTION.
BRAINIAC? SOMETHING'S WRONG. IF OLSEN WRECKED THE GENERATOR, WHY HASN'T THE FORCE-SCREEN COLLAPSED?
"ANALYSIS: YOU ARE CORRECT...EARTH'S CHAMPIONS REMAIN OUTSIDE...SOME UNKNOWN FORCE MAINTAINS THE SHIELD...
"PERHAPS...PERHAPS IT IS DESTINY. IN ANY EVENTUALITY...WE MUST MAKE USE OF IT...WHILE THIS FLUKE SITUATION ...ENDURES."
OUR FINAL ASSAULT... BEGINS...
PREPARE...FOR A NUCLEAR STRIKE...

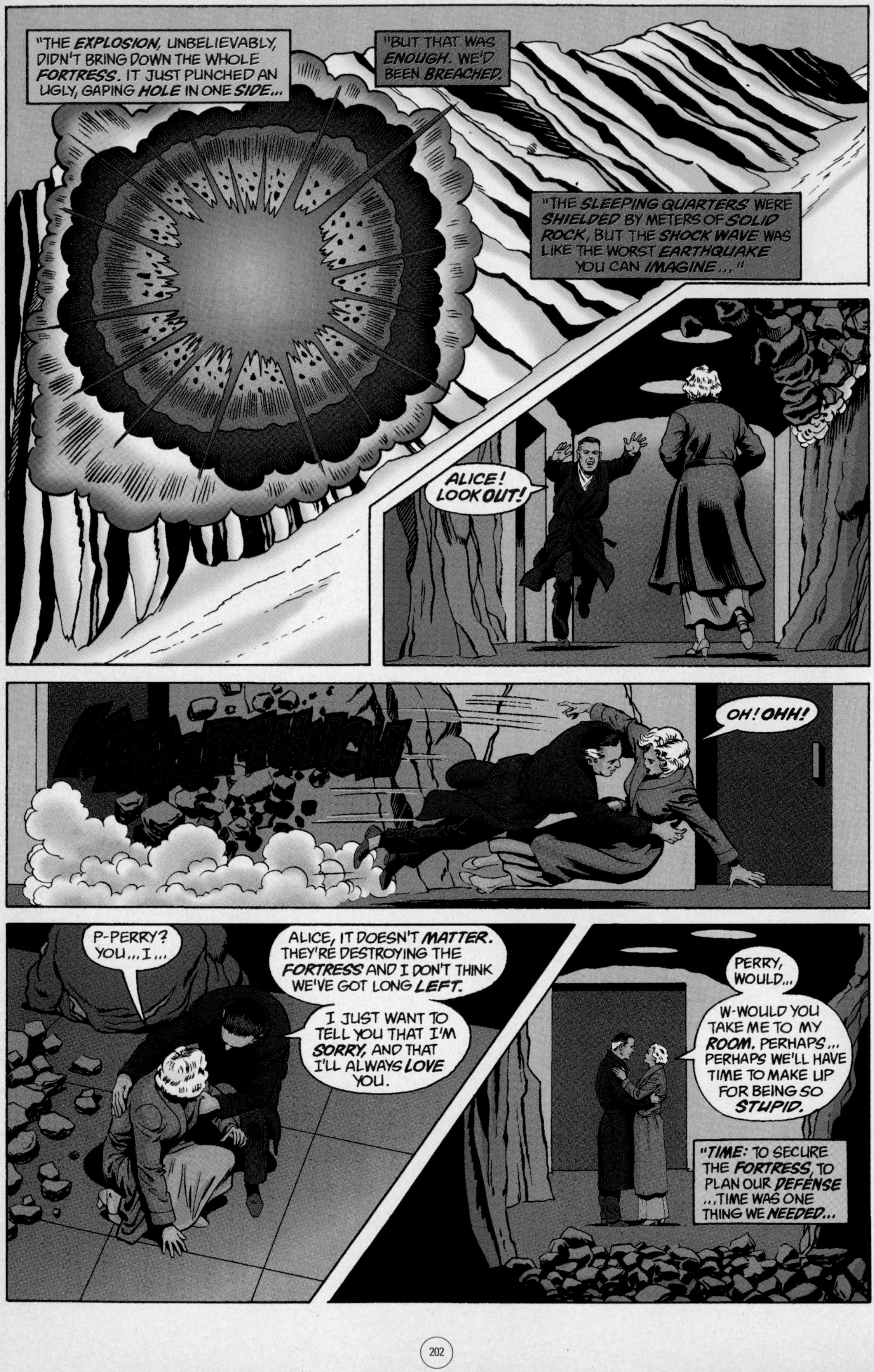
"THE EXPLOSION, UNBELIEVABLY, DIDN'T BRING DOWN THE WHOLE FORTRESS. IT JUST PUNCHED AN UGLY, GAPING HOLE IN ONE SIDE...
"BUT THAT WAS ENOUGH. WE'D BEEN BREACHED.
"THE SLEEPING QUARTERS WERE SHIELDED BY METERS OF SOLID ROCK, BUT THE SHOCK WAVE WAS LIKE THE WORST EARTHQUAKE YOU CAN IMAGINE..."
ALICE! LOOK OUT!
OH! OHH!
P-PERRY? YOU... I...
ALICE, IT DOESN'T MATTER. THEY'RE DESTROYING THE FORTRESS AND I DON'T THINK WE'VE GOT LONG LEFT.
I JUST WANT TO TELL YOU THAT I'M SORRY, AND THAT I'LL ALWAYS LOVE YOU.
PERRY, WOULD...
W-WOULD YOU TAKE ME TO MY ROOM. PERHAPS... PERHAPS WE'LL HAVE TIME TO MAKE UP FOR BEING SO STUPID.
"TIME: TO SECURE THE FORTRESS, TO PLAN OUR DEFENSE ...TIME WAS ONE THING WE NEEDED...

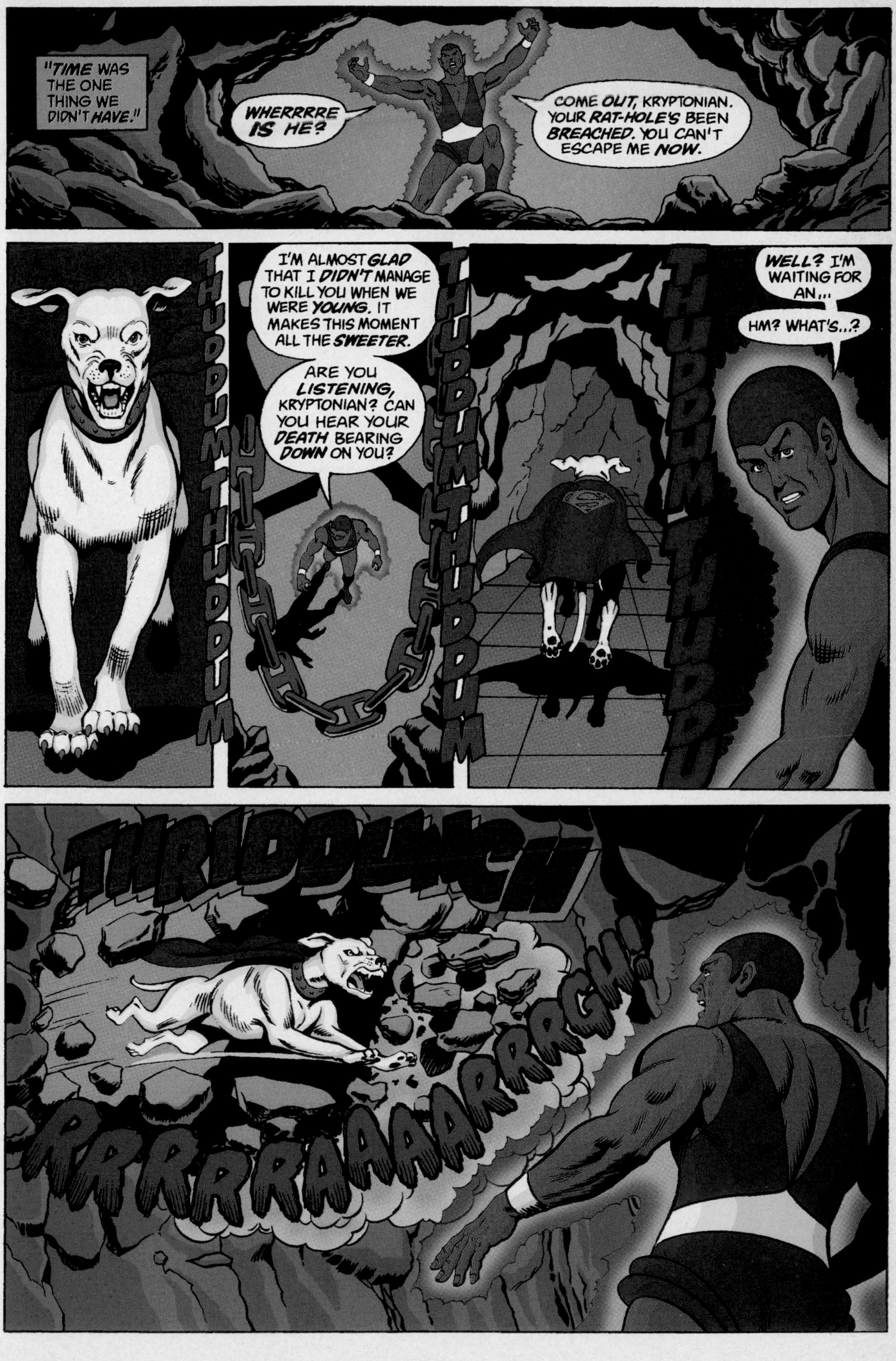
"TIME WAS THE ONE THING WE DIDN'T HAVE."
WHERRRRE IS HE?
COME OUT, KRYPTONIAN. YOUR RAT-HOLE'S BEEN BREACHED. YOU CAN'T ESCAPE ME NOW.
THUDDUM THUDDUM
I'M ALMOST GLAD THAT I DIDN'T MANAGE TO KILL YOU WHEN WE WERE YOUNG. IT MAKES THIS MOMENT ALL THE SWEETER.
ARE YOU LISTENING, KRYPTONIAN? CAN YOU HEAR YOUR DEATH BEARING DOWN ON YOU?
THUDDUM THUDDUM
THUDDUM THUDDU
WELL? I'M WAITING FOR AN...
HM? WHAT'S...?
THRIDDUNCH
RRRRAAAARRRGH!

NO! **NO!**

AAAAEEEEARRGH! STOP IT! GET OFF GET OFF GET **OFF!**

I'M **KILLING** YOU, YOU STUPID **ANIMAL!** DON'T YOU **UNDERSTAND?** I'M KILLING YAAAAAAAAAAAAAAA

AAAAF

SNOPF

AAAOOOOOOOOOOOO

"PETE ROSS, LANA, JIMMY... NOW **KRYPTO** WAS GONE AS WELL.

"I WAS WITH SUPERMAN WHEN HE HEARD HIS PET'S **DEATH-HOWL,** BUT WE **COULDN'T DO** ANYTHING...

204

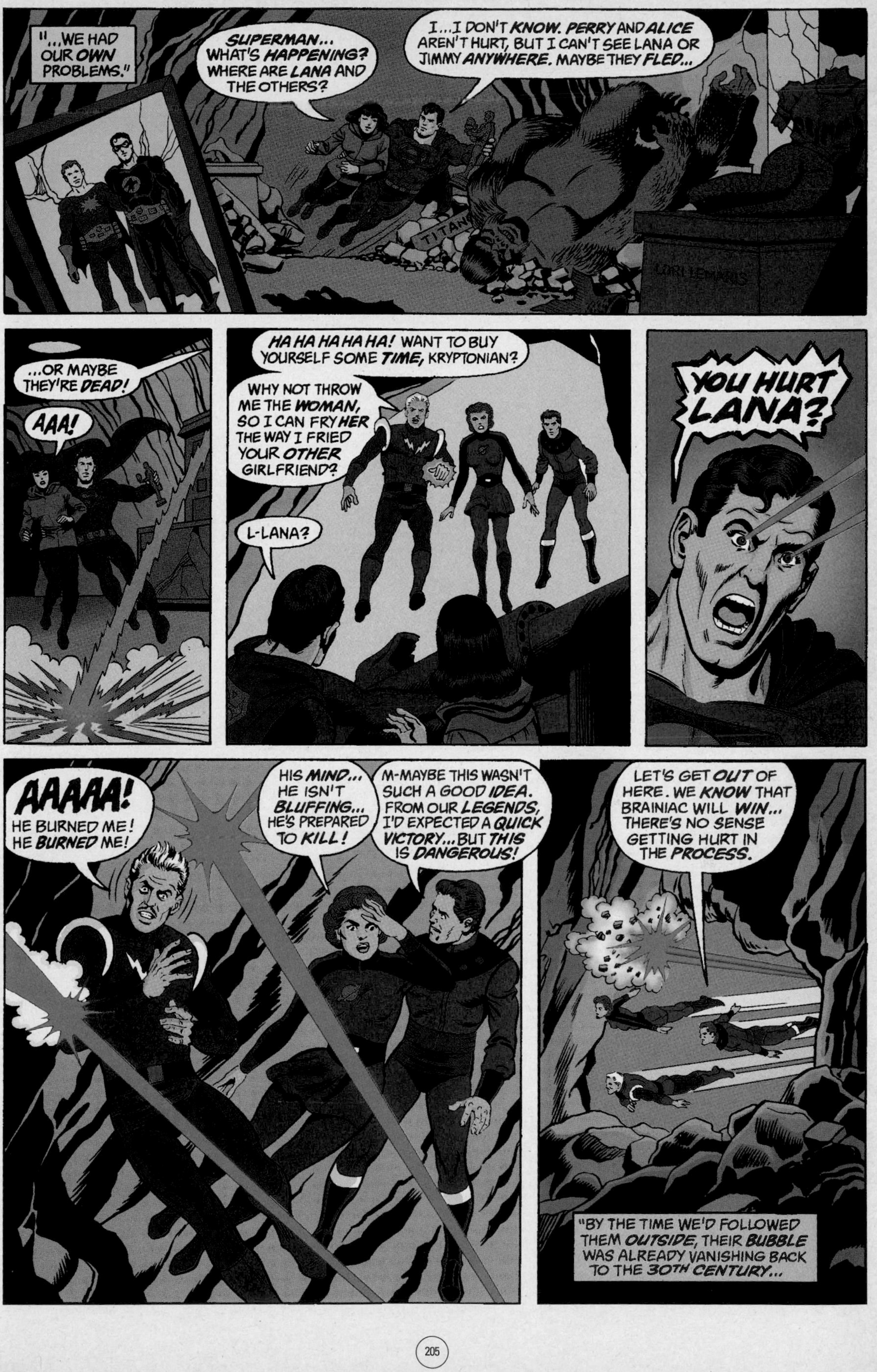
"...WE HAD OUR OWN PROBLEMS."
SUPERMAN... WHAT'S HAPPENING? WHERE ARE LANA AND THE OTHERS?
I...I DON'T KNOW. PERRY AND ALICE AREN'T HURT, BUT I CAN'T SEE LANA OR JIMMY ANYWHERE. MAYBE THEY FLED...
TITAN
LORI LEMARIS
...OR MAYBE THEY'RE DEAD!
AAA!
HA HA HA HA HA! WANT TO BUY YOURSELF SOME TIME, KRYPTONIAN?
WHY NOT THROW ME THE WOMAN, SO I CAN FRY HER THE WAY I FRIED YOUR OTHER GIRLFRIEND?
L-LANA?
YOU HURT LANA?
AAAAA! HE BURNED ME! HE BURNED ME!
HIS MIND... HE ISN'T BLUFFING... HE'S PREPARED TO KILL!
M-MAYBE THIS WASN'T SUCH A GOOD IDEA. FROM OUR LEGENDS, I'D EXPECTED A QUICK VICTORY... BUT THIS IS DANGEROUS!
LET'S GET OUT OF HERE. WE KNOW THAT BRAINIAC WILL WIN... THERE'S NO SENSE GETTING HURT IN THE PROCESS.
"BY THE TIME WE'D FOLLOWED THEM OUTSIDE, THEIR BUBBLE WAS ALREADY VANISHING BACK TO THE 30TH CENTURY...

"...AND THERE WAS ONLY ONE FOE LEFT TO *FACE*."

"OR MAYBE *TWO*."

ANALYSIS: STIFFENING...OF LIMBS...DIFFICULTY...IN MOVEMENT. *ASSESSMENT:* ONSET...OF RIGOR MORTIS... IN HOST BODY...IMMINENT.

OH, GOD, *LOOK* AT IT!

BUT...THE VILLAINS FROM THE FUTURE...THEY SAID YOU WOULD MEET...YOUR GREATEST FOE IN BATTLE... AND BE NO MORE. ME. BRAINIAC.YOUR GREATEST FOE...

I AM PREDESTINED... TO DESTROY YOU...

LOIS, GET *BACK!* HE'S *FALLING!*

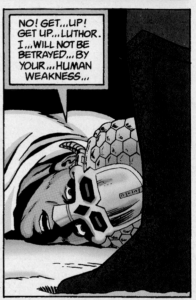

NO! GET...*UP!* GET UP...LUTHOR. I...WILL NOT BE BETRAYED...BY YOUR...HUMAN WEAKNESS...

WHERE...IS MY KRYPTONITE MAN...? WHY...IS MY FORCE-SCREEN...STILL STANDING..? I DON'T KNOW...I DON'T CARE...

I...AM COMING FOR YOU... KRYPTONIAN... MY VICTORY...IS INEVITABLE...

SUPERMAN? IT'S CRAWLING *OFF* HIM...

CLINK RINK PLITTINK

IT'S OKAY, LOIS. I... I DON'T THINK HE'S IN ANY CONDITION TO HARM US.

SHRING CHLINK KINGLE TING

"THE DISINTEGRATING COLLECTION OF PLATES AND CIRCUITS CRAWLED A COUPLE OF INCHES, PROPELLED BY SHEER MALICE, THEN STOPPED MOVING.

"BRAINIAC WAS *DEAD*.

"IT WAS ALL OVER...

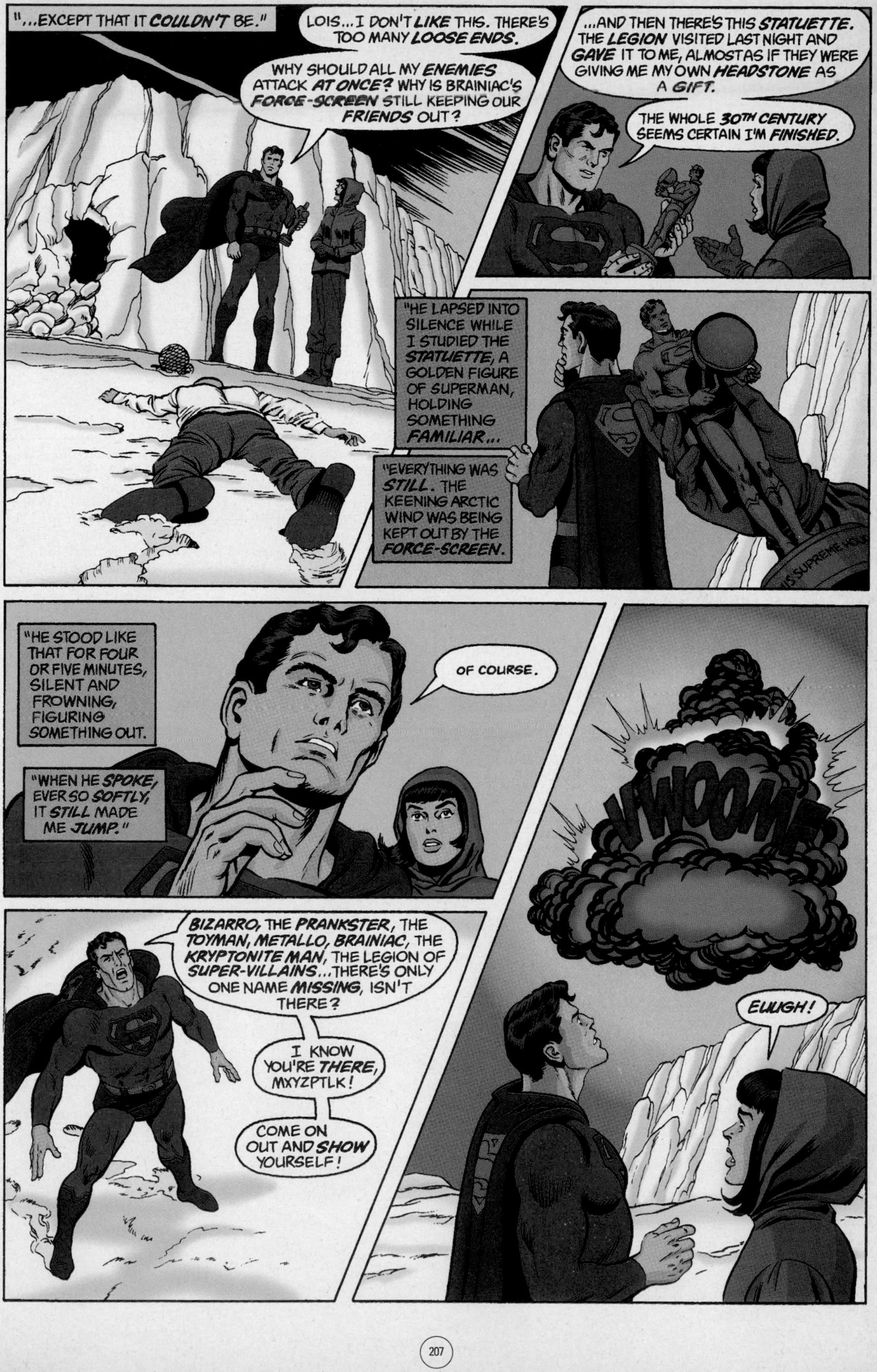
"...EXCEPT THAT IT COULDN'T BE."
LOIS... I DON'T LIKE THIS. THERE'S TOO MANY LOOSE ENDS.
WHY SHOULD ALL MY ENEMIES ATTACK AT ONCE? WHY IS BRAINIAC'S FORCE-SCREEN STILL KEEPING OUR FRIENDS OUT?
...AND THEN THERE'S THIS STATUETTE. THE LEGION VISITED LAST NIGHT AND GAVE IT TO ME, ALMOST AS IF THEY WERE GIVING ME MY OWN HEADSTONE AS A GIFT.
THE WHOLE 30TH CENTURY SEEMS CERTAIN I'M FINISHED.
"HE LAPSED INTO SILENCE WHILE I STUDIED THE STATUETTE, A GOLDEN FIGURE OF SUPERMAN, HOLDING SOMETHING FAMILIAR...
"EVERYTHING WAS STILL. THE KEENING ARCTIC WIND WAS BEING KEPT OUT BY THE FORCE-SCREEN.
"HE STOOD LIKE THAT FOR FOUR OR FIVE MINUTES, SILENT AND FROWNING, FIGURING SOMETHING OUT.
"WHEN HE SPOKE, EVER SO SOFTLY, IT STILL MADE ME JUMP."
OF COURSE.
BIZARRO, THE PRANKSTER, THE TOYMAN, METALLO, BRAINIAC, THE KRYPTONITE MAN, THE LEGION OF SUPER-VILLAINS... THERE'S ONLY ONE NAME MISSING, ISN'T THERE?
I KNOW YOU'RE THERE, MXYZPTLK!
COME ON OUT AND SHOW YOURSELF!
VWOOMF
EUUGH!

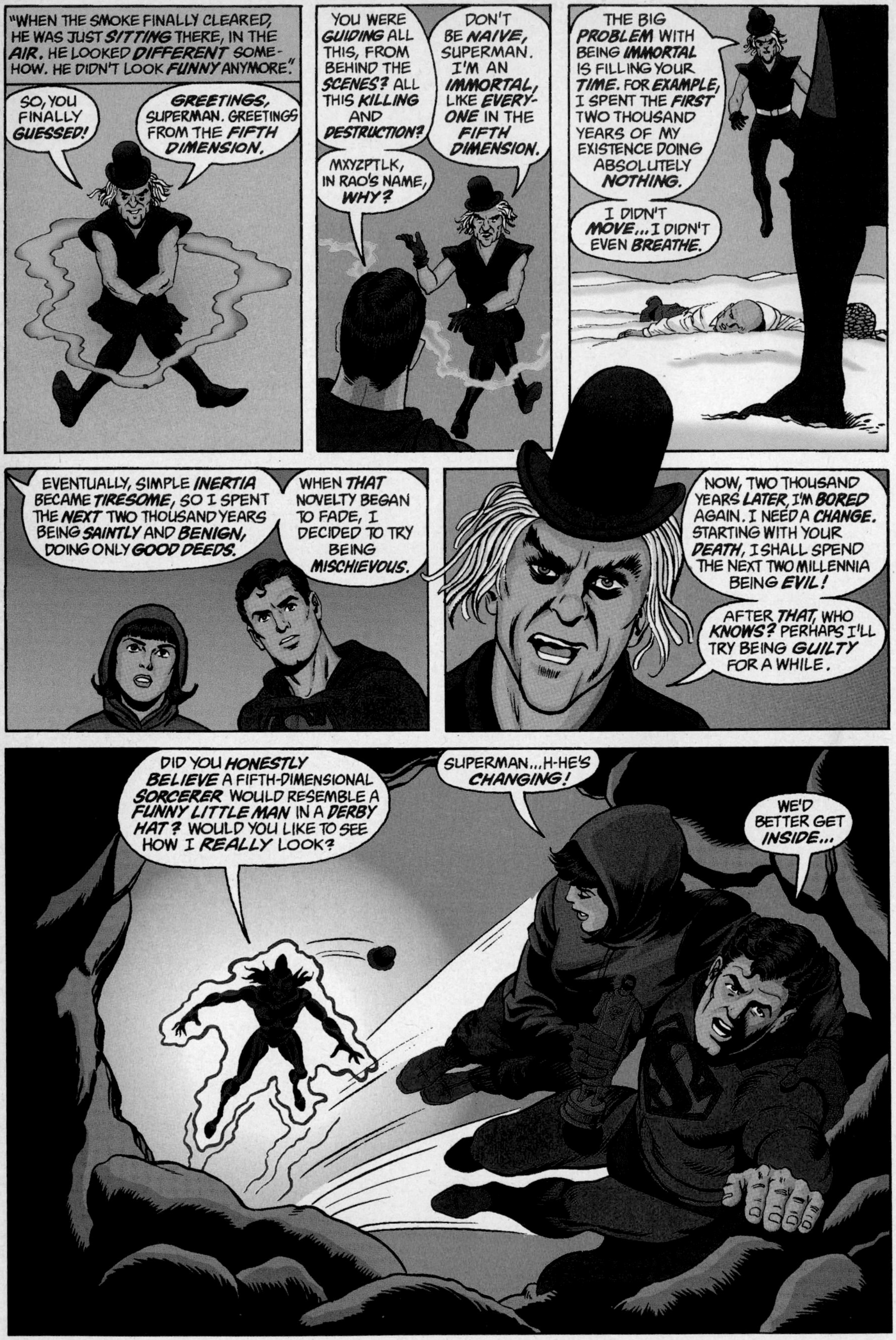
"WHEN THE SMOKE FINALLY CLEARED, HE WAS JUST SITTING THERE, IN THE AIR. HE LOOKED DIFFERENT SOMEHOW. HE DIDN'T LOOK FUNNY ANYMORE."
SO, YOU FINALLY GUESSED!
GREETINGS, SUPERMAN. GREETINGS FROM THE FIFTH DIMENSION.
YOU WERE GUIDING ALL THIS, FROM BEHIND THE SCENES? ALL THIS KILLING AND DESTRUCTION?
MXYZPTLK, IN RAO'S NAME, WHY?
DON'T BE NAIVE, SUPERMAN. I'M AN IMMORTAL, LIKE EVERYONE IN THE FIFTH DIMENSION.
THE BIG PROBLEM WITH BEING IMMORTAL IS FILLING YOUR TIME. FOR EXAMPLE, I SPENT THE FIRST TWO THOUSAND YEARS OF MY EXISTENCE DOING ABSOLUTELY NOTHING.
I DIDN'T MOVE... I DIDN'T EVEN BREATHE.
EVENTUALLY, SIMPLE INERTIA BECAME TIRESOME, SO I SPENT THE NEXT TWO THOUSAND YEARS BEING SAINTLY AND BENIGN, DOING ONLY GOOD DEEDS.
WHEN THAT NOVELTY BEGAN TO FADE, I DECIDED TO TRY BEING MISCHIEVOUS.
NOW, TWO THOUSAND YEARS LATER, I'M BORED AGAIN. I NEED A CHANGE. STARTING WITH YOUR DEATH, I SHALL SPEND THE NEXT TWO MILLENNIA BEING EVIL!
AFTER THAT, WHO KNOWS? PERHAPS I'LL TRY BEING GUILTY FOR A WHILE.
DID YOU HONESTLY BELIEVE A FIFTH-DIMENSIONAL SORCERER WOULD RESEMBLE A FUNNY LITTLE MAN IN A DERBY HAT? WOULD YOU LIKE TO SEE HOW I REALLY LOOK?
SUPERMAN... H-HE'S CHANGING!
WE'D BETTER GET INSIDE...

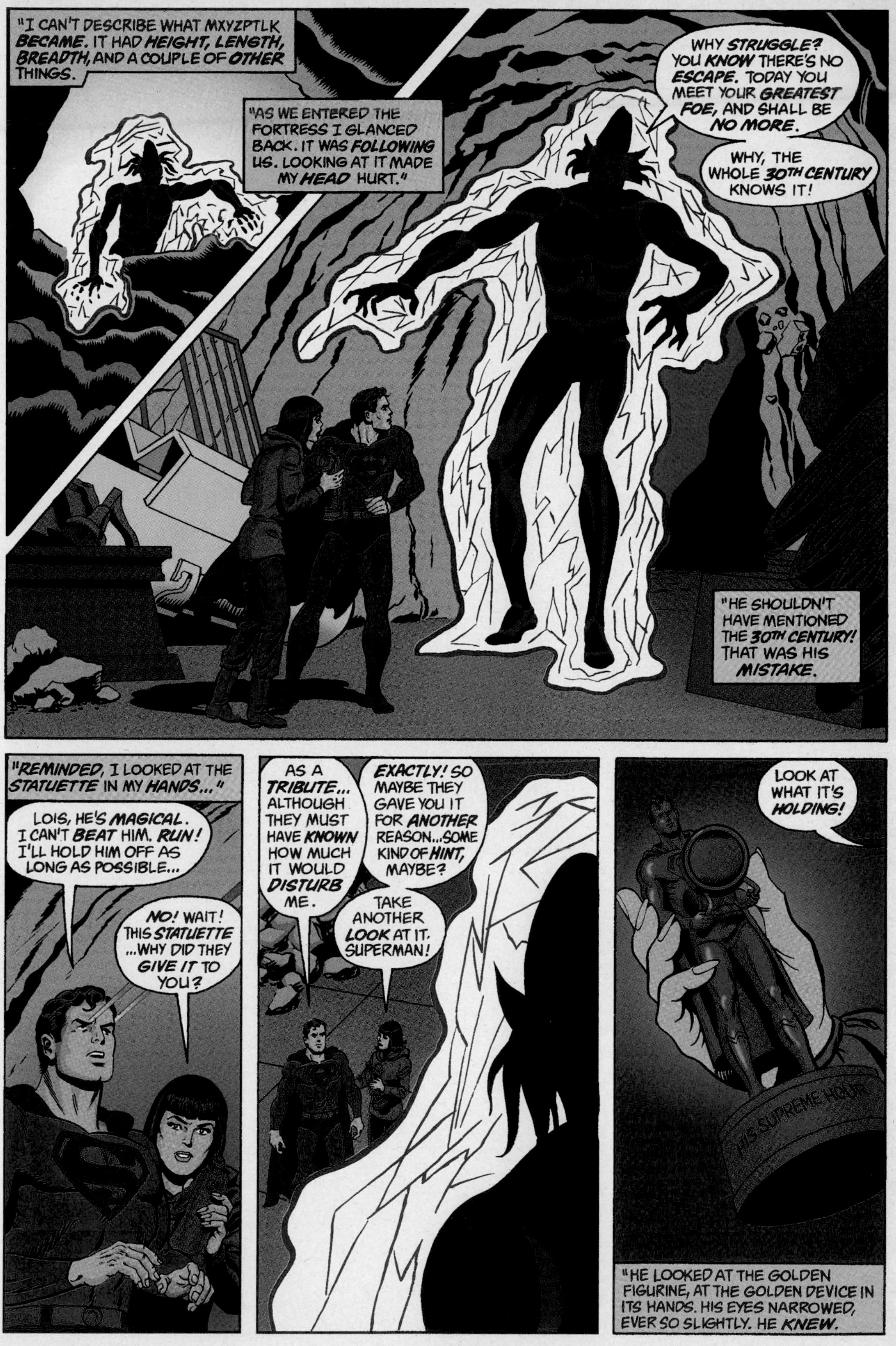
"I CAN'T DESCRIBE WHAT MXYZPTLK BECAME. IT HAD HEIGHT, LENGTH, BREADTH, AND A COUPLE OF OTHER THINGS.
"AS WE ENTERED THE FORTRESS I GLANCED BACK. IT WAS FOLLOWING US. LOOKING AT IT MADE MY HEAD HURT."
WHY STRUGGLE? YOU KNOW THERE'S NO ESCAPE. TODAY YOU MEET YOUR GREATEST FOE, AND SHALL BE NO MORE.
WHY, THE WHOLE 30TH CENTURY KNOWS IT!
"HE SHOULDN'T HAVE MENTIONED THE 30TH CENTURY! THAT WAS HIS MISTAKE.
"REMINDED, I LOOKED AT THE STATUETTE IN MY HANDS..."
LOIS, HE'S MAGICAL. I CAN'T BEAT HIM. RUN! I'LL HOLD HIM OFF AS LONG AS POSSIBLE...
NO! WAIT! THIS STATUETTE ...WHY DID THEY GIVE IT TO YOU?
AS A TRIBUTE... ALTHOUGH THEY MUST HAVE KNOWN HOW MUCH IT WOULD DISTURB ME.
EXACTLY! SO MAYBE THEY GAVE YOU IT FOR ANOTHER REASON...SOME KIND OF HINT, MAYBE?
TAKE ANOTHER LOOK AT IT, SUPERMAN!
LOOK AT WHAT IT'S HOLDING!
HIS SUPREME HOUR
"HE LOOKED AT THE GOLDEN FIGURINE, AT THE GOLDEN DEVICE IN ITS HANDS. HIS EYES NARROWED, EVER SO SLIGHTLY. HE KNEW.

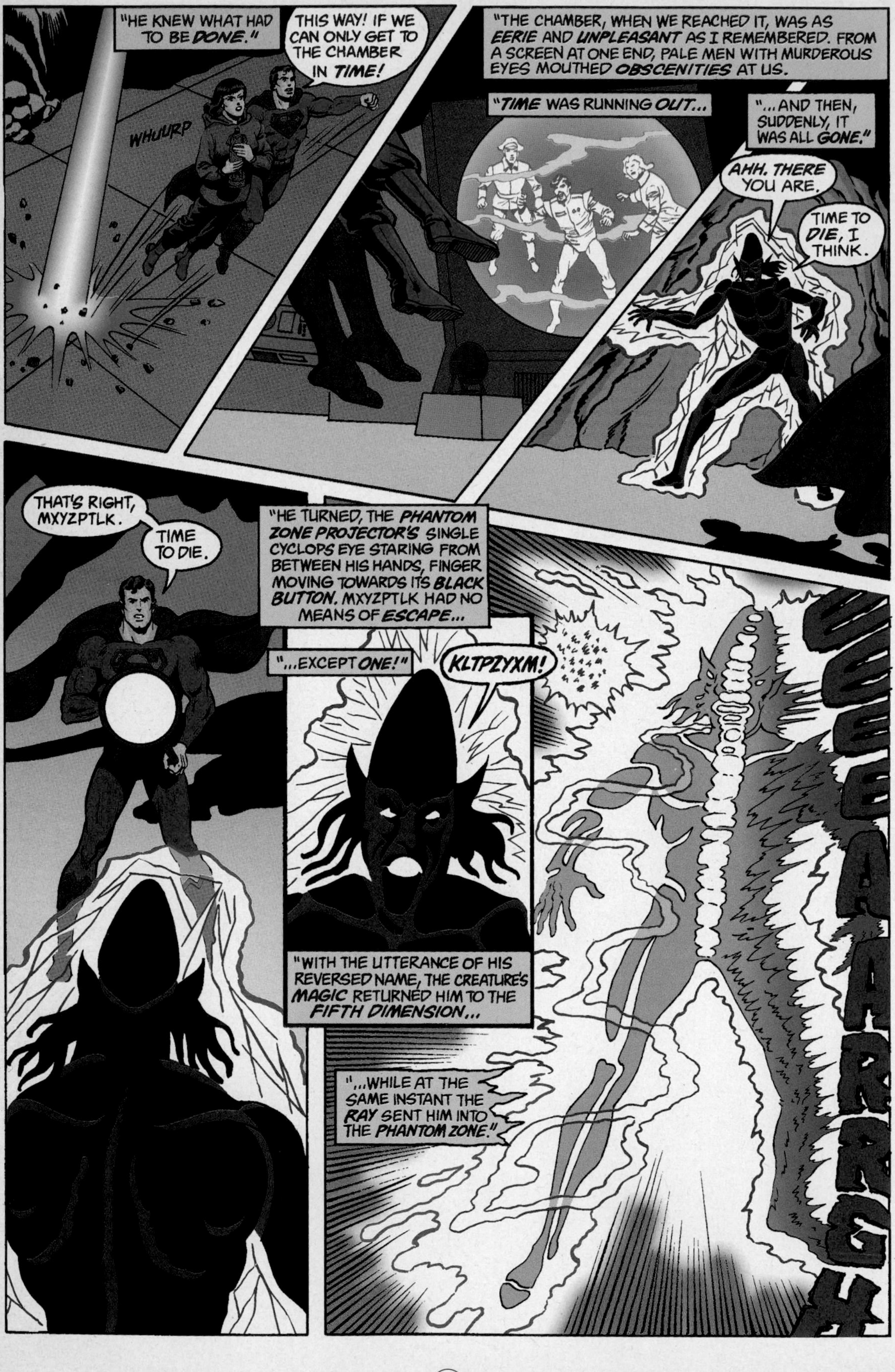
"HE KNEW WHAT HAD TO BE DONE."
THIS WAY! IF WE CAN ONLY GET TO THE CHAMBER IN TIME!
WHUURP
"THE CHAMBER, WHEN WE REACHED IT, WAS AS EERIE AND UNPLEASANT AS I REMEMBERED. FROM A SCREEN AT ONE END, PALE MEN WITH MURDEROUS EYES MOUTHED OBSCENITIES AT US.
"TIME WAS RUNNING OUT...
"...AND THEN, SUDDENLY, IT WAS ALL GONE."
AHH. THERE YOU ARE.
TIME TO DIE, I THINK.
THAT'S RIGHT, MXYZPTLK.
TIME TO DIE.
"HE TURNED, THE PHANTOM ZONE PROJECTOR'S SINGLE CYCLOPS EYE STARING FROM BETWEEN HIS HANDS, FINGER MOVING TOWARDS ITS BLACK BUTTON. MXYZPTLK HAD NO MEANS OF ESCAPE...
"...EXCEPT ONE!"
KLTPZYXM!
"WITH THE UTTERANCE OF HIS REVERSED NAME, THE CREATURE'S MAGIC RETURNED HIM TO THE FIFTH DIMENSION...
"...WHILE AT THE SAME INSTANT THE RAY SENT HIM INTO THE PHANTOM ZONE."
UUUEEAAARRRGH

THAT TERRIBLE *SCREAM*. IS HE...?

TORN IN *HALF*, BETWEEN *DIMENSIONS*. HE PANICKED WHEN HE SAW THE *RAY* AND MADE A *FATAL ERROR*. JUST AS I *KNEW* HE WOULD.

I *KILLED* HIM, LOIS! I *INTENDED* TO KILL HIM!

I JUST COULDN'T RISK LETTING ANYTHING THAT *POWERFUL* AND *MALIGNANT* SURVIVE, SO I MADE UP MY *MIND*, AND I *DID* IT.

I BROKE MY *OATH*. I *KILLED* HIM.

B-BUT YOU *HAD* TO! YOU HAVEN'T DONE ANYTHING *WRONG*...

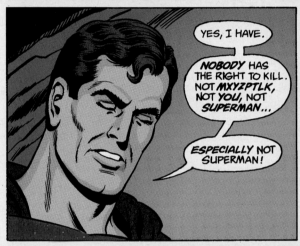

YES, I HAVE.

NOBODY HAS THE RIGHT TO KILL. NOT *MXYZPTLK*, NOT *YOU*, NOT *SUPERMAN*...

ESPECIALLY NOT SUPERMAN!

"HE TURNED AND WALKED AWAY, IN COMPLETE SILENCE. I RAN *AFTER* HIM, CALLING HIS *NAME*.

"HE DIDN'T *REPLY*...

"...AND BY THE TIME I REALIZED WHERE HE WAS *HEADING*, IT WAS *TOO LATE*.

GOLD KRYPTONITE

SAMPLE STORAGE CHAMBER

KEEP OUT!

"AS HE WALKED INTO THE BLINDING GOLDEN LIGHT HE *TURNED*, AND LOOKED BACK OVER HIS *SHOULDER*. HE *SMILED* AT ME...

"I NEVER SAW SUPERMAN AGAIN.

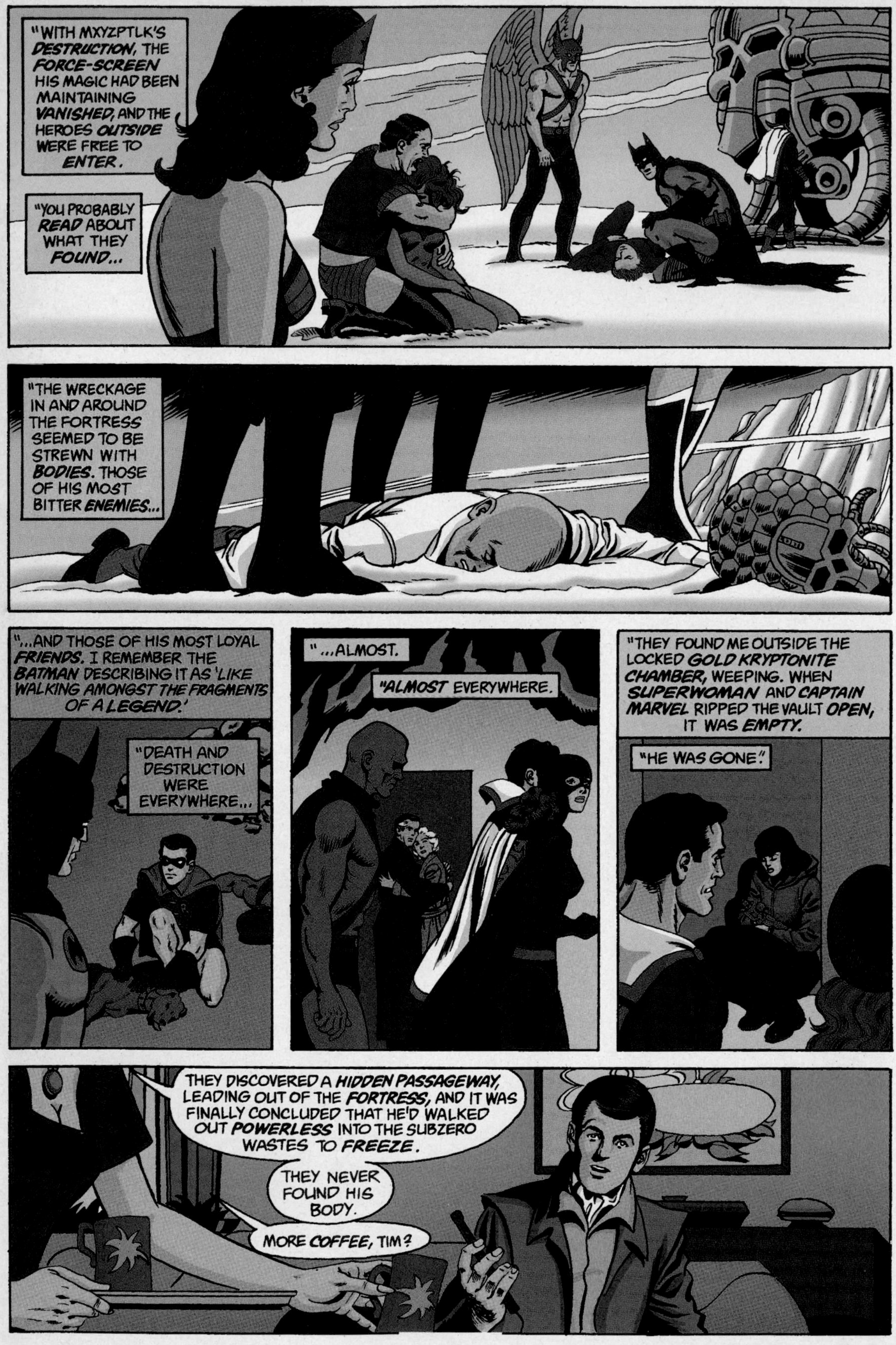
"WITH MXYZPTLK'S DESTRUCTION, THE FORCE-SCREEN HIS MAGIC HAD BEEN MAINTAINING VANISHED, AND THE HEROES OUTSIDE WERE FREE TO ENTER.
"YOU PROBABLY READ ABOUT WHAT THEY FOUND...
"THE WRECKAGE IN AND AROUND THE FORTRESS SEEMED TO BE STREWN WITH BODIES. THOSE OF HIS MOST BITTER ENEMIES...
"...AND THOSE OF HIS MOST LOYAL FRIENDS. I REMEMBER THE BATMAN DESCRIBING IT AS 'LIKE WALKING AMONGST THE FRAGMENTS OF A LEGEND.'
"DEATH AND DESTRUCTION WERE EVERYWHERE...
"...ALMOST.
"ALMOST EVERYWHERE.
"THEY FOUND ME OUTSIDE THE LOCKED GOLD KRYPTONITE CHAMBER, WEEPING. WHEN SUPERWOMAN AND CAPTAIN MARVEL RIPPED THE VAULT OPEN, IT WAS EMPTY.
"HE WAS GONE."
THEY DISCOVERED A HIDDEN PASSAGEWAY, LEADING OUT OF THE FORTRESS, AND IT WAS FINALLY CONCLUDED THAT HE'D WALKED OUT POWERLESS INTO THE SUBZERO WASTES TO FREEZE.
THEY NEVER FOUND HIS BODY.
MORE COFFEE, TIM?

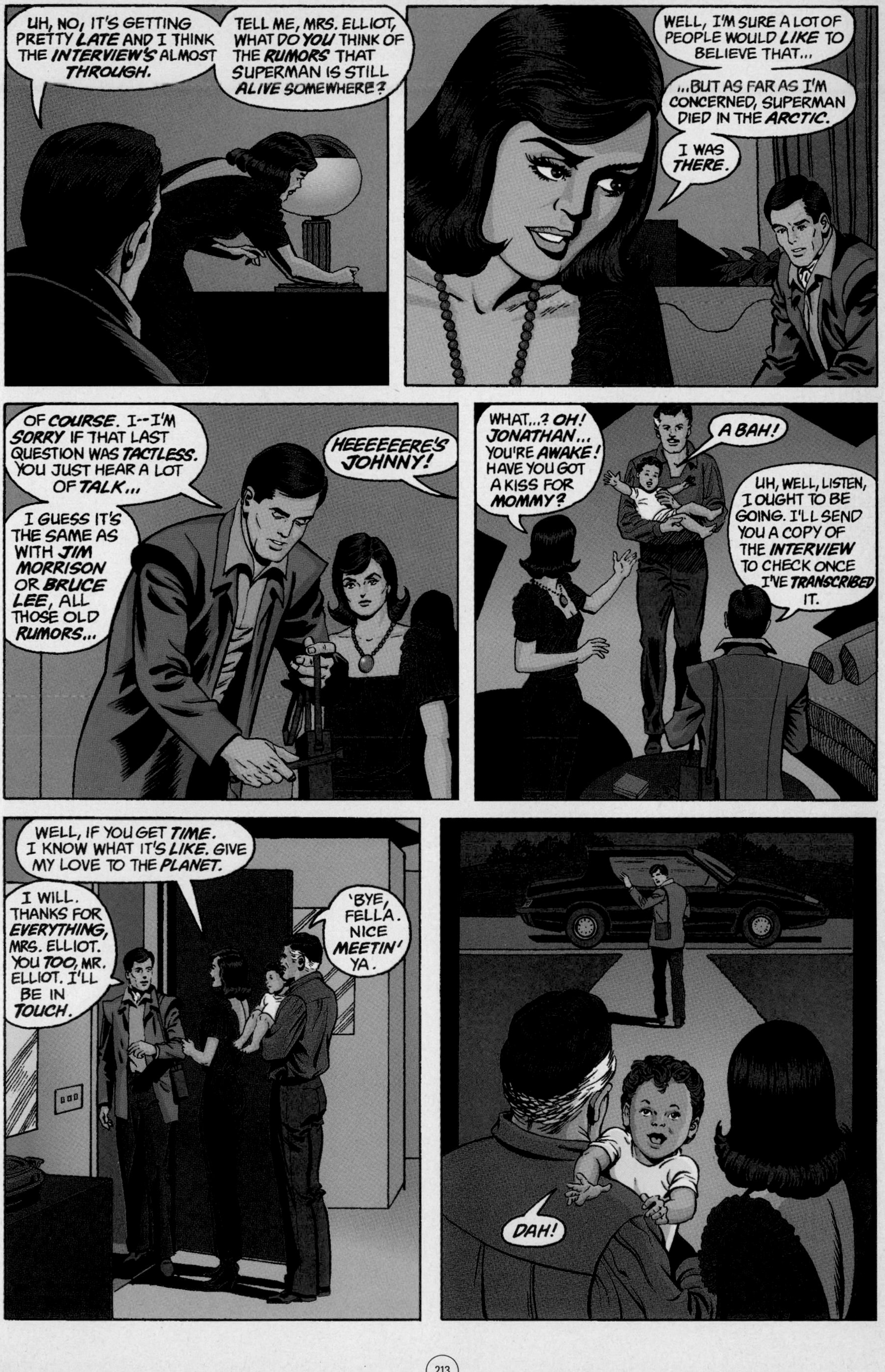
UH, NO, IT'S GETTING PRETTY LATE AND I THINK THE INTERVIEW'S ALMOST THROUGH.
TELL ME, MRS. ELLIOT, WHAT DO YOU THINK OF THE RUMORS THAT SUPERMAN IS STILL ALIVE SOMEWHERE?
WELL, I'M SURE A LOT OF PEOPLE WOULD LIKE TO BELIEVE THAT...
...BUT AS FAR AS I'M CONCERNED, SUPERMAN DIED IN THE ARCTIC.
I WAS THERE.
OF COURSE. I--I'M SORRY IF THAT LAST QUESTION WAS TACTLESS. YOU JUST HEAR A LOT OF TALK...
I GUESS IT'S THE SAME AS WITH JIM MORRISON OR BRUCE LEE, ALL THOSE OLD RUMORS...
HEEEEEERE'S JOHNNY!
WHAT...? OH! JONATHAN... YOU'RE AWAKE! HAVE YOU GOT A KISS FOR MOMMY?
A BAH!
UH, WELL, LISTEN, I OUGHT TO BE GOING. I'LL SEND YOU A COPY OF THE INTERVIEW TO CHECK ONCE I'VE TRANSCRIBED IT.
WELL, IF YOU GET TIME. I KNOW WHAT IT'S LIKE. GIVE MY LOVE TO THE PLANET.
I WILL. THANKS FOR EVERYTHING, MRS. ELLIOT. YOU TOO, MR. ELLIOT. I'LL BE IN TOUCH.
'BYE, FELLA. NICE MEETIN' YA.
DAH!

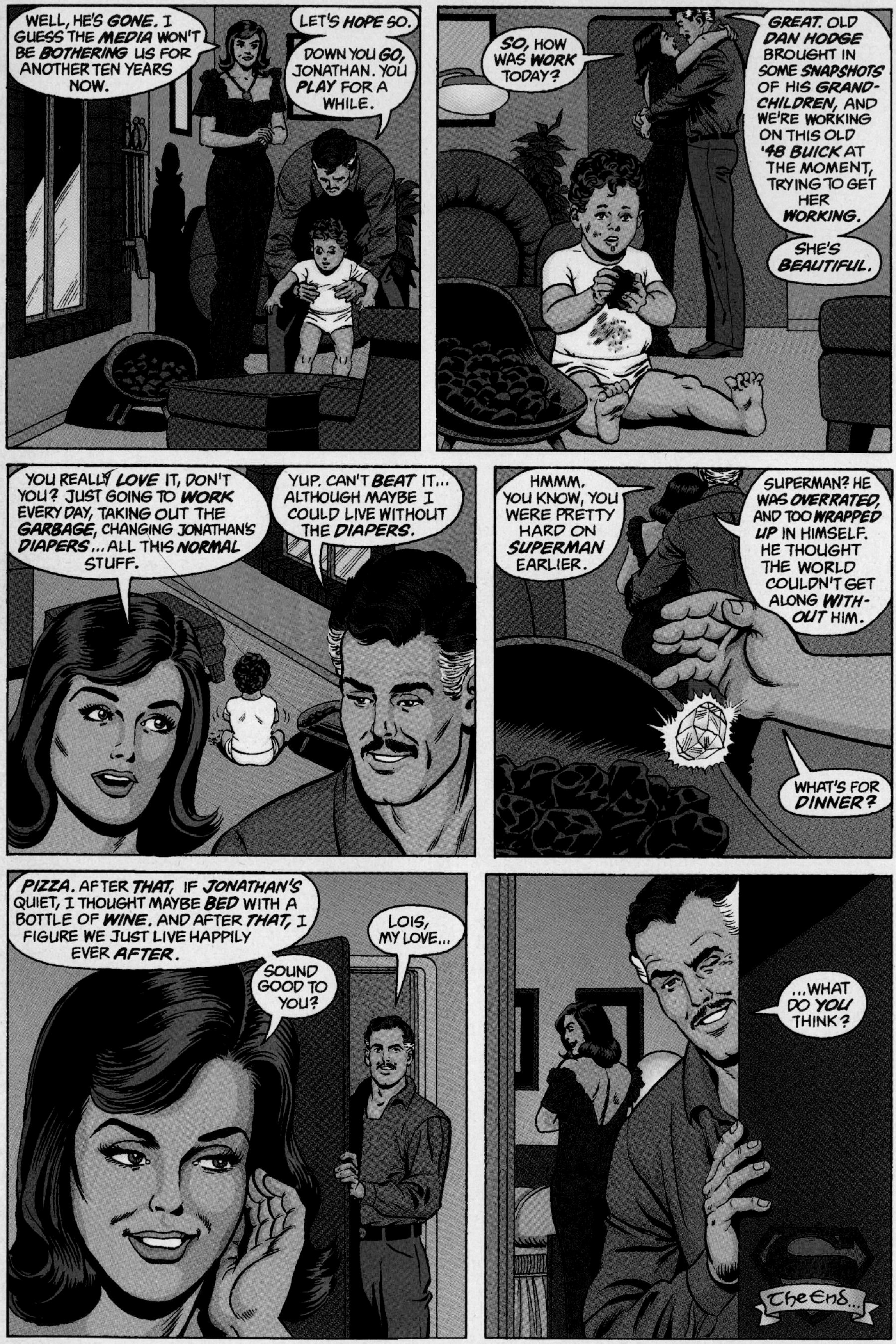
WELL, HE'S GONE. I GUESS THE MEDIA WON'T BE BOTHERING US FOR ANOTHER TEN YEARS NOW.
LET'S HOPE SO.
DOWN YOU GO, JONATHAN. YOU PLAY FOR A WHILE.
SO, HOW WAS WORK TODAY?
GREAT. OLD DAN HODGE BROUGHT IN SOME SNAPSHOTS OF HIS GRAND-CHILDREN, AND WE'RE WORKING ON THIS OLD '48 BUICK AT THE MOMENT, TRYING TO GET HER WORKING.
SHE'S BEAUTIFUL.
YOU REALLY LOVE IT, DON'T YOU? JUST GOING TO WORK EVERY DAY, TAKING OUT THE GARBAGE, CHANGING JONATHAN'S DIAPERS... ALL THIS NORMAL STUFF.
YUP. CAN'T BEAT IT... ALTHOUGH MAYBE I COULD LIVE WITHOUT THE DIAPERS.
HMMM. YOU KNOW, YOU WERE PRETTY HARD ON SUPERMAN EARLIER.
SUPERMAN? HE WAS OVERRATED, AND TOO WRAPPED UP IN HIMSELF. HE THOUGHT THE WORLD COULDN'T GET ALONG WITH-OUT HIM.
WHAT'S FOR DINNER?
PIZZA. AFTER THAT, IF JONATHAN'S QUIET, I THOUGHT MAYBE BED WITH A BOTTLE OF WINE. AND AFTER THAT, I FIGURE WE JUST LIVE HAPPILY EVER AFTER.
SOUND GOOD TO YOU?
LOIS, MY LOVE...
...WHAT DO YOU THINK?
The End...

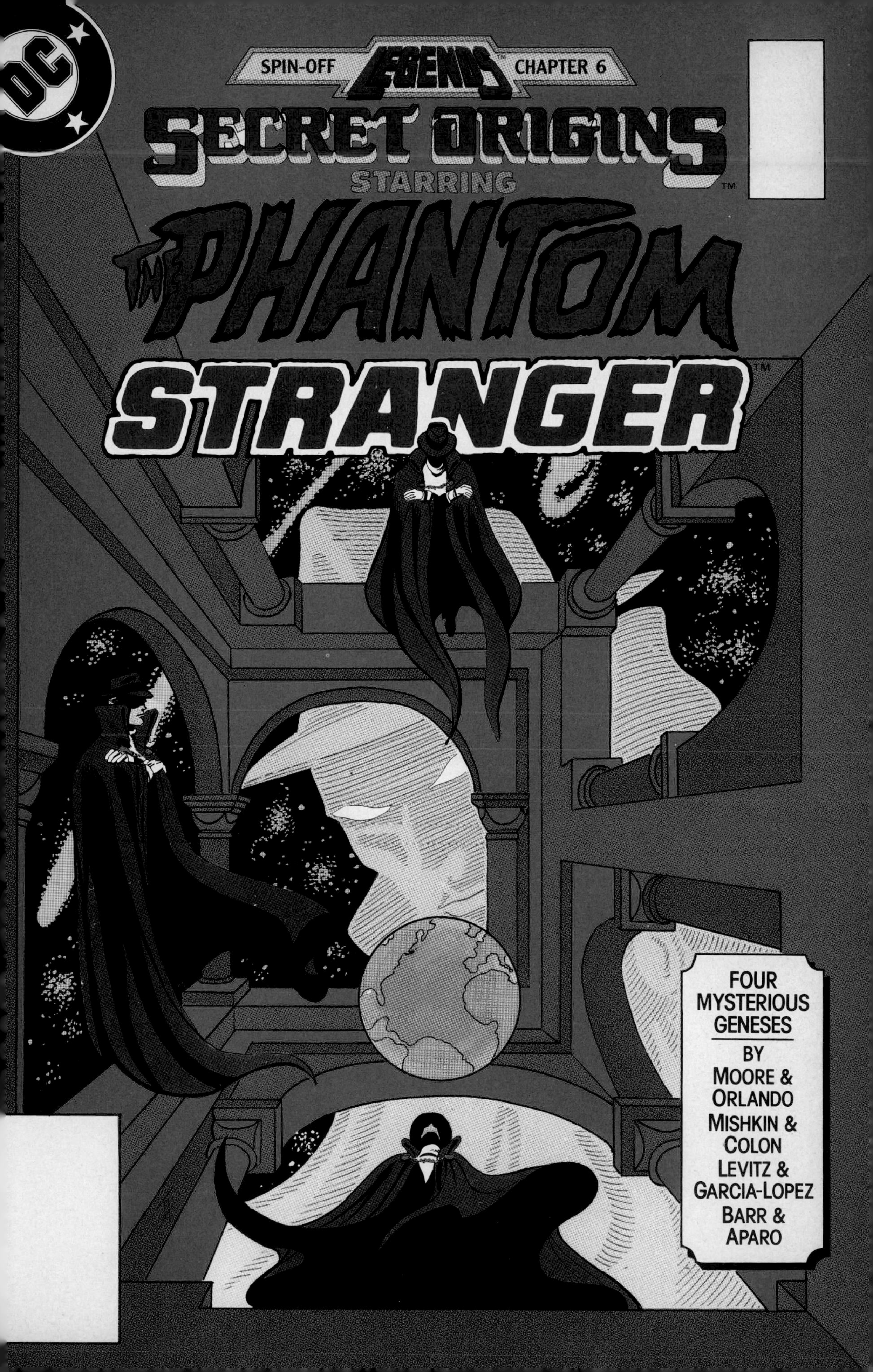
DC
SPIN-OFF LEGENDS CHAPTER 6
SECRET ORIGINS
STARRING
THE PHANTOM STRANGER
FOUR MYSTERIOUS GENESES
BY
MOORE & ORLANDO
MISHKIN & COLON
LEVITZ & GARCIA-LOPEZ
BARR & APARO

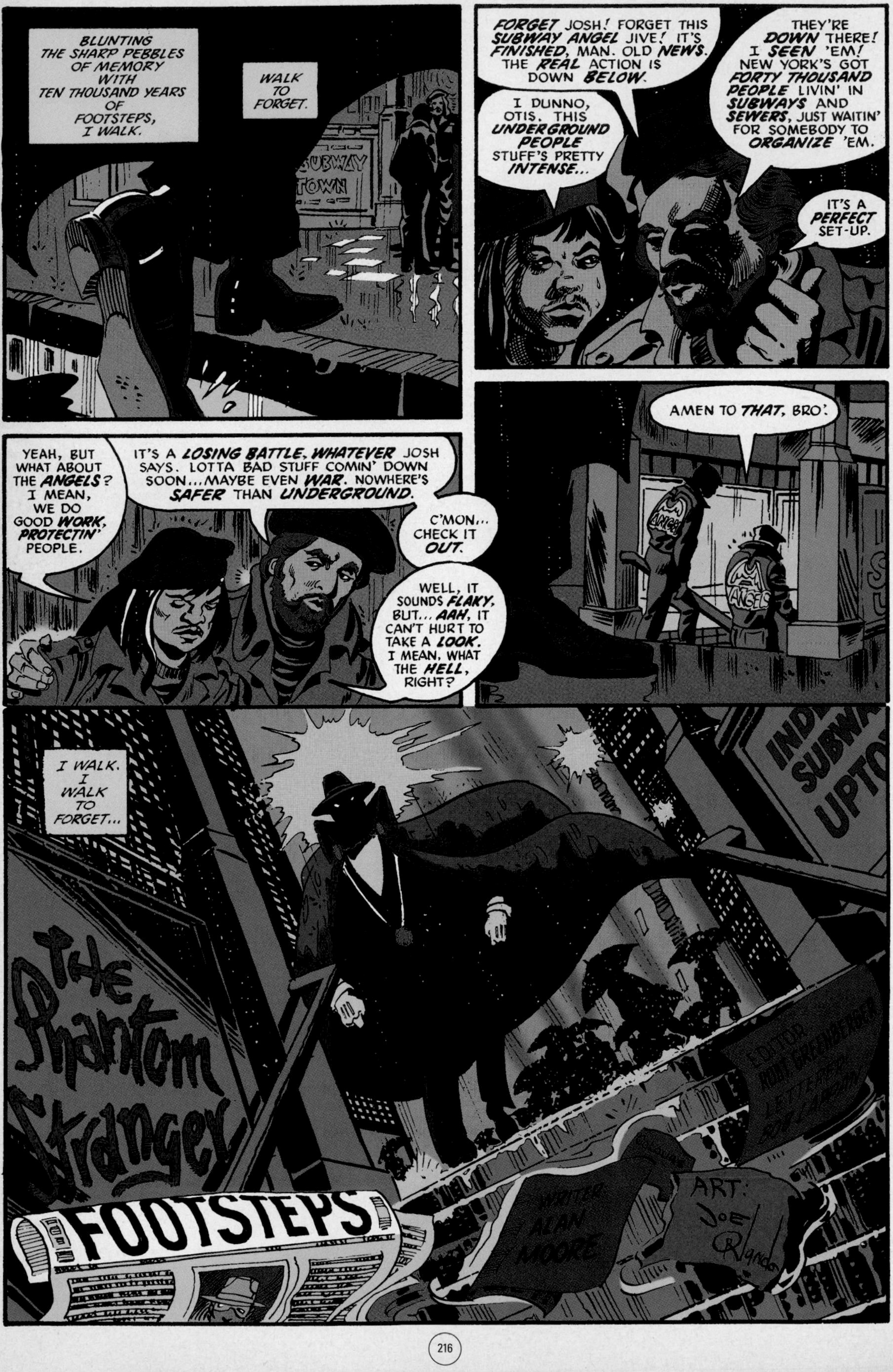
BLUNTING THE SHARP PEBBLES OF MEMORY WITH TEN THOUSAND YEARS OF FOOTSTEPS, I WALK.
WALK TO FORGET.
SUBWAY TOWN
FORGET JOSH! FORGET THIS SUBWAY ANGEL JIVE! IT'S FINISHED, MAN. OLD NEWS. THE REAL ACTION IS DOWN BELOW.
I DUNNO, OTIS. THIS UNDERGROUND PEOPLE STUFF'S PRETTY INTENSE...
THEY'RE DOWN THERE! I SEEN 'EM! NEW YORK'S GOT FORTY THOUSAND PEOPLE LIVIN' IN SUBWAYS AND SEWERS, JUST WAITIN' FOR SOMEBODY TO ORGANIZE 'EM.
IT'S A PERFECT SET-UP.
YEAH, BUT WHAT ABOUT THE ANGELS? I MEAN, WE DO GOOD WORK, PROTECTIN' PEOPLE.
IT'S A LOSING BATTLE. WHATEVER JOSH SAYS. LOTTA BAD STUFF COMIN' DOWN SOON... MAYBE EVEN WAR. NOWHERE'S SAFER THAN UNDERGROUND.
C'MON... CHECK IT OUT.
WELL, IT SOUNDS FLAKY, BUT... AAH, IT CAN'T HURT TO TAKE A LOOK. I MEAN, WHAT THE HELL, RIGHT?
AMEN TO THAT, BRO'.
ANGELS
I WALK. I WALK TO FORGET...
The Phantom Stranger
FOOTSTEPS
WRITER ALAN MOORE
ART: JOE ORLANDO

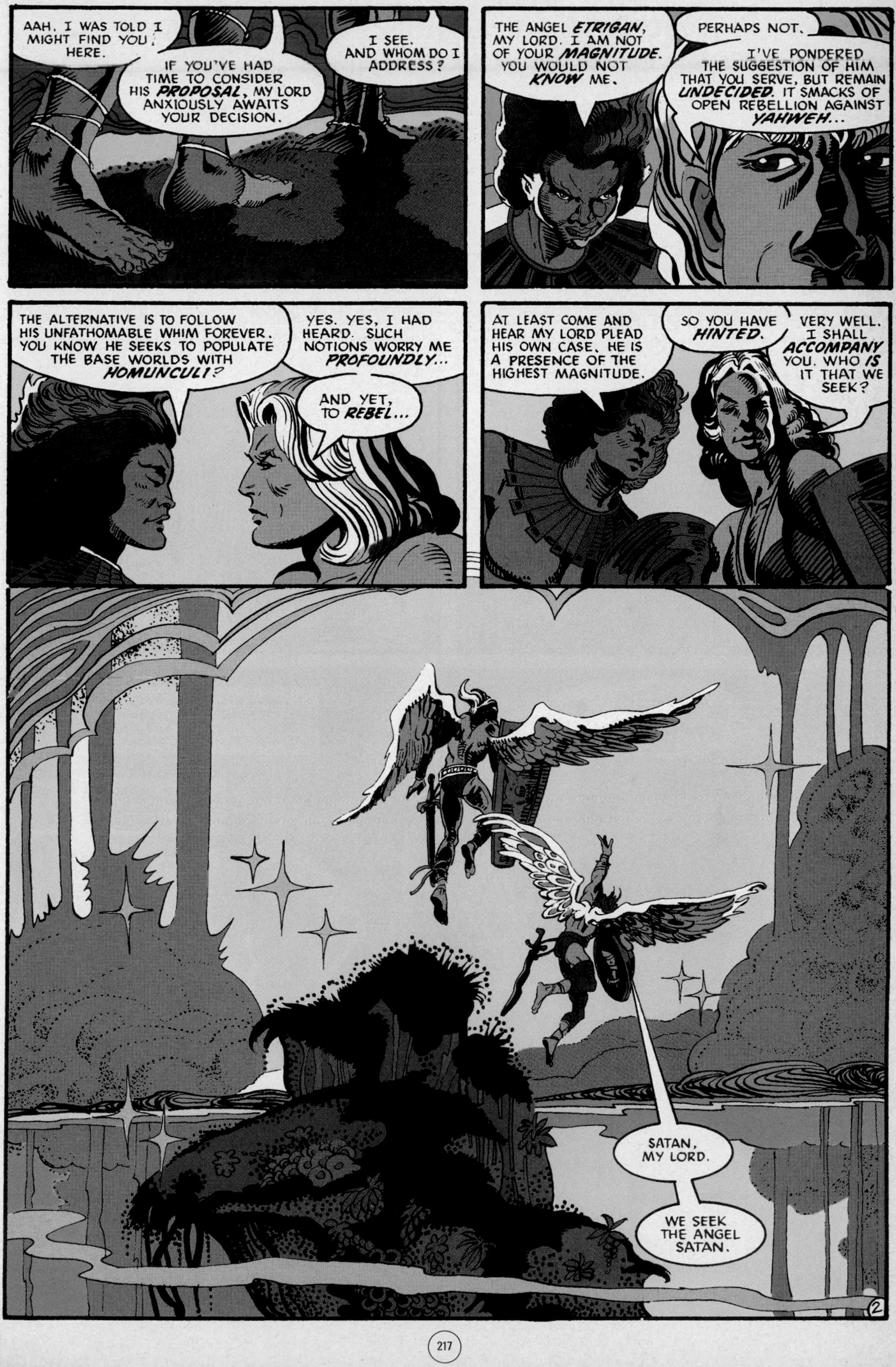

AAH, I WAS TOLD I MIGHT FIND YOU HERE.
IF YOU'VE HAD TIME TO CONSIDER HIS PROPOSAL, MY LORD ANXIOUSLY AWAITS YOUR DECISION.
I SEE. AND WHOM DO I ADDRESS?
THE ANGEL ETRIGAN, MY LORD. I AM NOT OF YOUR MAGNITUDE. YOU WOULD NOT KNOW ME.
PERHAPS NOT.
I'VE PONDERED THE SUGGESTION OF HIM THAT YOU SERVE, BUT REMAIN UNDECIDED. IT SMACKS OF OPEN REBELLION AGAINST YAHWEH...
THE ALTERNATIVE IS TO FOLLOW HIS UNFATHOMABLE WHIM FOREVER. YOU KNOW HE SEEKS TO POPULATE THE BASE WORLDS WITH HOMUNCULI?
YES. YES, I HAD HEARD. SUCH NOTIONS WORRY ME PROFOUNDLY...
AND YET, TO REBEL...
AT LEAST COME AND HEAR MY LORD PLEAD HIS OWN CASE. HE IS A PRESENCE OF THE HIGHEST MAGNITUDE.
SO YOU HAVE HINTED.
VERY WELL. I SHALL ACCOMPANY YOU. WHO IS IT THAT WE SEEK?
SATAN, MY LORD.
WE SEEK THE ANGEL SATAN.
2

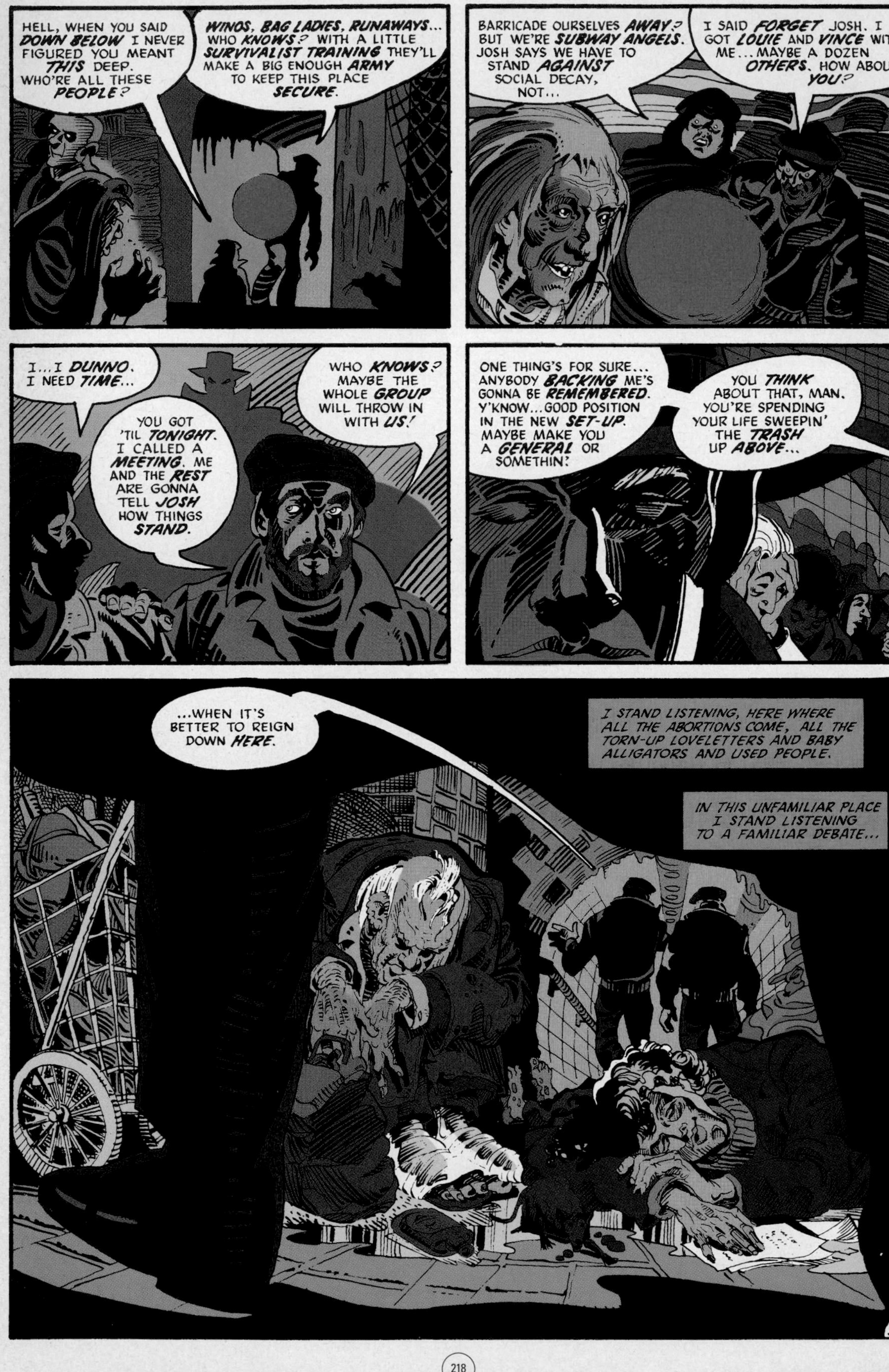
HELL, WHEN YOU SAID DOWN BELOW I NEVER FIGURED YOU MEANT THIS DEEP. WHO'RE ALL THESE PEOPLE?
WINOS, BAG LADIES, RUNAWAYS... WHO KNOWS? WITH A LITTLE SURVIVALIST TRAINING THEY'LL MAKE A BIG ENOUGH ARMY TO KEEP THIS PLACE SECURE.
BARRICADE OURSELVES AWAY? BUT WE'RE SUBWAY ANGELS. JOSH SAYS WE HAVE TO STAND AGAINST SOCIAL DECAY, NOT...
I SAID FORGET JOSH. I GOT LOUIE AND VINCE WITH ME... MAYBE A DOZEN OTHERS. HOW ABOUT YOU?
I... I DUNNO. I NEED TIME...
YOU GOT 'TIL TONIGHT. I CALLED A MEETING. ME AND THE REST ARE GONNA TELL JOSH HOW THINGS STAND.
WHO KNOWS? MAYBE THE WHOLE GROUP WILL THROW IN WITH US!
ONE THING'S FOR SURE... ANYBODY BACKING ME'S GONNA BE REMEMBERED. Y'KNOW... GOOD POSITION IN THE NEW SET-UP. MAYBE MAKE YOU A GENERAL OR SOMETHIN'.
YOU THINK ABOUT THAT, MAN. YOU'RE SPENDING YOUR LIFE SWEEPIN' THE TRASH UP ABOVE...
...WHEN IT'S BETTER TO REIGN DOWN HERE.
I STAND LISTENING, HERE WHERE ALL THE ABORTIONS COME, ALL THE TORN-UP LOVELETTERS AND BABY ALLIGATORS AND USED PEOPLE.
IN THIS UNFAMILIAR PLACE I STAND LISTENING TO A FAMILIAR DEBATE...
3

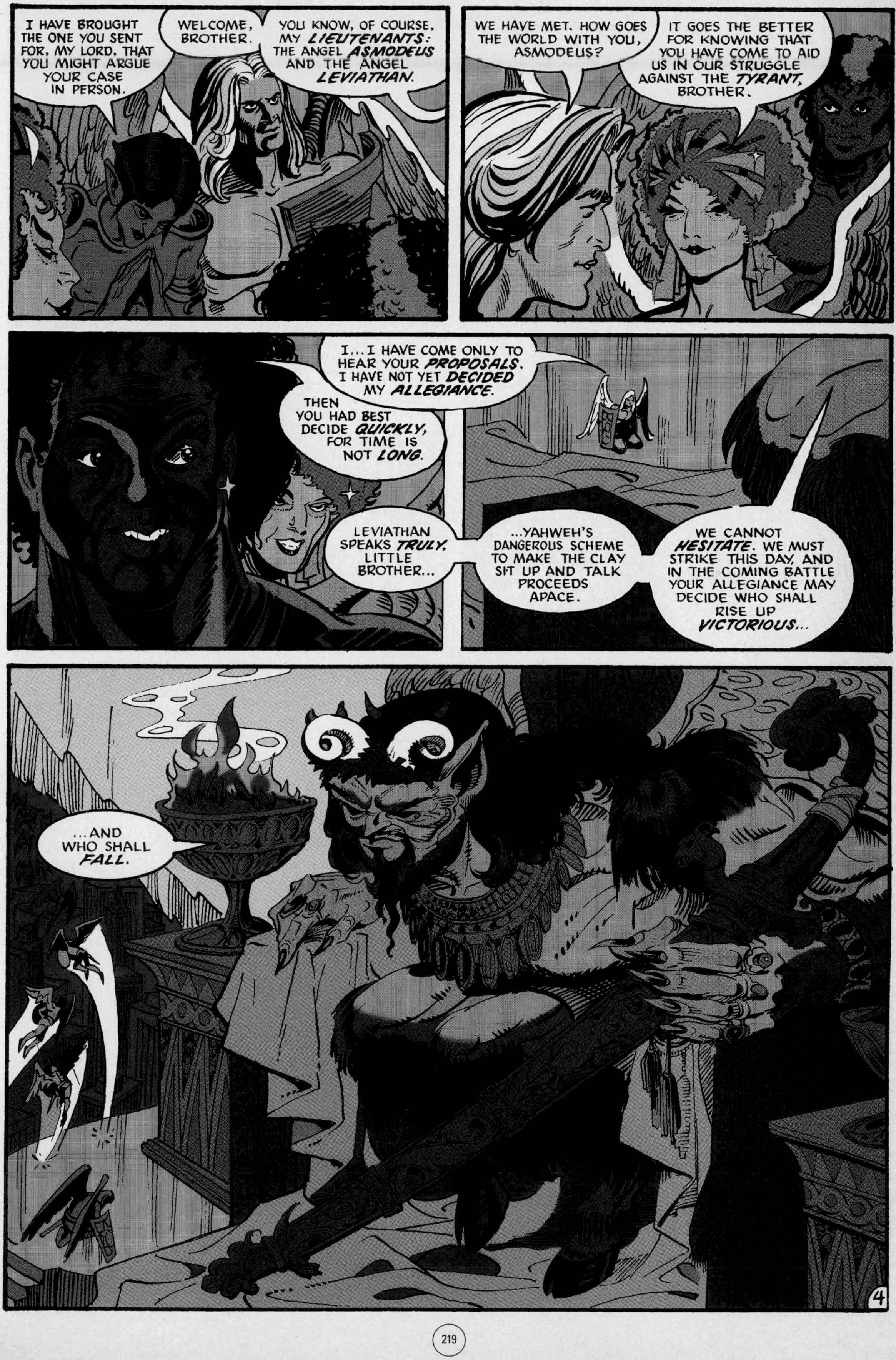
I HAVE BROUGHT THE ONE YOU SENT FOR, MY LORD, THAT YOU MIGHT ARGUE YOUR CASE IN PERSON.
WELCOME, BROTHER.
YOU KNOW, OF COURSE, MY LIEUTENANTS: THE ANGEL ASMODEUS AND THE ANGEL LEVIATHAN.
WE HAVE MET. HOW GOES THE WORLD WITH YOU, ASMODEUS?
IT GOES THE BETTER FOR KNOWING THAT YOU HAVE COME TO AID US IN OUR STRUGGLE AGAINST THE TYRANT, BROTHER.
I...I HAVE COME ONLY TO HEAR YOUR PROPOSALS. I HAVE NOT YET DECIDED MY ALLEGIANCE.
THEN YOU HAD BEST DECIDE QUICKLY, FOR TIME IS NOT LONG.
LEVIATHAN SPEAKS TRULY, LITTLE BROTHER...
...YAHWEH'S DANGEROUS SCHEME TO MAKE THE CLAY SIT UP AND TALK PROCEEDS APACE.
WE CANNOT HESITATE. WE MUST STRIKE THIS DAY, AND IN THE COMING BATTLE YOUR ALLEGIANCE MAY DECIDE WHO SHALL RISE UP VICTORIOUS...
...AND WHO SHALL FALL.
4

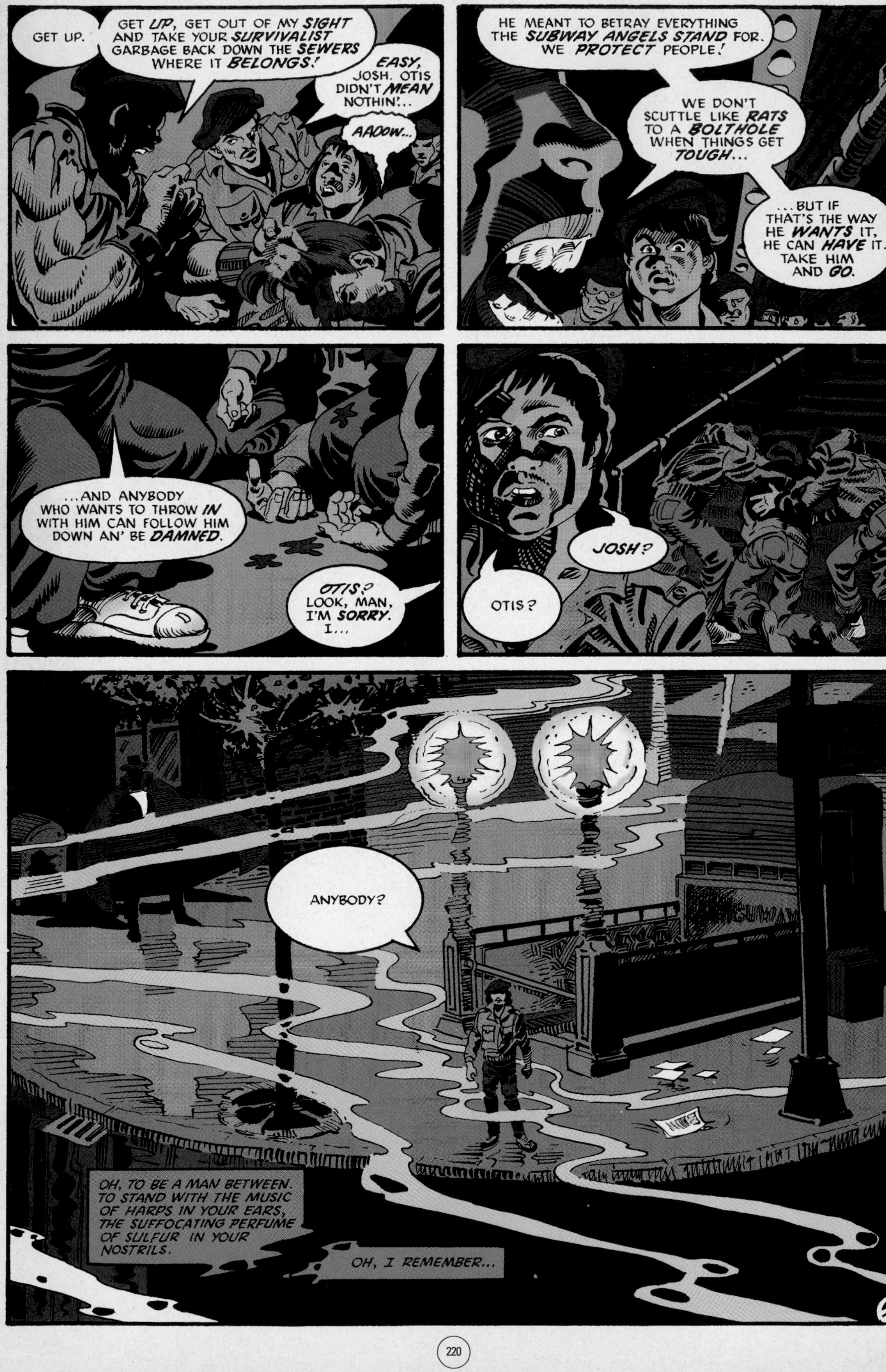
GET UP.
GET UP, GET OUT OF MY SIGHT AND TAKE YOUR SURVIVALIST GARBAGE BACK DOWN THE SEWERS WHERE IT BELONGS!
EASY, JOSH. OTIS DIDN'T MEAN NOTHIN'...
AAOOW...
HE MEANT TO BETRAY EVERYTHING THE SUBWAY ANGELS STAND FOR. WE PROTECT PEOPLE!
WE DON'T SCUTTLE LIKE RATS TO A BOLTHOLE WHEN THINGS GET TOUGH...
...BUT IF THAT'S THE WAY HE WANTS IT, HE CAN HAVE IT. TAKE HIM AND GO.
...AND ANYBODY WHO WANTS TO THROW IN WITH HIM CAN FOLLOW HIM DOWN AN' BE DAMNED.
OTIS? LOOK, MAN, I'M SORRY. I...
JOSH?
OTIS?
ANYBODY?
OH, TO BE A MAN BETWEEN. TO STAND WITH THE MUSIC OF HARPS IN YOUR EARS, THE SUFFOCATING PERFUME OF SULFUR IN YOUR NOSTRILS.
OH, I REMEMBER...
5

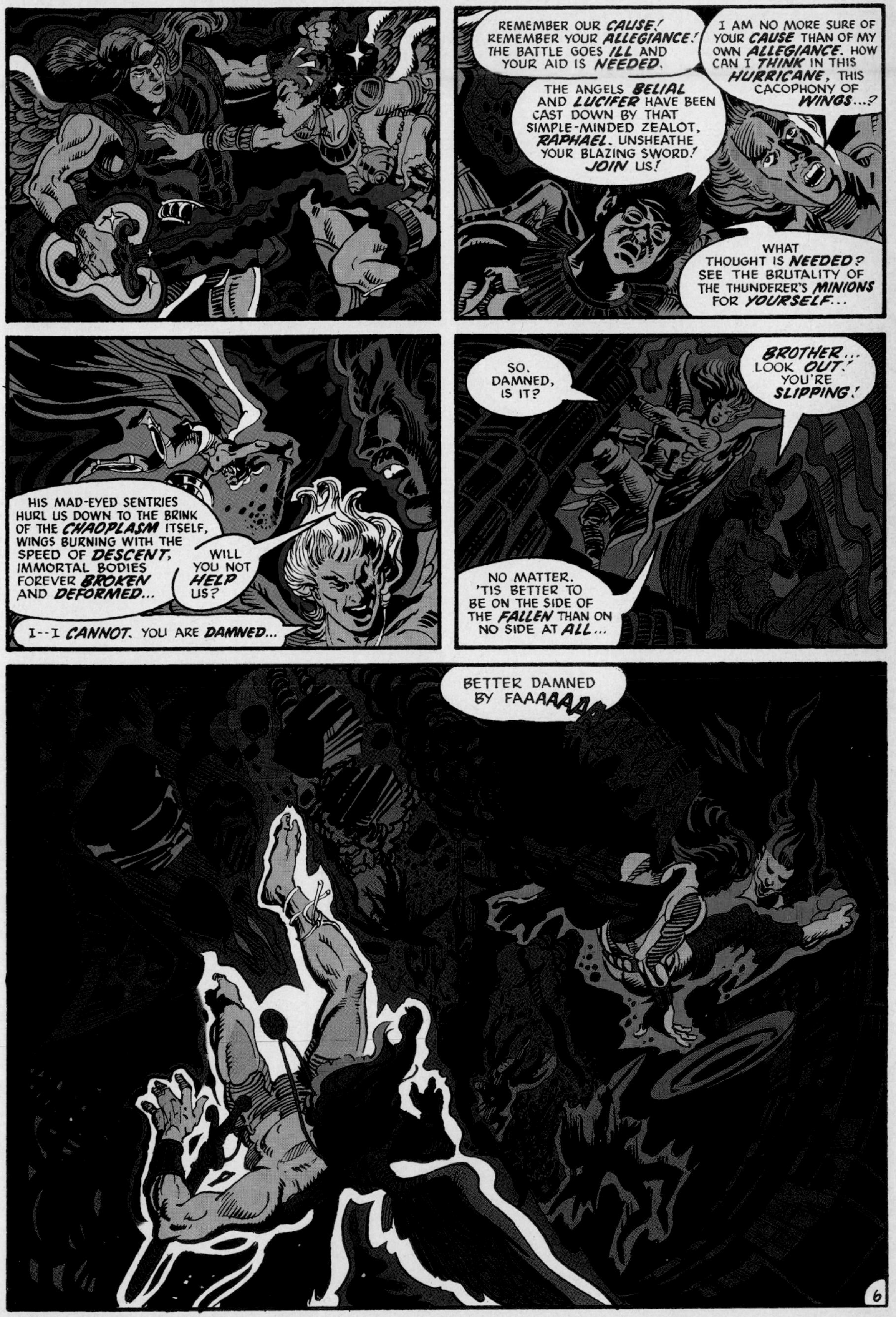
REMEMBER OUR CAUSE! REMEMBER YOUR ALLEGIANCE! THE BATTLE GOES ILL AND YOUR AID IS NEEDED.
THE ANGELS BELIAL AND LUCIFER HAVE BEEN CAST DOWN BY THAT SIMPLE-MINDED ZEALOT, RAPHAEL. UNSHEATHE YOUR BLAZING SWORD! JOIN US!
I AM NO MORE SURE OF YOUR CAUSE THAN OF MY OWN ALLEGIANCE. HOW CAN I THINK IN THIS HURRICANE, THIS CACOPHONY OF WINGS...?
WHAT THOUGHT IS NEEDED? SEE THE BRUTALITY OF THE THUNDERER'S MINIONS FOR YOURSELF...
HIS MAD-EYED SENTRIES HURL US DOWN TO THE BRINK OF THE CHAOPLASM ITSELF, WINGS BURNING WITH THE SPEED OF DESCENT, IMMORTAL BODIES FOREVER BROKEN AND DEFORMED...
WILL YOU NOT HELP US?
I--I CANNOT. YOU ARE DAMNED...
SO. DAMNED, IS IT?
BROTHER... LOOK OUT! YOU'RE SLIPPING!
NO MATTER. 'TIS BETTER TO BE ON THE SIDE OF THE FALLEN THAN ON NO SIDE AT ALL...
BETTER DAMNED BY FAAAAAAA
6

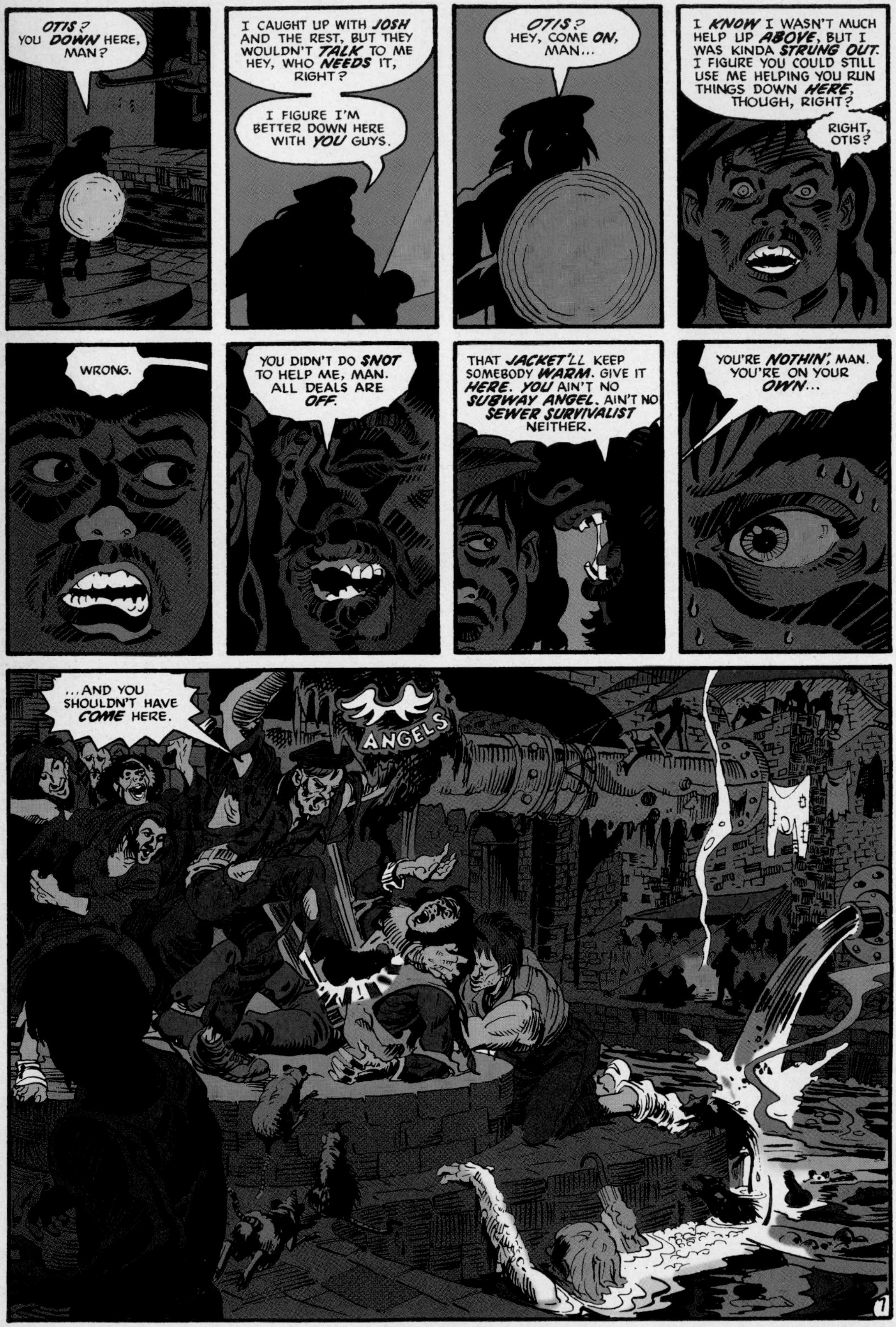
OTIS? YOU DOWN HERE, MAN?
I CAUGHT UP WITH JOSH AND THE REST, BUT THEY WOULDN'T TALK TO ME HEY, WHO NEEDS IT, RIGHT?
I FIGURE I'M BETTER DOWN HERE WITH YOU GUYS.
OTIS? HEY, COME ON, MAN...
I KNOW I WASN'T MUCH HELP UP ABOVE, BUT I WAS KINDA STRUNG OUT. I FIGURE YOU COULD STILL USE ME HELPING YOU RUN THINGS DOWN HERE, THOUGH, RIGHT?
RIGHT, OTIS?
WRONG.
YOU DIDN'T DO SNOT TO HELP ME, MAN. ALL DEALS ARE OFF.
THAT JACKET'LL KEEP SOMEBODY WARM. GIVE IT HERE. YOU AIN'T NO SUBWAY ANGEL. AIN'T NO SEWER SURVIVALIST NEITHER.
YOU'RE NOTHIN', MAN. YOU'RE ON YOUR OWN...
...AND YOU SHOULDN'T HAVE COME HERE.
ANGELS
7

BROTHERS? I HAVE FLOWN MANY DAYS TO *FIND* YOU AND WALKED ON SHARP CINDERS WHEN I WEARIED OF *FLIGHT*.

THE *POWERS* AND *THRONES* HAVE *DISOWNED* ME. SHALL THE *FALLEN* DISOWN ME *ALSO*?

DISOWN YOU? AFTER WALKING SO *FAR?* BROTHER, WE *WELCOME* YOUR HANDSOME FACE, IT MAKES OUR *OWN* DEFORMITY SO MUCH MORE *BEARABLE!*

AND ALL THAT *WALKING*: SO MUCH *SLOWER* AND MORE *TEDIOUS* THAN OUR *OWN* DESCENT.

I--I DID NOT MEAN...

FILTH! COWARD! HALF-FALLEN ONE!

FALL *NOW!* WALLOW IN THE *ORDURE* THAT IS YOUR ONLY *BROTHER!*

UUUUAAGH!

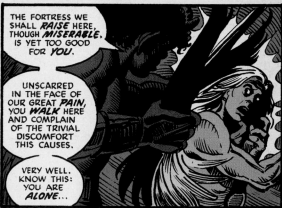

THE FORTRESS WE SHALL *RAISE* HERE, THOUGH *MISERABLE*, IS YET TOO GOOD FOR *YOU*.

UNSCARRED IN THE FACE OF OUR GREAT *PAIN*, YOU *WALK* HERE AND COMPLAIN OF THE TRIVIAL DISCOMFORT THIS CAUSES.

VERY WELL, KNOW THIS: YOU ARE *ALONE*...

...AND YOU SHALL *WALK* ALONE FOR ALL *ETERNITY*.

8

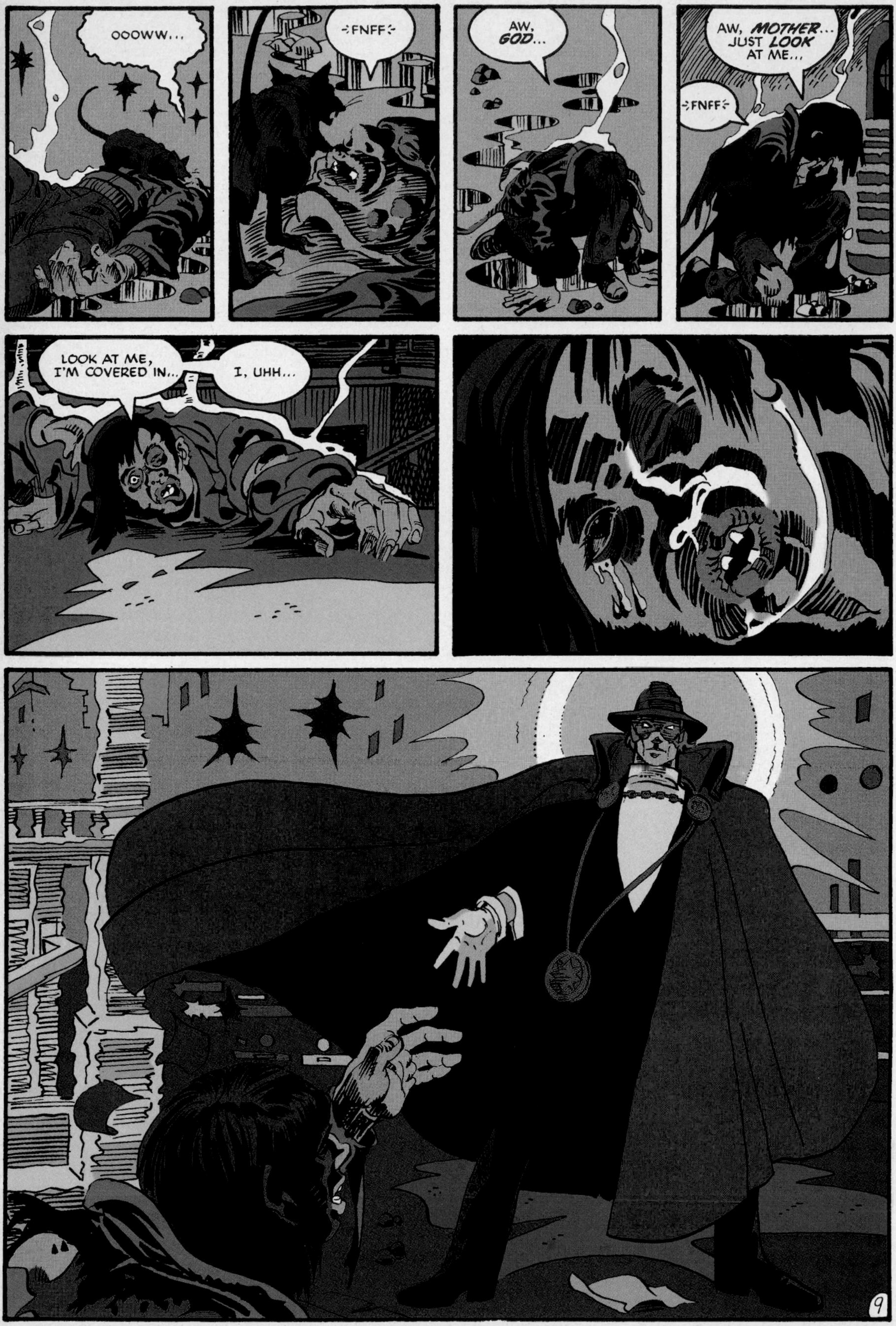
OOOWW...
FNFF
AW, GOD...
AW, MOTHER... JUST LOOK AT ME...
FNFF
LOOK AT ME, I'M COVERED IN...
I, UHH...
9

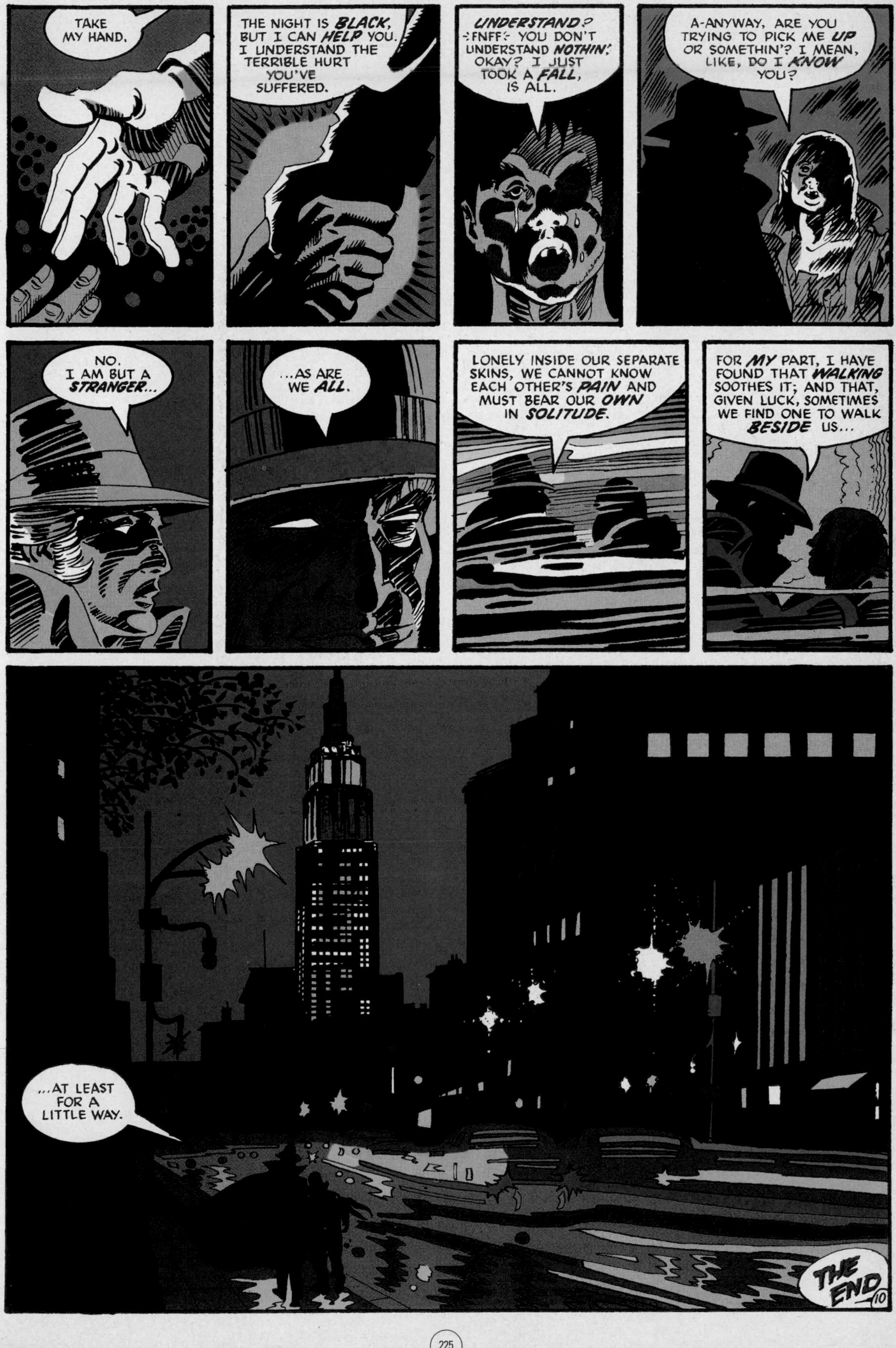

TAKE MY HAND.
THE NIGHT IS BLACK, BUT I CAN HELP YOU. I UNDERSTAND THE TERRIBLE HURT YOU'VE SUFFERED.
UNDERSTAND? -FNFF- YOU DON'T UNDERSTAND NOTHIN'! OKAY? I JUST TOOK A FALL, IS ALL.
A-ANYWAY, ARE YOU TRYING TO PICK ME UP OR SOMETHIN'? I MEAN, LIKE, DO I KNOW YOU?
NO. I AM BUT A STRANGER...
...AS ARE WE ALL.
LONELY INSIDE OUR SEPARATE SKINS, WE CANNOT KNOW EACH OTHER'S PAIN AND MUST BEAR OUR OWN IN SOLITUDE.
FOR MY PART, I HAVE FOUND THAT WALKING SOOTHES IT; AND THAT, GIVEN LUCK, SOMETIMES WE FIND ONE TO WALK BESIDE US...
...AT LEAST FOR A LITTLE WAY.
THE END
10

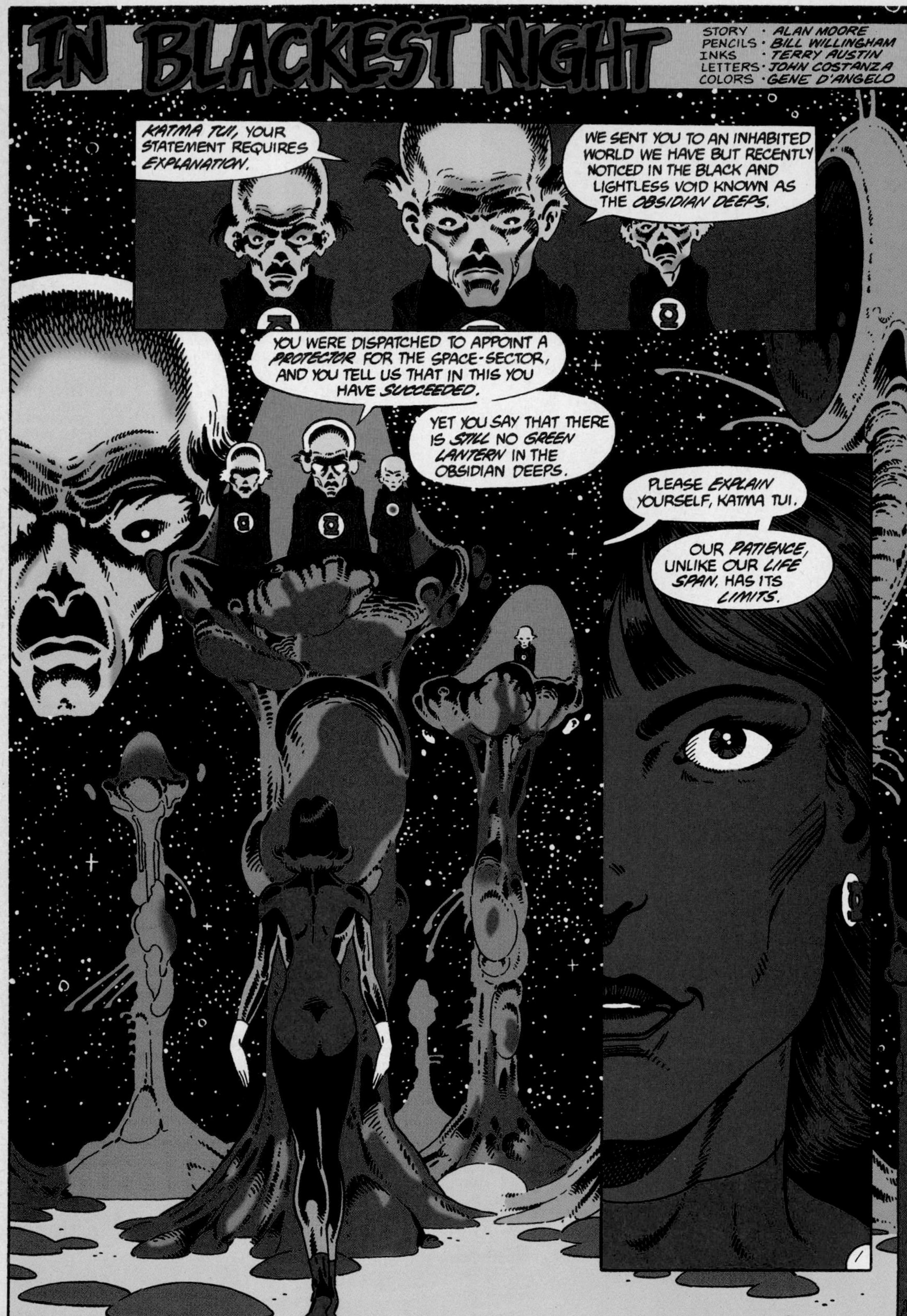
IN BLACKEST NIGHT
STORY · ALAN MOORE
PENCILS · BILL WILLINGHAM
INKS · TERRY AUSTIN
LETTERS · JOHN COSTANZA
COLORS · GENE D'ANGELO
KATMA TUI, YOUR STATEMENT REQUIRES EXPLANATION.
WE SENT YOU TO AN INHABITED WORLD WE HAVE BUT RECENTLY NOTICED IN THE BLACK AND LIGHTLESS VOID KNOWN AS THE OBSIDIAN DEEPS.
YOU WERE DISPATCHED TO APPOINT A PROTECTOR FOR THE SPACE-SECTOR, AND YOU TELL US THAT IN THIS YOU HAVE SUCCEEDED.
YET YOU SAY THAT THERE IS STILL NO GREEN LANTERN IN THE OBSIDIAN DEEPS.
PLEASE EXPLAIN YOURSELF, KATMA TUI.
OUR PATIENCE, UNLIKE OUR LIFE SPAN, HAS ITS LIMITS.
1

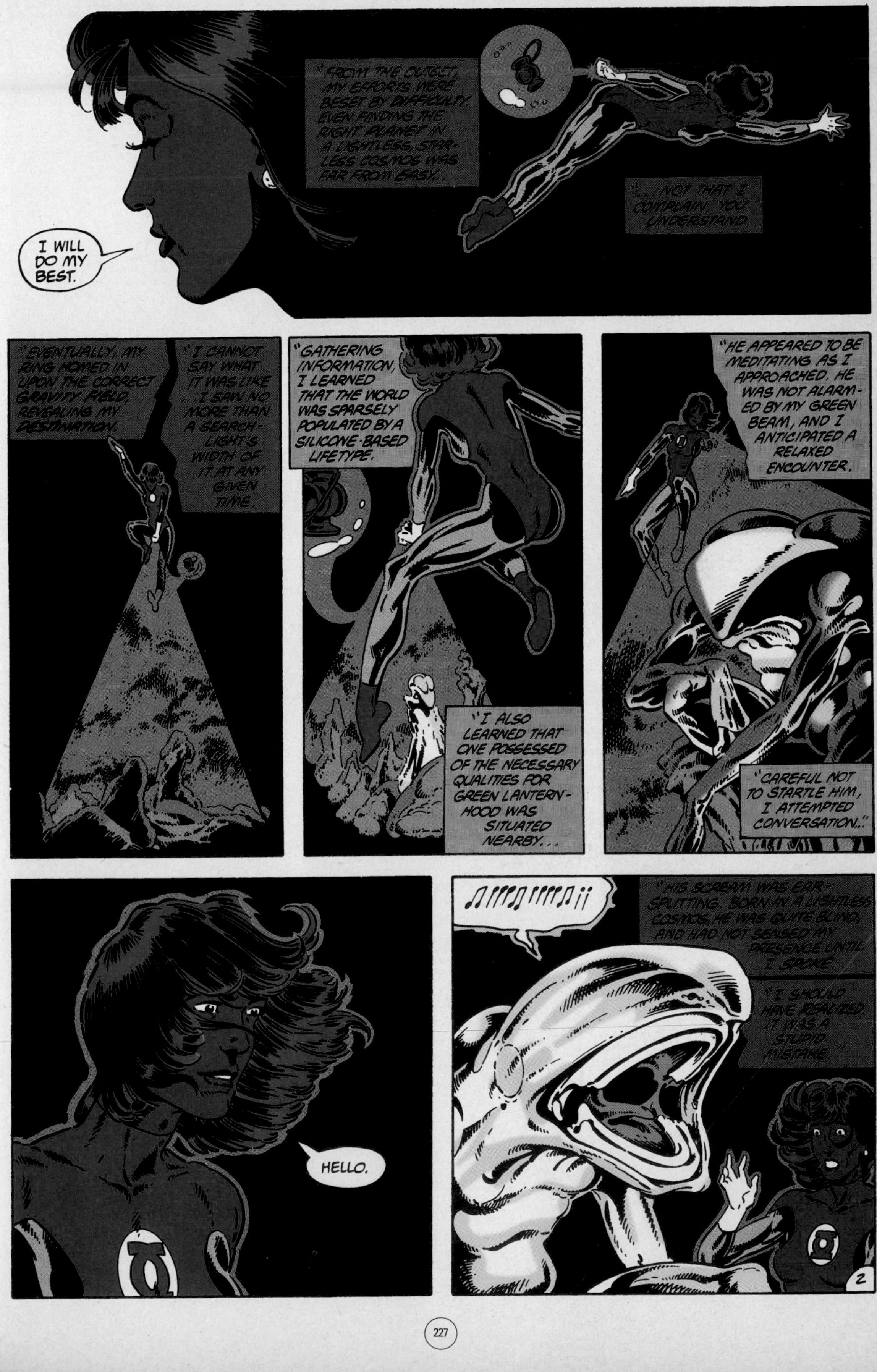

I WILL DO MY BEST.
"FROM THE OUTSET, MY EFFORTS WERE BESET BY DIFFICULTY. EVEN FINDING THE RIGHT PLANET IN A LIGHTLESS, STARLESS COSMOS WAS FAR FROM EASY...
"...NOT THAT I COMPLAIN, YOU UNDERSTAND.
"EVENTUALLY, MY RING HOMED IN UPON THE CORRECT GRAVITY FIELD, REVEALING MY DESTINATION.
"I CANNOT SAY WHAT IT WAS LIKE ...I SAW NO MORE THAN A SEARCHLIGHT'S WIDTH OF IT AT ANY GIVEN TIME.
"GATHERING INFORMATION, I LEARNED THAT THE WORLD WAS SPARSELY POPULATED BY A SILICONE-BASED LIFETYPE.
"I ALSO LEARNED THAT ONE POSSESSED OF THE NECESSARY QUALITIES FOR GREEN LANTERNHOOD WAS SITUATED NEARBY...
"HE APPEARED TO BE MEDITATING AS I APPROACHED. HE WAS NOT ALARMED BY MY GREEN BEAM, AND I ANTICIPATED A RELAXED ENCOUNTER.
"CAREFUL NOT TO STARTLE HIM, I ATTEMPTED CONVERSATION..."
HELLO.
"HIS SCREAM WAS EAR-SPLITTING. BORN IN A LIGHTLESS COSMOS, HE WAS QUITE BLIND, AND HAD NOT SENSED MY PRESENCE UNTIL I SPOKE.
"I SHOULD HAVE REALIZED IT WAS A STUPID MISTAKE.
2

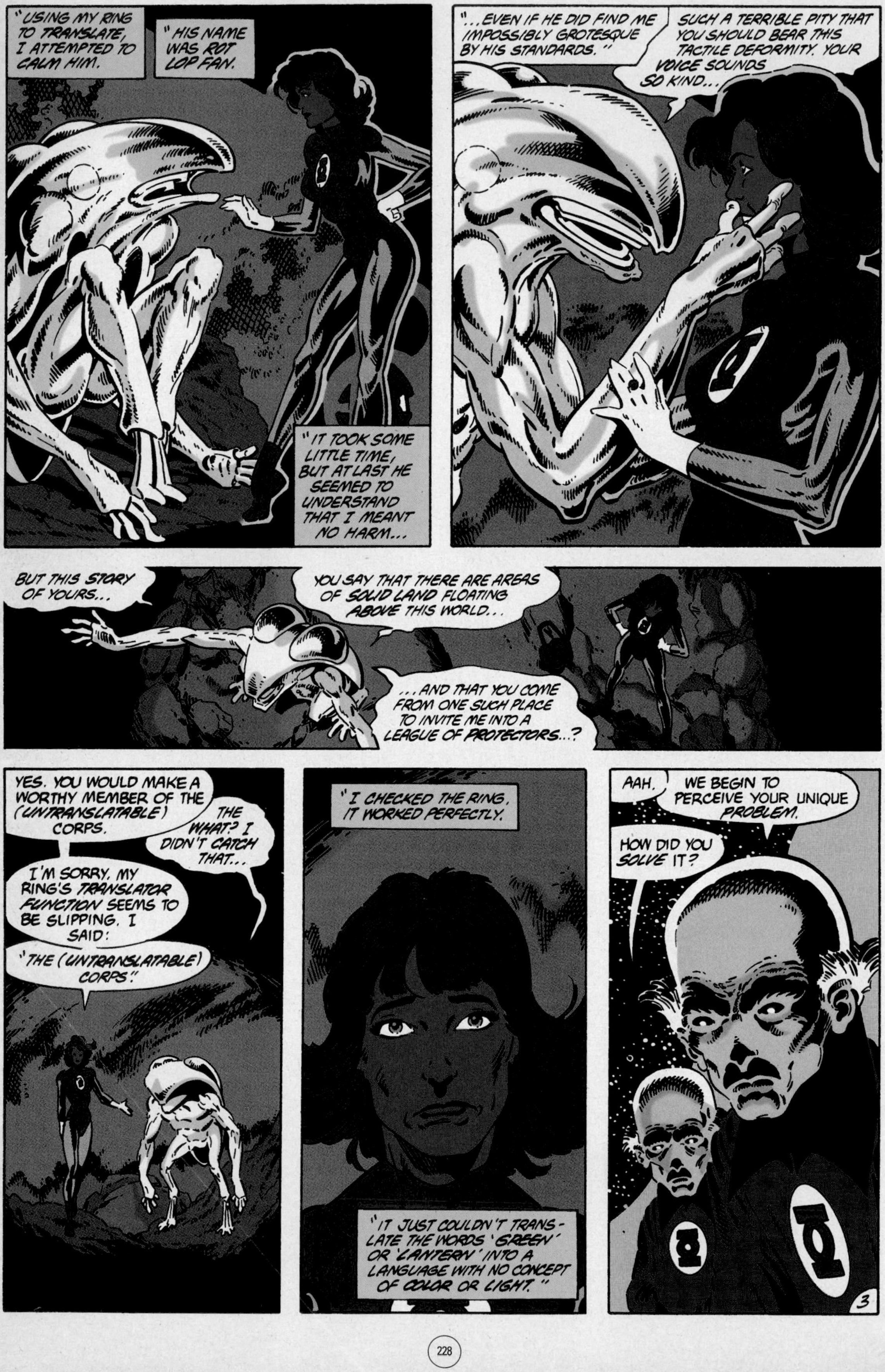
"USING MY RING TO TRANSLATE, I ATTEMPTED TO CALM HIM.
"HIS NAME WAS ROT LOP FAN.
"IT TOOK SOME LITTLE TIME, BUT AT LAST HE SEEMED TO UNDERSTAND THAT I MEANT NO HARM...
"...EVEN IF HE DID FIND ME IMPOSSIBLY GROTESQUE BY HIS STANDARDS."
SUCH A TERRIBLE PITY THAT YOU SHOULD BEAR THIS TACTILE DEFORMITY. YOUR VOICE SOUNDS SO KIND...
BUT THIS STORY OF YOURS...
YOU SAY THAT THERE ARE AREAS OF SOLID LAND FLOATING ABOVE THIS WORLD...
...AND THAT YOU COME FROM ONE SUCH PLACE TO INVITE ME INTO A LEAGUE OF PROTECTORS...?
YES. YOU WOULD MAKE A WORTHY MEMBER OF THE (UNTRANSLATABLE) CORPS.
THE WHAT? I DIDN'T CATCH THAT...
I'M SORRY. MY RING'S TRANSLATOR FUNCTION SEEMS TO BE SLIPPING. I SAID:
"THE (UNTRANSLATABLE) CORPS."
"I CHECKED THE RING. IT WORKED PERFECTLY.
"IT JUST COULDN'T TRANSLATE THE WORDS 'GREEN' OR 'LANTERN' INTO A LANGUAGE WITH NO CONCEPT OF COLOR OR LIGHT."
AAH.
WE BEGIN TO PERCEIVE YOUR UNIQUE PROBLEM.
HOW DID YOU SOLVE IT?
3

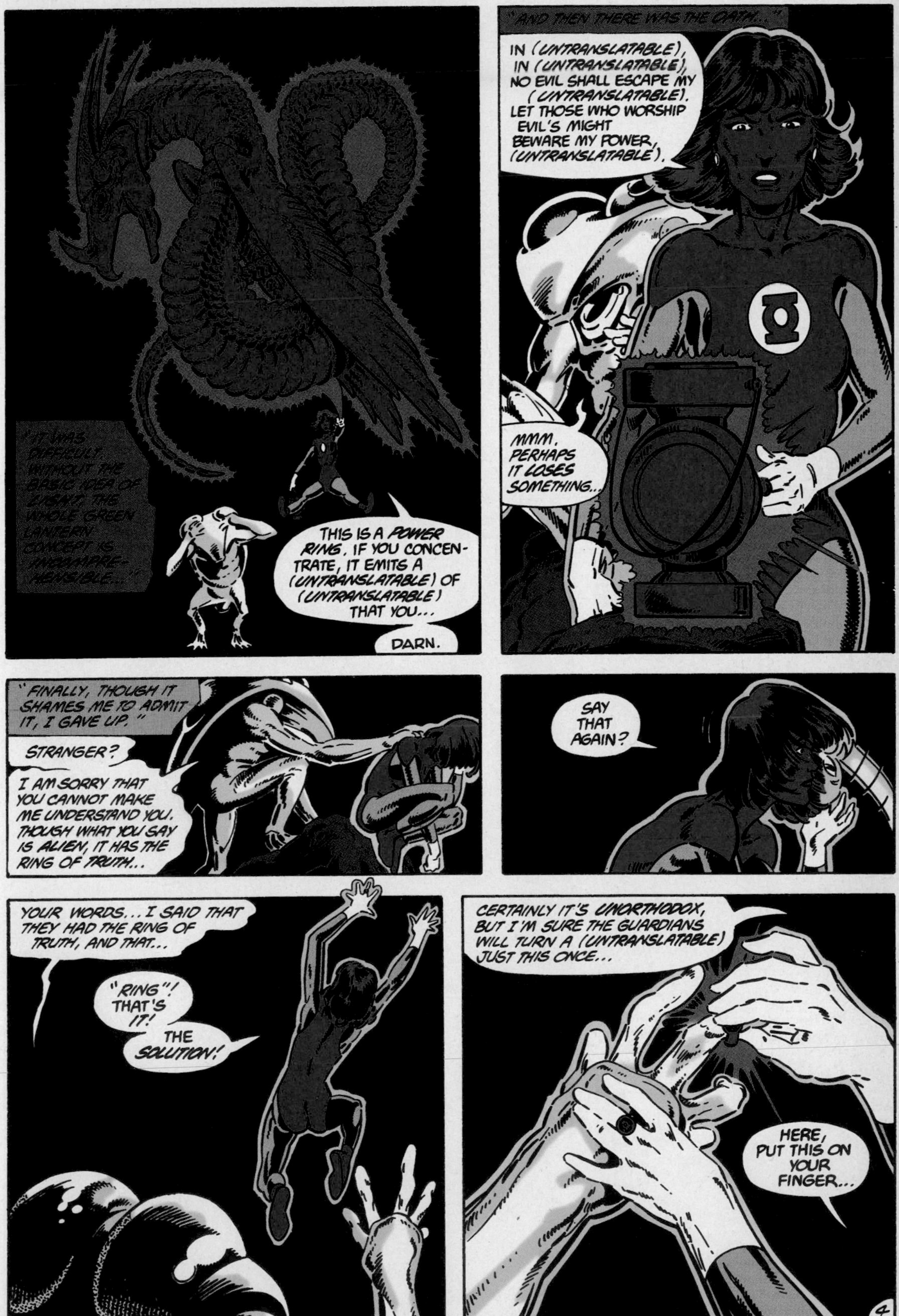
"IT WAS DIFFICULT. WITHOUT THE BASIC IDEA OF LIGHT, THE WHOLE GREEN LANTERN CONCEPT IS INCOMPRE-HENSIBLE..."
THIS IS A POWER RING. IF YOU CONCEN-TRATE, IT EMITS A (UNTRANSLATABLE) OF (UNTRANSLATABLE) THAT YOU...
DARN.
"AND THEN THERE WAS THE OATH..."
IN (UNTRANSLATABLE), IN (UNTRANSLATABLE), NO EVIL SHALL ESCAPE MY (UNTRANSLATABLE). LET THOSE WHO WORSHIP EVIL'S MIGHT BEWARE MY POWER, (UNTRANSLATABLE).
MMM. PERHAPS IT LOSES SOMETHING...
"FINALLY, THOUGH IT SHAMES ME TO ADMIT IT, I GAVE UP."
STRANGER?
I AM SORRY THAT YOU CANNOT MAKE ME UNDERSTAND YOU. THOUGH WHAT YOU SAY IS ALIEN, IT HAS THE RING OF TRUTH...
SAY THAT AGAIN?
YOUR WORDS... I SAID THAT THEY HAD THE RING OF TRUTH, AND THAT...
"RING"! THAT'S IT!
THE SOLUTION!
CERTAINLY IT'S UNORTHODOX, BUT I'M SURE THE GUARDIANS WILL TURN A (UNTRANSLATABLE) JUST THIS ONCE...
HERE, PUT THIS ON YOUR FINGER...
4

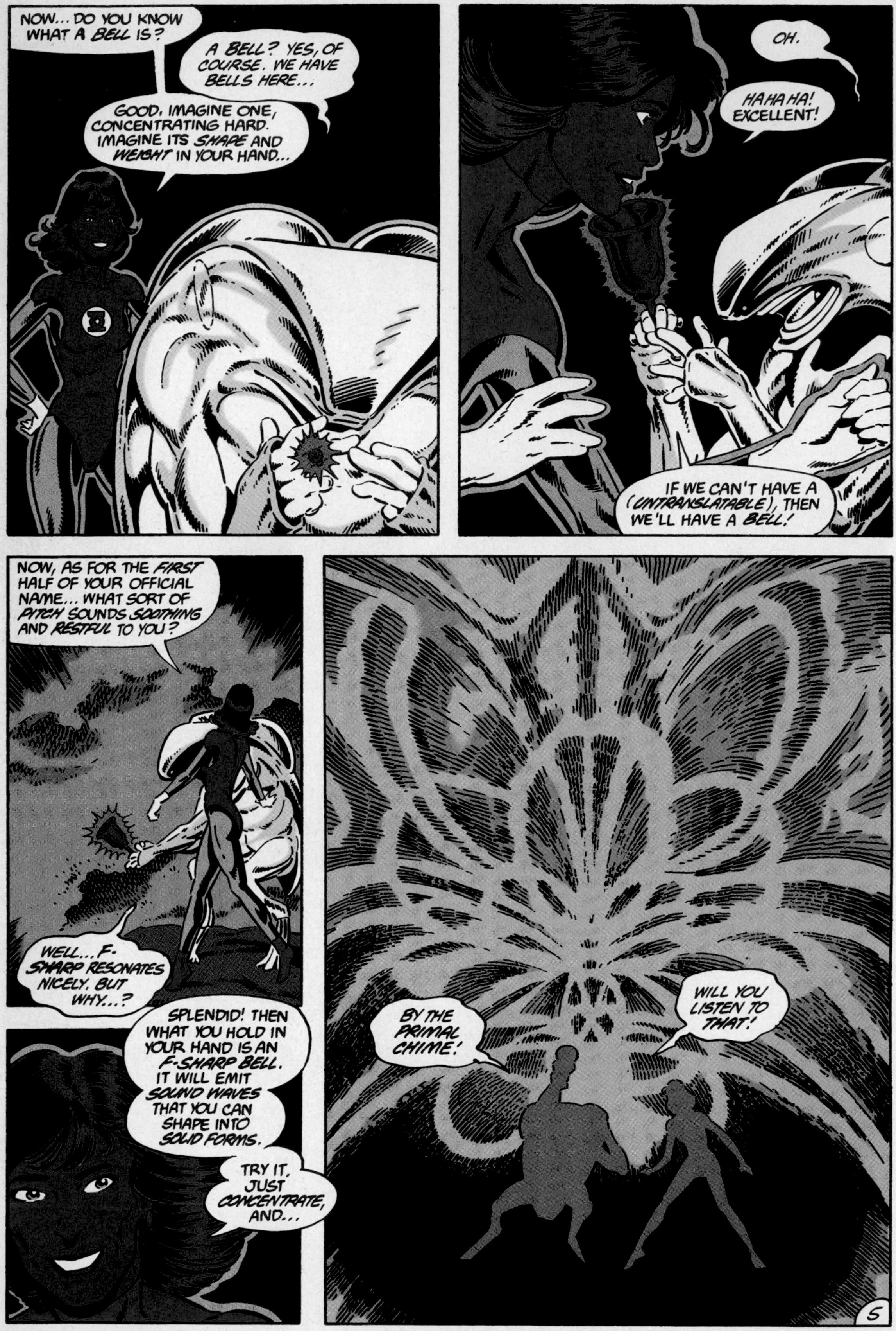
NOW... DO YOU KNOW WHAT A BELL IS?
A BELL? YES, OF COURSE. WE HAVE BELLS HERE...
GOOD. IMAGINE ONE, CONCENTRATING HARD. IMAGINE ITS SHAPE AND WEIGHT IN YOUR HAND...
OH.
HA HA HA! EXCELLENT!
IF WE CAN'T HAVE A (UNTRANSLATABLE), THEN WE'LL HAVE A BELL!
NOW, AS FOR THE FIRST HALF OF YOUR OFFICIAL NAME... WHAT SORT OF PITCH SOUNDS SOOTHING AND RESTFUL TO YOU?
WELL... F-SHARP RESONATES NICELY. BUT WHY...?
SPLENDID! THEN WHAT YOU HOLD IN YOUR HAND IS AN F-SHARP BELL. IT WILL EMIT SOUND WAVES THAT YOU CAN SHAPE INTO SOLID FORMS.
TRY IT. JUST CONCENTRATE, AND...
BY THE PRIMAL CHIME!
WILL YOU LISTEN TO THAT!
5

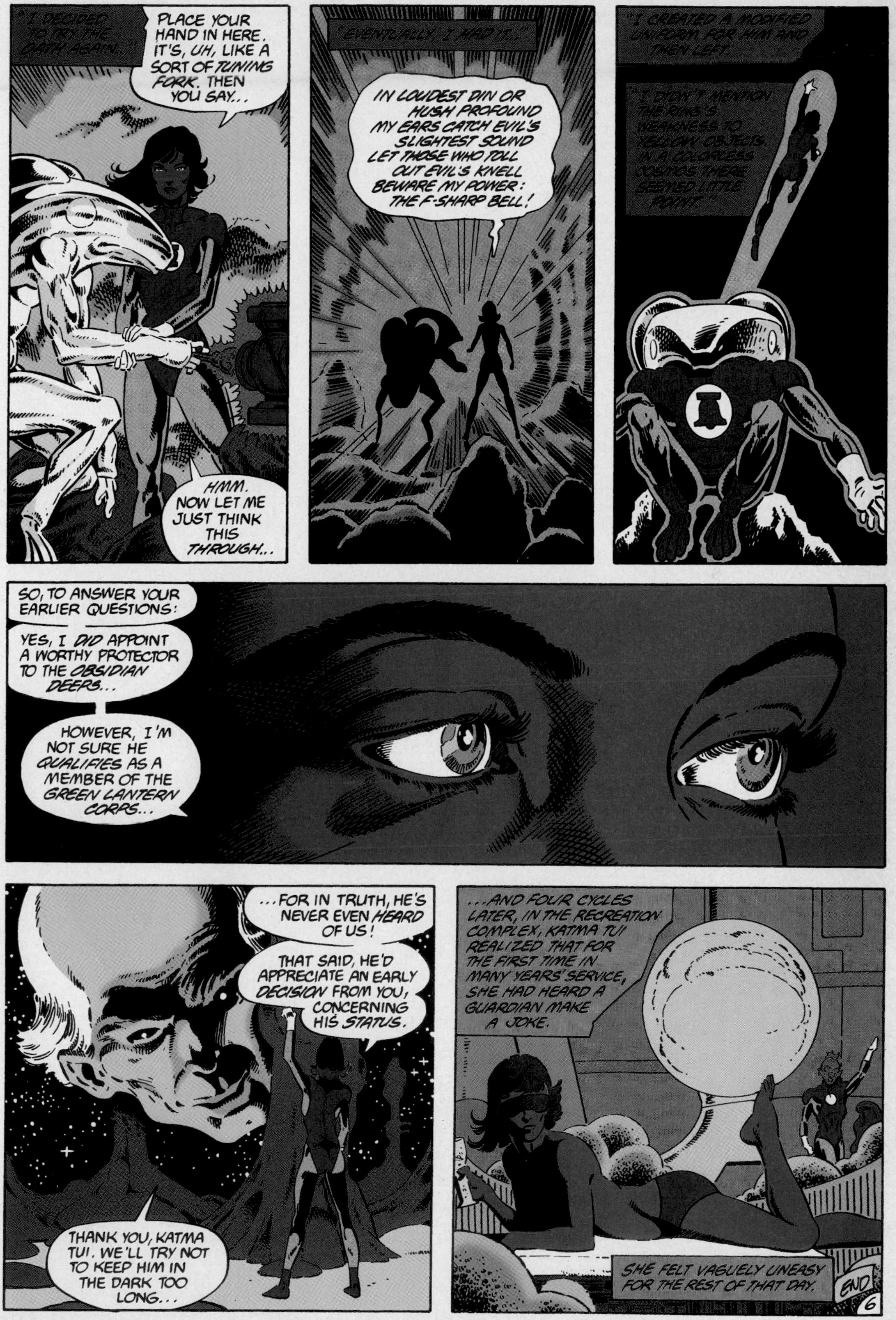

"I DECIDED TO TRY THE OATH AGAIN..."
PLACE YOUR HAND IN HERE. IT'S, UH, LIKE A SORT OF TUNING FORK. THEN YOU SAY...
HMM. NOW LET ME JUST THINK THIS THROUGH...
"EVENTUALLY, I HAD IT..."
IN LOUDEST DIN OR HUSH PROFOUND MY EARS CATCH EVIL'S SLIGHTEST SOUND LET THOSE WHO TOLL OUT EVIL'S KNELL BEWARE MY POWER: THE F-SHARP BELL!
"I CREATED A MODIFIED UNIFORM FOR HIM AND THEN LEFT."
"I DIDN'T MENTION THE RING'S WEAKNESS TO YELLOW OBJECTS. IN A COLORLESS COSMOS THERE SEEMED LITTLE POINT."
SO, TO ANSWER YOUR EARLIER QUESTIONS:
YES, I DID APPOINT A WORTHY PROTECTOR TO THE OBSIDIAN DEEPS...
HOWEVER, I'M NOT SURE HE QUALIFIES AS A MEMBER OF THE GREEN LANTERN CORPS...
...FOR IN TRUTH, HE'S NEVER EVEN HEARD OF US!
THAT SAID, HE'D APPRECIATE AN EARLY DECISION FROM YOU, CONCERNING HIS STATUS.
THANK YOU, KATMA TUI. WE'LL TRY NOT TO KEEP HIM IN THE DARK TOO LONG...
...AND FOUR CYCLES LATER, IN THE RECREATION COMPLEX, KATMA TUI REALIZED THAT FOR THE FIRST TIME IN MANY YEARS' SERVICE, SHE HAD HEARD A GUARDIAN MAKE A JOKE.
SHE FELT VAGUELY UNEASY FOR THE REST OF THAT DAY.
END
6

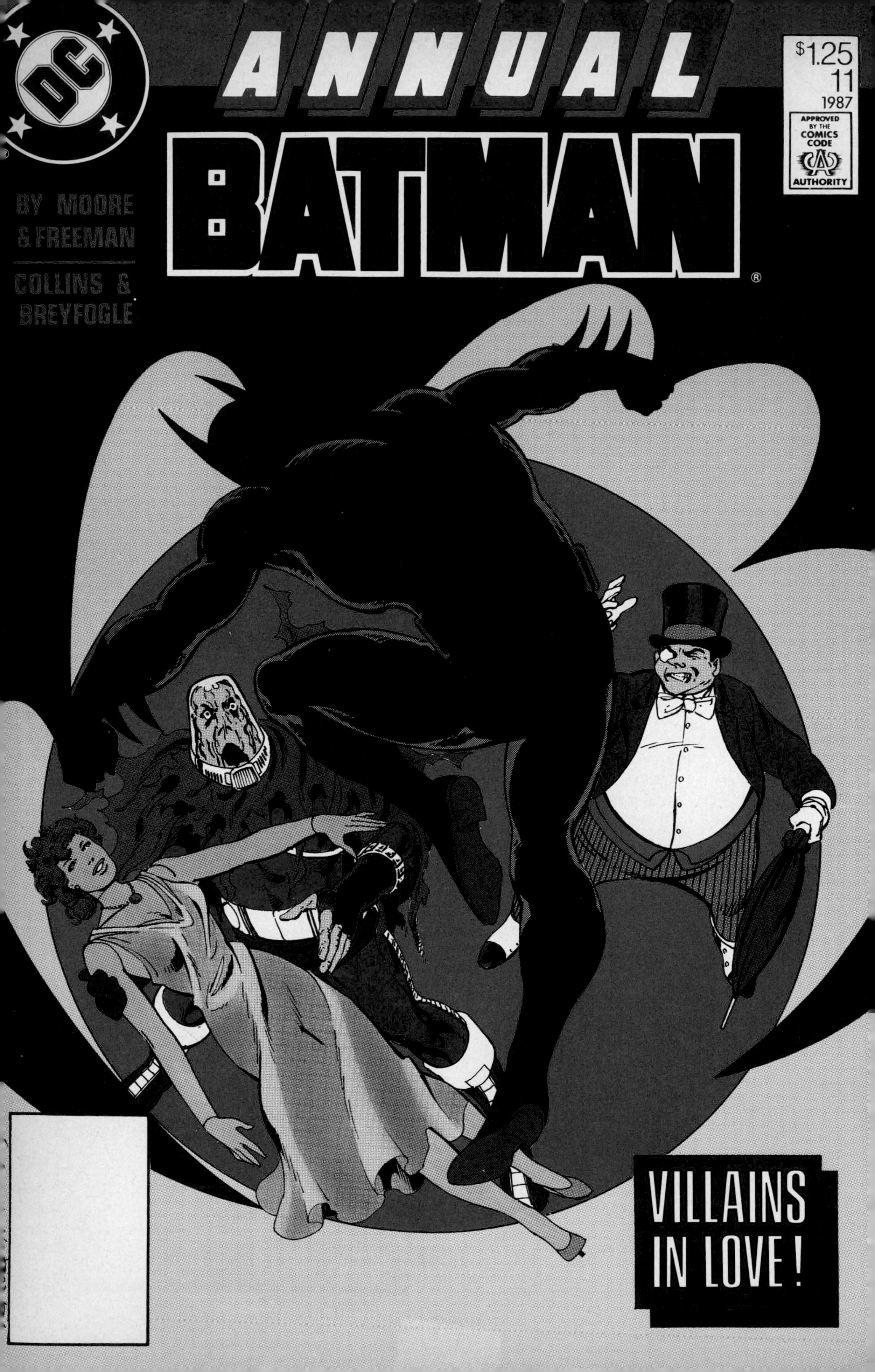
ANNUAL
$1.25
11
1987
APPROVED BY THE COMICS CODE AUTHORITY
BATMAN
BY MOORE & FREEMAN
COLLINS & BREYFOGLE
VILLAINS IN LOVE!

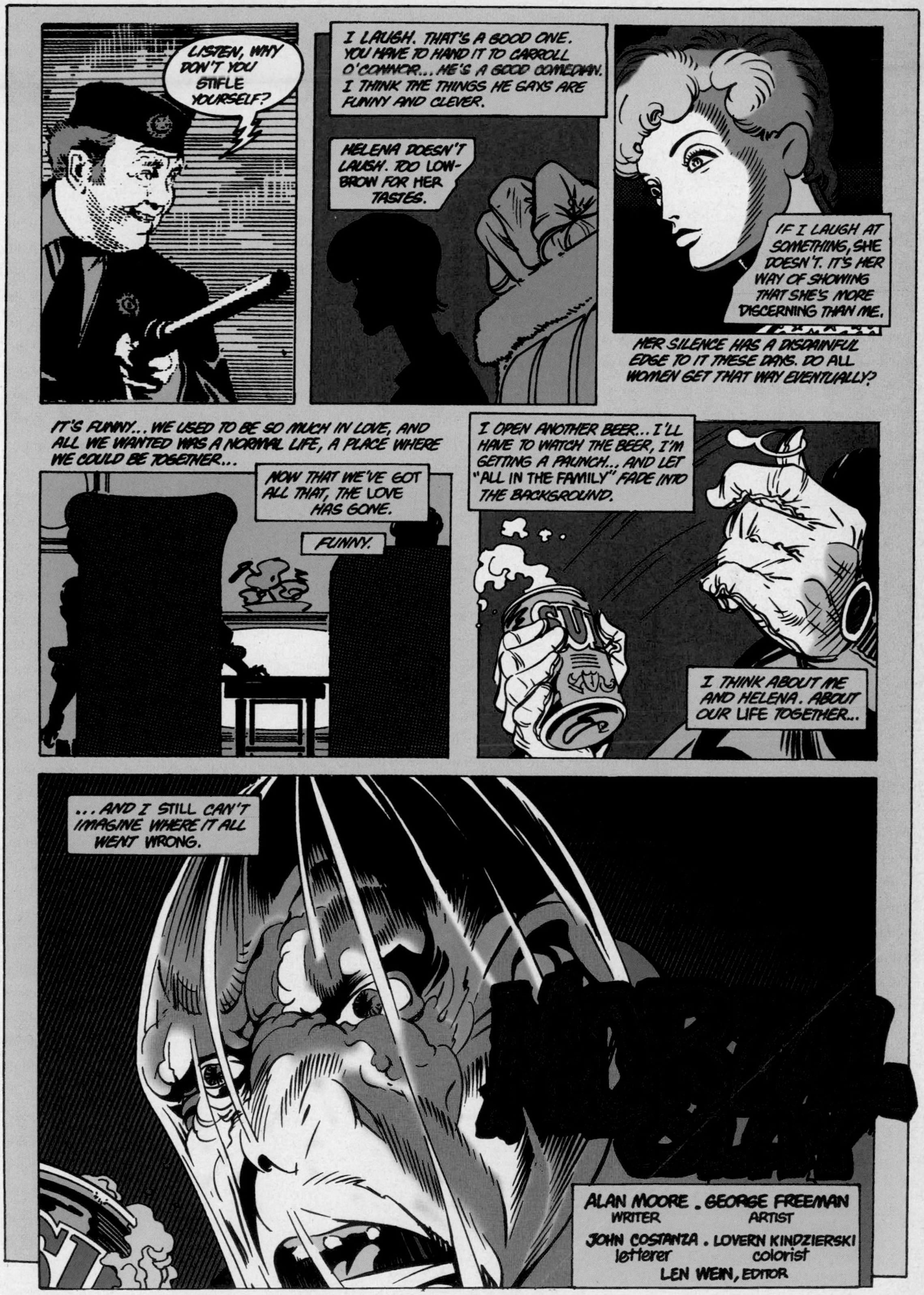

LISTEN, WHY DON'T YOU STIFLE YOURSELF?
I LAUGH. THAT'S A GOOD ONE. YOU HAVE TO HAND IT TO CARROLL O'CONNOR... HE'S A GOOD COMEDIAN. I THINK THE THINGS HE SAYS ARE FUNNY AND CLEVER.
HELENA DOESN'T LAUGH. TOO LOW-BROW FOR HER TASTES.
IF I LAUGH AT SOMETHING, SHE DOESN'T. IT'S HER WAY OF SHOWING THAT SHE'S MORE DISCERNING THAN ME.
HER SILENCE HAS A DISDAINFUL EDGE TO IT THESE DAYS. DO ALL WOMEN GET THAT WAY EVENTUALLY?
IT'S FUNNY... WE USED TO BE SO MUCH IN LOVE, AND ALL WE WANTED WAS A NORMAL LIFE, A PLACE WHERE WE COULD BE TOGETHER...
NOW THAT WE'VE GOT ALL THAT, THE LOVE HAS GONE.
FUNNY.
I OPEN ANOTHER BEER... I'LL HAVE TO WATCH THE BEER, I'M GETTING A PAUNCH... AND LET "ALL IN THE FAMILY" FADE INTO THE BACKGROUND.
I THINK ABOUT ME AND HELENA. ABOUT OUR LIFE TOGETHER...
...AND I STILL CAN'T IMAGINE WHERE IT ALL WENT WRONG.
ALAN MOORE . GEORGE FREEMAN
WRITER ARTIST
JOHN COSTANZA . LOVERN KINDZIERSKI
letterer colorist
LEN WEIN, EDITOR

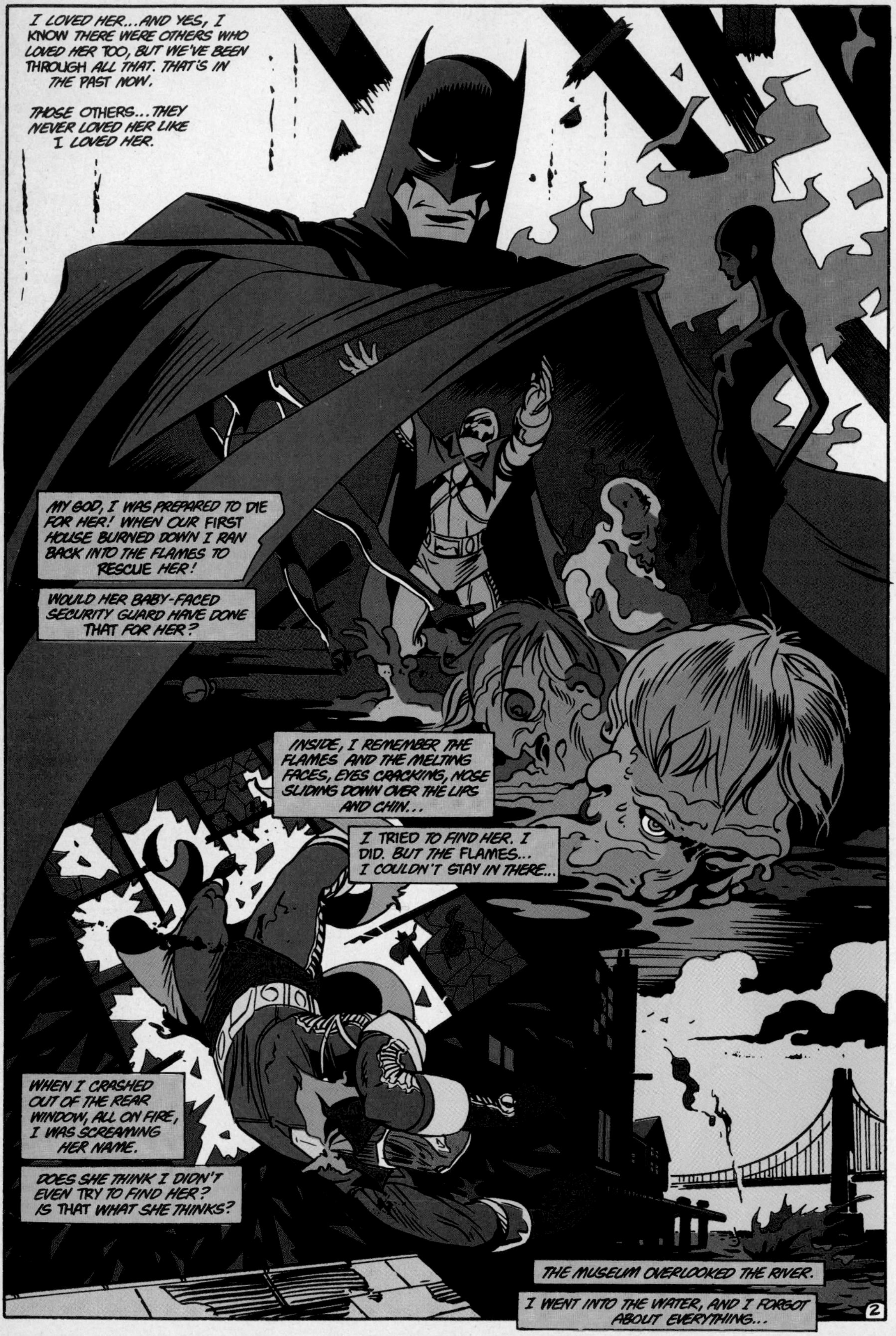
I LOVED HER...AND YES, I KNOW THERE WERE OTHERS WHO LOVED HER TOO, BUT WE'VE BEEN THROUGH ALL THAT. THAT'S IN THE PAST NOW.
THOSE OTHERS...THEY NEVER LOVED HER LIKE I LOVED HER.
MY GOD, I WAS PREPARED TO DIE FOR HER! WHEN OUR FIRST HOUSE BURNED DOWN I RAN BACK INTO THE FLAMES TO RESCUE HER!
WOULD HER BABY-FACED SECURITY GUARD HAVE DONE THAT FOR HER?
INSIDE, I REMEMBER THE FLAMES AND THE MELTING FACES, EYES CRACKING, NOSE SLIDING DOWN OVER THE LIPS AND CHIN...
I TRIED TO FIND HER. I DID. BUT THE FLAMES... I COULDN'T STAY IN THERE...
WHEN I CRASHED OUT OF THE REAR WINDOW, ALL ON FIRE, I WAS SCREAMING HER NAME.
DOES SHE THINK I DIDN'T EVEN TRY TO FIND HER? IS THAT WHAT SHE THINKS?
THE MUSEUM OVERLOOKED THE RIVER.
I WENT INTO THE WATER, AND I FORGOT ABOUT EVERYTHING...
2

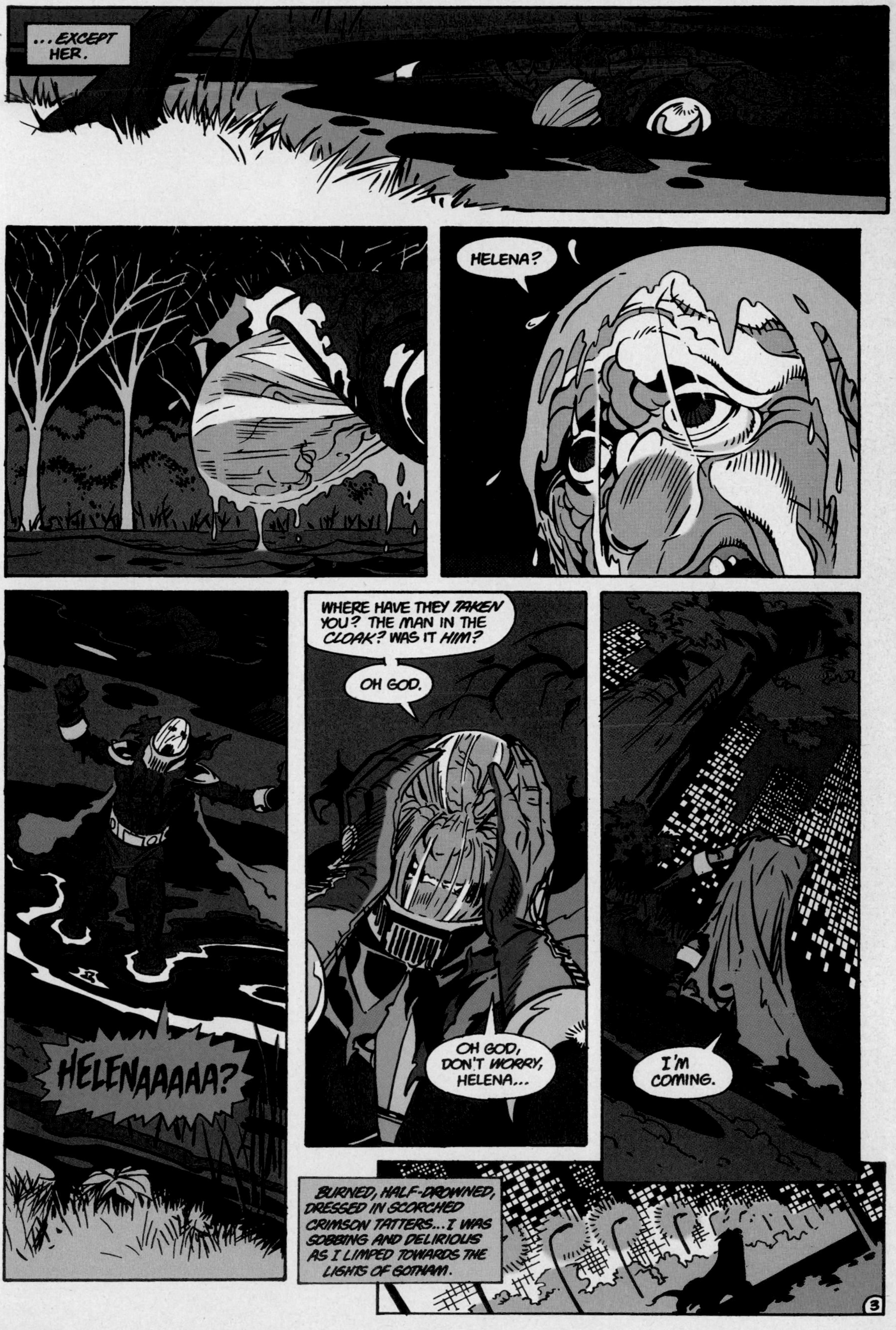

...EXCEPT HER.
HELENA?
HELENAAAAA?
WHERE HAVE THEY TAKEN YOU? THE MAN IN THE CLOAK? WAS IT HIM?
OH GOD.
OH GOD, DON'T WORRY, HELENA...
I'M COMING.
BURNED, HALF-DROWNED, DRESSED IN SCORCHED CRIMSON TATTERS... I WAS SOBBING AND DELIRIOUS AS I LIMPED TOWARDS THE LIGHTS OF GOTHAM.
3

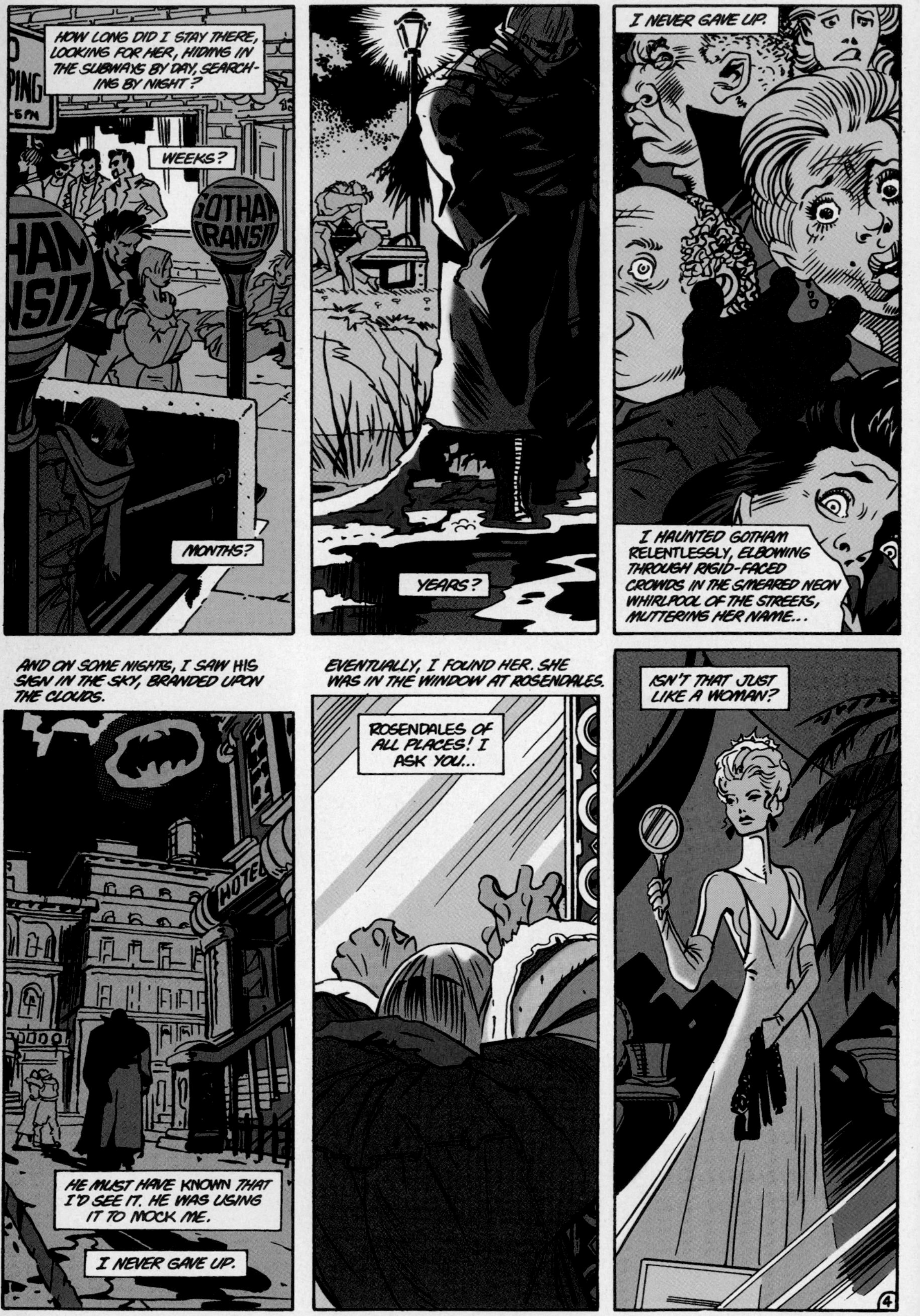
HOW LONG DID I STAY THERE, LOOKING FOR HER, HIDING IN THE SUBWAYS BY DAY, SEARCHING BY NIGHT?
WEEKS?
MONTHS?
YEARS?
I NEVER GAVE UP.
I HAUNTED GOTHAM RELENTLESSLY, ELBOWING THROUGH RIGID-FACED CROWDS IN THE SMEARED NEON WHIRLPOOL OF THE STREETS, MUTTERING HER NAME...
AND ON SOME NIGHTS, I SAW HIS SIGN IN THE SKY, BRANDED UPON THE CLOUDS.
HE MUST HAVE KNOWN THAT I'D SEE IT. HE WAS USING IT TO MOCK ME.
I NEVER GAVE UP.
EVENTUALLY, I FOUND HER. SHE WAS IN THE WINDOW AT ROSENDALES.
ROSENDALES OF ALL PLACES! I ASK YOU...
ISN'T THAT JUST LIKE A WOMAN?

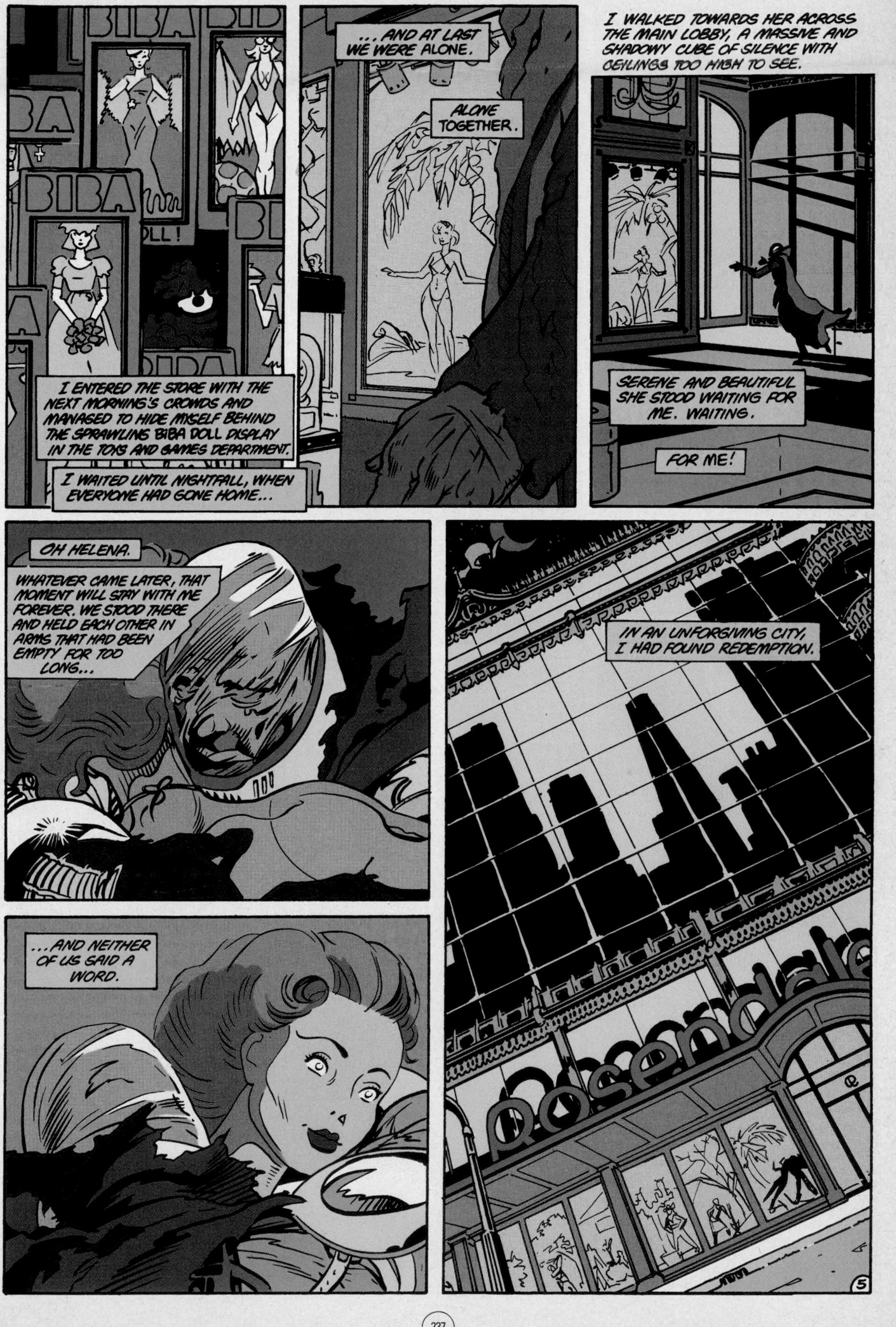

BIBA
I ENTERED THE STORE WITH THE NEXT MORNING'S CROWDS AND MANAGED TO HIDE MYSELF BEHIND THE SPRAWLING BIBA DOLL DISPLAY IN THE TOYS AND GAMES DEPARTMENT.
I WAITED UNTIL NIGHTFALL, WHEN EVERYONE HAD GONE HOME...
...AND AT LAST WE WERE ALONE.
ALONE TOGETHER.
I WALKED TOWARDS HER ACROSS THE MAIN LOBBY, A MASSIVE AND SHADOWY CUBE OF SILENCE WITH CEILINGS TOO HIGH TO SEE.
SERENE AND BEAUTIFUL SHE STOOD WAITING FOR ME. WAITING.
FOR ME!
OH HELENA.
WHATEVER CAME LATER, THAT MOMENT WILL STAY WITH ME FOREVER. WE STOOD THERE AND HELD EACH OTHER IN ARMS THAT HAD BEEN EMPTY FOR TOO LONG...
...AND NEITHER OF US SAID A WORD.
IN AN UNFORGIVING CITY, I HAD FOUND REDEMPTION.
Rosendale
5

MORE THAN THAT, I HAD FOUND A HOME.

HELENA WAS TRANSFERRED TO LADIES' EVENINGWEAR ON THE TWELFTH FLOOR, WHILE I TOOK UP RESIDENCE IN BEDROOM FURNISHINGS ON THE FLOOR BELOW.

IT WAS AN IDEAL EXISTENCE. ONCE I HAD GROWN USED TO SLEEPING IN CONCEALMENT BY DAY AND AVOIDING THE FEW SECURITY GUARDS BY NIGHT, OUR RELATIONSHIP BLOSSOMED.

AT NIGHT WE WOULD EAT FOOD THAT I HAD PREPARED IN THE FAMOUS BAYVIEW RESTAURANT, OUR EYES ONLY FOR EACH OTHER.

IT WAS AS IF THERE WERE NO ONE ELSE IN THE ROOM BUT US.

SOMETIMES, SO AS NOT TO BECOME FATIGUED BY EACH OTHER'S COMPANY, WE WOULD VISIT FRIENDS.

THEY WERE HELENA'S FRIENDS, OF COURSE, BUT I FOUND THEM EASY ENOUGH TO TALK TO.

I WAS LIVING WITH THE WOMAN I LOVED, IN A MANSION STOCKED WITH EVERYTHING WE SHOULD EVER NEED. WE HAD FRIENDS, WE WERE SOCIALLY ACTIVE...

WE HAD A NORMAL LIFE!

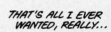

THAT'S ALL I EVER WANTED, REALLY...

A NORMAL LIFE.

⑥

WE HAD THREE MONTHS... THREE BLISSFULLY HAPPY MONTHS... AND THEN EVERYTHING STARTED TO GO WRONG.

THESE'S THE ONES?

UH... LEMME JUST TAKE A LOOK HERE...

YUP! THESE ARE THEY... "TWO F/M MANNIKINS, MOVE FROM L/ EVENINGWEAR TO L/LINGERIE, ONE DAY ONLY."

LINGERIE, HUH? Y'KNOW, WHEN YOU WERE A KID, YOU EVER GO DOWN TO THE STOREFRONT TO WATCH 'EM CHANGING THE DUMMIES?

HA HA HA! YEAH!

MAN, THAT AN' THE NATIONAL GEOGRAPHIC, THAT WAS MY EDUCATION! HA HA HA!

I REMEMBER WHEN IT ALL CHANGED: I WOKE A LITTLE AFTER TEN A.M. AND KNEW IMMEDIATELY THAT SOME- THING WAS DIFFERENT.

I RACED UP THE STAIRS TO LADIES' EVENINGWEAR, KNOWING IN THE PIT OF MY STOMACH WHAT I SHOULD FIND THERE...

HELENA?

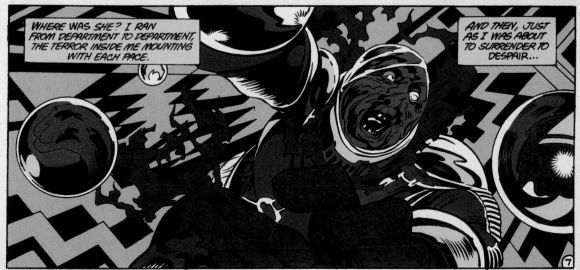

WHERE WAS SHE? I RAN FROM DEPARTMENT TO DEPARTMENT, THE TERROR INSIDE ME MOUNTING WITH EACH PACE.

AND THEN, JUST AS I WAS ABOUT TO SURRENDER TO DESPAIR...

7

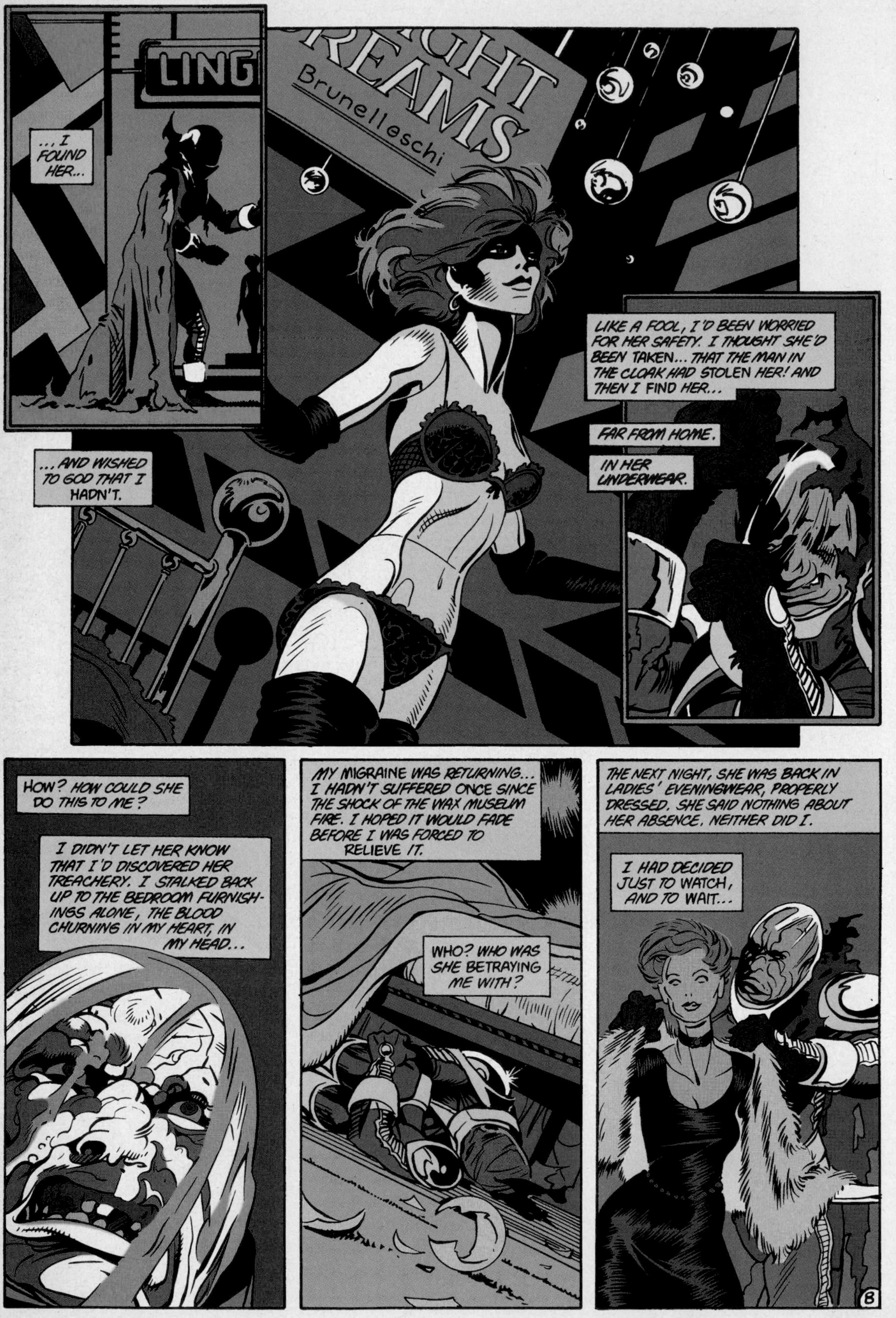
LING
...BRIGHT DREAMS
Brunelleschi
...I FOUND HER...
...AND WISHED TO GOD THAT I HADN'T.
LIKE A FOOL, I'D BEEN WORRIED FOR HER SAFETY. I THOUGHT SHE'D BEEN TAKEN... THAT THE MAN IN THE CLOAK HAD STOLEN HER! AND THEN I FIND HER...
FAR FROM HOME.
IN HER UNDERWEAR.
HOW? HOW COULD SHE DO THIS TO ME?
I DIDN'T LET HER KNOW THAT I'D DISCOVERED HER TREACHERY. I STALKED BACK UP TO THE BEDROOM FURNISHINGS ALONE, THE BLOOD CHURNING IN MY HEART, IN MY HEAD...
MY MIGRAINE WAS RETURNING... I HADN'T SUFFERED ONCE SINCE THE SHOCK OF THE WAX MUSEUM FIRE. I HOPED IT WOULD FADE BEFORE I WAS FORCED TO RELIEVE IT.
WHO? WHO WAS SHE BETRAYING ME WITH?
THE NEXT NIGHT, SHE WAS BACK IN LADIES' EVENINGWEAR, PROPERLY DRESSED. SHE SAID NOTHING ABOUT HER ABSENCE. NEITHER DID I.
I HAD DECIDED JUST TO WATCH, AND TO WAIT...
8

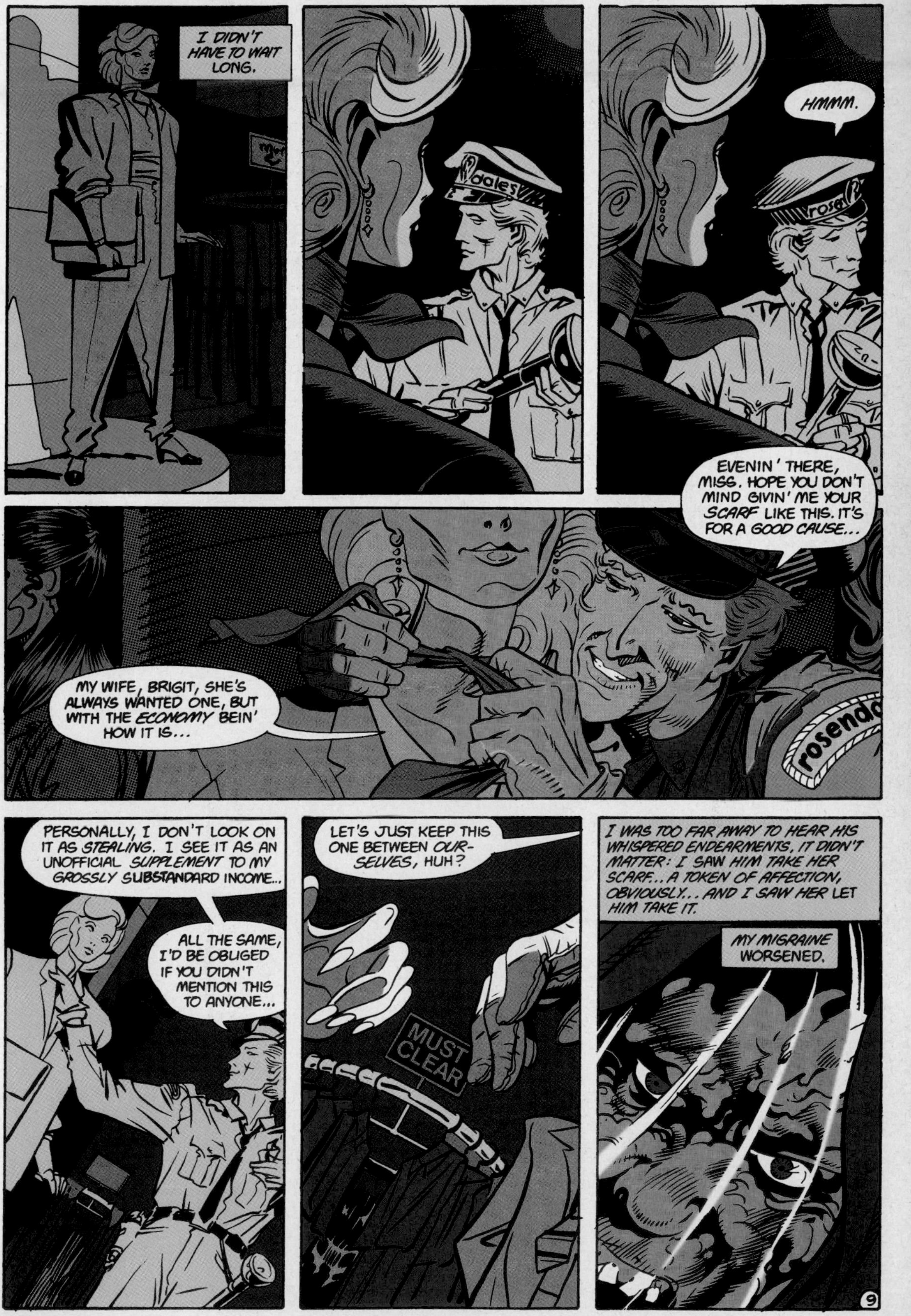
I DIDN'T HAVE TO WAIT LONG.
HMMM.
EVENIN' THERE, MISS. HOPE YOU DON'T MIND GIVIN' ME YOUR SCARF LIKE THIS. IT'S FOR A GOOD CAUSE...
MY WIFE, BRIGIT, SHE'S ALWAYS WANTED ONE, BUT WITH THE ECONOMY BEIN' HOW IT IS...
rosendo
PERSONALLY, I DON'T LOOK ON IT AS STEALING. I SEE IT AS AN UNOFFICIAL SUPPLEMENT TO MY GROSSLY SUBSTANDARD INCOME...
ALL THE SAME, I'D BE OBLIGED IF YOU DIDN'T MENTION THIS TO ANYONE...
LET'S JUST KEEP THIS ONE BETWEEN OURSELVES, HUH?
MUST CLEAR
I WAS TOO FAR AWAY TO HEAR HIS WHISPERED ENDEARMENTS. IT DIDN'T MATTER: I SAW HIM TAKE HER SCARF... A TOKEN OF AFFECTION, OBVIOUSLY... AND I SAW HER LET HIM TAKE IT.
MY MIGRAINE WORSENED.
9

I WAITED FOR HIM TO LEAVE, AND THEN I SLIPPED OUT UNOBSERVED. I DIDN'T WANT TO MAKE A SCENE IN FRONT OF HELENA.

ISN'T THAT RIDICULOUS? I STILL LOVED HER...

...AFTER ALL SHE'D DONE TO ME.

HEY... IS THERE SOMEBODY BACK THERE? RAY? IS THAT YOU BACK THERE, FOOLIN' AROUND?

HELLO?

ALL RIGHT... WHOEVER IT IS, YOU BETTER COME OUT NICE AN' EASY...

AND I WANTA BE ABLE TO SEE YOUR...

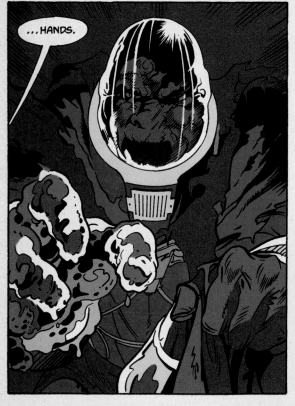

...HANDS.

AAAAAAAAA!

AAAAAAHHHH!

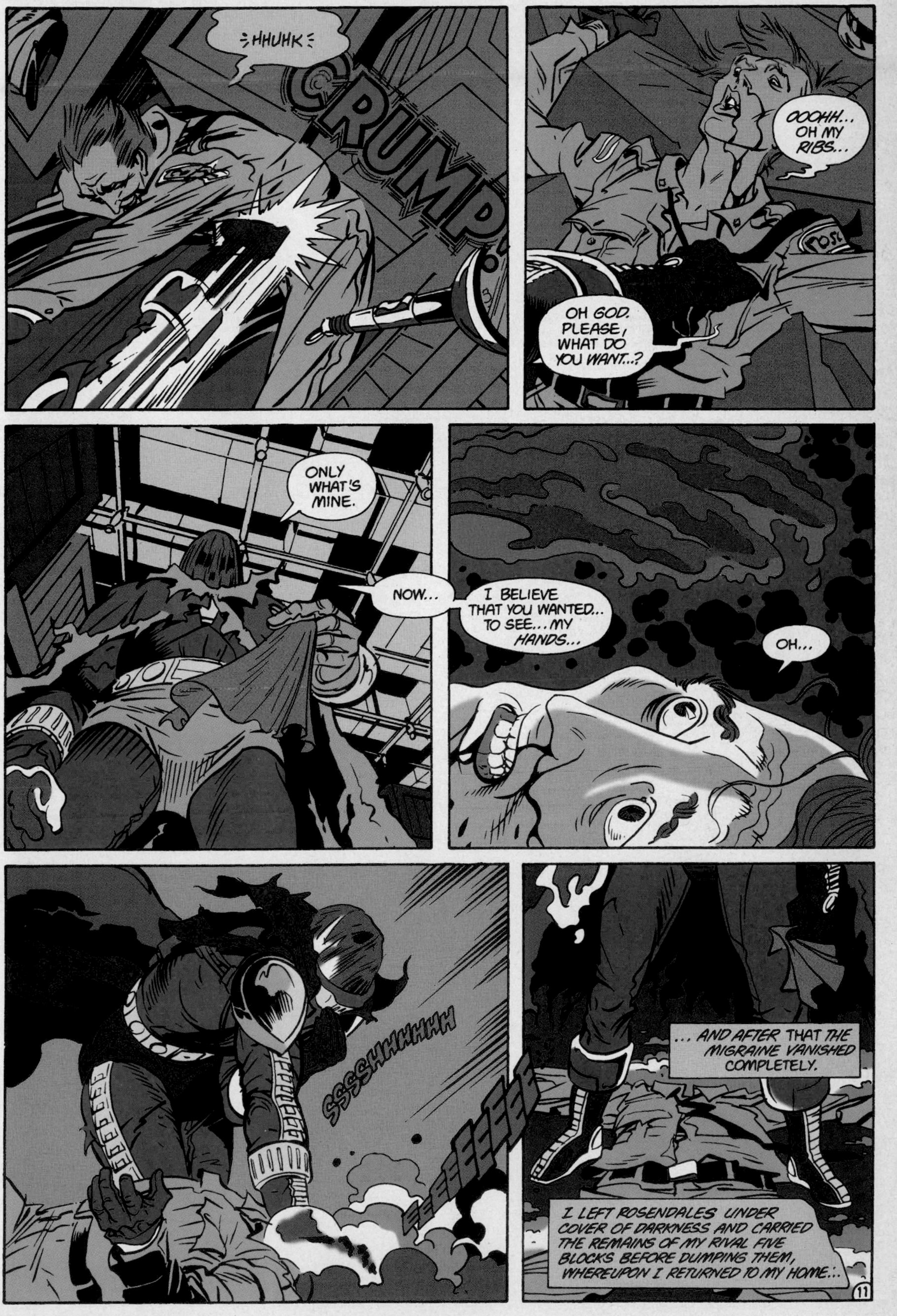

HHUHK
CRUMP
OOOHH... OH MY RIBS...
OH GOD. PLEASE, WHAT DO YOU WANT...?
ONLY WHAT'S MINE.
NOW...
I BELIEVE THAT YOU WANTED... TO SEE... MY HANDS...
OH...
SSSSHHHHHHH
EEEEEEEEE
... AND AFTER THAT THE MIGRAINE VANISHED COMPLETELY.
I LEFT ROSENDALES UNDER COVER OF DARKNESS AND CARRIED THE REMAINS OF MY RIVAL FIVE BLOCKS BEFORE DUMPING THEM, WHEREUPON I RETURNED TO MY HOME...
11

...AND TO MY WIFE.

WOMEN'S WEAR

NEITHER OF US EVER MENTIONED WHAT HAD HAPPENED. PERUSING A NEWSPAPER ONE NIGHT IN MAGAZINES, CIGARETTES AND CONFECTIONERY, I LEARNED THAT THE BODY HAD BEEN FOUND.

I HID THE PAPER FROM HELENA.

I'D ASSUMED THAT ONCE MY RIVAL STOPPED CALLING ON HER, SHE WOULD RETURN HER FULL AFFECTIONS TO ME. I WAS WRONG.

SHE SEEMED SUDDENLY DISTANT, AND THERE WERE LONG SILENCES AT MEALTIMES...

HAD SHE FOUND OUT ABOUT HER EX-LOVER? NO. IT WAS IMPOSSIBLE. THE BODY WOULD HAVE BEEN COMPLETELY UNIDENTIFIABLE.

IT HAD TO BE SOMETHING ELSE...

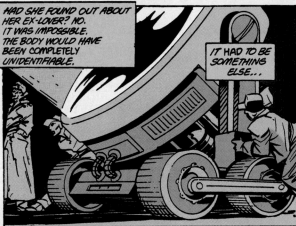

...OR PERHAPS SOMEBODY ELSE? ANOTHER LOVER? COULD IT BE? SHE'D BETRAYED ME BEFORE...

ONE NIGHT, AT DINNER, I NOTICED THAT HER GAZE WAS TRAINED UPON SOMETHING BEHIND ME, HER LOOK TENDER AND LOVING. I TURNED...

...AND I SAW.

SHE PRETENDED TO BE LOOKING AT SOMETHING ELSE, AND I CONFESS I BECAME UNCERTAIN.

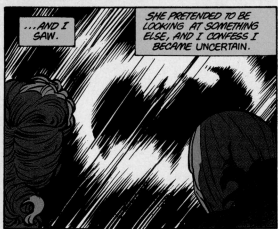

COULD IT BE THAT I WAS OVERSUSPICIOUS OF HER? COULD IT BE THAT I WAS IMAGINING THINGS?

YES. THAT HAD TO BE THE ANSWER. I MUST BE MISTAKEN. IT COULDN'T BE...

12

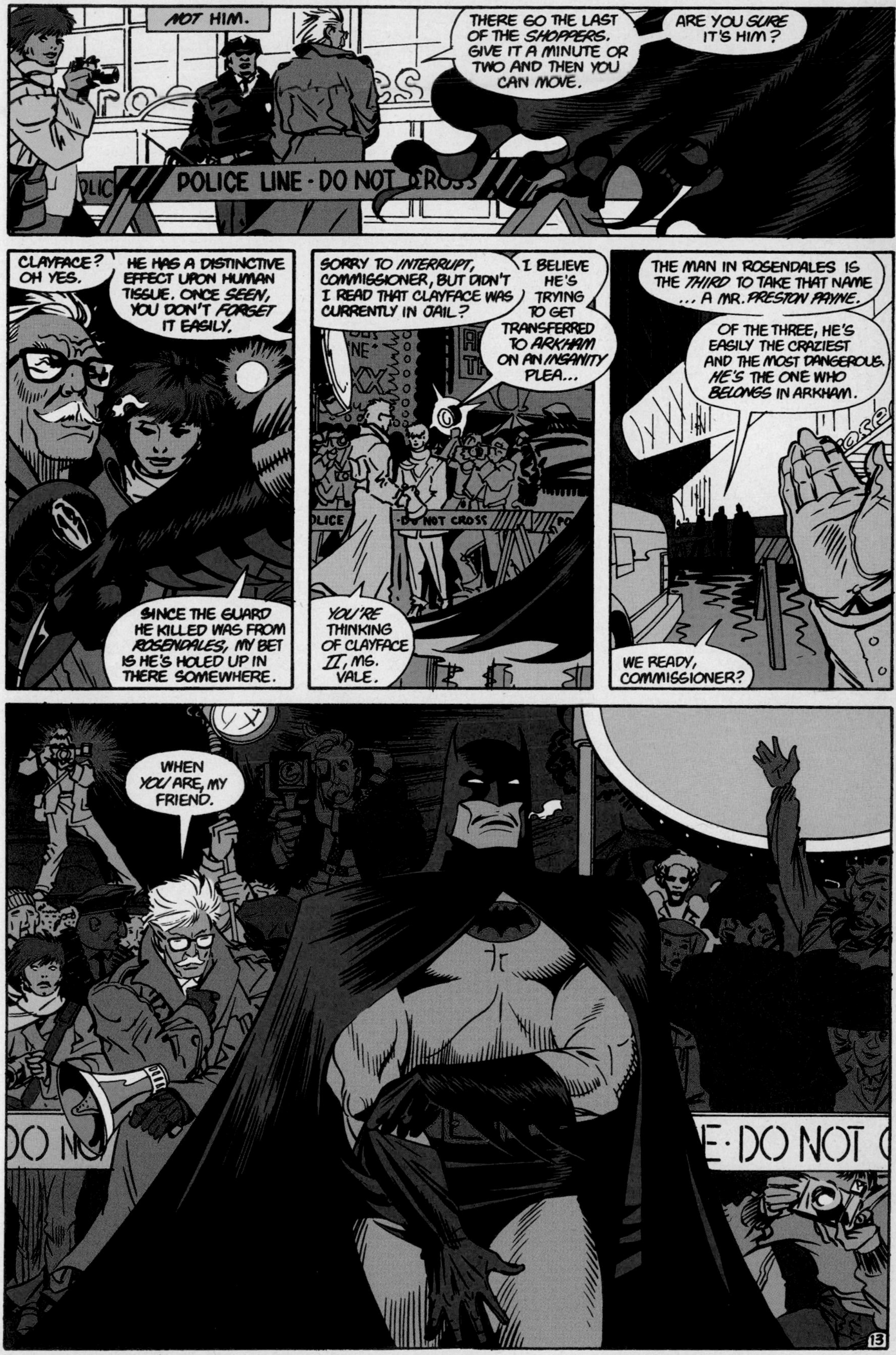
NOT HIM.
THERE GO THE LAST OF THE SHOPPERS. GIVE IT A MINUTE OR TWO AND THEN YOU CAN MOVE.
ARE YOU SURE IT'S HIM?
POLICE LINE - DO NOT CROSS
CLAYFACE? OH YES.
HE HAS A DISTINCTIVE EFFECT UPON HUMAN TISSUE. ONCE SEEN, YOU DON'T FORGET IT EASILY.
SINCE THE GUARD HE KILLED WAS FROM ROSENDALES, MY BET IS HE'S HOLED UP IN THERE SOMEWHERE.
SORRY TO INTERRUPT, COMMISSIONER, BUT DIDN'T I READ THAT CLAYFACE WAS CURRENTLY IN JAIL?
I BELIEVE HE'S TRYING TO GET TRANSFERRED TO ARKHAM ON AN INSANITY PLEA...
YOU'RE THINKING OF CLAYFACE II, MS. VALE.
DO NOT CROSS
THE MAN IN ROSENDALES IS THE THIRD TO TAKE THAT NAME ... A MR. PRESTON PAYNE.
OF THE THREE, HE'S EASILY THE CRAZIEST AND THE MOST DANGEROUS. HE'S THE ONE WHO BELONGS IN ARKHAM.
WE READY, COMMISSIONER?
WHEN YOU ARE, MY FRIEND.
DO NO
E · DO NOT
13

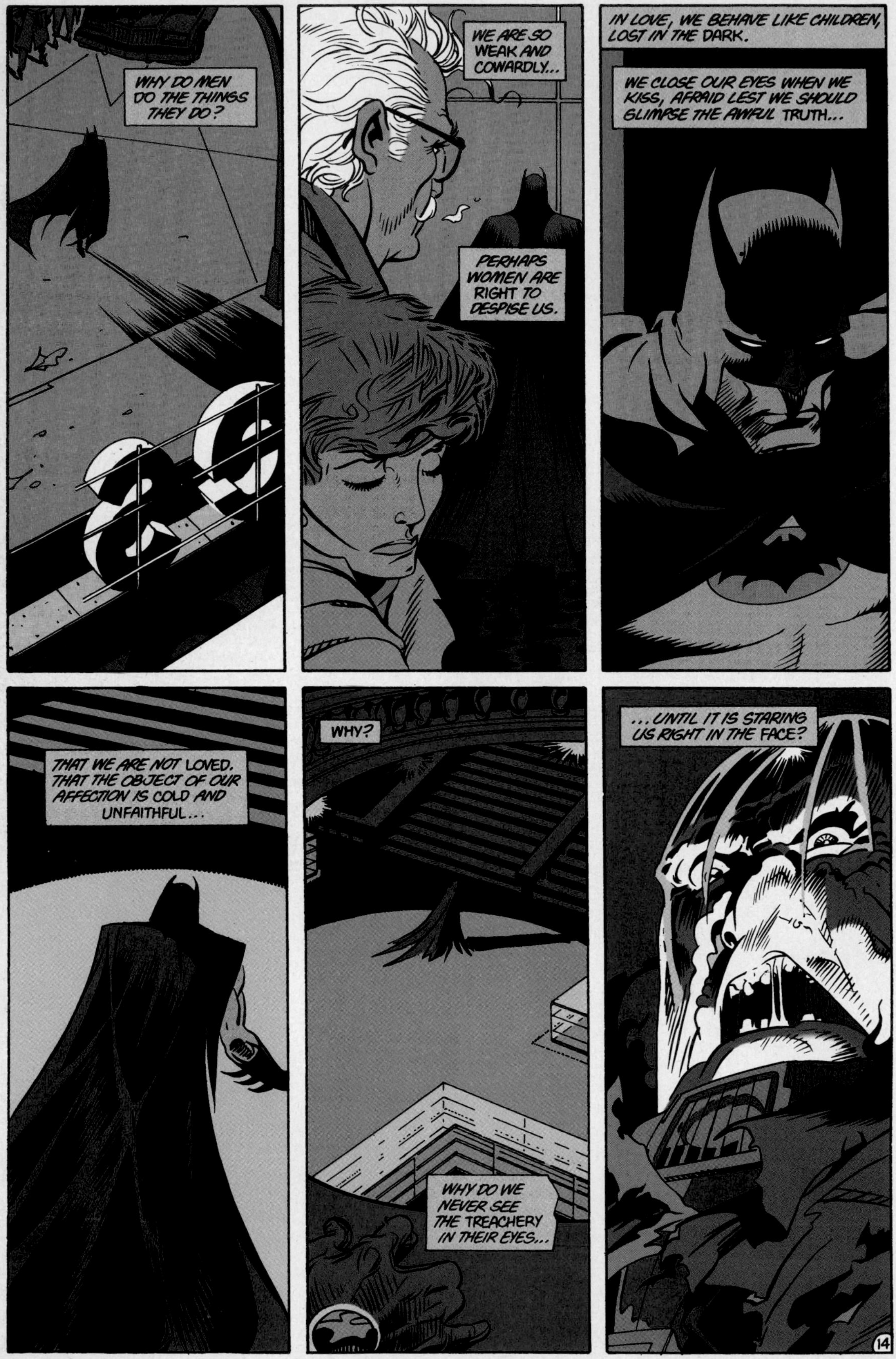
WHY DO MEN DO THE THINGS THEY DO?
WE ARE SO WEAK AND COWARDLY...
PERHAPS WOMEN ARE RIGHT TO DESPISE US.
IN LOVE, WE BEHAVE LIKE CHILDREN, LOST IN THE DARK.
WE CLOSE OUR EYES WHEN WE KISS, AFRAID LEST WE SHOULD GLIMPSE THE AWFUL TRUTH...
THAT WE ARE NOT LOVED. THAT THE OBJECT OF OUR AFFECTION IS COLD AND UNFAITHFUL...
WHY?
WHY DO WE NEVER SEE THE TREACHERY IN THEIR EYES...
...UNTIL IT IS STARING US RIGHT IN THE FACE?
14

I UNDERSTOOD EVERYTHING.

THEY'D BEEN SEEING EACH OTHER SINCE THE BEGINNING. THEY'D PROBABLY PLANNED THE WAX MUSEUM FIRE TO GET ME OUT OF THE WAY.

HOW MANY TIMES?

HOW MANY TIMES HAD HE STEALTHILY CLIMBED THESE STAIRS, FROM BOOKS AND STATIONERY TO GARDENING ACCESSORIES AND ON TO LADIES' EVENINGWEAR?

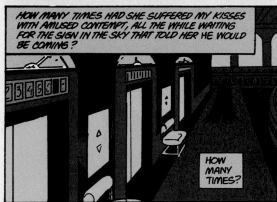

HOW MANY TIMES HAD SHE SUFFERED MY KISSES WITH AMUSED CONTEMPT, ALL THE WHILE WAITING FOR THE SIGN IN THE SKY THAT TOLD HER HE WOULD BE COMING?

HOW MANY TIMES?

"NEVER AGAIN."

TO BE HONEST, I NO LONGER CARED.

I NO LONGER CARED HOW MUCH OR HOW MANY OR HOW OFTEN...

I NO LONGER CARED ABOUT NUMBERS.

THERE WAS ONLY ONE THOUGHT IN MY MIND, ONE UNSHAKABLE RESOLUTION...

15

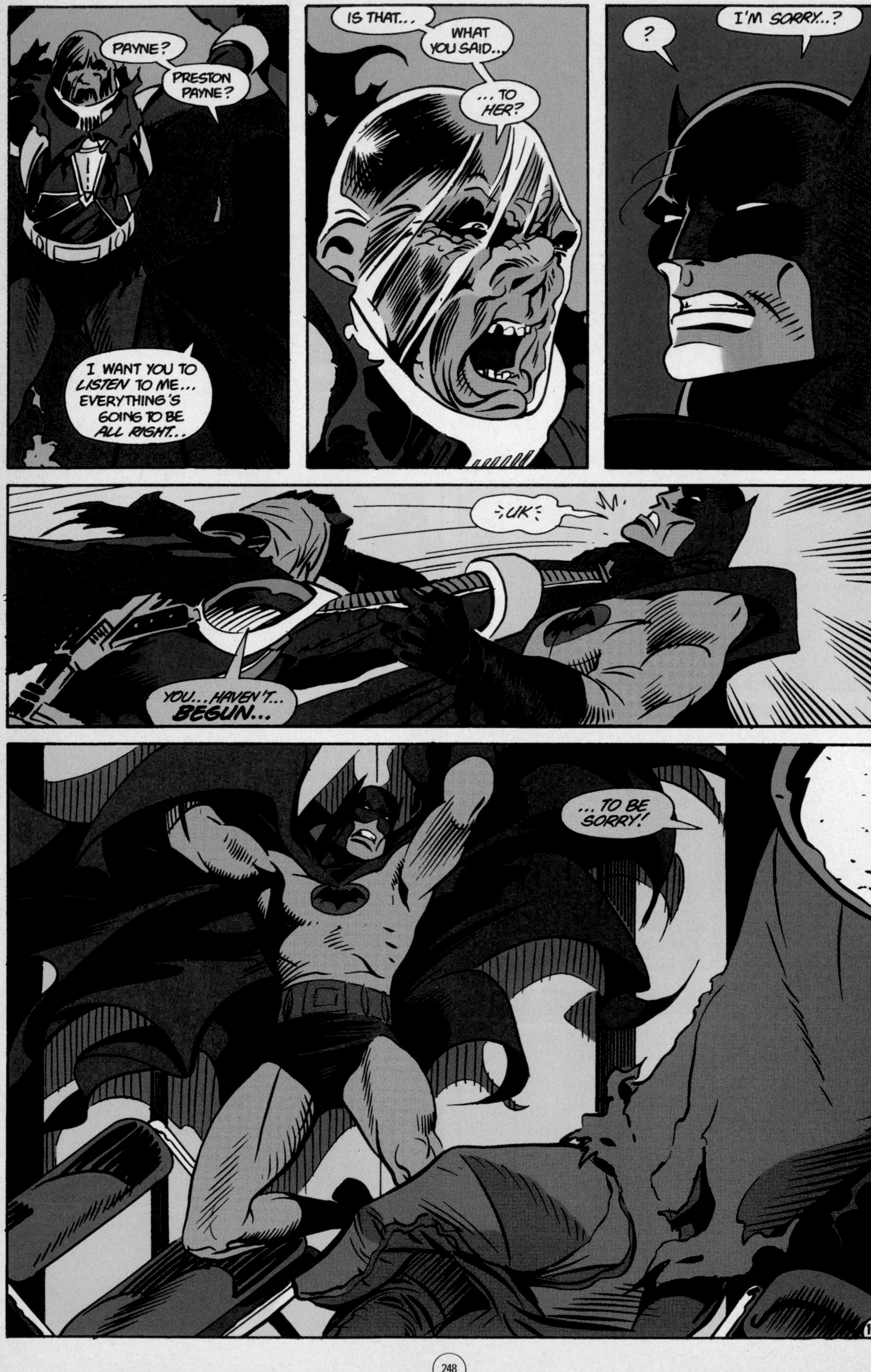

PAYNE?
PRESTON PAYNE?
I WANT YOU TO LISTEN TO ME... EVERYTHING'S GOING TO BE ALL RIGHT...
IS THAT...
WHAT YOU SAID...
...TO HER?
?
I'M SORRY...?
UK
YOU...HAVEN'T... BEGUN...
...TO BE SORRY!
15

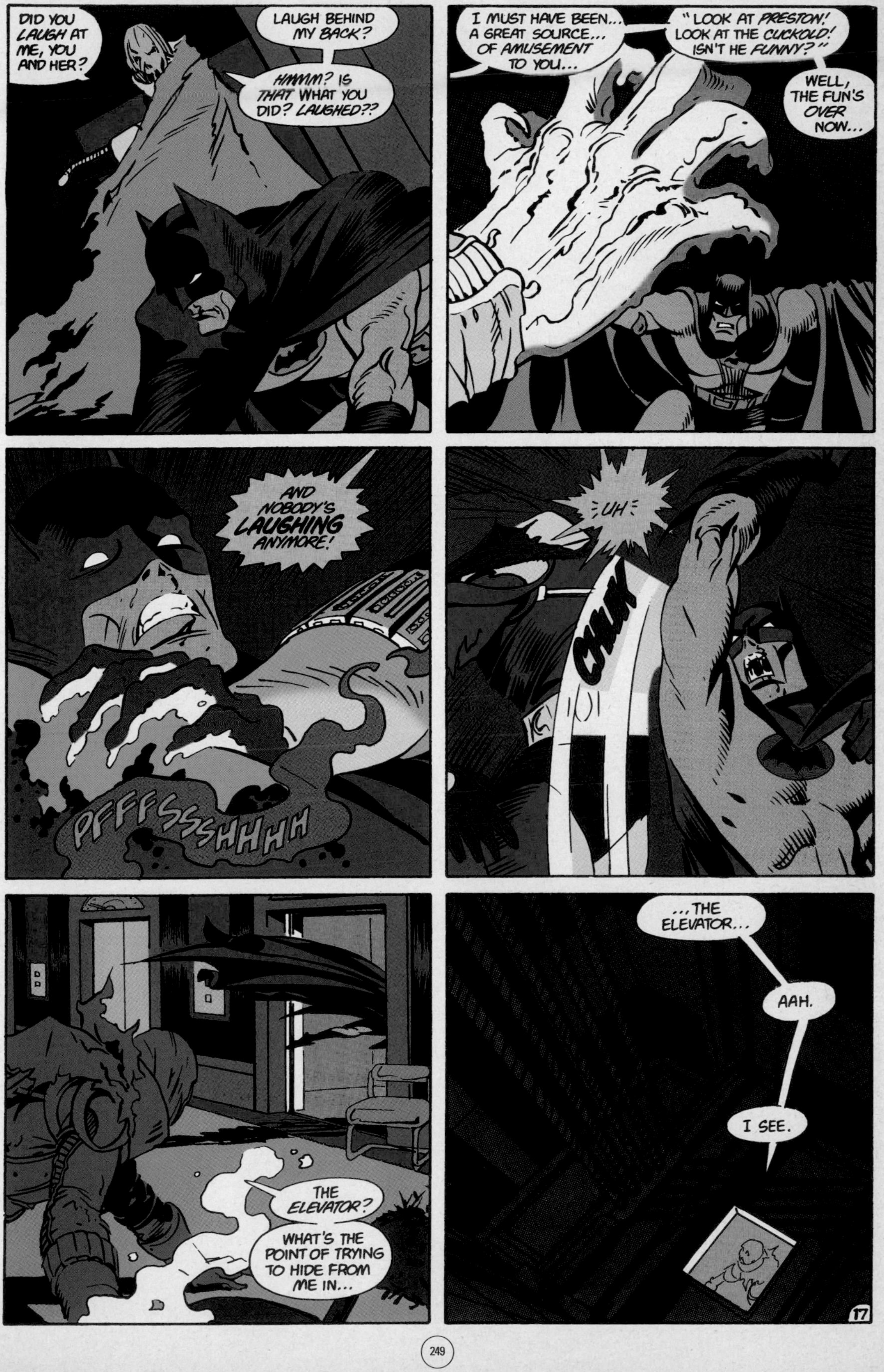
DID YOU LAUGH AT ME, YOU AND HER?
LAUGH BEHIND MY BACK?
HMMM? IS THAT WHAT YOU DID? LAUGHED??
I MUST HAVE BEEN... A GREAT SOURCE... OF AMUSEMENT TO YOU...
"LOOK AT PRESTON! LOOK AT THE CUCKOLD! ISN'T HE FUNNY?"
WELL, THE FUN'S OVER NOW...
AND NOBODY'S LAUGHING ANYMORE!
PFFFSSSHHHHH
UH
THE ELEVATOR?
WHAT'S THE POINT OF TRYING TO HIDE FROM ME IN...
...THE ELEVATOR...
AAH.
I SEE.
17

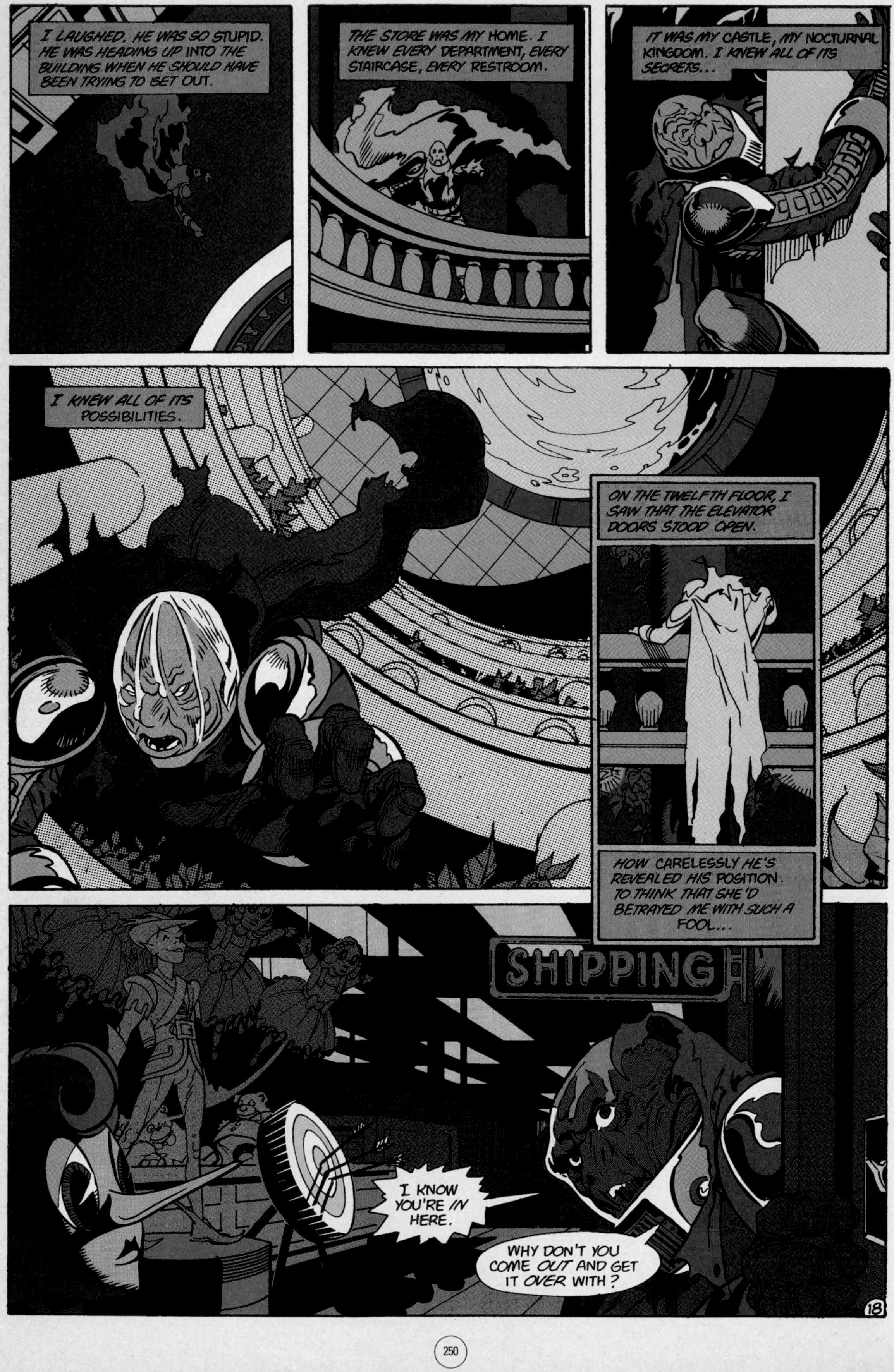
I LAUGHED. HE WAS SO STUPID. HE WAS HEADING UP INTO THE BUILDING WHEN HE SHOULD HAVE BEEN TRYING TO GET OUT.
THE STORE WAS MY HOME. I KNEW EVERY DEPARTMENT, EVERY STAIRCASE, EVERY RESTROOM.
IT WAS MY CASTLE, MY NOCTURNAL KINGDOM. I KNEW ALL OF ITS SECRETS...
I KNEW ALL OF ITS POSSIBILITIES.
ON THE TWELFTH FLOOR, I SAW THAT THE ELEVATOR DOORS STOOD OPEN.
HOW CARELESSLY HE'S REVEALED HIS POSITION. TO THINK THAT SHE'D BETRAYED ME WITH SUCH A FOOL...
SHIPPING
I KNOW YOU'RE IN HERE.
WHY DON'T YOU COME OUT AND GET IT OVER WITH?
18

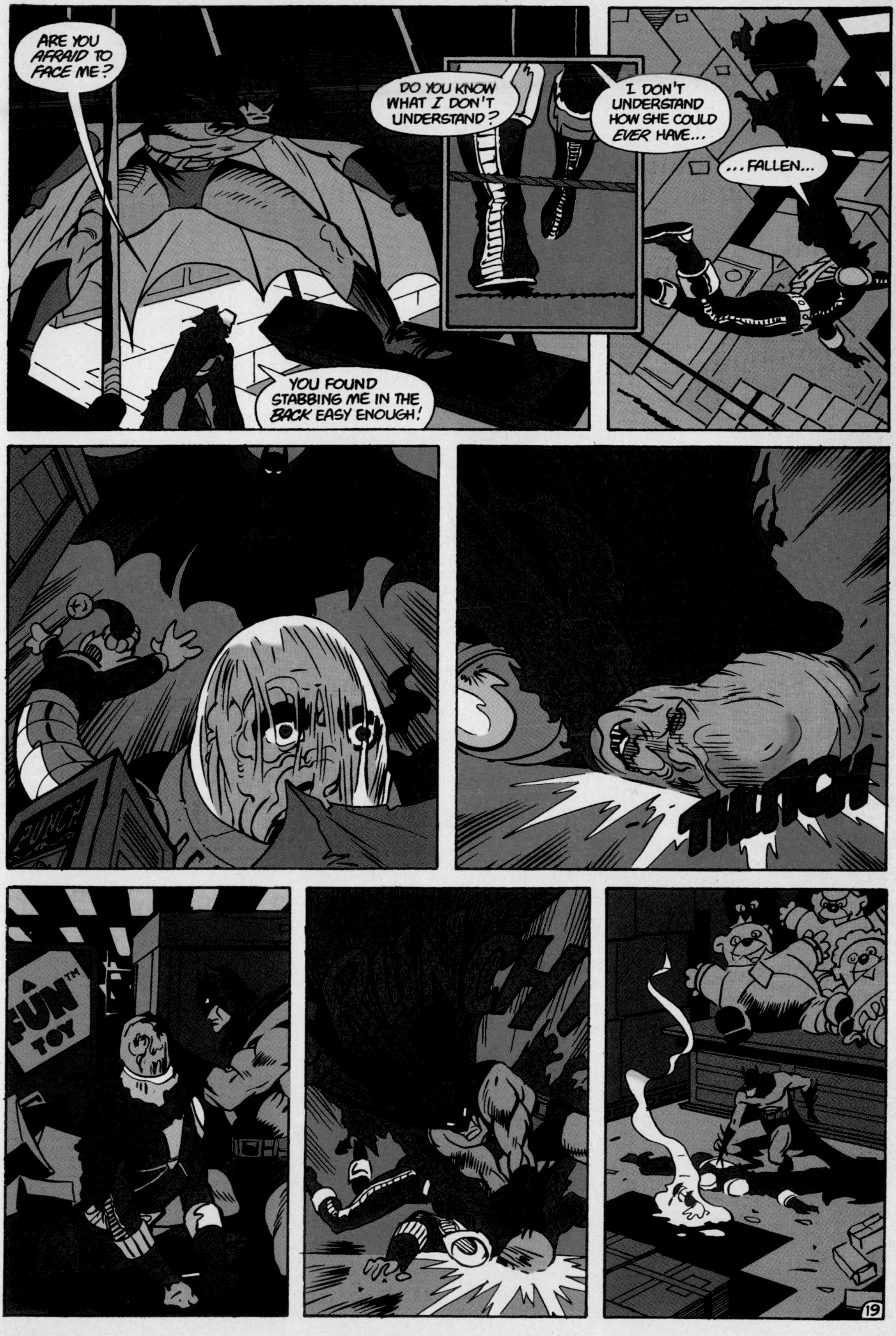
ARE YOU AFRAID TO FACE ME?
DO YOU KNOW WHAT I DON'T UNDERSTAND?
I DON'T UNDERSTAND HOW SHE COULD EVER HAVE...
...FALLEN...
YOU FOUND STABBING ME IN THE BACK EASY ENOUGH!
PUNCH
THUTCH
FUN TOY
19

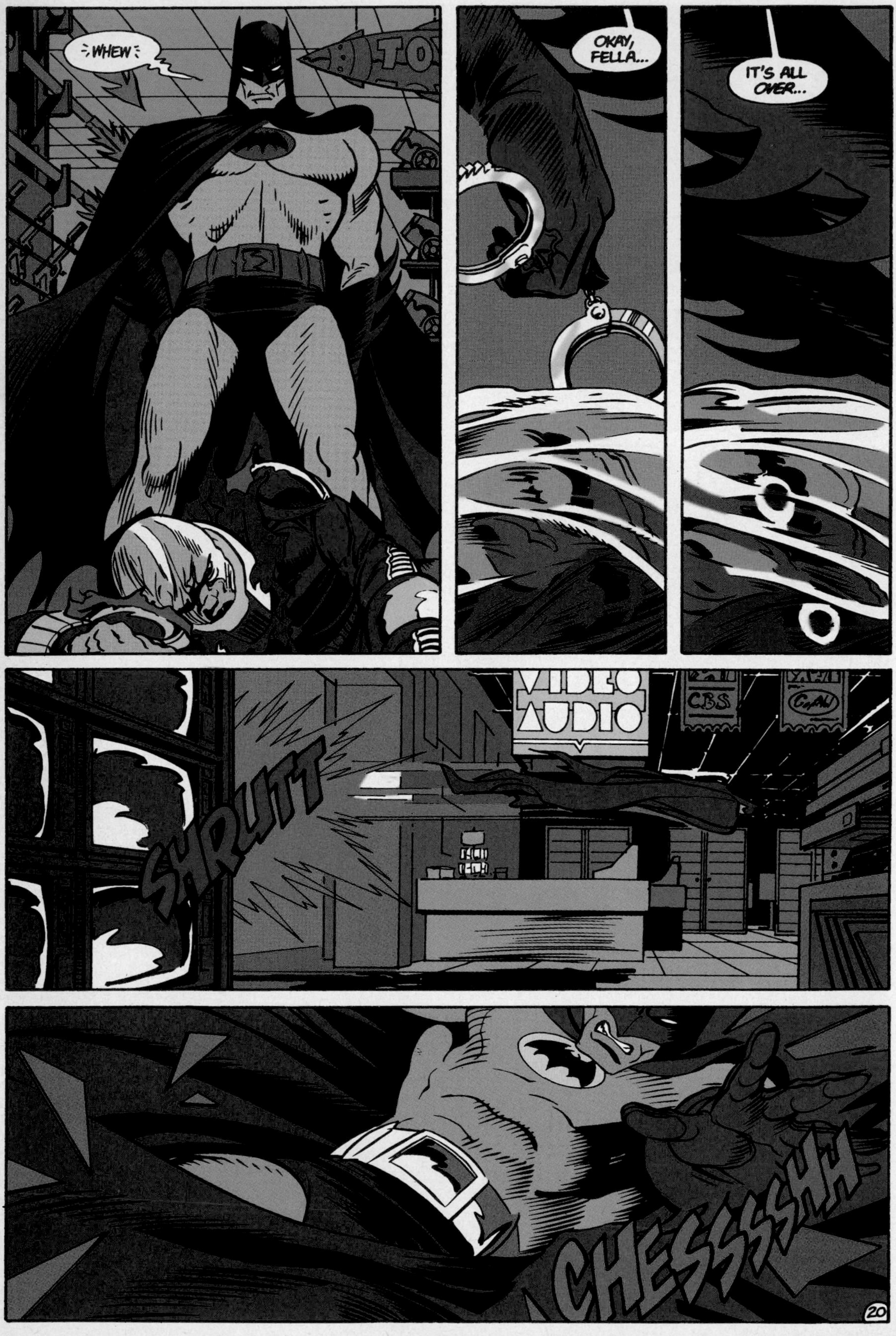
WHEW
TOY
OKAY, FELLA...
IT'S ALL OVER...
VIDEO AUDIO
CBS
SHRUTT
CHESSSSHH
20

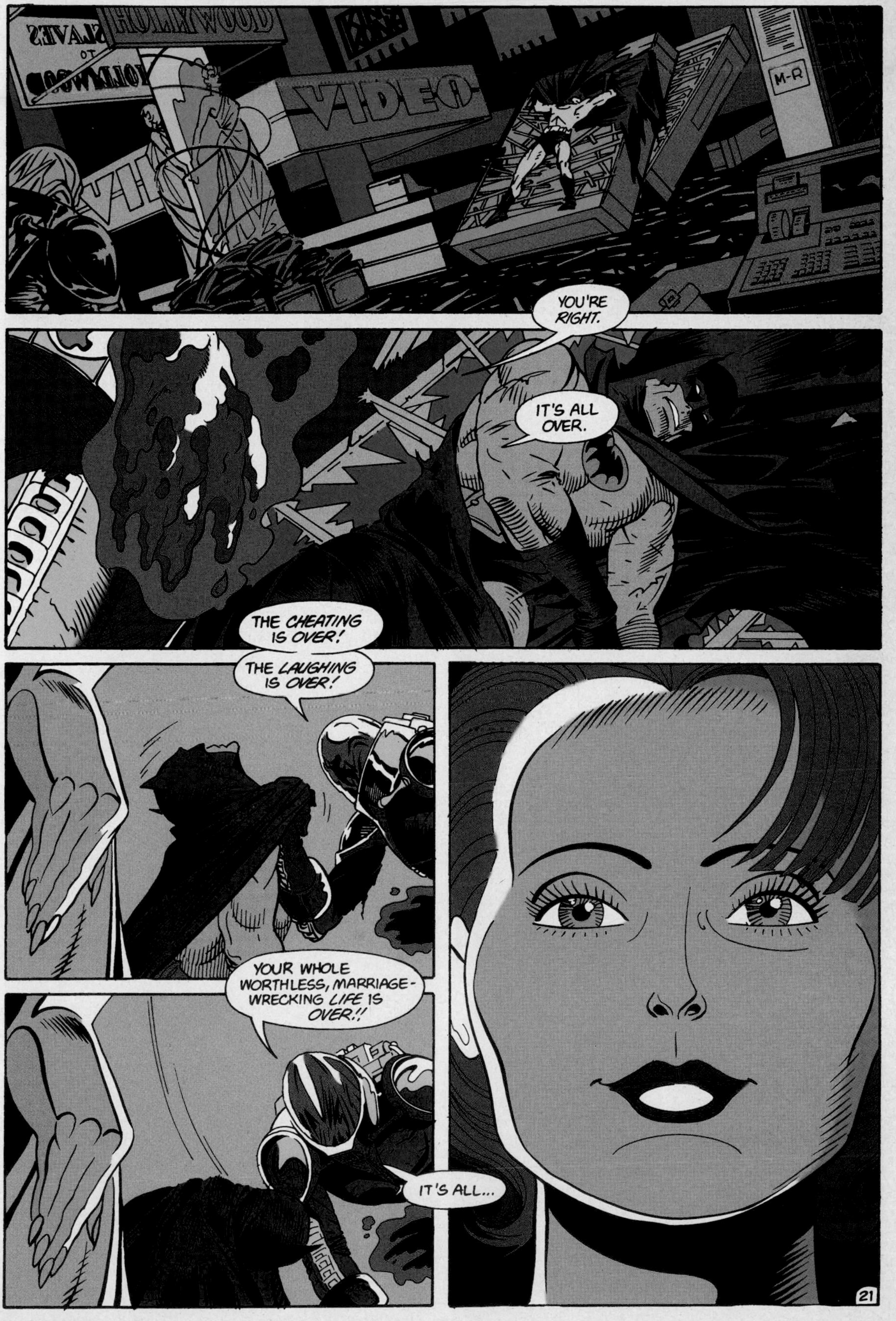
HOLLYWOOD
SLAVES TO HOLLYWOOD
VIDEO
M-R
YOU'RE RIGHT.
IT'S ALL OVER.
THE CHEATING IS OVER!
THE LAUGHING IS OVER!
YOUR WHOLE WORTHLESS, MARRIAGE-WRECKING LIFE IS OVER!!
IT'S ALL...
21

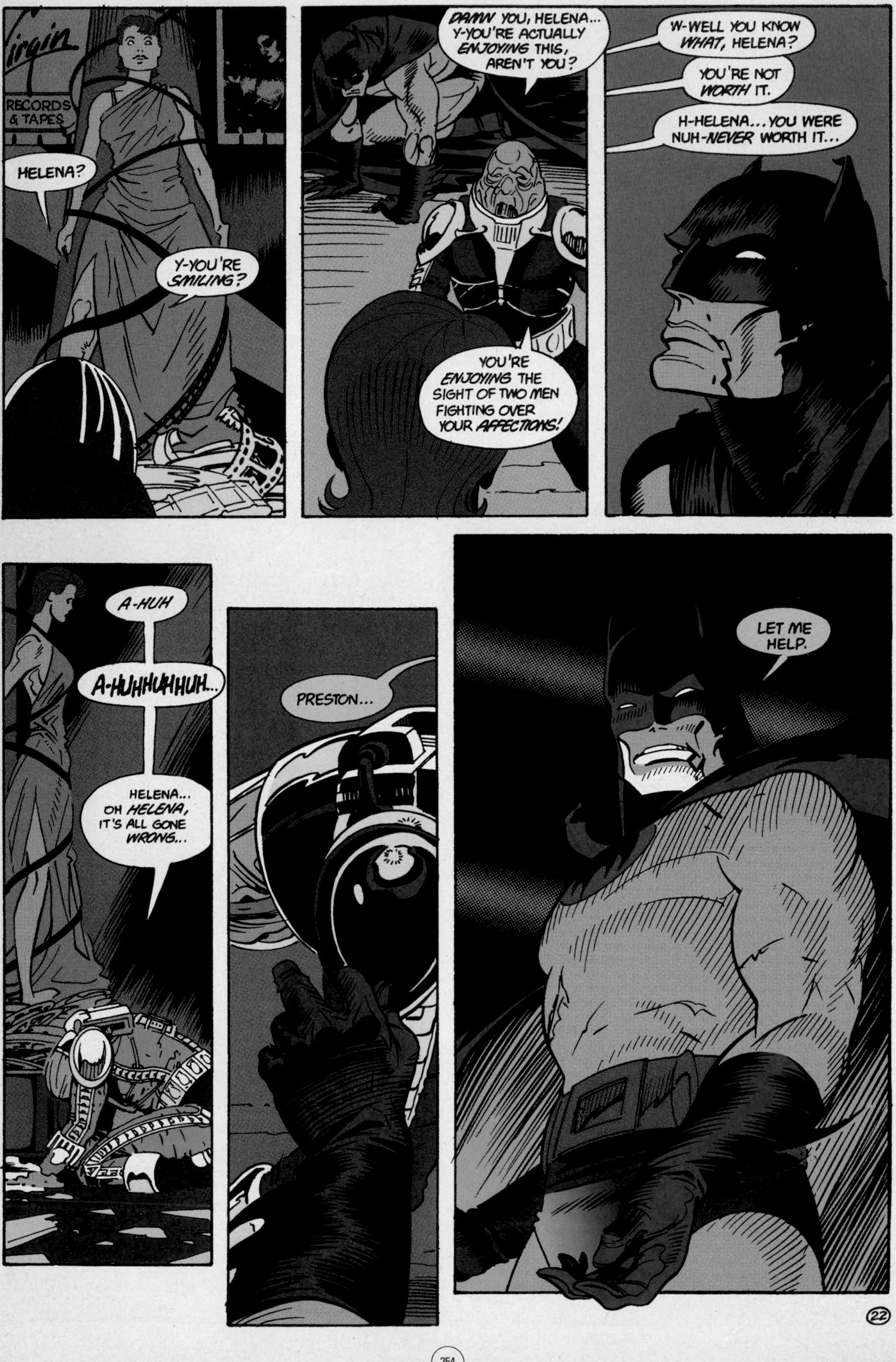
VIRGIN
RECORDS & TAPES
HELENA?
Y-YOU'RE SMILING?
DAMN YOU, HELENA... Y-YOU'RE ACTUALLY ENJOYING THIS, AREN'T YOU?
YOU'RE ENJOYING THE SIGHT OF TWO MEN FIGHTING OVER YOUR AFFECTIONS!
W-WELL YOU KNOW WHAT, HELENA?
YOU'RE NOT WORTH IT.
H-HELENA... YOU WERE NUH-NEVER WORTH IT...
A-HUH
A-HUHHUHHUH...
HELENA... OH HELENA, IT'S ALL GONE WRONG...
PRESTON...
LET ME HELP.
22

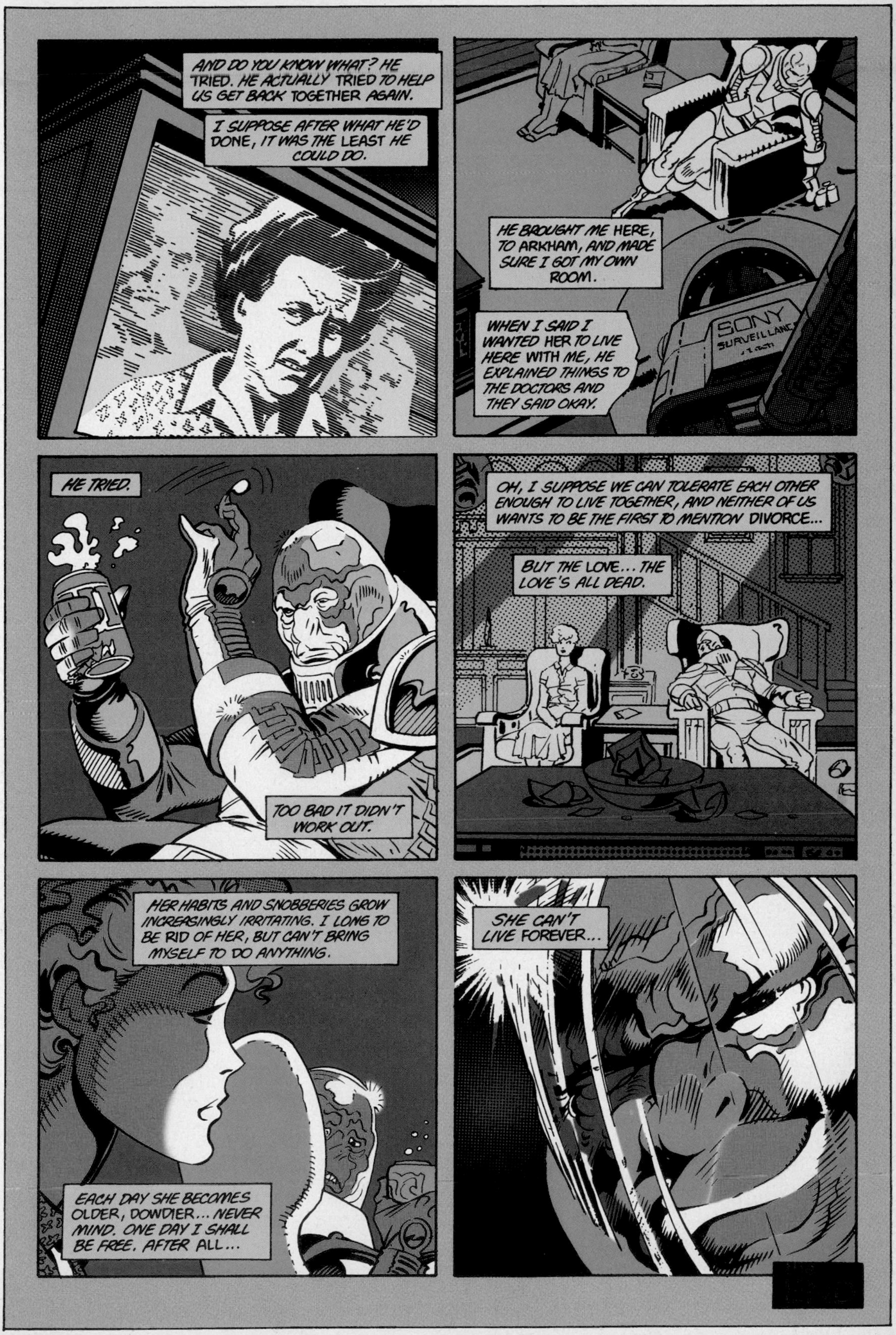
AND DO YOU KNOW WHAT? HE TRIED. HE ACTUALLY TRIED TO HELP US GET BACK TOGETHER AGAIN.
I SUPPOSE AFTER WHAT HE'D DONE, IT WAS THE LEAST HE COULD DO.
HE BROUGHT ME HERE, TO ARKHAM, AND MADE SURE I GOT MY OWN ROOM.
WHEN I SAID I WANTED HER TO LIVE HERE WITH ME, HE EXPLAINED THINGS TO THE DOCTORS AND THEY SAID OKAY.
SONY
HE TRIED.
TOO BAD IT DIDN'T WORK OUT.
OH, I SUPPOSE WE CAN TOLERATE EACH OTHER ENOUGH TO LIVE TOGETHER, AND NEITHER OF US WANTS TO BE THE FIRST TO MENTION DIVORCE...
BUT THE LOVE... THE LOVE'S ALL DEAD.
HER HABITS AND SNOBBERIES GROW INCREASINGLY IRRITATING. I LONG TO BE RID OF HER, BUT CAN'T BRING MYSELF TO DO ANYTHING.
EACH DAY SHE BECOMES OLDER, DOWDIER... NEVER MIND. ONE DAY I SHALL BE FREE. AFTER ALL...
SHE CAN'T LIVE FOREVER...

ON **BATMAN**

BRIAN **BOLLAND** RECALLS THE **KILLING** JOKE

There seem to have been a few misconceptions about THE KILLING JOKE. One is that it started off as a Batman annual story that somehow ended up in a Prestige Format book. That's not quite the way I remember it.

Alan's great talent is widely known and celebrated, deservedly so. With a writer of Alan's significance inevitably we consider everything he does to be part of the Alan Moore canon. THE KILLING JOKE is one such thing but it differs in that it started off as a project of the artist and not the writer. Back in 1984 I'd recently finished and wrapped up CAMELOT 3000, which was quite a success, I understand. After I got back from a month trekking around China I rang Dick Giordano and asked him what I could do next for DC. He said, "Anything you want, Brian." With a sudden rush of oxygen to the head I thought of my — at that time — favorite character, Batman, and my favorite writer, Alan Moore. Alan and I had got to know each other quite well in the preceding couple of years. We'd even talked about doing a Batman meets Judge Dredd one-off book together but the intercompany politics at the time made it impossible. A proposal and script exists somewhere, though.

My editor on CAMELOT 3000 had been Len Wein. Len asked Alan, just beginning work on WATCHMEN, if he'd like to do a prestige Batman book with me. He said yes. Pretty soon he was on the phone asking me what it was I wanted to draw. I'd already got some ideas sloshing around in my brain about what I wanted. Over the last couple of years I'd drawn quite a few pages featuring Judge Death. I'd become a bit obsessed with the rictus grin of the character. I'd even recently been to see the wonderful 1928 film *The Man Who Laughs* starring Conrad Veidt and Mary Philbin (yes, *the* Mary Philbin who three years earlier had been menaced by Lon Chaney Sr.'s Phantom of the Opera), a film which, lawyers advise me to say, played no part in the creation of the Joker. I think I had been limbering up to draw the Joker for some time.

I said to Alan that it would be great if our book could be about the Joker, and Batman could almost be an incidental character — hardly in it at all. Alan seemed to like the idea. From that point on I thought: I'm the artist, he's the writer and a brilliant one. I can trust him to get on and write it. Round about that time I met Frank Miller and Lynn Varley for a Japanese meal in New York. Frank asked me what I was working on. I told him a prestige Batman book. A shadow of concern flickered across his granite features — forgive me, I've been reading his *Sin City* — his features. Concern for me, I should think. He was just about to launch THE DARK KNIGHT RETURNS on an unsuspecting world. Back in England there was a brief interlude when Alan rang Len Wein and asked permission to do terrible things to poor Barbara. The exact wording of Len's reply can't be printed here but it has entered into folklore. Shortly after that Len left the job and THE KILLING JOKE was inherited by Denny O'Neil.

Alan's legendary typewritten script arrived after a while, with its famous first page suggesting I begin by making myself a cup o' coffee. Then everything at DC went quiet for almost two years and I got on with the business of drawing it. I once rang my editor and got no impression that THE KILLING JOKE was urgent or required at all by DC. Denny was a very relaxed editor and, I thought, was probably busy doing 101 other more important things. It was only right at the end, when the book was scheduled, that I was suddenly in a panic to get it done and, ashamed at how long I'd spent drawing it, I agreed reluctantly to let someone else color it.

The end result wasn't quite what I'd hoped. I don't think it rates with some of the groundbreaking highlights of Alan's career. There are things in the story I wouldn't have done, but it contains moments (my favorite being when the Joker's gun turns out to be empty) which are among Alan's greatest moments and some of the most chilling.

For all I know, Alan may have had the idea in his mind for a Batman annual long before I came along, but that's the way I remember it.

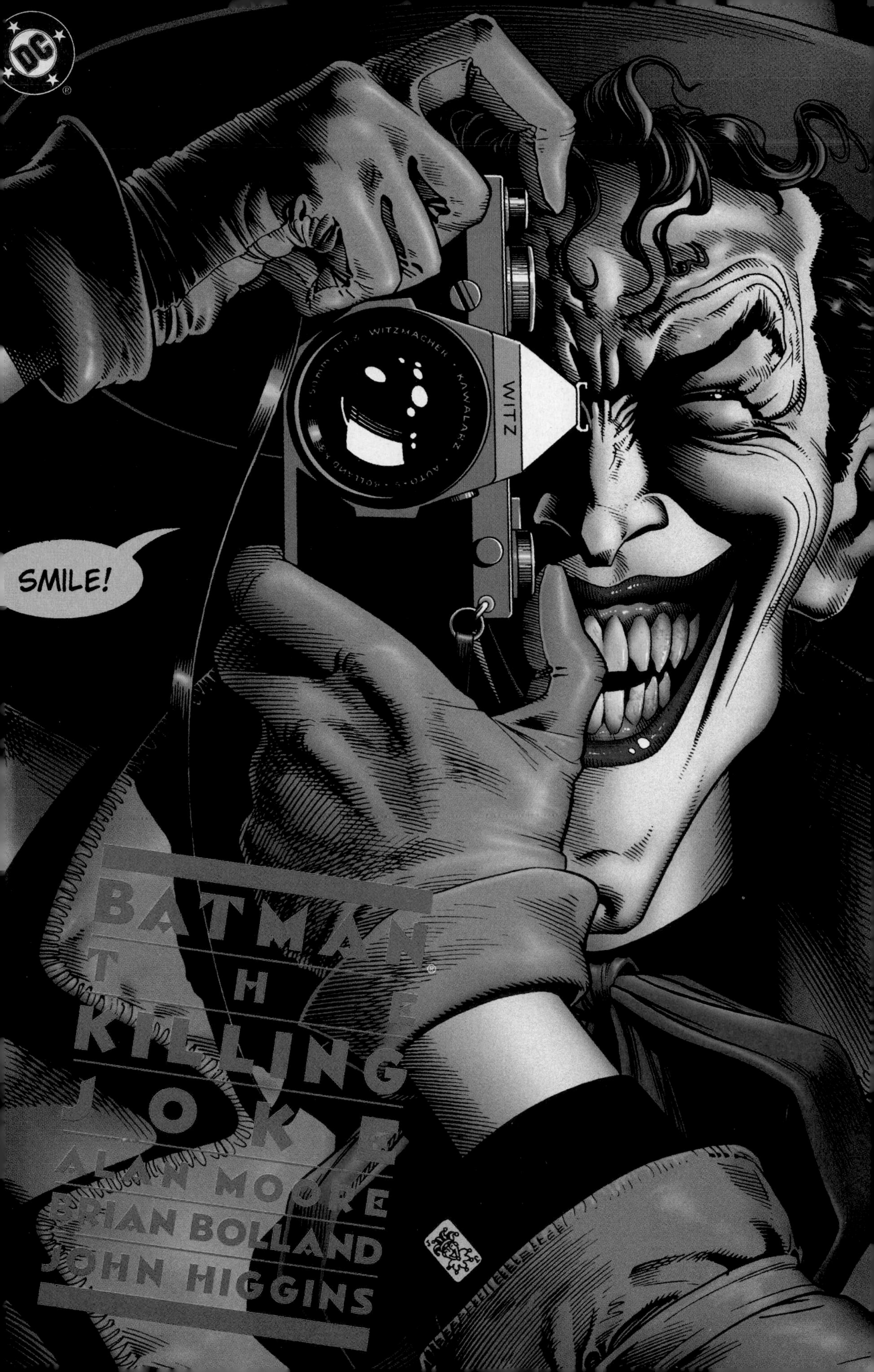

SMILE!
WITZ
BATMAN
THE
KILLING
JOKE
MOORE
BRIAN BOLLAND
JOHN HIGGINS

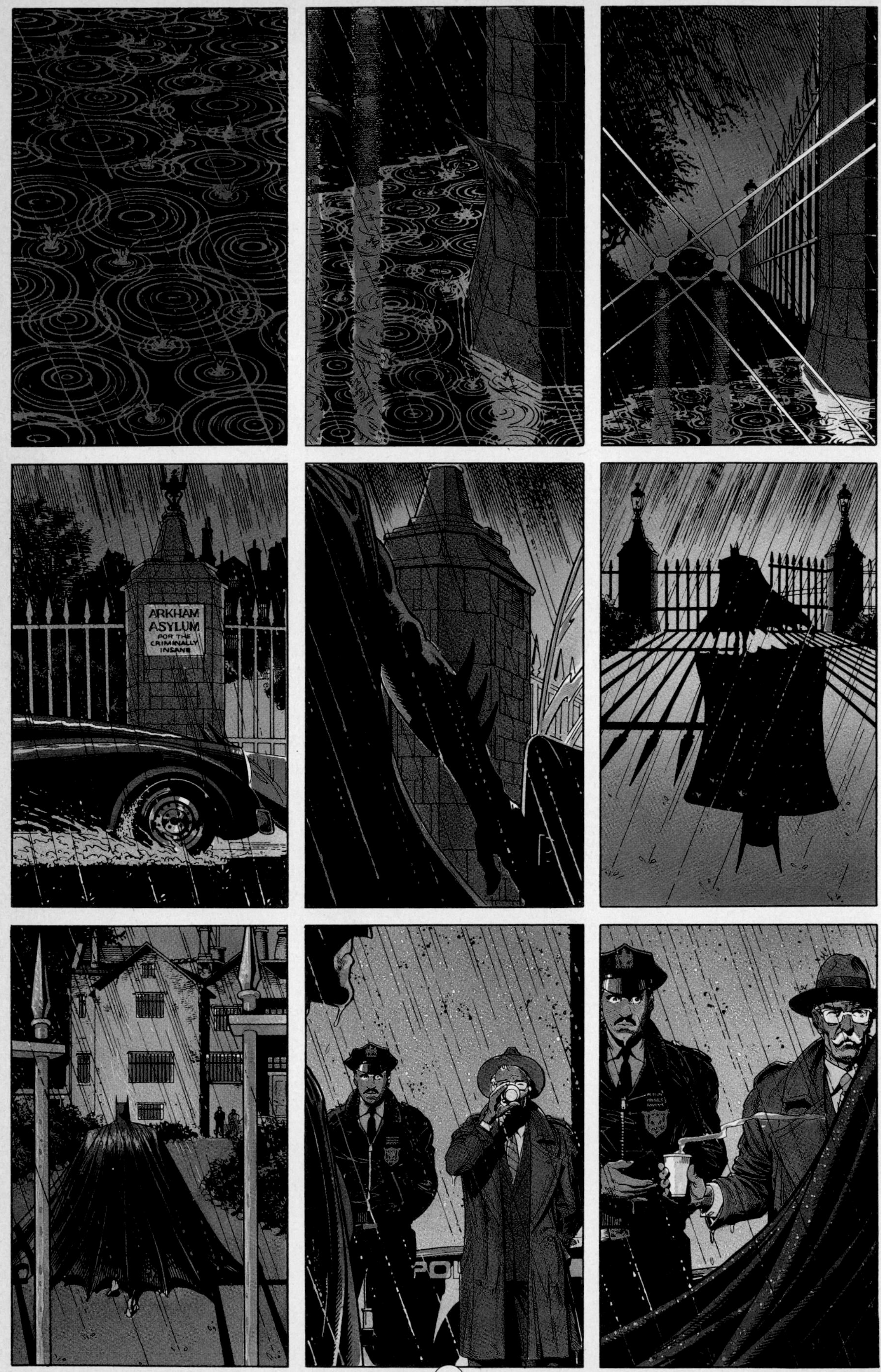
ARKHAM ASYLUM FOR THE CRIMINALLY INSANE
POLI

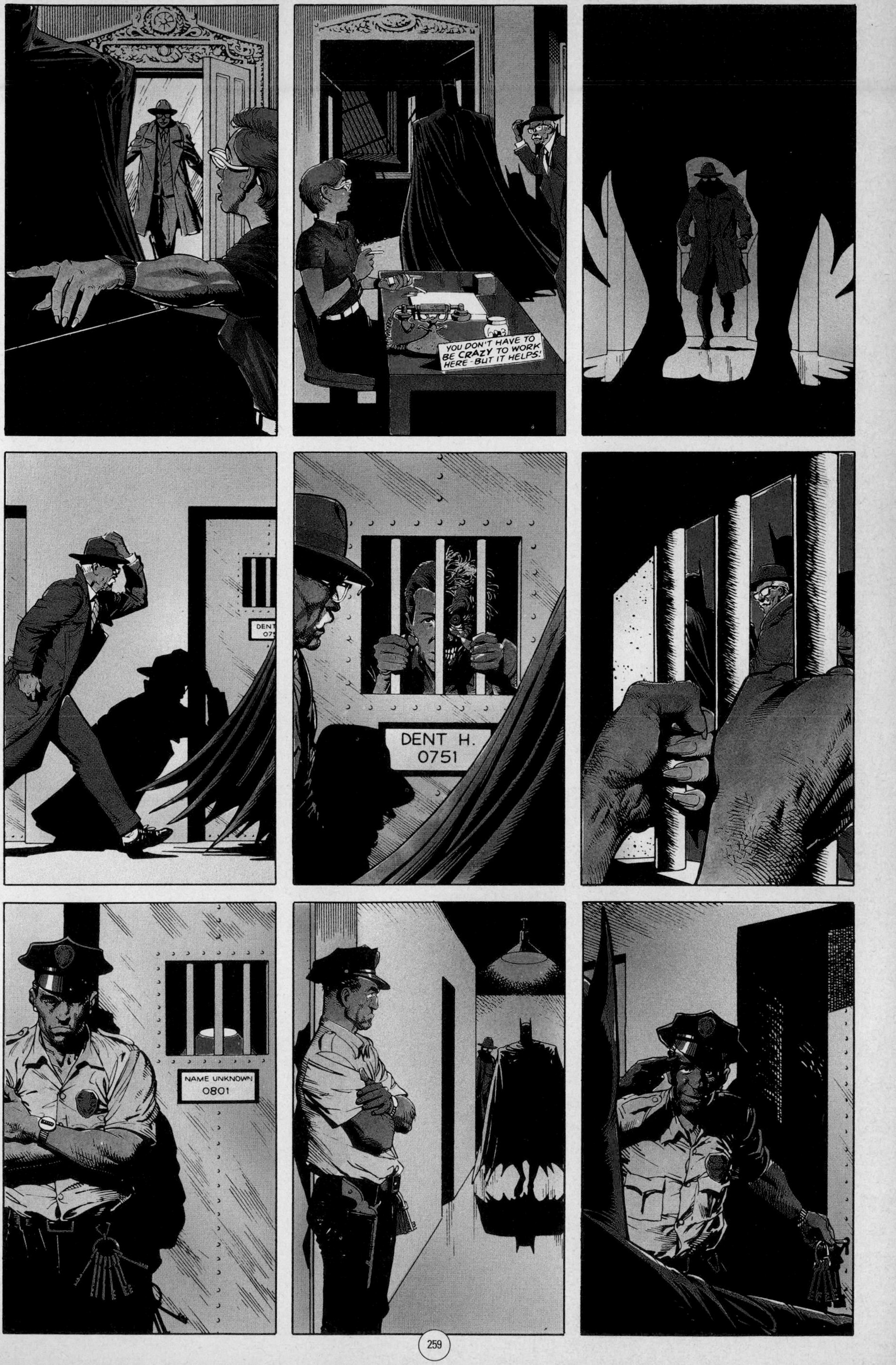
YOU DON'T HAVE TO BE CRAZY TO WORK HERE - BUT IT HELPS!
DENT H. 0751
NAME UNKNOWN 0801

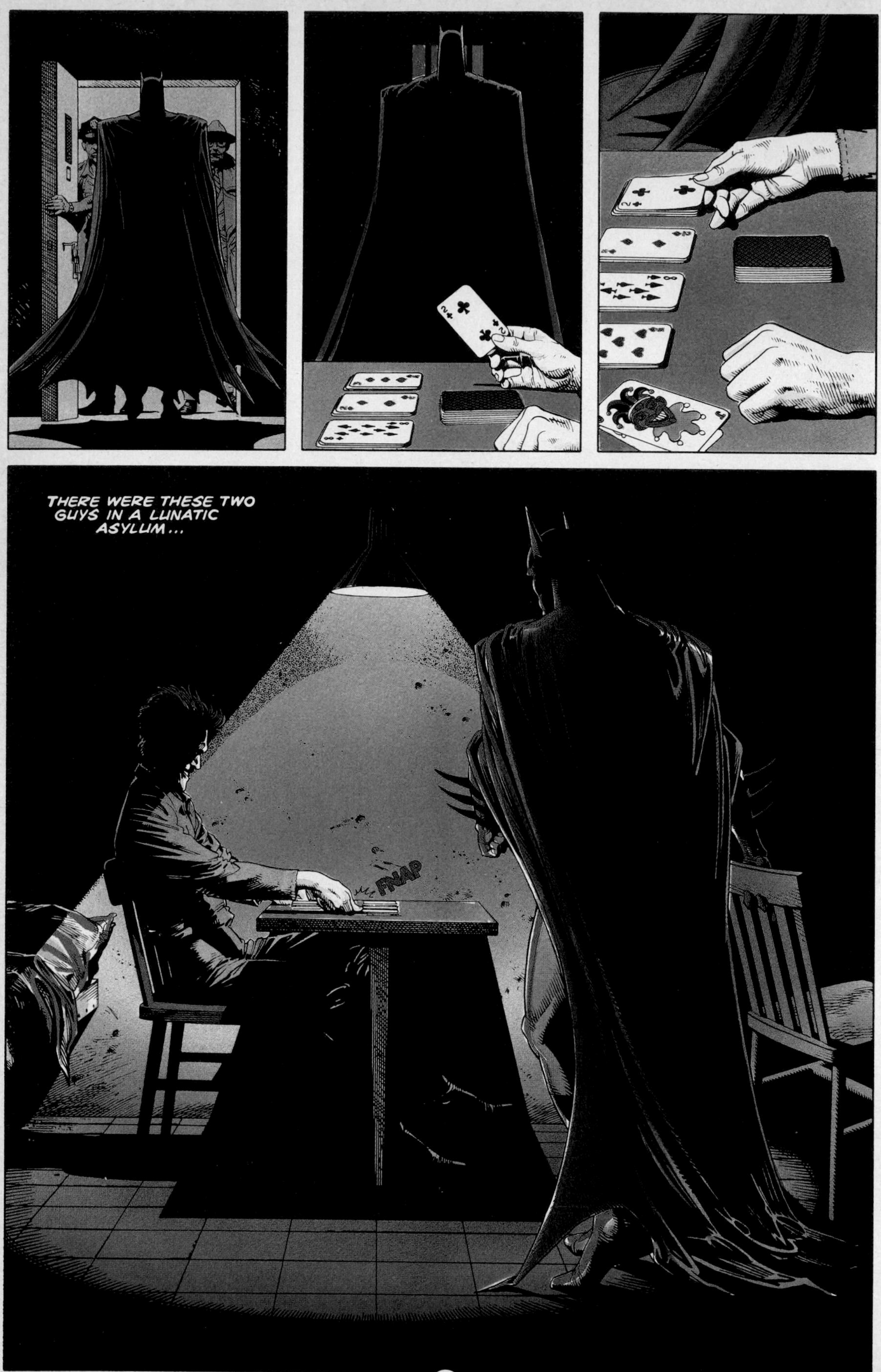
THERE WERE THESE TWO GUYS IN A LUNATIC ASYLUM...
FNAP

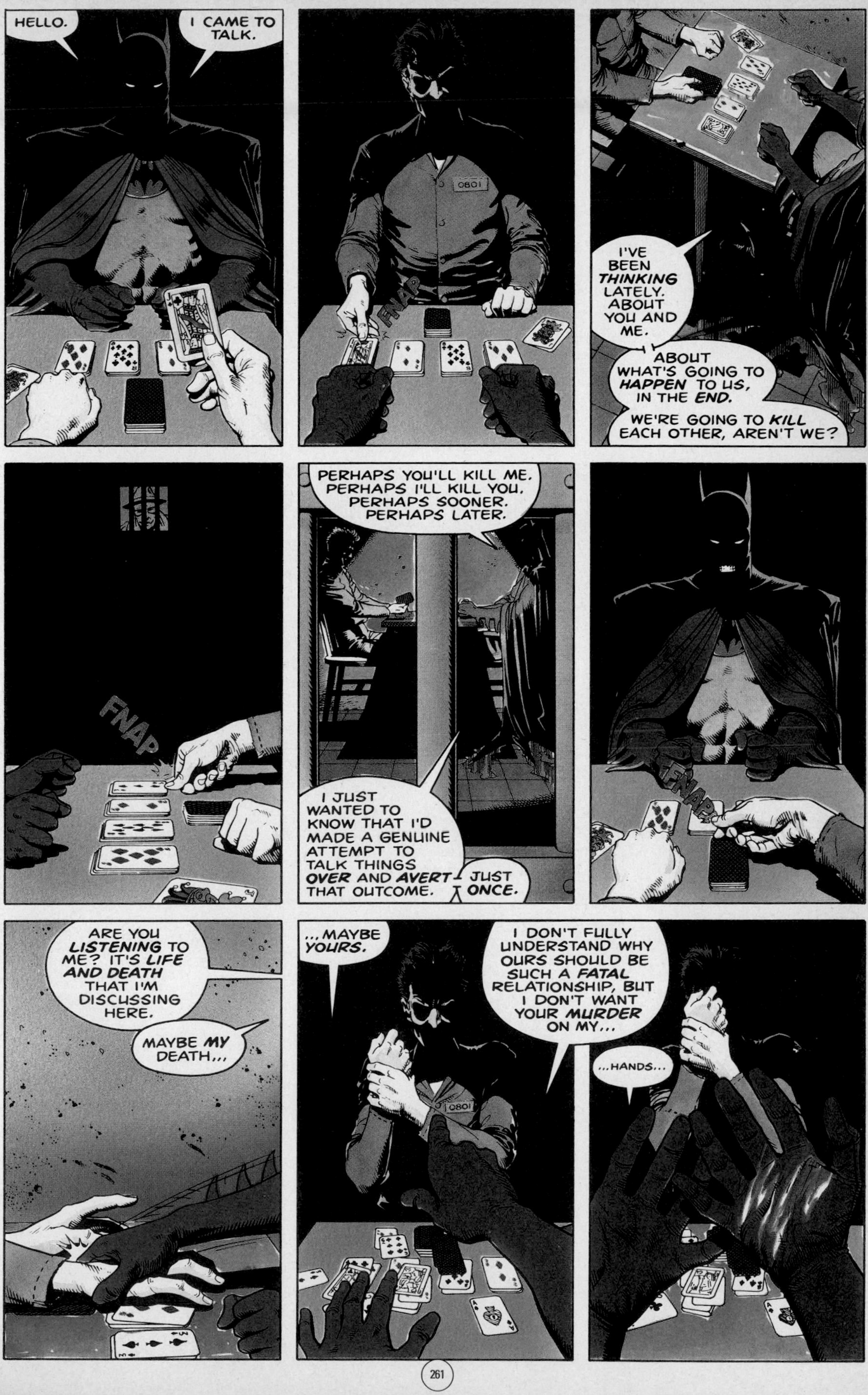
HELLO.
I CAME TO TALK.
FNAP
I'VE BEEN THINKING LATELY. ABOUT YOU AND ME.
ABOUT WHAT'S GOING TO HAPPEN TO US, IN THE END.
WE'RE GOING TO KILL EACH OTHER, AREN'T WE?
FNAP
PERHAPS YOU'LL KILL ME. PERHAPS I'LL KILL YOU. PERHAPS SOONER. PERHAPS LATER.
I JUST WANTED TO KNOW THAT I'D MADE A GENUINE ATTEMPT TO TALK THINGS OVER AND AVERT THAT OUTCOME.
JUST ONCE.
FNAP
ARE YOU LISTENING TO ME? IT'S LIFE AND DEATH THAT I'M DISCUSSING HERE.
MAYBE MY DEATH...
...MAYBE YOURS.
I DON'T FULLY UNDERSTAND WHY OURS SHOULD BE SUCH A FATAL RELATIONSHIP, BUT I DON'T WANT YOUR MURDER ON MY...
...HANDS...

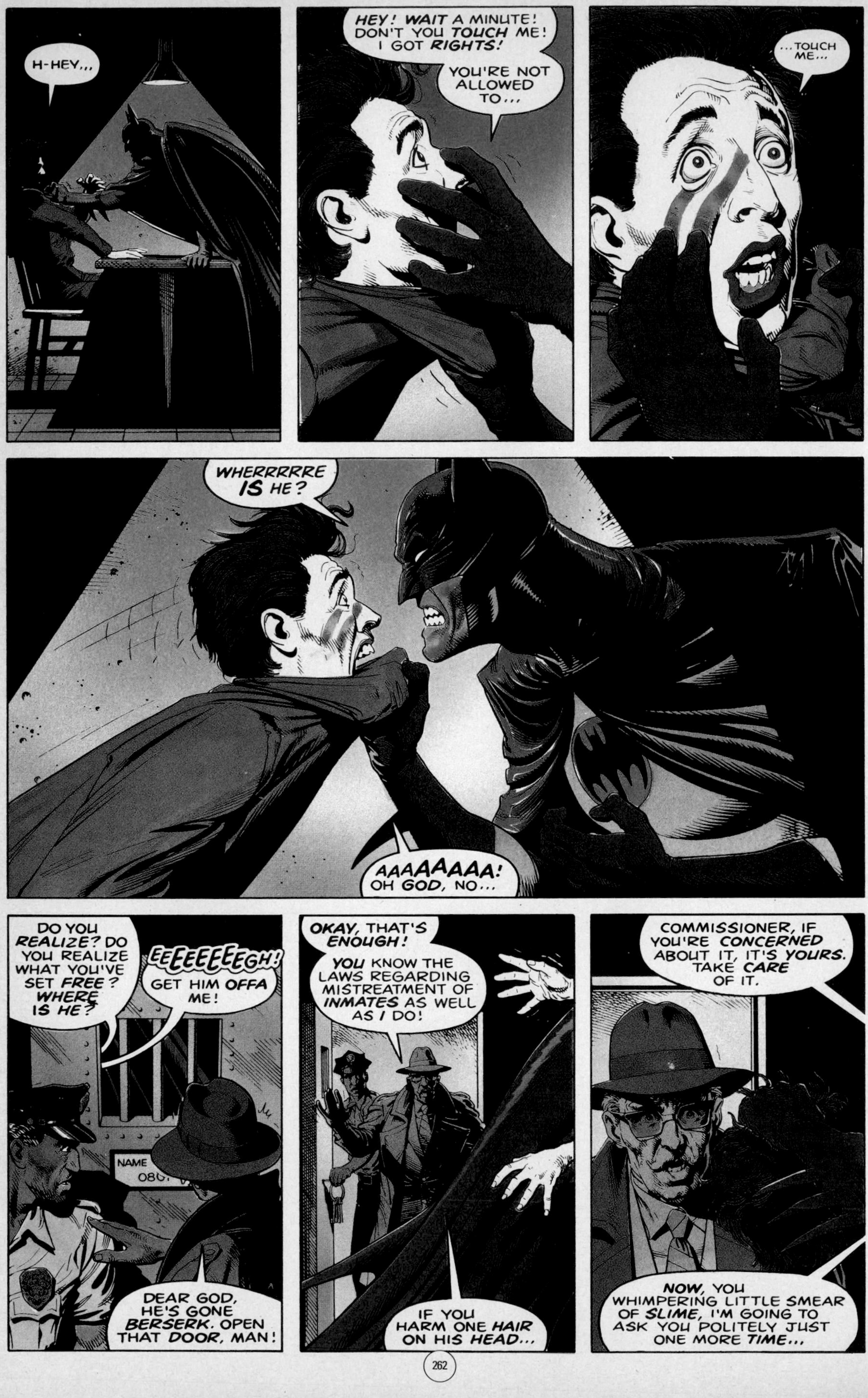
H-HEY...
HEY! WAIT A MINUTE! DON'T YOU TOUCH ME! I GOT RIGHTS!
YOU'RE NOT ALLOWED TO...
...TOUCH ME...
WHERRRRRE IS HE?
AAAAAAAA! OH GOD, NO...
DO YOU REALIZE? DO YOU REALIZE WHAT YOU'VE SET FREE? WHERE IS HE?
EEEEEEEEGH!
GET HIM OFFA ME!
NAME
DEAR GOD, HE'S GONE BERSERK. OPEN THAT DOOR, MAN!
OKAY, THAT'S ENOUGH!
YOU KNOW THE LAWS REGARDING MISTREATMENT OF INMATES AS WELL AS I DO!
IF YOU HARM ONE HAIR ON HIS HEAD...
COMMISSIONER, IF YOU'RE CONCERNED ABOUT IT, IT'S YOURS. TAKE CARE OF IT.
NOW, YOU WHIMPERING LITTLE SMEAR OF SLIME, I'M GOING TO ASK YOU POLITELY JUST ONE MORE TIME...

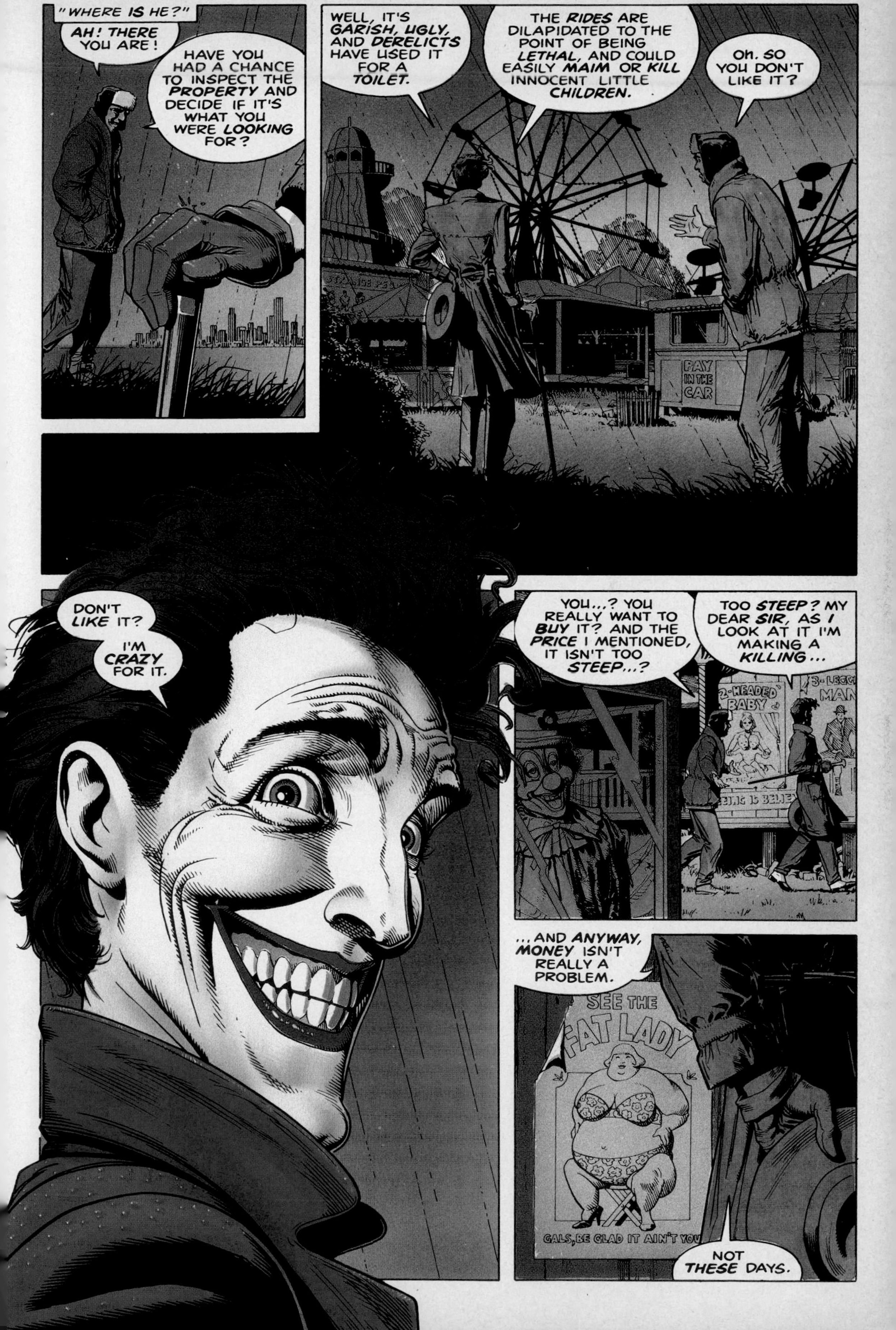
"WHERE IS HE?"
AH! THERE YOU ARE!
HAVE YOU HAD A CHANCE TO INSPECT THE PROPERTY AND DECIDE IF IT'S WHAT YOU WERE LOOKING FOR?
WELL, IT'S GARISH, UGLY, AND DERELICTS HAVE USED IT FOR A TOILET.
THE RIDES ARE DILAPIDATED TO THE POINT OF BEING LETHAL, AND COULD EASILY MAIM OR KILL INNOCENT LITTLE CHILDREN.
Oh. SO YOU DON'T LIKE IT?
PAY IN THE CAR
DON'T LIKE IT?
I'M CRAZY FOR IT.
YOU...? YOU REALLY WANT TO BUY IT? AND THE PRICE I MENTIONED, IT ISN'T TOO STEEP...?
TOO STEEP? MY DEAR SIR, AS I LOOK AT IT I'M MAKING A KILLING...
...AND ANYWAY, MONEY ISN'T REALLY A PROBLEM.
SEE THE FAT LADY
GALS, BE GLAD IT AIN'T YOU
NOT THESE DAYS.

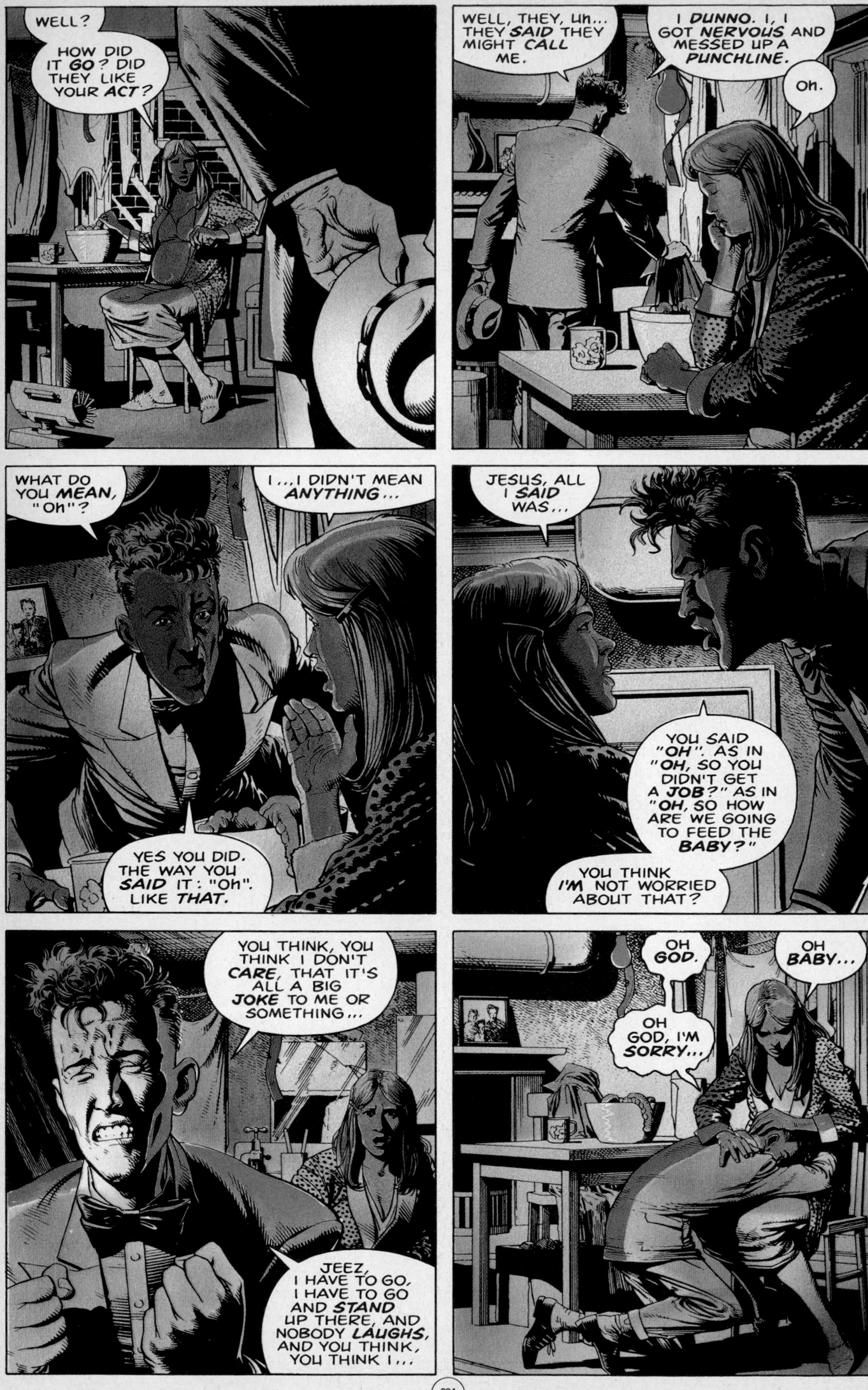
WELL?
HOW DID IT GO? DID THEY LIKE YOUR ACT?
WELL, THEY, uh... THEY SAID THEY MIGHT CALL ME.
I DUNNO. I, I GOT NERVOUS AND MESSED UP A PUNCHLINE.
Oh.
WHAT DO YOU MEAN, "Oh"?
I...I DIDN'T MEAN ANYTHING...
YES YOU DID. THE WAY YOU SAID IT: "Oh". LIKE THAT.
JESUS, ALL I SAID WAS...
YOU SAID "OH". AS IN "OH, SO YOU DIDN'T GET A JOB?" AS IN "OH, SO HOW ARE WE GOING TO FEED THE BABY?"
YOU THINK I'M NOT WORRIED ABOUT THAT?
YOU THINK, YOU THINK I DON'T CARE, THAT IT'S ALL A BIG JOKE TO ME OR SOMETHING...
JEEZ, I HAVE TO GO, I HAVE TO GO AND STAND UP THERE, AND NOBODY LAUGHS, AND YOU THINK, YOU THINK I...
OH GOD.
OH BABY...
OH GOD, I'M SORRY...

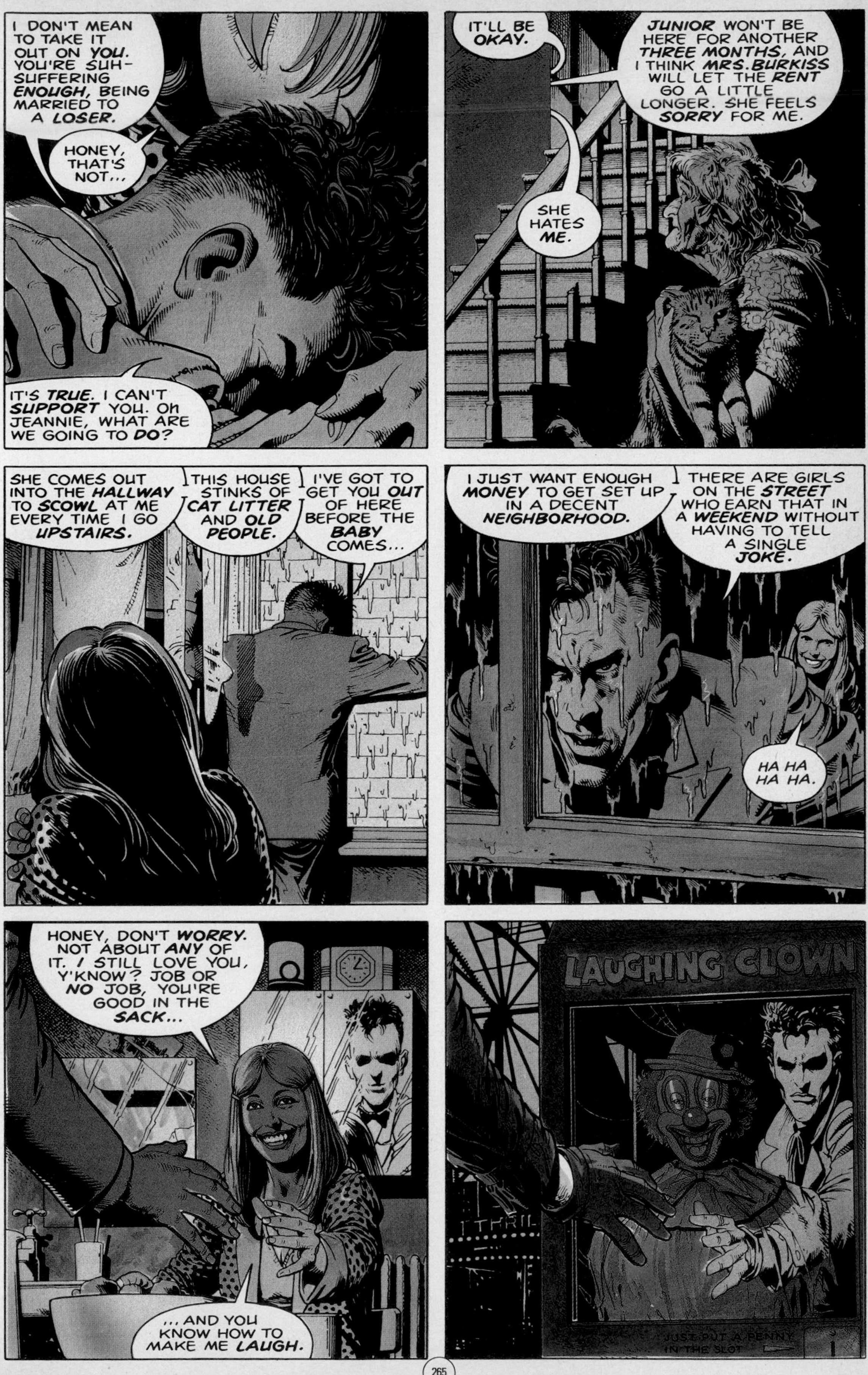
I DON'T MEAN TO TAKE IT OUT ON YOU. YOU'RE SUH-SUFFERING ENOUGH, BEING MARRIED TO A LOSER.
HONEY, THAT'S NOT...
IT'S TRUE. I CAN'T SUPPORT YOU. OH JEANNIE, WHAT ARE WE GOING TO DO?
IT'LL BE OKAY.
JUNIOR WON'T BE HERE FOR ANOTHER THREE MONTHS, AND I THINK MRS. BURKISS WILL LET THE RENT GO A LITTLE LONGER. SHE FEELS SORRY FOR ME.
SHE HATES ME.
SHE COMES OUT INTO THE HALLWAY TO SCOWL AT ME EVERY TIME I GO UPSTAIRS.
THIS HOUSE STINKS OF CAT LITTER AND OLD PEOPLE.
I'VE GOT TO GET YOU OUT OF HERE BEFORE THE BABY COMES...
I JUST WANT ENOUGH MONEY TO GET SET UP IN A DECENT NEIGHBORHOOD.
THERE ARE GIRLS ON THE STREET WHO EARN THAT IN A WEEKEND WITHOUT HAVING TO TELL A SINGLE JOKE.
HA HA HA HA.
HONEY, DON'T WORRY. NOT ABOUT ANY OF IT. I STILL LOVE YOU, Y'KNOW? JOB OR NO JOB, YOU'RE GOOD IN THE SACK...
...AND YOU KNOW HOW TO MAKE ME LAUGH.
LAUGHING CLOWN
JUST PUT A PENNY IN THE SLOT

Y'KNOW, I'M *POSITIVE* YOU WON'T *REGRET* THIS PURCHASE. THE PLACE ISN'T *THAT* DILAPIDATED. SOME OF THESE *RIDES* ARE STILL PRETTY *STURDY...*

REALLY, THIS COULD BE ONE *HELL* OF A CARNIVAL.

OH, YOU'RE *SO* RIGHT.

THANKS TO YOUR SMOOTH SALESMANSHIP AND YOUR SILVER TONGUE YOU'VE COMPLETELY *SOLD* ME ON THE PLACE. LET'S *SHAKE* ON IT.

UH..., WELL, SURE. IT'S MY *PRIVILEGE...*

INDEED IT *IS.*

NATURALLY, I WON'T BE *PAYING* YOU ANYTHING. MY *COLLEAGUES* PERSUADED YOUR *PARTNER* TO SIGN THE NECESSARY *DOCUMENTS* JUST OVER AN *HOUR* AGO. THE PROPERTY'S MINE *ALREADY.*

YOU'RE *HAPPY* WITH THAT, I TAKE IT?

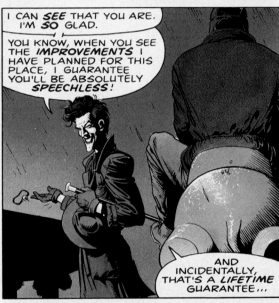

I CAN *SEE* THAT YOU ARE. I'M *SO* GLAD.

YOU KNOW, WHEN YOU SEE THE *IMPROVEMENTS* I HAVE PLANNED FOR THIS PLACE, I GUARANTEE YOU'LL BE ABSOLUTELY *SPEECHLESS!*

AND, INCIDENTALLY, THAT'S A *LIFETIME* GUARANTEE...

WELL, I MUST *DASH.* THERE'S *EQUIPMENT* TO HIRE, PLUS *WORKERS* WHO'LL SUIT THE GENERAL *TONE* OF THE ESTABLISHMENT...

...AND THEN, OF COURSE, I'VE YET TO SECURE MY *MAIN ATTRACTION.*

DO FEEL FREE TO STICK AROUND.

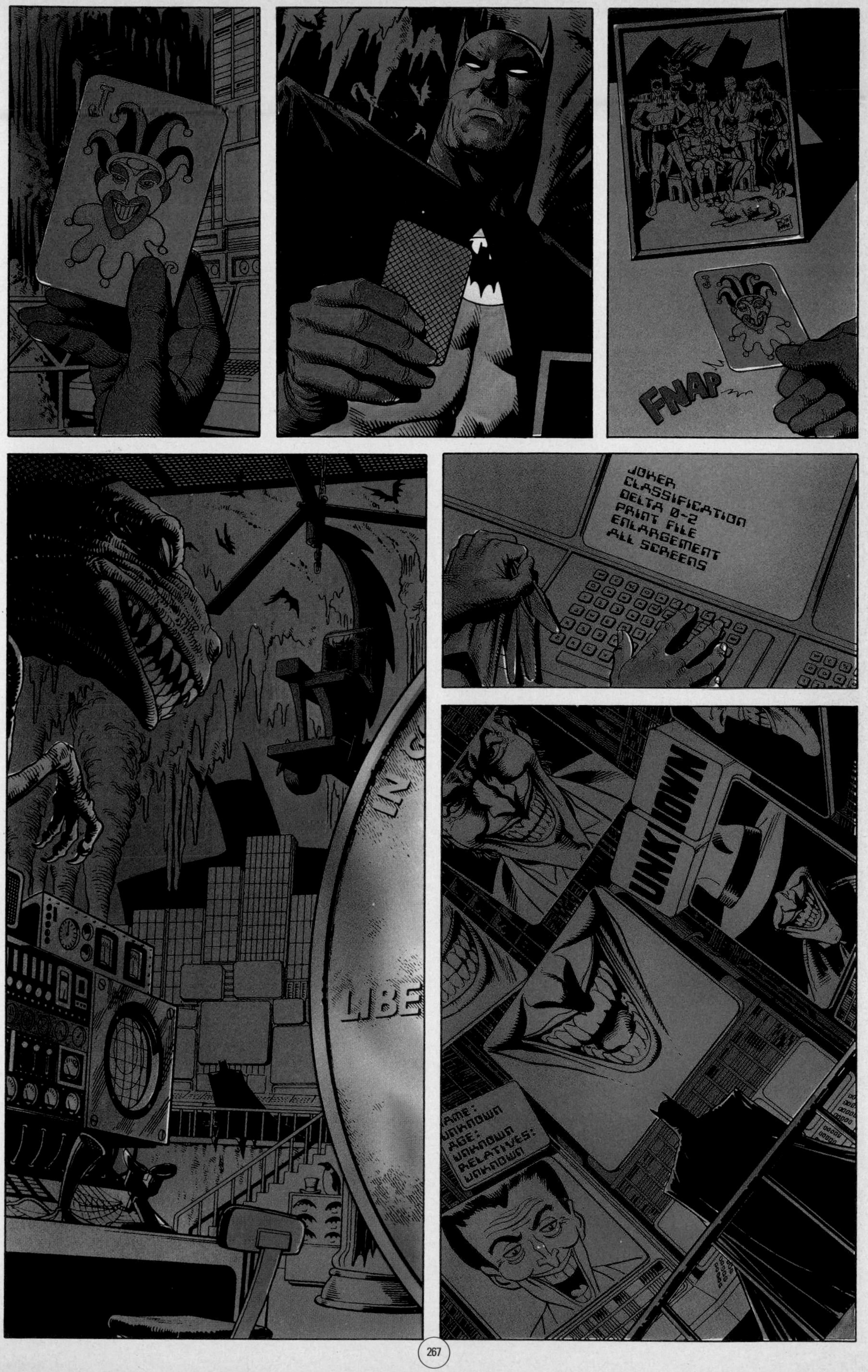
FNAP
JOKER
CLASSIFICATION
DELTA 0-2
PRINT FILE
ENLARGEMENT
ALL SCREENS
LIBE
UNKNOWN
AME:
UNKNOWN
AGE:
UNKNOWN
RELATIVES:
UNKNOWN

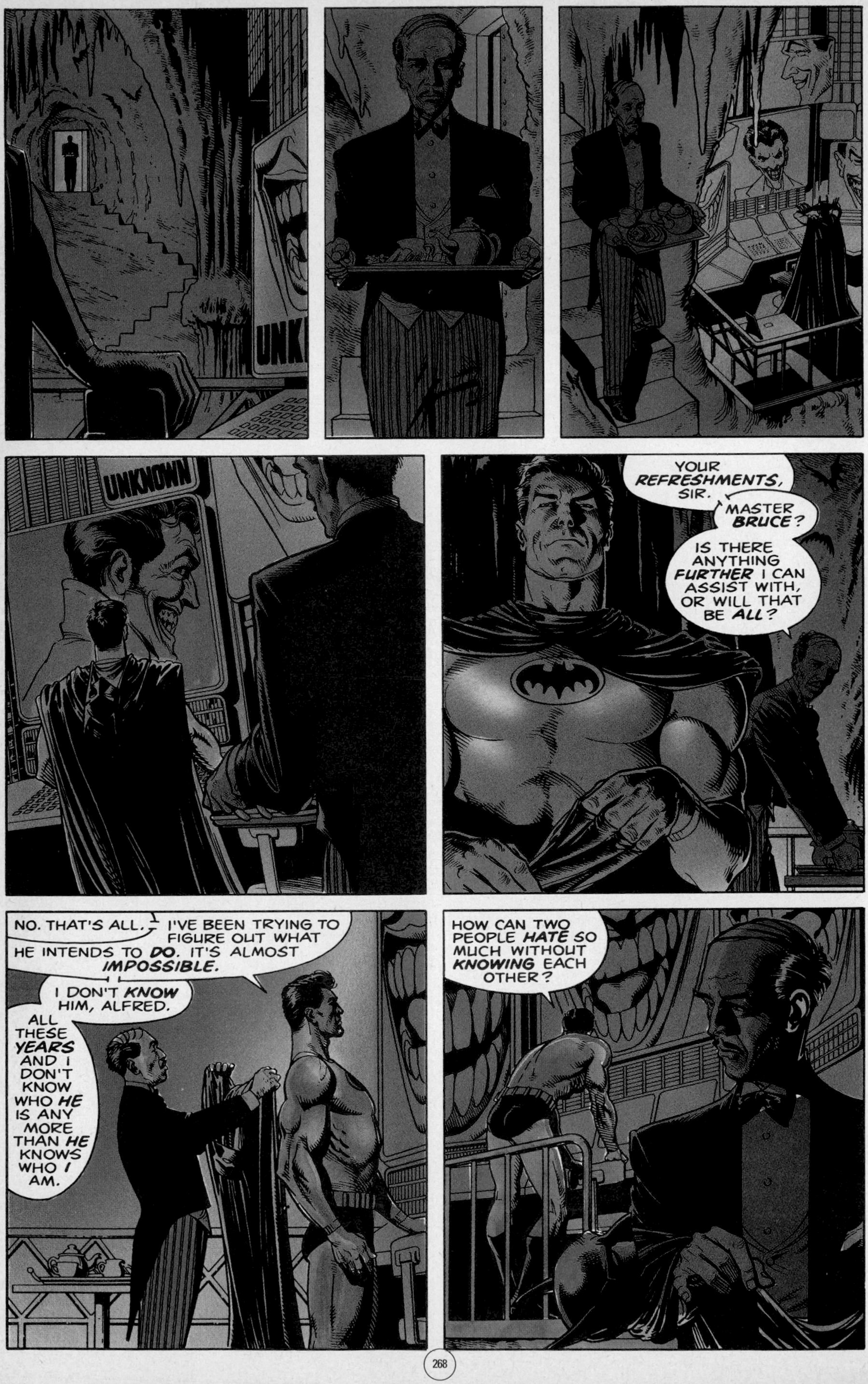
UNKNOWN
YOUR REFRESHMENTS, SIR.
MASTER BRUCE?
IS THERE ANYTHING FURTHER I CAN ASSIST WITH, OR WILL THAT BE ALL?
NO. THAT'S ALL.
I'VE BEEN TRYING TO FIGURE OUT WHAT HE INTENDS TO DO. IT'S ALMOST IMPOSSIBLE.
I DON'T KNOW HIM, ALFRED.
ALL THESE YEARS AND I DON'T KNOW WHO HE IS ANY MORE THAN HE KNOWS WHO I AM.
HOW CAN TWO PEOPLE HATE SO MUCH WITHOUT KNOWING EACH OTHER?

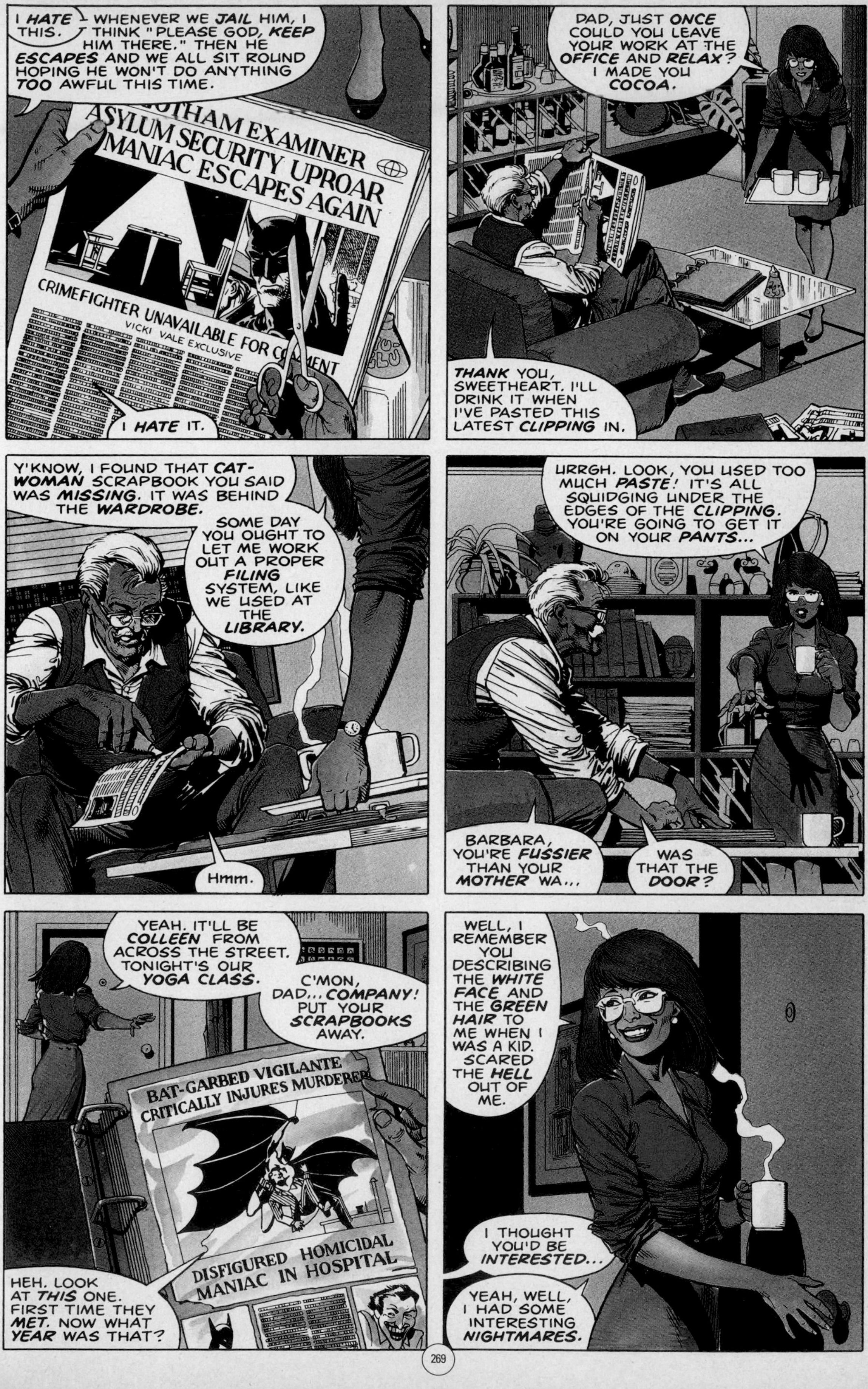
I HATE THIS.
- WHENEVER WE JAIL HIM, I THINK "PLEASE GOD, KEEP HIM THERE." THEN HE ESCAPES AND WE ALL SIT ROUND HOPING HE WON'T DO ANYTHING TOO AWFUL THIS TIME.
GOTHAM EXAMINER
ASYLUM SECURITY UPROAR
MANIAC ESCAPES AGAIN
CRIMEFIGHTER UNAVAILABLE FOR COMMENT
VICKI VALE EXCLUSIVE
I HATE IT.
DAD, JUST ONCE COULD YOU LEAVE YOUR WORK AT THE OFFICE AND RELAX? I MADE YOU COCOA.
THANK YOU, SWEETHEART. I'LL DRINK IT WHEN I'VE PASTED THIS LATEST CLIPPING IN.
Y'KNOW, I FOUND THAT CAT-WOMAN SCRAPBOOK YOU SAID WAS MISSING. IT WAS BEHIND THE WARDROBE.
SOME DAY YOU OUGHT TO LET ME WORK OUT A PROPER FILING SYSTEM, LIKE WE USED AT THE LIBRARY.
Hmm.
URRGH. LOOK, YOU USED TOO MUCH PASTE! IT'S ALL SQUIDGING UNDER THE EDGES OF THE CLIPPING. YOU'RE GOING TO GET IT ON YOUR PANTS...
BARBARA, YOU'RE FUSSIER THAN YOUR MOTHER WA...
WAS THAT THE DOOR?
YEAH. IT'LL BE COLLEEN FROM ACROSS THE STREET. TONIGHT'S OUR YOGA CLASS.
C'MON, DAD... COMPANY! PUT YOUR SCRAPBOOKS AWAY.
BAT-GARBED VIGILANTE CRITICALLY INJURES MURDERER
DISFIGURED HOMICIDAL MANIAC IN HOSPITAL
HEH. LOOK AT THIS ONE. FIRST TIME THEY MET. NOW WHAT YEAR WAS THAT?
WELL, I REMEMBER YOU DESCRIBING THE WHITE FACE AND THE GREEN HAIR TO ME WHEN I WAS A KID. SCARED THE HELL OUT OF ME.
I THOUGHT YOU'D BE INTERESTED...
YEAH, WELL, I HAD SOME INTERESTING NIGHTMARES.

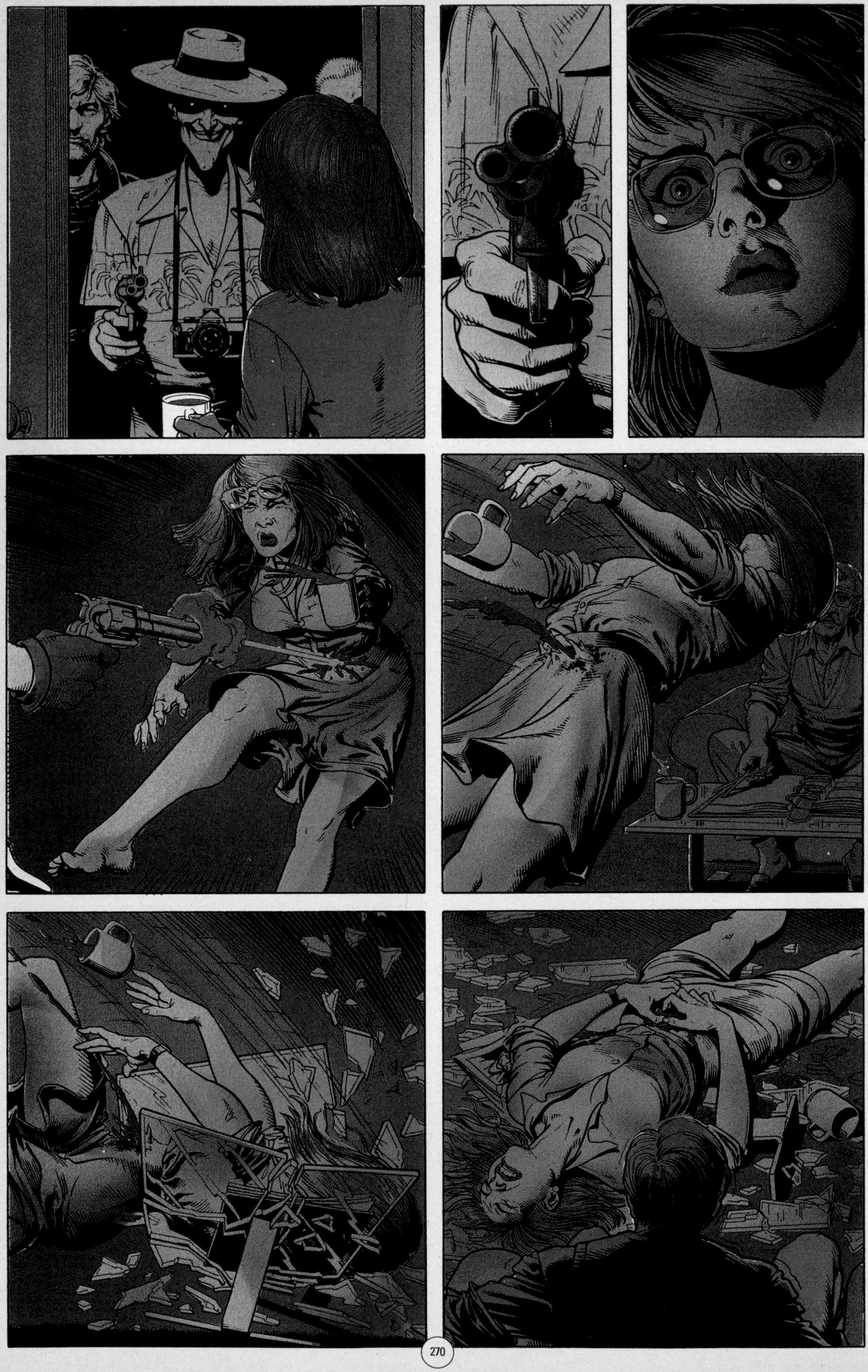

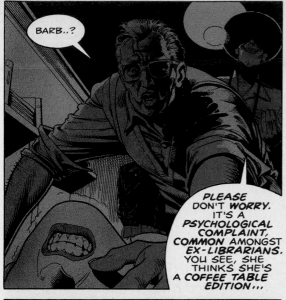

BARB..?

PLEASE DON'T *WORRY.* IT'S A *PSYCHOLOGICAL* COMPLAINT, *COMMON* AMONGST *EX-LIBRARIANS.* YOU SEE, SHE THINKS SHE'S A *COFFEE TABLE EDITION...*

MIND *YOU,* I CAN'T SAY MUCH FOR THE VOLUME'S *CONDITION.*

I *MEAN,* THERE'S A *HOLE* IN THE *JACKET* AND THE *SPINE* APPEARS TO BE DAMAGED.

YOU, YOU *SCUM,* MY *DAUGHTER,* I'LL...

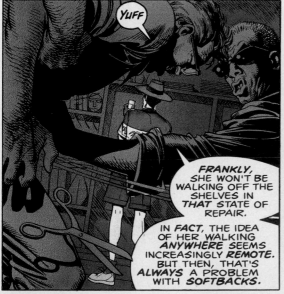

YUFF

FRANKLY, SHE WON'T BE WALKING OFF THE SHELVES IN *THAT* STATE OF REPAIR.

IN *FACT,* THE IDEA OF HER WALKING *ANYWHERE* SEEMS INCREASINGLY *REMOTE.* BUT THEN, THAT'S *ALWAYS* A PROBLEM WITH *SOFTBACKS.*

GOD, THESE *LITERARY DISCUSSIONS* ARE SO *DRY.* WHEN YOU'VE *FINISHED* WITH THE OLD BOY, YOU KNOW WHERE TO *TAKE* HIM.

AND *PLEASE... DO BE CAREFUL!* AFTER ALL, HE *IS* TOPPING THE *BILL.*

YOU KNOW, IT'S *SUCH* A *SHAME* YOU'LL MISS YOUR FATHER'S *DEBUT,* MISS GORDON.

SADLY, OUR *VENUE* WASN'T *BUILT* WITH THE *DISABLED* IN MIND. BUT DON'T *WORRY...,* I'LL TAKE SOME *SNAPSHOTS* TO *REMIND* HIM OF *YOU.*

WUH... WUH...,WHY..., ARE YOU...

DUH..., *DOING* THIS..?

TO PROVE A *POINT.*

HERE'S TO *CRIME.*

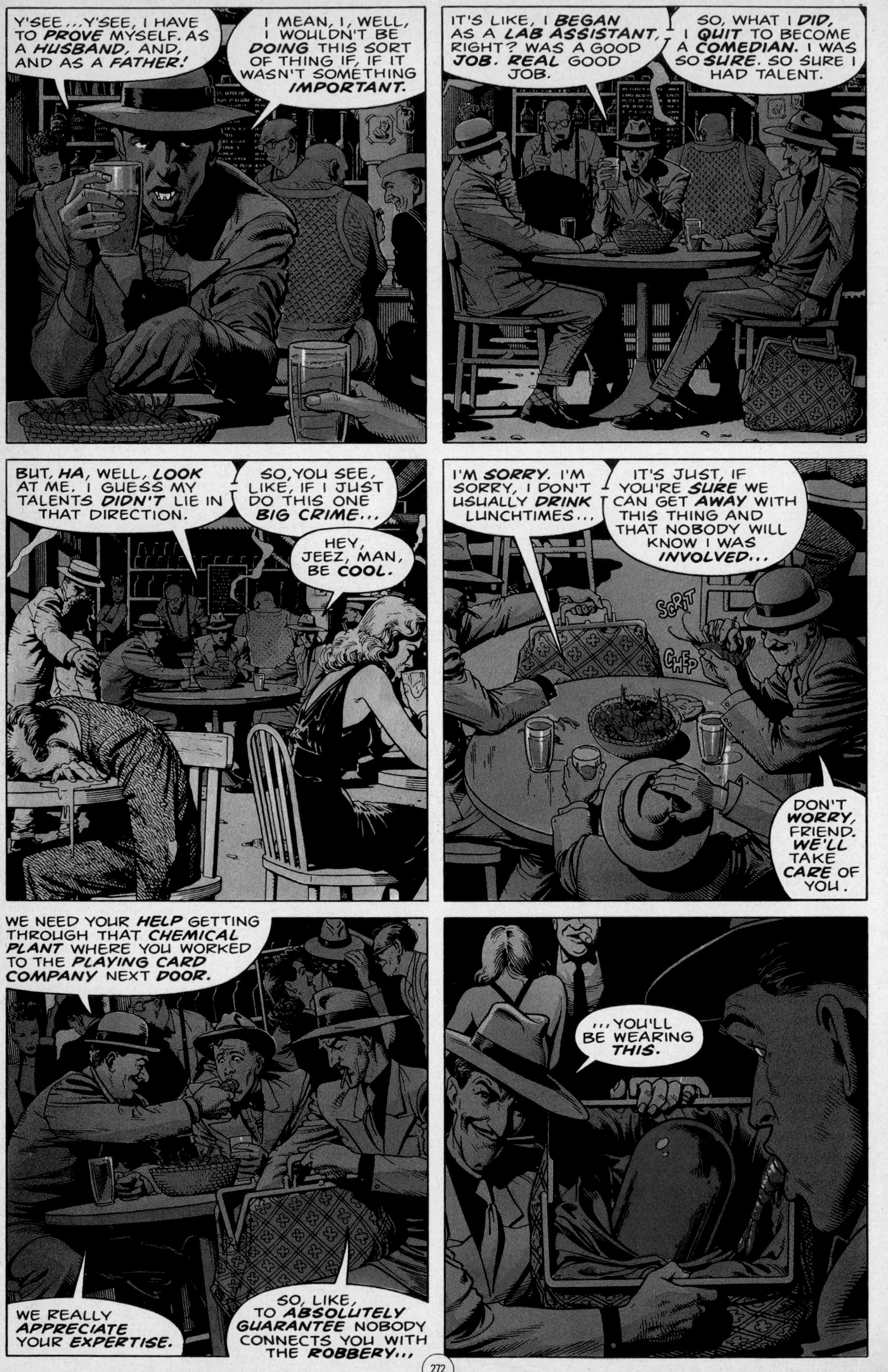

Y'SEE...Y'SEE, I HAVE TO PROVE MYSELF. AS A HUSBAND, AND, AND AS A FATHER!
I MEAN, I, WELL, I WOULDN'T BE DOING THIS SORT OF THING IF, IF IT WASN'T SOMETHING IMPORTANT.
IT'S LIKE, I BEGAN AS A LAB ASSISTANT, RIGHT? WAS A GOOD JOB. REAL GOOD JOB.
SO, WHAT I DID, I QUIT TO BECOME A COMEDIAN. I WAS SO SURE. SO SURE I HAD TALENT.
BUT, HA, WELL, LOOK AT ME. I GUESS MY TALENTS DIDN'T LIE IN THAT DIRECTION.
SO, YOU SEE, LIKE, IF I JUST DO THIS ONE BIG CRIME...
HEY, JEEZ, MAN, BE COOL.
I'M SORRY. I'M SORRY, I DON'T USUALLY DRINK LUNCHTIMES...
IT'S JUST, IF YOU'RE SURE WE CAN GET AWAY WITH THIS THING AND THAT NOBODY WILL KNOW I WAS INVOLVED...
SCRT
CHEP
DON'T WORRY, FRIEND. WE'LL TAKE CARE OF YOU.
WE NEED YOUR HELP GETTING THROUGH THAT CHEMICAL PLANT WHERE YOU WORKED TO THE PLAYING CARD COMPANY NEXT DOOR.
WE REALLY APPRECIATE YOUR EXPERTISE.
SO, LIKE, TO ABSOLUTELY GUARANTEE NOBODY CONNECTS YOU WITH THE ROBBERY...
...YOU'LL BE WEARING THIS.

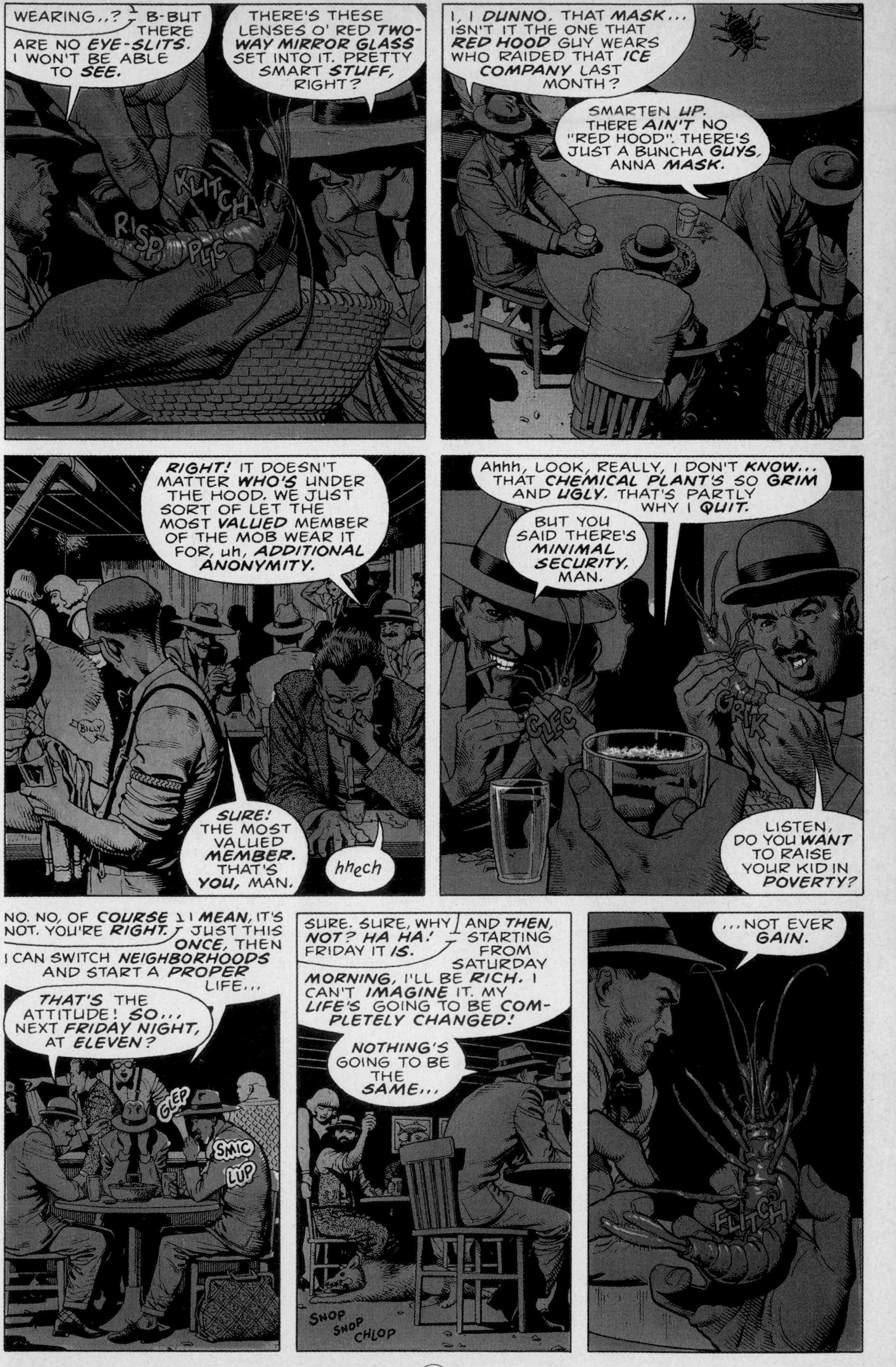
WEARING..? B-BUT THERE ARE NO EYE-SLITS. I WON'T BE ABLE TO SEE.
THERE'S THESE LENSES O' RED TWO-WAY MIRROR GLASS SET INTO IT. PRETTY SMART STUFF, RIGHT?
KLITCH
RISP
PLIC
I, I DUNNO. THAT MASK... ISN'T IT THE ONE THAT RED HOOD GUY WEARS WHO RAIDED THAT ICE COMPANY LAST MONTH?
SMARTEN UP. THERE AIN'T NO "RED HOOD". THERE'S JUST A BUNCHA GUYS, ANNA MASK.
RIGHT! IT DOESN'T MATTER WHO'S UNDER THE HOOD. WE JUST SORT OF LET THE MOST VALUED MEMBER OF THE MOB WEAR IT FOR, uh, ADDITIONAL ANONYMITY.
SURE! THE MOST VALUED MEMBER. THAT'S YOU, MAN.
hhech
Ahhh, LOOK, REALLY, I DON'T KNOW... THAT CHEMICAL PLANT'S SO GRIM AND UGLY. THAT'S PARTLY WHY I QUIT.
BUT YOU SAID THERE'S MINIMAL SECURITY, MAN.
LISTEN, DO YOU WANT TO RAISE YOUR KID IN POVERTY?
NO. NO, OF COURSE NOT. YOU'RE RIGHT. I MEAN, IT'S JUST THIS ONCE, THEN I CAN SWITCH NEIGHBORHOODS AND START A PROPER LIFE...
THAT'S THE ATTITUDE! SO... NEXT FRIDAY NIGHT, AT ELEVEN?
GLEP
SMIC
LUP
SURE. SURE, WHY NOT? HA HA! FRIDAY IT IS. AND THEN, STARTING FROM SATURDAY MORNING, I'LL BE RICH. I CAN'T IMAGINE IT. MY LIFE'S GOING TO BE COMPLETELY CHANGED!
NOTHING'S GOING TO BE THE SAME...
SNOP SNOP CHLOP
...NOT EVER GAIN.
FLITCH

THE BULLET WENT THROUGH HER *SPINE.*

I'M AFRAID HER *LEGS* ARE COMPLETELY *USELESS.*

PUTTING IT *BLUNTLY,* SHE MAY WELL BE IN A *CHAIR* FOR THE REMAINDER OF HER *LIFE.*

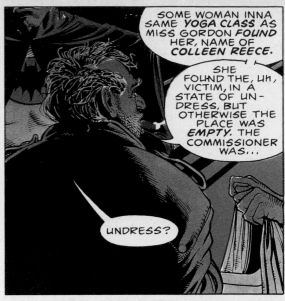

SOME WOMAN INNA SAME *YOGA CLASS* AS MISS GORDON *FOUND* HER, NAME OF *COLLEEN REECE.*

SHE FOUND THE, UH, VICTIM, IN A STATE OF UN-*DRESS,* BUT OTHERWISE THE PLACE WAS *EMPTY.* THE COMMISSIONER WAS...

UNDRESS?

THEY DIDN'T *TELL* YOU? HE'D REMOVED HER *CLOTHING* AFTER *SHOOTING* HER. WE, UH... WELL, WE FOUND A *LENS-CAP* ON THE FLOOR THAT DIDN'T FIT ANY CAMERA IN THE PLACE. WE BELIEVE THAT, UHH...

WELL, THAT HE TOOK SOME *PICTURES.*

OF HER.

JEEZ, LOOK, REALLY, I'M *SORRY.* I THOUGHT YOU *KNEW.* IT'S PRETTY *SICK,* AIN'T IT?

YES.

PRETTY SICK.

PLEASE LEAVE US ALONE FOR A MOMENT.

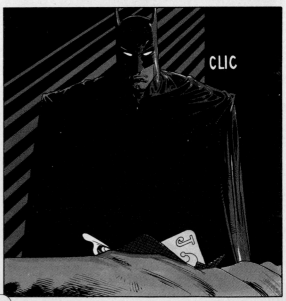

CLIC

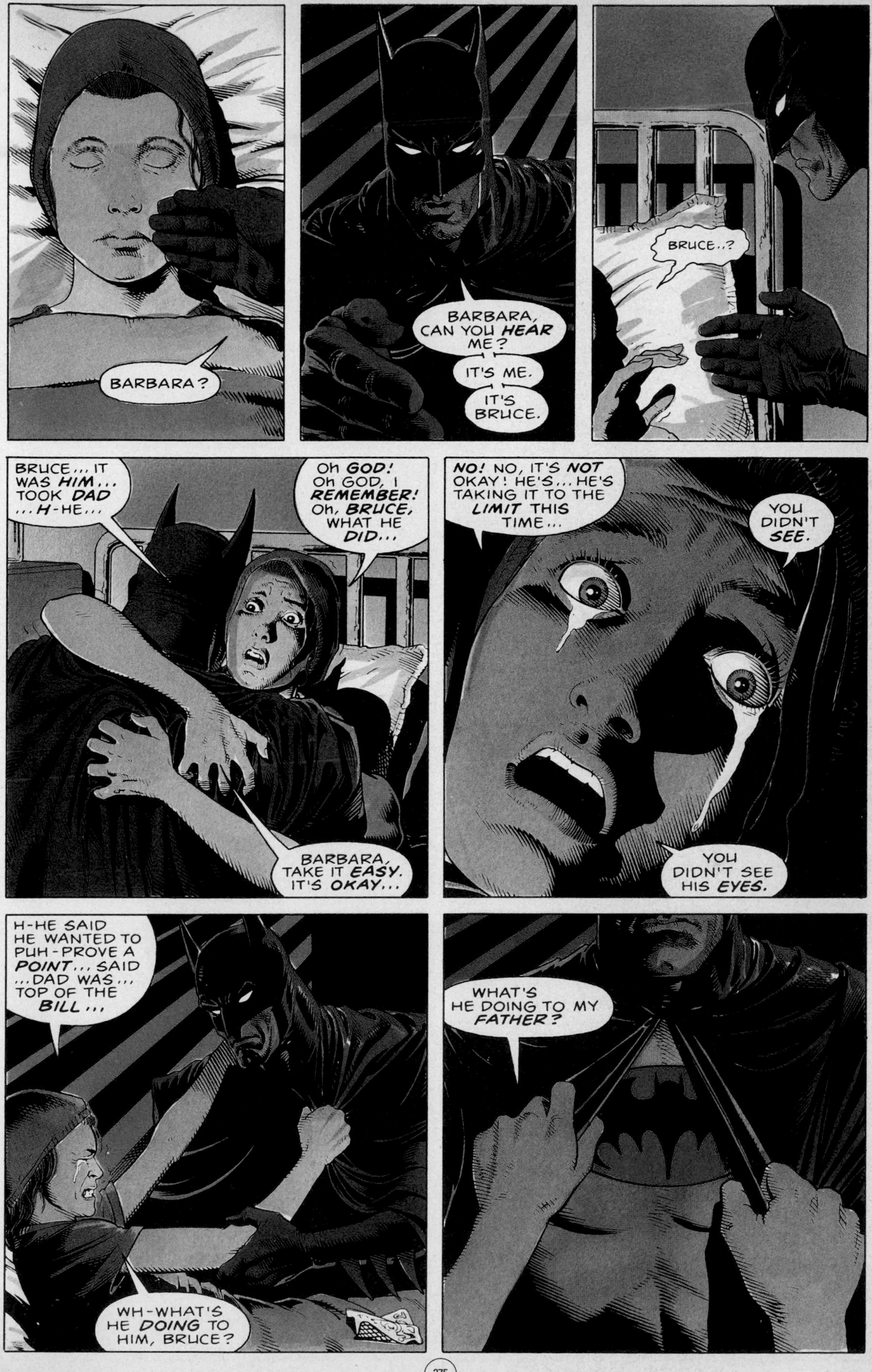
BARBARA?
BARBARA, CAN YOU HEAR ME?
IT'S ME.
IT'S BRUCE.
BRUCE..?
BRUCE... IT WAS HIM... TOOK DAD ...H-HE...
Oh GOD! Oh GOD, I REMEMBER! Oh, BRUCE, WHAT HE DID...
BARBARA, TAKE IT EASY. IT'S OKAY...
NO! NO, IT'S NOT OKAY! HE'S... HE'S TAKING IT TO THE LIMIT THIS TIME...
YOU DIDN'T SEE.
YOU DIDN'T SEE HIS EYES.
H-HE SAID HE WANTED TO PUH-PROVE A POINT... SAID ...DAD WAS... TOP OF THE BILL...
WH-WHAT'S HE DOING TO HIM, BRUCE?
WHAT'S HE DOING TO MY FATHER?

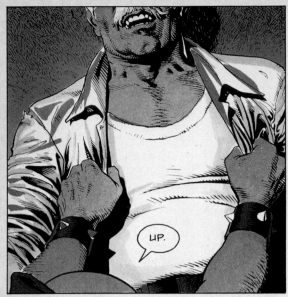

UP.

UP.

UP!

UNH?

WUH... WAIT... WAZZISS..?

WH-WHAT ARE YOU *DOING?* YOU CAN'T DO *THAT!* STOP...

OAAAAAH!

TZZSP

OUHH... OH NO.

OH *NO.* DON'T. DON'T *DO* THIS...

I WON'T... HUU-HUKK

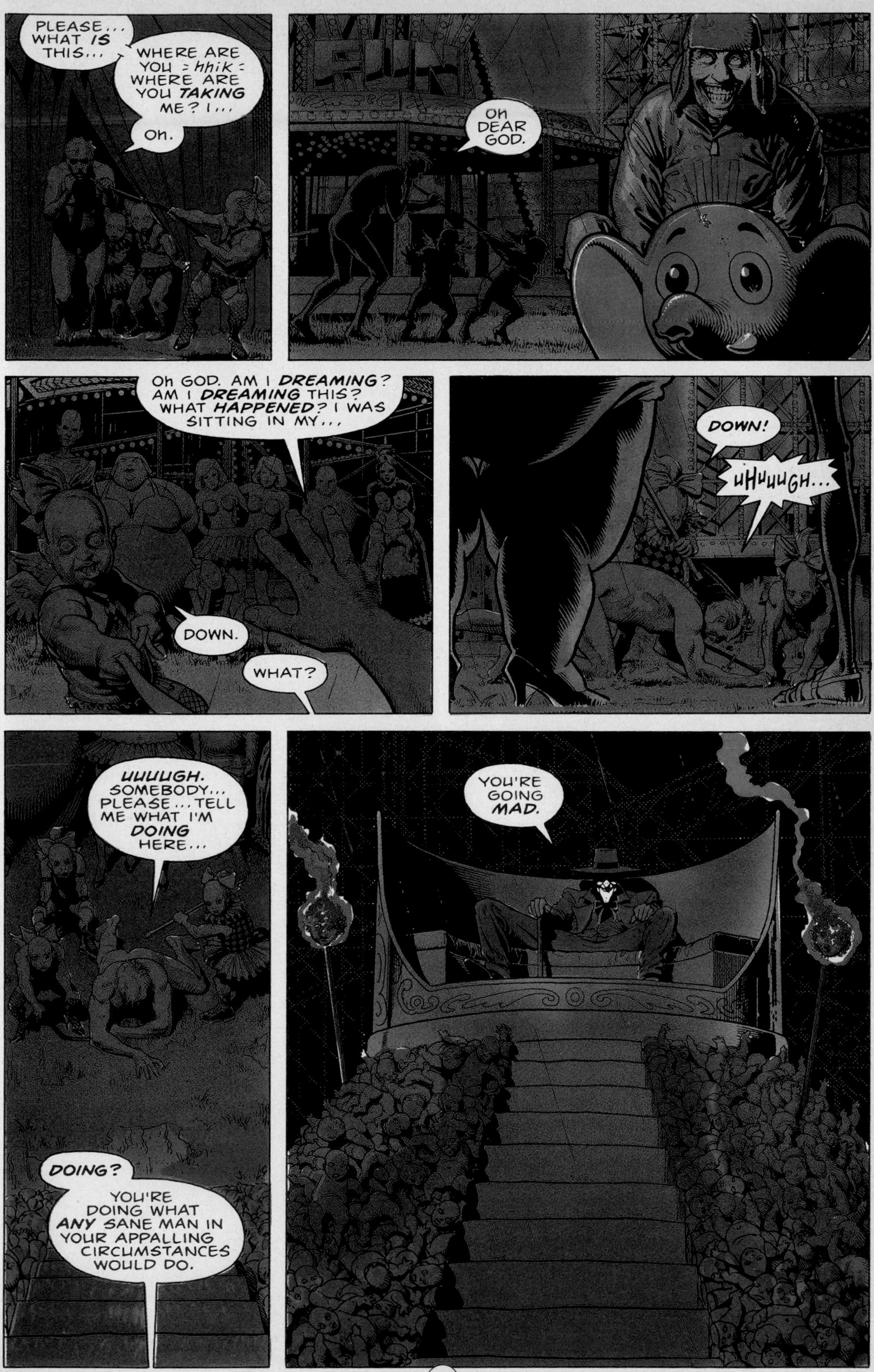

PLEASE... WHAT IS THIS...
WHERE ARE YOU =hhik= WHERE ARE YOU TAKING ME? I...
Oh.
Oh DEAR GOD.
Oh GOD. AM I DREAMING? AM I DREAMING THIS? WHAT HAPPENED? I WAS SITTING IN MY...
DOWN.
WHAT?
DOWN!
uHuuuGH...
UUUUGH. SOMEBODY... PLEASE... TELL ME WHAT I'M DOING HERE...
DOING?
YOU'RE DOING WHAT ANY SANE MAN IN YOUR APPALLING CIRCUMSTANCES WOULD DO.
YOU'RE GOING MAD.

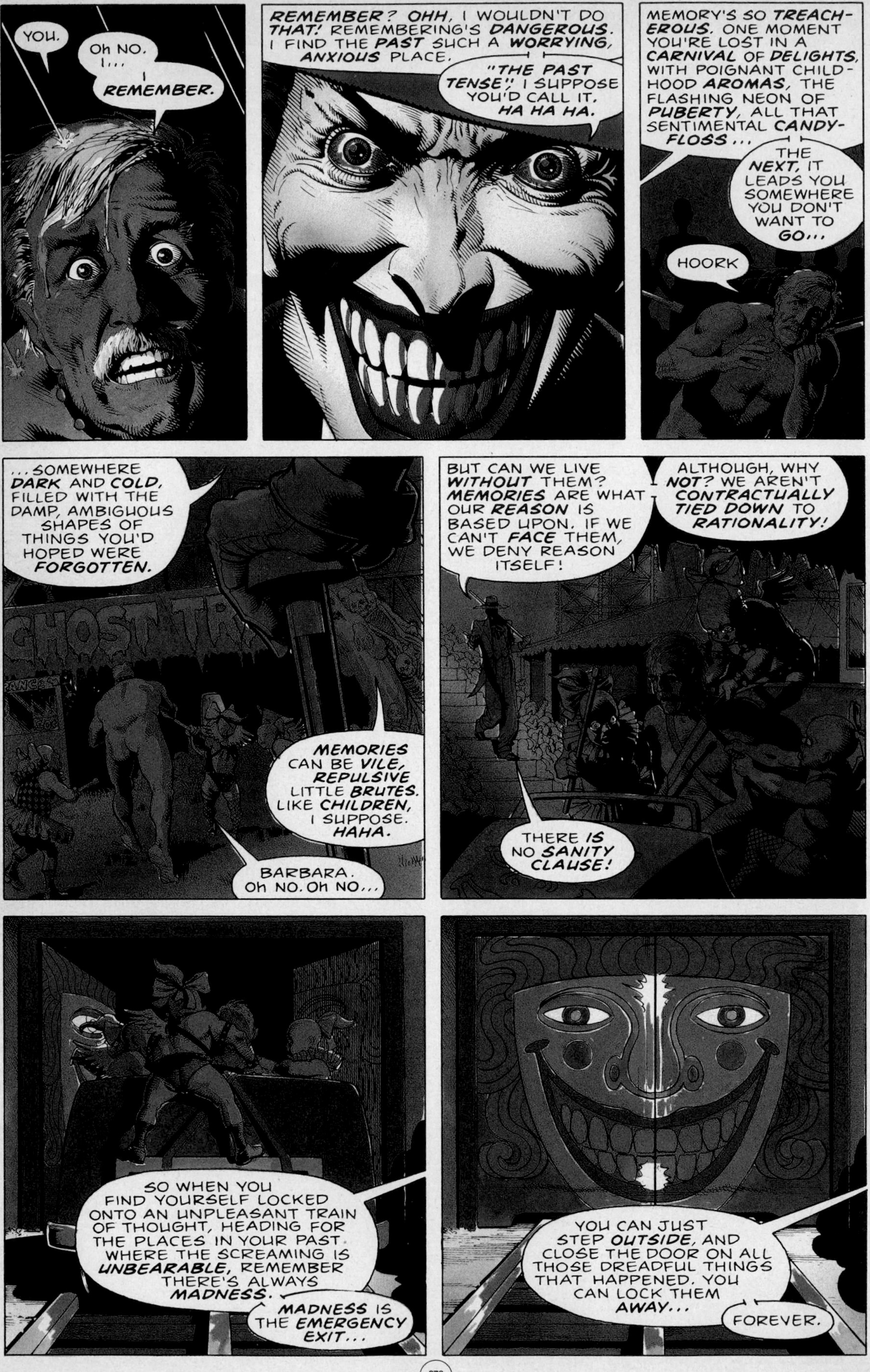
YOU.
Oh NO. I... I REMEMBER.
REMEMBER? OHH, I WOULDN'T DO THAT! REMEMBERING'S DANGEROUS. I FIND THE PAST SUCH A WORRYING, ANXIOUS PLACE.
"THE PAST TENSE," I SUPPOSE YOU'D CALL IT. HA HA HA.
MEMORY'S SO TREACHEROUS. ONE MOMENT YOU'RE LOST IN A CARNIVAL OF DELIGHTS, WITH POIGNANT CHILDHOOD AROMAS, THE FLASHING NEON OF PUBERTY, ALL THAT SENTIMENTAL CANDY-FLOSS...
THE NEXT, IT LEADS YOU SOMEWHERE YOU DON'T WANT TO GO...
HOORK
...SOMEWHERE DARK AND COLD, FILLED WITH THE DAMP, AMBIGUOUS SHAPES OF THINGS YOU'D HOPED WERE FORGOTTEN.
GHOST TR
MEMORIES CAN BE VILE, REPULSIVE LITTLE BRUTES. LIKE CHILDREN, I SUPPOSE. HAHA.
BARBARA. Oh NO. Oh NO...
BUT CAN WE LIVE WITHOUT THEM? MEMORIES ARE WHAT OUR REASON IS BASED UPON. IF WE CAN'T FACE THEM, WE DENY REASON ITSELF!
ALTHOUGH, WHY NOT? WE AREN'T CONTRACTUALLY TIED DOWN TO RATIONALITY!
THERE IS NO SANITY CLAUSE!
SO WHEN YOU FIND YOURSELF LOCKED ONTO AN UNPLEASANT TRAIN OF THOUGHT, HEADING FOR THE PLACES IN YOUR PAST WHERE THE SCREAMING IS UNBEARABLE, REMEMBER THERE'S ALWAYS MADNESS.
MADNESS IS THE EMERGENCY EXIT...
YOU CAN JUST STEP OUTSIDE, AND CLOSE THE DOOR ON ALL THOSE DREADFUL THINGS THAT HAPPENED. YOU CAN LOCK THEM AWAY...
FOREVER.

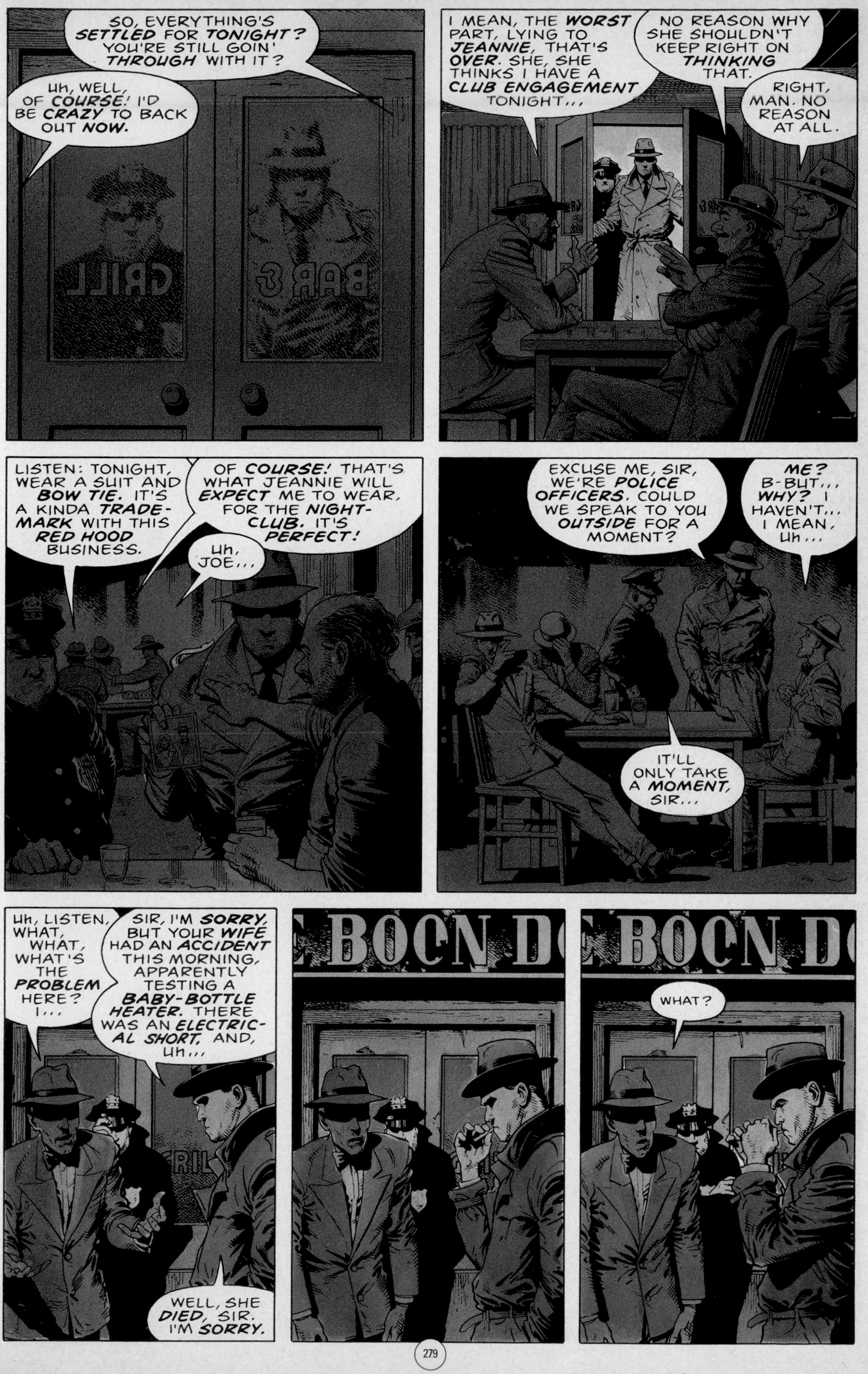
SO, EVERYTHING'S SETTLED FOR TONIGHT? YOU'RE STILL GOIN' THROUGH WITH IT?
UH, WELL, OF COURSE! I'D BE CRAZY TO BACK OUT NOW.
GRILL
BAR 3
I MEAN, THE WORST PART, LYING TO JEANNIE, THAT'S OVER. SHE, SHE THINKS I HAVE A CLUB ENGAGEMENT TONIGHT...
NO REASON WHY SHE SHOULDN'T KEEP RIGHT ON THINKING THAT.
RIGHT, MAN. NO REASON AT ALL.
LISTEN: TONIGHT, WEAR A SUIT AND BOW TIE. IT'S A KINDA TRADE-MARK WITH THIS RED HOOD BUSINESS.
OF COURSE! THAT'S WHAT JEANNIE WILL EXPECT ME TO WEAR, FOR THE NIGHT-CLUB. IT'S PERFECT!
UH, JOE...
EXCUSE ME, SIR, WE'RE POLICE OFFICERS. COULD WE SPEAK TO YOU OUTSIDE FOR A MOMENT?
ME? B-BUT... WHY? I HAVEN'T... I MEAN, UH...
IT'LL ONLY TAKE A MOMENT, SIR...
UH, LISTEN, WHAT, WHAT, WHAT'S THE PROBLEM HERE? I...
SIR, I'M SORRY, BUT YOUR WIFE HAD AN ACCIDENT THIS MORNING, APPARENTLY TESTING A BABY-BOTTLE HEATER. THERE WAS AN ELECTRICAL SHORT, AND, UH...
WELL, SHE DIED, SIR. I'M SORRY.
BOON DO
BOON DO
WHAT?

LISTEN, I *HATE* TO *BREAK* IT TO YOU LIKE THIS. IT WAS A *MILLION* TO ONE ACCIDENT! THEY HAVE *FULL DETAILS* WAITING FOR YOU AT THE *HOSPITAL*.

THERE'S NO *HURRY*.

IF I WAS YOU, I'D HAVE ANOTHER *DRINK*.

MY *WIFE*. SHE'S *DEAD*. MY *WIFE...*,

GEE, THAT'S *TERRIBLE*. WE'RE REALLY *SORRY*.

YEAH. HEY, LISTEN, MAN, YOU PROBABLY WANNA BE LEFT *ALONE* RIGHT NOW, HUH? WE'LL SEE YOU HERE *TONIGHT*, OKAY?

TONIGHT? BUT..., BUT I CAN'T DO ANYTHING *TONIGHT*. TH—THERE'S NO *REASON* ANYMORE. JEANNIE..., JEANNIE..., JEANNIE'S *DEAD*. YOU DON'T *UNDERSTAND...*,

NO, NO, NO. NO, I'M *SORRY* ABOUT YOUR *WIFE*, BUT IT'S *YOU* THAT DON'T *UNDERSTAND*.

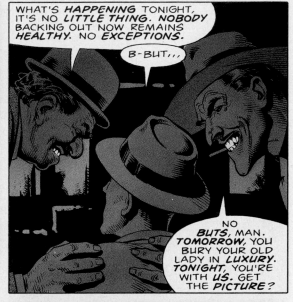

WHAT'S *HAPPENING* TONIGHT, IT'S NO *LITTLE THING*. NOBODY BACKING OUT NOW REMAINS *HEALTHY*. NO *EXCEPTIONS*.

B—BUT...,

NO *BUTS*, MAN. *TOMORROW*, YOU BURY YOUR OLD LADY IN *LUXURY*. *TONIGHT*, YOU'RE WITH *US*. GET THE *PICTURE?*

YES. YES, I GET THE PICTURE.

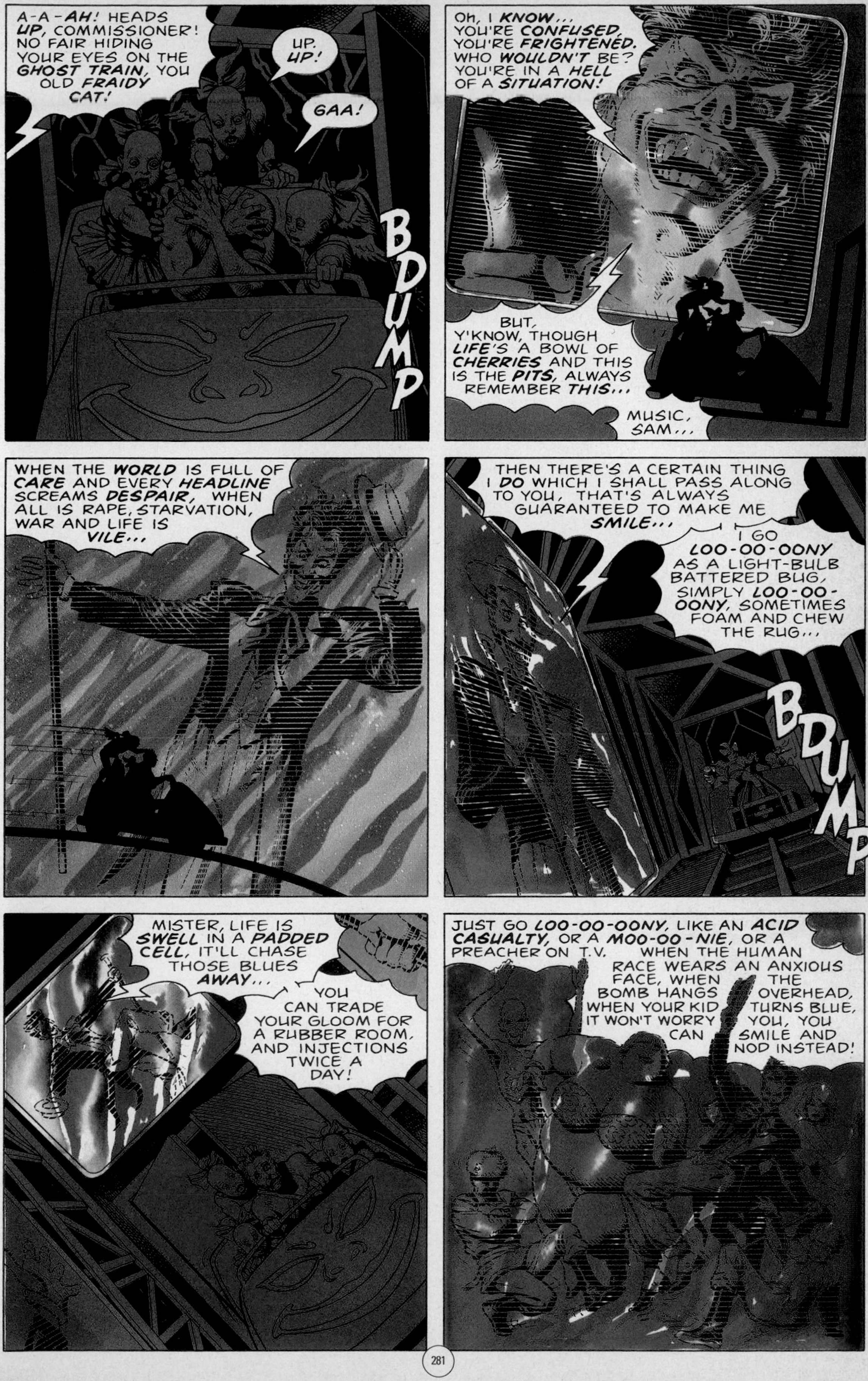

A-A-AH! HEADS UP, COMMISSIONER! NO FAIR HIDING YOUR EYES ON THE GHOST TRAIN, YOU OLD FRAIDY CAT!
UP. UP!
GAA!
BDUMP
Oh, I KNOW... YOU'RE CONFUSED. YOU'RE FRIGHTENED. WHO WOULDN'T BE? YOU'RE IN A HELL OF A SITUATION!
BUT, Y'KNOW, THOUGH LIFE'S A BOWL OF CHERRIES AND THIS IS THE PITS, ALWAYS REMEMBER THIS...
MUSIC, SAM...
WHEN THE WORLD IS FULL OF CARE AND EVERY HEADLINE SCREAMS DESPAIR, WHEN ALL IS RAPE, STARVATION, WAR AND LIFE IS VILE...
THEN THERE'S A CERTAIN THING I DO WHICH I SHALL PASS ALONG TO YOU, THAT'S ALWAYS GUARANTEED TO MAKE ME SMILE...
I GO LOO-OO-OONY AS A LIGHT-BULB BATTERED BUG, SIMPLY LOO-OO-OONY, SOMETIMES FOAM AND CHEW THE RUG...
BDUMP
MISTER, LIFE IS SWELL IN A PADDED CELL, IT'LL CHASE THOSE BLUES AWAY...
YOU CAN TRADE YOUR GLOOM FOR A RUBBER ROOM, AND INJECTIONS TWICE A DAY!
JUST GO LOO-OO-OONY, LIKE AN ACID CASUALTY, OR A MOO-OO-NIE, OR A PREACHER ON T.V. WHEN THE HUMAN RACE WEARS AN ANXIOUS FACE, WHEN THE BOMB HANGS OVERHEAD, WHEN YOUR KID TURNS BLUE, IT WON'T WORRY YOU, YOU CAN SMILE AND NOD INSTEAD!

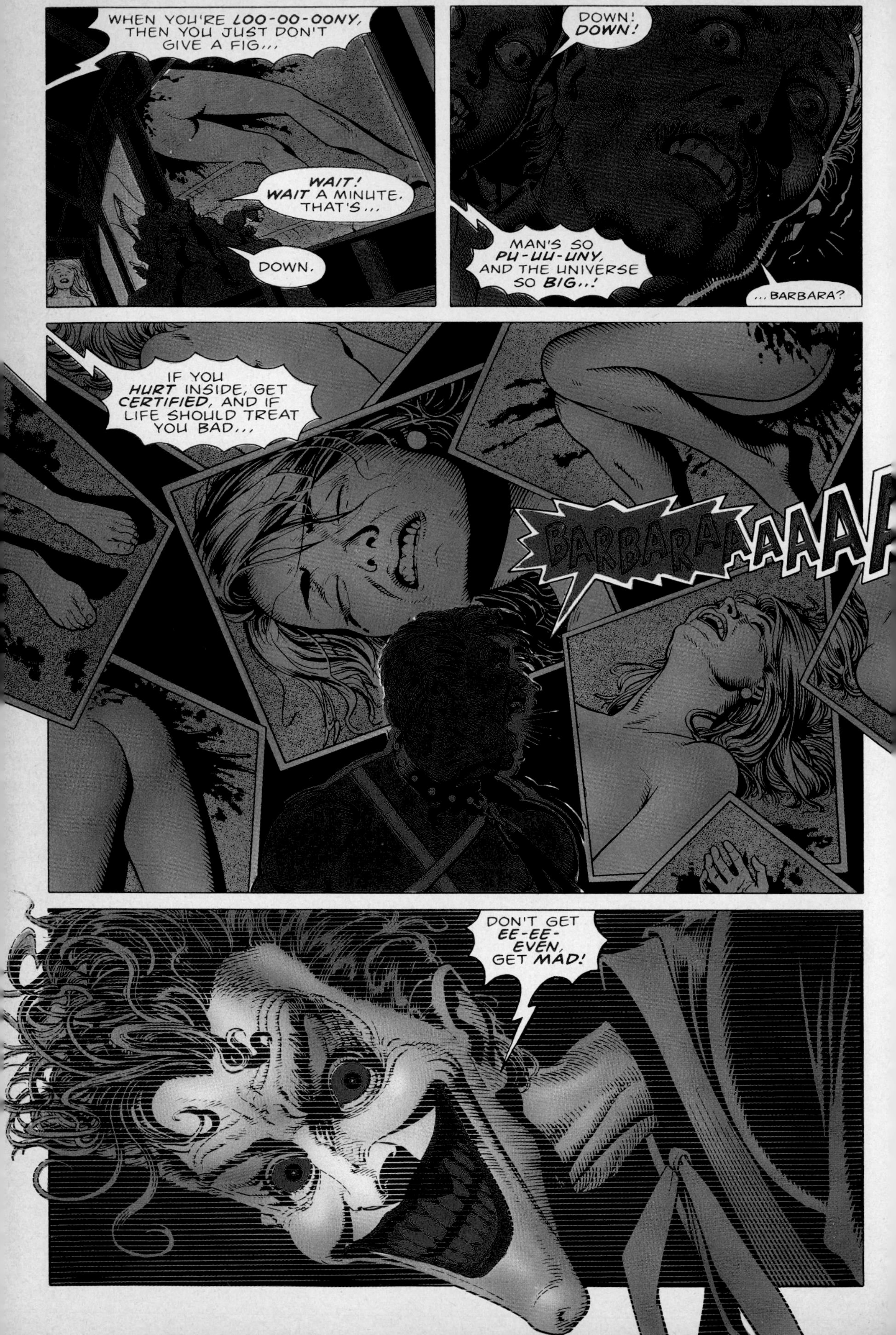

WHEN YOU'RE LOO-OO-OONY, THEN YOU JUST DON'T GIVE A FIG...
WAIT! WAIT A MINUTE. THAT'S...
DOWN.
DOWN! DOWN!
MAN'S SO PU-UU-UNY, AND THE UNIVERSE SO BIG...!
...BARBARA?
IF YOU HURT INSIDE, GET CERTIFIED, AND IF LIFE SHOULD TREAT YOU BAD...
BARBARAAAAAA
DON'T GET EE-EE-EVEN, GET MAD!

BDUMP

DANGEROUS
DO NOT APPROACH

BDUMP

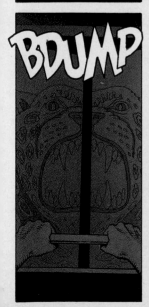

BDUMP

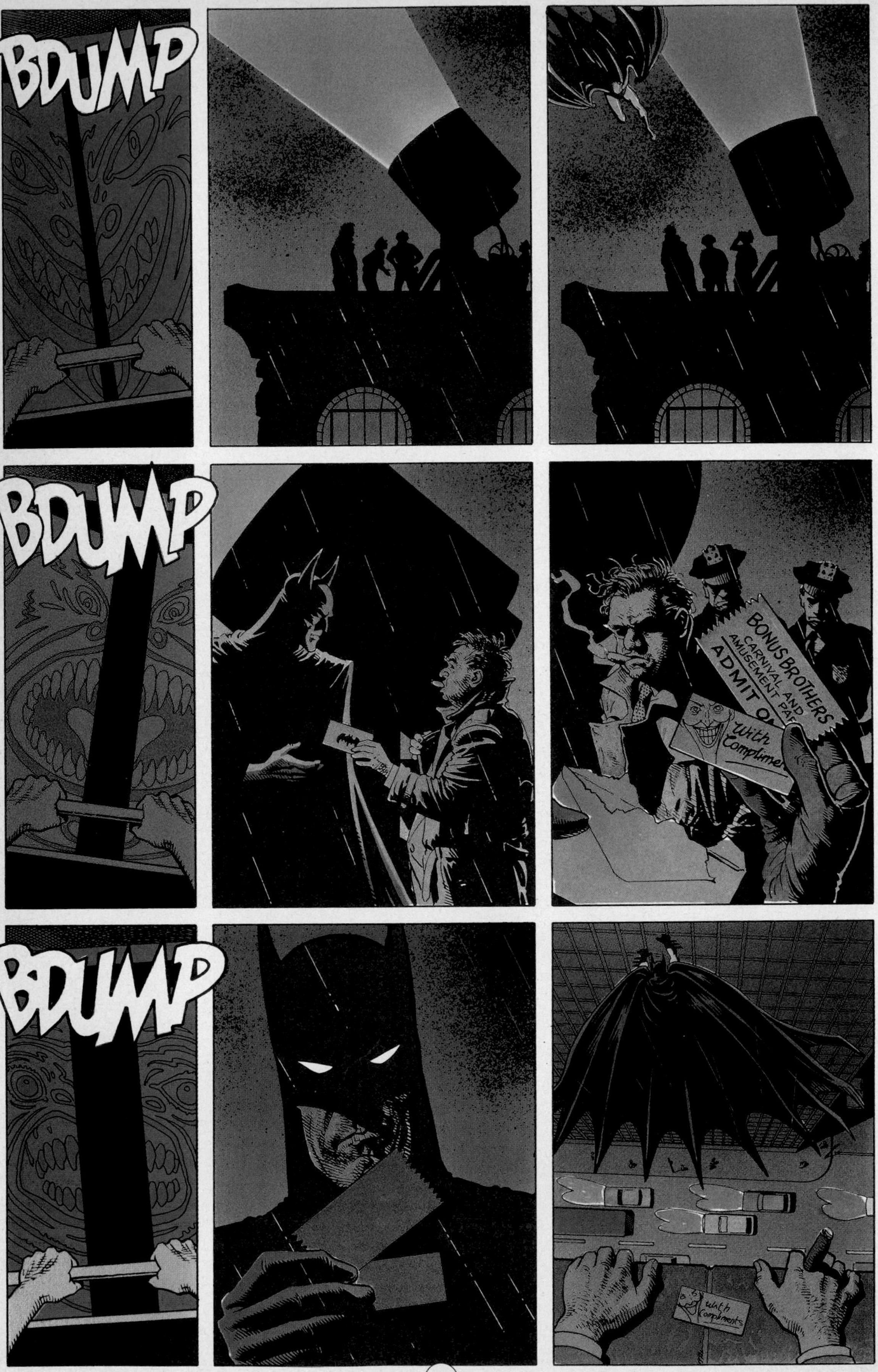
BDUMP
BDUMP
BONUS BROTHERS
CARNIVAL AND
With
BDUMP
With
Compliments

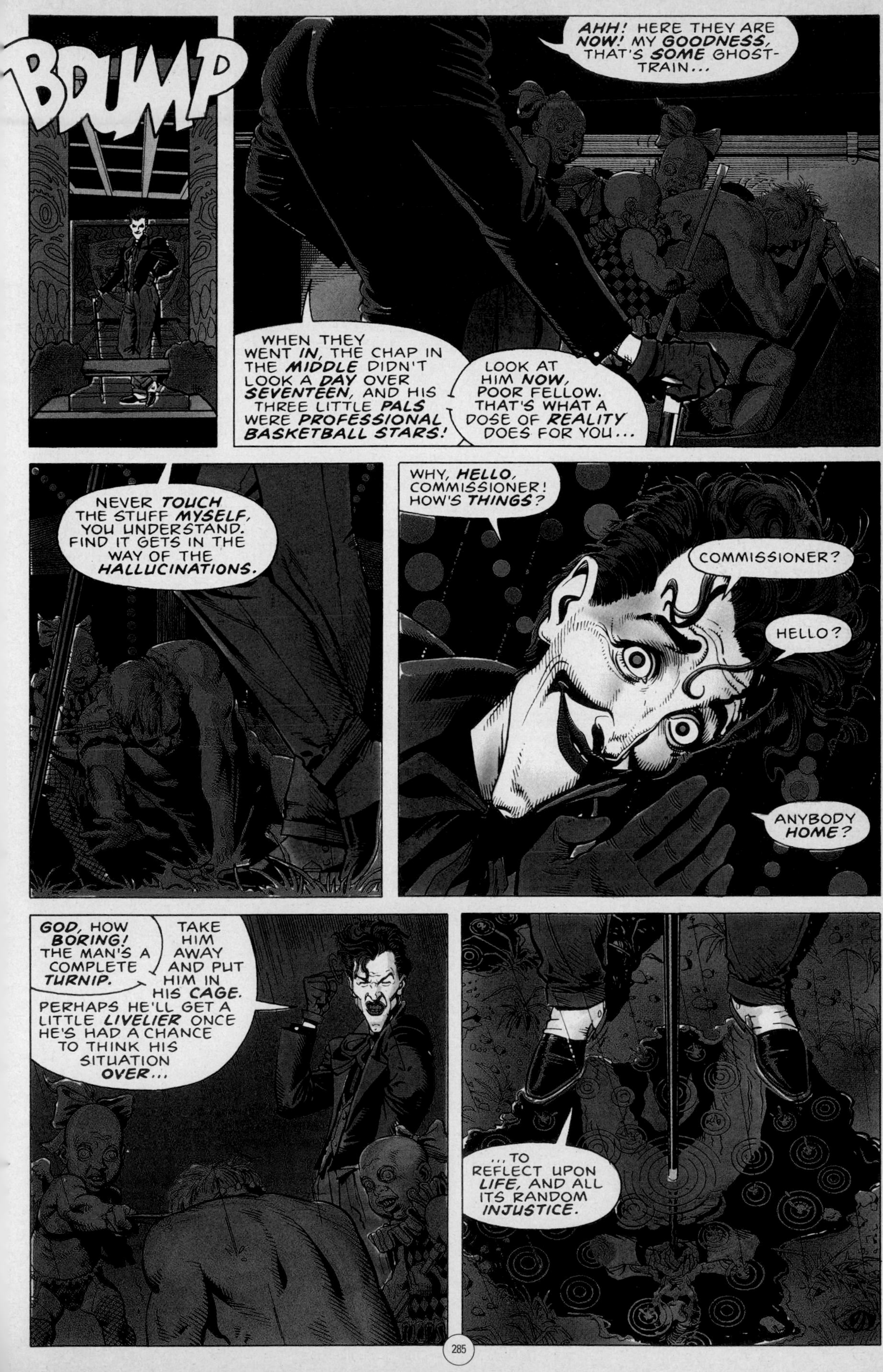
BDUMP
AHH! HERE THEY ARE NOW! MY GOODNESS, THAT'S SOME GHOST-TRAIN...
WHEN THEY WENT IN, THE CHAP IN THE MIDDLE DIDN'T LOOK A DAY OVER SEVENTEEN, AND HIS THREE LITTLE PALS WERE PROFESSIONAL BASKETBALL STARS!
LOOK AT HIM NOW, POOR FELLOW. THAT'S WHAT A DOSE OF REALITY DOES FOR YOU...
NEVER TOUCH THE STUFF MYSELF, YOU UNDERSTAND. FIND IT GETS IN THE WAY OF THE HALLUCINATIONS.
WHY, HELLO, COMMISSIONER! HOW'S THINGS?
COMMISSIONER?
HELLO?
ANYBODY HOME?
GOD, HOW BORING! THE MAN'S A COMPLETE TURNIP.
TAKE HIM AWAY AND PUT HIM IN HIS CAGE.
PERHAPS HE'LL GET A LITTLE LIVELIER ONCE HE'S HAD A CHANCE TO THINK HIS SITUATION OVER...
...TO REFLECT UPON LIFE, AND ALL ITS RANDOM INJUSTICE.

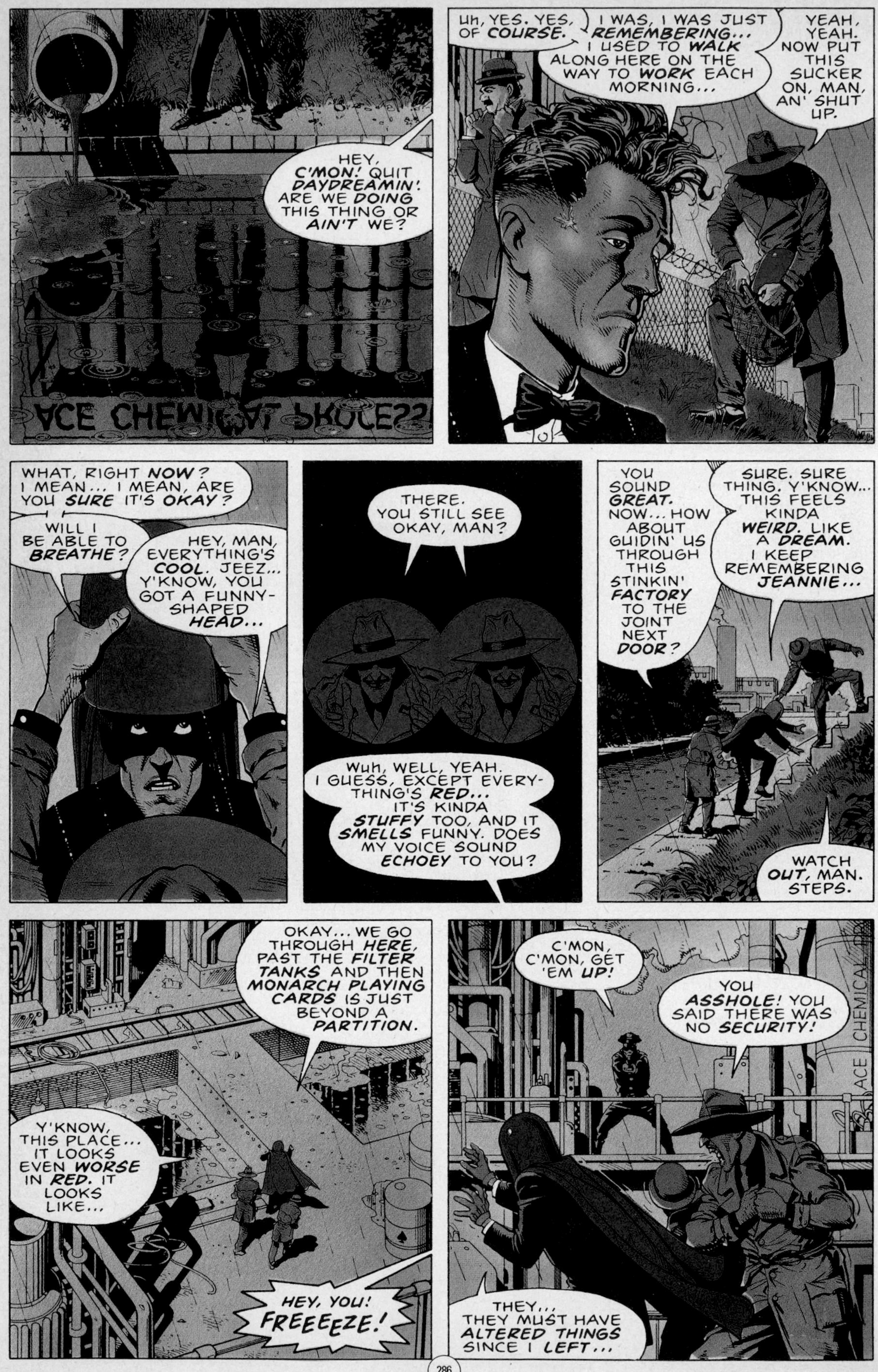

HEY, C'MON! QUIT DAYDREAMIN'. ARE WE DOING THIS THING OR AIN'T WE?
UH, YES. YES, OF COURSE.
I WAS, I WAS JUST REMEMBERING... I USED TO WALK ALONG HERE ON THE WAY TO WORK EACH MORNING...
YEAH, YEAH. NOW PUT THIS SUCKER ON, MAN, AN' SHUT UP.
WHAT, RIGHT NOW? I MEAN... I MEAN, ARE YOU SURE IT'S OKAY?
WILL I BE ABLE TO BREATHE?
HEY, MAN, EVERYTHING'S COOL. JEEZ... Y'KNOW, YOU GOT A FUNNY-SHAPED HEAD...
THERE. YOU STILL SEE OKAY, MAN?
WUH, WELL, YEAH. I GUESS, EXCEPT EVERYTHING'S RED... IT'S KINDA STUFFY TOO, AND IT SMELLS FUNNY. DOES MY VOICE SOUND ECHOEY TO YOU?
YOU SOUND GREAT. NOW... HOW ABOUT GUIDIN' US THROUGH THIS STINKIN' FACTORY TO THE JOINT NEXT DOOR?
SURE. SURE THING. Y'KNOW... THIS FEELS KINDA WEIRD. LIKE A DREAM. I KEEP REMEMBERING JEANNIE...
WATCH OUT, MAN. STEPS.
OKAY... WE GO THROUGH HERE, PAST THE FILTER TANKS AND THEN MONARCH PLAYING CARDS IS JUST BEYOND A PARTITION.
Y'KNOW, THIS PLACE... IT LOOKS EVEN WORSE IN RED. IT LOOKS LIKE...
HEY, YOU! FREEEEZE!
C'MON, C'MON, GET 'EM UP!
YOU ASSHOLE! YOU SAID THERE WAS NO SECURITY!
ACE CHEMICAL
THEY... THEY MUST HAVE ALTERED THINGS SINCE I LEFT...

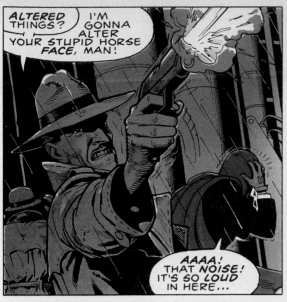

ALTERED THINGS? I'M GONNA ALTER YOUR STUPID HORSE FACE, MAN!

AAAA! THAT NOISE! IT'S SO LOUD IN HERE...

FOR GOD'S SAKE, RUN! THIS IS ALL SCREWED UP!

MURPH, GET SOME MEN OVER TO THE REAR BAYS. WE GOT THE RED HOOD MOB IN HERE.

Oh JESUS! WHICH WAY IS IT? HOW DO WE GET OUT?

I...I DON'T KNOW! THIS MASK...CAN'T SEE WHERE I'M GOING...

I'M GONNA KILL YOU, YOU USELESS SON OF A BITCH! WHEN WE GET OUTTA HERE, I'M GONNA...

AW HELL. AW HELL...

YOU GUYS... YOU DON'T WANT ME. YOU WANT HIM. HE'S THE RING-LEADER. HE'S THE RED HOOD...

WHAT? WHAT IS IT? WHAT IS IT, IT'S ALL OVER ME...

WATCH OUT! HE'S PULLING A GUN!

AAAAAAAAA Oh NO. NO, NO, NO, NO...

THE RING-LEADER'S TAKING OFF ACROSS THE CAT-WALK...

HE'S STILL IN RANGE...

NO. NO MORE SHOOTING.

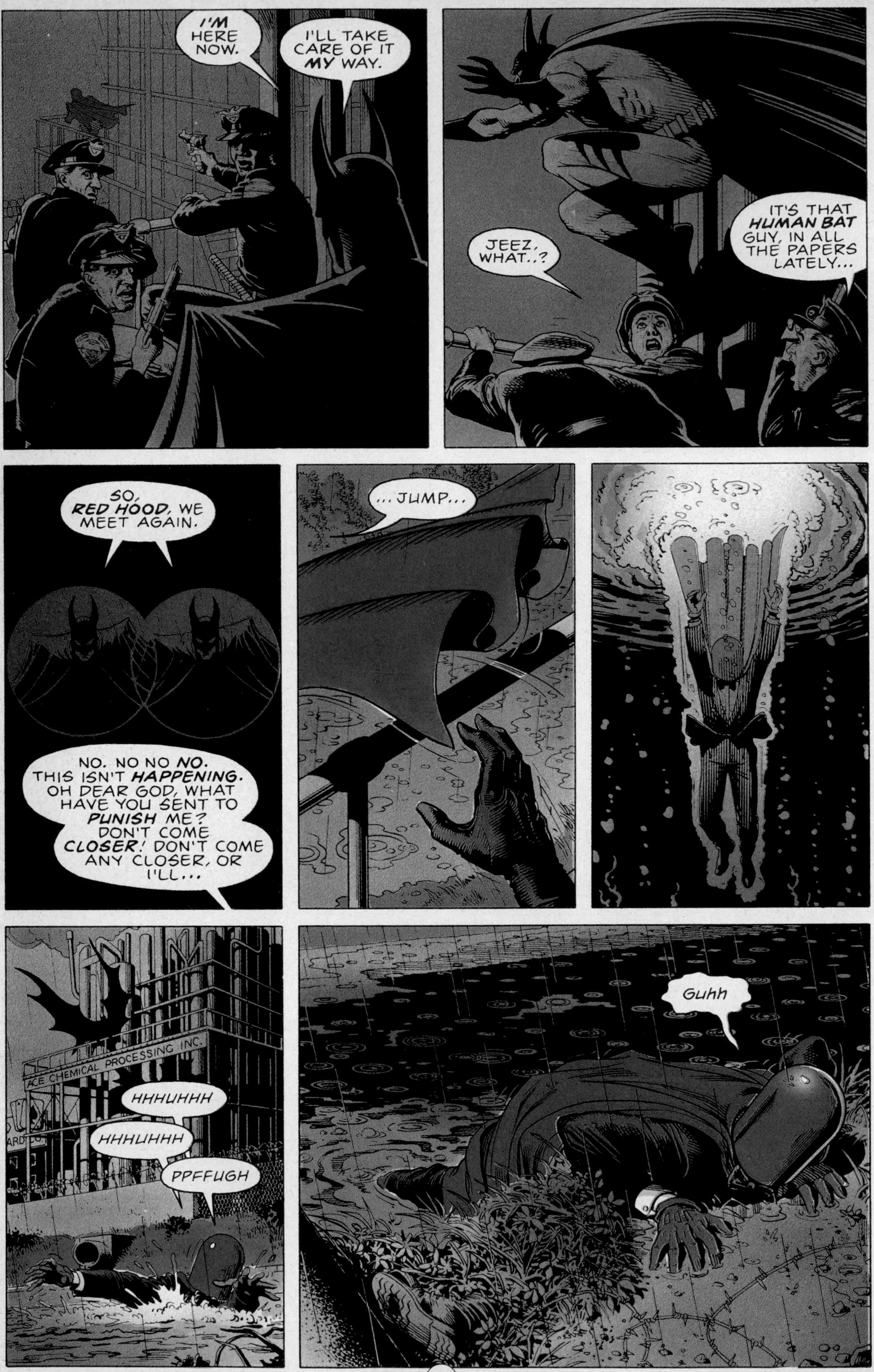
I'M HERE NOW.
I'LL TAKE CARE OF IT MY WAY.
JEEZ, WHAT..?
IT'S THAT HUMAN BAT GUY, IN ALL THE PAPERS LATELY...
SO, RED HOOD, WE MEET AGAIN.
NO. NO NO NO. THIS ISN'T HAPPENING. OH DEAR GOD, WHAT HAVE YOU SENT TO PUNISH ME? DON'T COME CLOSER! DON'T COME ANY CLOSER, OR I'LL...
...JUMP...
ACE CHEMICAL PROCESSING INC.
HHHUHHH
HHHUHHH
PPFFUGH
Guhh

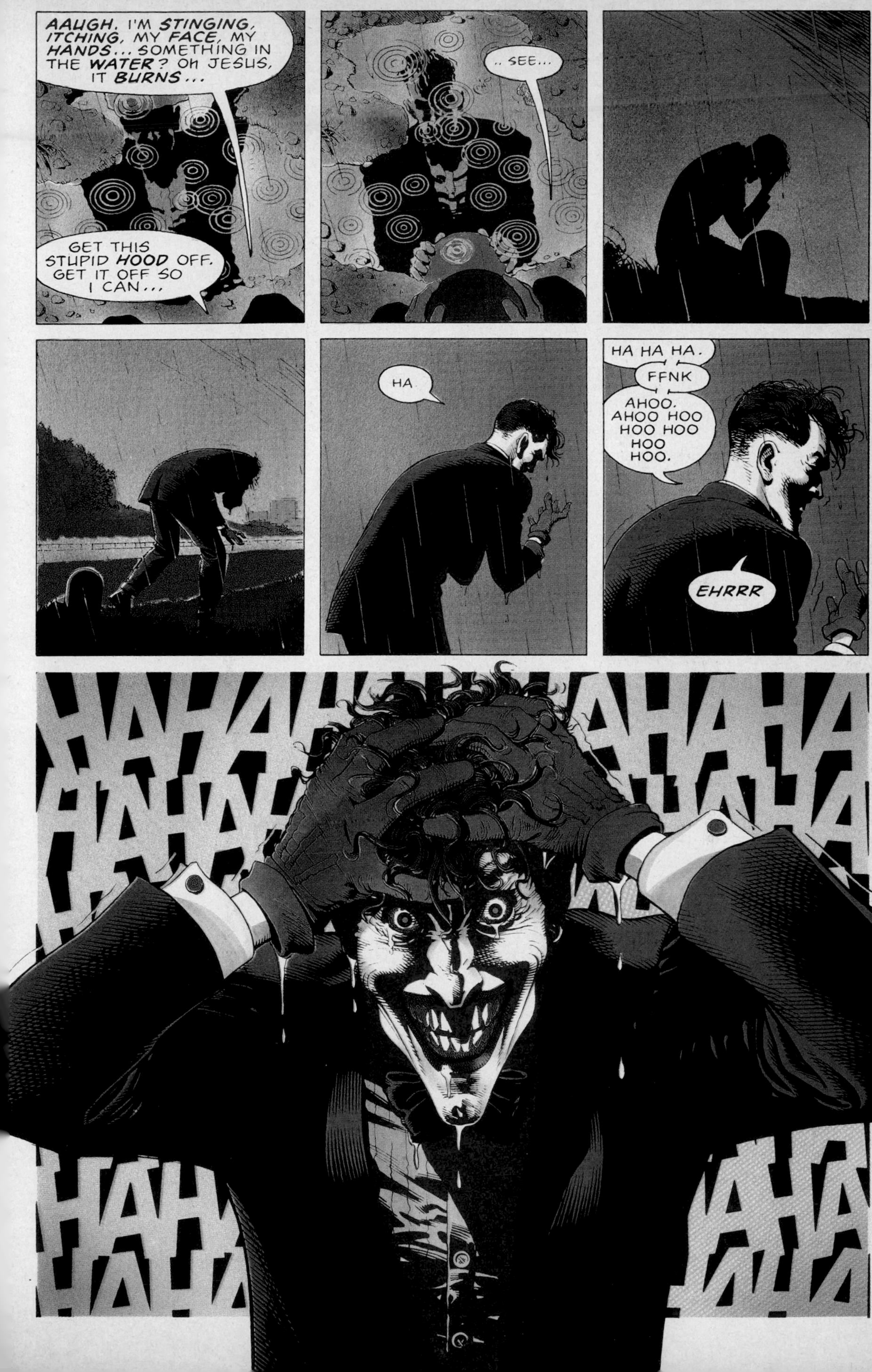
AAUGH. I'M STINGING, ITCHING, MY FACE, MY HANDS... SOMETHING IN THE WATER? Oh JESUS, IT BURNS...
GET THIS STUPID HOOD OFF. GET IT OFF SO I CAN...
.. SEE...
HA.
HA HA HA.
FFNK
AHOO. AHOO HOO HOO HOO HOO HOO.
EHRRR

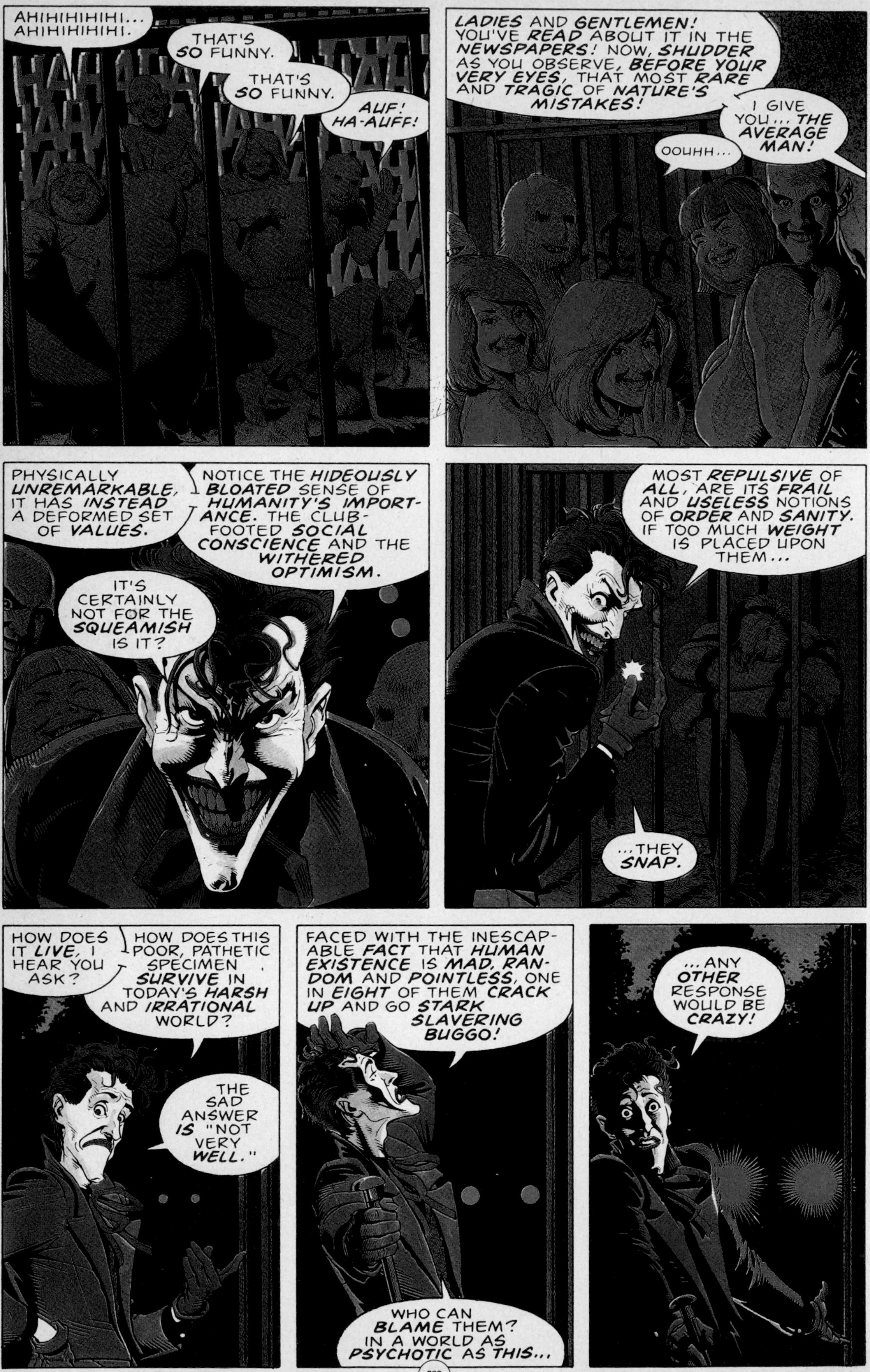

AHIHIHIHIHI... AHIHIHIHIHI.
THAT'S SO FUNNY.
THAT'S SO FUNNY.
AUF! HA-AUFF!
LADIES AND GENTLEMEN! YOU'VE READ ABOUT IT IN THE NEWSPAPERS! NOW, SHUDDER AS YOU OBSERVE, BEFORE YOUR VERY EYES, THAT MOST RARE AND TRAGIC OF NATURE'S MISTAKES!
I GIVE YOU... THE AVERAGE MAN!
OOUHH...
PHYSICALLY UNREMARKABLE, IT HAS INSTEAD A DEFORMED SET OF VALUES.
NOTICE THE HIDEOUSLY BLOATED SENSE OF HUMANITY'S IMPORTANCE. THE CLUB-FOOTED SOCIAL CONSCIENCE AND THE WITHERED OPTIMISM.
IT'S CERTAINLY NOT FOR THE SQUEAMISH IS IT?
MOST REPULSIVE OF ALL, ARE ITS FRAIL AND USELESS NOTIONS OF ORDER AND SANITY. IF TOO MUCH WEIGHT IS PLACED UPON THEM...
...THEY SNAP.
HOW DOES IT LIVE, I HEAR YOU ASK?
HOW DOES THIS POOR, PATHETIC SPECIMEN SURVIVE IN TODAY'S HARSH AND IRRATIONAL WORLD?
THE SAD ANSWER IS "NOT VERY WELL."
FACED WITH THE INESCAPABLE FACT THAT HUMAN EXISTENCE IS MAD, RANDOM AND POINTLESS, ONE IN EIGHT OF THEM CRACK UP AND GO STARK SLAVERING BUGGO!
WHO CAN BLAME THEM? IN A WORLD AS PSYCHOTIC AS THIS...
...ANY OTHER RESPONSE WOULD BE CRAZY!

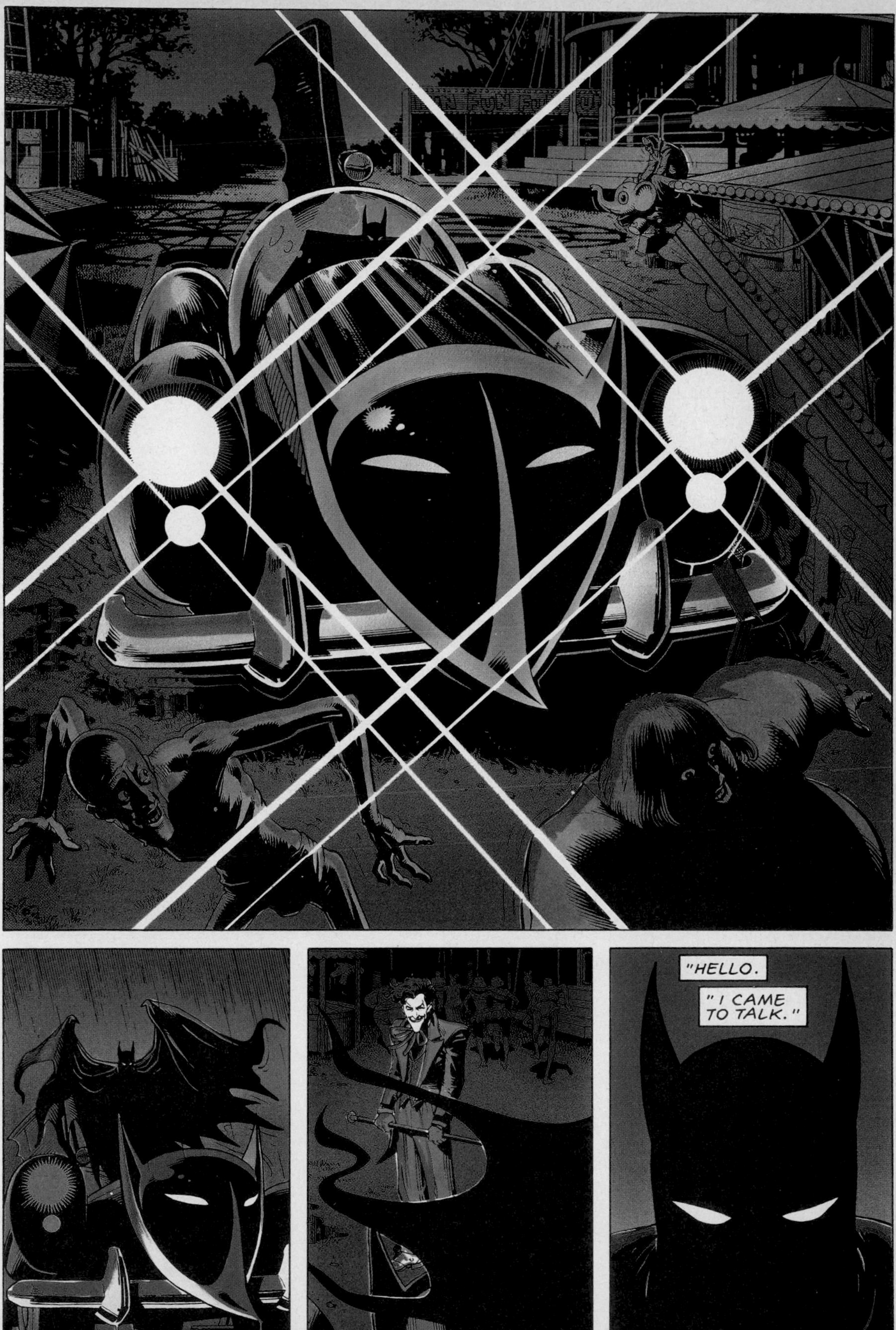
"HELLO.
"I CAME TO TALK."

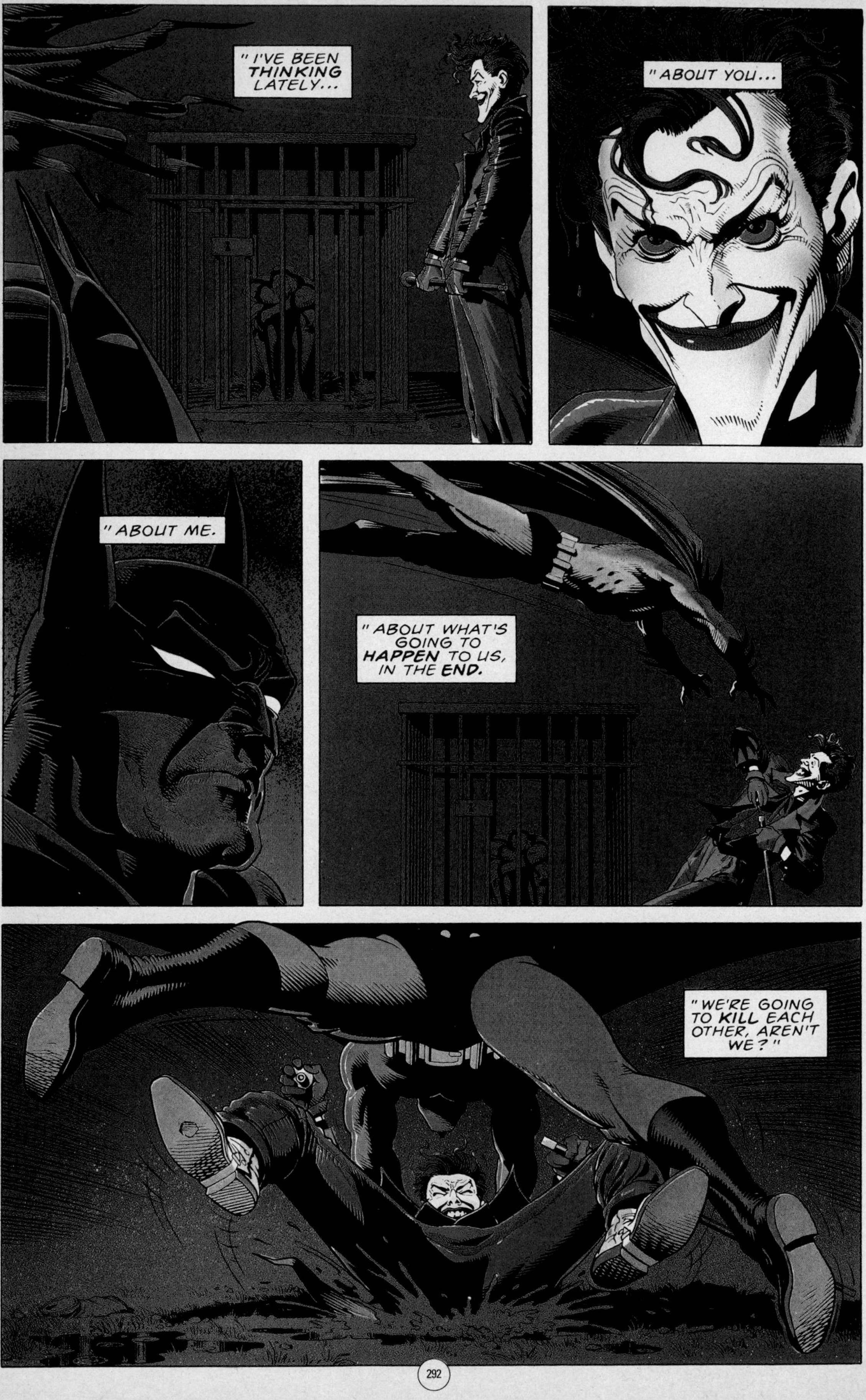
"I'VE BEEN THINKING LATELY...
"ABOUT YOU...
"ABOUT ME.
"ABOUT WHAT'S GOING TO HAPPEN TO US, IN THE END.
"WE'RE GOING TO KILL EACH OTHER, AREN'T WE?"

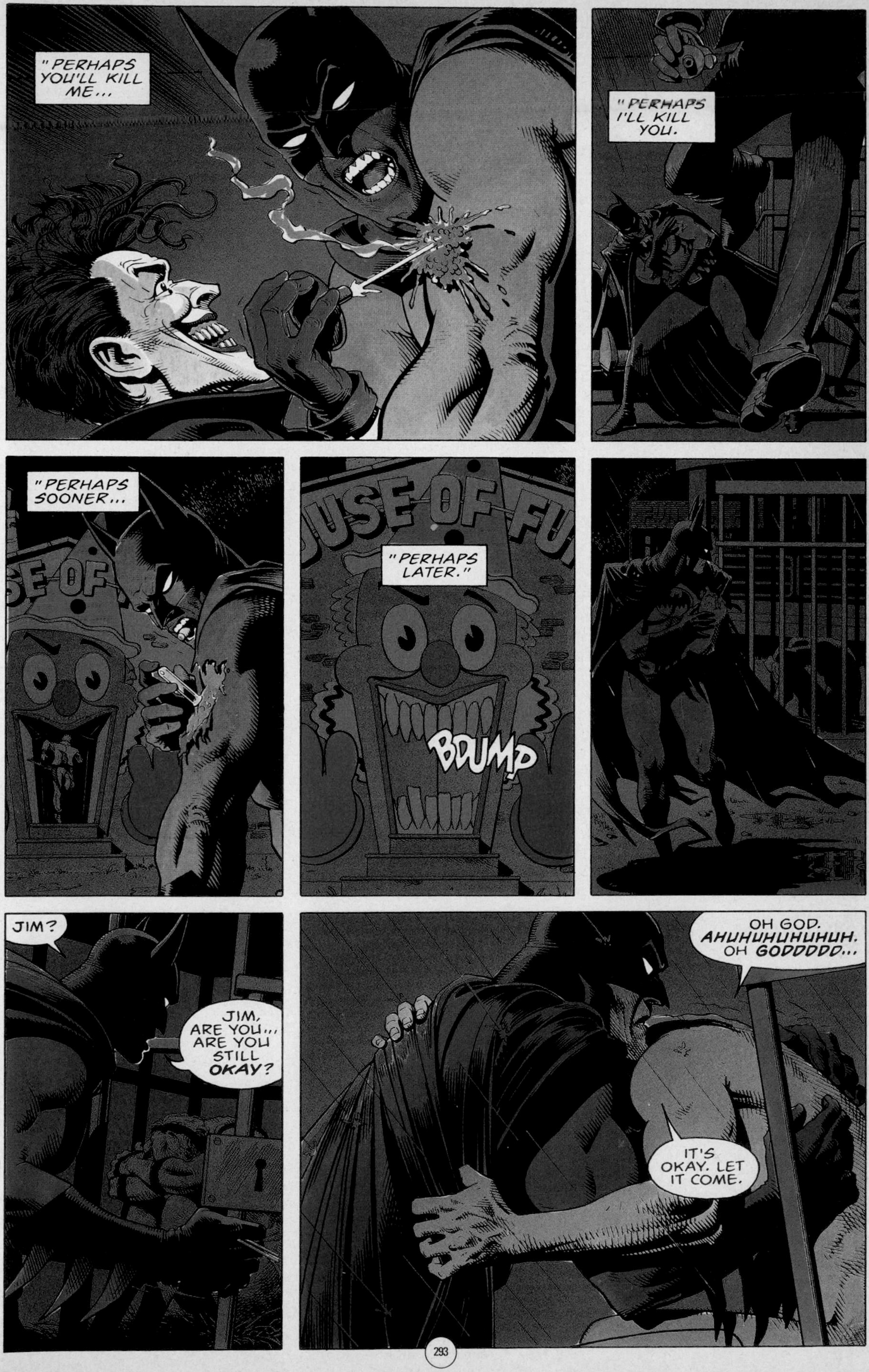
"PERHAPS YOU'LL KILL ME...
"PERHAPS I'LL KILL YOU.
"PERHAPS SOONER...
"PERHAPS LATER."
BDUMP
JIM?
JIM, ARE YOU... ARE YOU STILL OKAY?
OH GOD. AHUHUHUHUHUH. OH GODDDDD...
IT'S OKAY. LET IT COME.

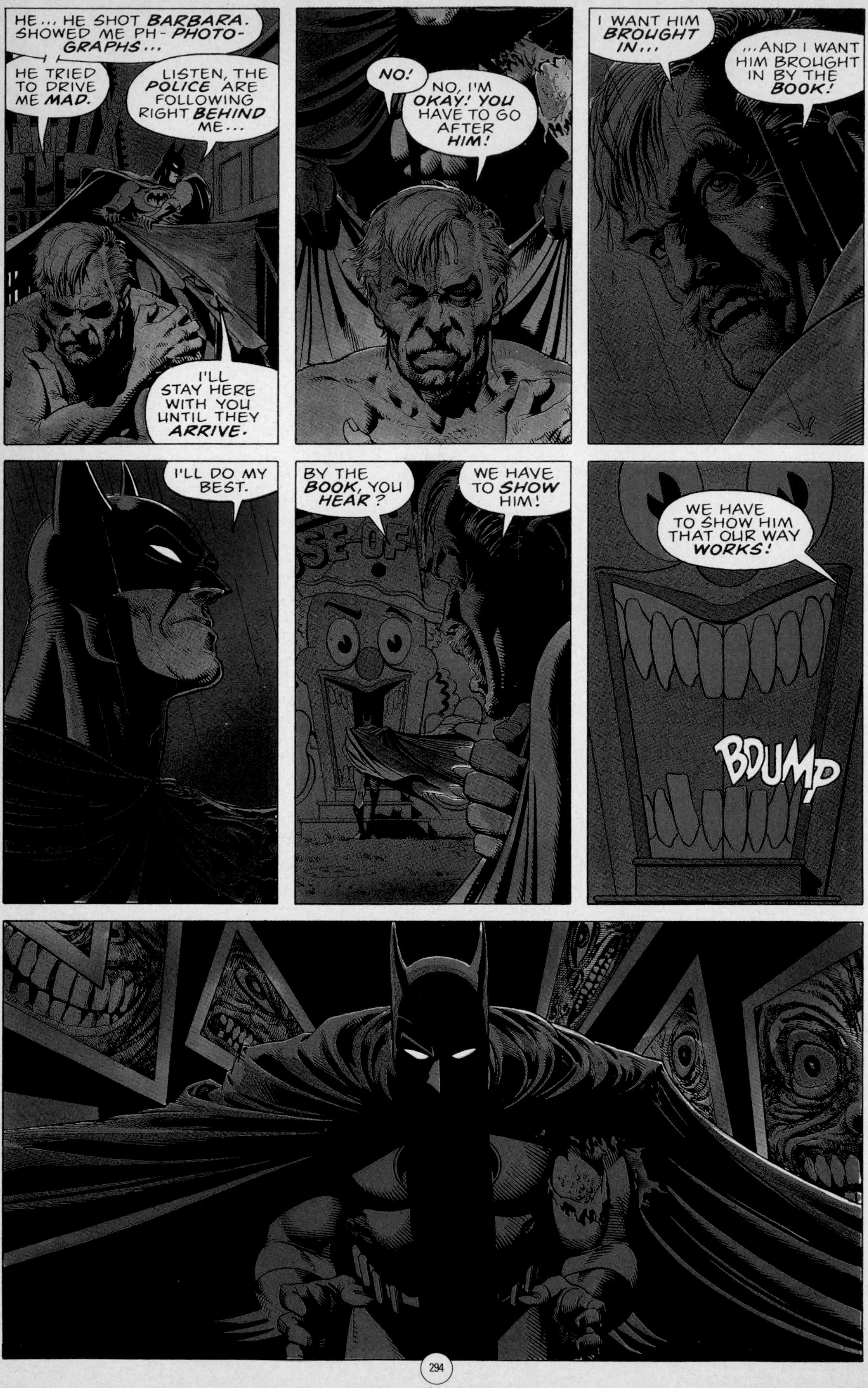

HE... HE SHOT BARBARA. SHOWED ME PH-PHOTOGRAPHS...
HE TRIED TO DRIVE ME MAD.
LISTEN, THE POLICE ARE FOLLOWING RIGHT BEHIND ME...
I'LL STAY HERE WITH YOU UNTIL THEY ARRIVE.
NO!
NO, I'M OKAY! YOU HAVE TO GO AFTER HIM!
I WANT HIM BROUGHT IN...
...AND I WANT HIM BROUGHT IN BY THE BOOK!
I'LL DO MY BEST.
BY THE BOOK, YOU HEAR?
WE HAVE TO SHOW HIM!
WE HAVE TO SHOW HIM THAT OUR WAY WORKS!
BDUMP

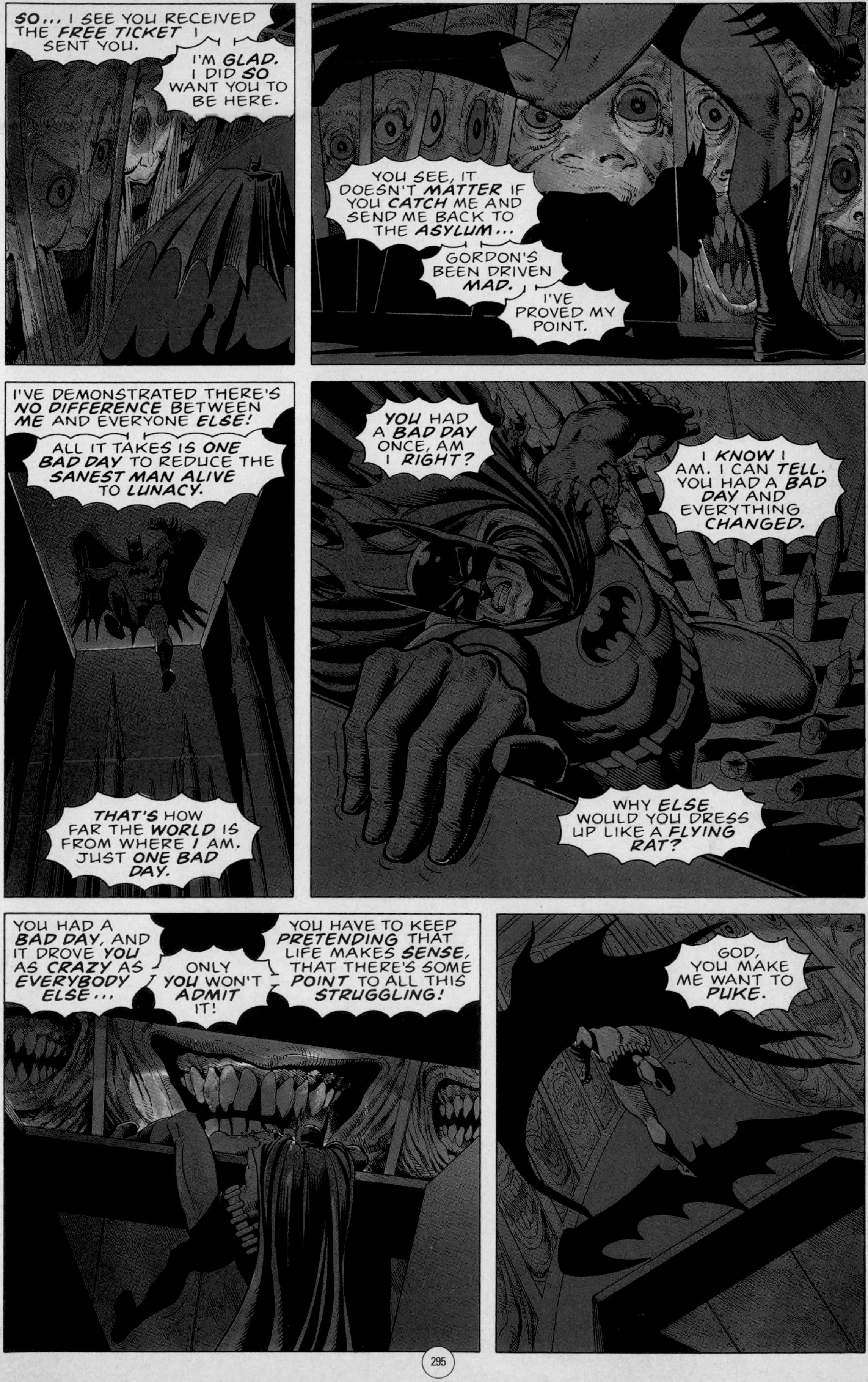
SO... I SEE YOU RECEIVED THE FREE TICKET I SENT YOU.
I'M GLAD. I DID SO WANT YOU TO BE HERE.
YOU SEE, IT DOESN'T MATTER IF YOU CATCH ME AND SEND ME BACK TO THE ASYLUM...
GORDON'S BEEN DRIVEN MAD.
I'VE PROVED MY POINT.
I'VE DEMONSTRATED THERE'S NO DIFFERENCE BETWEEN ME AND EVERYONE ELSE!
ALL IT TAKES IS ONE BAD DAY TO REDUCE THE SANEST MAN ALIVE TO LUNACY.
THAT'S HOW FAR THE WORLD IS FROM WHERE I AM. JUST ONE BAD DAY.
YOU HAD A BAD DAY ONCE, AM I RIGHT?
I KNOW I AM. I CAN TELL. YOU HAD A BAD DAY AND EVERYTHING CHANGED.
WHY ELSE WOULD YOU DRESS UP LIKE A FLYING RAT?
YOU HAD A BAD DAY, AND IT DROVE YOU AS CRAZY AS EVERYBODY ELSE...
ONLY YOU WON'T ADMIT IT!
YOU HAVE TO KEEP PRETENDING THAT LIFE MAKES SENSE, THAT THERE'S SOME POINT TO ALL THIS STRUGGLING!
GOD, YOU MAKE ME WANT TO PUKE.

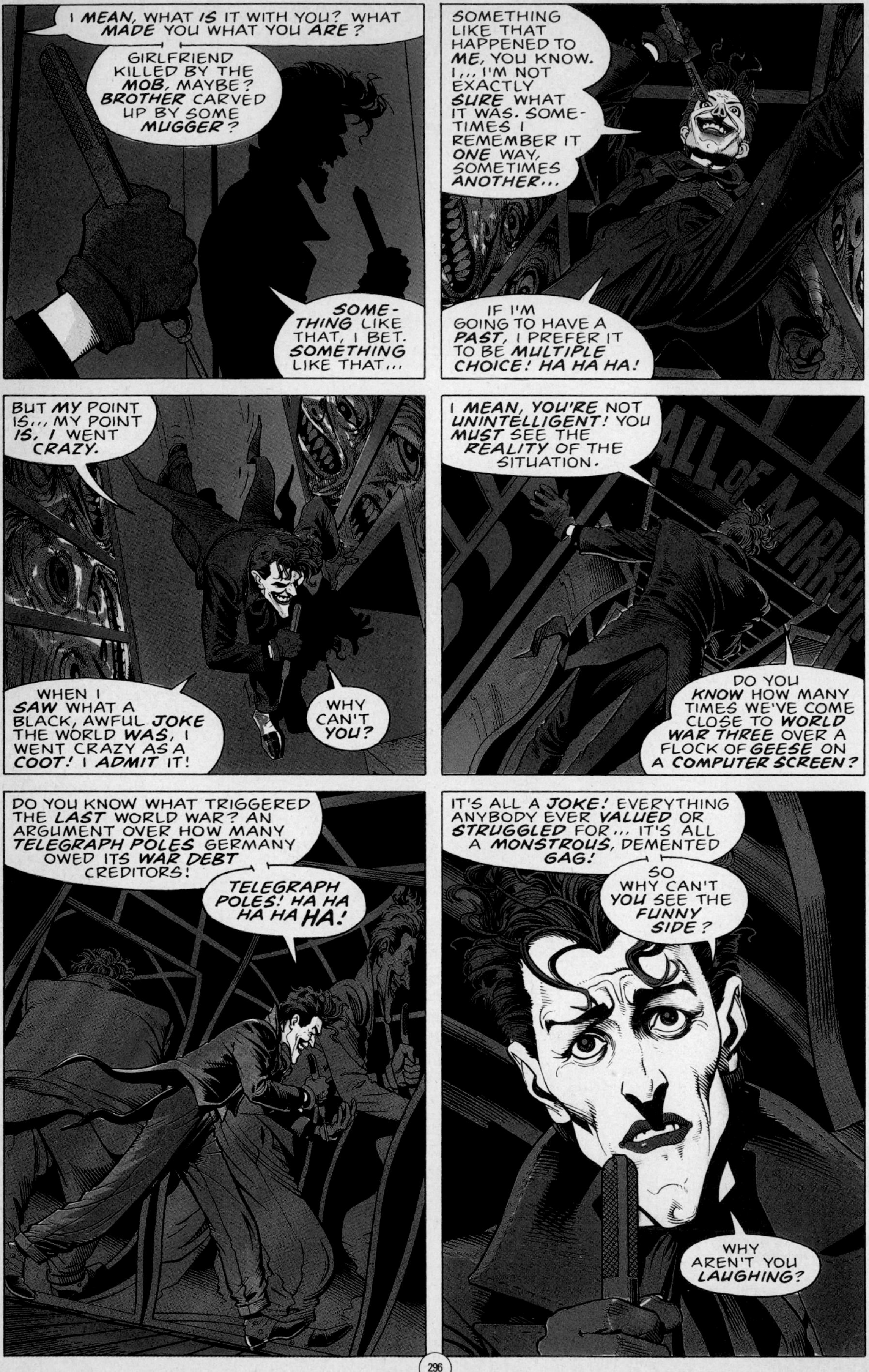

I MEAN, WHAT IS IT WITH YOU? WHAT MADE YOU WHAT YOU ARE?
GIRLFRIEND KILLED BY THE MOB, MAYBE? BROTHER CARVED UP BY SOME MUGGER?
SOME-THING LIKE THAT, I BET. SOMETHING LIKE THAT...
SOMETHING LIKE THAT HAPPENED TO ME, YOU KNOW. I... I'M NOT EXACTLY SURE WHAT IT WAS. SOME-TIMES I REMEMBER IT ONE WAY, SOMETIMES ANOTHER...
IF I'M GOING TO HAVE A PAST, I PREFER IT TO BE MULTIPLE CHOICE! HA HA HA!
BUT MY POINT IS... MY POINT IS, I WENT CRAZY.
WHEN I SAW WHAT A BLACK, AWFUL JOKE THE WORLD WAS, I WENT CRAZY AS A COOT! I ADMIT IT!
WHY CAN'T YOU?
I MEAN, YOU'RE NOT UNINTELLIGENT! YOU MUST SEE THE REALITY OF THE SITUATION.
ALL OF MIRR
DO YOU KNOW HOW MANY TIMES WE'VE COME CLOSE TO WORLD WAR THREE OVER A FLOCK OF GEESE ON A COMPUTER SCREEN?
DO YOU KNOW WHAT TRIGGERED THE LAST WORLD WAR? AN ARGUMENT OVER HOW MANY TELEGRAPH POLES GERMANY OWED ITS WAR DEBT CREDITORS!
TELEGRAPH POLES! HA HA HA HA HA!
IT'S ALL A JOKE! EVERYTHING ANYBODY EVER VALUED OR STRUGGLED FOR... IT'S ALL A MONSTROUS, DEMENTED GAG!
SO WHY CAN'T YOU SEE THE FUNNY SIDE?
WHY AREN'T YOU LAUGHING?

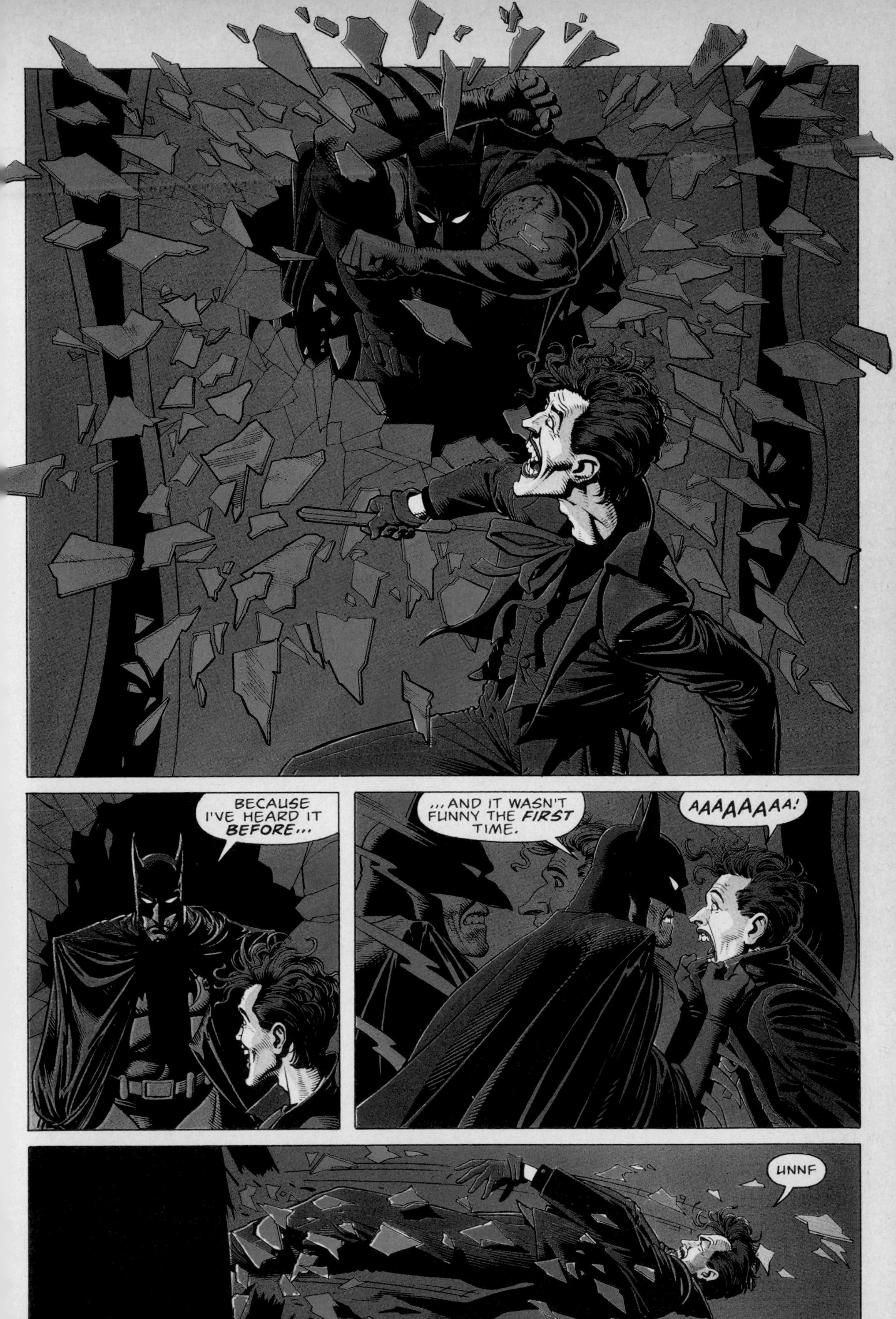
BECAUSE I'VE HEARD IT BEFORE...
...AND IT WASN'T FUNNY THE FIRST TIME.
AAAAAAAA!
UNNF

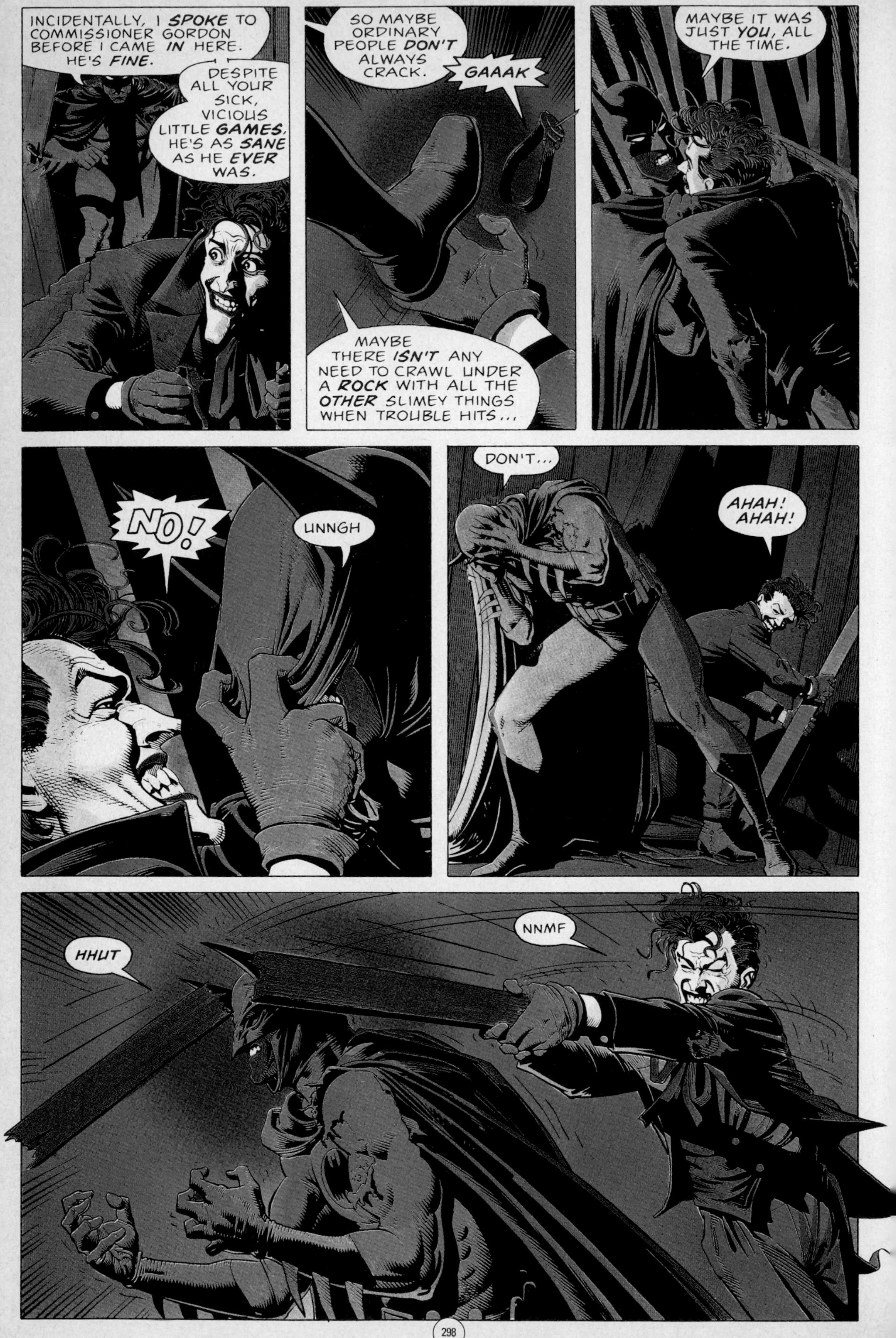
INCIDENTALLY, I SPOKE TO COMMISSIONER GORDON BEFORE I CAME IN HERE. HE'S FINE.
DESPITE ALL YOUR SICK, VICIOUS LITTLE GAMES, HE'S AS SANE AS HE EVER WAS.
SO MAYBE ORDINARY PEOPLE DON'T ALWAYS CRACK.
GAAAK
MAYBE THERE ISN'T ANY NEED TO CRAWL UNDER A ROCK WITH ALL THE OTHER SLIMEY THINGS WHEN TROUBLE HITS...
MAYBE IT WAS JUST YOU, ALL THE TIME.
NO!
UNNGH
DON'T...
AHAH! AHAH!
HHUT
NNMF

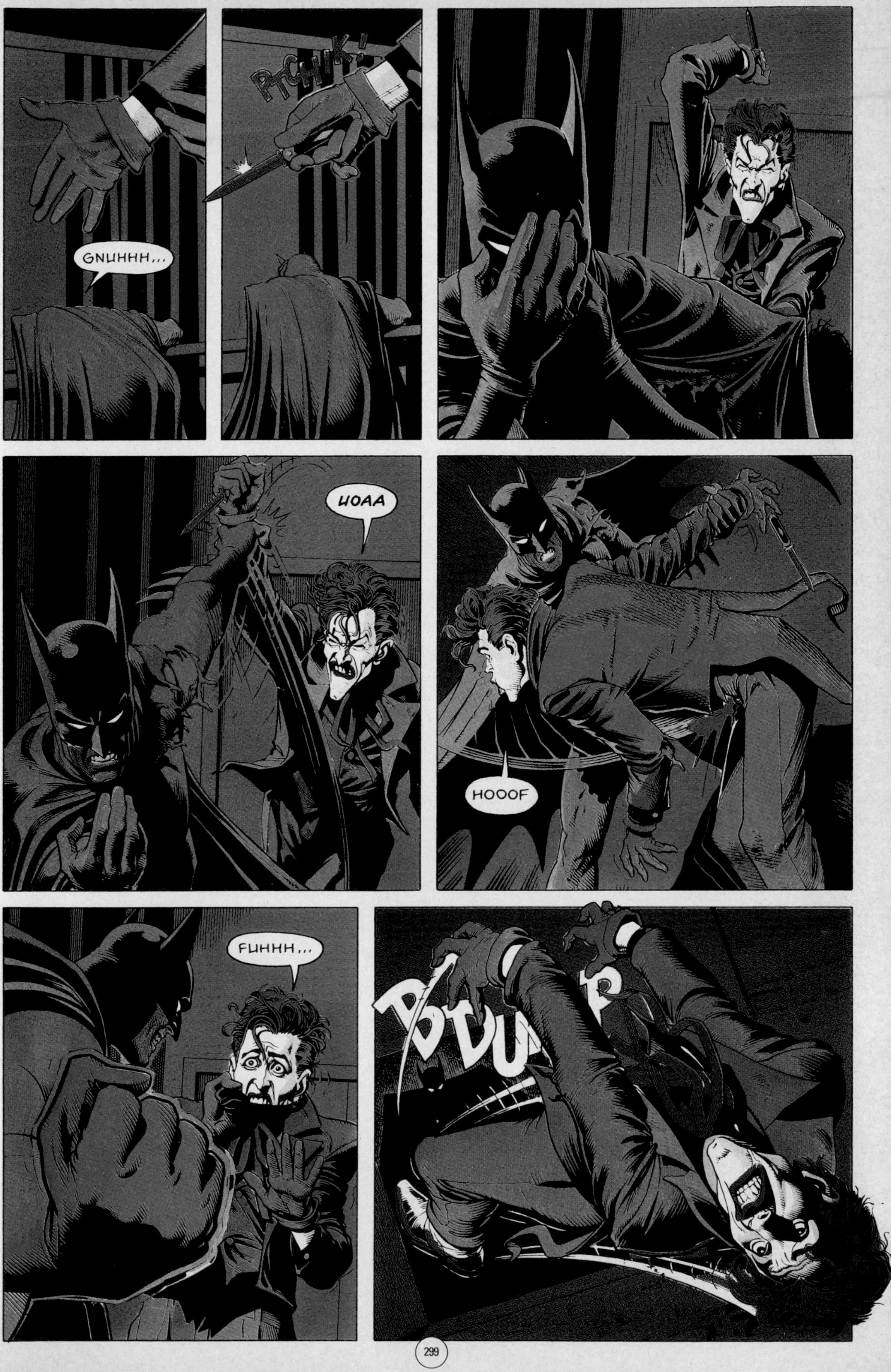
GNUHHH,,,
PTCHIK!
UOAA
HOOOF
FUHHH,,,
BDUMP

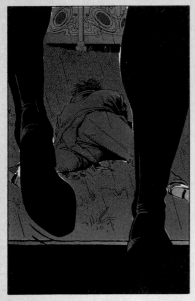

CLICK
CLICK
CLICK

GOD *DAMN* IT...

IT'S *EMPTY!*

CLICK CLICK CLICK

WELL? WHAT ARE YOU *WAITING* FOR?

I SHOT A *DEFENSELESS GIRL.* I *TERRORIZED* AN *OLD MAN.*

WHY DON'T YOU KICK THE *HELL* OUT OF ME AND GET A *STANDING OVATION* FROM THE *PUBLIC GALLERY?*

BECAUSE I'M DOING THIS ONE BY THE *BOOK...*

...AND BECAUSE I DON'T *WANT* TO.

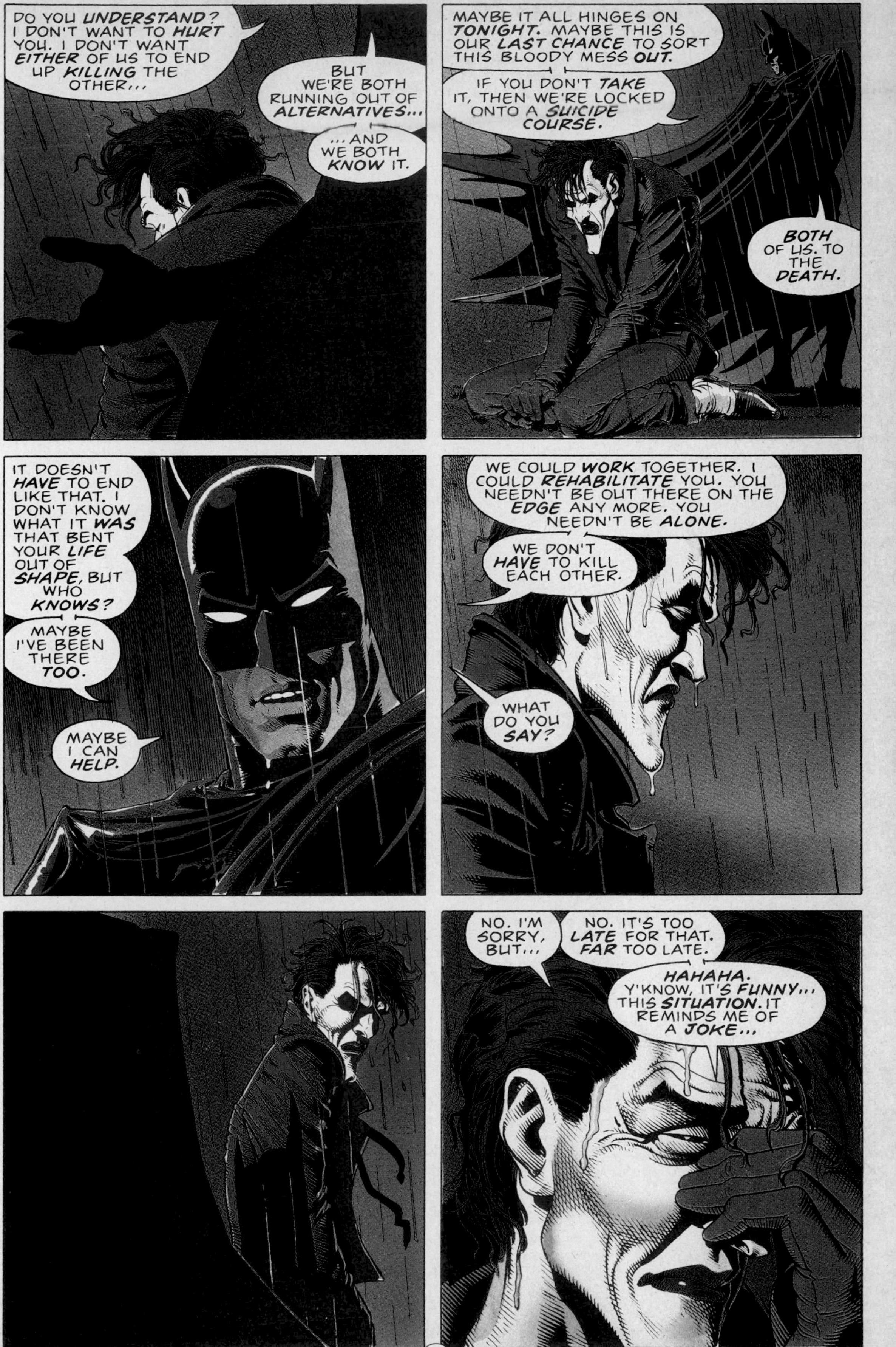
DO YOU UNDERSTAND? I DON'T WANT TO HURT YOU. I DON'T WANT EITHER OF US TO END UP KILLING THE OTHER...
BUT WE'RE BOTH RUNNING OUT OF ALTERNATIVES...
...AND WE BOTH KNOW IT.
MAYBE IT ALL HINGES ON TONIGHT. MAYBE THIS IS OUR LAST CHANCE TO SORT THIS BLOODY MESS OUT.
IF YOU DON'T TAKE IT, THEN WE'RE LOCKED ONTO A SUICIDE COURSE.
BOTH OF US. TO THE DEATH.
IT DOESN'T HAVE TO END LIKE THAT. I DON'T KNOW WHAT IT WAS THAT BENT YOUR LIFE OUT OF SHAPE, BUT WHO KNOWS?
MAYBE I'VE BEEN THERE TOO.
MAYBE I CAN HELP.
WE COULD WORK TOGETHER. I COULD REHABILITATE YOU. YOU NEEDN'T BE OUT THERE ON THE EDGE ANY MORE. YOU NEEDN'T BE ALONE.
WE DON'T HAVE TO KILL EACH OTHER.
WHAT DO YOU SAY?
NO. I'M SORRY, BUT...
NO. IT'S TOO LATE FOR THAT. FAR TOO LATE.
HAHAHA. Y'KNOW, IT'S FUNNY... THIS SITUATION. IT REMINDS ME OF A JOKE...

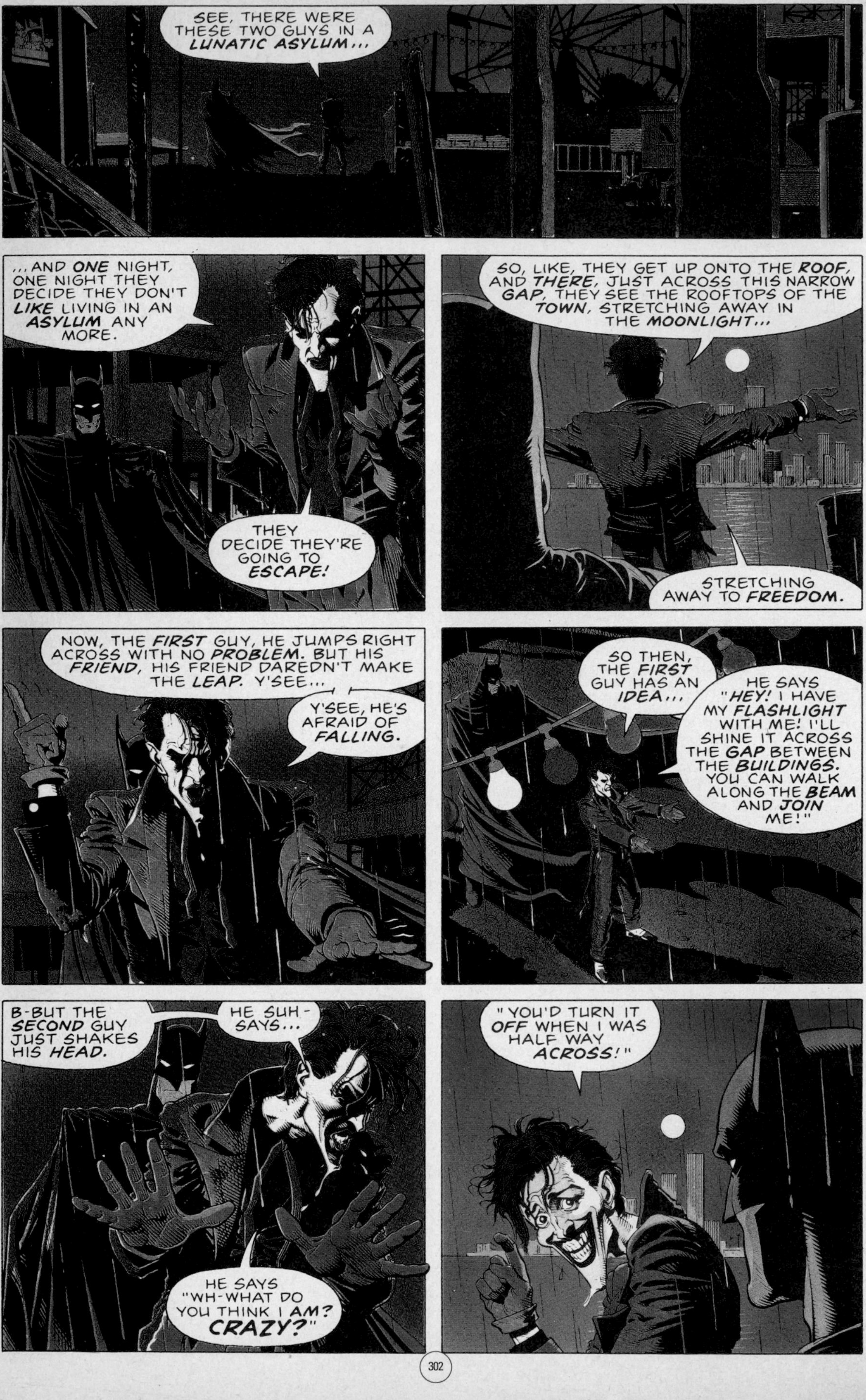
SEE, THERE WERE THESE TWO GUYS IN A LUNATIC ASYLUM...
...AND ONE NIGHT, ONE NIGHT THEY DECIDE THEY DON'T LIKE LIVING IN AN ASYLUM ANY MORE.
THEY DECIDE THEY'RE GOING TO ESCAPE!
SO, LIKE, THEY GET UP ONTO THE ROOF, AND THERE, JUST ACROSS THIS NARROW GAP, THEY SEE THE ROOFTOPS OF THE TOWN, STRETCHING AWAY IN THE MOONLIGHT...
STRETCHING AWAY TO FREEDOM.
NOW, THE FIRST GUY, HE JUMPS RIGHT ACROSS WITH NO PROBLEM. BUT HIS FRIEND, HIS FRIEND DAREDN'T MAKE THE LEAP. Y'SEE...
Y'SEE, HE'S AFRAID OF FALLING.
SO THEN, THE FIRST GUY HAS AN IDEA...
HE SAYS "HEY! I HAVE MY FLASHLIGHT WITH ME! I'LL SHINE IT ACROSS THE GAP BETWEEN THE BUILDINGS. YOU CAN WALK ALONG THE BEAM AND JOIN ME!"
B-BUT THE SECOND GUY JUST SHAKES HIS HEAD.
HE SUH-SAYS...
HE SAYS "WH-WHAT DO YOU THINK I AM? CRAZY?"
"YOU'D TURN IT OFF WHEN I WAS HALF WAY ACROSS!"

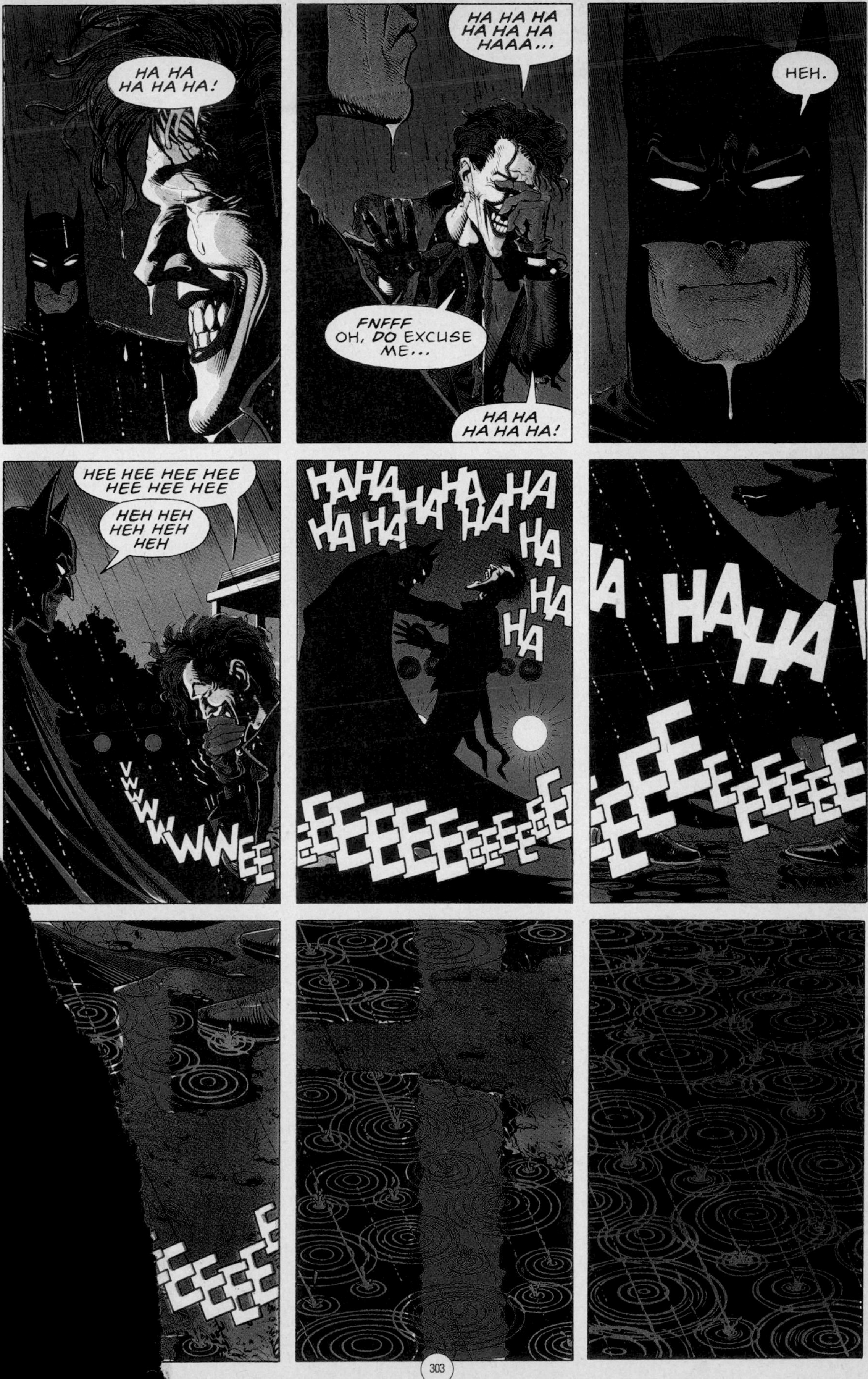

HA HA
HA HA HA!
HA HA HA
HA HA HA HA
HAAA...
FNFFF
OH, DO EXCUSE
ME...
HA HA
HA HA HA!
HEH.
HEE HEE HEE HEE
HEE HEE HEE
HEH HEH
HEH HEH
HEH
VWWWWWEEEEEEEEEEEEEEEEEE
HAHAHAHAHAHA
HAHAHAHAHA
HA
HA
HA
HA
HA
HAHA
EEEEEEEEEEEE
EEEEEEE

OTHER BOOKS BY ALAN MOORE

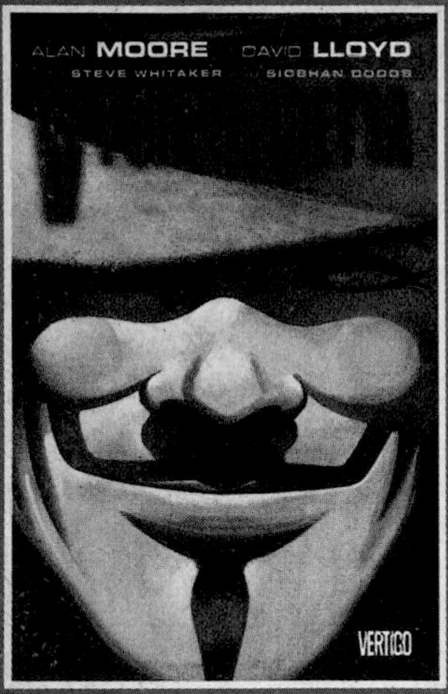
ALAN MOORE
DAVID LLOYD
STEVE WHITAKER
SIOBHAN DODDS
VERTIGO

V FOR VENDETTA
WITH DAVID LLOYD

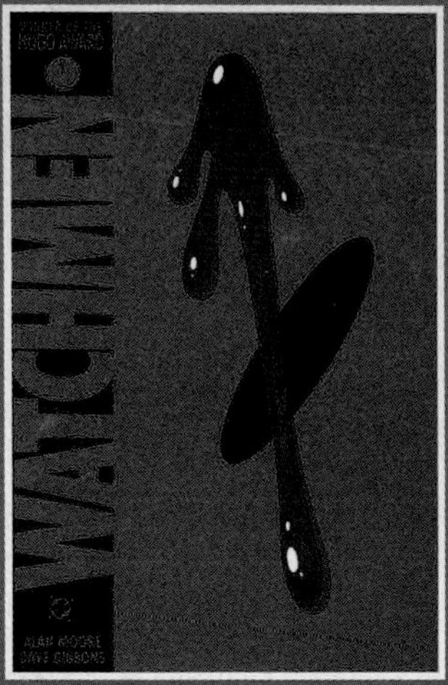
WATCHMEN
ALAN MOORE
DAVE GIBBONS

WATCHMEN
WITH DAVE GIBBONS

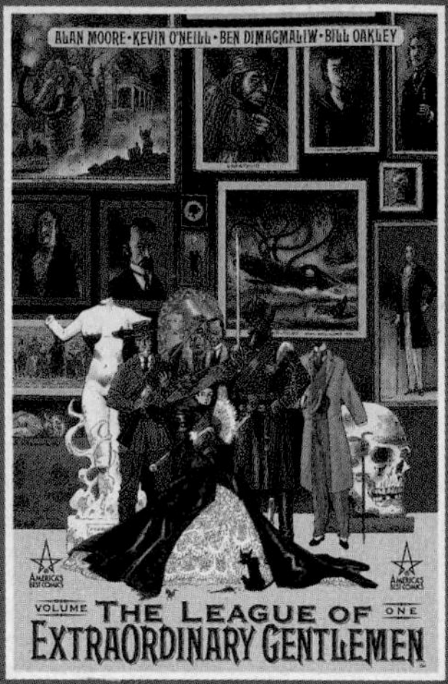
ALAN MOORE · KEVIN O'NEILL · BEN DIMAGMALIW · BILL OAKLEY
VOLUME ONE
THE LEAGUE OF EXTRAORDINARY GENTLEMEN

THE LEAGUE OF EXTRAORDINARY GENTLEMEN WITH KEVIN O'NEILL

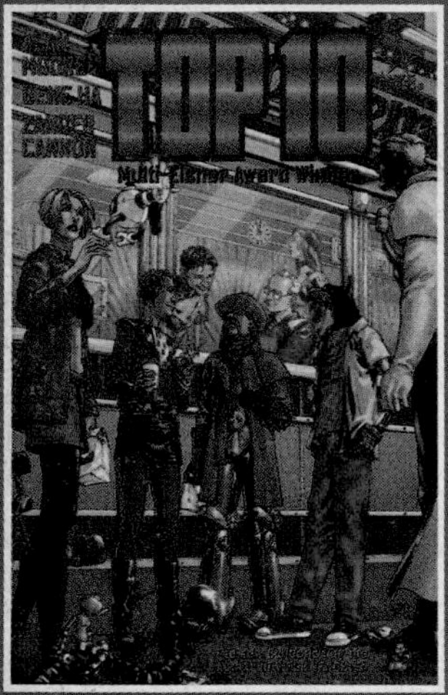
TOP 10

TOP TEN: BOOK ONE
WITH GENE HA AND ZANDER CANNON

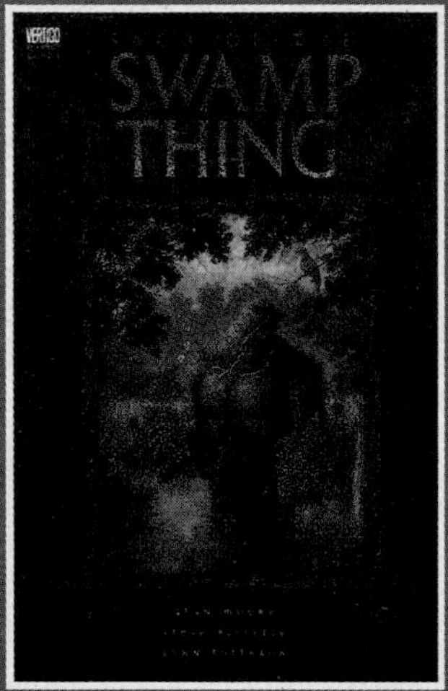
VERTIGO
SWAMP THING

SAGA OF THE SWAMP THING
WITH STEVE BISSETTE, JOHN TOTLEBEN AND VARIOUS

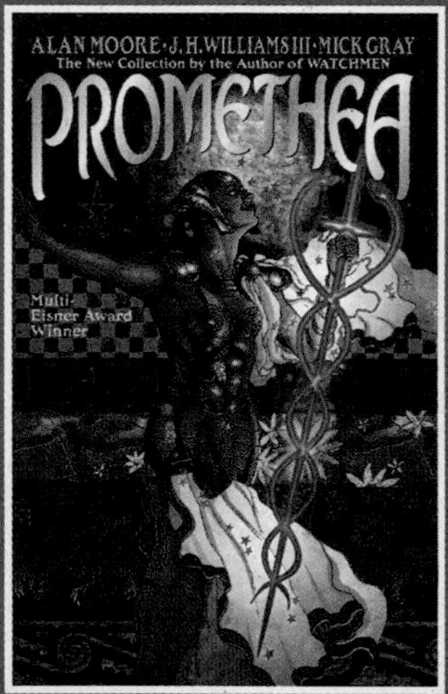
ALAN MOORE · J.H. WILLIAMS III · MICK GRAY
The New Collection by the Author of WATCHMEN
PROMETHEA
Multi-Eisner Award Winner

PROMETHEA BOOK ONE
WITH J.H. WILLIAMS III AND MICK GRAY

ALSO FROM VERTIGO

SWAMP THING: LOVE AND DEATH
BOOK TWO
with S. Bissette/J. Totleben/S. McManus

SWAMP THING: THE CURSE
BOOK THREE
with S. Bissette/J. Totleben

SWAMP THING: A MURDER OF CROWS
BOOK FOUR
with S. Bissette/J. Totleben/various

SWAMP THING: EARTH TO EARTH
BOOK FIVE
with S. Bissette/J. Totleben/various

SWAMP THING: REUNION
BOOK SIX
with S. Bissette/J. Totleben/various

ALSO FROM AMERICA'S BEST COMI

TOM STRONG
BOOK ONE
with Chris Sprouse/Alan Gordon/various

TOM STRONG
BOOK TWO
with Chris Sprouse/Alan Gordon/various

TOM STRONG
BOOK THREE
with Chris Sprouse/Alan Gordon/various

PROMETHEA
BOOK TWO
with J.H. Williams III/Mick Gray

PROMETHEA
BOOK THREE
with J.H. Williams III/Mick Gray

PROMETHEA
BOOK FOUR
with J.H. Williams III/Mick Gray

SMAX
with Zander Cannon/Andrew

TOP 10
BOOK TWO
with Gene Ha/Zand

TOP 10: THE
with Gene Ha

TOMORRO
BOOK ONE
with K.

TOMO
BOOK
with

LEA
GEN
BOOK
with